WRISTWATCH ANNUAL

2023

THE CATALOG

of

PRODUCERS, PRICES, MODELS,

and

SPECIFICATIONS

BY PETER BRAUN

WITH MARTON RADKAI

ABBEVILLE PRESS PUBLISHERS

New York London

Mr Roboto Bronzo

CONTENTS

Dear Reader,

If you haven't heard it yet from some other source, here it is again: something happened to the watch industry during the pandemic episode, something that shook up the market and opened new vistas. You'll find it right in the lede of Elizabeth Doerr's article on the independent scene (p. 10). After years of hard work trying to get recognition from the watch lovers who have been drawn, like moths to the flame, to Big Names, many small brands and independents, those freethinking and often freewheeling horologists, suddenly started attracting some very welcome attention. Those of us covering the industry were no longer hearing about their sometimes-frustrating attempts to explain to people why there is great value in owning a watch that is not being sold by famous "ambassadors" or at big and noisy events. Indeed, many have been discovered by new fans who were eager to stock up on some never-seen, intriguing, unusual timepieces. The only challenge: With supply lines stymied by the pandemic, the problem was actually getting those watches made and assembled while everything was shut down and maintaining the stringently high quality that small brands must deliver at all costs.

One CEO told me excitedly how, during the lockdown, he drove up hill and down dale through watch country in the canton of Neuchâtel to deliver parts to the artisans working away in their ateliers. A smallish brand, like Czapek, which used to produce a few hundred very high-end watches for its fans, even decided this year it had to find the space to set up more workbenches. "Until then, our cash burn was like a prairie fire in our backs," Czapek CEO Xavier de Roquemaurel told me in June, briefly mentioning the goal of a few thousand watches a year in the next five to ten years.

There is some head-scratching about how this burst of interest in smaller and at times recondite brands came to be. One possible explanation is, of course, that some markets are maturing and becoming bolder. Fine timepieces are being considered an investment, and with the collapse of the crypto market, maybe that idea will solidify further. This could also explain why the secondhand market is also swelling. A casual polling of executives and keen observers during the watch fairs I attended suggested that many people had time to surf the Internet during the lockdowns and bit by bit they discovered alternatives to the bigger brands.

Of course, the big brands make some superb timepieces in all price categories that will make your heart beat a little faster. See, for example, Grand Seiko's Kodo (p. 161), a magical tourbillon whose ticking sound is tuned to sound like a heartbeat (*kodo* in Japanese). Van Cleef & Arpels's Heures Florales (p. 317) is a veritable tour de force, with opening flowers telling the hours. The Shooting Star (p. 185) of Jaeger-LeCoultre is magical.

But the smaller brands and independents have managed to carve out a niche for themselves thanks to their aura of intimacy, the care given to each timepiece, and the love of the craft that they pour into each product. When you contact, say, Stefan Kudoke, or Itay Noy, or even Roland Murphy at RGM, you can speak to the creator, you will hear the dedication, and if you tap a little deeper, you might even get the full story, with the bells, the whistles, the warts, and the triumphs.

There are many dedicated journalists—like the aforementioned Elizabeth Doerr—who, of course, go out in the field to search for and listen to these brilliant watch wizards, who get the skinny straight from the source, and keep at it year after year. That's why, in this book, I decided to give some space to those who are trying their hand at unusual watchmaking, the "Mavericks and Meddlers" (p. 18). I've added a small reminder of accessories that collectors might need (p. 28). On page 30, you'll find a portrait of Antoine Preziuso, who has infected his entire family with his passion. And finally, watch tech and design combine in an exploration of the art and technique of skeletonization and why there is a lot more there than meets the eye, quite literally.

The catalogue section reflects to some extent what is happening in the industry. Some of the large brands have had to be cut back to make space for such names as Milus and Perrelet (back after a brief hiatus). New to these pages are ROBOT from the Czech Republic, as well as three models from Kleynod at the Kyiv Ukrainian Watch factory, still producing while the missiles are falling.

A word of thanks to close: Cindi Barton, Kourtnay King, Erin Morris, Stephanie Sarkany, and others across the pond from me helped to review the text, manage the workflow in difficult times, and lay out the chapters, and who remained calm under pressure. Thanks, too, to Elizabeth Doerr for her annual contributions. And thanks to the brands that advertise with *Wristwatch Annual* and who trust in the power of a real book filled with images and original copy—no copy-pasting here. Errors do occur, and if you run into one, please make gentle note of it so we can correct it. And then enjoy everything else. We'd love to hear from you.

Marton Radkai

This year's *Wristwatch Annual* cover features the **Ball Engineer M Skindiver III Beyond**. It comes in a 41.5-millimeter stainless-steel case with a height of 13.8 millimeters. It runs on Ball's own COSC-certified Caliber 7309-C delivering 80 hours of power reserve. This diver's watch, with a magnified date, is a genuine tool watch, with 5,000 G-shock resistance thanks to the Amortiser patented anti-shock system. Visibility is guaranteed by micro gas tubes on the unidirectional bezel, on the indices, and on the three hands. The Engineer Skindiver III Beyond can resist a magnetic field to 4,800 m/A and is water-resistant to 30 atm thanks to a screw-in crown. It comes in a limited edition of 1,000 pieces.

JS WATCH CO. REYKJAVIK
Probably the World's Smallest Watch Manufacturer
g
With his legendary concentration and over 50 years of experience our Master Watchmaker and renowned craftsman, Gilbert O. Gudjonsson, inspects every single timepiece before it leaves our workshop in Reykjavik, Iceland.
JS Watch co. REYKJAVIK
SIF NART 1948
JS Watch co.
REYKJAVIK
Learn more
www.jswatch.com

1

THE INDEPENDENT SCENE 2022

2

3

1. Natural stones used by Beauregard

2. and 3. Rexhep and Rexhepi and his prize-winning Chronomètre Contemporain II

BY ELIZABETH DOERR

Independent makers and brands experienced a nearly unmanageable uptick in not only business and sales during these pandemic years, but also in recognition, respect, and understanding. This is a new position for these makers of elite and unusually artisanal watches to be in, but it is also one that encourages new faces and talents. So, it is probably no wonder that our world of ticks and tocks is now graced with more "independents" than ever before. Here is a selection of new watches by independents introduced in 2022.

CLASSIC WATCHMAKING

Fans of **Akrivia** have probably been waiting with bated breath for the **Rexhep Rexhepi Chronomètre Contemporain II**, and they weren't disappointed with what is essentially a new watch crafted as a follow-up to the sensational timepiece released in 2018 that sealed the reputation of its maker and took home an award at the 2018 Grand Prix d'Horlogerie de Genève (GPHG). The RRCC II, as it is known, may seem like the same watch as the sold-out model it has replaced, but it is definitely not the same. It resembles the original RRCC in one respect only: the way it looks from the front, crisp and traditional with nothing confusing or "progressive." I mention the word "progressive" because Rexhepi's Akrivia brand is normally all about being progressive. At its debut in 2018, the RRCC represented a major deviation in Akrivia's style, marking a new line, the "Rexhep Rexhepi collection."

It is entirely like Rexhepi to not be satisfied with just repeating something, even if that "something" was beyond successful. So, aside from its looks, this watch is different in magnificent ways. "Built on the same principles, but taken to the next level," the press release states, it finds its roots in Rexhepi's vision of high-quality nineteenth-century pocket watch dials adorned with high-fire enamel combined with "a modern twist" based on "sector" dials of the 1930s and 1940s. The RRCC II is powered by an entirely new caliber that is as focused on chronometric precision as the first model was. It is outfitted with two gear trains and twin barrels arranged symmetrically to ensure a precise and consistent motion of the deadbeat second hand, which makes one quartz-like jump per second. At any rate,

1

2

3

1. Theo Auffret's Tourbillon Grand Sport, "younger and hipper"

2. and 3. Massena Lab "school watch" keeps it simple but effective.

4. and 5. Unique jewelry watches by Canadian Alexandre Beauregard

4

the Rehxepi's second "RRCC" clinched the Men's Watch award at the GPHG in 2022, proof that he must be onto something.

There are two variations of the RRCC II to choose from: platinum with black enamel dial and pink gold with white enamel dial.

Theo Auffret is a young Paris-based watchmaker versed in restoration. He was the winner of the 2018 F.P.Journe Young Talent Competition with a prototype of his Tourbillon à Paris. This evolved into his **Tourbillon Grand Sport**, a four-piece subscription watch that retains the tourbillon and handmade look of the predecessor timepiece, but which is upgraded in many dial details. Above all, the case and strap make it look a bit younger and hipper (yet still classic). And it succeeded.

Old School by **Massena LAB** and **Luca Soprana** is a fresh take on the *montre d'école* concept, the pieces that watchmaking students complete prior to graduation to display their newly acquired skills. The hallmarks of a high-quality school watch include handmade, high-quality decoration, and Old School delivers, beginning with the hand-frosted German silver dial. While the movement handmade by Luca Soprana looks quite straightforward at first inspection, a closer look reveals several lovely "old-school" touches to like the stylized swan-neck regulating spring, the bimetallic split escapement, and outstanding hand-finishing.

Massena LAB, the brainchild of collector and former TimeZone CEO William Massena, is a collaboration-based entity that works primarily with independent creators.

BEAUTIFUL WATCHMAKING

Alexandre **Beauregard**'s eponymous firm invites us to fall in love with its creations at first sight, so enchanting are these wonderfully crafted horological objects that also happen to be highly sophisticated yet wholly unpretentious pieces of jewelry art. Beauregard's latest is called **Lili Candy** and its most prominent feature is the set of stones including white opal, carnelian, Fanta opal, yellow opal, chrysoprase, topaz, and amethyst fashioned to resemble a good old-fashioned lollipop. The petite 33-millimeter case with crown on the back is available in a choice of 18-karat white gold or platinum and crafted only upon order. It is set with 150 flawless VVS DEF diamonds forming two rows encircling the precious lollipop and comes on a satin strap.

The fraternal Dutch duo **Grönefeld** introduced the **1941 Grönograaf** in a (sold-out) limited edition of 25 pieces in tantalum cases and a 188-piece limited edition in stainless steel. While the tantalum case is much harder (and harder to machine and finish) than stainless steel, the two versions are visually indistinguishable until turned over (where the engraving reveals the edition).

This is an extremely nicely executed, relatively discreet, traditional two-pusher chronograph, but it is also much more as the unusual regulator mechanism visible at 6 o'clock reveals: this component dampens the excessive speed of the chronograph's flying resetting central hand as well as the smaller 30-minute hand, virtually eliminating the shock and wear undergone by all other chronograph movements when resetting.

5

MILITARY EDITION
HONOR THAT WILL NOT FADE WITH TIME
G.C.T.
VORTIC WATCH COMPANY 20 13
THE MILITARY EDITION
Antique American pocket watches built for the US Army Air Corps during World War II converted into limited edition wristwatches aptly named The Military Edition.
VORTICWATCHES.COM | INFO@VORTICWATCHES.COM | 324 JEFFERSON STREET, FORT COLLINS, CO 80524 | 855-285-7884

1

2

ASTRONOMICAL WATCHMAKING

Krayon, the brainchild of Rémi Maillat, specializes in astronomical complications. And after the success of the ultra-complicated Everywhere, Krayon introduces the artistic and efficient **Anywhere**, which very intuitively displays sunrise and sunset nearly anywhere on the planet. The visuals are a perfect distillation of the core concept and take what was an awesome yet rather technical watch and turn it into something that is more ephemeral, ethereal, and emotional, just like sunrise and sunset are.

Stepan Sarpaneva's latest watch is called **Nocturne** and it is an ode to the night with his massive iconic moon behind a scene designed by Finnish illustrator Ville Tietäväinen. The Sarpaneva Nocturne teems with stunning imagery: an almost eerie midnight scene with a stern owl overlooking water while the clouds roll in, with stars and a fiery comet in the sky.

There are two versions of the Nocturne: White Glow Moon and Orange Glow Moon, the latter nicknamed "Harvest Moon." The dial is strewn with a total of nine different colors of Super-LumiNova applied to the six different components that make up the dial side.

The Nocturne White Glow Moon and Orange Glow Moon (Harvest Moon) are each limited to 30 pieces and require a lead time of two to six months to be manufactured and delivered.

1. Rémi Maillat's Anywhere shows the sunrise and sunset anywhere.

2. Sarpaneva's Nocturne brings back his hallmark moon.

3. Another world timer is Sven Andersen's Heures du Monde.

A.H.C.I. NEWS

The heart of the independent scene is—and always has been in the modern era—the A.H.C.I. (Académie Horlogère des Créateurs Indépendants/Horological Academy of Independent Creators), a group of independent creators founded in 1985. The way of these individualistic watchmaker-inventors is indeed anachronistic, and though the products that emerge may not be everyone's cup of tea all of the time, they do attract the attention of collectors of rare taste who follow not only the horological escapades of these 30-odd men of varying age and nationality, but also the passion and personality that goes into each extremely limited-edition timepiece.

MING
MING
CELEBRATING FIVE YEARS OF THE ILLUMINATINGLY UNCONSTRAI
WWW.MING.WATC

1. and 2. Raul Pagès and Massena LAB collaborated for the classically streamlined Régulateur à détente.

The latest by A.H.C.I. cofounder Svend Andersen is the **Andersen Genève x Asprey Heures du Monde**, which is chock-full of inspiration from Andersen's past. One of the most important of these characteristics are the beautiful triangular lugs that Andersen originally designed for the case of 1996's Secular Perpetual Calendar, a design at that time carried out by famed Genevan case maker Jean-Pierre Hagmann to Andersen's specifications.

Another inspired element is the 21-karat blue gold that the boutique maker has been using since 2005. Here it forms the center of the three-part dial that also includes the reference city ring and day/night ring. The guilloché pattern on the blue-gold dial and rotor was inspired by historical Asprey perfume bottles. Andersen Genève confirms that this pattern has until now never been used on a watch dial. It is available in an edition of 24 pieces only from Asprey.

Raul Pagès was busy this year with his own watch, the **Régulateur à détente**, and a Massena LAB collaboration called **Magraph**. The haute horlogerie Régulateur is a clean and minimally designed watch that introduces Pagès's take on the detent escapement. The beautifully finished movement is entirely handmade by Pagès with no visible connection between the balance and escapement and the rest of the going train in a horological magic trick. The Magraph, on the other hand, is a mid-priced watch that is simultaneously Pagès's first collaboration with another "brand," and it features for the first time ever a Massena LAB proprietary movement: the M660, designed by Pagès in Switzerland. "For me, the idea of doing a collaboration, my first ever, was an exciting and rewarding challenge," said Pagès. "I am proud to have worked with Massena LAB on the design of the new caliber M660."

Elizabeth Doerr is a freelance journalist specialized in watches and was senior editor of Wristwatch Annual *until the 2010 edition. She is now the editor-in-chief of* Quill & Pad*, an online magazine that keeps a watch on time (www.quillandpad.com).*

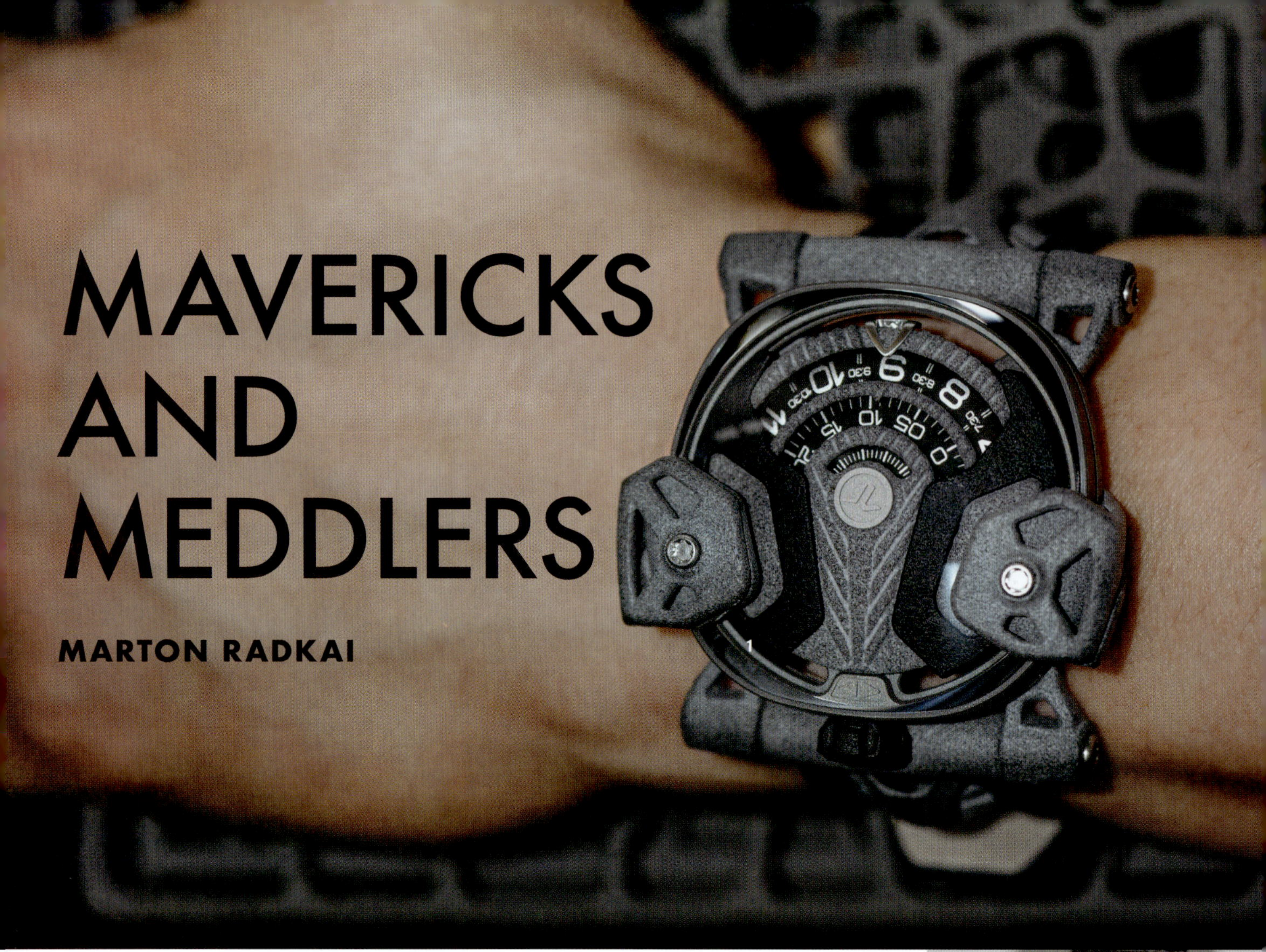

MAVERICKS AND MEDDLERS

MARTON RADKAI

Like many industries trading in product and emotion, watchmaking attracts all sorts, including imaginative or passionate individuals who, at times, are not necessarily from the industry itself and do not fit into any clean-cut category. The vagaries of the market determine staying power. Here are some "*objets trouvés*," not necessarily new, but that deserve a showing.

The insistent emails announcing the release of the Gyro Dial at the Geneva Watch Days were a bit irritating, and nevertheless, as a chess fan, the name **Byrne** just remained stuck in my mind (Donald and Robert Byrne were American grandmasters). So, I decided to drop in and see what John Byrne had to show. Byrne is a young Frenchman living in Paris. In 2015, he was watching a ballet at the Opéra when he saw four dancers line up as one and then fall out of line to the right and left. For someone who has worked in watchmaking all his career, it was an epiphany. Byrne saw a single watch that could change its dial. "So, it's never the same watch," he told me triumphantly.

What Byrne had in mind was a mechanism that would switch the cardinal numerals at midnight, producing four different visuals. It was obvious that the 12, 3, 6, and 9 would have to be placed on a satellite cube of sorts that would all jump smoothly at the same time. And the numerals were perfectly flush with the dial. The solution was an ETA 2894 caliber minus the chronograph module and mainplate and dial with carefully cut out windows. The rest was all about filing for patents, finding a company that could implement his ideas, like Le Cercle des Horlogers in the Jura mountains north of Neuchâtel, and lots of trial and error. The case itself needed to be perfect. It took all of seven years, but the Gyro Dial is now on the market. (byrnewatch.com)

1

2

1. and 2. Now you see it, then it changes: Byrne's four dials in one watch.

STERNGLAS
ZEITMESSER
MADE IN GERMANY
The watch start-up from Germany
German watchmaking with a Bauhaus design.
We are taking the watch world by storm by
offering high-quality timepieces at a fair price
In our world, good design should not be a luxury.
Honest, functional and to the point. That's STERNGLAS.
rilliant Nuevo Diamonds Pittsburgh, PA | Cornerstone Fine Jewelry Springfield, MO | Humes Jewelers Hopkinsville, KY | Mark Peters Diamond Designs Plainfield, IL |
Midwest Estate Buyers Zionsville, IN | Reiner's Fine Jewelry Houston, TX | Sink Jewelers Arcanum, OH | Spratford Fine Jewelry Overland Park, KS |Vierk's Fine Jewelry
fayette, IN | Jaqueline's Fine Jewelry Morgantown, WV | Alexanders of Atlanta Lawrenceville, GA | Bassano Jewelry New York, NY | Brentwood Jewelry Brentwood, TN
hadwick's Jewelers St. Simons Island, GA | Danson Jewelers Allendale, NJ | Gold Galore Diamond Center Hudson, FL Lamon Jewelers Gatlinburg, TN | Old Northeast
ewelers Tampa & St. Petersburg, FL | O'Neils Cape May, NJ Orlando Watch Co. Winter Park, FL | State Street Jewelers Greensboro, NC | Stonehaven Jewelry Cary, NC |
The Watch & Jewelry Hospital Port St. Lucie, FL | Worthmore Jewelers Atlanta, GA | Whitten's Fine Jewelers Wilmington, DE | Your Favorite Jewelers Tallahassee, FL |
Garrick Jewelers Hanover, PA | Radisson Jewels Maho, Sint Maarten | Arctic G&G Anchorage, AK | Joshua's Watch Repair & Timepieces Yorba Linda, CA | JP Diamond
Designs Pismo Beach, CA | Mimi's Jewelry Fountain Valley, CA | Right Time Highlands Ranch, CO | Huntington Jewelers Las Vegas, NV
Sternglas USA 727-896-4278

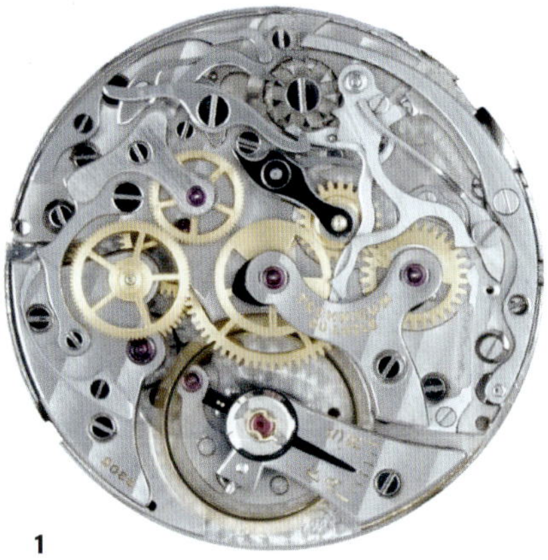

1

2

ABSOLUTELY CLASSIC

During a casual conversation, Paul Gerber, perhaps the most self-effacing genius in this industry, decried the fact that when watchmakers die, the treasures they leave behind are often misunderstood as disparate junk collected by someone on the brink of dementia. Among these treasures is the Valjoux 88, a very fine caliber dating to 1947 that has been used by many brands as a base. It features three dates, a moon phase, and a chronograph with a thirty-minute and an hour totalizer. The engine runs at 18,000 vph.

At this year's Watches and Wonders, too, I spotted Carole Harlé-Voutaz at a solitary table. She heads **Berney**, a small watchmaking company in l'Abbaye, in the Joux Valley, where you also find Breguet and Claude Meylan, for example. Among the products on display were several Valjoux 88-based watches, including one skeleton. What struck me with the VJ88 G was how the designers had created a very orderly dial, which can otherwise become a bit messy, with all the hands turning and pointing. The watch in gold goes for around $18,000. (berneywatch.ch)

SQUARING THE CIRCLE

One definition of quaintness, according to Webster's Dictionary, is "uncommon, old-fashioned, or unfamiliar, but often agreeable or attractive in character... ." Does that sound like vintage? Yes, according to the late British art historian and museum curator James Laver (1899-1975), who determined that a fashion being resurrected fifty years on is indeed "quaint." So, unsurprisingly, square watches seem to be appearing on the radar in recent times. The shape is a little awkward at times. The 1970s were, admittedly, more angular and monochromatic than the wild and flowery 1960s, just as Bauhaus followed Art Nouveau. Besides the electronic watches with digital displays, many brands produced square timepieces, from Patek Philippe to Seiko, Chopard (the Happy Diamonds), Piaget, and Casio, of course. Some models never really lost their popularity, like TAG Heuer's Monaco, which is still a favorite and has reemerged to even win a prize at the Grand Prix d'Horlogerie in Geneva.

Unlike the eternal circle on the wrist, squares are not easy spaces to fill with time indicators. The orphaned corners need to be integrated somehow with a round hour track, and most movements happen to be round. But brands do manage with some imagination.

In fall 2022, I received a number of alerts from **Charles Zuber**, a Genevan brand that had been dormant for some time. The eponymous founder, jeweler, and designer Charles Zuber (1932-2012), had worked for many big brands, including Piaget, Harry Winston, and Audemars Piguet. Three fellows (gem-setter Vincent Perego, jeweler Aram Garabetian, and businessman Mohamed Hilal), owners of another watchmaking company, decided it was time to revive the brand and its flashy DNA. For their first

3

4

1. The Valjoux 88 skeletonized (source Clinique Horlogère Porrentruy)

2. Berney Watch with a streamlined rendering of the Valjoux 88

3. and 4. The 1970s, TAG Heuer's remake of the Monaco, an original Seiko

German Design
Swiss Made
Single-hand
PRIMATIC
MEISTERSINGER
Primatic,
_etting go and trusting time.
Single-hand watch with
swiss automatic movement
and power reserve indicator.
08 09 10 11 12

1

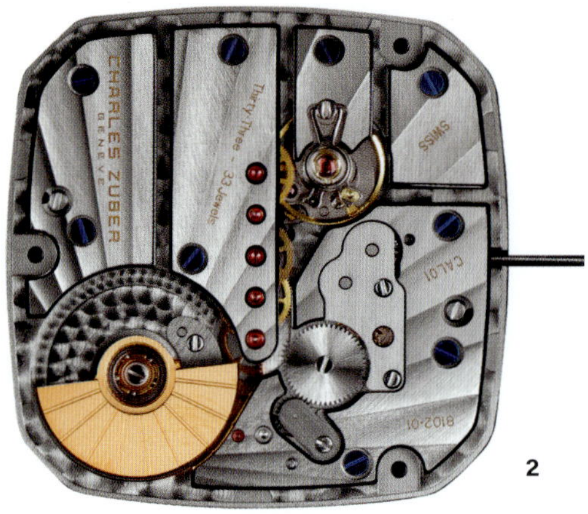

2

3

4

watch, the Perfos, they wisely chose to work with Eric Giroud. The result is an elegant, square automatic, with an equally square movement inside. The dial features sixty sprightly rhodium-plated indices around a simple, circular track. The case, in three parts and carefully beveled to avoid sharp edges, is subtly contemporary. The '70s feel is merely a faint visual redolence. It comes in three sizes to adapt perfectly to different wrists. The hues are kept elegant. Interestingly, when Perego went to Zuber's widow to find some images of her late husband, he also found sketches of a similar design. Apparently, the idea needed incarnation.

One doesn't have to spend a fortune for a retro look, however. The portfolio of the French company **Depancel** includes the F-series, for example, an almost square watch (43 mm x 36 mm) for under $1,000. What looks like a chronograph from a distance is in fact a calendar spread out over subdials, including a GMT function. It runs on an automatic Miyota 9120 and is guaranteed for life.

A little more expensive, and also more frankly 1970s, is the first mechanical to come out of **Shinola**. The Mackinac is named after a tough regatta that goes from Port Huron to Mackinac Island. The dial is an eye-catching light orange, a little blonder than the notorious orange of the '70s, and the main complication justifying the $3,500 price tag is the subdial with a chronograph yacht race complication. (shinola.com)

TIME AND ART

If you are doing squares, then go all the way. This bold idea was implemented by Nicolas Mertenat, who launched his **Blancarré** (White Square) watch after leaving Omega. His brother Claude is on board but handles the finances. It is in a black-and-white pattern with indices and a subsidiary dial all repeating the squareness of the watch itself. "I was inspired by minimal art and cubic sculptures," Nicolas told a newspaper in 2016. Getting the project off the ground was not easy, due mainly to the pandemic hitting at the wrong moment. But now this unique set of timepieces is beginning to catch on,

5

6

1. and 2. Charles Zuber revived: hints of the past and a dedicated rectangular movement (below)

3. Depancel's F-series, almost retro, certainly affordable

4. Shinola's throwback to the 1970s has a mechanical heart.

5. and 6. Blancarré's black-and-white squares, inspired by Op Art

REACH YOUR SUMMIT
Alpina
1883 GENEVE
ALPINER EXTREME REGULATOR AUTOMATIC
Swiss Professional Alpine Watch
INDEPENDENCE, PERSEVERANCE, HERITAGE.
us.alpinawatches.com

thanks to a new and more dynamic marketing strategy. There are six versions in black, white, and grey patterns. The 37x37-millimeter case is made of titanium. Besides the three hands, each watch has a second time zone and a large date. (blancarre.com)

NOT-SO-SQUARE LIFESTYLE

If you have ever dreamed of owning one of those large rectangular talking pieces designed by Hautlence, for instance, but you couldn't afford them, **SevenFriday** has a solution. Founder Dan Niederer (a Dutchman living in Zurich) worked in the industry for many years before setting off on his own in 2012. He will tell you that his company manufactures square watches (with rounded corners), because he heard they don't sell well. They are, of course, unabashed lifestyle products giving off the aura of easy, breezy living. He also sells accessories, like ultra-cool frames for glasses. The name alone suggests that every day is Friday, and you're getting ready for a weekend of fun every day.

The keys to the watches' draw with the fan base are the complex dials that suggest a lot more than the Miyota movements inside, which do the work and allow Niederer to keep low prices. Modern technology is also used to enhance the look and functionality. Each watch is equipped with NFC technology to identify the owner, track watches, and prevent counterfeiting. The most recent innovation is using 3D printing and a castor oil base to make straps and a very modernistic box to deliver the watch to the new owner.

Big, bold, fun is the recipe for SevenFriday watches.

For some masterpieces,
it's all in the name.
JUNGHANS
FRI 25
CHRONOSCOPE
MADE IN GERMANY
Junghans
MEISTER

1

2

CLOCKING OUT

The name SevenFriday is itself quite an eyecatcher. And there is another brand that also has a day of the week in its name and is also devoted to lifestyle, according to the founder, but not in the same extroverted manner. In the old watch country, the term "blue Mondays" referred to the day that the most skilled watchmakers would take off to to get over any heavy-duty weekend partying, knowing that they could catch up on their work later on in the week. This tradition ended in the 1920s, apparently. The logo of the **Lundis Bleus** watches is therefore a stylized version of an ethanol molecule. Founder Bastien Vuilliomenet, an industrial designer, has created two distinct lines. Either there are unique pieces, like the Viper, in cloisonné enamel (at around $12,000), or he offers the Color Spectrum collection, in his words: "The dial is grand feu enamel on gold leaf. The latter makes it possible to obtain extremely vivid colors. The idea of this collection is to recreate the color spectrum with seven watches in red, orange, yellow, green, cyan, blue and violet." These watches sell at around $4,000 a piece. (lundis-bleus.com).

Finally, no collection of found objects would be complete without mentioning the great **Miki Eleta**, who comes up with the most hair-raising ways to give time a physical manifestation. His "Passage of Time," is, as usual, an extraordinary feat of engineering and finishing using bronze, gold-plating, lapis lazuli, and steel. The functions include a retrograde minute and days of the week represented by their Roman planets, moons, and suns—in short, a galactic jumble, perfectly organized and with a human figure in the middle, which, like each of us on earth, cannot move from the spot, but does raise his arm and drop his head every twenty seconds in order to read time. It's more than a clock: it's a machine that philosophizes about our abject subjugation to the arrow of time. (mikieleta.ch)

3

1. and 2. Lundis Bleus makes uncomplicated watches with superb grand-feu dials.

3. The fantastic world of Miki Eleta

1

COLLECTOR'S DELIGHTS

Every industry, especially one based on passion, will have a peripheral circle of enterprises that have spotted needs for customers that are either not met, or are truly part of the spirit of the original.

If you have a nice collection of automatics, and if those automatics have complications that depend on the watch being wound at all times, you will be in a pickle if you don't have a watch winder. Perpetual calendars and moonphases, for instance, do not like to be wound down, and setting them again can lead to damage if not done just right. The second challenge is travel. Fortunately, there are companies that have thought about all the possibilities and offer some solid solutions.

THE LIFE

CEO Simon Wolf of Wolf 1834 is conscious of the changing generation of watch owners. The company offers a wide range of products, from trendy winders with skulls whose eye sockets light up in red, to modular winder batteries. At any rate, Wolf likes the idea of lifestyle and fun as collector qualities. "We do not take ourselves too seriously and always err on the side of making it fun," says Wolf. So, if you are on the road, you do want to carry your watches with you. The self-winders present another problem. One of the latest Wolf products is called The Rocket: small, efficient, fits easily into a suitcase for the journey. It will do up to 900 turns per day, so it will wind your watch and then return it to its original position. The cuff is adjustable to the size of the watch and clicks easily into place.

CLASSIC ELEGANCE

Another travel option are the elegant products made by Scatola del Tempo. Their Pochette ("little pocket" in French) can carry up to four watches. The inside is built for modularity, so you can also shift things around for larger watches, or use it for transporting other items, from make-up, to straps, USB sticks, or shaving paraphernalia. It has its price ($515), but you'll have a leather product made by fine artisans in Italy. And watches are worth the extra mile.

Scatola del Tempo also makes the little handmade leather Toolkit, which can come in very handy for small repairs, as well as carrying things around. If you have attended a watchmaking seminar, you may even be able to use it to delve deeper into the innards of your watch, or any watch you'll have found at a junk store or flea market, or at the bottom of a drawer. The Toolkit comes in brown, black, and chestnut ($440).

2

3

LITTLE THINGS

There are two more items you should bring along. The first is a pair of light cotton jeweler's gloves. They are not expensive, so buying a few pairs is a good idea in case you are showing your collection to a friend at home. They prevent you from leaving your fingerprints on the watches, especially the crystal. Also, the oils on your hands can over time etch the metal a bit. Anyone showing you a watch will be thankful.

The other tool is a loupe—a jeweler's magnifying glass. They are cheap as well and readily available. Some can be easily clamped into your eye socket, leaving your hands free. What you stare at for long minutes, while the owner of the watch counts to 100 and back, is up to you. I tend to look at the finishing, the clean lines, the quality of an enamel dial, the incredible ballet of a complicated watch's workings. Staring too long at the pallet fork going back and forth can have a hypnotic effect.

LIGHTS

Increasingly, brands are making use of luminescent materials. Full-lume dials, bright hands, and numerals have always been popular, and nothing is more fun than showing up the details, like where the brand has placed the material. To do this, you will need a UV flashlight. They are usually small and light, so traveling with them is not a burden. You don't need a powerful one (320-400 nm is quite enough) and you can use the light for other things, like checking for pet urine. You won't regret it.

CLASS WRITING

A watch friend recently noticed that I was holding a small object in my hand and asked me what it was. A pen, I replied. A Kaweco. This old German brand, which dates to the 1880s, makes some delightful Bauhaus travel pens that fit in the hand. The screwed cap, which ensures no leakage, extends the little pen to a fair length. In fact, much of this book is prepared on paper using such pens. These are not ostentatious writing implements. They are elegant (they co-brand with Nomos) and discreet, and they fit the image of the serious collector. Sure, we can rely on a keyboard, but putting pen to paper is a special act, almost revolutionary. And if you want a truly unique pen that is not expensive, I found a small one-man operation in France called Wagner Stylos (wagner-stylos.com). Gerhard Wagner, a guitarist, became a passionate maker of writing implments. My Wagner fountain pen is wrapped in leather, closes with a magnetic cap, and cost around $60.

1. Wolf 1834's Rocket for travelers with automatics

2. and 3. Scatola del Tempo's Pochette (above) for watches or paraphernalia; the elegant Toolkit (below), for little repairs

4., 5., 6. Watch examination requires gloves (top), magnifying loupes (middle), and a UV light (bottom) to highlight luminescent mass.

7., 8., 9. Bauhaus Kaweco pens are excellent travel companions; Wagner Stylos offers rare handmade fountain pens for outstanding value.

7

AGENT OF TIME

BY MARTON RADKAI

Watchmakers are strange creatures. They walk the fine line between being artists and being engineers, two professions that might seem incompatible. Antoine Preziuso has walked this tightrope since childhood and never tires of it.

2. and 3. Spontaneous inspiration: The Torre de Mangia (top) turns into a watch (below).

4. A glimpse of New York became the Urban Square.

5. Tiret and Preziuso teamed up for high-end bling: the Day and Night Tourbillon.

Creativity has many formulas. One of them is the intuitive ability to spot potential in some serendipitous snapshot of life, trite or glorious, and then build a story, a tableau, a piece of music, or, in this case, a watch, around it. Antoine Preziuso has that ability and it has served him well throughout his career.

Sometimes, the flash is simple. There is, for instance, the great clock on the fourteenth-century Torre de Mangia in Siena, Italy, a one-hand time-keeper, which inspired one of Preziuso's most enduring timepieces, the appropriately named Siena, which was the first to actually sport his name on the dial. At other times the snapshot has to be transformed and fine-tuned by his orderly and systematic mind to find a rendering that pays tribute to the original while making horological sense. This is how the minimalistic Urban Square was born: "I was in a plane landing in New York city, when I looked down and saw a square."

His calm, slightly lilting speech belies his untamed imagination, which is limited only by the engineering requirements of his vision. The physical shape of his timepieces is not the primary issue, though there is a feel to his watches, a certain heft. It is more as if everything must be shown, and if there is no place on the dial for some complication, well, there is always the rear. He has made tonneau watches, round watches, square watches, crazy watches, sober watches. The world of watchmaking, so imbued with Calvinistic self-effacement, might deplore bling as a touch vulgar, but in Preziuso's hands in 2005, when brands were competing for who could make the most extravagant watch, it translated as a sixty-five-millimeter watch for Jay-Z via Tiret, with a tourbillon on the dial side *and* the movement side.

He does not take his work lightly. Every watch is like a child he has to nurture in every aspect. While some watchmakers focus heavily on the mechanics, Preziuso always pays attention to the aesthetics as well. After that, it is all about, in his words, "the three Ps, which are passion, patience, and perseverance. You need this when you spend twelve hours a day working in an area of a few square centimeters."

EARLY PASSIONS

He was born in 1957 in Geneva to Italian parents. His name, which translates as "precious," may well have predestined him to work in the luxury industry. But besides a natural gift, there was the circumstance of living in the Plainpalais-Jonction quarter in Geneva of the 1960s. It was home to many street-level workshops devoted to various crafts, including watchmaking. He would hang around and observe these men at work and receive various components and other scraps that would supplement a collection his father was giving him, too. He had found his calling and one day, with teenage boldness, he asked one of those watchmakers if he could work with him. "No, kid," the man answered crisply, "first you go to watchmaking school." The man was none other than Gérald Genta, the genius behind such legendary collections as Patek Philippe's Nautilus, Audemars Piguet's Royal Oak, IWC's Ingenieur, and many others.

AT THE WORKBENCH

Preziuso followed that advice and learned all the steps for making a good watch, from the cutting, filing, and polishing, to getting its heart to beat precisely. He graduated top of his class in 1978, in the midst of the quartz crisis, and was promptly picked up by Patek Philippe. "That was magic, like a second school," he remembers fondly of his time at the venerable *manufacture*. "I worked in the 'cardiology' department, on the balance, the escapement, and such. They were very punctilious." He also found the cabinets where they kept their spare parts and would dig up old movements that his supervisor would let him tinker with.

His next great learning experience was at the Antiquorum auction house, where he prepared and restored the watches and clocks being put on the block. "They would bring me shopping bags full of watches collected from around the world and tell me to get them ready for the end of the week." It was a hard deadline, but, he tells me, he was exposed to all sorts of movements and systems. One of the strangest tasks he had was having to rebuild a little moving bird on a clock. It no longer had any feathers, so he chased around Geneva from one bird-seller to the next collecting feathers from cages. "Everything worked perfectly," he recalls, "but the bird I had made looked scary!" Seeing this, his boss almost fired him. But the auction proceeded, the clock brought in a pretty penny, and the boss returned on the following Monday with a bottle of champagne. There was no more mention of a pink slip.

SETTING SAIL

A lively, imaginative mind like that of Antoine Preziuso was not made for employment, however, and he soon set up his own workshop in Geneva. It was 1981. He could now give birth to his own visions of watchmaking, while continuing to freelance as a restorer and developer of complications for major brands. Among his triumphs of that period was a minute repeater with a perpetual calendar for Breguet, which came with a pocket watch. It was considered the most complicated watch at the time.

Needless to say, he was also working on his own pieces, but watchmakers, ironically, need time, especially if their concepts go beyond just three-handers with a standard movement. After two years of hard research, in 1989, he came out with the Répétition à quart, a quarter-hour repeater armed by rotating the bezel. It was a system that he would return to again in 1991, with the Minute Repeater & Perpetual Calendar, a feat that earned him the coveted *Poinçon de Genève* (Geneva Seal). And seventeen years later, he used the arming mechanism on a square watch (the Mystery Minute Repeater), which looks especially impressive as the bezel, when turned, breaks up the angularity of the case.

1

2

3

4

1. The iconic Patek Philippe Nautilus by Gérald Genta, who told Preziuso to go to watchmaking school

2. Antoine Preziuso restored clocks and watches for the Antiquorum auction house.

3. The coveted Geneva Seal, one of the highest certifications

4. The Mystery Minute Repeater has a rotating bezel to arm the chimes.

Ernst Benz
PRECISION INSTRUMENTS FOR TIMEKEEPING
Ernst Benz
CHRONOLUNAR
AUTOMATIC
SWISS MADE
CHRONOLUNAR OFFICER
Blue Sunburst Dial with Raised Numerals, White Luminous and Polished Matching Hands. Polished Stainless Steel Case, Exhibition Back with Sapphire Glass.
Automatic Chronograph with Hours, Minutes and Seconds. Calender Indicating the Day, Date, Month and Phases of the Moon.
Available in 47mm & 44mm
GREAT CIRCLE
Ernst Benz
SWITZERLAND
www.ernstbenz.com

Like many genuine artists, Preziuso knows a winner when he sees one. Case in point: the entrance to the Harry Winston boutique on Fifth Avenue in New York, which, in his inner eye, became a tourbillon gyrating at the base of a tall arch sunken into the dial. He made one for himself and then pitched it to the company. They bit, and the watch then became a skeleton watch, giving it the depth it had in real life, with a hinged back cover opening onto a perpetual calendar. "So I got my foot in the stirrup there and it turned into a beautiful adventure," he says, mentioning in passing Harry Winston's successful Wall Street collection, which he also had a hand in. And soon other high-end brands were knocking at his door, like Bedat & Co. and the now-defunct de Grisogono. "They were looking for architectural watches with a clear visual effect, complicated but without excesses."

Leaving well-enough alone, however, is not a Preziuso trait. His Harry Winston watch gradually transformed into the cool-school Stardust with a diamond-studded bezel, and then the Pop Art and Pop Star, with bezels set with separated stones or diamonds that appear to blister up from the bezel. The effect is remarkable and not easy to achieve: "Each stone has to be set into the case without soldering, and all have to be at exactly the same level." The watch also came as the Tourbillon Météor Gibeon model, using sections of the Gibeon meteorite found in Namibia in 1836. It is a material he would keep returning to over the years.

FAMILY AFFAIR

In addition to founding a business, Preziuso also had a private life. May, his wife, was a paramedical nurse. She is part Swiss, part Syrian. No doubt, the Mediterranean spirit nourished their affinity to one another. "When I was going through watchmaking school, she would help me cram for the lessons," he recalls. They traveled the world together, and by osmosis she became infected by the watchmaking bug and started assisting where she could, doing those small jobs of putting order in parts. "She worked a lot faster than me," he says with a smile. "For me it's meditative work, I go tic-tac," a reference to that steady beating of the balance. May also handles the business end because, as she readily admits, "watchmakers do not sell themselves very well." She has a point, because they tend to think that their product will do the work for them.

And so they had two children, Florian, born in 1987 and Laura, born in 1992. May worked as a paramedic nurse and was outside the home, so the children were often exposed to the world of watch parts and a

2. and 3. Harry Winston's New York boutique (top) became Preziuso's watch (below) and a collaboration.

4. Meet the Preziusos, from left to right: May, Laura, Antoine and Florian.

5. The workbench, where Antoine Preziuso implements his visions

The Authentic Choice.
The Sustainable Choice.
The Attainable Choice.
ZENITH
EL PRIMERO
AUTOMATIC
SHOPWORN
shopworn.com | @theshopworn

1. and 2.: The B-Side can be turned around without taking off the watch.

3. The tools of Preziuso's trade and various collector's items

4. and 5. Sensual mechanics: Laura Preziuso's Tourbillon of Love

5. Laura Preziuso's Moonlight steeps a moon phase in mystery.

father passionate about assembling those parts into mechanical marvels. At one point, Florian wanted to become a motorcycle mechanic, but Antoine convinced him that it was hard work that left your hands black with oil. And soon Florian was in the same school of watchmaking as his father and graduated at the top of his class. They have worked on several projects together, notably the Tourbillon des Tourbillons, and a remarkable piece called the B-Side. It is encased in a mechanism that allows the wearer to turn the watch upside down without having to remove it from the bracelet.

As for Laura, by her early twenties, she was designing and making "mechanical jewelry" together with her father. The Moonlight, for example, is a pendant with a real moon phase. The Tourbillon of Love, for its part, features a tourbillon surrounded by a sprinkling of rubies in the shape of a heart, a romantic idea with a very sensual effect.

With the growing family and the uncertainties of urban life (his shop was burgled three times, the last time using an SUV as a battering ram), the couple decided to move into an old farmhouse near Geneva, which they renovated from top to bottom.

I visited on a chilly autumn day. The mountains around Geneva had just received their first snow toppings. The furnishings are a mix of modern, very comfortable—I spotted a couch that seemed to be an acre in size—made for conviviality. His own domain, his "temple of watchmaking," as he calls it, is upstairs in a small apartment under the eaves. There is enough space for a small kitchen, where he likes to entertain occasionally. He likes to cook. The act of cutting up the ingredients, putting in the spices, and so forth, make it sound very much the same as assembling a watch, "it all goes tic-tac." Like most watchmakers, Preziuso is a dyed-in-the-wool collector. Whenever traveling, he visits flea markets and junkshops, looking for anything related to watchmaking that he likes or could use. His work area is liberally decorated with clocks, pocket watches, wristwatches, wall clocks, posters. Old watches are treasures; for him, each movement he finds holds the potential for greatness.

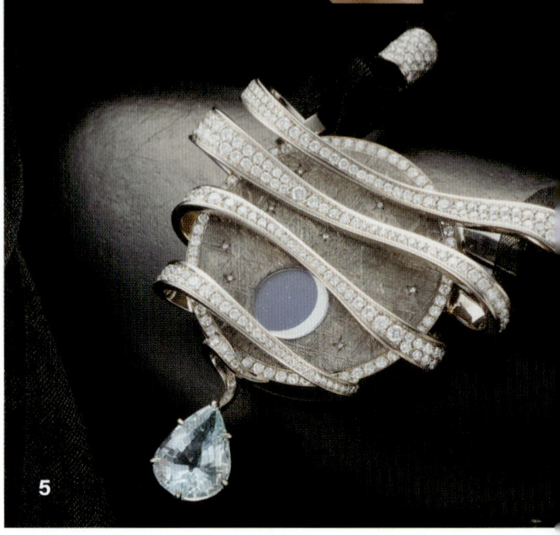

On the way up, I spot an oddity, a tableau of a manga figure. It is mostly in light colors, except for a big, prominent wristwatch on the figure's arm, the famous Tourbillon des Tourbillons. Preziuso has a very loyal fanbase in Japan, a country he visits often. He attributes this loyalty to the culture: "They know that each model has a story behind its creation, and that my personality, which reflects the passion of an independent watchmaker who works in the family. They respect the work of a master craftsman and cultivate the idea of the *sensei*."

His workbench is the inner sanctum of his space. It has a plunging view of the garden. He shows me his large collection of nineteenth-century pocket watches with hand-painted enamel dials advertising businesses, like an underwear store, or simply figures holding the subsidiary dials. "I don't buy watches with soldiers," he points out.

The workbench itself is the usual riot of tools, but I notice he is working on the one watch that is something of an obsession with him: the Tourbillon des Tourbillons. When I first met Preziuso, it was still in the trial-

A STRONG CHARACTER CAN BE
IDENTIFIED BY THE WRIST.
The Wempe Iron Walker GMT. At home on
Fifth Avenue and in all time zones.
WEMPE
IRON WALKER
Glashütte I/SA | self-winding GMT | stainless steel
certified chronometer | water-resistant to 30 bar | $4,440
700 FIFTH AVENUE & 55TH STREET • NEW YORK • 212.397.9000 • WEMPE.COM

and-error stage. He still didn't know if this "monster" with three tourbillons on a revolving plate would do what he thought it would. The idea germinated in 2004. As an inveterate maker of tourbillons, he realized that Breguet's invention was made for pocket watches, so it didn't really serve much purpose in a wristwatch. "Basically, if you flick your wrist every minute like this, you will get the same effect as a normal tourbillon." He moves his wrist about. "I wanted to find out if the three tourbillons would resonate," he tells me. "Because with everything will find its harmony and become more stable, more precise." And so he applied for the patents, a key in watchmaking, and launched the project. And he invited his son to join him, since Florian had already designed quite a few tourbillons for other brands. In fact, when I met Preziuso for the first time, he proudly spoke of his son's vital contribution: a triple-differential for the center of the watch to collect the energy from the three tourbillons.

The Tourbillon des Tourbillons took ten years to finish. When he finally assembled the watch, he immediately saw the little miracle: "One of the three tourbillons 'gives' its beat to a second one, and then the third one chimes in." Needless to say, this mechanical gem in a relatively small case (39.4 millimeters) picked up the Public Prize and the Innovation Prize at the 2015 Grand Prix d'Horlogerie in Geneva. For Antoine Preziuso, though, it was just the beginning. On his workbench I see that he has filled the ogee-shaped corners of the bridge holding the tourbillons with a metal that turned out to be from a meteorite. "These are asteroids," he tells me, "they traveled here from outer space!" Looking through his life's work, which is still ongoing, I realize that he has just described metaphorically, his own modus operandi: let the ideas, visions, snapshots come whenever, however, wherever, and turn them into ticking engines and artworks that do that hallowed job of counting off the seconds, minutes, and hours of our earthly existence.

1. and 2. A special collection of hand-painted, nineteenth-century enamel pocket watches

3. Preziuso's pride: a unique, decorated marine chronometer

4. From Japan with love: a manga figure wearing the Tourbillon des Tourbillons

5. Antoine and his son Florian accept the Innovation Prize at the 2015 GPHG.

6. and 7. Ten years of work went into the Tourbillon des Tourbillons.

LEAN MACHINES

BY MARTON RADKAI

When the marketing people say "Less is more," they often mean that what they have to offer might not be meeting any expectations of abundance. This bromidic little cliché does actually apply in many cases, however, and nowhere more than in the watchmaker's most challenging and purely aesthetic complication: skeletonization.

1. Surgically reducing a bridge

2. The Matterhorn appears in ArtyA's Son of Alps.

3. Claude Meylan's cutting reveals a skull.

You may have noticed that when you show your favorite watches to friends who are not really fans, they will look at the dial and give it a thumbs up or a non-committal nod. The afficionado, on the other hand, will turn it upside down to gaze at the movement. Indeed, the exhibition case back, a development of modern times, allows for a viewing of the best part of the watch, its engine. Not surprisingly, there are quite a few watchmakers and brands that have decided to go further and reveal as much of the movement as possible by skeletonizing some of their models.

Yvan Arpa, the bad boy of the watch world and, by many accounts, one of its genuine creative heads, calls watches a "black box" for many wearers. "They see the hands, but that's all," he told me over lunch. "When you skeletonize the watch, people understand a lot more about what's happening inside. They see the spring barrel tightening up and releasing its energy, they see the escapement, the gear wheels, and suddenly they have the feeling of really sharing in the world of watchmaking and understanding how these timepieces work." Arpa believes that a skeleton watch could well be one of the first luxury watches a person will buy.

2

ArtyA is notorious for producing a wide range of unusual watches, with lightning-blasted bezels and dials featuring bullets, electronic junk, cut up money, butterfly wings, pigments, tobacco leaves. Skeletonizing is not a major focus. Nevertheless, Arpa has produced numerous watches with bridges cut to look like the Matterhorn, or a snowflake, or a star.

BARE BONES

The term open-worked is often used as an alternative to skeletonizing. The difference can stump even some well-versed members of the community. Most people I have spoken to suggest its more a question of volume. Philippe Belais, on the other hand, owner of Claude Meylan (see page 120), a brand specializing in skeleton watches, believes it is a semantic point. "The term skeleton has negative connotations," he told me in an interview, "so 'open-worked' has become an alternative description."

At any rate, the term itself may sound strange to the newcomer, but it simply means removing as much material as possible from the movement and dial to reveal the mechanism. It is a fairly old technique, in fact, though it has gained favor in recent times. One could almost argue that the clocks in church towers, from which the watch movement originated, were often exposed because they were hidden up in the belfries and it made them easier to repair and adjust. Desk clocks, too, often reveal their mechanisms. For pocket watches, and later wristwatches, the dial was the most important visual magnet, since it was used not only to tell time but in some cases to serve as a backdrop for artwork or special decorations.

THE LEADER

Some brands, like the abovementioned Claude Meylan, have made skeletonizing one of their main techniques. If there is any name spoken on whispers whenever skeletonizing is discussed, however, it is Armin Strom, who, for decades, patiently worked the fretsaw and very fine files with enormous skill, to produce genuine works of art. Other brands even tapped him to transform their models since he had more or less cornered the market. Legend has it that he began skeletonizing while waiting for customers to buy his watches, and soon found that they had a lot of appeal.

I met Strom at my first Baselworld, a stocky man with a genial smile under a dense chevron moustache. He explained how he does his work, noting that it is not like cutting out cookies. You can't just remove material from metal parts and think the job has been finished. Doing so will change the tensile strength of the metal, which can jeopardize the functioning of the watch. And here is the clincher: the watchmaker will only find out once the parts have been assembled. In other words, skeletonization requires deep knowledge of the materials being cut away and lots of testing.

Armin Strom's own watches had a Rococo quality about them. Every bridge or remaining sections of the mainplate were well chamfered and polished, decoration and engraving were stunning and perhaps a little too effusive for some tastes. A younger generation bought the company in 2009, verticalized the business by creating in-house movements, and proceeded to modernize the aesthetics. "The opportunity to develop our watches ourselves has opened new ways for us to produce our skeleton watches," says Claude Greisler, co-founder of Armin Strom (see page 64) and master watchmaker at the company. "We now take the shapes of the individual components into consideration during the design."

ENGINEERING THE LOOK

Maintaining the integrity of the original movement is one of the most important goals of the skeletonizer. Alexander Klingbeil, CEO of Blaken, a German customization specialist, had his baptism of fire when a customer came to the company requesting them to redo his Rolex Daytona, including skeletonizing. The busy watchmakers at Blaken took apart the movement piece by piece, determined what they would be doing using software, and then started experimenting on real movements in 3D. "We wanted a special 'language' for this movement, so we did it with a lot of straight, orderly lines," he told me, "but what we found out was that Rolex really does manufacture the best movements, and when customizing them, we had to make sure we respected that. The final product had to be

1. Transparent table clocks as kinetic art (here MB& Orb)

2. Claude Meylan's skeletonization connects the m important dots.

3., 4., 5., 6. Armin Strom at work; the evolution of th brand's skeletons, from Baroqu-ish to clear lines

7. and 8. Blaken "improves" a Rolex with skeletoniz and other techniques.

1

2

1., 2., 3. From a motorcycle wheel rim to the Excalibur with the iconic bridge

4., 5., 6., 7. Watchmaker and artist Stefan Kudoke hand-skeletonizes and decorates a movement.

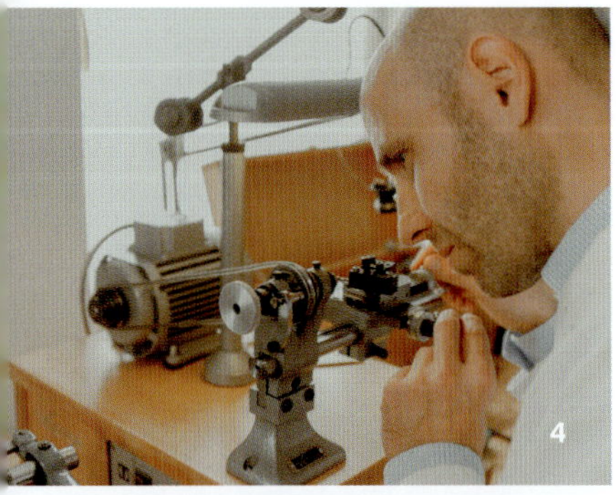

just as precise and stable." Once they had their design, they tried out their concept on real 4130s to see how it would hold up. All in all, the job took two years, but the customer was happy.

The staff at Roger Dubuis also faced the integrity issue, especially since their watches are ultra-technical and often come with tourbillons and other modules that strain the bridges. Gregory Bruttin, product strategy director at Roger Dubuis and known for large, ultra-technical watches, described how the idea of skeletonizing came about at the Geneva-based brand. The watches produced at Roger Dubuis were being awarded the coveted *Poinçon de Genève*, the Geneva Seal, which applies not only to the mechanics, but also the finishing (*habillage*). The designers started questioning why one would cover up such terrific movements with a dial. "We had a lot of discussions with Roger Dubuis about skeletonization," Bruttin told me. "His idea was to create a perfect aesthetic whole, because basically we were constrained by the technical work, we had to revolve around the elements of the movement. His idea was to do the technical work and the aesthetic work in parallel. So we will have to move certain elements around to fit the design."

The result was the striking, star-shaped bridges that grip the movement and give Roger Dubuis watches their characteristic visual vigor. However, there is no way to reinforce the brass used for these bridges, Bruttin told me, so they had to search for technological alloys that delivered greater rigidity. "The challenge was above all to decorate these materials in the same way as the brass in order to have the most homogeneous and perfect result possible."

DEVILISH DETAILS

Beyond surgically removing material from the plates, bridges, or dials, skeletonization is often performed on the gearwheels and hands. Each of these parts must then be subjected to careful finishing, since they are now all visible—parts inside regular watches are also finished, but they are not visible. For both artisan and buyer, there is still more to consider. The dial, for example. Removing it means that hands will often be competing for supremacy with all the other thinned out metal parts, yet the wearer still needs to be able to read the time. This is where some skeleton watches do go overboard, though the genuine lover of mechanics will usually not mind.

A CANVAS FOR THE ARTIST

Most skeleton watches aim to reveal the mechanism. Others go a step further and use the emptied case as a backdrop for miniature sculptures. One of the leading lights of this technique is Stefan Kudoke. A loner

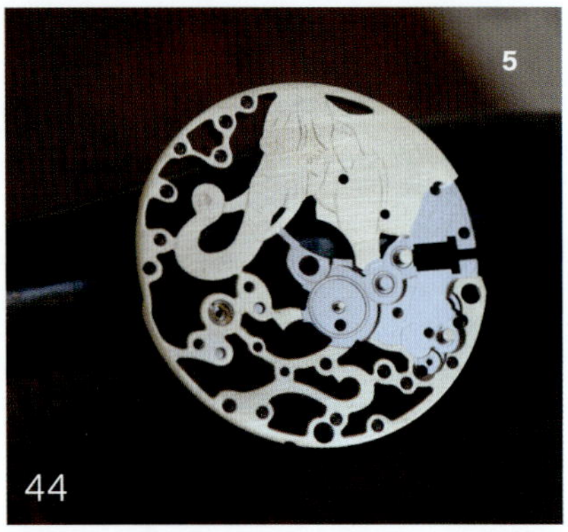

MON 1
AUTOMATIC
200M
MON 1
AUTOMATIC
200M

out on Germany's eastern border with Poland, he is both an engraving artist as well as a watchmaker. His first encounter with the art of skeletonizing was at Glashütte Original. He was asked to assemble a particularly beautiful limited edition of skeleton watches, an activity that was not part of the training curriculum. "I found the subject exciting, because you could work the parts in such an artistic and filigree manner," he said in an interview. "The inside of the movement is then exposed and you can watch the individual components at work. I continued to work with this particular craft and to push for perfection."

In the twenty-four years since that discovery, Kudoke has refined his technique and developed a style blending sure-fingeredness, imagination, and a keen sense of humor with a touch of romanticism. First and foremost, skeletonizing is a technical process, which can also be done by machines and is also operated in this way by most manufacturers of skeleton watches. The high school is then skeletonizing by hand with a small fretsaw and many filigree files. In the process, the actual function and stability of the movement must not be compromised. You must know exactly how the forces act in the movement and where to take material from the movement parts. Combining that with creativity and special motives lets unique works of art develop. These are then also not to be compared with the machine skeleton clocks from mass production.

THE FULL MONTY

The French have a saying: "Impossible is not French!" This bit of Gallic boasting is debatable, generally, but when it comes to watchmakers there are truly no bounds to their envelope pushing. ArtyA has a number of very fine skeleton watches, with bridges shaped like snowflakes, edelweiss flowers, even the Matterhorn. "It's kind of fun," Yvan Arpa says, "because you can take the base movement, you have your screws, pinions, your wheels, and the idea is to remove material as elegantly as possible around these parts. It's like those games where you had to connect the dots." But he didn't stop there. The charm of ArtyA's recent Purity collection is that it takes a whole movement, with two barrel springs and a flying tourbillon, and encases it in sapphire crystal. The circular bridge delicately holding the movement suggests some sort of religious artifact. To top it off, Arpa went out of his way to dig up a product called NanoSapphire, which is extra hard and changes color when in daylight or artificial light. It is called the Chameleon, of course.

There is another step before making the watch disappear altogether, and that is the mystérieuse idea, which might be off-topic, but should be mentioned nonetheless. There is Thomas Prescher's Mysterious Automatic Double Axis Tourbillon, which has been featured a few times in this book. Then there is Cartier, which has gone to great lengths to explore the possibilities of this style. The idea is no longer to cut out material, but rather to park the mechanism of the watch somewhere in the case and have time revealed on invisible sapphire discs or in midair, as it were. In the Prescher timepiece, the engine is in the frame, while the time, date, and moon phase are on rollers. The double-axis tourbillon gyrates in the middle of nowhere, as if by magic. As for Cartier, in 2022 it presented a new and clever solution for this magic trick—the origins of which back to the nineteenth century and the magician Houdin, later known as Houdini. The entire mechanism is tucked into a delicately skeletonized rotor/oscillating mass. It is another brilliant way to watch the time pass, distracted by the animation, so you do not have to count the hours, which is exactly what a luxurious watch should do, namely focus on the beauty, forget the passage of time.

1

2

3

1. Total exposure of the movement with ArtyA'a Purity

2. Cartier's Masse Mystérieuse turns the movement into a rotor.

3. Prescher's Double Axis Tourbillon disappears the movement into the frame.

WILLIAM
HENRY
WILLIAM HENRY
WILLIAMHENRY.COM

SKELETON SAMPLE

BY MARTON RADKAI

When purchasing a skeleton watch, you should first check your personal "like" button. Then look at a few details. Is the finishing well-done? How is the coating on the remaining bridges? Remember that enamel, for example, is very finicky. Check all the chamfering and beveling. Can you read the time properly, or is that not your primary purpose? You should carry around a good loupe, so you can check any purchases carefully, be that in the store or at the flea market. Never let yourself be rushed: buying a watch takes time. What follows is a small selection of skeleton watches that might help you hone your appreciation of this special complication.

The inspiration for the Roger Dubuis Excalibur was originally a motorcycle wheel rim. Continuous stylizing and integration of the movement to make everything fit gives the model a particularly dynamic look, with the garish star-shaped bridge.

The Amadeo Amadeo Skeleton Tourbillon by Bovet is made to show the company's extreme skill in decoration, which includes skeletonizing, and it serves as a kind of backdrop for the tourbillon anchoring the watch face.

Skeletons mean bones, and Kudoke decided to create the Real Skeleton watch with rhodium-plated bone hands, and bones, some in gold, serving as bridges. The skull has diamond eyes. Everything is hand-crafted.

The emptiness of Hysek's new Skeleton Tourbillon reveals a fairly simple movement (barring the tourbillon, of course). Winding up the watch will set the flange, which is studded with black diamonds, in motion.

Classic skeletonizing of the Valjoux 88 by a small Swiss company Berney located in L'Abbaye, Switzerland, in the Joux Valley.

The skeletonizing on the Waltz No. 1 by Carl Suchy & Söhne is special. "The discreet skeletonizing of the dial recalls the inspiration for the watch: Viennese Modernism led by Alfred Loos in the early twentieth century," says Robert Punkenhofer, brand CEO. "The watch's skeletonized seconds disk turning creates a hypnotic animation on the dial."

An oddity because Corum's Golden Bridge is not really a skeleton watch. However, due to the unique, narrow linear movement, the watch face can remain empty or be filled with other elements.

For H. Moser & Cie, skeletonizing the Pioneer Cylindrical Skeleton was the best way to show off the depth of the movement and especially the cylindrical hairspring on the tourbillon, an occasional on ancient marine clocks.

The watch designed by Pia de Chefdebien is one of the fine so-called ladies' watches on the market. The idea is to break the stereotype that women do not see the aesthetics of engineering. Claude Meylan proves them wrong.

Like Roger Dubuis's Excalibur, the movement of Ulysse Nardin's Blast is essentially purpose-built to be a skeleton.

ACCUTRON

Well before quartz regulars blew up the watch market, engineers were tinkering with the idea of building an electric watch. There is some debate as to who succeeded first, but it was probably the Elgin 725, a collaboration with the French company Lip, that was the first. It had a traditional mechanical movement with a button cell battery-run mechanism. It failed to thrill the market, however. But it did get another company, Bulova Watch Company, interested in the technology. Over the next few years, with the aid of a Swiss engineer named Max Hetzel, the company came up with a clever system using a tiny 360 Hertz tuning fork and a transistor. The Accutron, a combination of the terms accurate and electronic, was unveiled in 1960 as the world's first fully electronic watch. It was an instant success and even attracted NASA, among others.

Today, Accutron has been resurrected as a separate brand, and with its iconic watch. The company's design and engineering team based in Tokyo reworked the engine and the look to create a brand-new proprietary electrostatic energy movement. It is run by twin turbines that rotate very fast between two electrodes using the wearer's movements. The energy, stored in an accumulator, powers two motors. One drives the sweep second hand, and a step motor powers the hour and minute hands. Both motors are synchronized through integrated circuits to provide accuracy to +/- 5 seconds a month.

Accutron decided to steer close to the original when it comes to design. Fans will easily recognize the cherished dial-less model with its green accents. As for the Spaceview, it was in its time a landmark achievement, with its case stripped down to expose the unique tuning fork movement. And to prove that it can also make fine mechanical watches as well, the company has come out with a number of models based on Sellita calibers.

Accutron c/o Citizen Watch America
Empire State Building
350 Fifth Avenue, 29th Floor
New York, NY 10118

Website:
https://www.accutronwatch.com/

Founded:
1960 (relaunched in 2020)

Distribution:
Accutron
customercare@accutronwatch.com
866-419-84-63

Most important collections/price range:
Spaceview 2020 and Accutron DNA / $3,300 to $5,000; Legacy / $1,290 to $1,550 / Astronaut $3,500

Spaceview 2020 x La Palina Luxury Set

Reference number: 2ES6A007
Movement: Accutron caliber NS30; quartz resonator with dual stepper motor and electrostatic drive system for the hands; ø 36 mm, height 6.48 mm; 28 jewels
Functions: hours, minutes, sweep seconds
Case: stainless steel, ø 43.5 mm, height 15.9 mm; sapphire crystal; water resistant to 5 atm
Band: reptile skin, double folding clasp
Remarks: the set includes a humidor with ten Accutron blend cigars
Price: $5,000; limited edition of 222 pieces

Spaceview 2020

Reference number: 2ES6A005
Movement: Accutron caliber NS30; quartz resonator with dual stepper motor and electrostatic drive system for the hands; ø 36 mm, height 6.48 mm; 28 jewels
Functions: hours, minutes, sweep seconds
Case: stainless steel, ø 43.5 mm, height 15.9 mm; sapphire crystal; water resistant to 5 atm
Band: calfskin, double folding clasp
Price: $3,450

Spaceview 2020

Reference number: 2ES6A006
Movement: Accutron caliber NS30; quartz resonator with dual stepper motor and electrostatic drive system for the hands; ø 36 mm, height 6.48 mm; 28 jewels
Functions: hours, minutes, sweep seconds
Case: stainless steel, ø 43.5 mm, height 15.9 mm; sapphire crystal; water resistant to 5 atm
Band: stainless steel, double folding clasp
Price: $3,850

Accutron DNA

Reference number: 2ES8A004
Movement: Accutron caliber NS30; quartz resonator with dual stepper motor and electrostatic drive system for the hands; ø 36 mm, height 6.48 mm; 28 jewels
Functions: hours, minutes, sweep seconds
Case: stainless steel, ø 45.1 mm, height 15.6 mm; sapphire crystal; water resistant to 5 atm
Band: rubber strap, double folding clasp
Price: $3,300

Accutron DNA

Reference number: 2ES8A001
Movement: Accutron caliber NS30; quartz resonator with dual stepper motor and electrostatic drive system for the hands; ø 36 mm, height 6.48 mm; 28 jewels
Functions: hours, minutes, sweep seconds
Case: stainless steel, ø 45.1 mm, height 15.6 mm; sapphire crystal; water resistant to 5 atm
Band: rubber strap, double folding clasp
Price: $3,300

Accutron Astronaut

Reference number: 2SW8A002
Movement: automatic, Sellita Caliber SW330, ø 26.20 mm, height 4.10 mm; 25 jewels; 28,800 vph; 42-hour power reserve
Functions: hours, minutes, sweep seconds; second time zone with GMT hand
Case: stainless steel, ø 34 mm, height 12.5 mm; railroad case design and crown placement at 4 o'clock; sapphire crystal; transparent case back; water-resistant to 3 atm
Band: stainless steel, double folding clasp
Remarks: the Astronaut "T" design first launched in 1968 features a distinctive day/night bezel.
Price: $3,500; limited to 300 numbered pieces

Accutron Legacy

Reference number: 2SW6B001RD
Movement: automatic, Sellita Caliber SW200-1, ø 25.60 mm, height 4.6 mm; 26 jewels; 28,800 vph; 42-hour power reserve
Functions: hours, minutes, seconds, date
Case: stainless steel, ø 34 mm, height 12.5 mm; railroad case design and crown placement at 4 o'clock; sapphire crystal; transparent case back; water-resistant to 3 atm
Band: reptile skin, double folding clasp
Remarks: the "R.R.-0" design first launched in 1970 with a 0 at the 12-hour mark to meet Canadian Railroad specs, and a red second hand for accurate monitoring
Price: $1,290; limited to 600 numbered pieces

Accutron Legacy

Reference number: 2SW6A002GN
Movement: automatic, Sellita Caliber SW200-1, ø 25.60 mm, height 4.6 mm; 26 jewels; 28,800 vph; 42-hour power reserve
Functions: hours, minutes, seconds
Case: stainless steel, ø 34 mm, height 12.6 mm; railroad case design and crown placement at 4 o'clock; sapphire crystal; transparent case back; water-resistant to 3 atm
Band: reptile skin, double folding clasp
Remarks: 565 of 600 pieces known as the Football Cross Hatch watch in 1966
Price: $1,390; limited to 600 numbered pieces

Accutron Legacy

Reference number: 2SW7A001OR
Movement: automatic, Sellita Caliber SW200-1, ø 25.60 mm, height 4.6 mm; 26 jewels; 28,800 vph; 42-hour power reserve
Functions: hours, minutes, sweep seconds
Case: stainless steel with gold PVD, ø 34 mm, height 12.6m; crown placement at 4 o'clock; sapphire crystal; transparent case back; water-resistant to 3 atm
Band: calfskin, double folding clasp
Remarks: replicate of the 1960s "521" model
Price: $1,450; limited to 600 numbered pieces

A. LANGE & SÖHNE

A. Lange & Söhne exemplifies the steady, careful, and effective way Germans tend to develop their businesses, in particular family-run ones. Walter Lange, who died in January 2017, actually re-registered the brand A. Lange & Söhne in its old hometown of Glashütte. He did so on December 7, 1990, on the exact day 145 years after the firm was originally founded by his great-grandfather, Ferdinand Adolph Lange. Ferdinand Adolph had originally launched the company to provide work to the local population. And shortly after German reunification in 1990, that is exactly what Glashütte needed again.

Lange is known for its unique aesthetic and mechanical codes, which are at the heart of the Glashütte tradition. There is the three-quarter plate made of German silver (an alloy that looks like silver but is harder and more durable) and or the hand-engraved balance cock. The company's growing inventory of outstanding calibers number sixty-nine now and have all been developed and manufactured in-house. They are decorated and assembled by hand with the fine adjustment done in five positions. Patented innovations include the Lange large date, the automatic "zero reset" for the second hand, and the three different patented constant force escapements, notably one for the Lange 31, whose mainspring provides a power reserve of 744 hours. Materials for the cases have grown as well and now include platinum, white, pink, yellow and "honey" gold, stainless steel, and titanium.

Lange's products, which are designed with great care, always surprise. The entry-level family is the classic, visually balanced, three-hand Saxonia, while the Lange 1, introduced in 1994, is considered the collection flagship. In 2019, the company created a stir among watch fans when the Odysseus, with a custom automatic movement and weekday and date display, staked a claim in the sports watch club. A wealth of novelties appeared in 2020, notably several inside "honey gold" cases, including a Zeitwerk with a minute repeater. And the Odysseus's stainless-steel model has now been joined by a titanium version, as well as a white gold model with an integrated leather or rubber strap, taking daily sports routine to the high end, as it were.

Lange Uhren GmbH
Ferdinand-A.-Lange-Platz 1
D-01768 Glashütte
Germany

Tel.:
+49-35053-44-0

E-mail:
info@lange-soehne.com

Website:
www.alange-soehne.com

Founded:
1990

Number of employees:
750 employees, almost half of whom are watchmakers

U.S. distributor:
A. Lange & Söhne
645 Fifth Avenue
New York, NY 10022
800-408-8147

Most important collections/price range:
Lange 1 / $40,300 to $359,400; Saxonia / $19,700 to $287,800; 1815 / $27,300 to $253,500; Richard Lange / $36,800 to $247,800; Zeitwerk / $89,200 to $141,300; Odysseus / $34,900 to $56,500

Odysseus

Reference number: 363.117
Movement: automatic, Lange Caliber L155.1 Datomatic; ø 32.9 mm, height 6.2 mm; 31 jewels; 28,800 vph; hand-engraved balance cock, 1 screw-mounted gold chaton, swan-neck fine adjustment; parts finished and assembled by hand; 50-hour power reserve
Functions: hours, minutes, subsidiary seconds; large date, weekday
Case: titanium, ø 40.5 mm, height 11.1 mm; sapphire crystal; transparent case back; water-resistant to 12 atm
Band: titanium, folding clasp
Price: $56,500; limited to 250 pieces (boutique edition)
Variations: In stainless steel ($34,900)

Odysseus

Reference number: 363.038
Movement: automatic, Lange Caliber L155.1 Datomatic; ø 32.9 mm, height 6.2 mm; 31 jewels; 28,800 vph; hand-engraved balance cock, 1 screw-mounted gold chaton, swan-neck fine adjustment; parts finished and assembled by hand; 50-hour power reserve
Functions: hours, minutes, subsidiary seconds; large date, weekday
Case: white gold, ø 40.5 mm, height 11.1 mm; sapphire crystal; transparent case back; water-resistant to 12 atm
Band: calf leather, buckle
Price: $47,400
Variations: with rubber strap ($47,400)

Lange 1

Reference: 191.039
Movement: manually wound, Lange Caliber L121.3; ø 30.6 mm, height 5.7 mm; 47 jewels; 21,600 vph; 8 screw-mounted gold chatons, swan-neck fine adjustment, hand-engraved balance cock, parts finished and assembled by hand; 72-hour power reserve
Functions: hours, minutes, subsidiary seconds; power reserve indicator; large date
Case: white gold, ø 38.5 mm, height 9.8 mm; sapphire crystal; transparent case back; water-resistant to 3 atm
Band: reptile skin, buckle
Price: $40,300
Variations: in pink gold ($40,300); platinum ($53,000)

Grand Lange 1

Reference number: 137.033
Movement: manually wound, Lange Caliber L095.1; ø 34.1 mm, height 4.7 mm; 42 jewels; 21,600 vph; 7 screw-mounted gold chatons, swan-neck fine adjustment, hand-engraved balance cock, parts finished and assembled by hand; 72-hour power reserve
Functions: hours, minutes, subsidiary seconds; power reserve indicator; large date
Case: pink gold, ø 41 mm, height 8.2 mm; sapphire crystal; transparent case back; water-resistant to 3 atm
Band: reptile skin, buckle
Price: $48,100
Variations: in white gold ($48,100)

Little Lange 1 Moon Phase

Reference number: 182.086
Movement: manually wound, Lange Caliber L121.2; ø 30.6 mm, height 6 mm; 44 jewels; 21,600 vph; 8 screw-mounted gold chatons, swan-neck fine adjustment, hand-engraved balance cock, parts finished and assembled by hand; 72-hour power reserve
Functions: hours, minutes, subsidiary seconds; power reserve indication, large date, moon phase
Case: white gold, ø 36.8 mm, height 9.5 mm; sapphire crystal; transparent case back; water-resistant to 3 atm
Band: reptile skin, buckle
Remarks: dial covered in dark blue aventurine
Price: $49,400
Variations: with diamond bezel ($62,300)

Lange 1 Time Zone

Reference number: 136.029
Movement: manually wound, Lange Caliber 141.1; ø 34.1 mm, height 6.7 mm; 38 jewels; 21,600 vph; 3 screw-mounted gold chatons; parts finished and assembled by hand; 38-hour power reserve
Functions: hours, minutes, subsidiary seconds; additional 12-hour display (second time zone) day/night indication (double), power reserve indicator, daylight savings indication; large date
Case: white gold, ø 41.9 mm, height 10.9 mm; sapphire crystal; transparent case back; water-resistant to 3 atm
Band: reptile skin, buckle
Price: $57,800
Variation: in pink gold ($57,800)

Lange 1 Perpetual Calendar

Reference number: 345.033
Movement: automatic, Lange Caliber L021.3; ø 35.8 mm, height 8.8 mm; 63 jewels; 21,600 vph; off-center balance, 5 screw-mounted gold chatons, hand-engraved balance cock, gold rotor with platinum oscillating mass; 50-hour power reserve
Functions: hours, minutes, subsidiary seconds; day/night indication; perpetual calendar with large date, weekday, month, moon phase, leap year
Case: pink gold, ø 41.9 mm, height 12.1 mm; sapphire crystal; transparent case back; water-resistant to 3 atm
Band: reptile skin, buckle
Price: $113,400
Variations: white gold with pink gold dial ($116,000), limited to 150 pieces

Saxonia Thin

Reference number: 205.086
Movement: manually wound, Lange Caliber L093.1; ø 28 mm, height 2.9 mm; 21 jewels; 21,600 vph; screw balance, swan-neck fine adjustment, hand-engraved balance cock, 3 gold chatons; 72-hour power reserve
Functions: hours, minutes
Case: white gold, ø 39 mm, height 6.2 mm; sapphire crystal; transparent case back
Band: reptile skin, buckle
Remarks: copper-blue aventurine dial
Price: $26,400
Variations: in pink or white gold in a 37-millimeter case with silver-colored dial ($21,200)

Saxonia Outsize Date

Reference number: 381.032
Movement: automatic; Lange Caliber L086.8; ø 30.4 mm, height 5.2 mm; 40 jewels; 21,600 vph; hand-engraved balance cock, screw balance, swan-neck fine adjustment; 72-hour power reserve
Functions: hours, minutes, subsidiary seconds; large date
Case: pink gold, ø 38.5 mm, height 9.6 mm; sapphire crystal; transparent case back; water-resistant to 3 atm
Band: reptile skin, buckle
Price: $30,800
Variations: white gold ($30,800); with black dial

Saxonia Moon Phase

Reference number: 384.026
Movement: automatic, Lange Caliber L086.5; ø 30.4 mm, height 5.2 mm; 40 jewels; 21,600 vph; hand-engraved balance cock, screw balance, swan-neck fine adjustment; 72-hour power reserve
Functions: hours, minutes, subsidiary seconds; large date, moon phase
Case: white gold, ø 40 mm, height 9.8 mm; sapphire crystal; transparent case back; water-resistant to 3 atm
Band: reptile skin
Price: $34,900
Variations: in pink gold ($34,900)

Datograph Up/Down

Reference number: 405.035
Movement: manually wound, Lange Caliber L951.7; ø 30.6 mm, height 8.1 mm; 46 jewels; 18,000 vph; 4 screw-mounted gold chatons, swan-neck fine adjustment, hand-engraved balance cock; 60-hour power reserve
Functions: hours, minutes, subsidiary seconds; power reserve indicator; flyback chronograph with precisely jumping minute counter; large date
Case: platinum, ø 41 mm, height 13.4 mm; sapphire crystal; transparent case back; water-resistant to 3 atm
Band: reptile skin, buckle
Price: $110,300
Variations: in pink gold ($94,400)

Datograph Perpetual Tourbillon

Reference number: 410.038
Movement: manually wound, Lange Caliber L952.1; ø 32 mm, height 8 mm; 45 jewels; 18,000 vph; off-center balance; in-house balance spring, column wheel control of the chronograph functions; 4 screw-mounted gold chatons, 36-hour power reserve
Functions: hours, minutes, subsidiary seconds; day/night indicator; flyback chronograph with precisely jumping minute counter; perpetual calendar with large date, weekday, months moon phase, leap year
Case: white gold, ø 41 mm, height 13.5 mm; sapphire crystal; transparent case back; water-resistant to 3 atm
Band: reptile skin, buckle
Price: $158,900

Zeitwerk Date

Reference number: 148.038
Movement: manually wound, Lange Caliber L043.8; ø 37 mm, height 8.9 mm; 70 jewels; 18,000 vph; 2 screw-mounted gold chatons, constant force mechanism (remontoir), hand-engraved balance cock; 72-hour power reserve
Functions: hours and minutes (digital, jumping), subsidiary seconds; power reserve indicator; date
Case: white gold, ø 44.2 mm, height 12.3 mm; sapphire crystal; transparent case back; water-resistant to 3 atm
Band: reptile skin, buckle
Price: $115,000

Zeitwerk Striking Time

Reference number: 145.032
Movement: manually wound, Lange Caliber L043.2; ø 36 mm, height 10 mm; 78 jewels; 18,000 vph; 2 screw-mounted gold chatons, constant force mechanism (remontoir), hand-engraved balance cock, acoustic signal at the top of the hour and every quarter hour; 36-hour power reserve
Functions: hours and minutes (digital, jumping), subsidiary seconds; power reserve indicator
Case: pink gold, ø 44.2 mm, height 13.1 mm; sapphire crystal; transparent case back; water-resistant to 3 atm
Band: reptile skin, folding clasp
Price: $141,300
Variations: in white gold ($141,300)

1815 Up/Down

Reference number: 234.032
Movement: manually wound, Lange Caliber L051.2; ø 30.6 mm, height 4.6 mm; 29 jewels; 21,600 vph; 7 screw-mounted gold chatons, three-quarter plate, screw balance, hand-engraved balance cock, parts finished and assembled by hand; 55-hour power reserve
Functions: hours, minutes, subsidiary seconds; power reserve indicator
Case: pink gold, ø 39 mm, height 8.7 mm; sapphire crystal; transparent case back; water-resistant to 3 atm
Band: reptile skin, buckle
Price: $31,800
Variations: white gold ($31,800)

1815 Annual Calendar

Reference number: 238.032
Movement: manually wound, Lange Caliber L051.3; ø 30.6 mm, height 5.7 mm; 26 jewels; 21,600 vph; 3 screw-mounted gold chatons, hand-engraved balance cock, parts finished and assembled by hand; 72-hour power reserve
Functions: hours, minutes, subsidiary seconds; annual calendar with date, weekday, month, moon phase
Case: pink gold, ø 40 mm, height 10.1 mm; sapphire crystal; transparent case back; water-resistant to 3 atm
Band: reptile skin, buckle
Price: $48,000
Variations: white gold ($48,000)

1815 Chronograph

Reference number: 414.028
Movement: manually wound, Lange Caliber L951.5; ø 30.6 mm, height 6.1 mm; 34 jewels; 21,600 vph; 4 screw-mounted gold chatons, hand-engraved balance cock, parts finished and assembled by hand; 60-hour power reserve
Functions: hours, minutes, subsidiary seconds; flyback chronograph
Case: white gold, ø 39.5 mm, height 11 mm; sapphire crystal; transparent case back; water-resistant to 3 atm
Band: reptile skin, buckle
Price: $67,800
Variations: in pink gold ($67,800), white gold "boutique exclusive"

1815 Rattrapante Perpetual Calendar

Reference number: 421.025
Movement: manually wound, Lange Caliber L101.1; ø 32.6 mm, height 9.1 mm; 43 jewels; 21,600 vph; 4 screw-mounted gold chatons; hand-engraved balance cock, parts finished and assembled by hand; 42-hour power reserve
Functions: hours, minutes, subsidiary seconds; power reserve indicator; split-seconds chronograph; perpetual calendar with date, weekday, months moon phase, leap year
Case: platinum, ø 41.9 mm, height 14.7 mm; sapphire crystal; transparent case back; water-resistant to 3 atm
Band: reptile skin, folding clasp
Price: $253,500

Richard Lange

Reference number: 232.032
Movement: manually wound, Lange Caliber L041.2; ø 30.6 mm, height 6 mm; 26 jewels; 21,600 vph; hand-engraved balance cock, 2 screw-mounted gold chatons, parts finished and assembled by hand; in-house manufactured balance spring with a patented anchoring clip; 38-hour power reserve
Functions: hours, minutes, sweep seconds
Case: pink gold, ø 40.5 mm, height 10.5 mm; sapphire crystal; transparent case back; water-resistant to 3 atm
Band: reptile skin, buckle
Price: $36,800
Variations: In white gold (boutique edition, $36,800)

Richard Lange Minute Repeater

Reference number: 606.079
Movement: manually wound, Lange Caliber L122.1; ø 30 mm, height 5.4 mm; 40 jewels; 21,600 vph; 4 screw-mounted gold chatons, hand-engraved balance cock, parts finished and assembled by hand; 72-hour power reserve
Functions: hours, minutes, subsidiary seconds; minute Repeater
Case: platinum, ø 39 mm, height 9.7 mm; sapphire crystal; transparent case back; water-resistant to 2 atm
Band: reptile skin, folding clasp
Price: on request; limited to 50 pieces (boutique edition)

Richard Lange Jumping Seconds

Reference number: 252.029
Movement: manually wound, Lange Caliber L094.1; ø 33.6 mm, height 6 mm; 50 jewels; 21,600 vph; zero-reset mechanism, constant force escapement (remontoir); 42-hour power reserve
Functions: off-center hours and minutes, large seconds (jumping); winding reminder
Case: white gold, ø 39.9 mm, height 10.6 mm; sapphire crystal; transparent case back; water-resistant to 3 atm
Band: reptile skin, buckle
Price: $88,600
Variations: pink gold with silver-colored dial, limited to 100 pieces ($88,300); platinum ($84,200)

Caliber L155.1 Datomatic

Automatic; swan-neck fine adjustment; second stop mechanism, platinum oscillating mass; single spring barrel; 50-hour power reserve
Functions: hours, minutes, subsidiary seconds; date, weekday
Diameter: 32.9 mm
Height: 6.2 mm
Jewels: 31, including a screw-mounted gold chaton
Balance: glucydur with regulating screws
Frequency: 28,800 vph
Balance spring: made in-house
Remarks: components hand-finished and -assembled; 312 parts

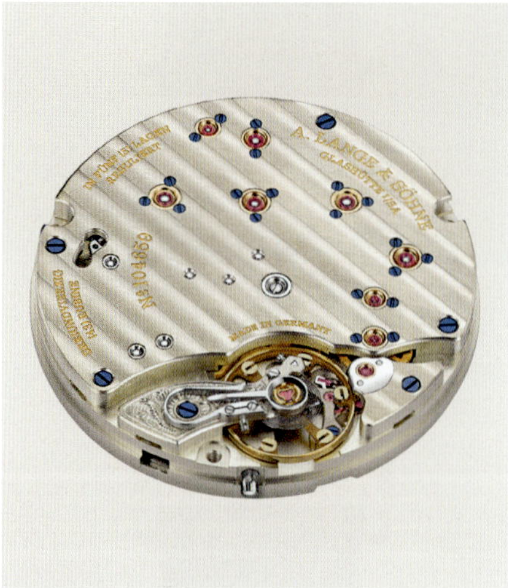

Caliber L121.1

Manually wound; stop-seconds mechanism, 8 screw-mounted gold chatons, swan-neck fine adjustment; double spring barrel; 72-hour power reserve
Functions: hours, minutes, subsidiary seconds; power reserve indicator; large date
Diameter: 30.6 mm
Height: 5.7 mm
Jewels: 43
Balance: glucydur with eccentric adjustment cams
Frequency: 21,600 vph
Balance spring: made in-house
Shock protection: Kif
Remarks: plates and bridges of untreated German silver, decorated and assembled mostly by hand, hand-engraved balance cock

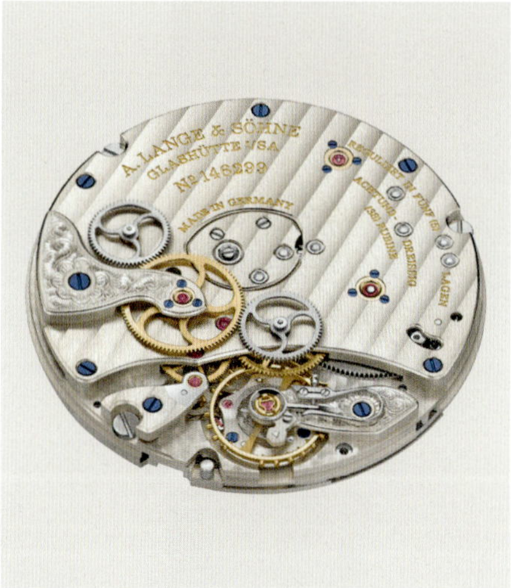

Caliber L141.1

Manually wound; stop-seconds mechanism, 3 screw-mounted gold chatons, swan-neck fine adjustment; single spring barrel; 38-hour power reserve
Functions: hours, minutes, subsidiary seconds; 2nd time zone, 2 day/night indicators, power reserve indicator, daylight saving time
Diameter: 34.1 mm
Height: 6.7 mm
Jewels: 38
Balance: glucydur with eccentric adjustment cams
Frequency: 21,600 vph
Hairspring: made in-house Kif
Remarks: German silver plates and bridges, hand-finished and assembled, hand-engraved balance cock

Caliber L021.3

Automatic; unidirectional gold rotor with a platinum oscillating mass; single spring barrel, 50-hour power reserve
Functions: hours, minutes, subsidiary seconds; day/night indicator; perpetual calendar with large date, weekday, month, moon phase, leap year
Diameter: 35.8 mm
Height: 8.8 mm
Jewels: 63, including 5 screw-mounted gold chatons
Balance: glucydur with eccentric regulating cams 21,600 vph
Balance spring: in-house manufacture
Remarks: assembled and decorated by hand, hand-engraved balance cock; 621 components

Caliber L086.5

Automatic; single spring barrel; 72-hour power reserve
Functions: hours, minutes, subsidiary seconds; large date, moon phase
Diameter: 30.4 mm
Height: 5.2 mm
Jewels: 40
Balance: glucydur
Frequency: 21,600 vph;
Balance spring: made in-house
Remarks: German silver plates, hand-engraved balance cock; 325 parts

Caliber L951.6

Manually wound; stop-seconds mechanism, jumping minute counter; single spring barrel; 60-hour power reserve
Functions: hours, minutes, subsidiary seconds; power reserve indicator; flyback chronograph; large date
Diameter: 30.6 mm **Height:** 7.9 mm **Jewels:** 46
Balance: glucydur with weighted screws
Frequency: 18,000 vph
Hairspring: made in-house
Shock protection: Incabloc
Remarks: three-quarter plate of untreated German silver, hand-assembled and decorated according to highest quality standards, hand-engraved balance cock; 451 parts

Caliber L952.1

Manually wound; single spring barrel; 36-hour power reserve
Functions: subsidiary seconds; day/night indicator; flyback chronograph with exactly jumping minute counter, perpetual calendar with large date, weekday, months moon phase, leap year
Diameter: 32 mm
Height: 8 mm
Jewels: 45, including 4 screw-mounted gold chatons
Balance: glucydur with eccentric regulating cams
Frequency: 18,000 vph
Balance spring: in-house manufacture
Remarks: parts finished and assembled by hand, hand-engraved balance cock; 556 parts

Caliber L132.1

Manually wound; column-wheel control of chronograph functions; single spring barrel; 55-hour power reserve
Functions: hours, minutes, subsidiary seconds; power reserve indicator; flyback chronograph, with triple flyback for comparative time measurements up to 12 hours, precisely jumping chrono and flyback minute counter, continuous chrono and split-second hour counter
Diameter: 30.6 mm **Height:** 9.4 mm
Jewels: 46, including 5 screw-mounted gold chatons, glucydur with eccentric adjustment cams
Frequency: 21,600 vph
Balance spring: made in-house
Remarks: German silver plates and bridges, hand-engraved balance cock; 567 parts

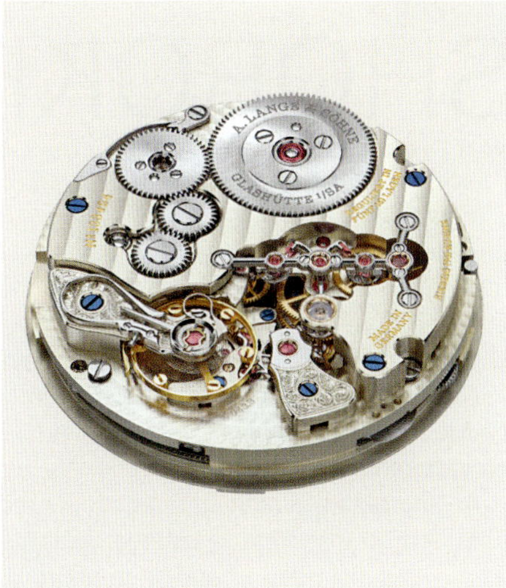

Caliber L043.8

Manually wound; jumping minute, constant force mechanism (remontoir), patented barrel spring mechanism, stop-seconds mechanism; single spring barrel; 72-hour power reserve
Functions: hours, minutes (digital, jumping), subsidiary seconds; power reserve indicator, acoustic signal every 10 minutes and on the hour (with switch-off mechanism); date
Diameter: 37 mm **Height:** 8.9 mm **Jewels:** 70
Balance: glucydur with eccentric adjustment cams
Frequency: 18,000 vph
Balance spring: made in-house with hairspring clamp
Shock protection: Incabloc
Remarks: three-quarter plate of German silver; 516 parts

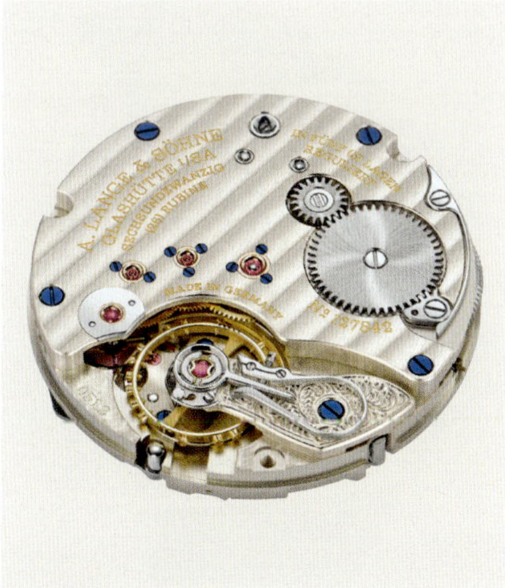

Caliber L051.3

Manually wound; swan-neck fine adjustment, stop-seconds, German silver mainplate and bridges; single spring barrel, 72-hour power reserve
Functions: hours, minutes, subsidiary seconds; annual calendar with date, weekday, months, moon phase
Diameter: 30.6 mm
Height: 5.7 mm
Jewels: 26, including 3 screw-mounted gold chatons
Balance: glucydur with weighted screws
Frequency: 21,600 vph
Balance spring: in-house manufacture
Remarks: parts finished and assembled by hand, hand-engraved balance cock; 345 parts

Caliber L101.1

Manually wound; stop-second system; single spring barrel, 42-hour power reserve
Functions: hours, minutes, subsidiary seconds; power reserve indicator; split-seconds chronograph; perpetual calendar with date, weekday, months moon phase, leap year
Diameter: 32.6 mm
Height: 9.1 mm
Jewels: 43, including 4 screw-mounted gold chatons
Balance: glucydur with weighted screws
Frequency: 21,600 vph
Balance spring: in-house manufacture
Shock protection: Kif
Remarks: parts finished and assembled by hand, hand-engraved balance cock; 528 parts

Caliber L122.1

Manually wound; stop-second system; single spring barrel, 72-hour power reserve
Functions: hours, minutes, subsidiary seconds; minute repeater
Diameter: 30 mm
Height: 5.4 mm
Jewels: 40, including 4 screw-mounted gold chatons
Balance: glucydur with weighted screws Frequency: 21,600 vph
Balance spring: in-house manufacture
Shock protection: Kif
Remarks: parts finished and assembled by hand, hand-engraved balance cock; 414 parts

ALEXANDER SHOROKHOFF

The ultimate goal for the watch connoisseur may be realizing one's own ideas for timepieces. In the first stages of his life, Alexander Shorokhoff, born in Moscow in 1960, was an engineer and then an architect with his own construction company. This turned out to be an excellent platform to begin expanding into the field of fine timepieces. In 1992, shortly after the demise of the Soviet Union, Shorokhoff founded a distribution company in Germany to market Russia's own Poljot watches. This gave him the insight and practice needed to launch phase two of his plan: establishing his own manufacturing facilities for an independent watch brand under his own name.

At Shorokhoff Watches, three main creative lines are bundled under the general concept "Art on the Wrist": Heritage, Avantgarde, and Vintage. The three lines share a design with a distinctly artistic orientation. They all focus on technical quality, sophisticated hand-engraving, and the cultural backdrop. "We consider watches not only as timekeepers, but also as works of art," says Alexander Shorokhoff. It's a statement that can be seen in the watches. The brand is at home in the world of international and Russian art and culture. Each dial is designed down to the smallest detail. The engraving and finishing of the movements are unique as well.

All of them are taken apart in Alzenau, reworked, and then reassembled with great care, which is why the brand has stamped each watch with "Handmade in Germany." Some of the modules used in these timepieces were developed by the company itself. Before a watch leaves the manufacture, it is subjected to strict quality control. The timepiece's functionality must be given the cleanest bill of health before it can be sent out to jewelers around the world.

Alexander Shorokhoff Uhrenmanufaktur
Hanauer Strasse 25
63755 Alzenau
Germany

Tel.:
+49-6023-919-93

E-mail:
info@alexander-shorokhoff.de

Website:
www.alexander-shorokhoff.de

Founded:
2003

Number of employees:
16

Annual production:
approx. 1,500 watches

Distributor:
About Time Luxury Group
210 Bellevue Avenue
Newport, RI 02840
401-846-0598

Most important collections/price range:
Heritage / starting at approx. $4,500; Avantgarde / starting at approx. $1,500; Vintage / starting at approx. $800

Avantgarde "Neva Chrono"

Reference number: AS.CA05-NEV3
Movement: automatic, Caliber 2030.AS (base Dubois Dépraz 2030); ø 30 mm, height 7.5 mm; 49 jewels; 28,800 vph; 38-hour power reserve
Functions: hours, minutes, subsidiary seconds; chronograph
Case: stainless steel, ø 43.5 mm, height 14.4 mm; sapphire crystal; transparent case back; water-resistant to 5 atm
Band: calfskin, buckle
Price: $3,100; limited to 100 pieces

Avantgarde "Crazy Balls"

Reference number: AS.CB01-1
Movement: automatic, Sellita Caliber SW200-1; ø 25.6 mm, height 4.6 mm; 26 jewels; 28,800 vph; 38-hour power reserve
Functions: hours, minutes, sweep seconds; date
Case: stainless steel, ø 39 mm, height 10.6 mm; sapphire crystal; transparent case back; water-resistant to 5 atm
Band: ray skin, buckle
Price: $1,900; limited to 88 pieces

Avantgarde "Square & Round"

Reference number: AS.SR02-6
Movement: automatic, ETA Caliber 7753; ø 30 mm, height 7.9 mm; 27 jewels; 28,800 vph; 42-hour power reserve
Functions: hours, minutes, subsidiary seconds; chronograph;
Case: stainless steel, 44.5 x 44.5 mm, height 14.75 mm; sapphire crystal; transparent case back; water-resistant to 3 atm
Band: reptile skin, buckle
Price: $3,500; limited to 30 pieces

Avantgarde "Shar"

Reference number: AS.SH01-1
Movement: automatic, Caliber 2671.AS (base ETA 2671); ø 17.5 mm, height 4.8 mm; 25 jewels; 28,800 vph; hand-engraved oscillating mass; 42-hour power reserve
Functions: hours, minutes, sweep seconds; date
Case: stainless steel, ø 25 mm, height 25.8 mm; sapphire crystal; water-resistant to 3 atm
Band: reptile skin, buckle
Remarks: hand-engraved dial; hemispherical case; limited to 30 pieces
Price: $1,900

Avantgarde "Deep Ding 2"

Reference number: AS.DD03-RSR
Movement: automatic, ETA Caliber 2824-2 or Sellita SW200-1; ø 25.6 mm, height 4.6 mm; 25 or 26 jewels; 28,800 vph; 49- or 38-hour power reserve
Functions: hours, minutes, sweep seconds; date
Case: stainless steel, ø 45 mm, height 13.75 mm; crown-adjustable inner bezel with 0-60 scale; sapphire crystal; water-resistant to 10 atm
Band: rubber, folding clasp
Remarks: comes with additional stainless-steel protective grille for the case; limited to 37 pieces
Price: $2,200

Avantgarde "Arrow"

Reference number: AS.C01-ARW
Movement: manually wound, Caliber 31379.AS (base Poljot 3133); ø 31 mm, height 7.35 mm; 23 jewels; 21,600 vph; 42-hour power reserve
Functions: hours, minutes, subsidiary seconds; chronograph; date, moon phase
Case: stainless steel, ø 43.5 mm, height 14.4 mm; sapphire crystal; water-resistant to 5 atm
Band: calfskin, buckle
Price: on request; limited to 48 pieces

Avantgarde Tourbillon Picassini

Reference number: AS.TU-PCSN
Movement: manually wound, Caliber MU 8950; ø 30.4 mm, height 5.8 mm; 27 jewels; 28,800 vph; 1-minute tourbillon; hand-engraved and finished movement; 60-hour power reserve
Functions: hours, minutes, subsidiary seconds (on the tourbillon cage)
Case: stainless steel with red-gold inlays, 41 x 41 mm, height 12.5 mm; sapphire crystal; transparent case back; water-resistant to 3 atm
Band: reptile skin, buckle
Price: $33,000; limited to 5 pieces

Avantgarde "Neva"

Reference number: AS.NEV02-4
Movement: manually wound, Caliber 3105.AS (base Poljot 3105); ø 31 mm, height 5.28 mm; 17 jewels; 21,600 vph; finely finished movement; 42-hour power reserve
Functions: hours, minutes, subsidiary seconds; date
Case: stainless steel with red-gold plating, ø 43.5 mm, height 11.5 mm; sapphire crystal; transparent case back; water-resistant to 5 atm
Band: reptile skin, buckle
Price: $1,450; limited to 98 pieces

Avantgarde "Autumn"

Reference number: AS.LA-AMN-10
Movement: automatic, ETA Caliber 2824-2 or Sellita SW200-1; ø 25.6 mm, height 4.6 mm; 25 or 26 jewels; 28,800 vph; 49- or 38-hour power reserve
Functions: hours, minutes, sweep seconds; date
Case: stainless steel with brown PVD, ø 39 mm, height 10.6 mm; sapphire crystal; transparent case back; water-resistant to 5 atm
Band: ray skin, buckle
Price: $2,150

ALPINA

Alpina essentially grew out of a confederation of watchmakers known as the Alpina Union Horlogère, founded by Gottlieb Hauser. The group expanded quickly to reach beyond Swiss borders into Germany, where it opened a factory in Glashütte. For a while in the 1930s, it even merged with Gruen, one of the most important watch companies in the United States at the time.

After World War II, the Allied Forces decreed that the name Alpina could no longer be used in Germany, and so that brand was renamed "Dugena" for Deutsche Uhrmacher-Genossenschaft Alpina, or the German Watchmaker Cooperative Alpina.

Today, Geneva-based Alpina is no longer associated with that watchmaker cooperative of yore. Now a sister brand of Frédérique Constant, it has a decidedly modern collection enhanced with a series of movements designed, built, and assembled in-house: the Tourbillon AL-980, the World Timer AL-718, the Automatic Regulator AL-950, the Small Date Automatic AL-710, and, more recently, the Flyback Chronograph Automatic AL-760, which features the patented Direct Flyback technology. Owners Peter and Aletta Stas sold it to Citizen Group in 2016.

Alpina has a history of pioneering advances in watchmaking. Its iconic Block Uhr of 1933 and the Alpina 4 of 1938, with an in-house automatic movement, set the pace for all sports watches, with a waterproof stainless-steel case and an amagnetic movement. In 2015, together with its sister company Frédérique Constant, the company introduced its Swiss-made "Horological Smartwatch." In June 2020, it contributed the Alpiner X Alive to the trend toward health monitoring. The watch features, among other things, a pulsometer. And its contribution to World Oceans Day in 2022 was the Seastrong Diver 300 Automatic Calanda with a case made of 100 percent recycled stainless steel and a strap made of recycled plastic. The PuReSteel recycled steel, manufactured by Thyssen Krupp, is of the highest quality and originates from the maritime sector.

Alpina Watch International SA
Route de la Galaise, 8
CH-1228 Plan-les-Ouates, Geneva
Switzerland

Tel.:
+41-0-22-860-87-40

E-mail:
info@alpina-watches.com

Website:
www.alpina-watches.com

Founded:
1883

Number of employees:
100

U.S. distributor:
Alpina Frederique Constant USA
350 5th Avenue, 29th Floor
New York, NY 10118
310-532-8463
customercare@alpinawatches.com

Most important collections/price range:
AlpinerX / from approx. $995 to $1,295; Seastrong Diver 300 GMT / from approx. $795 to $995; Startimer Pilot Automatic / from approx. $995 to $1,295

Seastrong Diver 300 Automatic Calanda

Reference number: AL-525BBG4VR6
Movement: automatic, Caliber AL-525 (base Sellita SW200-1); ø 25.6 mm, height 4.6 mm; 26 jewels; 28,800 vph; 38-hour power reserve
Functions: hours, minutes, sweep seconds; date
Case: "PuReSteel" (recycled stainless steel), ø 42 mm, height 12.66 mm; unidirectional bevel with 0-60 scale; sapphire crystal; screw-in crown; water resistant to 30 atm
Band: textile from recycled PET bottles, buckle
Price: $1,895; limited to 300 pieces

Startimer Pilot Automatic

Reference number: AL-525BBG4S26
Movement: automatic, Caliber AL-525 (base Sellita SW200-1); ø 25.6 mm, height 4.6 mm; 26 jewels; 28,800 vph; 38-hour power reserve
Functions: hours, minutes, sweep seconds; date
Case: stainless steel, ø 41 mm, height 11.5 mm; unidirectional bezel with 0-60 scale; sapphire crystal; water-resistant to 10 atm
Band: calf leather, buckle
Price: $1,195

Alpiner Regulator Automatic

Reference number: AL-650DGN4AE6
Movement: automatic, Alpina Caliber AL-650 (based on a Unitas movement), ø 30.5 mm, height 4.5 mm; 31 jewels; 28,800 vph; 38-hour power reserve
Functions: hours (off-center), minutes, subsidiary seconds
Case: stainless steel, 41 mm x 42.5 mm, height 12 mm; sapphire crystal; water-resistant to 20 atm
Band: rubber, buckle
Price: $2,195; limited to 888 pieces

Angelus
Manufacture La Joux-Perret SA
Boulevard des Eplatures 38
2300 La Chaux-de-Fonds
Switzerland

Tel:
+41-32-967-97-97

E-mail:
info@angelus-watches.com

Website:
www.angelus-watches.com

Founded:
1891; relaunched 2011

Number of employees:
about 100, including at the La Joux-Perret manufacture

Distributor:
Angelus USA
510 West 6th Street, Suite 309
Los Angeles, CA 90014
213-622-1133
info@arnoldandsonusa.com

Most important collections/price range:
U23 / U30 / U41 / U50 / U51 / U53 / $32,000; various tourbillons / $28,000 to $110,000

ANGELUS

The watch landscape in Switzerland has always been rich in small, vital brands. Many are no longer active, but their names still make for weepy eyes with connoisseurs and collectors. And every now and then, an older company is revived with varying degrees of success. It its day, Angelus, founded by Gustave and Albert Stolz in Le Locle in 1891, quickly forged a reputation for complicated watches, notably repeaters and chronographs. The brothers, Catholics, named the brand after the first word of a standard Catholic prayer and the midday church bells.

One of the brand's claims to fame was a two-handed chronograph, which became a hit in the thirties, culminating in a contract with the Hungarian air force in 1940. The company then built a chronograph with a date, and later one of the first digital dates. Meanwhile, it was creating excellent movements, one of which drove Panerai's Mare Nostrum in the fifties. Among its most iconic models was the waterproof repeater/alarm called the Tinkler—a very limited series, hence extremely rare—and, in the seventies, a five-minute repeater, which never really got off the ground due to the quartz crisis, which brought Angelus to its knees...

In 2011, La Joux-Perret, a company known for movements and modules and behind Arnold & Son, relaunched the brand. The breakout watch in 2015, designed by Sébastien Chaulmontet, was the Tourbillon Lumière, a modern, television-shaped behemoth recalling the travel clocks the company produced at one time. The tourbillon turns in one window, time appears in the other. In 2017, this eyebrow-raising format was used for a skull watch.

Nevertheless, Angelus has gone on to produce series of round watches based on their in-house movements, notably a very high-end diver (the U53) and a series of fun, colorful tourbillons based on the A-250. The recent Chronodate is a revised version of a vintage Angelus. And the recent Gold & Carbon Flying Tourbillon has no real dial, so it can reveal its clever, minimalistic architecture.

U53 Tourbillon Skeleton

Reference number: 0.TDDT.G01A.T008G
Movement: manually wound, Caliber A- 300; ø 32.8 mm, height 4.3 mm; 23 jewels; 28,800 vph; flying 1-minute tourbillon; black DLC-coated, snailed and beveled mainplate and bridges; skeletonized titanium bridges; 60-hour power reserve
Functions: hours, minutes, subsidiary seconds
Case: titanium, ø 46 mm, height 12.47 mm; crown-adjustable unidirectional 60-minute timing bezel; double crown guards; sapphire crystal; transparent case back; water-resistant to 30 atm
Band: rubber, buckle
Remarks: comes with an additional textile strap
Price: $42,800; limited to 25 pieces

Chronodate Titanium

Reference number: 0CDZF.U01A.K009H
Movement: automatic, Caliber A-500; ø 30 mm, height 7.9 mm; 26 jewels; 28,800 vph; finely finished movement with sandblasted or microbeaded parts, NAC-coated mainplate and bridges; tungsten and red-gold rotor; 45-hour power reserve
Functions: hours, minutes, seconds; chronograph; power reserve indicator
Case: titanium monobloc, ø 42.5 mm, height 14.25 mm; sapphire crystal; carbon composite pushers and case back; water-resistant to 3 atm
Band: rubber, folding clasp
Remarks: blue PVD, frosted dial center
Price: $23,100
Variations: with white dial ($23,100); in red gold ($43,300); limited to 25 pieces per model

Gold & Carbon Flying Tourbillon

Reference number: 0TCDB.B01A.K009B
Movement: manually wound, Caliber A-250; ø 32.6 mm, height 5.78 mm; 18 jewels in gold chatons; 21,600 vph; 1-minute flying tourbillon; sandblasted titanium bridges with red gold-colored PVD; 90-hour power reserve
Functions: hours, minutes
Case: red gold and carbon composite, ø 42.5 mm, height 11.7 mm; black PVD on flange; white-gold hour markers; sapphire crystal; transparent case back; water-resistant to 3 atm
Band: "ballistic" rubber, folding clasp
Price: $72,080; limited to 18 pieces

ANONIMO

Anonimo SA
Chemin des Tourelles 4
CH-2400 Le Locle
Switzerland

Tel.:
+41-22-566-06-06

E-mail:
info@anonimo.com

Website:
anonimo.com

Founded:
1997; moved to Switzerland in 2013

U.S. distributor:
BeauGeste Luxury Brands
697 Third Avenue
New York, NY 10017
212-847-1371
www.beaugesteluxury.com

Most important collections/price range:
Epurato, Militare, Nautilo / $2,300 to $5,700

The brand Anonimo was launched in Florence, Italy. Watchmaking has a long history in Florence, going back to such innovators as Giovanni de Dondi (1318–1389), who built his first planetarium around 1368, and architect and goldsmith Lorenzo della Volpaia (1446–1512), who worked with calendars and astronomical instruments. And finally, there were the likes of the mathematician Galileo and the incomparable Leonardo da Vinci.

In more recent times, the Italian watch industry has been equipping submarine crews and frogmen with timepieces. The key technology comes from Switzerland, but the specialized know-how for making robust, water-resistant timepieces sprang from small enterprises with special competencies in building cases, notably of bronze. The founders of Anonimo understood this strength and decided to put it in the service of their "anonymous" brand—a name chosen to "hide" the fact that many small, discreet companies are involved in their superbly finished watches.

In 2013, armed with some fresh capital and a new management team, Anonimo came out with three watch families running on Swiss technology: the mechanical movements are a combination of Dubois Dépraz modules and tried-and-true Sellita movements. On the whole, though, the collections reflect exquisite conception and manufacturing, and the quality of the materials is unimpeachable: corrosion-resistant stainless steel, fine bronze, and titanium. The design is definitely vintage, a bit 1960s with a hint of a cushion case, but use of only three numerals—4, 8, and 12, which sketch an A on the dial—is quite modern. On the military models, the crown has been placed in a protected area between the two upper lugs. Thanks to a clever hinge system, that crown can be pressed onto the case for an impermeable fit or released for time setting. The Militare line is also home to a special-edition chronograph to celebrate Anonimo's status as official timer of the World Rally Championship, Italy section. Fans seeking a simpler dial have the Epurato line, including a number of different-colored dials, each with characteristic sunray effect. The Nautilo series was conceived for divers, chic and sportive and able to descend beyond 600 feet. The latest models look back to older Dino Zei Nautilos of the past, with hints of '60s-style cushion cases.

Militare Chrono DLC

Reference number: AM-1128.22.721.T74
Movement: automatic, Sellita Caliber SW300 with Dubois Dépraz 2035M module; ø 26.2 mm, height 6.5 mm; 49 jewels; 28,800 vph; 42-hour power reserve
Functions: hours, minutes, subsidiary seconds; chronograph
Case: stainless steel with black DLC, ø 43.5 mm, height 14.5 mm; sapphire crystal; transparent case back; water-resistant to 12 atm
Band: textile, buckle
Remarks: crown is pressed onto the case by upper lug for water-tight seal.
Price: $4,650

Nautilo 42mm Satin Blue

Reference number: AM-5009.09.103.M01
Movement: automatic, Sellita Caliber SW200-1; ø 25.6 mm, height 4.6 mm; 26 jewels; 28,800 vph; oscillating weight with côtes de Genève; 38-hour power reserve
Functions: hours, minutes, sweep seconds; date
Case: stainless steel, ø 42 mm, height 11.8 mm; unidirectional bezel with ceramic insert, with 0-60 scale; sapphire crystal; transparent case back; screw-in crown; water-resistant to 20 atm
Band: stainless steel, folding clasp with safety catch
Price: $2,980
Variations: with calfskin or rubber strap ($2,780)

Militare Chrono Bronze

Reference number: AM-1120.04.001.A01
Movement: automatic, Sellita Caliber SW300 with Dubois Dépraz 2035M module; ø 26.2 mm, height 6.5 mm; 49 jewels; 28,800 vph; 42-hour power reserve
Functions: hours, minutes, subsidiary seconds; chronograph
Case: bronze, ø 43.5 mm, height 14.5 mm; sapphire crystal; transparent case back; water-resistant to 12 atm
Band: calf leather, buckle
Remarks: crown is pressed onto the case by upper lug for water-tight seal.
Price: $5,400

ARMIN STROM

For more than thirty years, Armin Strom's name was associated mainly with the art of skeletonizing. But this "grandmaster of skeletonizers" then decided to entrust his life's work to the next generation, which turned out to be the Swiss industrialist and art patron Willy Michel.

Michel had the wherewithal to expand the one-man show into a full-blown *manufacture* able to conceive, design, and produce its own mechanical movements. The endeavor attracted Claude Greisler, a very skilled designer, and Michel's own son, Serge, who became business manager. When this triumvirate joined forces, it was able to come up with a technically fascinating movement at the quaint little *manufacture* in the Biel suburb of Bözingen within a brief period.

The new movement went on to grow into a family of ten, which forms the backbone of a new collection, including a tourbillon with microrotor—no mean feat for a small firm. The ARF15 caliber of the Mirrored Force Resonance, for example, features two balance wheels placed close enough to influence each other (resonance) and give the movement greater stability. The two oscillating systems are connected by a clutch spring. A similar movement is used in an exclusive, new, minute repeater. The company has innovated in many other directions, notably, in its System 78 line with a clever stop-work mechanism for an automatic movement, and development of a motor barrel, whereby the pivot is the driver of the movement.

This essential portfolio has given the *manufacture* the industrial autonomy to implement its projects quickly and independently. Armin Strom has additionally created an online configurator (on its homepage) giving fans and collectors the opportunity to personalize their watches. All components can be selected individually and combined, from the dial, hands, and finishing to the straps. The finished product can be picked up at a local dealership or at the manufacturer in Biel/Bienne, including a tour of the place.

Armin Strom AG
Bözingenstrasse 46
CH-2502 Biel/Bienne
Switzerland

Tel.:
+41-32-343-3344

E-mail:
info@arminstrom.com

Website:
www.arminstrom.com

Founded:
2006 (first company 1967)

Number of employees:
22

Annual production:
approx. 1000 watches

U.S. representative:
Jean-Marc Bories
Head of North America
929-353-5395
Jean-marc@arminstrom.com

Most important collections/price range:
Masterpiece Collection, Resonance Collection, Skeleton Collection, System 78 Collection / $9,900 to $100,000 plus

Orbit – First Edition

Reference number: ST22-GEFD.75.ST
Movement: automatic, Armin Strom Caliber ASS20; ø 35.52 mm, height 8.42 mm; 30 jewels; 25,200 vph; micro-rotor; spring barrel with constant and limited force mechanism with Maltese cross escapement; finely finished movement; 72-hour power reserve
Functions: hours and minutes (off-center), subsidiary seconds; date
Case: stainless steel, ø 43.4 mm, height 12.6 mm; ceramic bezel, with date division; sapphire crystal; transparent case back; water-resistant to 5 atm
Band: stainless steel, double folding clasp
Price: $29,500; limited to 25 pieces

Mirrored Force Resonance First Edition

Reference number: ST22-RF.75
Movement: manually wound, Caliber ARF21_ZG; ø 36.6 mm, height 7 mm; 39 jewels; 25,200 vph; two independent regulating mechanisms connected by a resonance clutch spring that stabilize each other mutually; finely finishing on movement; 48-hour power reserve
Functions: hours and minutes (off-center), double subsidiary seconds
Case: stainless steel, ø 37.20 mm, height 6.70 mm; sapphire crystal; transparent case back; water-resistant to 5 atm
Band: reptile skin, buckle
Price: $59,000; limited to 25 pieces

Tribute 1 California

Reference number: ST21-TNS.05.AL.M.35
Movement: manually wound, Armin Strom Caliber AMW21; ø 33.5 mm, height 4.2 mm; 21 jewels; 25,200 vph; variable inertia balance; finely finished movement; 100-hour power reserve
Functions: off-center hours, minutes, and sweep seconds
Case: stainless steel, ø 38 mm, height 9 mm; sapphire crystal; transparent case back; water-resistant to 5 atm
Band: reptile skin, double folding clasp
Price: $17,900; limited to 5 pieces per dial color (25 pieces in all)
Variations: four other dial colors

Gravity Equal Force Ultimate Sapphire

Reference number: ST21-GEF.SA.VE.M.30
Movement: automatic, Armin Strom Caliber ASB19; ø 35.52 mm, height 11.67 mm; 28 jewels; 25,200 vph; micro-rotor; spring barrel with constant and limited force mechanism with Maltese cross escapement; finely finished movement; 72-hour power reserve
Functions: hours and minutes (off-center), subsidiary seconds; power reserve indicator
Case: stainless steel, ø 41 mm, height 12.65 mm; sapphire crystal; transparent case back; water-resistant to 3 atm
Band: textile, double folding clasp
Price: $22,900

Tribute 1 Black Edition

Reference number: ST21-TRI.90
Movement: manually wound, Armin Strom Caliber AMW21; ø 33.5 mm, height 4.2 mm; 21 jewels; 25,200 vph; balance with variable inertia; finely finished movement; 100-hour power reserve
Functions: off-center hours, minutes, and sweep seconds
Case: stainless steel, ø 38 mm, height 9 mm; sapphire crystal; transparent case back; water-resistant to 5 atm
Band: reptile skin, double folding clasp
Price: $13,900; limited to 100 pieces
Variations: with a blue dial limited to 100 pieces, in rose gold ($23,900)

Tribute 1 Rose Gold

Reference number: RG21-TRI.70
Movement: manually wound, Caliber AMW21; ø 33.5 mm, height 4.02 mm; 21 jewels; 25,200 vph; 100-hour power reserve
Functions: off-center hours, minutes, and sweep seconds
Case: rose gold, ø 38 mm, height 9 mm; sapphire crystal; transparent case back; water-resistant to 5 atm
Band: reptile skin, double folding clasp
Price: $23,900; limited to 100 pieces
Variations: in stainless steel (13,900); with blue dial

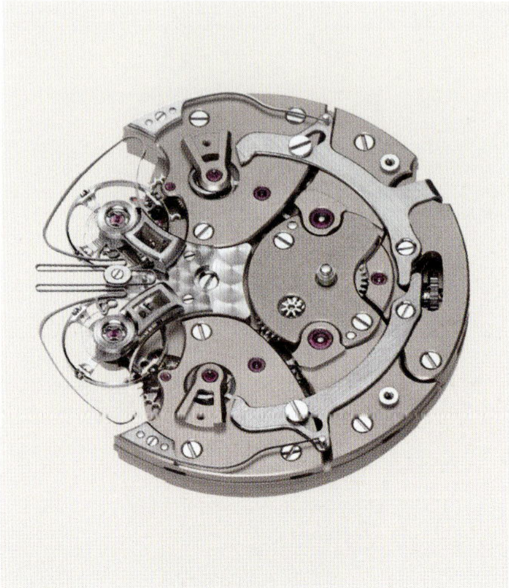

Caliber ARF21 ZG

Manually wound; 2 separate regulating systems are connected by a resonance clutch spring and mutually stabilize each other; double spring barrel, 80-hour power reserve
Functions: hours and minutes (off-center), 2 independent, symmetrically mirrored subsidiary seconds
Diameter: 36.6 mm
Height: 7 mm
Jewels: 39
Balance: 2 balance wheels oscillating in opposite directions on a single hairspring
Frequency: 25,200 vph
Remarks: hand-decorated movement; 260 parts

Caliber ARF15

Manually wound; 2 separate regulating systems are connected by a resonance clutch spring and mutually stabilize each other; single spring barrel, 48-hour power reserve
Functions: hours and minutes (off-center), 2 independent symmetrically mirrored subsidiary seconds
Diameter: 36.6 mm
Height: 7.7 mm
Jewels: 43
Balance: 2 balance wheels oscillating in opposite directions on a single hairspring
Frequency: 25,200 vph
Remarks: 226 components; fine, hand-decorated movement

Caliber ASB19

Automatic; micro-rotor; spring barrel with constant force escapement (Maltese cross); single spring barrel; 72-hour power reserve
Functions: hours, minutes, subsidiary seconds; power reserve indicator
Diameter: 35.52 mm
Height: 11.67 mm
Jewels: 28
Balance: screw balance with variable inertia
Frequency: 25,200 vph
Remarks: movement decorated by hand; 202 parts

ARNOLD & SON

John Arnold holds a special place among the British watchmakers of the eighteenth and nineteenth centuries because he was the first to organize the production of his chronometers along industrial lines. He developed his own standards and employed numerous watchmakers. During his lifetime, he is said to have manufactured around 5,000 marine chronometers, which he sold at reasonable prices to the Royal Navy and the West Indies merchant fleet. Arnold chronometers were packed in the trunks of some of the greatest explorers, from John Franklin and Ernest Shackleton to Captain Cook and Dr. Livingstone.

As Arnold & Son was once synonymous with precision timekeeping on the high seas, it stands to reason, then, that the modern brand should also focus its design policies on the interplay of time and geography as well as the basic functions of navigation. Independence from The British Masters Group has meant that the venerable English chronometer brand has been reorienting itself, setting its sights on classic, elegant watchmaking. With the expertise of watch manufacturer La Joux-Perret behind it (and the expertise housed in the building behind the complex on the main road between La Chaux-de-Fonds and Le Locle), the brand has been able to implement several new ideas.

Keeping it modern is, perhaps, the biggest challenge for any brand, and here Arnold shows remarkable skill. The characteristic bridge over the dial of the Globetrotter has been streamlined, somewhat, and the colors offered are bolder. The same applies to the Double Tourbillon Escapement, which now comes in a brilliant green. As for the Ultrathin Tourbillon, it runs on a movement that is less than 3 millimeters high. Perhaps the most striking models of late are the moon phase displays on the Luna Magna by way of a decorated 12-millimeter sculptural moon, or the Perpetual Moon collection, which also displays a prominent moon crossing the dial.

Arnold & Son
38, boulevard des Eplatures
CH-2300 La Chaux-de-Fonds
Switzerland

Tel.:
+41-32-967-9797

E-mail:
info@arnoldandson.com

Website:
www.arnoldandson.com

Founded:
1995

Number of employees:
approx. 30

U.S. distributor:
Arnold & Son USA
510 West 6th Street, Suite 309
Los Angeles, CA 90014
213-622-1133

Most important collections/price range:
Eight-Day / Globetrotter / Nebula / TB88, TBR, TE8 (Tourbillon), Time Pyramid, UTTE / from approx. $10,000 to $325,000

Luna Magna Ultimate I

Reference number: 1LMMW.Z01A.C177A
Movement: manually wound, Arnold & Son Caliber a&s1021; ø 37.60 mm, height 4.75 mm; 12 mm 3D moon; 35 jewels; 21,600 vph; 90-hour power reserve; COSC-certified chronometer
Functions: hours, minutes; moon phase (1-day correction every 122 years); moon phase on the movement side
Case: white gold, ø 44 mm, height 15.90 mm; sapphire crystal; transparent case back; water-resistant to 3 atm
Band: reptile skin, buckle set with 26 baguette-cut diamonds
Remarks: 12-mm moon set with 161 diamonds and 161 sapphires
Price: on request; limited to 8 pieces

Luna Magna Ultimate II

Reference number: 1LMM.WZ04A.C213A
Movement: manually wound, Arnold & Son Caliber a&s1021; ø 37.60 mm, height 4.75 mm, 12 mm 3D moon; 35 jewels; 21,600 vph; 90-hour power reserve; circular graining and côtes de Genève decoration; COSC-certified chronometer
Functions: hours, minutes; moon phase (1-day correction every 122 years); moon phase on the movement side
Case: grey gold, ø 44 mm, height 15.90 mm; sapphire crystal; transparent case back; water-resistant to 3 atm
Band: reptile skin, buckle set with 26 baguette-cut diamonds
Remarks: ruthenium crystal with lagoon-blue PVD; lugs set with 112 diamonds; 12-millimeter moon with 161 diamonds and 161 tourmalines
Price: $214,000; limited to 8 pieces

Luna Magna Platinum I

Reference number: 1LMAX.Z01A.C233C
Movement: manually wound, Arnold & Son Caliber a&s1021; ø 37.60 mm, height 4.75 mm, 12 mm 3D moon; 35 jewels; 21,600 vph; 90-hour power reserve; circular graining and côtes de Genève decoration; COSC-certified chronometer
Functions: hours, minutes; moon phase (1-day correction every 122 years); moon phase on the movement side
Case: platinum, ø 44 mm, height 15.90 mm; sapphire crystal; transparent case back; water-resistant to 3 atm
Band: reptile skin, buckle set with 26 baguette-cut diamonds
Remarks: meteorite dial and sand-colored PVD
Price: $71,700; limited to 8 pieces

HM Perpetual Obsidian

Reference number: 1GLAR.Z01A.C154A
Movement: manually wound, Arnold & Son Caliber 1512; ø 34 mm, height 5.35 mm; 27 jewels; 21,600 vph; astronomically precise 122-year moon phase; 90-hour power reserve
Functions: hours, minutes; moon phase
Case: pink gold, ø 42 mm, height 11.43 mm; sapphire crystal; transparent case back; water-resistant to 3 atm
Band: reptile skin, buckle
Remarks: blue aventurine dial, blue lacquered moon disk, hand-engraved sculptural red gold moon and stars
Price: $33,650; limited to 28 pieces

Perpetual Moon Celestial Rays

Reference number: 1GLBX.P01A.C200W
Movement: manually wound, Arnold & Son Caliber 1512; ø 34 mm, height 5.35 mm; 27 jewels; 21,600 vph; astronomically precise 122-year moon phase; 90-hour power reserve
Functions: hours, minutes; moon phase
Case: platinum, ø 41.5 mm, height 11.30 mm; sapphire crystal; transparent case back; water-resistant to 3 atm
Band: reptile skin, buckle
Remarks: special "stellar rays" finishing on dial; mother-of-pearl moon, with blue PVD backdrop of the sky with the Big Dipper and Cassiopeia
Price: $47,500
Variations: case in red gold

Double Tourbillon Jade

Reference number: 1DTAR.Z01A.C120R
Movement: manually wound, Arnold & Son Caliber 8513; ø 37.30 mm, height 8.35 mm; 42 jewels; 21,600 vph; NAC-treated mainplate; 1-minute tourbillon with white gold bridges; finely finished parts, skeletonized movement; double spring barrel; 90-hour power reserve
Functions: hours, minutes, seconds on tourbillon; double power reserve indicator
Case: white gold, ø 43.5 mm, height 12.67 mm; sapphire crystal; transparent case back; water-resistant to 3 atm
Band: reptile skin, buckle
Price: $215,800; unique piece

Ultrathin Tourbillon Dragon & Phoenix

Reference number: 1ETAS.B01A.C113S
Movement: manually wound, Arnold & Son Caliber 8200; ø 32 mm, height 2.97 mm; 29 jewels; 28,800 vph; 1-minute flying tourbillon; mainplate with côtes de Genève, hand-engraved tourbillon bridge; 90-hour power reserve; COSC-certified chronometer
Functions: hours, minutes
Case: stainless steel, ø 42 mm, height 12.23 mm; sapphire crystal; transparent case back; water-resistant to 3 atm
Band: reptile skin, buckle
Remarks: eudialyte dial; miniature painting on black mother-of-pearl, painting engraved by hand
Price: $112,000; limited to 5 individual pieces
Variations: comes with bronzite, marcassite, pietersite or verdite dial; with simple dial ($73,900)

Double Tourbillon Escapement

Reference number: 1DTAW.Z01A.C121W
Movement: manually wound, Arnold & Son Caliber 8513; ø 37.30 mm, height 8.35 mm; 42 jewels; 21,600 vph; NAC-treated mainplate; 1-minute tourbillon with white gold bridges; finely finished parts, skeletonized movement; double spring barrel; 90-hour power reserve
Functions: hours, minutes, seconds on tourbillon; double power reserve indicator
Case: white gold, ø 43.5 mm, height 12.67 mm; sapphire crystal; transparent case back; water-resistant to 3 atm
Band: reptile skin, buckle
Price: $215,800; limited to 28 pieces

Globetrotter

Reference number: 1WTAS.U01C.C155S
Movement: automatic, Arnold & Son Caliber 6022; ø 38 mm, height 6.55 mm (14 mm includes arched bridge and hemisphere); 29 jewels; 28,800 vph; 3D world time display in sculptural hemisphere design; coastlines lined In Superluminova for special effect in the dark; 45-hour power reserve
Functions: hours, minutes; world time indicator (on 24-hour ring)
Case: stainless steel, ø 45 mm, height 17.2 mm; sapphire crystal; transparent case back; water-resistant to 3 atm
Band: reptile skin, buckle
Price: $20,000; limited to 88 pieces
Variations: with blue dial

ARTYA

Business gurus like to invent words for their processes like "agility," and "disruptive," and even "innovative," to describe more of the same with a few small changes. In watchmaking, the approach often involves small engineering advances and a noisy campaign. Yvan Arpa, founder of ArtyA watches, does it differently.

This refreshingly candid personality who spent his *Wanderjahre* crossing Papua New Guinea on foot and practicing Thai boxing in its native land, lives, breathes, and garrulously posts his lived horology online, be it the diving trip to test his divers' watches, or some trek up a mountain.

After various trials and tribulations in the industry, Arpa founded ArtyA, where he could get his "monster" off the slab as it were, with a divine spark. "I had worked with water, rust, dust, and other elements, and then I really caught fire," says Arpa. Indeed, among his first creations were steel cases struck by artificial lightning from a Tesla generator.

Arpa's watches hit nerves and drew a gamut of emotional responses. His dials shake up the owner and are often unique in the real sense of the word. No two ones are alike.

Thinking outside of the box is not enough for Arpa. He thinks out of the dial, as illustrated by the Son of Finance Raptor, which features a sleeve-ripping bird of prey staring down from the bezel onto a dial strewn with cut up banknotes. His most recent exploration is with an artificial sapphire that changes color and which he uses not only to create mysterious watches but also bracelets. The Depth Gauge is another clever concept: the arched colored bands on the dial disappear as the watch reaches depths that certain color frequencies can no longer reach.

One of Arpa's not-so-secret weapons in the fight for market share is his artist wife, Dominique Arpa-Cirpka, who delivers dreamier dials that carefully mix textures and pigments or use real butterfly wings and collages of earth, shells, pigments, or fish scales. A simple tobacco leaf immediately carries one to a tropical island and the aromas of cigars, coffee, and rum.

Luxury Artpieces ArtyA SA
Route de Gy, 27
1252 Meinier
Switzerland

Tel.:
+41-22-752-4940

Website:
www.artya.com

Founded:
2010

Number of employees:
12

U.S. distributor:
Beau Geste Luxury Brands:
https://www.beaugesteluxury.com/

Most important collections/price range:
ArtyA Complications / $90,000 to $500,000;
Son of a Gun / $8,800 to $167,000;
Son of Art / $3,800 to $21,000;
Son of Earth / $4,300 to $183,000;
Son of Sound / $4,300 to $22,110;
Son of Gears / $6,550 to $16,550;
Race / $7000 to $19,000

Purity Tourbillon Chameleon

Movement: manually wound, ArtyA exclusive tourbillon; ø 35 mm, height 10 mm; 28,800 vph; 17 jewels; 2 parallel-mounted spring barrels; 1-minute, 17-millimeter flying tourbillon; fully skeletonized movement; 70-hour power reserve
Functions: hours, minutes, seconds on tourbillon cage
Case: extra-hard "Nano-Sapphire" case, crown, and lugs; ø 46 mm, height 13.4 mm; water-resistant to 3 atm
Band: reptile skin, buckle
Remarks: case changes hues depending on the heat of the light
Price: $180,000; unique piece
Variations: with calfskin strap ($150,000)

ArtyA Gold Purity Tourbillon

Movement: manually wound, ArtyA exclusive tourbillon; ø 35 mm, height 10 mm; 28,800 vph; 17 jewels; 2 parallel-mounted spring barrels; 1-minute, 17-millimeter flying tourbillon; fully skeletonized movement; 70-hour power reserve
Functions: hours, minutes, seconds on tourbillon cage
Case: pink gold; ø 44 mm, height 13.4 mm; screwed-down transparent case back; water-resistant to 3 atm
Band: reptile skin, buckle
Remarks: case changes hues when exposed to light
Price: $120,000; limited to 9 pieces

Purity Chiaroscuro

Movement: manually wound, ArtyA exclusive tourbillon; ø 35 mm, height 10 mm; 28,800 vph; 17 jewels; 2 parallel-mounted spring barrels; 1-minute, 17-millimeter flying tourbillon; fully skeletonized movement; 70-hour power reserve
Functions: hours, minutes, seconds on tourbillon cage
Case: stainless steel with black PVD; ø 46 mm, height 13.4 mm; water-resistant to 3 atm
Band: reptile skin, buckle
Remarks: case changes hues when exposed to light
Price: $99,900; unique piece

Diver

Movement: automatic, exclusive ArtyA Aion Caliber; ø 26.20 mm, height 3.60 mm; 25 jewels; 28,800 vph; with côtes de Genève; grey NAC coating on bridges; rhodium-plated gold oscillator; COSC-certified; 42-hour power reserve
Functions: hours, minutes, sweep seconds; date
Case: lab-made sapphire, ø 41 mm, height 12,45 mm; sapphire bezel transparent case back; water-resistant to 10 atm
Band: rubber, folding clasp
Remarks: aventurine dial
Price: $29,900
Variations: comes in sapphire of different colors ($39,900-$45,000); different dials

Depth Gauge

Movement: automatic, exclusive ArtyA Aion Caliber; ø 26.20 mm, height 3.60 mm; 25 jewels; 28,800 vph; with côtes de Genève; grey NAC coating on bridges; rhodium-plated gold oscillator; COSC-certified; 42-hour power reserve
Functions: hours, minutes, sweep seconds
Case: stainless steel with black DLC, ø 44 mm, height 14 mm; transparent case back; water-resistant to 3 atm
Band: leather
Remarks: depth gauge on dial with colored arches that disappear one by one the deeper the diver goes due to light wavelengths no longer reaching the dial
Price: $7,900
Variations: in 41-mm case and with full sapphire case

The Wave

Movement: automatic, exclusive ArtyA Aion Caliber; ø 26.20 mm, height 3.60 mm; 25 jewels; 28,800 vph; with côtes de Genève; grey NAC coating on bridges; rhodium-plated gold oscillator; COSC-certified; 42-hour power reserve
Functions: hours, minutes, sweep seconds; date
Case: stainless steel with black DLC, ø 43 mm, height 14 mm; unidirectional bezel with ceramic insert; transparent case back; water-resistant to 30 atm
Band: rubber, folding clasp
Remarks: special 3D enamel design looks like ripples made by a pebble thrown into the water
Price: $7,900
Variations: black enamel dial

Son of Earth Crystal

Movement: automatic, ArtyA Aion; ø 26.20 mm, height 3.60 mm; 25 jewels; 28,800 vph; with côtes de Genève; rhodium-plated gold oscillator; COSC-certified; 42-hour power reserve
Functions: hours, minutes, sweep seconds
Case: sapphire case, ø 39 mm, height 11 mm; engraved and screwed-down case back; water-resistant to 3 atm
Band: leather, buckle
Remarks: dial with real butterfly wings
Price: $28,900

Butterfly Nanosapphire Bicolor

Movement: automatic Lajoux Perret G100; ø 25.6 mm, height 4.45 mm; 24 jewels; 28,800 vph; 60-hour power reserve
Functions: hours, minutes, sweep seconds
Case: two-tone nanosapphire, ø 39 mm, height 11 mm; full sapphire case back; water-resistant to 3 atm
Band: leather, buckle
Remarks: hand-made dial of real butterfly wings and natural pigments, by Dominique Arpa-Cirpka
Price: $ 69,100; unique piece

ArtyA White Enamel

Movement: automatic ArtyA A82, modified; ø 26.2 mm, height 3.6 mm; movement; 50-hour power reserve
Functions: hours, minutes, subsidiary seconds; date
Case: stainless steel, ø 41 mm, height 12 mm; engraved and screwed-down transparent case back; water-resistant to 3 atm
Band: reptile skin, buckle
Price: $9,900; limited to 9 pieces
Variations: multiple enamel colors

AUDEMARS PIGUET

Manufacture d'Horlogerie Audemars Piguet
Route de France 16
CH- 1348 Le Brassus
Switzerland

Tel.:
+41-21-642-3900

E-mail:
info@audemarspiguet.com

Website:
www.audemarspiguet.com

Founded:
1875

Number of employees:
approx. 1,300

Annual production:
40,000 watches

U.S. distributor:
Audemars Piguet (North America) Inc.
Service Center of the Americas
3040 Gulf to Bay Boulevard
Clearwater, FL 33759

Most important collections/price range:
CODE 11.59 / from approx. $26,000; Millenary / from approx. $28,400; Royal Oak / from approx. $17,800; special concept watches

Jules-Louis Audemars (b. 1851) and Edward-Auguste Piguet (b. 1853) knew they would follow in the footsteps of their fathers and grandfathers and become watchmakers. They were members of the same sports association, sang in the same choir, attended the same vocational school—and both became outstandingly talented watchmakers. The *manufacture*, founded over 140 years ago by these two, is still in family hands, and it has become one of the leading names in the industry.

In the history of watchmaking, only a handful of watches have really achieved cult status. One of them is the Royal Oak by Audemars Piguet. It was born as a radical answer to the global invasion of the quartz watch. Audemars Piguet contacted the designer Gérald Genta to create a watch for a new generation of customers, a sportive luxury timepiece with a modern look, which could be worn every day. The result was a luxurious watch of stainless steel. The octagonal bezel held down with boldly "industrial" hexagonal bolts onto a 39-millimeter case was provocatively big and was nicknamed "Jumbo." It ran on what was then the thinnest automatic movement, a slice 3.05 millimeters high. This iconic piece, designed by Gérald Genta, is celebrating its fiftieth birthday this year, and the explosion in demand underscores the importance of the design of the century.

The second key to the brand's enduring success was no doubt the acquisition of the atelier Renaud et Papi in 1992. APRP, as it is known, specializes in creating and executing complex complications, a skill it lets other brands share in as well.

As for the "Code 11.59," a marketing name that suggests deep brand codes cloaked in modern garb, it was presented with lots of fireworks at the 2019 SIHH. There is the round bezel and case with an octagonal barrel. The sapphire crystal is specially shaped with a double vault. The dials are particularly clever. They feature a variety of different surface techniques. Among the new movements, the first in-house integrated flyback chronograph (caliber 4401) is noteworthy.

Royal Oak "Jumbo" Extra-Thin "50th Anniversary"

Reference number: 16202ST.OO.1240ST.01
Movement: automatic, AP Caliber 7121; ø 29.6 mm, height 3.2 mm; 33 jewels; 28,800 vph; white gold oscillating weight; 55-hour power reserve
Functions: hours, minutes, date
Case: stainless steel, ø 39 mm, height 8 mm; bezel screwed to case with 8 white-gold screws; sapphire crystal; transparent case back; water-resistant to 5 atm
Band: stainless steel, folding clasp
Price: $34,900

Royal Oak "Jumbo" Openworked "50th Anniversary"

Reference number: 16204OR.OO.1240OR.01
Movement: automatic, AP Caliber 7124; ø 29.6 mm, height 2.7 mm; 31 jewels; 28,800 vph; skeletonized and blackened movement; 55-hour power reserve
Functions: hours, minutes
Case: rose gold, ø 39 mm, height 8 mm; bezel screwed to case with 8 white-gold screws; sapphire crystal; transparent case back; water-resistant to 5 atm
Band: rose gold, folding clasp
Remarks: skeletonized dial
Price: on request

Royal Oak "Jumbo" Extra-Thin "50th Anniversary"

Reference number: 16202PT.OO.1240PT.01
Movement: automatic, AP Caliber 7121; ø 29.6 mm, height 3.2 mm; 33 jewels; 28,800 vph; white gold oscillating weight; 55-hour power reserve
Functions: hours, minutes, date
Case: platinum, ø 39 mm, height 8 mm; bezel screwed to case with 8 white-gold screws; sapphire crystal; transparent case back; water-resistant to 5 atm
Band: platinum, folding clasp
Price: $119,800

Royal Oak Black Ceramic

Reference number: 77350CE.00.1266CE.01
Movement: automatic, AP Caliber 5800; ø 23.3 mm, height 3.9 mm; 28 jewels; 28,800 vph; 50-hour power reserve
Functions: hours, minutes, sweep seconds; date
Case: ceramic, ø 34 mm, height 9 mm; bezel screwed to case with 8 rose-gold screws; sapphire crystal; transparent case back; screw-in crown; water-resistant to 5 atm
Band: ceramic, folding clasp
Price: $45,000

Royal Oak Flying Tourbillon Openworked

Reference number: 26735ST.00.1320ST.01
Movement: automatic, AP Caliber 2972; ø 31.5 mm, height 6.8 mm; 27 jewels; 21,600 vph; 1-minute flying tourbillon; skeletonized movement; 65-hour power reserve
Functions: hours, minutes
Case: stainless steel, ø 41 mm, height 10.6 mm; bezel screwed to case with 8 white-gold screws; sapphire crystal; transparent case back; water-resistant to 5 atm
Band: stainless steel, folding clasp
Price: on request

Royal Oak Selfwinding Flying Tourbillon

Reference number: 26730TI.00.1320TI.01
Movement: automatic, AP Caliber 2950; ø 30.9 mm, height 6.24 mm; 27 jewels; 21,600 vph; 1-minute flying tourbillon; 65-hour power reserve
Functions: hours, minutes
Case: titanium, ø 41 mm, height 11 mm; bezel screwed to case with 8 white-gold screws; sapphire crystal; transparent case back; screw-in crown; water-resistant to 5 atm
Band: stainless steel, folding clasp
Price: on request

Royal Oak Chronograph

Reference number: 26240OR.OO.1320OR.04
Movement: automatic, AP Caliber 4401; ø 32 mm, height 6.8 mm; 40 jewels; 28,800 vph; movement entirely hand-decorated; 70-hour power reserve
Functions: hours, minutes, subsidiary seconds; chronograph; date
Case: rose gold, ø 41 mm, height 12.4 mm; bezel screwed to case with 8 white-gold screws; sapphire crystal; transparent case back; screw-in crown and pushers; water-resistant to 5 atm
Band: rose gold, folding clasp
Price: $260,000
Variations: various cases, bands, and dials

Royal Oak Selfwinding Chronograph

Reference number: 26715ST.00.1356ST.01
Movement: automatic, AP Caliber 2385; ø 26.2 mm, height 5.5 mm; 37 jewels; 21,600 vph; movement entirely hand-decorated; 40-hour power reserve
Functions: hours, minutes, subsidiary seconds; chronograph; date
Case: stainless steel, ø 38 mm, height 11 mm; bezel screwed to case with 8 white-gold screws; sapphire crystal; screw-in crown and pusher; water-resistant to 5 atm
Band: stainless steel, folding clasp
Price: $34,200
Variations: various cases, bands, and dials

Royal Oak Selfwinding "50th Anniversary"

Reference number: 15550ST.00.1356ST.04
Movement: automatic, AP Caliber 5900; ø 26.2 mm, height 3.9 mm; 29 jewels; 28,800 vph; fine finishing on movement; 60-hour power reserve
Functions: hours, minutes, sweep seconds; date
Case: stainless steel, ø 37 mm, height 9 mm; bezel screwed to case with 8 white-gold screws; sapphire crystal; transparent case back; water-resistant to 5 atm
Band: stainless steel, folding clasp
Price: $25,300

Royal Oak Offshore Chronograph

Reference number: 26420RO.OO.A002CA.01
Movement: automatic, AP Caliber 4401; ø 32 mm, height 6.8 mm; 40 jewels; 28,800 vph; hand-decorated movement; 70-hour power reserve
Functions: hours, minutes, subsidiary seconds; chronograph; date
Case: pink gold, ø 43 mm, height 14.4 mm; ceramic bezel screwed to case back with 8 white-gold screws; sapphire crystal; ceramic crown and pushers; water-resistant to 10 atm
Band: rubber, buckle
Remarks: comes with additional rubber strap
Price: $63,700

Royal Oak Minute Repeater Supersonnerie

Reference number: 26591TI.OO.1252TI.03
Movement: manually wound, AP Caliber 2953; ø 30 mm, height 6 mm; 32 jewels; 21,600 vph; fine finishing on movement; 72-hour power reserve
Functions: hours, minutes, subsidiary seconds; minute repeater
Case: titanium, ø 42 mm, height 14 mm; bezel screwed to case with 8 white-gold screws; sapphire crystal; screw-in crown
Band: titanium, folding clasp
Price: on request

Royal Oak Offshore Diver

Reference number: 15720ST.OO.A052CA.01
Movement: automatic, AP Caliber 4308; ø 32 mm, height 5.2 mm; 32 jewels; 28,800 vph; 60-hour power reserve
Functions: hours, minutes, sweep seconds; date
Case: stainless steel, ø 42 mm, height 14.2 mm; bezel screwed to case back with 8 white-gold screws, crown-activated scale ring with 0-60 scale; sapphire crystal; screw-in crown; water-resistant to 30 atm
Band: rubber, buckle
Price: $29,000
Variations: comes in various colors

CODE 11.59 Chronograph

Reference number: 26393NB.OO.A002KB.01
Movement: automatic, AP Caliber 4401; ø 32 mm, height 6.8 mm; 40 jewels; 28,800 vph; skeletonized gold rotor, finely finished movement; 70-hour power reserve
Functions: hours, minutes, subsidiary seconds; flyback-chronograph; date
Case: white gold, ø 41 mm, height 12.6 mm; sapphire crystal; transparent case back; water-resistant to 3 atm
Band: textile with rubber coating, buckle
Price: $51,400
Variations: in rose gold ($51,400)

CODE 11.59 Chronograph

Reference number: 26393NR.OO.A002KB.01
Movement: automatic, AP Caliber 4401; ø 32 mm, height 6.8 mm; 40 jewels; 28,800 vph; skeletonized gold rotor, finely finished movement; 70-hour power reserve
Functions: hours, minutes, subsidiary seconds; flyback chronograph; date
Case: rose gold, ø 41 mm, height 12.6 mm; sapphire crystal; transparent case back; water-resistant to 3 atm
Band: textile with rubber coating, buckle
Price: $51,400
Variations: in white gold ($51,400)

CODE 11.59 Perpetual Calendar

Reference number: 26394OR.OO.D027KB.01
Movement: automatic, AP Caliber 5134; ø 29 mm, height 4.31 mm; 38 jewels; 19,800 vph; skeletonized gold rotor, finely finished movement; 40-hour power reserve
Functions: hours, minutes; perpetual calendar with date, weekday, calendar week, month, moon phase, leap year
Case: rose gold, ø 41 mm, height 10.9 mm; sapphire crystal; transparent case back
Band: rubber with, folding clasp
Remarks: aventurine dial
Price: $99,400

Caliber 4302

Automatic; bidirectionally winding gold rotor; single spring barrel, 70-hour power reserve
Functions: hours, minutes, sweep seconds; date
Diameter: 32 mm
Height: 4.8 mm
Jewels: 32
Balance: with variable inertia
Frequency: 28,800 vph
Remarks: beveled and polished steel parts, plate with perlage, bridges with côtes de Genève; 257 parts

Caliber 4401

Automatic; column-wheel control of chronograph functions; skeletonized gold rotor; single spring barrel, 70-hour power reserve
Functions: hours, minutes, subsidiary seconds; flyback chronograph; date
Diameter: 32 mm
Height: 6.8 mm
Jewels: 40
Balance: with variable inertia
Frequency: 28,800 vph
Remarks: beveled and polished steel parts, plate with perlage, bridges with côtes de Genève; 367 parts

Caliber 5134

Automatic; flying spring barrel; 40-hour power reserve
Functions: hours, minutes; perpetual calendar with date, weekday, calendar week, month, moon phase, leap year
Diameter: 29 mm
Height: 4.31 mm
Jewels: 38
Balance: with variable inertia
Frequency: 19,800 vph
Balance spring: flat hairspring
Remarks: hand-decorated movement; gold rotor; 374 parts

Caliber 2950

Automatic; 1-minute flying tourbillon; skeletonized rotor; single spring barrel, 65-hour power reserve
Functions: hours, minutes
Diameter: 30.9 mm
Height: 6.24 mm
Jewels: 27
Frequency: 21,600 vph
Remarks: 270 parts

Caliber 2956

Manually wound; two separate spring barrels for movement and chiming mechanism (grand and small strike, minute repeater); 48-hour power reserve
Functions: hours, minutes; minute repeater, grand and small strike with carillon (three gongs)
Diameter: 29.9 mm
Height: 5.88 mm
Jewels: 53
Balance: with variable inertia
Frequency: 21,600 vph
Remarks: beveled and polished steel parts, perlage on mainplate, bridges with côtes de Genève

Caliber 2965

Manually wound; 1-minute flying tourbillon; single spring barrel, 72-hour power reserve
Functions: hours, minutes
Diameter: 31 mm
Height: 3.85 mm
Jewels: 17
Frequency: 21,600 vph
Remarks: hand-painted 3-D-Marvel Comics superhero "Black Panther" in white gold Integrated in the movement; 242 parts

AZIMUTH

Creativity can take on all forms and accept all forms as well. This appears to be the philosophy behind Azimuth, an independent watch brand that has sprouted an eclectic and surprising bouquet of watch designs. For the company, the path is by no means well-beaten: Azimuth always guarantees a raised eyebrow with avant-garde designs for luxury timepieces, with several iconic models like the Mr. Roboto, the Spaceship series, the automobile series and the TT and GT enjoying cult status.

Azimuth consistently explores the worlds of sci-fi with a few nods to pop culture, but it always does so boldly, sparing no expense to shape the watch cases themselves if need be. Dials featuring Astro Boy or the world's favorite cat Garfield mingle with iconic car-inspired pieces, like the Twin Turbo. And 2023 being the brand's twentieth anniversary, the followers of this unconventional company can expect some surprises. Mr. Roboto has been rebuilt using a block of sapphire crystal. The 3-dimensional eyes and mouth are visible from all angles, creating a perception of depth and intricacies. The complex CNC operation to cut the sapphire crystal makes this model by far the rarest Mr. Roboto ever created.

As for the Spaceship Predator, it appears in the form of the PVD Lava OverLand. It is in the Spaceship collection lineage, one of the company's most popular collections. It now comes in a titanium case and features enamel dial depicting a fierce flow of molten lava over land. Each dial is meticulously hand painted, meaning that no two dials are exactly alike.

Like all great artists, though, Azimuth is capable of doing "serious watches," and for that they purchased a venerable Swiss brand in 2013 called Montres Choisi (see page 220).

Azimuth Watch Co. Sàrl
Rue des Draizes 5
CH-2000 Neuchâtel
Switzerland

Tel.:
+41-79-765-1466

E-mail:
gpi@azimuthwatch.com
chrislong@azimuthwatch.com

Website:
www.azimuthwatch.com

Founded:
2003

Number of employees:
6

U.S. distributor:
About Time Luxury Group
210 Bellevue Avenue
Newport RI 02840
401-952-4684

Most important collection/price range:
SP-1 / from $1,750

SP-1 Mr. Roboto Bronzo Artist Series

Reference number: SP.BR.MRB.L002
Movement: automatic, Caliber ETA 2836 in-house modified, ø 32.5mm, height 6.70mm; 28,800 vph; 36-hour power reserve
Functions: regulator hours, retrograde minutes; second time zone
Case: bronze, 43 x 50 mm; sapphire crystal, water-resistant to 3 atm
Band: calf leather, bronze buckle
Remarks: unique piece; individually hand-engraved bezel with a unique motif
Price: $9,850

SP-1 Mr. Roboto R2

Reference number: SP.SS.ROT.N001
Movement: automatic, in-house modified; ø 32.5 mm, height 6.70 mm; 28,800 vph; sapphire rotor; 36-hour power reserve
Functions: regulator hours, retrograde minutes; second time zone
Case: stainless steel, 47 x 55 mm, sapphire crystal, water-resistant to 3 atm
Band: calf leather, folding clasp
Price: $6,000
Variations: mid-case in titanium with blue PVD treatment

Azimuth Garfield BITCOIN PIZZA! Back-In-Time

Reference number: RN.BT.BR.N003
Movement: automatic, in-house modified; ø 34.4 mm, height 4.50 mm; 28,800 vph, 36-hour power reserve
Functions: hands in counterclockwise motion
Case: bronze, ø 42 mm, height 14.4 mm; domed sapphire crystal, water-resistant to 3 atm
Band: calf leather, bronze tang buckle
Remarks: special Singapore edition to commemorate the creation of Bitcoin
Price: $2,650; limited to 100 pieces

SP-1 Predator 2.0

Reference number: SP.TI.PR.N001
Movement: manual winding, AZM 769; ø 36.6 mm, height 4.50 mm; 21,600 vph; modified and skeletonized aluminum plates, 40-hour power reserve
Functions: jumping hours, minutes, seconds
Case: titanium and stainless steel, ø 44 mm, domed sapphire crystal, water-resistant to 3atm
Band: rubber, folding clasp
Remarks: 3-dimensional titanium minute hand
Price: $5,850
Variations: movement plates in various colors

SP-1 Spaceship Predator Lava OverLand

Reference number: SP.BR.PR.N002
Movement: manual winding, Caliber 6497; ø 36.6 mm, height 4.50 mm; 21,600 vph; 40-hour power reserve
Functions: jumping hours, minutes
Case: bronze and stainless steel, ø 44 mm, domed sapphire crystal, water-resistant to 3atm
Band: rubber, bronze tang buckle
Remarks: hand-painted dial
Price: $5,500; limited to 100 pieces

SP-1 Spaceship Predator PVD Lava OverLand

Reference number: SP.TI.PR.N003
Movement: manual winding, Caliber 6497; ø 36.6 mm, height 4.50 mm; 21,600 vph; 40-hour power reserve
Functions: jumping hours, minutes
Case: titanium with PVD treatment and stainless steel, ø 44 mm, domed sapphire crystal, water-resistant to 3 atm
Band: rubber, folding clasp
Price: $5,500

SP-1 Gran Turismo

Reference number: SP.SS.GT.N003
Movement: automatic, ETA 2671; ø 17.2 mm, height 4.80 mm; 25 jewels; 28,800 vph; 44-hour power reserve
Functions: hour, minutes, seconds
Case: stainless steel with black PVD treatment, 50 mm x 45 mm, water-resistant to 3 atm
Band: calfskin, folding clasp
Price: $4,850; limited to 100 pieces
Variations: top case in stainless steel, gold PVD treatment or camo

SP-1 Twin Turbo

Reference number: SP.SS.TT.N001
Movement: manually wound, ETA 2512-1; ø 17.2 mm, height 2.85 mm; 21,600 vph; 17 jewels; 44-hour power reserve
Functions: hour, minutes, 2 time zones
Case: stainless steel and aluminum, 51 mm x 50 mm, water-resistant to 3 atm
Band: calfskin, folding clasp
Remarks: 2 vintage movements
Price: $6,000; limited to 88 pieces
Variations: top hood in grey, anthracite or red (red version limited to 50 pieces)

SP-1 Crazy Rider

Reference number: SP.SS.CR.N004
Movement: automatic, in-house modified; length 47.7 mm, height 4.35 mm; 28,800 vph
Functions: 24-hour chain-drive hour system, minutes
Case: stainless steel with PVD treatment, titanium bezel with black PVD treatment, 55 mm x 36 mm, sapphire crystal, water-resistant to 3 atm
Band: calfskin, folding clasp
Price: $5,250
Variations: brown dial

BALL WATCH CO.

Ball Watch Co. collections trace back to the company's origins and evoke the glorious age when trains puffing smoke and steam crisscrossed America. The General Railroads Timepiece Standards back then included such norms as regulation in at least five positions, precision to within thirty seconds per week, Breguet hairsprings, and so on. One of the chief players in developing the standards was Webster Clay Ball, a farm boy-turned-watchmaker from Fredericktown, Ohio. He decided to leave the homestead and apprentice as a watchmaker. He worked as a sales rep for Dueber watch cases and finally opened the Webb C. Ball Company in Cleveland. In 1891, he added the position of chief inspector of the Lake Shore Lines to his CV. His defining moment came when a hogshead's watch stopped for a few minutes, resulting in a lethal crash near Kipton, Ohio. Ball decided to establish quality benchmarks for watch manufacturing that included amagnetic technology. He also set up an inspection system for the timepieces. This standardized timekeeping tool gave rise to an expression in the American vernacular, to "be on the Ball." It also inspired the future Swiss Society of Chronometry (COSC), which governs the highest watch timing certification standards today.

Today, Ball Watch Co. still produces tool-like watches, including divers, although now the manufacturing is done in Switzerland. These rugged, durable watches aim to be "accurate in adverse conditions," so says the company tagline—and at a very good price. Since functionality is a top priority, Ball has developed several mechanisms like the patented SpringLOCK anti-shock system that prevents the balance spring from unfurling when jostled. Ball has also developed special oils for cold temperatures, and it is one of few brands to use tritium gas tubes to light up dials, hands, and markers. For those who need to read the time accurately in dark places—divers, pilots, commandos, hunters, etc.—this is essential.

BALL Watch Company SA
Rue du Châtelot 21
CH-2300 La Chaux-de-Fonds
Switzerland

Tel.:
0041-32-724-53-00

E-mail:
info@ballwatch.ch

Website:
www.ballwatch.com

Founded:
1891

U.S. distribution:
BALL Watch USA
888-660-0691

Most important collections/price range:
Engineer, Fireman, Trainmaster / $1,300 to $6,500

Engineer Hydrocarbon Original

Reference number: DM2218B-S2CJ-GR, Ball Caliber
Movement: automatic RR1102-CSL; ø 25.6 mm, height 5.05 mm; 25 or 26 jewels; 28,800 vph; 38-hour power reserve; COSC-certified chronometer; SpringLOCK antishock system; SpringSEAL patented regulator anti-shock system
Functions: hours, minutes, sweep seconds; day, date
Case: stainless steel, ø 43 mm, height 15.3 mm; sapphire unidirectional bezel with micro gas tubes; Mu-metal shield; sapphire crystal; crown protection system; water-resistant to 20 atm; Amortiser anti-shock system
Band: stainless steel, folding buckle and extension
Remarks: micro gas tube illumination; shock-resistant; anti-magnetic
Price: $3,349
Variations: blue or black dial; rubber strap

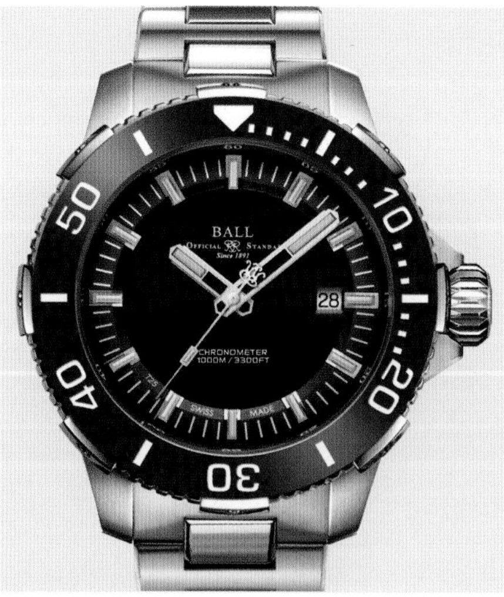

Engineer Hydrocarbon DeepQUEST Ceramic

Reference number: DM3002A-S4CJ-BK
Movement: automatic, Ball Caliber RR1101-C; ø 25.6 mm, height 3.6 mm; 25 jewels; 28,800 vph; 42-hour power reserve; COSC-certified chronometer
Functions: hours, minutes, sweep seconds; date; patented automatic helium release valve crown
Case: titanium, ø 42 mm, height 15.5 mm; ceramic unidirectional bezel; sapphire crystal; screwed-in crown; water-resistant to 100 atm
Band: tapered titanium and stainless steel, folding buckle and extension
Remarks: micro gas tube illumination; shock-resistant; anti-magnetic
Price: $3,999
Variations: rubber strap; green dial; black bezel

Engineer Hydrocarbon NEDU

Reference number: DC3026A-S3C-BE
Movement: automatic, Ball Caliber RR1402-C; ø 30 mm, height 7.9 mm; 25 jewels; 28,800 vph; 48-hour power reserve; COSC-certified chronometer
Functions: hours, minutes, subsidiary seconds; day, date; 12-hour chronograph operable underwater
Case: titanium, ø 42 mm, height 17.3 mm; patented helium system; ceramic unidirectional bezel; sapphire crystal; crown protection system; water-resistant to 60 atm
Band: titanium/stainless steel, folding buckle and extension
Remarks: micro gas tube illumination; shock-resistant; anti-magnetic
Price: $4,649
Variations: blue dial; rubber strap

Engineer Master II Worldtime

Reference number: DG2232A-SC-GR
Movement: automatic, Ball Caliber RR1501-C; ø 31.4 mm, height 6.95 mm; 25 or 26 jewels; 28,800 vph; 38-hour power reserve; COSC-certified chronometer
Functions: hours, minutes, sweep seconds; day and date; world time indication; unidirectional diving bezel
Case: stainless steel, ø 42 mm, height 14.4 mm; sapphire crystal; transparent case back; screwed-in crown; water-resistant to 30 atm
Band: tapered stainless steel, folding buckle
Remarks: micro gas tube illumination; shock-resistant; anti-magnetic
Price: $3,399
Variations: black dial; rubber strap

Engineer Master II Diver Chronometer

Reference number: DM2280A-S1C-BKR
Movement: automatic, Ball Caliber; RR1101-C; ø 25.6 mm, height 3.6 mm; 25 jewels; 28,800 vph; 42-hour power reserve; COSC-certified chronometer
Functions: hours, minutes, sweep seconds; date
Case: stainless steel, ø 42 mm, height 13.5 mm; inner bezel with micro gas tube illumination; Mu-metal shield; sapphire crystal; screwed-in crown; water-resistant to 30 atm
Band: stainless steel, folding buckle
Remarks: micro gas tube illumination; shock-resistant; anti-magnetic
Price: $2,599
Variations: blue dial; standard tubes colors; rubber strap

Engineer II Moon Calendar

Reference number: NM3016C-S1J-CH
Movement: automatic, Ball Caliber; RR1807; ø 26.2 mm, height 5.2 mm; 25 jewels; 28,800 vph; 38-hour power reserve
Functions: hours, minutes and sweep seconds; month, day and date; moon phase
Case: stainless steel, ø 40 mm, height 13.4 mm; sapphire crystal; transparent case back; screwed-in crown; water-resistant to 10 atm; Amortiser anti-shock system
Band: stainless steel, folding buckle
Remarks: micro gas tube illumination; shock-resistant; anti-magnetic
Price: $3,049
Variations: white dial; blue dial; green dial; silver dial; ice blue dial

Engineer II Skindiver Heritage Manufacture Chronometer

Reference number: DD3208B-S2C-BKR
Movement: automatic, Ball Caliber RRM7309-C; ø 34.24 mm, height 5.16 mm; 25 jewels; 28,800 vph; 80-hour power reserve; COSC-certified chronometer
Functions: hours, minutes, sweep seconds; date
Case: stainless steel with TiC coating, ø 42 mm, height 15.2 mm; sapphire unidirectional bezel; sapphire crystal; transparent case back; screwed-in crown; water-resistant to 20 atm
Band: TiC coated stainless steel, folding buckle
Remarks: micro gas tube illumination; shock-resistant; anti-magnetic
Price: $3,449
Variations: blue dial; standard tubes colors; rubber strap

Engineer III Outlier

Reference number: DG9000B-S1C-BK
Movement: automatic, Ball Caliber RRM7337-C; ø 26.2 mm, height 4.5 mm; 25 jewels; 28,800 vph; 42-hour power reserve; COSC-certified chronometer
Functions: hours, minutes, sweep second; magnified date; quick-set local 12-hour hand; three time zone indication
Case: stainless steel, ø 40 mm, height 13.8 mm; bidirectional steel bezel; mu-metal shield; sapphire crystal; screwed-in crown; water-resistant to 20 atm; Amortiser anti-shock system
Band: stainless steel, folding buckle
Remarks: micro gas tube illumination; shock-resistant; anti-magnetic
Price: $3,449

Engineer III Legend II

Reference number: NM2126C-S5C-BE2
Movement: automatic, Ball Caliber RR1101-C; ø 25.6 mm, height 3.6 mm; 25 jewels; 28,800 vph; 42-hour power reserve; COSC-certified chronometer
Functions: hours, minutes, sweep seconds; magnified date
Case: stainless steel, ø 40 mm, height 11.5 mm; mu-metal shield; sapphire crystal; screwed-in crown; water-resistant to 10 atm
Band: stainless steel, folding buckle
Remarks: micro gas tube illumination; shock-resistant; anti-magnetic
Price: $2,449
Variations: black dial; standard tubes colors

Engineer III Maverick GMT

Reference number: DG3028C-S1CJ-BE
Movement: automatic, Ball Caliber RRM7337-C; ø 26.2 mm, height 4.5 mm; 25 jewels; 28,800 vph; 42-hour power reserve; COSC-certified chronometer
Functions: hours, minutes, sweep second; magnified date; quick-set local 12-hour hand; three time zone indication
Case: stainless steel, ø 40 mm, height 12.8 mm; sapphire bidirectional bezel; mu-metal shield; sapphire crystal; screwed-in crown; water-resistant to 10 atm; Amortiser anti-shock system
Band: stainless steel, folding buckle
Remarks: micro gas tube illumination; shock-resistant; anti-magnetic
Price: $3,599
Variations: black dial; ice blue dial

Engineer III Endurance 1917 GMT

Reference number: GM9100C-S2C-IBER
Movement: automatic, Ball Caliber RRM7337-C; ø 26.2 mm, height 4.5 mm; 25 jewels; 28,800 vph; 42-hour power reserve; COSC-certified chronometer; Special movement oil to endure -45°C / -49°F
Functions: hours, minutes, sweep second; magnified date; quick-set local 12-hour hand; second time zone indication
Case: stainless steel, ø 41 mm, height 13.15 mm; mu-metal shield; sapphire crystal; screwed-in crown; water-resistant to 10 atm; Amortiser anti-shock system
Band: stainless steel, folding buckle
Remarks: micro gas tube illumination; shock-resistant; anti-magnetic
Price: $3,199
Variations: gray dial; blue dial; standard tubes colors

Engineer III Marvelight Chronometer

Reference number: NM9026C-S6CJ-RD
Movement: automatic, Ball Caliber RR1103-C; ø 25.6 mm, height 4.6 mm; 25 or 26 jewels; 28,800 vph; 38-hour power reserve; COSC-certified chronometer
Functions: hours, minutes, sweep seconds; magnified date
Case: stainless steel, ø 40 mm, height 13.15 mm; mu-metal shield; sapphire crystal; screwed-in crown; water-resistant to 10 atm
Band: stainless steel, folding buckle
Remarks: micro gas tube illumination; shock-resistant; anti-magnetic
Price: $2,349
Variations: black dial; blue dial; green dial; ice blue dial; gray dial

Engineer M Skindiver III Beyond

Reference number: DD3100A-S2C-BE
Movement: automatic, Ball Caliber RRM7309-C; ø 34.24 mm, height 5.16 mm; 25 jewels; 28,800 vph; 80-hour power reserve; COSC-certified chronometer
Functions: hours, minutes, sweep seconds; magnified date
Case: stainless steel, ø 41.5 mm, height 13.8 mm; sapphire unidirectional bezel; sapphire crystal; screwed-in crown; water-resistant to 30 atm; Amortiser anti-shock system
Band: stainless steel, folding buckle
Remarks: micro gas tube illumination; shock-resistant; anti-magnetic
Price: $3,699

Engineer M Pioneer

Reference number: NM9032C-S2C-BK2
Movement: automatic, Ball Caliber RRM7309-CS; ø 34.24 mm, height 5.16 mm; 25 jewels; 28,800 vph; 80-hour power reserve; COSC-certified chronometer
Functions: hours, minutes, sweep seconds; magnified date
Case: stainless steel, ø 40 mm, height 13 mm; sapphire crystal; transparent case back; screwed-in crown; water-resistant to 10 atm; Amortiser anti-shock system
Band: stainless steel, folding buckle
Remarks: micro gas tube illumination; shock-resistant; anti-magnetic
Price: $3,849
Variations: blue dial; green dial

Roadmaster Rescue Chronograph

Reference number: DC3030C-S1-WH
Movement: automatic, Ball Caliber RR1402; ø 30 mm, height 7.9 mm; 25 jewels; 28,800 vph; 48-hour power reserve; special movement oil to endure -45°C / -49°F
Functions: hours, minutes, subsidiary seconds; day and date; 12-hour chronograph; pulsometer
Case: titanium, ø 41 mm, height 14.8 mm; ceramic unidirectional bezel; sapphire crystal; screwed-in crown; water-resistant to 10 atm; Amortiser anti-shock system
Band: titanium and stainless steel bracelet with folding buckle
Remarks: micro gas tube illumination; shock-resistant; anti-magnetic
Price: $2,599
Variations: blue dial; ice blue dial

Roadmaster Marine GMT

Reference number: DG3000A-S4C-BK
Movement: automatic, Ball Caliber RR1203-C; ø 31.4 mm, height 5.75 mm; 25 or 26 jewels; 28,800 vph; 38-hour power reserve; COSC-certified chronometer
Functions: hours, minutes, sweep seconds; day and date
Case: titanium, ø 40 mm, height 14 mm; bidirectional ceramic bezel; sapphire crystal; screwed-in crown; transparent case back; water-resistant to 20 atm
Band: titanium and stainless steel bracelet with folding buckle
Remarks: micro gas tube illumination; shock-resistant; anti-magnetic
Price: $3,249
Variations: blue dial

Roadmaster Pilot GMT

Reference number: DG3038A-S3C-BK
Movement: automatic, Ball Caliber RR1204-C; ø 31.4 mm, height 5.75 mm; 25 jewels; 28,800 vph; 38-hour power reserve; COSC-certified chronometer
Functions: hours, minutes, sweep seconds; magnified date; patented quick set mechanism for local 12-hour hand; three time zone indication
Case: titanium, ø 40 mm, height 14 mm; ceramic bidirectional bezel; sapphire crystal; transparent case back; screwed-in crown; water-resistant to 30 atm
Band: titanium and stainless steel bracelet with folding buckle
Remarks: micro gas tube illumination; shock-resistant; anti-magnetic
Price: $3,249
Variations: blue dial; white dial

Roadmaster Ocean Explorer

Reference number: DM3120C-SCJ-BE
Movement: automatic, Ball Caliber RR1803-C; ø 31.4 mm, height 5.75 mm; 25 or 26 jewels; 28,800 vph; 38-hour power reserve; COSC-certified chronometer
Functions: hours, minutes, sweep seconds; magnified date; high and low tide indication; moon phase; spring and neap tide indication
Case: ø 41 mm, height 12.95 mm; aluminum bidirectional bezel; sapphire crystal; transparent case back; screwed-in crown; water-resistant to 10 atm
Band: stainless steel, folding buckle
Remarks: micro gas tube illumination; shock-resistant; anti-magnetic
Price: $3,299
Variations: black dial; green dial

Trainmaster Legend

Reference number: NM9080D-L1J-BE
Movement: automatic, Ball Caliber RR1103; ø 25.6 mm, height 4.6 mm; 25 or 26 jewels; 28,800 vph; 38-hour power reserve
Functions: hours, minutes, sweep seconds; date
Case: stainless steel, ø 40 mm, height 11.45 mm; sapphire crystal; transparent case back; push crown; water-resistant to 3 atm
Band: calf leather NATO style, buckle
Remarks: micro gas tube illumination; shock-resistant; anti-magnetic
Price: $1,849
Variations: black dial; silver dial; stainless steel bracelet

Trainmaster Railroad Standard 130 Anniversary

Reference number: NM3888D-S4CJ-WH
Movement: automatic, Ball Caliber RR1105-C; ø 25.6 mm, height 4.35 mm; 27 jewels; 28,800 vph; 42-hour power reserve; COSC-certified chronometer
Functions: hours, minutes, subsidiary seconds; date
Case: stainless steel, ø 40 mm, height 12 mm; sapphire crystal; transparent case back; screwed-in crown; water-resistant to 3 atm
Band: stainless steel bracelet, folding buckle
Remarks: micro gas tube illumination; shock-resistant; anti-magnetic
Price: $2,649
Variations: reptile skin strap

Fireman Victory

Reference number: NM2098C-S5J-SL
Movement: automatic, Ball Caliber RR1103; ø 25.6 mm, height 4.6 mm; 25 or 26 jewels; 28,800 vph; 38-hour power reserve
Functions: hours, minutes, sweep seconds; date
Case: stainless steel, ø 40 mm, height 11.3 mm; sapphire crystal; screwed-in crowns; water-resistant to 10 atm
Band: stainless steel bracelet, folding buckle
Remarks: micro gas tube illumination; shock-resistant; anti-magnetic
Price: $1,499
Variations: black dial; blue dial; calf leather

BAUME & MERCIER

Baume & Mercier, a company founded in 1830, has staked a claim on the market by its ability to keep a finger on the pulse of stylish, urban fashionistas, who are looking for affordable yet remarkable timepieces. Since the early 2000s, it has created a number of noteworthy—and often copied—classics, like the Riviera and the Catwalk.

Joining the Richemont Group has boosted the brand's technical value. In 2018, after four years of development with ValFleurier, the Group's movement manufacturer, and the RIMS research and innovation team, Baume & Mercier released its first in-house *manufacture* movement, the Baumatic Caliber BM12-1975A. In 2020, it added two new complications to the in-house caliber. Models using the caliber boast a five-day power reserve and accuracy of just −4/+6 seconds per day and amagnetism that is about twenty-five times higher than the current ISO norm.

The new BM14.1975 AC1/AC2 caliber is used in four of the Clifton models and drives a moon phase plus, in two models, a weekday and date display. In order to make way for the subsidiary dials and apertures, the crosshairs that "ordered" the dial of the simpler three-handers were removed.

The Hampton line was also extended with a series of watches whose rectangular shape recalls Art Deco predecessors. Two models come on Milanese bracelets, for a little retro look, and colors have become more exuberant. Most recently, the company rebooted the Riviera collection, which will be celebrating its fiftieth anniversary in 2023. This iconic model now comes in different colored dials and different sizes, including a 33-millimeter case. And thanks to a tool-free fastening system, all bracelets can be easily interchanged. Baume & Mercier offers a wide variety of classic colors here.

Baume & Mercier
Rue André de Garrini 4
CH-1217 Meyrin
Switzerland

Tel.:
+41-022-580-2948

Website:
www.baume-et-mercier.com

Founded:
1830

Annual production:
100,000 (estimated)

U.S. distributor:
Baume & Mercier
Richemont North America
New York, NY 10022
800-637-2437

Most important collections/price range:
Clifton (men) / $3,250 o $26,800;
Riviera (men and women) / $1,900 to $6,400;
Classima (men and women) / $1,050 to $4,700;
Hampton (men and women) / $1,600 to $4,350

Riviera Baumatic

Reference number: M0A10702
Movement: automatic, Caliber Baumatic BM13.1975A; ø 28.2 mm, height 4.2 mm; 21 jewels; 28,800 vph; silicon anchor and escape wheel; balance with variable inertia; skeletonized rotor; 120-hour power reserve
Functions: hours, minutes, sweep seconds; date
Case: stainless steel, ø 42 mm, height 10.7 mm; sapphire crystal; transparent case back; water-resistant to 10 atm
Band: stainless steel, triple folding clasp
Price: $3,700
Variations: various bands and dials

Riviera

Reference number: M0A10660
Movement: automatic, Sellita Caliber SW200-1; ø 25.2 mm, height 4.6 mm; 26 jewels; 28,800 vph; 38-hour power reserve
Functions: hours, minutes, sweep seconds; date
Case: stainless steel, ø 42 mm, height 10.7 mm; titanium bezel; sapphire crystal; transparent case back; water-resistant to 10 atm
Band: rubber, triple folding clasp
Price: $3,000
Variations: various bands and dials

Riviera

Reference number: M0A10679
Movement: automatic, Sellita Caliber SW200-1; ø 25.2 mm, height 4.6 mm; 26 jewels; 28,800 vph; 38-hour power reserve
Functions: hours, minutes, sweep seconds; date
Case: stainless steel, ø 36 mm, height, 9.6 mm. sapphire crystal; transparent case back; water-resistant to 5 atm
Band: stainless steel, triple folding clasp
Price: $2,750
Variations: various bands and dials

Riviera

Reference number: M0A10661
Movement: automatic, Sellita Caliber SW200-1; ø 25.2 mm, height 4.6 mm; 26 jewels; 28,800 vph; 38-hour power reserve
Functions: hours, minutes, sweep seconds; date
Case: stainless steel, ø 36 mm, height 9.6 mm; titanium bezel; sapphire crystal; transparent case back; water-resistant to 5 atm
Band: stainless steel, triple folding clasp
Price: $3,150
Variations: various bands and dials

Riviera Chronograph

Reference number: M0A10625
Movement: automatic, ETA Caliber 7750; ø 30 mm, height 7.9 mm; 25 jewels; 28,800 vph; 42-hour power reserve
Functions: hours, minutes, subsidiary seconds; chronograph; date und weekday
Case: stainless steel with black DLC, ø 42 mm, height 14.1 mm; sapphire crystal; transparent case back; water-resistant to 10 atm
Band: rubber, triple folding clasp
Price: $4,400

Riviera

Reference number: M0A10675
Movement: automatic, Sellita Caliber SW200-1; ø 25.2 mm, height 4.6 mm; 26 jewels; 28,800 vph; 38-hour power reserve
Functions: hours, minutes, sweep seconds; date
Case: stainless steel, ø 36 mm, height 9.6 mm; sapphire crystal; transparent case back; water-resistant to 5 atm
Band: stainless steel, triple folding clasp
Price: $2,750

Hampton

Reference number: M0A10672
Movement: automatic, ETA Caliber 2671; ø 17.5 mm, height 4.8 mm; 25 jewels; 28,800 vph; 38-hour power reserve
Functions: hours, minutes, sweep seconds
Case: stainless steel, 27.5 mm x 43 mm, height 10 mm; sapphire crystal; water-resistant to 5 atm
Band: stainless steel Milanese bracelet, double folding clasp
Price: $2,800

Hampton

Reference number: M0A10670
Movement: quartz
Functions: hours, minutes
Case: stainless steel, 27.5 mm x 43 mm, height 8.9 mm; sapphire crystal; water-resistant to 5 atm
Band: calfskin, buckle
Price: $1,600

Classima

Reference number: M0A10695
Movement: automatic, Sellita Caliber SW200-1; ø 25.6 mm, height 4.6 mm; 26 jewels; 28,800 vph; 38-hour power reserve
Functions: hours, minutes, sweep seconds; date
Case: stainless steel, ø 42 mm, height 8.93 mm; sapphire crystal; water-resistant to 5 atm
Band: textile, buckle
Price: $1,950

BELL & ROSS

If there is such a class as "military chic," Bell & Ross is undoubtedly one of the leaders. The Paris-headquartered brand develops, manufactures, assembles, and regulates its timepieces in a modern factory in La Chaux-de-Fonds in the Jura mountains of Switzerland. The early models had a certain stringency that one might associate with soldierly life, but in the past years, working with outside specialists, the company has ventured into even more complicated watches such as tourbillons and wristwatches with uncommon shapes. This kind of ambitious innovation has only been possible since perfume and fashion specialist Chanel—which also maintains a successful watch line in its own right—became a significant Bell & Ross shareholder and brought the watchmaker access to the production facilities where designers Bruno Belamich and team can create more complicated, more interesting designs for their aesthetically unusual "instrument" watches.

What sets Bell & Ross timepieces apart from those of other, more traditional professional luxury makers is their special, roguish look: a delicate balance between striking, martial, and poetic—think Lawrence of Arabia, the gallivanting warrior. And it is this beauty for the eye to behold that makes the company's wares popular with style-conscious "civilians" as well as with the pilots, divers, astronauts, sappers, and other hard-riding professionals drawn to Bell & Ross timepieces for their superior functionality. The latest line, the BR 05, connects two geometric forms, the circle and the square. The result is a watch that gravitates more toward everyday usage, or what the brand calls "Urban Explorers," a modern version of the elemental being that slumbers in everyone.

Bell & Ross Ltd.
8 rue Copernic
F-75116 Paris
France

Tel.:
+33-1-73-73-93-00

E-mail:
sav@bellross.com

Website:
www.bellross.com

Founded:
1992

U.S. distributor:
Bell & Ross, Inc.
605 Lincoln Road, Suite 300
Miami Beach, FL 33139
888-307-7887
information@bellross.com
www.bellross.com

Most important collections/price range:
Instrument BR-X1, BR 01, BR 03, and BR 05 / approx. $3,100 to $450,000

BR 03-92 Diver Brown Bronze

Reference number: BR0392-D-BR-BR/SCA
Movement: automatic, Caliber BR-CAL.302 (Base ETA 2892-A2); ø 25.6 mm, height 3.6 mm; 21 jewels; 28,800 vph; 42-hour power reserve
Functions: hours, minutes, sweep seconds; date
Case: bronze, 42 x 42 mm, height 12.05 mm; unidirectional bezel with aluminum insert and 0-60 scale; sapphire crystal; screw-in crown; water resistant to 30 atm
Band: calf leather, buckle
Remarks: comes with rubber strap
Price: $4,700; limited to 999 pieces

BR 03-92 Diver White

Reference number: BR0392-D-WH-ST/SRB
Movement: automatic, Caliber BR-CAL.302 (Base ETA 2892-A2); ø 25.6 mm, height 3.6 mm; 21 jewels; 28,800 vph; 42-hour power reserve
Functions: hours, minutes, sweep seconds; date
Case: stainless steel, 42 x 42 mm, height 12.05 mm; unidirectional bezel with aluminum insert and 0-60 scale; sapphire crystal; screw-in crown; water resistant to 30 atm
Band: rubber, buckle
Remarks: comes with additional textile strap
Price: $3,990

BR 05 Chrono Edición Limitada

Reference number: BR05C-LDA/SSG
Movement: automatic, Caliber BR-CAL.301 (Base ETA 2894); ø 28.6 mm, height 6.1 mm; 37 jewels; 28,800 vph; 42-hour power reserve
Functions: hours, minutes, subsidiary seconds; chronograph; date
Case: stainless steel, 42 x 42 mm, height 12.4 mm; rose-gold bezel crewed to the monocoque case with 4 screws; sapphire crystal; transparent case back; screw-in crown; water resistant to 10 atm
Band: stainless steel with rose-gold elements, folding clasp
Remarks: third limited special edition for cigar lovers
Price: $13,000
Variations: with rubber strap ($8,600)

BR 03-94 Multimeter

Reference number: BR0394-SW-CE/SRB
Movement: automatic, Caliber BR-CAL.301 (Base ETA 2894-2); ø 28.6 mm, height 6.1 mm; 37 jewels; 28,800 vph; 42-hour power reserve
Functions: hours, minutes, subsidiary seconds; chronograph; date
Case: ceramic, 42 x 42 mm, height 12.8 mm; bezel screwed to the monocoque case with 4 screws; sapphire crystal; water-resistant to 10 atm
Band: rubber, buckle
Remarks: dial with tachymeter, pulsometer and asthmometer scale
Price: $5,800

BR V2-92 Full Lum

Reference number: BRV292-LUM-ST/SRB
Movement: automatic, Caliber BR-CAL.302 (Base ETA 2892-A2); ø 25.6 mm, height 3.6 mm; 21 jewels; 28,800 vph; 42-hour power reserve
Functions: hours, minutes, sweep seconds; date
Case: stainless steel, ø 41 mm, height 11.5 mm; unidirectional bezel with aluminum insert, and 0-60 scale; sapphire crystal; transparent case back; screw-in crown; water resistant to 10 atm
Band: rubber, buckle
Remarks: full-lume dial; limited to 500 pieces
Price: $3,800

BR V2-92 Orange Steel

Reference number: BRV292-O-ST/SRB
Movement: automatic, Caliber BR-CAL.302 (Base ETA 2892-A2); ø 25.6 mm, height 3.6 mm; 21 jewels; 28,800 vph; 42-hour power reserve
Functions: hours, minutes, sweep seconds; date
Case: stainless steel, ø 41 mm, height 11.5 mm; unidirectional bezel with aluminum insert, and 0-60 scale; sapphire crystal; transparent case back; screw-in crown; water resistant to 10 atm
Band: rubber, buckle
Price: $3,500; limited to 500 pieces
Variations: with stainless steel bracelet ($3,800)

BR 05 Skeleton Green

Reference number: BR05A-GN-SKST/SST
Movement: automatic, Caliber BR-CAL.322 (base ETA 2892-A2); ø 25.6 mm, height 3.6 mm; 21 jewels; 28,800 vph; movement components galvanized green 42-hour power reserve
Functions: hours, minutes, sweep seconds
Case: stainless steel, 40 x 40 mm, height 10.33 mm; bezel screwed to monocoque case with 4 screws; sapphire crystal; transparent case back; screw-in crown; water resistant to 10 atm
Band: stainless steel, folding clasp
Remarks: skeletonized dial
Price: $7,000; limited to 500 pieces
Variations: with rubber strap ($6,500)

BR 03-92 Radiocompass

Reference number: BR0392-RCO-CE/SRB
Movement: automatic, Caliber BR-CAL.302 (Base ETA 2892-A2); ø 25.6 mm, height 3.6 mm; 21 jewels; 28,800 vph; 42-hour power reserve
Functions: hours, minutes, sweep seconds; date
Case: ceramic, 42 x 42 mm, height 10.4 mm; bezel screwed to the monocoque case with 4 screws; sapphire crystal; screw-in crown; water resistant to 10 atm
Band: rubber, buckle
Price: $4,100

BR 05 GMT White

Reference number: BR05C-BU-ST/SST
Movement: automatic, Caliber BR-CAL.303 (Base ETA 2893-2); ø 25.6 mm, height 4.1 mm; 21 jewels; 28,800 vph; 42-hour power reserve
Functions: hours, minutes, sweep seconds; additional 24-hour display (second time zone), chronograph; date
Case: stainless steel, 40 x 40 mm, height 11.07 mm; bezel screwed to the monocoque case with 4 screws; sapphire crystal; transparent case back; screw-in crown; water resistant to 10 atm
Band: rubber, buckle
Price: $5,000
Variations: with stainless steel bracelet ($5,500)

BLANCPAIN

Blancpain SA
Le Rocher 12
CH-1348 Le Brassus
Switzerland

Tel.:
+41-21-796-3636

Website:
www.blancpain.com

Founded:
1735

U.S. distributor:
Blancpain
The Swatch Group (U.S.), Inc.
1200 Harbor Boulevard
Weehawken, NJ 07086
201-271-4680

Most important collections/price range:
Villeret, Fifty Fathoms, Ladybird, Air Command, Métiers d'Art / $9,800 to $400,000

In its advertising, the Blancpain watch brand has always proudly declared that, since 1735, the company has never made quartz watches and never will. Indeed, Blancpain is Switzerland's oldest watchmaker, and by sticking to its ideals, the company was put out of business by the "quartz boom" of the 1970s.

The Blancpain brand we know today came into being in the mid-eighties, when Jean-Claude Biver and Jacques Piguet purchased the venerable name. The company was subsequently moved to the Frédéric Piguet watch factory in Le Brassus, where it quickly became largely responsible for the renaissance of the mechanical wristwatch. This success caught the attention of the Swatch Group—known at that time as SMH. In 1992, it swooped in and purchased both companies to add to its portfolio. Movement fabrication and watch production were melded to form the Blancpain Manufacture in mid-2010.

But being quartz-less does not mean being old-fashioned. Over the past several years, Blancpain president Marc A. Hayek has put a great deal of energy into developing the company's technical originality. In terms of complications, Blancpain watches have always been in a class of their own. The product families were all consolidated into four families: the Villeret; the legendary Fifty Fathoms diver's watches; Ladybird, a graceful series for women; and Metiers d'art, a collection of unique pieces that express the brand's artistic and watchmaking prowess.

The strong focus on diver's watches has also had an impact on the company's environmental efforts. For almost twenty years, Blancpain has sponsored various initiatives aimed at protecting the oceans. Hayek is a passionate diver and particularly concerned about marine protected areas (MPAs). Human activity of all kind is banned or at least severely restricted in these areas so that corals and fish stocks can recover. In 2022, Blancpain announced support for a new initiative to promote the renaturation of the affected marine and coastal sections on the island of Pangatalan (Philippines).

Villeret Carrousel Répétition Minutes

Reference number: 00235-3631-55B
Movement: automatic, Blancpain Caliber 235; ø 32.8 mm, height 9.1 mm; 54 jewels; 21,600 vph; escapement with 1-minute flying carrousel
Functions: hours, minutes; minute repeater
Case: pink gold, ø 45 mm, height 15.35 mm; sapphire crystal; transparent case back
Band: reptile skin, folding clasp
Remarks: enamel dial
Price: $412,100

Villeret Tourbillon Carrousel

Reference number: 2322-3631-55B
Movement: manually wound, Blancpain Caliber 2322; ø 35.3 mm, height 5.85 mm; 70 jewels; 21,600 vph; escapement with flying 1-minute tourbillon and 1-minute carousel with differential compensation; 3 spring barrels, 168-hour power reserve
Functions: hours minutes, power reserve indicator (on the movement side); date
Case: red gold, ø 44.6 mm, height 11.94 mm; sapphire crystal; transparent case back; water-resistant to 3 atm
Band: reptile skin, folding clasp
Remarks: enamel dial
Price: $319,000

Villeret Tourbillon Volant Une Minute 12 Jours

Reference number: 66240-3431-55B
Movement: automatic, Blancpain Caliber 242; ø 30.6 mm, height 6.1 mm; 43 jewels; 28,800 vph; 1-minute flying tourbillon; 288-hour power reserve
Functions: hours, minutes; power reserve display (on rear)
Case: platinum, ø 42 mm, height 11.65 mm; sapphire crystal; transparent case back; water-resistant to3 atm
Band: reptile skin, folding clasp
Remarks: enamel dial
Price: $148,800; limited to 188 pieces
Variations: in red gold ($127,400)

Villeret Carrousel Phases de Lune

Reference number: 6622L-3631-55B
Movement: automatic, Blancpain Caliber 225L; ø 31.9 mm, height 6.86 mm; 40 jewels; 28,800 vph; flying 1-minute carousel; 120-hour power reserve
Functions: hours, minutes; date, moon phase
Case: red gold, ø 42 mm, height 12.74 mm; sapphire crystal; transparent case back; water-resistant to 3 atm
Band: reptile skin, folding clasp
Remarks: enamel dial
Price: $129,600
Variations: in platinum (limited to 88 pieces, $151,000)

Villeret Tourbillon Volant Heure Sautante Minute Rétrograde

Reference number: 66260-3633-55B
Movement: manually wound, Blancpain Caliber 260MR; ø 32 mm, height 5.85 mm; 39 jewels; 21,600 vph; one-minute flying tourbillon; 144-hour power reserve
Functions: hours (digital, jumping), minutes (retrograde)
Case: red gold, ø 42 mm, height 11 mm; sapphire crystal; transparent case back; water-resistant to 3 atm
Band: reptile skin, folding clasp
Remarks: enameled dial
Price: $148,800
Variations: red gold Bracelet: $167,400; platinum ($180,900, limited to 50 pieces)

Villeret Quantième Perpétuel

Reference number: 6656-3642-55B
Movement: automatic, Blancpain Caliber 5954; ø 32 mm, height 4.97 mm; 32 jewels; 28,800 vph; 72-hour power reserve
Functions: hours, minutes, sweep seconds; perpetual calendar with date, weekday, month, moon phase, leap year
Case: red gold, ø 40 mm, height 11.1 mm; sapphire crystal; transparent case back; water-resistant to 3 atm
Band: reptile skin, folding clasp
Remarks: opaline dial
Price: $45,000
Variations: with red gold Milanese mesh bracelet ($64,100)

Villeret Quantième Complet GMT

Reference number: 6676-1127-55B
Movement: automatic, Blancpain Caliber 67A5; ø 27 mm, height 6 mm; 28 jewels; 28,800 vph; 2 spring barrels; 72-hour power reserve
Functions: hours, minutes; additional 24-hour power reserve display (second time zone); full calendar with date, weekday, month, moon phase
Case: stainless steel, ø 40 mm, height 11.8 mm; sapphire crystal; transparent case back; water-resistant to 3 atm
Band: reptile skin, folding clasp
Price: $15,900

Villeret Quantième Complet

Reference number: 6654-3640-55B
Movement: automatic, Blancpain Caliber 6654; ø 32 mm, height 5.5 mm; 28 jewels; 28,800 vph; 2 spring barrels, 72-hour power reserve
Functions: hours, minutes, sweep seconds; full calendar with date, weekday, month, moon phase
Case: red gold, ø 40 mm, height 10.94 mm; sapphire crystal; transparent case back; water-resistant to 3 atm
Band: reptile skin, folding clasp
Price: $25,700
Variations: with red gold Milanese mesh bracelet ($45,000)

Villeret Grande Date Jour Retrograde

Reference number: 6668-3642-55B
Movement: automatic, Blancpain Caliber 6950GJ; ø 32 mm, height 5.27 mm; 40 jewels; 28,800 vph; 72-hour power reserve
Functions: hours, minutes, sweep seconds; large date, weekday (retrograde)
Case: red gold, ø 40 mm, height 11.1 mm; sapphire crystal; transparent case back; water-resistant to 3 atm
Band: reptile skin, folding clasp
Remarks: opaline dial
Price: $24,500

Villeret Extraplate

Reference number: 6224-3642-55B
Movement: automatic, Blancpain Caliber 1150; ø 26.2 mm, height 3.25 mm; 21 jewels; 28,800 vph; 100-hour power reserve
Functions: hours, minutes, sweep seconds; date
Case: red gold, ø 38 mm, height 8.35 mm; sapphire crystal; transparent case back; water-resistant to 3 atm
Band: reptile skin, folding clasp
Price: $18,800
Variations: in red gold with "mille mailles" mesh bracelet ($39,100); stainless steel ($10,100)

Villeret Ultraplate

Reference number: 6605-1127-55B
Movement: manually wound, Blancpain Caliber 11A4B; ø 27.4 mm, height 2.8 mm; 21 jewels; 21,600 vph; 100-hour power reserve
Functions: hours, minutes; power reserve display (on rear)
Case: stainless steel, ø 40 mm, height 7.39 mm; sapphire crystal; transparent case back; water-resistant to 3 atm
Band: reptile skin, folding clasp
Price: $10,100

Fifty Fathoms Tourbillon 8 Jours

Reference number: 5025-12B40-052A
Movement: automatic, Blancpain Caliber 25C; ø 26.2 mm, height 4.85 mm; 29 jewels; 28,800 vph; one-minute flying tourbillon; 192-hour power reserve
Functions: hours, minutes, subsidiary seconds (on the tourbillon cage)
Case: titanium, ø 45 mm, height 14.8 mm; unidirectional bezel with sapphire crystal insert, with 0-60 scale; sapphire crystal; transparent case back; water-resistant to 30 atm
Band: textile, buckle
Price: $116,600
Variations: in rose gold ($132,500)

Fifty Fathoms Automatique

Reference number: 5015-12B40-052A
Movement: automatic, Blancpain Caliber 1315; ø 30.6 mm, height 5.65 mm; 35 jewels; 28,800 vph; silicon spring; 120-hour power reserve
Functions: hours, minutes, sweep seconds; date
Case: titanium, ø 45 mm, height 15.4 mm; unidirectional bezel with sapphire crystal insert, with 0-60 scale; sapphire crystal; transparent case back; water-resistant to 30 atm
Band: textile, buckle
Price: $15,700
Variations: various bands and dials

Fifty Fathoms Automatique

Reference number: 5015-12B30-98
Movement: automatic, Blancpain Caliber 1315; ø 30.6 mm, height 5.65 mm; 35 jewels; 28,800 vph; silicon spring; 120-hour power reserve
Functions: hours, minutes, sweep seconds; date
Case: titanium, ø 45 mm, height 15.4 mm; unidirectional bezel with sapphire crystal insert, with 0-60 scale; sapphire crystal; transparent case back; water-resistant to 30 atm
Band: titanium, folding clasp
Price: $18,300
Variations: blue dial and bezel $18,300

Fifty Fathoms Bathyscaphe Chronograph Flyback

Reference number: 5200-0153-B52A
Movement: automatic, Blancpain Caliber F385; ø 31.8 mm, height 6.65 mm; 37 jewels; 36,000 vph; silicon hairspring; 50-hour power reserve
Functions: hours, minutes, subsidiary seconds; flyback chronograph; date
Case: ceramic, ø 43.6 mm, height 15.25 mm; unidirectional bezel with ceramic insert, with 0-60 scale; sapphire crystal; transparent case back; water-resistant to 30 atm
Band: textile, buckle
Price: $17,200

Fifty Fathoms Bathyscaphe Titanium

Reference number: 5000-1210-G52A
Movement: automatic, Blancpain Caliber 1315; ø 30.6 mm, height 5.65 mm; 35 jewels; 28,800 vph; silicon spring; 120-hour power reserve
Functions: hours, minutes, sweep seconds; date
Case: titanium, ø 43 mm, height 13.4 mm; unidirectionally rotating bezel with ceramic inlay and 60-minute divisions; sapphire crystal; transparent case back; screw-in crown; water-resistant to 30 atm
Band: textile, buckle
Price: $15,800

Fifty Fathoms Bathyscaphe Sedna Gold

Reference number: 5000-36S40-052A
Movement: automatic, Blancpain Caliber 1315; ø 30.6 mm, height 5.65 mm; 35 jewels; 28,800 vph; silicon hairspring; 120-hour power reserve
Functions: hours, minutes, sweep seconds; date
Case: rose gold ("Sedna gold"), ø 43 mm, height 13.4 mm; unidirectional bezel with ceramic insert with 0-60 scale; sapphire crystal; transparent case back; screw-in crown; water-resistant to 30 atm
Band: textile, buckle
Remarks: special corrosion-resistant gold alloy
Price: $25,200

Air Command

Reference number: AC02-12B40-63
Movement: automatic, Blancpain Caliber F388B; ø 31.8 mm, height 6.65 mm; 35 jewels; 28,800 vph; 50-hour power reserve
Functions: hours, minutes, flyback chronograph
Case: titanium, ø 42.5 mm, height 13.77 mm; bidirectionally rotating bezel with ceramic inlay, with 0-60 scale; sapphire crystal; transparent case back; water-resistant to 3 atm
Band: calfskin, buckle
Price: $18,500
Variations: in rose gold $29,100

Villeret Women Quantième Phase de Lune

Reference number: 6126-2987-55B
Movement: automatic, Blancpain Caliber 913QL.P; ø 23.7 mm, height 4.65 mm; 20 jewels; 28,800 vph; 40-hour power reserve
Functions: hours, minutes, sweep seconds; date, moon phase
Case: red gold, ø 33.2 mm, height 10.2 mm; bezel with set with 48 diamonds; sapphire crystal; transparent case back; water-resistant to 3 atm
Band: reptile skin, folding clasp
Remarks: dial set with 8 diamonds
Price: $22,900

Villeret Women Date

Reference number: 6127-4628-55B
Movement: automatic, Blancpain Caliber 1151; ø 27.4 mm, height 3.25 mm; 28 jewels; 28,800 vph; 100-hour power reserve
Functions: hours, minutes, sweep seconds; date
Case: stainless steel, ø 33.2 mm, height 9.15 mm; bezel with set with diamonds; sapphire crystal; transparent case back; water-resistant to 3 atm
Band: reptile skin, buckle
Remarks: dial set with 8 diamond indices
Price: $14,100
Variations: various strap colors

Ladybird Complete Calendar Moon Phase

Reference number: 3663-2954-55B
Movement: automatic, Blancpain Caliber 6763; ø 27 mm, height 4.9 mm; 30 jewels; 28,800 vph; 100-hour power reserve
Functions: hours, minutes, subsidiary seconds; full calendar with date, weekday, months, moon phase
Case: red gold, ø 35 mm, height 10.57 mm; bezel set with diamonds; sapphire crystal; transparent case back; water-resistant to 3 atm
Band: reptile skin, buckle
Remarks: mother-of-pearl dial set with 9 diamonds
Price: $28,900

BOVET

If any brand can claim real connections to China, it is Bovet, founded by Swiss businessman Edouard Bovet. Bovet emigrated to Canton, China, in 1818 and sold four watches of his own design there. On his return to Switzerland in 1822, he set up a company for shipping his Fleurier-made watches to China. The company name, pronounced "Bo Wei" in Mandarin, became a synonym for "watch" in Asia and at one point had offices in Canton. For more than eighty years, Bovet and his successors supplied the Chinese ruling class with valuable timepieces.

In 2001, the brand was bought by entrepreneur Pascal Raffy. He ensured the company's industrial independence by acquiring several other companies as well, notably the high-end watchmaker Swiss Time Technology (STT) in Tramelan, which he renamed Dimier 1738. In addition to creating its own line of watches, this *manufacture* produces complex technical components such as tourbillons for Bovet watches. Assembly of Bovet creations takes place at the headquarters in the thirteenth-century Castle of Môtiers in Val-de-Travers not far from Fleurier.

Bovet is an equal opportunity manufacturer of fine watches for men and women. These high-end timekeepers do have several distinctive features. The first is intricate dial work, featuring not only complex architecture in the men's series, but also intricate guilloché patterns and very fine enameling techniques. Bovet has even collaborated with car manufacturers like Pininfarina, celebrating its ninetieth anniversary, and Rolls-Royce, for which it manufactured a bespoke dashboard clock that can be used as a table clock or wristwatch thanks to the Amadéo conversion system. This allows the wristbands to be easily attached or removed from the watch. Some models convert to table clocks, and the Amadeo Fleurier Miss Audrey series can even be worn as a necklace. One of the recent developments of this unusual brand is the use of sugar to form a bed of colored beads for the dial appropriately named Sweet Art.

Bovet Fleurier S.A.
Le Château, CP20
CH-2112 Môtiers
Switzerland

Tel.:
+41-32-862-0808

E-mail:
info@bovet.com

Website:
www.bovet.com

Founded:
1822

Annual production:
around 1,000 timepieces

U.S. distributor:
Bovet LLC North America
305-974-4826

Most important collections/price range:
Amadeo Fleurier, Dimier, Pininfarina, Récital, Virtuoso / $18,500 to $1,000,000

Fleurier 19Thirty Orbis Mundi

Reference number: NTHU012
Movement: manually wound, Bovet Caliber 15BM01HU; ø 35.97 mm, height 5.30 mm; 18,000 vph; with côtes de Genève; 1-minute tourbillon; 7-day power reserve
Functions: hours, minutes, seconds; world time display with 24 city references; power reserve indicator
Case: red gold, ø 42 mm, height 11.25 mm; transparent case back; water-resistant to 3 atm
Band: leather, buckle
Price: $53,000; limited to 60 pieces

Recital 29

Reference number: R290001
Movement: manually wound, Bovet Caliber 13DM04; ø 30.45, with 36.09 mm module, height: 15.70 mm; 21,600 vph; 1-minute, double-sided flying tourbillon; 5-day power reserve
Functions: hours, minutes; moon phase; power reserve indicator
Case: stainless steel ø 42 mm, height 10.3 mm; sapphire crystal; transparent case back; water-resistant to 3 atm
Remarks: "slant-top desk" case; green guilloché dial
Band: calfskin, buckle
Price: $29,456
Variations: blue guilloché dial

Recital 21

Reference number: R210009
Movement: manually wound, Bovet Caliber 13DM05-QPR; ø 30.40 height: 6.75 mm; 37 jewels; 21,600 vph; 1-minute tourbillon; 5-day power reserve
Functions: hours, minutes, coaxial seconds; perpetual calendar, day, date (retrograde), month, leap year; power reserve indicator
Case: titanium, ø 44.4 mm, height 15.5 mm; sapphire crystal; transparent case back; water-resistant to 3 atm
Band: rubber, buckle
Price: $86,000
Variations: red gold ($96,000)

Fleurier Tourbillon Virtuoso III Perpetual Calendar

Reference number: AIQPR030
Movement: manually wound, Bovet Caliber 17BM01AI-QPR; ø 38 mm, height 12.41 mm; 21,600 vph; 1-minute tourbillon; 5-day power reserve
Functions: hours, minutes, seconds (on tourbillon cage); calendar (retrograde), month, leap year; power reserve indicator, reversed hand-fitting (hours, minutes, seconds)
Case: red gold, ø 46 mm, height 18.3 mm; sapphire crystal; transparent case back; water-resistant to 3 atm
Band: reptile skin, buckle
Price: $347,000
Variations: white dial; chain in red or white gold

Amadeo Fleurier Virtuoso V Salmon

Reference number: ACHS041
Movement: automatic, Bovet Caliber 13BM11AIHSMR; ø 31.00 mm, height 5.09 mm; 21,600 vph; 5-day power reserve
Functions: jumping hours, minutes (retrograde); hours, minutes, seconds on the rear
Case: white gold, ø 43.5 mm, height 15.70 mm; sapphire crystal; transparent case back; water-resistant to 3 atm
Band: as wristwatch with reptile skin, buckle
Remarks: reversed hand fitting
Price: $77,000

Amadéo Tourbillon

Reference number: AIFSQ035-G123467
Movement: manually wound, Bovet Caliber 14BM02A1; ø 29.10 mm, height 3.6 mm; 21,600 vph; 7-day power reserve
Functions: hours, minutes, seconds on tourbillon, reversed hand-fitting, power reserve indicator
Case: red gold, ø 45 mm, height 14.30 mm; Amadéo convertible system sapphire crystal; transparent case back; water-resistant to 3 atm
Band: reptile skin, buckle
Remarks: hand-engraved case, bezel and bow with floral motif (*fleurisannes*); Amadéo system lets wearer turn the watch into a table clock, pendant, or pocket watch without tools
Price: $304,000; unique piece

19Thirty Great Guilloché Turquoise

Reference number: NTS0054
Movement: manually wound, Bovet Caliber 15BM04; ø 35 mm, height: 3.80 mm; 21,600 vph; 7-day power reserve
Functions: hours, minutes, subsidiary seconds; power reserve indicator
Case: stainless steel, ø 42 mm, height 9.05 mm; sapphire crystal; transparent case back; water-resistant to 3 atm
Band: reptile skin, buckle
Remarks: pinwheel guilloché dials
Price: $24,000

Miss Audrey Sweet Art

Reference number: AS36027-SD12
Movement: automatic, Bovet Caliber 11BA15; ø 26.20mm, height 3.60 mm; 28,800 vph; 42-hour power reserve
Functions: hours, minutes
Case: stainless steel, ø 36 mm, 11 mm; crown and strap bolts with sapphire cabochon; transparent case back; water-resistant to 3 atm
Band: reptile skin, buckle
Remarks: dial made of specially processed sugar crystals; comes with convertible system turn the watch into a table clock, pendant, or wristwatch
Price: $31,000
Variations: sugar crystals come in the colors purple, blue, black, gray, pink, yellow or a gradient of colors

Amadeo Fleurier 36 Miss Audrey

Reference number: AS36012-SD12
Movement: automatic, Bovet Caliber 11BA13; ø 26.20 mm, height 5.09 mm; 28,800 vph; 42-hour power reserve
Functions: hours, minutes
Case: stainless steel, ø 36 mm, height 11.25 mm; sapphire crystal; bezel set with 60 round diamonds; water-resistant to 3 atm
Band: synthetic satin with calfskin lining, buckle
Remarks: 4 diamond indices; necklace bowset with diamonds
Price: $27,000
Variations: green guilloché dial

BREGUET

Abraham-Louis Breguet (1747–1823), who hailed from Switzerland, brought his craft to Paris in the *Sturm und Drang* atmosphere of the late eighteenth century. It was fertile ground for one of the most inventive watchmakers in the history of horology, and his products soon found favor with the highest levels of society.

Little has changed two centuries later. After a few years of drifting, in 1999 the brand carrying this illustrious name became the prize possession of the Swatch Group and came under the personal management of Nicolas G. Hayek, CEO. Hayek worked assiduously to restore the brand's roots, going as far as rebuilding the legendary Marie Antoinette pocket watch and contributing to the restoration of the Petit Trianon at Versailles.

Breguet is a full-fledged *manufacture*, and this has allowed it to forge ahead uncompromisingly with upscale watches and even jewelry. In modern facilities on the shores of Lake Joux, traditional craftsmanship still plays a significant role in the production of its fine watches, but at the same time, Breguet is one of the few brands to work with modern materials for its movements.

2021 was dominated by the 220th anniversary of the tourbillon, for which its inventor Abraham-Louis Breguet is still revered today. This company located in the famed watchmaking hub of the Vallée de Joux has now turned its attention to other complications, for example, the display of two time zones. The time zone function already known from the Classique line, the Marine GMT, now appears as the Marine Hora Mundi. Unlike the old complication with an additional subdial for the second time zone, the Hora Mundi, which boasts four patents, uses a window display with the reference city names of the twenty-four world time zones. An ingenious switching mechanism allows the times in two set locations to be displayed via a single pair of hands, changing between the two time zones at will via the crown at 8 o'clock, which also functions as a pusher, causing the hour hand to jump over as well.

Montres Breguet SA
CH-1344 L'Abbaye
Switzerland

Tel.:
+41-21-841-9090

Website:
www.breguet.com

Founded:
1775 (Swatch Group since 1999)

Number of Employees:
1,000

U.S. distributor:
Breguet
The Swatch Group (U.S.), Inc.
1200 Harbor Boulevard, 7th Floor
Weehawken, NJ 07087
201-271-1400

Most important collections:
Classique, Tradition, Héritage, Marine, Reine de Naples, Type XX, Type XXI, Type XXII

Tourbillon Extra Thin 5367

Reference number: 5367PT 29 9WU
Movement: automatic, Breguet Caliber 581; ø 36 mm, 33 jewels; 28,800 vph; 1-minute tourbillon; silicon pallet lever and hairspring; 80-hour power reserve
Functions: hours, minutes, subsidiary seconds (on tourbillon cage)
Case: platinum, ø 41 mm, height 7.45 mm; sapphire crystal; transparent case back; water-resistant to 3 atm
Band: reptile skin, triple folding clasp
Remarks: enamel dial
Price: $161,800
Variations: in rose gold ($147,500)

Classique Tourbillon Extra-Thin Skeleton 5395

Reference number: 5395PT RS 9WU
Movement: automatic, Breguet Caliber 581SQ; ø 36 mm, 33 jewels; 28,800 vph; 1-minute tourbillon; silicon anchor and lever escapement; fully skeletonized movement; 80-hour power reserve
Functions: hours, minutes, subsidiary seconds (on tourbillon cage)
Case: platinum, ø 41 mm, height 7.7 mm; sapphire crystal; transparent case back; water-resistant to 3 atm
Band: reptile skin, folding clasp
Price: $240,600
Variations: in rose gold ($225,200)

Classique 7147

Reference number: 7147BR 12 9WU
Movement: automatic, Breguet Caliber 502.3SD; ø 24.9 mm, height 2.4 mm; 35 jewels; 21,600 vph; silicon pallet lever and hairspring; 45-hour power reserve
Functions: hours, minutes, subsidiary seconds
Case: rose gold, ø 40 mm, height 6.1 mm; sapphire crystal; transparent case back; water-resistant to 3 atm
Band: reptile skin, buckle
Remarks: hand guilloché gold dial
Price: $21,000
Variations: in white gold ($21,500)

Classique Full Calendar

Reference number: 7337BB Y5 9VU
Movement: automatic, Breguet Caliber 502.3 QSE1; ø 31 mm, height 3.8 mm; 35 jewels; 21,600 vph; silicon hairspring, rose gold hand guilloché oscillating mass, numbered and signed movement
Functions: hours, minutes, subsidiary seconds; full calendar with date, weekday, moon phase and age
Case: white gold, ø 39 mm, height 9.9 mm; sapphire crystal; transparent case back; water-resistant to 3 atm
Band: reptile skin, folding clasp
Remarks: silvered, hand guilloché gold dial
Price: $43,000
Variations: in rose gold ($43,000)

Classique 7137

Reference number: 7137BR 15 9VU
Movement: automatic, Breguet Caliber 502.3 DR1; ø 27.1 mm, height 3.65 mm; 37 jewels; 21,600 vph; Breguet silicon spring and escapement; gold oscillating weight; 46-hour power reserve
Functions: hours, minutes, power reserve indicator; date, moon phase and age
Case: rose gold, ø 39 mm, height 8.65 mm; sapphire crystal; transparent case back; water-resistant to 3 atm
Band: reptile skin, folding clasp
Remarks: hand guilloché gold dial
Price: $40,000
Variations: in white gold ($40,000)

Classique 5177

Reference number: 5177 BB 2Y 9V6
Movement: automatic, Breguet Caliber 777Q; ø 27.1 mm, 26 jewels; 28,800 vph; silicon pallet lever, escape wheel and hairspring; 55-hour power reserve
Functions: hours, minutes, sweep seconds; date
Case: white gold, ø 38 mm, height 8.8 mm; sapphire crystal; transparent case back; water-resistant to 3 atm
Band: reptile skin, buckle
Remarks: blue enamel dial
Price: $23,700

Classique 7787

Reference number: 7787 BB 29 9V6
Movement: automatic, Breguet Caliber 591 DRL; ø 25.6 mm, height 10.2 mm; 25 jewels; 28,800 vph; Breguet silicon spring and escapement; 38-hour power reserve
Functions: hours, minutes, sweep seconds; power reserve indicator, moon phase
Case: white gold, ø 39 mm, height 10.2 mm; sapphire crystal; transparent case back; water-resistant to 3 atm
Band: reptile skin, folding clasp
Remarks: hand guilloché gold dial with grand-feu enamel
Price: $30,200

Marine Équation Marchante

Reference number: 5887PT Y2 9WV
Movement: automatic, Breguet Caliber 581DPE; ø 37.2 mm, 57 jewels; 28,800 vph; 1-minute tourbillon; silicon anchor, anchor escape wheel and hairspring; 80-hour power reserve
Functions: hours, minutes, subsidiary seconds, (on the tourbillon cage); "running" equation of time; perpetual calendar with date (retrograde) weekday, months, leap year
Case: platinum, ø 43.9 mm, height 11.75 mm; sapphire crystal; transparent case back; water-resistant to 10 atm
Band: reptile skin, triple folding clasp
Price: $230,400
Variations: in rose gold ($215,000)

Marine Hora Mundi

Reference number: 5557BR YS 9WV
Movement: automatic, Breguet Caliber 77F1; 40 jewels; 28,800 vph; silicon anchor, anchor escape wheel, and hairspring; 55-hour power reserve
Functions: hours, minutes, sweep seconds; world-time display (two time zones, pusher-activated); day/night indicator; date
Case: rose gold, ø 43.9 mm, height 13.8 mm; sapphire crystal; transparent case back; water-resistant to 10 atm
Band: reptile skin, triple folding clasp
Remarks: hand guilloché dial with continents made of sapphire
Price: $72,700
Variations: in white gold ($72,700)

Marine Date

Reference number: 5517TI Y1 5ZU
Movement: automatic, Breguet Caliber 777A; ø 33.8 mm, 26 jewels; 28,800 vph; silicon pallet lever and hairspring; 55-hour power reserve
Functions: hours, minutes, sweep seconds; date
Case: titanium, ø 40 mm, height 11.5 mm; sapphire crystal; transparent case back
Band: rubber, folding clasp with safety pushers
Remarks: dial with sunburst
Price: $17,300
Variations: with reptile skin band ($17,300). in rose gold ($28,600); in white gold ($28,600)

Marine Chronograph

Reference number: 5527BR G3 RW0
Movement: automatic, Breguet Caliber 582QA; ø 32.7 mm, 28 jewels; 28,800 vph; silicon pallet lever and hairspring; 48-hour power reserve
Functions: hours, minutes, subsidiary seconds; chronograph; date
Case: rose gold, ø 42.3 mm, height 13.85 mm; sapphire crystal; transparent case back; screw-in crown; water-resistant to 10 atm
Band: rose gold folding clasp with safety catch
Price: $56,300
Variations: with rubber or reptile skin strap ($33,800) in white gold ($33,800) in titanium ($21,500)

Marine Alarme Musicale

Reference number: 5547BB Y2 9ZU
Movement: automatic, Breguet Caliber 518F/1; ø 27.1 mm, 36 jewels; 28,800 vph; silicon pallet lever and hairspring 45-hour power reserve
Functions: hours, minutes, sweep seconds; additional 24-hour display (second time zone), power reserve for the chiming mechanism; alarm (set to the minute) date
Case: white gold, ø 40 mm, height 13.05 mm; sapphire crystal; transparent case back; water-resistant to 5 atm
Band: reptile skin, folding clasp with safety catch
Price: $39,900
Variations: with a rubber strap ($39,00); in titanium with titanium bracelet ($31,200)

Marine Lady 9518

Reference number: 9518BB V2 584 D000
Movement: automatic, Breguet Caliber 591A; ø 25.6 mm, 25 jewels; 28,800 vph; Breguet silicon spring and escapement, gold oscillating mass set with 31 diamonds; 38-hour power reserve
Functions: hours, minutes, sweep seconds; date
Case: white gold, ø 38.8 mm, height 9.89 mm; bezel set with 50 diamonds; sapphire crystal; transparent case back; water-resistant to 5 atm
Band: rubber, folding clasp
Remarks: hand guilloché mother-of-pearl dial
Price: $34,900
Variations: in rose gold ($34,900)

Tradition Dame 7035

Reference number: 7035BR8D9V6_D00D
Movement: automatic, Breguet Caliber 505J; ø 33 mm, 38 jewels; 21,600 vph; silicon hairspring, gold mainplate and bridges set with 190 diamonds; 50-hour power reserve
Functions: hours and minutes (off-center); subsidiary seconds (retrograde)
Case: rose gold, ø 37 mm, height 11.85 mm; bezel set with diamonds; sapphire crystal; transparent case back; water-resistant to 3 atm
Band: reptile skin, buckle
Remarks: decentral gold dial, movement plate and cocks set with 74 diamonds
Price: $79,900

Tradition Quantième Retrograde

Reference number: 7597BRG19WU
Movement: automatic, Breguet Caliber 505 Q; ø 33 mm, 38 jewels; 21,600 vph; silicon Breguet-hairspring and anchor pallets; 50-hour power reserve
Functions: hours and minutes (off-center); date, (retrograde)
Case: rose gold, ø 40 mm, height 12.1 mm; sapphire crystal; transparent case back; water-resistant to 3 atm
Band: reptile skin, folding clasp
Remarks: hand guilloché and silver-plated gold dial
Price: $37,800
Variations: in white gold ($38,600)

Tradition Seconde Retrograde

Reference number: 7097BB GY 9WU
Movement: automatic, Breguet Caliber 505 SR1; ø 33 mm, 38 jewels; 21,600 vph; silicon Breguet-hairspring and anchor pallets; 50-hour power reserve
Functions: hours and minutes (off-center), subsidiary seconds (retrograde)
Case: white gold, ø 40 mm, height 11.8 mm; sapphire crystal; transparent case back; water-resistant to 3 atm
Band: reptile skin, folding clasp
Remarks: hand guilloché gold dial; exclusively available in Breguet boutiques
Price: $36,100
Variations: in rose gold ($32,700)

Type XXI Chrono Cadran Vintage

Reference number: 3817ST X2 3ZU
Movement: automatic, Breguet Caliber 584 Q/2; ø 30 mm, 26 jewels; 28,800 vph; silicon hairspring and escapement, sweep minute counter; 48-hour power reserve
Functions: hours, minutes, subsidiary seconds; additional 12-hour display (second time zone); flyback chronograph; date
Case: stainless steel, ø 42 mm, height 15.2 mm; unidirectional bezel with 60-minute scale; sapphire crystal; transparent case back; water-resistant to 10 atm
Band: calfskin, folding clasp
Price: $13,900

Type XXII Chronograph

Reference number: 3880BR Z2 9XV
Movement: automatic, Breguet Caliber 589F; ø 30 mm, height 8.3 mm; 28 jewels; 72,000 vph; high-frequency silicon escapement, sweep minute counter; 40-hour power reserve
Functions: hours, minutes, subsidiary seconds (on a 30-second base); additional 12-hour display (second time zone); flyback chronograph; date
Case: rose gold, ø 44 mm, height 18.5 mm; bidirectional bezel with 0-60 scale; sapphire crystal; transparent case back; screw-in crown; water-resistant to 10 atm
Band: calfskin, folding clasp
Price: $35,500

Reine de Naples

Reference number: 8918BB 5P 964 D00D
Movement: automatic, Breguet Caliber 537/3; ø 19.7 mm; 26 jewels; 21,600 vph; silicon balance wheel, escapement, and hairspring; 45-hour power reserve
Functions: hours, minutes
Case: white gold, 28.45 x 36 mm, height 10.05 mm; bezel and flange set with 117 diamonds; sapphire crystal; transparent case back; crown with diamond cabochon; water-resistant to 3 atm
Band: reptile skin, folding clasp set with 26 diamonds
Remarks: enamel dial with drop-shaped diamonds
Price: $36,100
Variations: rose gold ($35,100); yellow gold ($36,100)

Reine de Naples

Reference number: 8928BR 5W 944 DD0D
Movement: automatic, Breguet Caliber 586/1; ø 19.7 mm, 29 jewels; 21,600 vph; silicon anchor and lever escapement; 38-hour power reserve
Functions: hours, minutes,
Case: rose gold, 24.95 mm x 33 mm, height 8.5 mm; bezel and flange set with 139 diamonds; sapphire crystal; transparent case back; crown with diamond cabochon; water-resistant to 3 atm
Band: reptile skin, folding clasp set with 26 diamonds
Remarks: mother-of-pearl dial
Price: $35,100

Reine de Naples

Reference number: 8938BB 8D 964 DD0D
Movement: automatic, Breguet Caliber 537/3; ø 19.7 mm, 26 jewels; 21,600 vph; silicon anchor and lever escapement, platinum oscillating mass; 45-hour power reserve
Functions: hours, minutes
Case: white gold, 28.45 mm x 36 mm, height 10.05 mm; bezel and flange set with 161 diamonds; sapphire crystal; transparent case back; crown with diamond cabochon; water-resistant to 3 atm
Band: reptile skin, folding clasp set with 28 diamonds
Remarks: gold dial set with 384 diamonds
Price: $50,700

BREITLING

When Léon Breitling opened his workshop in St. Imier in the Jura Mountains in 1884, he set a course focusing consistently on instrument watches with a distinctive design. High quality standards and the rise of aviation completed the picture.

Today, Breitling's relationship with air sports and commercial and military aviation is clear from its brand identity. The unveiling of its own, modern chronograph movement at Basel in 2009 was a major milestone in the company's history and also a return to its roots. The new design was to be "100 percent Breitling" and industrially produced in large numbers at a reasonable cost. Although Breitling's operations in Grenchen and in La Chaux-de-Fonds both boast state-of-the-art equipment, the contract for the new chronograph was awarded to a small team in Geneva. In 2006, the brand-new Caliber B01 made the COSC grade and has enjoyed great popularity ever since. For the team of designers, the innovative centering system on the reset mechanism that requires no manual adjustment was one of the great achievements.

Under CEO Georges Kern—of IWC fame—Breitling expanded beyond the pilot watch niche and tapped markets in the Far East. The new collections were streamlined and given more defined profiles, a recipe he brought in from his IWC days. The winged logo was replaced mostly with a coquettish "B."

The brand has also introduced a new hypoallergenic material called Breitlight and is boldly using scintillating colors, like bright red straps. But of course, the models of the past still have top billing. For its seventieth birthday, the Navitimer was equipped with the in-house Caliber B01, which is housed in a newly redesigned case. The new design did nothing to change the water resistance, which is modest for a sports watch: 3 atm, primarily due to the sealing of the rotating bezel—i.e., the slide rule—which the designers definitely did not want to dispense with.

Breitling
Léon Breitling-Strasse 2
2540 Grenchen
Switzerland

Tel.:
+41-32-654-5454

E-mail:
info.US@breitling.com

Website:
www.breitling.com

Founded:
1884

Annual production:
700,000 (estimated)

U.S. distributor:
Breitling U.S.A. Inc.
206 Danbury Road
Wilton, CT 06897
203-762-1180
www.breitling.com

Most important collections:
Navitimer, Avenger, Premier, Chronomat, Top Time, Superocean Heritage, Superocean, Professional, Classic Avi

Navitimer B01 Chronograph 46

Reference number: AB0137241L1P1
Movement: automatic, Breitling Caliber B01; ø 30 mm, height 7.2 mm; 47 jewels; 28,800 vph; column-wheel control of chronograph functions; 70-hour power reserve; COSC-certified chronometer
Functions: hours, minutes, subsidiary seconds; chronograph; date
Case: stainless steel, ø 46 mm, height 13.9 mm; bidirectional bezel with integrated slide rule and tachymeter scale; sapphire crystal; transparent case back; water-resistant to 3 atm
Band: reptile skin, folding clasp
Price: $9,200
Variations: various cases, bands, and dials

Navitimer B01 Chronograph 43

Reference number: RB0138211B1R1
Movement: automatic, Breitling Caliber B01; ø 30 mm, height 7.2 mm; 47 jewels; 28,800 vph; column wheel control of the chronograph functions; 70 hours power reserve; COSC-certified chronometer
Functions: hours, minutes, subsidiary seconds; chronograph; date
Case: red gold, ø 43 mm, height 13.6 mm; bidirectional bezel with integrated slide rule and tachymeter scale; sapphire crystal; transparent case back; water-resistant to 3 atm
Band: red gold, folding clasp
Price: $37,500
Variations: various cases, bands, and dials

Navitimer B01 Chronograph 43

Reference number: AB0138211B1A1
Movement: automatic, Breitling Caliber B01; ø 30 mm, height 7.2 mm; 47 jewels; 28,800 vph; column-wheel control of chronograph functions; 70-hour power reserve; COSC-certified chronometer
Functions: hours, minutes, subsidiary seconds; chronograph; date
Case: stainless steel, ø 43 mm, height 13.6 mm; bidirectional bezel with integrated slide rule and tachymeter scale; sapphire crystal; transparent case back; water-resistant to 3 atm
Band: stainless steel, folding clasp
Price: $9,500
Variations: various cases, bands, and dials

Navitimer B01 Chronograph 43

Reference number: AB0138241C1P1
Movement: automatic, Breitling Caliber B01; ø 30 mm, height 7.2 mm; 47 jewels; 28,800 vph; column-wheel control of chronograph functions; 70-hour power reserve; COSC-certified chronometer
Functions: hours, minutes, subsidiary seconds; chronograph; date
Case: stainless steel, ø 43 mm, height 13.6 mm; bidirectional bezel with integrated slide rule and tachymeter scale; sapphire crystal; transparent case back; water-resistant to 3 atm
Band: reptile skin, folding clasp
Price: $8,500
Variations: various cases, bands, and dials

Navitimer B01 Chronograph 41

Reference number: AB0139241C1P1
Movement: automatic, Breitling Caliber B01; ø 30 mm, height 7.2 mm; 47 jewels; 28,800 vph; column-wheel control of chronograph functions; 70-hour power reserve; COSC-certified chronometer
Functions: hours, minutes, subsidiary seconds; chronograph; date
Case: stainless steel, ø 41 mm, height 13.6 mm; bidirectional bezel with integrated slide rule and tachymeter scale; sapphire crystal; transparent case back; water-resistant to 3 atm
Band: reptile skin, folding clasp
Price: $9,000
Variations: various cases, bands, and dials

Superocean Heritage B01 Chronograph 44

Reference number: AB0162121G1A1
Movement: automatic, Breitling Caliber B01; ø 30 mm, height 7.2 mm; 47 jewels; 28,800 vph; column-wheel control of chronograph functions; 70-hour power reserve; COSC-certified chronometer
Functions: hours, minutes, subsidiary seconds; chronograph; date
Case: stainless steel, ø 44 mm, height 15.5 mm; unidirectional bezel with ceramic insert; sapphire crystal; screw-in crown; water-resistant to 20 atm
Band: stainless steel Milanese mesh, folding clasp
Price: $8,300
Variations: various bands and dials

Superocean Heritage B20 Automatic 44

Reference number: AB2030121B1S1
Movement: automatic, Breitling Caliber B20 (base Tudor MT 5612); ø 31.8 mm, height 6.5 mm; 28 jewels; 28,800 vph; 70-hour power reserve; COSC-certified chronometer
Functions: hours, minutes, sweep seconds; date
Case: stainless steel, ø 44 mm, height 14.55 mm; unidirectional bezel with ceramic insert; sapphire crystal; screw-in crown; water-resistant to 20 atm
Band: rubber, folding clasp
Price: $5,000
Variations: various cases, bands, and dials

Superocean Heritage B20 Automatic 42

Reference number: AB2010121L1S1
Movement: automatic, Breitling Caliber B20 (base Tudor MT 5612); ø 31.8 mm, height 6.5 mm; 28 jewels; 28,800 vph; 70-hour power reserve; COSC-certified chronometer
Functions: hours, minutes, sweep seconds; date
Case: stainless steel, ø 42 mm, height 14.3 mm; unidirectional bezel with ceramic insert; sapphire crystal; screw-in crown; water-resistant to 20 atm
Band: rubber, folding clasp
Price: $9,100
Variations: various cases, bands, and dials

Superocean Heritage B20 Automatic 46

Reference number: AB2020161C1S1
Movement: automatic, Breitling Caliber B20 (base Tudor MT 5612); ø 31.8 mm, height 6.5 mm; 28 jewels; 28,800 vph; 70-hour power reserve; COSC-certified chronometer
Functions: hours, minutes, sweep seconds; date
Case: stainless steel, ø 46 mm, height 14.9 mm; unidirectional bezel with ceramic insert; sapphire crystal; screw-in crown; water-resistant to 20 atm
Band: rubber, folding clasp
Price: $5,100
Variations: various cases, bands, and dials

Super Chronomat B01 44

Reference number: AB0136251B1S1
Movement: automatic, Breitling Caliber B01; ø 30 mm, height 7.2 mm; 47 jewels; 28,800 vph; column wheel control of chronograph functions; 70-hour power reserve; COSC-certified chronometer
Functions: hours, minutes, subsidiary seconds; chronograph; date
Case: stainless steel, ø 44 mm, height 14.4 mm; unidirectional bezel with 0-60 scale; sapphire crystal; transparent case back; screw-in crown; water-resistant to 20 atm
Band: rubber, folding clasp
Price: $8,950

Super Chronomat B01 44

Reference number: RB0136E31Q1S1
Movement: automatic, Breitling Caliber B01; ø 30 mm, height 7.2 mm; 47 jewels; 28,800 vph; column wheel control of chronograph functions; 70-hour power reserve; COSC-certified chronometer
Functions: hours, minutes, subsidiary seconds; chronograph; date
Case: red gold, ø 44 mm, height 14.4 mm; unidirectional bezel with 0-60 scale; sapphire crystal; transparent case back; screw-in crown; water-resistant to 20 atm
Band: rubber, folding clasp
Price: $23,650
Variations: various cases, bands, and dials

Chronomat B01 42

Reference number: AB0134101L1A1
Movement: automatic, Breitling Caliber B01; ø 30 mm, height 7.2 mm; 47 jewels; 28,800 vph; column wheel control of chronograph functions; 70-hour power reserve; COSC-certified chronometer
Functions: hours, minutes, subsidiary seconds; chronograph; date
Case: stainless steel, ø 42 mm, height 15.1 mm; unidirectionally rotating bezel with 0-60 scale; sapphire crystal; transparent case back; screw-in crown; water-resistant to 20 atm
Band: stainless steel, folding clasp
Price: $4,900
Variations: various cases, bands, and dials

Chronomat B01 42

Reference number: PB0134101C1S1
Movement: automatic, Breitling Caliber B01; ø 30 mm, height 7.2 mm; 47 jewels; 28,800 vph; column wheel control of chronograph functions; 70-hour power reserve; COSC-certified chronometer
Functions: hours, minutes, subsidiary seconds; chronograph; date
Case: stainless steel, ø 42 mm, height 15.1 mm; unidirectional platinum bezel with 0-60 scale; sapphire crystal; transparent case back; screw-in crown; water-resistant to 20 atm
Band: rubber, folding clasp
Price: $9,750
Variations: various cases, bands, and dials

Chronomat Automatic 36

Reference number: U10380101A1U1
Movement: automatic, Breitling Caliber 10 (base ETA 2892-A2); ø 25.6 mm, height 3.6 mm; 21 jewels; 28,800 vph; 42-hour power reserve; COSC-certified chronometer
Functions: hours, minutes, sweep seconds; date
Case: stainless steel, ø 36 mm, height 10 mm; unidirectional pink gold bezel, with 0-60 scale; sapphire crystal; water-resistant to 10 atm
Band: stainless steel with pink gold elements, double folding clasp
Price: $8,550
Variations: various cases, bands, and dials

Chronomat Automatic 36

Reference number: A10380101L1A1
Movement: automatic, Breitling Caliber 10 (base ETA 2892-A2); ø 25.6 mm, height 3.6 mm; 21 jewels; 28,800 vph; 42-hour power reserve; COSC-certified chronometer
Functions: hours, minutes, sweep seconds; date
Case: stainless steel, ø 36 mm, height 10 mm; unidirectional bezel with 0-60 scale; sapphire crystal; water-resistant to 10 atm
Band: stainless steel, double folding clasp
Price: $4,850
Variations: various cases, bands, and dials

Chronomat 32

Reference number: R77310101A1R1
Movement: quartz, Breitling Caliber 77, COSC-certified chronometer
Functions: hours, minutes, sweep seconds; date
Case: red gold, ø 32 mm, height 8.5 mm; sapphire crystal; water-resistant to 10 atm
Band: red gold, double folding clasp
Price: $8,500
Variations: various cases, bands, and dials

Endurance Pro

Reference number: X82310281B1S1
Movement: quartz, Breitling Caliber 77, COSC-certified chronometer
Functions: hours, minutes, subsidiary seconds; chronograph; date
Case: composite material ("Breitlight"), ø 44 mm, height 12.5 mm; sapphire crystal; water-resistant to 10 atm
Band: rubber, buckle
Price: $3,300
Variations: various bands and dials

Endurance Pro

Reference number: X82310A51B1S1
Movement: quartz, Breitling Caliber 77, COSC-certified chronometer
Functions: hours, minutes, subsidiary seconds; chronograph; date
Case: composite material ("Breitlight"), ø 44 mm, height 12.5 mm; sapphire crystal; water-resistant to 10 atm
Band: rubber, buckle
Price: $3,300
Variations: various bands and dials

Caliber B01

Automatic; column-wheel control of chronograph functions; vertical clutch; single spring barrel; COSC-certified chronometer; 70-hour power reserve
Functions: hours, minutes, subsidiary seconds; chronograph; date
Diameter: 30 mm
Height: 7.2 mm
Jewels: 47
Balance: glucydur
Frequency: 28,800 vph

Caliber B04

Automatic; column-wheel control of chronograph functions; vertical clutch; single spring barrel; COSC-certified chronometer; 70-hour power reserve
Functions: hours, minutes, subsidiary seconds; additional 24-hour display (2nd time zone); chronograph; date
Diameter: 30 mm
Height: 7.4 mm
Jewels: 47
Balance: glucydur
Frequency: 28,800 vph

Caliber B05

Automatic; column-wheel control of chronograph functions; vertical clutch; time zone disk connected to hand mechanism by planetary transmission; single spring barrel; COSC-certified chronometer; 70-hour power reserve
Functions: hours, minutes, subsidiary seconds; world time display (crown-set 2nd time zone); chronograph; date
Diameter: 30 mm
Height: 8.1 mm
Jewels: 56
Balance: glucydur
Frequency: 28,800 vph

BREMONT

Bremont watches have adventure in their DNA, as it were, but adventure with a bit of Anglo-Saxon understatement. They have been worn by a number of people who have exhibited their taste for derring-do, like polar explorer Ben Saunders or Levison Wood, who was the first person to walk the length of the Nile. And it's hardly any wonder, since the brand is the brainchild of brothers Nick and Giles English, themselves dyed-in-the-wool pilots and restorers of vintage airplanes. The brand name has a wild story as well: to avoid a storm, the brothers were forced to land their vintage biplane in a field in southern France. The farmer, a former World War II pilot, was more than happy to put them up for the night. His name: Antoine Bremont.

These British-made timepieces hit the market in 2007 and hit a nerve in those seeking a watch that tells the time and expresses some smoldering attraction to danger, perhaps. They use sturdy, COSC- or ISO-3159-certified automatic movements; extensively modified, hardened steel; a patented shock-absorbing system; and a rotor whose design recalls a flight of planes. The brand has steadily increased its production and programmatic scope. Bremont has sought its inspiration from such British icons as the Spitfire, Bletchley Park (where the German codes were broken during World War II), and Jaguar sports cars. The brand also partnered with Boeing to produce an elegant range of watches on an organic polymer strap. Water sport is another area Bremont has explored, with models inspired by the legendary J-Class yachts, like the ladies' model AC I 32, and a special set devoted to the America's Cup. The Argonaut series is dedicated to the British navy and provides water-resistance to about 300 meters.

The watches have been manufactured in Henley-on-Thames since 2010. In 2017, Bremont became the first official timekeeper for the Henley Royal Regatta, one of Great Britain's top rowing events.

Bremont Watch Company
P.O. Box 4741
Henley-on-Thames
RG9 9BZ Oxfordshire
United Kingdom

Tel.:
+44-800-817-4281

E-mail:
info@bremont.com

Website:
www.bremont.com

Founded:
2002

Number of employees:
100+

Annual production:
several thousand watches

U.S. distributor:
Michael Pearson
Michael.Pearson@bremont.com
Anthony Kozlowsky
Anthony.kozlowsky@bremont.com
Bremont Inc.
501 Madison Avenue, New York, NY 10022
855-273-6668

Most important collections/price range:
ALT1, Armed Forces collection, Bremont Boeing, Bremont Jaguar, MB, SOLO, Supermarine, U-2, and limited editions / $3,600 to $42,500

Argonaut Bronze

Movement: automatic, Caliber BE-92AV (base Sellita SW300); ø 25.6 mm, height 3.6 mm; 25 jewels; 28,800 vph; ISO.3159-certified chronometer; 38-hour power reserve
Functions: hours, minutes, sweep seconds; date
Case: bronze, ø 43 mm, height 12.7 mm; crown-activated scale ring with 0-60 scale; sapphire crystal; water-resistant to 30 atm
Band: textile (sail cloth) buckle
Price: $3,995
Variations: with black dial

Supermarine Descent II

Movement: automatic, Caliber BE-93-2AV (base Sellita SW330-1); ø 25.6 mm, height 4.1 mm; 25 jewels; 28,800 vph; ISO 3159-certified chronometer; 38-hour power reserve
Functions: hours, minutes, sweep seconds; additional 24-hour display (second time zone); date
Case: titanium, ø 43 mm, height 16.5 mm; unidirectional bronze bezel with 0-60 scale; sapphire crystal; transparent case back; screw-in crown; water resistant to 50 atm
Band: rubber, folding clasp
Remarks: "Supermarine" collection named after the manufacturer of the legendary Spitfire
Price: $4,495
Variations: with black rubber strap

Jaguar C-Type

Movement: automatic, Caliber BE-50AV (Sellita base SW500-1); ø 30 mm, height 7.9 mm; 27 jewels; 28,800 vph; ISO 3159-certified chronometer; 42-hour power reserve
Functions: hours, minutes, subsidiary seconds; chronograph; date
Case: stainless steel, ø 43 mm, height 15.8 mm; unidirectional bezel with tachymeter scale; sapphire crystal; screw-in crown and pushers; water resistant to 20 atm
Band: calf leather, folding clasp
Price: $6,495

BRM
(Bernard Richards Manufacture)
2 Impasse de L'Aubette
ZA des Aulnaies
F-95420 Magny-en-Vexin
France

Tel.:
+33-1-61-02-00-25

Fax:
+33-1-61-02-00-14

Website:
www.brm-chronographes.com

Founded:
2003

Number of employees:
20

Annual production:
approx. 2,000 pieces

U.S. distributor:
BRM Manufacture North America
25 Highland Park Village, Suite 100-777
Dallas, TX 75205
214-231-0144
usa@brm-manufacture.com

Price range:
$3,000 to $150,000

BRM

For Bernard Richards, the true sign of luxury lies in "technical skills and perfection in all stages of manufacture." The exterior of the product is of course crucial, but all of BRM's major operations for making a wristwatch—such as encasing, assembling, setting, and polishing—are performed by hand in his little garage-like factory located outside Paris in Magny-sur-Vexin.

BRM is devoted to the ultra-mechanical look with the *haute-horlogerie* feel of high-end materials. His inspiration at the start came from the 1940s, the age of axle grease, pinups, real pilots, and a can-do attitude. The design: three dimensions visible to the naked eye, big mechanical landscapes. The inside: custom-designed components, fitting perfectly into Richards's automotive ideal. Gradually, though, Richards has been modernizing.

BRM's unusual timepieces have mainly been based on the tried and trusted ETA movements. The new GTM, featuring a printed and UV-treated world on the dial, runs on one, for example. But Richards has set lofty goals for himself and his young venture, for he intends to set up a true *manufacture* in his French factory. His BiRotor model is thus outfitted with the Precitime, a caliber conceived and manufactured on French soil. The movement features BRM's shock absorbers mounted on the conical springs of its so-called Isolastic system. Plates and bridges are crafted in ARCAP, rotors are made of Fortale and tantalum. The twin rotors, found at 12 and 6 o'clock, are mounted on double rows of ceramic bearings that require no lubrication.

As any expert watchmaker would, Richards focuses as much attention on the inside as he does the outside. His golf series watch comes in a light apple green and has a unique golf-ball-like crown. And among the latest crop of watches, one finds the Art Car series, which boasts movements, dials, and cases with daubs of bright—not to say idiosyncratic—colors.

GF6-44-SA-SQ-AVP

Movement: automatic, ETA Caliber 2824/2 modified in-house; ø 25.6 mm, height 4.6 mm; 25 jewels; 28,800 vph; casing ring mounted on shock absorbers; skeletonized dial; 38-hour power reserve
Functions: hours, minutes, sweep seconds; 24-hour time zone (numbers printed on bezel rim); date
Case: stainless steel with green lacquer, ø 44 mm, height 10.8 mm; stainless steel and ceramic crown; crystal sapphire; transparent case back; screw-in crown; water-resistant to 10 atm
Band: technical fabric, buckle
Remarks: golf ball design dial and crown, crown on the left, full-floating technology, hand painted shock absorbers
Price: $5,795
Variations: options with configurator

DDF12-46-SQ-ABLF

Movement: automatic, ETA Valjoux Caliber 7753 modified in-house; ø 30 mm, height 7.90 mm; 27 jewels; 28,800 vph; skeletonized dial with hand painted automation bridge and hands; shock absorbers connected to block; 46-hour power reserve
Functions: hours, minutes, subsidiary seconds with stop-second device; chronograph
Case: titanium, ø 46 mm, height 14.5; sapphire crystal; screw-in crown; anti reflective on both sides; transparent case back; water-resistant to 10 atm
Remarks: "brake disc" design,
Price: $13,390 ($11,900)
Variations: options with configurator

V7-38-N-ART CAR

Movement: automatic, ETA Caliber 2824/2; ø 25.6 mm, height 4.6 mm; 25 jewels; 28,800 vph; casing ring mounted on shock absorbers; skeletonized dial; 38-hour power reserve
Functions: hours, minutes, sweep seconds
Case: stainless steel with black PVD, 38 mm, height 10.7 mm; domed sapphire crystal; anti reflective on both sides; domed sapphire crystal transparent case back; water-resistant to 10 atm
Band: leather with "Art Car" double stitching, buckle
Remarks: Art Car design
Price: $5,762
Variations: options with configurator

BRUNO SÖHNLE

Bruno Söhnle GmbH
Dresdner Str. 14
D-01768 Glashütte/Saxony
Germany

Tel.:
+49-35053-321-390

Email:
onlineshop@brunosoehnle.de

Website:
brunosoehnle-glashuette.com

Founded:
2000

Distribution:
retail in Europe and online

Most important collections:
Rondo, Stuttgart, München, Hamburg

Germany has two big cradles of watchmaking. One is in the southwest, in and around the Black Forest, in the region known as Swabia. The other is the famous Glashütte in Saxony, in the east, where nine brands share a few square miles of space to produce watches with a reputation that stretches around the world. All Germans will recognize the Swabian ending of Bruno Söhnle's name. As a young man, in the 1950s, he was introduced to watchmaking at his brother's business, Heges, in Wurmberg, Swabia, which produced mostly bigger clocks.

Fast forward forty plus years... East Germany is no more, and there is space in Glashütte for more watchmaking. For his sixtieth birthday in 2000, now-entrepreneur Bruno Söhnle gifted himself his own watch brand. In quiet, Swabian style, Söhnle came out with simple and affordable quartz watches. In 2010, he moved into mechanical watch with the first "Mechanik Edition," which cemented the company's reputation as an entry-level brand in Glashütte watchmaking. The key to this brand's success was not only price, but also modern, elegant design and light, skin-friendly titanium.

The product gained traction and soon he had purchased the venerable Assmann house in town, which had belonged at one time to one of the founding fathers of Glashütte's watch industry.

One of the model families is called "Stuttgart" and is a symbol for the perfect symbiosis of Swabian entrepreneurial spirit and Saxon watchmaking art. Stuttgart, the home of certain very high-end cars, is in fact about twenty-five miles from Söhnle's native Wurmberg. It may be a bit of an odd connection, but for the Bruno Söhnle watch atelier, the value-creation factor is of existential importance, because anyone who wants to paste the coveted "Made in Glashütte" label on their watches must demonstrably generate added value in Glashütte.

Mechanic Edition X

Reference number: 17-11100-228
Movement: manually wound, ETA Caliber 6498; ø 36.6 mm, height 4.5 mm; 17 jewels; 21,600 vph; 42-hour power reserve
Functions: hours, minutes, subsidiary seconds
Case: stainless steel, ø 42 mm, height 10.75 mm; sapphire crystal; water-resistant to 5 atm
Band: calfskin, folding clasp
Price: $2,950; limited to 125 pieces

Rondo Automatic Regulator

Reference number: 17-12198-360
Movement: automatic, Caliber BS 509R (based on Sellita SW200-1); ø 25.6 mm, height 4.6 mm; 26 jewels; 28,800 vph; 38-hour power reserve
Functions: hours (off-center), minutes, subsidiary seconds; date
Case: stainless steel, ø 42 mm, height 12 mm; sapphire crystal; transparent case back; water-resistant to 5 atm
Band: stainless steel Milanese mesh, folding clasp
Price: $2,660
Variations: various bands and dials

Stuttgart Automatic II Big

Reference number: 17-12173-361
Movement: automatic, Caliber BS 175 (based on Sellita SW200-1); ø 25.6 mm, height 4.6 mm; 26 jewels; 28,800 vph; 38-hour power reserve
Functions: hours, minutes, sweep seconds; date
Case: stainless steel, ø 42 mm, height 10.9 mm; sapphire crystal; transparent case back; water-resistant to 5 atm
Band: calfskin, buckle
Price: $1,300
Variations: various bands and dials

Bulgari Horlogerie SA
Rue de Monruz 34
CH-2000 Neuchâtel
Switzerland

Tel.:
+41-32-722-7878

E-mail:
info@bulgari.com

Website:
www.bulgari.com

Founded:
1884 (Bulgari Horlogerie was founded in the early 1980s as Bulgari Time)

U.S. distributor:
Bulgari Corporation of America
555 Madison Avenue
New York, NY 10022
212-315-9700

Most important collections/price range:
Bulgari-Bulgari / from approx. $4,700 to $30,300; Diagono / from approx. $3,200; Octo / from approx. $9,500 to $690,000 and above; Daniel Roth and Gérald Genta collections

BULGARI

Although Bulgari is one of the largest jewelry manufacturers in the world, watches have always played an important role for the brand. The purchase of Daniel Roth and Gérald Genta in the Vallée de Joux opened new perspectives for its timepieces, thanks to specialized production facilities and the watchmaking talent in the Vallée de Joux—especially where complicated timepieces are concerned. In March 2011, luxury goods giant Louis Vuitton Moët Hennessy (LVMH) secured all the Bulgari family shares in exchange for 16.5 million LVMH shares and a say in the group's future. The financial backing of the mega-group boosted the company's strategy to become fully independent.

Under the bold leadership of Guido Terrini, the watch division continued pushing the envelope with a series of increasingly thin and complicated automatics. After the tourbillon in 2014 came a minute repeater in 2016, which is 3.12 millimeters high and whose dial features slotted indices for better sound transmission. It was followed by the 5.15-millimeter-high Octo Finissimo Automatic run on the Caliber BVL 138. The Chronograph GMT (2019) was another record in streamlining. It is 6.9 millimeters high, and runs on the BVL 318, featuring a hubless peripheral rotor and an hour hand that can be quickly and easily clicked through the time zones.

The sixth world record came in 2020 with the Octo Finissimo Tourbillon Chronograph Skeleton Automatic, which combines the essential complications of modern watchmaking in the thinnest possible case. And in November 2021, Bulgari picked up the coveted Aiguille d'Or of the Grand Prix d'Horlogerie de Genève for the Octo Finissimo Perpetual Calendar, which measures 5.8 millimeters. Most recently the Octo Finissimo Ultra held the record for thinnest mechanical watch, with a total height of 1.8 millimeters. That record has since been broken, but rumor has it that the workshop in Neuchâtel will be setting a new record soon.

Octo Finissimo S Chronograph GMT Titanium

Reference number: 103661
Movement: automatic, Bulgari Caliber BVL 318 Finissimo; ø 36 mm, height 3.3 mm; 37 jewels; 28,800 vph; winding rotor with platinum oscillating mass; column wheel control of the chronograph functions; finely finished with côtes de Genève; 55-hour power reserve
Functions: hours, minutes, subsidiary seconds; additional 24-hour display (second time zone); chronograph
Case: titanium, ø 43 mm, height 6.9 mm; sapphire crystal; transparent case back; screw-in crown; water-resistant to 3 atm
Band: titanium, folding clasp
Remarks: ceramic dial; currently the thinnest GMT chronograph movement with automatic winding
Price: $17,600

Octo Finissimo Minute Repeater

Reference number: 103015
Movement: manually wound, Bulgari Caliber BVL 362; ø 28.5 mm, height 3.12 mm; 21,600 vph; 42-hour power reserve
Functions: hours, minutes, subsidiary seconds; minute repeater
Case: titanium, ø 40 mm, height 6.85 mm; sapphire crystal; transparent case back; water-resistant to 3 atm
Band: titanium, double folding clasp
Price: on request; limited to 50 pieces

Octo Finissimo Tourbillon Automatic

Reference number: BGO42CCXTSKAUTO
Movement: automatic, Bulgari Caliber BVL 288; ø 36 mm, height 1,95 mm; 24 jewels; 21,600 vph; 1-minute flying tourbillon; hubless peripheral rotor; 52-hour power reserve
Functions: hours, minutes
Case: carbon, ø 42 mm, height 3.95 mm; sapphire crystal; transparent case back; water-resistant to 3 atm
Band: carbon, double folding clasp
Remarks: currently the thinnest automatic mechanical watch, despite the tourbillon!
Price: $130,000

Octo Finissimo Perpetual Calendar Titanium

Reference number: 103200
Movement: automatic, Bulgari Caliber BVL 305; ø 36 mm, height 2.75 mm; 30 jewels; 21,600 vph; micro-rotor in platinum; finely finished with côtes de Genève; 60-hour power reserve
Functions: hours, minutes; perpetual calendar with date(retrograde), weekday, month, leap year display (retrograde)
Case: titanium, ø 40 mm, height 5.8 mm; sapphire crystal; water-resistant to 3 atm
Band: titanium, folding clasp
Remarks: currently the thinnest perpetual calendar
Price: $59,000
Variations: in platinum ($89,000)

Octo Finissimo Tourbillon Chronograph

Reference number: 103295
Movement: automatic, Bulgari Caliber BVL 388 Finissimo; height 3.5 mm; 21,600 vph; 1-minute tourbillon single pusher for chronograph functions, hubless rotor with platinum oscillating weight; 52-hour power reserve
Functions: hours, minutes, subsidiary seconds; chronograph
Case: titanium, ø 43 mm, height 7.4 mm; sapphire crystal; transparent case back; water-resistant to 3 atm
Band: titanium, folding clasp
Price: $170,000; limited to 50 pieces

Octo Finissimo Tourbillon Chronograph

Reference number: 103510
Movement: automatic, Bulgari Caliber BVL 388 Finissimo; height 3.5 mm; 21,600 vph; 1-minute tourbillon, single pusher for chronograph functions, hubless rotor with platinum oscillating weight; 52-hour power reserve
Functions: hours, minutes, subsidiary seconds; chronograph
Case: titanium, ø 43 mm, height 7.4 mm; sapphire crystal; transparent case back; water-resistant to 3 atm
Band: reptile skin, folding clasp
Price: $213,000; limited to 50 pieces

Octo Finissimo Ultra

Reference number: 103611
Movement: manually wound, Bulgari Caliber BVL 180; height 1.8 mm; 28,800 vph; tungsten carbide mainplate, stainless steel ratchet wheel with engraved QR code, which is connected with an exclusive non-fungible token artwork; 50-hour power reserve
Functions: hours (off-center), minutes (off-center)
Case: titanium, ø 40 mm, height 1.8 mm; sapphire crystal; transparent case back
Band: titanium, folding clasp
Price: $426,000; limited to 10 pieces

Octo Finissimo Automatic

Reference number: 102713
Movement: automatic, Bulgari Caliber BVL 138 Finissimo; ø 36 mm, height 2.23 mm; 23 jewels; 21,600 vph; platinum micro-rotor; finely finished with côtes de Genève; 60-hour power reserve
Functions: hours, minutes, subsidiary seconds
Case: titanium, ø 40 mm, height 6.9 mm; sapphire crystal; transparent case back; screw-in crown; water-resistant to 3 atm
Band: titanium, folding clasp
Price: $14,700

Octo Finissimo Chronograph GMT

Reference number: BGO43C14TTXTCHGMT
Movement: automatic, Bulgari Caliber BVL 318; ø 36 mm, height 3.3 mm; 37 jewels; 28,800 vph; hubless peripheral rotor with platinum oscillating mass; column wheel control of chronograph functions; finely finished with côtes de Genève; 55-hour power reserve
Functions: hours, minutes, subsidiary seconds; additional 24-hour display (second time zone); chronograph
Case: stainless steel, ø 42 mm, height 6.9 mm; sapphire crystal; transparent case back; screw-in crown; water-resistant to 10 atm
Band: stainless steel, folding clasp
Remarks: currently the thinnest automatic GMT-chronograph movement
Price: $18,000

Octo Finissimo Automatic S

Reference number: BGO40BPSSXTAUTO
Movement: automatic, Bulgari Caliber BVL 138 Finissimo; ø 36 mm, height 2.23 mm; 23 jewels; 21,600 vph; platinum micro-rotor; finely finished with côtes de Genève; 60-hour power reserve
Functions: hours, minutes, subsidiary seconds
Case: stainless steel, ø 40 mm, height 6.4 mm; sapphire crystal; transparent case back
Band: stainless steel, folding clasp
Price: $13,900
Variations: various dials

Octo Finissimo Automatic Steel Grey

Reference number: 102711
Movement: automatic, Bulgari Caliber BVL 138 Finissimo; ø 36 mm, height 2.23 mm; 23 jewels; 21,600 vph; platinum micro-rotor; finely finished with côtes de Genève; 60-hour power reserve
Functions: hours, minutes, subsidiary seconds
Case: titanium, ø 40 mm, height 6.4 mm; sapphire crystal; transparent case back; screw-in crown; water-resistant to 10 atm
Band: reptile skin, folding clasp
Price: $13,800

Bulgari Aluminum Chronograph

Reference number: 103383
Movement: automatic, ETA Caliber 2894; ø 28.6 mm, height 6.1 mm; 37 jewels; 28,800 vph; 42-hour power reserve
Functions: hours, minutes, subsidiary seconds; chronograph; date
Case: aluminum, ø 40 mm, height 13.8 mm; titanium bezel with rubber coating; sapphire crystal; water-resistant to 10 atm
Band: rubber, buckle
Price: $4,250

Bulgari Aluminum

Reference number: 103445
Movement: automatic, ETA Caliber 2892-A2; ø 25.6 mm, height 3.6 mm; 21 jewels; 28,800 vph; 42-hour power reserve
Functions: hours, minutes, sweep seconds; date
Case: aluminum, ø 40 mm, height 11.8 mm; titanium bezel with rubber coating; sapphire crystal; water-resistant to 10 atm
Band: rubber, buckle
Price: $2,950

Bulgari Aluminum

Reference number: 103445
Movement: automatic, ETA Caliber 2892-A2; ø 25.6 mm, height 3.6 mm; 21 jewels; 28,800 vph; 42-hour power reserve
Functions: hours, minutes, sweep seconds; date
Case: aluminum, ø 40 mm, height 11.8 mm; titanium bezel with rubber coating; sapphire crystal; water-resistant to 10 atm
Band: rubber, buckle
Price: $2,950
Variations: with black dial

Bulgari Aluminum Chronograph Ducati Edition

Reference number: 103701
Movement: automatic, ETA Caliber 2894; ø 28.6 mm, height 6.1 mm; 37 jewels; 28,800 vph; 42-hour power reserve
Functions: hours, minutes, subsidiary seconds; chronograph; date
Case: aluminum, ø 40 mm, height 13.8 mm; titanium bezel with rubber coating; sapphire crystal; water-resistant to 10 atm
Band: rubber, buckle
Price: $5,000; limited to 1000 pieces

CARL F. BUCHERER

While luxury watch brand Carl F. Bucherer is still rather young, the Lucerne-based Bucherer jewelry dynasty behind it draws its vast know-how from more than a century of experience in the conception and design of fine wristwatches, and over 130 years of experience in the sale of watches. Today, Carl F. Bucherer has worldwide presence and is one of the few independent Swiss watch *manufactures* that is still in the hands of the founding family. It is led these days by Jörg G. Bucherer, the grandson of the founder.

In 2005, Bucherer joined its Sainte-Croix-headquartered partner, Techniques Horlogères Appliquées SA (THA), to manufacture its own movement. THA was integrated into the Bucherer Group and the watch company renamed Carl F. Bucherer Technologies SA (CFBT).

The Swiss company also expanded its Lengnau location to create a competence center that can focus on manufacturing its own movements as well as in-house watches. The famed automatic caliber with the peripheral rotor went through a thorough revamping process with the idea of industrializing it. For its 130th birthday, in 2018, the company decided to create a special "floating" tourbillon for its Manero collection. Not only does it feature a hubless peripheral rotor but the power transmission to the tourbillon is done from the side, making it invisible to the observer, a very subtle technology that has greatly contributed to the brand's fame. Another pioneering mechanism in the field of peripheral technology is the minute repeater with a hubless regulating mechanism. All three innovations have been packed into the new Manero Minute Repeater "Symphony," to create a genuine masterpiece of watchmaking technology.

Bucherer AG
Carl F. Bucherer
Langensandstrasse 27
CH-6002 Lucerne
Switzerland

Tel.:
+41-41-369-7070

E-mail:
info@carl-f-bucherer.com

Website:
www.carl-f-bucherer.com

Founded:
1919; repositioned under the name Carl F. Bucherer in 2001

Number of employees:
approx. 200

Annual production:
approx. 30,000 watches

U.S. distributor:
Carl F. Bucherer North America
1805 South Metro Parkway
Dayton, OH 45459
937-291-4366
info@cfbna.com;
www.carl-f-bucherer.com

Most important collections/price range:
Patravi, Manero, Heritage, Alacria, and Pathos / core price segment $5,000 to $30,000

Manero Minute Repeater Symphony

Reference number: 00.10925.03.63.01
Movement: automatic, Caliber CFB MR3000; ø 35.7 mm, height 8.59 mm; 47 jewels; 21,600 vph; silicon escapement; floating 1-minute tourbillon with invisible peripheral drive; repeater mechanism with peripheral speed regulator; hubless peripheral rotor with rose-gold oscillating mass; 65-hour power reserve; COSC-certified chronometer
Functions: hours, minutes, subsidiary seconds (on the tourbillon cage); minute repeater
Case: rose gold, ø 43.8 mm, height 12.47 mm; sapphire crystal; transparent case back
Band: reptile skin, folding clasp
Price: on request

Manero Tourbillon Double Peripheral

Reference number: 00.10920.03.93.01
Movement: automatic, Caliber CFB T3000; ø 36.5 mm, height 4.6 mm; 32 jewels; 21,600 vph; silicon escapement; floating 1-minute tourbillon with invisible peripheral drive, hubless peripheral with rose-gold oscillating mass; 65-hour power reserve; COSC-certified chronometer
Functions: hours, minutes, subsidiary seconds (on the tourbillon cage)
Case: rose gold, ø 43.1 mm, height 11.57 mm; sapphire crystal; transparent case back; water-resistant to 3 atm
Band: reptile skin, folding clasp
Price: $72,500

Heritage Tourbillon Double Peripheral

Reference number: 00.10802.03.13.01
Movement: automatic, Caliber CFB T3000; ø 36.5 mm, height 4.6 mm; 32 jewels; 21,600 vph; silicon escapement; floating 1-minute tourbillon with invisible peripheral drive, hubless peripheral rotor with rose gold oscillating mass; hand-engraved white gold bridge; 65-hour power reserve; COSC-certified chronometer
Functions: hours, minutes, subsidiary seconds (on tourbillon cage)
Case: white gold, ø 42.5mm, height 11.9 mm; sapphire crystal; transparent case back; water-resistant to 3 atm
Band: reptile skin, folding clasp
Price: $90,000; limited to 88 pieces

Manero Peripheral BigDate

Reference number: 00.10926.08.53.01
Movement: automatic, Caliber CFB A2011; ø 30.6 mm, height 6.3 mm; 33 jewels; 28,800 vph; hubless peripheral rotor with tungsten oscillating mass; 55-hour power reserve; COSC-certified chronometer
Functions: hours, minutes, subsidiary seconds; power reserve indicator; large date and weekday
Case: stainless steel, ø 41.6 mm, height 12.21 mm; sapphire crystal; transparent case back; water-resistant to 3 atm
Band: textile, folding buckle
Price: $9,400

Heritage BiCompax Annual Hometown Editions "Berlin"

Reference number: 00.10803.08.92.86
Movement: automatic, Caliber CFB 1972; ø 30 mm, height 7.3 mm; 47 jewels; 28,800 vph; 42-hour power reserve
Functions: hours, minutes, subsidiary seconds; chronograph; annual calendar with large date, month
Case: stainless steel, ø 41 mm, height 14.15 mm; sapphire crystal; transparent case back with engraving of local landmark; water-resistant to 3 atm
Band: calfskin, folding clasp
Price: $7,800; limited to 88 pieces
Variations: 15 other limited city editions

Heritage BiCompax Annual Hometown Editions "Vienna"

Reference number: 00.10803.08.92.95
Movement: automatic, Caliber CFB 1972; ø 30 mm, height 7.3 mm; 47 jewels; 28,800 vph; 42-hour power reserve
Functions: hours, minutes, subsidiary seconds; chronograph; annual calendar with large date, month
Case: stainless steel, ø 41 mm, height 14.15 mm; sapphire crystal; transparent case back with engraving of local landmark; water-resistant to 3 atm
Band: calfskin, folding clasp
Price: $7,800; limited to 88 pieces
Variations: 15 other limited city editions

Heritage BiCompax Annual Hometown Editions "Lucerne"

Reference number: 00.10803.08.92.85
Movement: automatic, Caliber CFB 1972; ø 30 mm, height 7.3 mm; 47 jewels; 28,800 vph; 42-hour power reserve
Functions: hours, minutes, subsidiary seconds; chronograph; annual calendar with large date, month
Case: stainless steel, ø 41 mm, height 14.15 mm; sapphire crystal; transparent case back with engraving of local landmark; water-resistant to 3 atm
Band: calfskin, folding clasp
Price: $7,800; limited to 88 pieces
Variations: 15 other limited city editions

Manero Flyback Green

Reference number: 00.10919.08.93.98
Movement: automatic, Caliber CFB 1970; ø 30.4 mm, height 7.9 mm; 25 jewels; 28,800 vph; 42-hour power reserve
Functions: hours, minutes, subsidiary seconds; flyback chronograph; date
Case: stainless steel, ø 43 mm, height 14.45 mm; sapphire crystal; transparent case back; water-resistant to 3 atm
Band: textile, folding clasp
Price: $7,100
Variations: various case, bands, and dials

Manero Flyback Blue

Reference number: 00.10919.08.53.01
Movement: automatic, Caliber CFB 1970; ø 30.4 mm, height 7.9 mm; 25 jewels; 28,800 vph; 42-hour power reserve
Functions: hours, minutes, subsidiary seconds; flyback chronograph; date
Case: stainless steel, ø 43 mm, height 14.45 mm; sapphire crystal; transparent case back; water-resistant to 3 atm
Band: textile, folding clasp
Price: $7,100
Variations: various case, bands, and dials

Patravi ScubaTec Maldives

Reference number: 00.10632.23.53.02
Movement: automatic, Caliber CFB 1950.1; ø 26.2 mm, height 4.6 mm; 25 jewels; 28,800 vph; 38-hour power reserve; COSC-certified chronometer
Functions: hours, minutes, sweep seconds; date
Case: stainless steel, ø 44.6 mm, height 13.45 mm; unidirectional bezel with ceramic insert, with 0-60 scale; sapphire crystal; screw-in crown, helium valve; water-resistant to 50 atm
Band: rubber with recycled textile inlay, folding clasp with extension link
Price: $6,900

Patravi ScubaTec Black

Reference number: 00.10632.28.33.01
Movement: automatic, Caliber CFB 1950.1; ø 26.2 mm, height 4.6 mm; 25 jewels; 28,800 vph; 38-hour power reserve; COSC-certified chronometer
Functions: hours, minutes, sweep seconds; date
Case: titanium with black DLC coating, ø 44.6 mm, height 13.45 mm; unidirectional bezel with ceramic insert, with 0-60 scale; sapphire crystal; screw-in crown, helium valve; water-resistant to 50 atm
Band: rubber with recycled textile inlay, folding clasp with extension link
Price: $7,900
Variations: stainless steel with stainless steel bracelet ($7,400); stainless steel with rubber band ($6,900)

Patravi TravelTec Color Edition "Four Seasons" (Summer)

Reference number: 00.10620.08.93.01
Movement: automatic, Caliber CFB 1901.1; ø 28.6 mm, height 7.3 mm; 39 jewels; 28,800 vph; 42-hour power reserve; COSC-certified chronometer
Functions: hours, minutes, subsidiary seconds; additional 24-hour indicator (second time zone); chronograph; date
Case: stainless steel, ø 46.6 mm, height 15.5 mm; pusher-activated inner bezel with 24-hour division (third time zone); sapphire crystal; screw-in crown; water-resistant to 5 atm
Band: rubber, folding clasp with extension link
Price: $11,900
Variations: in green ("Spring"), turquoise ("Winter"), and orange ("Autumn")

Caliber CFB MR3000

Automatic; floating one-minute tourbillon; silicon escapement; bidirectional rotor, stainless-steel and rose-gold peripheral rotor on the outer edge with spring-mounted support bearings; precision fine adjustment; single spring barrel, 65-hour power reserve; COSC-certified chronometer
Functions: hours, minutes, subsidiary seconds; minute repeater
Diameter: 35.7 mm
Height: 8.59 mm
Jewels: 47
Frequency: 21,600 vph;
Hairspring: flat hairspring
Shock protection: Incabloc

Caliber CFB T3000

Automatic; floating one-minute tourbillon; silicon escapement; bidirectional rotor, tungsten or rose gold peripheral rotor on the outer edge with spring-mounted support bearings; precision fine adjustment; single spring barrel, 38-hour power reserve; COSC-certified chronometer
Functions: hours, minutes, subsidiary seconds
Diameter: 36.5 mm
Height: 7.6 mm including the tourbillon cage
Jewels: 32
Balance: glucydur
Frequency: 21,600 vph
Hairspring: flat hairspring
Shock protection: Incabloc

Caliber CFB A2011

Automatic; bidirectional rotor, peripheral tungsten rotor on the edge of the movement with spring-held support bearings; precision fine adjustment; single spring barrel, 55-hour power reserve; COSC-certified chronometer
Base caliber: CFB A2000
Functions: hours, minutes, subsidiary seconds; power reserve indicator; large date, weekday
Diameter: 30.6 mm
Height: 6.3 mm
Jewels: 33
Balance: glucydur
Frequency: 28,800 vph;
Hairspring: flat hairspring
Shock protection: Incabloc

Carl Suchy & Söhne
Prinz-Eugen-Strasse 48/Top 3
A-1010 Wien
Austria

Tel.:
+43-660-75-24-331

E-mail:
office@carlsuchy.com

Website:
www.carlsuchy.com

Founded:
1822/2017

Distribution:
Retail

Most important collection:
Waltz N°1, Waltz N°1 Skeleton

CARL SUCHY & SÖHNE

Reviving an old and venerable brand of anything can be a risky enterprise. Carl Suchy & Söhne, founded in 1822, was a clock and pocket-watch maker with a presence in Vienna and Prague and workshops in La Chaux-de-Fonds. The products were the ultimate in fashion at the time, made in the somewhat restrained, bourgeois Biedermeier style, which found favor well beyond Vienna's borders.

In 2016, a Viennese businessman with experience in "curating art" decided it was time for Vienna to have a watch brand again. The new Carl Suchy, however, would be in the timeless look of the Viennese Modern ushered in by architect Alfred Loos, whose main idea was encapsulated in a 1910 essay entitled "Ornament and Crime," in which he formulated his basic tenet: "Cultural evolution is equivalent to the removal of ornament from articles in daily use."

The Waltz N°1 was designed in a dialogue between CEO Robert Punkenhofer and a young graduate from the ECAL in Lausanne, Miloš Ristin. It was to express "Viennese elegance and savoir vivre," says the CEO. The final product was supervised by the outstanding Swiss watchmaker Marc Jenni. It is not a spectacular watch at first glance. All the value is in the detailed finishings of the thin case, the lugs, and the silk-leather strap. The dial features a calming geometric pattern with perpendicular guilloché on one half and a vertical guilloché on the other. It's not a static visual: at 6 o'clock, a small second disk turns, breaking up the pattern, but "clicking in place" twice each minute. This is the core of the model, since *walzen* in German means "to roll." Time for the Waltz N°1 is driven by a Vaucher Fleurier automatic caliber.

The model was skeletonized for the second version, giving the dial face a peculiar look, as if the movement, a Vaucher 5401/180, was covered by a shutter. It was followed up by a limited edition in gold, but without the skeletonization. The dial has since been skeletonized and painted in different colors. At the time of writing, a second line is about to come out, inspired by one of Vienna's great palaces. Stay tuned. . . .

Waltz N°1 Day & Night

Reference number: 200059
Movement: automatic, Vaucher Caliber VMF 5401; ø 30 mm, height 2.6 mm; 29 jewels; 21,600 vph; micro-rotor; finely finished movement with côtes de Genève; 48-hour power reserve
Functions: hours, minutes, subsidiary seconds (on a revolving disk)
Case: stainless steel with black PVD, ø 41.5 mm, height 9.3 mm; sapphire crystal; transparent case back; crown with ceramic insert; water-resistant to 3 atm
Band: leather, buckle
Remarks: silver and black dial with horizontal and vertical guilloché pattern
Price: $11,800; limited yearly production series of 10 pieces
Variations: with reptile skin strap

Waltz N°1

Reference number: 200052
Movement: automatic, Vaucher Caliber VMF 5401; ø 30 mm, height 2.6 mm; 29 jewels; 21,600 vph; micro-rotor; finely finished movement; 48-hour power reserve
Functions: hours, minutes, subsidiary seconds (on a revolving disk)
Case: stainless steel, ø 41.5 mm, height 9.3 mm; sapphire crystal; transparent case back; crown with black lacquer; water-resistant to 3 atm
Band: genuine leather (optional: alligator leather), double folding clasp
Remarks: dial with horizontal and vertical guilloché pattern
Price: $10,300
Variations: with black or blue dial; with case with black ADLC

Waltz N°1 Skeleton Gold

Reference number: 200058
Movement: automatic, Vaucher Caliber VMF 5401/180; ø 30 mm, height 2.6 mm; 29 jewels; 21,600 vph; micro-rotor; fully skeletonized dial; 42-hour power reserve
Functions: hours, minutes, subsidiary seconds (on a revolving disk)
Case: pink gold, ø 41.3 mm, height 9.3 mm; sapphire crystal; transparent case back; crown with ceramic insert; water-resistant to 3 atm
Band: reptile skin, double folding clasp
Remarks: skeletonized dial along the vertical and horizontal guilloché lines, with black PVD
Price: $37,500
Variations: blue or white dials

CARTIER

Since the Richemont Group's founding, Cartier has played an important role in the luxury concern as its premier brand and instigator of turnover. Although it took a while for Cartier to find its footing and convince the male market of its masculinity, any concerns about Cartier's seriousness and potential are being dispelled by facts. Carole Forestier-Kasapi —now at TAG Heuer—headed the watchmaking division that drove the company's vertical integration with a host of outstanding calibers, beginning with the 1904 MC, a reference to the year in which Louis Cartier developed the first wristwatch made for men—a pilot's watch custom designed for his friend and early pioneer of aviation, Alberto Santos-Dumont.

The automatic movement is a largely unadorned yet efficient machine, powered by twin barrels. The central rotor sits on ceramic ball bearings, and the adjustment of the conventional escapement is by an excenter screw. It is available for chronographs or diver's watches. But mainly, it has positioned Cartier as one of the most effective makers of high-end watches in a very competitive industry. It is also now just one of a family of outstanding calibers that continue to push Cartier to the top rung of *haute horlogerie*.

In a period that values vintage, the Cartier brand has an advantage. More than a century of watchmaking has provided it with a steady stream of models to revive and modernize. The Pasha, Santos, Tank, Rotonde, Drive, and Calibre de Cartier are among the best-known and most successful watches in the world and have become legends in the industry. And there is the series of "mystérieuse" watches, which in fine watchmaking stands for the invisible drive of an indicator or function. It refers to the oscillating weight of the automatic winding mechanism—or rather, the finely skeletonized movement housed within it, as is the case of the novelty Masse Mystérieuse for 2022. Enclosed between two sapphire crystal discs, the halved movement, moving by gravity and centrifugal force, appears to rotate freely in the watch case. A differential compensates for the relative movement and ensures that the time is always correctly displayed along the vertical axis of the watch.

Cartier
1201 Genève
Switzerland

E-mail:
contact.na@cartier.com

Website:
https://www.cartier.com

Founded:
1847

Number of employees:
approx. 1,300 (watch manufacturing)

U.S. distributor:
Cartier North America
645 Fifth Avenue
New York, NY 10022
1-800-CARTIER
www.cartier.us

Most important collections:
Santos de Cartier, Panthère de Cartier, Baignoire, Tank, Ballon Bleu de Cartier, Drive de Cartier, Calibre de Cartier, Clé de Cartier, Ronde de Cartier, Pasha de Cartier, Mystérieuse

Masse Mystérieuse

Reference number: WHRO0078
Movement: automatic, Cartier Caliber 9801 MC; ø 39.6 mm, height 7.3 mm; 43 jewels; 28,800 vph; entire movement "mysteriously" contained in the rotor, revolves around the central axis; 42-hour power reserve
Functions: hours, minutes
Case: platinum, ø 43.5 mm, height 12.64 mm; sapphire crystal; transparent case back; crown with ruby cabochon
Band: reptile skin, buckle
Price: on request; limited to 30 pieces

Cartier Privé Tank Chinoise

Reference number: CRWGTA0088
Movement: manually wound, Cartier Caliber 430 MC; ø 20.55 mm, height 2.1 mm; 18 jewels; 21,600 vph; 38-hour power reserve
Functions: hours minutes
Case: yellow gold, 29.2 mm x 39.49 mm, height 6.09 mm; sapphire crystal; crown with sapphire cabochon
Band: reptile skin, buckle
Price: $28,300; limited to 150 pieces

Cartier Privé Tank Chinoise

Reference number: CRWHTA0016
Movement: manually wound, Cartier Caliber 9627 MC; ø 26.1 mm, height 3.9 mm; 23 jewels; 21,600 vph; skeletonized movement with integrated decorative elements; 38-hour power reserve
Functions: hours minutes
Case: yellow gold, 29.2 mm x 39.5 mm, height 6.09 mm; sapphire crystal; crown with sapphire cabochon
Band: reptile skin, buckle
Price: $65,500; limited to 100 pieces

Tank Louis Cartier

Reference number: CRWGTA0093
Movement: manually wound, Cartier Caliber 1917 MC; 16 x 12.95 mm, height 2.9 mm; 19 jewels; 21,600 vph; 38-hour power reserve
Functions: hours minutes
Case: yellow gold, 25.5 mm x 33.7 mm, height 6.6 mm; sapphire crystal; crown with sapphire cabochon; water-resistant to 3 atm
Band: reptile skin, buckle
Price: $13,100
Variations: various cases and colors

Tank Louis Cartier

Reference number: CRWGTA0092
Movement: manually wound, Cartier Caliber 1917 MC; 16 x 12.95 mm, height 2.9 mm; 19 jewels; 21,600 vph; 38-hour power reserve
Functions: hours, minutes
Case: rose gold, 25.5 mm x 33.7 mm, height 6.6 mm; sapphire crystal; crown with sapphire cabochon; water-resistant to 3 atm
Band: reptile skin, buckle
Price: $13,100
Variations: various cases and colors

Tank Louis Cartier

Reference number: CRWGTA0091
Movement: manually wound, Cartier Caliber 1917 MC; 16 x 12.95 mm, height 2.9 mm; 19 jewels; 21,600 vph; 38-hour power reserve
Functions: hours, minutes
Case: yellow gold, 25.5 mm x 33.7 mm, height 6.6 mm; sapphire crystal; crown with sapphire cabochon; water-resistant to 3 atm
Band: reptile skin, buckle
Price: $12,800
Variations: various cases and colors

Pasha de Cartier

Reference number: CRWGPA0019
Movement: automatic, Cartier Caliber 1847 MC; ø 25.6 mm, 23 jewels; 28,800 vph; 40-hour power reserve
Functions: hours, minutes, sweep seconds;
Case: yellow gold, ø 41 mm, height 9.55 mm; sapphire crystal; crown with screw-in cap and sapphire cabochon; water-resistant to 10 atm
Band: reptile skin, folding clasp
Remarks: removable grid; comes with additional reptile-skin band
Price: $18,900

Pasha de Cartier Chronograph

Reference number: CRWSPA0027
Movement: automatic, Cartier Caliber 1904-CH MC; ø 25.58 mm, height 5.72 mm; 37 jewels; 28,800 vph; 47-hour power reserve
Functions: hours, minutes, subsidiary seconds; chronograph; date
Case: stainless steel, ø 41 mm, height 11.97 mm; sapphire crystal; capped crown and pushers and spinel cabochon; water-resistant to 10 atm
Band: reptile skin, buckle
Remarks: comes with additional stainless-steel bracelet
Price: $9,900

Pasha de Cartier Moon Phases

Reference number: CRWSPA0030
Movement: automatic, Cartier Caliber 1904-LU MC; ø 25.6 mm, height 4.2 mm; 25 jewels; 28,800 vph; 48-hour power reserve
Functions: hours, minutes, moon phase
Case: stainless steel, ø 41 mm, height 9.55 mm; sapphire crystal; crown with screw-in cap and spinel cabochon; water-resistant to 10 atm
Band: reptile skin, folding clasp
Remarks: comes with additional reptile-skin band
Price: $8,900

Santos Dumont

Reference number: CRWGSA0053
Movement: manually wound, Cartier Caliber 430 MC; ø 20.55 mm, height 2.1 mm; 18 jewels; 21,600 vph; 38-hour power reserve
Functions: hours, minutes
Case: platinum, with red paint, 31.4 mm x 43.5 mm, height 7.3 mm; sapphire crystal; crown with ruby cabochon
Band: reptile skin, buckle
Price: $18,800; limited to 150 pieces

Santos Dumont

Reference number: CRWGSA0054
Movement: manually wound, Cartier Caliber 430 MC; ø 20.55 mm, height 2.1 mm; 18 jewels; 21,600 vph; 38-hour power reserve
Functions: hours, minutes
Case: rose gold, with beige paint, 31.4 mm x 43.5 mm, height 7.3 mm; sapphire crystal; crown with sapphire cabochon
Band: reptile skin, buckle
Price: $14,100; limited to 250 pieces

Santos Dumont XL

Reference number: CRWSSA0032, CRW2SA0017
Movement: manually wound, Cartier Caliber 430 MC; ø 20.55 mm, height 2.1 mm; 18 jewels; 21,600 vph; 38-hour power reserve
Functions: hours, minutes
Case: rose gold, 33.9 x 46.6 mm, height 7.5 mm; sapphire crystal; crown with spinel cabochon
Band: reptile skin, buckle
Variations: in stainless steel ($6,000); in stainless steel with rose gold bezel ($8,450)

Santos de Cartier

Reference number: CRWSSA0047
Movement: automatic, Cartier Caliber 1847 MC; ø 25.6 mm, height 3.77 mm; 23 jewels; 28,800 vph; 40-hour power reserve
Functions: hours, minutes, sweep seconds; date
Case: stainless steel, 39.8 mm x 47.5 mm, height 9.37 mm; bezel with blue ADLC coating; sapphire crystal; spinel cabochon; water-resistant to 10 atm
Band: stainless steel, double folding clasp
Remarks: comes with additional rubber strap with QuickSwitch strap-changing system
Price: $7,800

Santos de Cartier

Reference number: CRWSSA0048
Movement: automatic, Cartier Caliber 1847 MC; ø 25.6 mm, height 3.77 mm; 23 jewels; 28,800 vph; 40-hour power reserve
Functions: hours, minutes, sweep seconds; date
Case: stainless steel, 39.8 mm x 47.5 mm, height 9.37 mm; bezel with blue ADLC coating; sapphire crystal; spinel cabochon; water-resistant to 10 atm
Band: stainless steel, double folding clasp
Remarks: comes with additional rubber strap with QuickSwitch strap-changing system
Price: $7,800

Santos de Cartier Squelette

Reference number: WHSA0026
Movement: manually wound, Cartier Caliber 9612 MC; 28.6 x 28.6 mm, height 3.97 mm; 20 jewels; 28,800 vph; skeleton movement with integrated Roman hour numerals; 2 spring barrels; 72-hour power reserve
Functions: hours, minutes
Case: stainless steel with blue DLC-coating, ø 39.8 mm, height 9.08 mm; bezel screwed to case back with 8 screws; sapphire crystal; transparent case back; crown with sapphire cabochon; water-resistant to 10 atm
Band: stainless steel with blue DLC-coating, double folding clasp
Remarks: comes with additional rubber strap with QuickSwitch strap-changing system
Price: $30,100

Chanel
135, avenue Charles de Gaulle
F-92521 Neuilly-sur-Seine Cedex
France

Tel.:
+33-1-41-92-08-33

Website:
www.chanel.com

Founded:
1914

Distribution:
retail and 200 Chanel boutiques worldwide

U.S. distributor:
Chanel Fine Jewelry and Watches
600 Madison Avenue, 19th Floor
New York, NY 10022
212-715-4741
www.chanel.com

Most important collections:
J12, Première, Boy.Friend, Monsieur de Chanel

CHANEL

After putting the occasional jewelry watch onto the market earlier, family-owned Chanel opened its own horology division in 1987, a move that gave the brand instant access to the world of watchmaking art. While the brand's first collections were directed exclusively at its female clientele, it was actually with the rather simple and masculine J12 that Chanel finally achieved a breakthrough. That was in 1999, over twenty years ago. The designer was Jacques Helleu. The J12 collection showpiece, the Rétrograde Mystérieuse, was a stroke of genius—courtesy of the innovative think tank Renaud et Papi. Its sleek ceramic case and complex mechanics instantly propelled Chanel into the world of haute *horlogerie*.

It was designer Arnaud Chastaingt who created the new J12.1. It still comes in brilliant white ceramic, but a black limited edition has been added as well. Inside is a new movement built by Kenissi, a joint venture Chanel shares with Tudor and Breitling. It no longer has a silicon hairspring, and it has returned to the soft iron cage to protect from magnetic fields.

In the past few years, the brand turned its attention to a younger, dynamic crowd with models like the prize-winning "Vendôme" rectangular Boy.Friend with diamonds, a watch that would fit any wrist on the male-female spectrum. The brand-new Superleggera is again equipped with the exclusive Caliber 1. The jumping hour display above the "6" relieves the dial of one hand, so that the retrograde minute hand can claim the space for itself, like a sports car speedometer, and the small seconds hand moves to the center like a fuel gauge. And in 2022, the brand came out with a new movement for the J12 series, which can now be had with a diamond-studded tourbillon, not an easy feat, since tourbillon cages should be light.

J12 Caliber 12.2

Reference number: H5696
Movement: automatic, Chanel Caliber 12.2; ø 26 mm, height 4.99 mm; 26 jewels; 28,800 vph; Winding rotor with tungsten oscillating mass; 50-hour power reserve; COSC-certified chronometer
Functions: hours, minutes, sweep seconds
Case: ceramic, ø 33 mm, height 12.94 mm; stainless steel bezel with ceramic insert and 0-60 scale; sapphire crystal; transparent case back; Stainless steel screw-in crown with Ceramic cabochon; water-resistant to 20 atm
Band: ceramic, triple folding clasp (stainless steel)
Price: $7,150; limited to 555 pieces
Variations: in white ceramic ($7,150, limited to 555 pieces)

J12 Diamond Tourbillon

Reference number: H7381
Movement: manually wound, Chanel Caliber 5; ø 28.4 mm, height 6.25 mm; 29 jewels; 28,800 vph; flying one-minute tourbillon with a 20-mm diameter; 48-hour power reserve
Functions: hours and minutes (off-center)
Case: ceramic, ø 38 mm; white gold bezel, bezel set with 34 baguette diamonds; sapphire crystal; transparent case back; crown with a diamond; water-resistant to 5 atm
Band: ceramic, triple folding clasp (in white gold)
Remarks: skeletonized dial and hands set with 49 diamonds
Price: $179,700; limited to 55 pieces
Variations: without diamonds on the bezel (limited to 55 pieces, $99,800)

Monsieur Superleggera Edition

Reference number: H6823
Movement: manually wound, Chanel Caliber I; ø 32 mm, height 5.5 mm; 30 jewels; 28,800 vph; 2 spring barrels; skeletonized and blackened bridges; 72-hour power reserve
Functions: hours (digital, jumping), minutes (retrograde), subsidiary seconds
Case: ceramic, ø 42 mm, height 12 mm; sapphire crystal; transparent case back; water-resistant to 3 atm
Band: textile with calfskin overlay, folding clasp
Remarks: guilloché dial
Price: $39,400

CHOPARD

The Chopard *manufacture* was founded by Louis-Ulysse Chopard in 1860 in the tiny village of Sonvillier in the Jura mountains of Switzerland. In 1963, it was purchased by Karl Scheufele, a goldsmith from Pforzheim, Germany, and revived as a producer of fine watches and jewelry.

The past seventeen years have seen a breathtaking development, when Karl Scheufele's son, Karl-Friedrich, and his sister, Caroline, decided to create watches with in-house movements, thus restoring the old business launched by Louis-Ulysse back in the nineteenth century.

In 1996, out of nowhere, Chopard opened up its watchmaking *manufacture* in the sleepy town of Fleurier in the Val-de-Travers, which had not yet experienced the revival of the mechanical watch. Focus on vertical integration drove the opening of a second building, Fleurier Ebauches SA, a hub of movement kits, including the L.U.C series. Chopard now has a line-up of eleven calibers, ranging from simple three-hander automatics to a tourbillon; a perpetual calendar; chronographs; an ultra-high-frequency chronometer; and a minute repeater, now with sapphire gongs that produce a very clear sound.

The company's Alpine Eagle collection is a modernized version of the St. Moritz from the 1980s. The latter is the first watch project by then co-president Karl-Friedrich Scheufele, who had to convince his father, Karl, to actually manufacture the watch. For the new version, it was his son's turn to do the convincing. And he got vigorous support from his grandfather.

Chopard & Cie. SA
8, rue de Veyrot
CH-1217 Meyrin (Geneva)
Switzerland

Tel.:
+41-22-719-3131

E-mail:
info@chopard.ch

Website:
www.chopard.ch

Founded:
1860

Distribution:
149 boutiques

U.S. distributor:
Chopard USA
75 Valencia Ave, Suite 1200
Coral Gables, FL 33134
1-800-CHOPARD
www.chopard.com/en-us

Most important collections/price range:
L.U.C / from $8,110; Happy Sport / from $4,420; Imperiale / from $5,780; Classic Racing / from $5,910; Alpine Eagle / from $9,810

Mille Miglia Classic Chronograph

Reference number: 168589-3028
Movement: automatic, ETA Caliber 2894-2; ø 28.6 mm, height 6.1 mm; 37 jewels; 28,800 vph; 42-hour power reserve; COSC-certified chronometer
Functions: hours, minutes, subsidiary seconds; chronograph; date
Case: stainless steel, with black DLC coating, ø 42 mm, height 12.67 mm; sapphire crystal; transparent case back, screw-in crown; water-resistant to 5 atm
Band: calfskin, folding clasp
Price: $6,940; limited to 1000 pieces

Mille Miglia GTS Race Edition 2022

Reference number: 168571-3010
Movement: automatic, ETA Caliber 7750; ø 30.4 mm, height 7.9 mm; 25 jewels; 28,800 vph; 48-hour power reserve; COSC-certified chronometer
Functions: hours, minutes, subsidiary seconds; chronograph; date
Case: stainless steel, ø 44 mm, height 13.79 mm; sapphire crystal; water-resistant to 10 atm
Band: calfskin, folding clasp
Price: $7,770; limited to 1000 pieces

Alpine Eagle Large Tourbillon

Reference number: 298616-3001
Movement: automatic, L.U.C Caliber 96.24-L; ø 27.4 mm, height 3.3 mm; 25 jewels; 25,200 vph; flying 1-minute tourbillon, 2 spring barrels, micro-rotor; 65-hour power reserve; Geneva Seal, COSC-certified chronometer
Functions: hours, minutes, subsidiary seconds (on the tourbillon cage)
Case: stainless steel, ø 41 mm, height 9.7 mm; bezel screwed to case with 8 screws; sapphire crystal; transparent case back; water-resistant to 10 atm
Band: stainless steel, folding clasp
Price: on request

Alpine Eagle Large

Reference number: 298600-3001
Movement: automatic, L.U.C Caliber 01.01-C; ø 28.8 mm, height 4.95 mm; 31 jewels; 28,800 vph; 60-hour power reserve; COSC-certified chronometer
Functions: hours, minutes, sweep seconds; date
Case: stainless steel, ø 41 mm, height 9.7 mm; bezel screwed to case with 8 screws; sapphire crystal; transparent case back; water-resistant to 10 atm
Band: stainless steel, folding clasp
Price: $13,400
Variations: rose gold bezel ($21,200); various dial colors

Alpine Eagle Large

Reference number: 298600-3002
Movement: automatic, L.U.C Caliber 01.01-C; ø 28.8 mm, height 4.95 mm; 31 jewels; 28,800 vph; 60-hour power reserve; COSC-certified chronometer
Functions: hours, minutes, sweep seconds; date
Case: stainless steel, ø 41 mm, height 9.7 mm; bezel screwed to case with 8 screws; sapphire crystal; transparent case back; water-resistant to 10 atm
Band: stainless steel, folding clasp
Price: $13,400
Variations: rose gold bezel ($21,200); various dial colors

Alpine Eagle Large

Reference number: 298600-6001
Movement: automatic, L.U.C Caliber 01.01-C; ø 28.8 mm, height 4.95 mm; 31 jewels; 28,800 vph; 60-hour power reserve; COSC-certified chronometer
Functions: hours, minutes, sweep seconds; date
Case: stainless steel, ø 41 mm, height 9.7 mm; rose-gold bezel screwed to case with 8 screws; sapphire crystal; transparent case back; water-resistant to 10 atm
Band: stainless steel with rose gold elements, folding clasp
Price: $21,200
Variations: various case materials

Alpine Eagle Large

Reference number: 295363-5001
Movement: automatic, L.U.C Caliber 01.01-C; ø 28.8 mm, height 4.95 mm; 31 jewels; 28,800 vph; 60-hour power reserve; COSC-certified chronometer
Functions: hours, minutes, sweep seconds; date
Case: rose gold, ø 41 mm, height 9.7 mm; rose-gold bezel screwed to case with 8 screws; sapphire crystal; transparent case back; water-resistant to 10 atm
Band: rose gold, folding clasp
Price: $50,000
Variations: stainless steel ($13,400)

Alpine Eagle Chronograph

Reference number: 298609-3001
Movement: automatic, L.U.C Caliber 03.05-C; ø 28.8 mm, height 7.6 mm; 45 jewels; 28,800 vph; 60-hour power reserve; COSC-certified chronometer
Functions: hours, minutes, subsidiary seconds; flyback chronograph; date
Case: stainless steel, ø 44 mm, height 14 mm; bezel screwed to case with 8 screws; sapphire crystal; transparent case back; water-resistant to 10 atm
Band: stainless steel, folding clasp
Price: $19,600
Variations: various cases, bands, and dials

Alpine Eagle Chronograph

Reference number: 298609-3004
Movement: automatic, L.U.C Caliber 03.05-C; ø 28.8 mm, height 7.6 mm; 45 jewels; 28,800 vph; 60-hour power reserve; COSC-certified chronometer
Functions: hours, minutes, subsidiary seconds; flyback chronograph; date
Case: stainless steel, ø 44 mm, height 14 mm; bezel screwed to case with 8 screws; sapphire crystal; transparent case back; water-resistant to 10 atm
Band: rubber, folding clasp
Price: $18,200

L.U.C Full Strike Tourbillon

Reference number: 161987-5001
Movement: manually wound, L.U.C Caliber 08.01-L; ø 37.2 mm, height 7.97 mm; 63 jewels; 28,800 vph; 1-minute tourbillon; sapphire gong; 60-hour power reserve; Geneva Seal, COSC certified chronometer
Functions: hours, minutes, subsidiary seconds; power reserve display, minute repeater
Case: rose gold, ø 42.5 mm, height 11.55 mm; sapphire crystal; transparent case back
Band: reptile skin, folding clasp
Price: on request; limited to 20 pieces

L.U.C XPS Flying T Twin

Reference number: 161978-5001
Movement: automatic, L.U.C Caliber 96.24-L; ø 27.4 mm, height 3.3 mm; 25 jewels; 25,200 vph; flying 1-minute tourbillon, 2 spring barrels; micro-rotor; 65-hour power reserve; Geneva Seal, COSC-certified chronometer
Functions: hours, minutes, subsidiary seconds (on the tourbillon cage)
Case: rose gold, ø 40 mm, height 7.2 mm; sapphire crystal; transparent case back; water-resistant to 3 atm
Band: reptile skin, buckle
Remarks: case manufactured of certified fair mined gold; hand-guilloché rose-gold dial
Price: on request; limited to 50 pieces

L.U.C Perpetual Chrono

Reference number: 168611-3001
Movement: manually wound, L.U.C Caliber 03.10-L; ø 33 mm, height 8.32 mm; 42 jewels; 28,800 vph; mainplate and balance cock of German silver; 60-hour power reserve; Geneva Seal, COSC certified chronometer
Functions: hours, minutes, sweep seconds; day/night indicator; flyback chronograph; perpetual calendar with large date, weekday, months, moon phase, leap year
Case: titanium, ø 45 mm, height 15.06 mm; sapphire crystal; transparent case back; water-resistant to 3 atm
Band: calfskin, folding clasp
Price: $76,400; limited to 20 pieces

L.U.C Time Traveler One

Reference number: 161942-5001
Movement: automatic, L.U.C Caliber 01.05-L; ø 35.3 mm, height 6.52 mm; 39 jewels; 28,800 vph; 60-hour power reserve; COSC-certified chronometer
Functions: hours, minutes, sweep seconds; world time (2nd time zone); date
Case: rose gold, ø 42 mm, height 12.09 mm; crown-activated scale ring, with reference city names; sapphire crystal; transparent case back; water-resistant to 5 atm
Band: reptile skin, buckle
Price: $25,800
Variations: in titanium ($15,900)

L.U.C Quattro Spirit

Reference number: 161977-5001
Movement: manually wound, L.U.C Caliber 98.06-L; ø 28.6 mm, height 4.85 mm; 42 jewels; 28,800 vph; 4 spring barrels, balance spring with Philips terminal curve; 192-hour power reserve; Geneva Seal
Functions: hours (digital, jumping), minutes, power reserve indicator (on the movement side)
Case: rose gold, ø 40 mm, height 10.3 mm; sapphire crystal; transparent case back
Band: reptile skin, buckle
Remarks: enamel dial; case manufactured of certified fair mined gold
Price: $46,100; limited to 100 pieces

L.U.C XPS Flying T Twin

Reference number: 161978-1001
Movement: automatic, L.U.C Caliber 96.24-L; ø 27.4 mm, height 3.3 mm; 25 jewels; 25.200 vph; 1-minute flying tourbillon 2 spring barrels; micro-rotor; 65-hour power reserve; Geneva seal, COSC-certified chronometer
Functions: hours, minutes, subsidiary seconds (on the tourbillon cage)
Case: white gold, ø 40 mm, height 7.2 mm; sapphire crystal; transparent case back; water-resistant to 3 atm
Band: reptile skin, buckle
Remarks: case made of certified fair mined gold; hand-guilloché white-gold dial
Price: upon request; limited to 50 pieces

L.U.C XPS 1860 Officer

Reference number: 161242-0001
Movement: automatic, L.U.C Caliber 96.01-L; ø 27.4 mm, height 3.3 mm; 29 jewels; 28,800 vph; 65-hour power reserve; Geneva Seal, COSC certified chronometer
Functions: hours, minutes, subsidiary seconds; date
Case: yellow gold, ø 40 mm, height 7.7 mm; sapphire crystal; transparent case back; water-resistant to 3 atm
Band: reptile skin, buckle
Remarks: hinged case back cover
Price: $33,500

L.U.C Perpetual Twin

Reference number: 168561-3001
Movement: automatic, L.U.C Caliber 96.22-L; ø 33 mm, height 6 mm; 29 jewels; 28,800 vph; 2 spring barrels; gold micro-rotor with heavy metal oscillating mass; with côtes de Genève; 65-hour power reserve; COSC-certified chronometer
Functions: hours, minutes, subsidiary seconds; perpetual calendar with large date, weekday, month, leap year
Case: stainless steel, ø 43 mm, height 11.47 mm; sapphire crystal; transparent case back; water-resistant to 3 atm
Band: calf leather, buckle
Price: $25,200

L.U.C Lunar One

Reference number: 161927-5001
Movement: automatic, L.U.C Caliber 96.13-L; ø 33 mm, height 6 mm; 32 jewels; 28,800 vph; 65-hour power reserve; Geneva Seal, COSC-certified chronometer
Functions: hours, minutes, subsidiary seconds; additional 24-hour display (2nd time zone); perpetual calendar with large date, weekday, month, orbital moon phase display, leap year
Case: rose gold, ø 43 mm, height 11.47 mm; sapphire crystal; transparent case back; water-resistant to 5 atm
Band: reptile skin, folding clasp
Price: $63,500
Variations: white gold ($63,500); platinum ($67,900)

L.U.C XP Skeletec

Reference number: 161984-1001
Movement: automatic, L.U.C Caliber 96.17-S; ø 27.4 mm, height 3.3 mm; 29 jewels; 28,800 vph; 2 spring barrels, gold rotor, bridges with côtes de Genève; completely skeletonized movement; 65-hour power reserve; COSC-certified chronometer
Functions: hours, minutes
Case: white gold, ø 40 mm, height 7.2 mm; sapphire crystal; transparent case back; water-resistant to 3 atm
Band: calfskin, buckle
Remarks: skeletonized dial; case made of gold with fair mined certification
Price: $27,100; limited to 50 pieces

L.U.C Time Traveller One

Reference number: 168574-3008
Movement: automatic, L.U.C Caliber 01.05-L; ø 35.3 mm, height 6.52 mm; 39 jewels; 28,800 vph; 60-hour power reserve; COSC-certified chronometer
Functions: hours, minutes, sweep seconds; world time (2nd time zone); date
Case: ceramized titanium, ø 42 mm, height 12.09 mm; crown rotates inner ring with reference city names; sapphire crystal; transparent case back; water-resistant to 5 atm
Band: textile, buckle
Price: $15,900; limited to 250 pieces

L.U.C XPS

Reference number: 171948-5001
Movement: automatic, L.U.C Caliber 96.12-L; ø 27.4 mm, height 3.3 mm; 29 jewels; 28,800 vph; gold rotor, bridges with côtes de Genève; 65-hour power reserve; COSC-certified chronometer
Functions: hours, minutes, subsidiary seconds
Case: rose gold, ø 40 mm, height 7.2 mm; bezel set with 58 diamonds; sapphire crystal; transparent case back; water-resistant to 3 atm
Band: reptile skin, buckle
Price: $35,300

Caliber L.U.C 96.24-L

Automatic; flying 1-minute tourbillon; gold micro-rotor; double spring barrel, 65-hour power reserve; Geneva Seal, COSC-certified chronometer
Functions: hours, minutes
Diameter: 27.4 mm
Height: 3.3 mm
Jewels: 25
Balance: glucydur
Frequency: 25,200 vph
Balance spring: flat hairspring, Nivarox 1
Remarks: 190 parts

Caliber L.U.C 98.06-L

Manually wound; swan-neck fine regulation; quadruple spring barrel running in twin series barrel springs, 192-hour power reserve; Geneva Seal
Functions: hours (digital, jumping), minutes; power reserve display (on the rear)
Diameter: 28.6 mm
Height: 4.85 mm
Jewels: 42
Frequency: 28,800 vph
Hairspring: Breguet hairspring with Phillips end curve
Remarks: 240 parts

Caliber L.U.C 96.01-L

Automatic; gold micro-rotor; double spring barrel, 65-hour power reserve; Geneva Seal, COSC-certified chronometer
Functions: hours, minutes, subsidiary seconds; date
Diameter: 27.4 mm
Height: 3.3 mm
Jewels: 29
Balance: glucydur
Frequency: 28,800 vph
Balance spring: flat hairspring, Nivarox 1

Caliber L.U.C 03.05-C

Automatic; column-wheel control of chronograph functions, vertical chronograph clutch; single spring barrel, 60-hour power reserve; COSC-certified chronometer
Functions: hours, minutes, subsidiary seconds; flyback chronograph; date
Diameter: 28.8 mm
Height: 7.6 mm
Jewels: 45
Balance: glucydur
Frequency: 28,800 vph; Hairspring: flat hairspring
Remarks: slitted movement bridges; grey finishing; rose gold skeletonized winding rotor

Caliber L.U.C 03.10-L

Manually wound; mainplate and balance cock of German silver; single spring barrel, 60-hour power reserve; Geneva Seal, COSC-certified chronometer
Functions: hours, minutes, sweep seconds; day/night indicator; flyback chronograph; perpetual calendar with large date, weekday, month, moon phase, leap year
Diameter: 33 mm
Height: 8.32 mm
Jewels: 42
Balance: Variner balance with 4 weighted screws
Frequency: 28,800 vph
Balance spring: flat hairspring

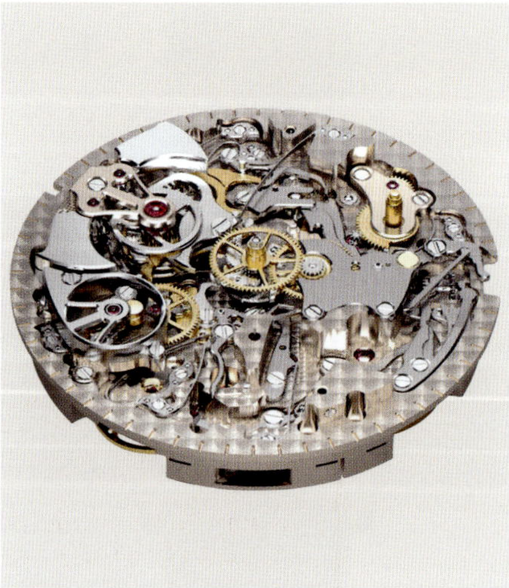

Caliber L.U.C 08.01-L

Manually wound; sapphire gongs for repeating mechanism; single spring barrel, 60-hour power reserve; Geneva Seal, COSC certified chronometer
Functions: hours, minutes, subsidiary seconds; power reserve display, minute repeater
Diameter: 37.2 mm
Height: 7.97 mm
Jewels: 63
Frequency: 28,800 vph
Balance spring: hairspring with Phillips end curve
Remarks: mainplate and balance cock of German silver; 533 parts

Christophe Claret SA
Route du Soleil d'Or 2
CH-2400 Le Locle
Switzerland

Tel.:
+41-32-933-0000

E-mail:
info@christopheclaret.com

Website:
www.christopheclaret.com

Founded:
manufacture 1989, brand 2009

Number of employees:
70

Distribution:
Contact the *manufacture* directly.

Most important collections:
Traditional complications (Maestro/Mecca/Allegro/Aventicum/Maestoso/Kantharos/Soprano/Concertino), Extreme line (X-TREM-1), gaming watches (Poker/Baccara/Blackjack), and ladies' complications line (Margot, Layla, Marguerite)
Prices are given in Swiss francs at near parity.

CHRISTOPHE CLARET

Individuals like Christophe Claret eat, drink, and breathe watchmaking and have developed careers based on pushing the envelope to the very edge of what's possible.

By the age of twenty-three, the Lyon-born Claret was in Basel, where he was spotted by the late Rolf Schnyder of Ulysse Nardin and commissioned to make a minute repeater with jacquemarts. In 1989, he opened his *manufacture*, a nineteenth-century mansion extended with a state-of-the-art machining area. Indeed, Claret embraces wholeheartedly the potential in modern tools to create the precise pieces needed to give physical expression to exceedingly complex ideas.

Over the years, Claret created complications and movements for many major brands, like Ulysse Nardin and Harry Winston.

Twenty years after establishing his business, Claret finally launched his own complex watches: models like the DualTow, turbocharged as the X-TREM-1, are perennial favorites of Claret. It has hours and minutes on two tracks, a minute repeater, and a complete view of the great ballet of cams and levers inside. Then came the Adagio, again a minute repeater, with a clear dial that has room for a second time zone and large date. In 2011, Claret wowed the watch world with a humorous, on-the-wrist gambling machine, telling time and allowing the wearer to play blackjack, craps, or roulette.

The list goes on and on. In the recent Al-Ula, Claret returned to his Aventicum's mechanism to highlight a hologram in the center of the watch; in this case, the center highlights the archeological site of Mada'in Salih in Al-Ula, Saudi Arabia. Even when exhibiting pure engineering art, as with the Maestro, though, Christophe Claret always manages to slip in a special complication, like the "memo," which lets the wearer set a small reminder of some upcoming date, for example. As for the Legend series, it reappears as Monaco: a tourbillon with a minute repeater pealing with Westminster chimes to celebrate a famous wedding in classy Monaco, that of Grace Kelly and Prince Rainier III.

Monaco

Reference number: MTR.NBC98.937
Movement: manually wound, Christophe Claret Caliber NBC98; ø 37 mm, height 9.03 mm; 36 jewels; 21,600 vph; striking mechanism (gong) with 4 melodies and 4 jaquemart automatons; 1-minute tourbillon with the princely family emblem; 60-hour power reserve
Functions: hours, minutes; minute, quarter and hourly repeater with Westminster chimes (on demand)
Case: titanium, 47 mm, height 15 mm; sapphire crystal; transparent case back; water-resistant to 3 atm
Remarks: hand-painted dial by André Martinez featuring a Monaco Grand Prix in the 60s
Band: reptile skin, folding clasp
Price: CHF 650,000; unique piece
Variation: gold case (CHF 680,000)

Maestro Indian

Reference number: MTR.DMC16.330-337
Movement: manually wound, Christophe Claret Caliber DMC16; ø 36.25 mm, height 10.50 mm; 33 jewels; 21,600 vph; skeletonized and step-shaped "Charles X" bridges; inverted movement construction with balance on the dial; 2 serial spring barrels;168-hour power reserve
Functions: hours, minutes, manually activated memo display (pusher switches sapphire at 4 o'clock to a ruby or diamond; two stones of same color means the owner has something coming up); large date (double digit) on a cone
Case: titanium, ø 42 mm, height 16.06 mm; sapphire crystal; transparent case back; water-resistant to 3 atm
Band: reptile skin, folding clasp
Price: CHF 72,000; limited to 7 pieces

Al-Ula

Reference number: MTR.AVE15.600-617
Movement: automatic, Christophe Claret Caliber AVE 15; ø 26.2 mm, height 3.37 mm; 28 jewels; 28,800 vph; invisible sapphire crystal rotor with five weights; 72 hours power reserve
Functions: hours (with anticorodal anodized aluminum pointers for lighter weight), minutes
Case: titanium, ø 44 mm, height 18.5 mm; sapphire crystal; transparent case back
Band: reptile skin, folding clasp
Remarks: mirascope optics that make a sculptural, hologram projection of a miniature of the famous archeological site of Mada'in Saleh micro-engraved in the middle of the dial
Price: CHF 69,000; limited to 17 pieces
Variations: in rose gold (CHF 77,000), limited to 17 pieces

CHRONOSWISS

Chronoswiss AG
Löwenstrasse 16b
CH-6004 Lucerne
Switzerland

Tel.:
+41-41-552-21-80

E-mail:
luzern@chronoswiss.com

Website:
www.chronoswiss.com

Founded:
1983

Number of employees:
approx. 20

Annual production:
up to 1,500 wristwatches

U.S. distributor:
Chronoswiss US Service Office
Shami Fine Watchmaking
372 Fairfield Rd
Fairfield, NJ 07004
973-785-0004

Most important collections/price range:
Approx. 30 models including, Space Timer, Flying Regulator, Open Gear ReSec, Lunar Chronograph, Opus Chronograph, SkelTec, Sirius Artist, (no current collection) approx. $5,800 to $47,000

Chronoswiss has been assembling its signature watches—which boast such features as coin edge bezels and onion crowns—since 1983. Founder Gerd-Rüdiger Lang loved to joke about having "the only Swiss watch factory in Germany," as the brand used Swiss technology with concepts and designs "made in Germany," in Karlsfeld, near Munich, to be precise.

Lang also created regulator watches in the 1980s, a pioneering idea that found many fans of new ways to tell the time. Whether in a rectangular or round case, with a tourbillon or without, the off-center dial became the absolute identity of Chronoswiss watches and remains so to this day. It was a remarkable bit of inspiration and somewhat anachronistic back then.

Chronoswiss has always been a little on the edge of the industry in terms of style and technical developments. It created the enduring *manufacture* caliber C.122—based on an old Enicar automatic movement with a patented rattrapante mechanism—and its Chronoscope chronograph has earned a solid reputation for technical prowess. The Pacific and Sirius models, additions to the classic collection, point the company in a new stylistic direction designed to help win new buyers and the attention of the international market.

In March 2012, a Swiss couple, Oliver and Eva Ebstein, purchased Chronoswiss and moved the company headquarters to Lucerne, Switzerland. They decided to remain faithful to the brand's codes. In-house calibers beat inside, and increasingly the staid look is giving way to modern designs, daring skeletonizing feats, and bold colors. The new tagline, "Modern Mechanical," suggests the brand's direction. Take such models as the SkelTec Pitch Black, whose components have been reduced to an absolute minimum. The geometrically cut bridges and deep black of the case and parts further underline the contemporary design.

Space Timer Jupiter

Reference number: CH-9343.2-CUBK
Movement: automatic, Chronoswiss Caliber C.308; ø 32.8 mm; 33 jewels; 28,800 vph; hands module (transmission gear) visible on dial side; finely finished movement; 42-hour power reserve
Functions: hours (off-center), minutes, sweep seconds; date
Case: stainless steel, ø 44 mm, height 15.2 mm; sapphire crystal; transparent case back; water-resistant to 10 atm
Band: reptile skin, folding clasp
Price: $17,900; limited to 50 pieces
Variations: with textile strap

Space Timer Moonwalk

Reference number: CH-9343.2-GRBL
Movement: automatic, Chronoswiss Caliber C.308; ø 32.8 mm; 33 jewels; 28,800 vph; hands module (transmission gear) visible on dial side; finely finished movement; 42-hour power reserve
Functions: hours (off-center), minutes, sweep seconds; date, moon phase
Case: stainless steel, ø 44 mm, height 15.2 mm; sapphire crystal; transparent case back; water-resistant to 10 atm
Band: reptile skin, folding clasp
Price: $17,900; limited to 50 pieces
Variations: with textile strap

Open Gear ReSec Electric Blue

Reference number: CH-6926-BLSI
Movement: automatic, Chronoswiss Caliber C.301; ø 36.5 mm; 28,800 vph; dial-side hands gear train (transmission wheel); finely finished movement; 42-hour power reserve
Functions: hours (off-center), minutes, subsidiary seconds (retrograde)
Case: stainless steel with blue CVD coating, ø 44 mm, height 13.35 mm; sapphire crystal; transparent case back; water-resistant to 10 atm
Band: reptile skin, folding clasp
Price: $12,000; limited to 50 pieces

Open Gear ReSec Chameleon

Reference number: CH-6923-PABK
Movement: automatic, Chronoswiss Caliber C.301; ø 36.5 mm; 28,800 vph; dial-side hands gear train (transmission wheel); finely finished movement; 42-hour power reserve
Functions: hours (off-center), minutes, subsidiary seconds (retrograde)
Case: stainless steel, ø 44 mm, height 13.35 mm; sapphire crystal; transparent case back; water-resistant to 10 atm
Band: textile, folding clasp
Price: $11,000; limited to 50 pieces

Open Gear ReSec Kingfisher

Reference number: CH-6923-BLOR
Movement: automatic, Chronoswiss Caliber C.301; ø 36.5 mm; 28,800 vph; dial-side hands gear train (transmission wheel); finely finished movement; 42-hour power reserve
Functions: hours (off-center), minutes, subsidiary seconds (retrograde)
Case: stainless steel, ø 44 mm, height 13.35 mm; sapphire crystal; transparent case back; water-resistant to 10 atm
Band: textile, folding clasp
Price: $11,000; limited to 50 pieces

Flying Regulator Open Gear Purple Haze

Reference number: CH-8758.1-PUBK
Movement: automatic, Chronoswiss Caliber C.299; ø 35.2 mm; height 6.11 mm; 31 jewels; 28,800 vph; hands module (transmission gear) visible on dial side; finely finished movement; 42-hour power reserve
Functions: hours (off-center), minutes, subsidiary seconds
Case: stainless steel with violet CVD coating, ø 41 mm, height 12.7 mm; sapphire crystal; transparent case back; water-resistant to 10 atm
Band: textile, folding clasp
Remarks: hand-guillochéed dial
Price: $11,900; limited to 50 pieces

Open Gear Flying Tourbillon Sunset

Reference number: CH-3123-ORBL
Movement: manually wound, Chronoswiss Caliber C.303; ø 32.8 mm; height 4.4 mm; 23 jewels; 28,800 vph; 1-minute flying tourbillon; plate and bridges with blue CVD coating; 60-hour power reserve
Functions: hours (off-center), minutes
Case: stainless steel, ø 44 mm, height 13.1 mm; sapphire crystal; transparent case back; water-resistant to 10 atm
Band: reptile skin, folding clasp
Remarks: hand-guillochéed dial
Price: $44,400; limited to 15 pieces

Open Gear Flying Tourbillon Paraiba

Reference number: CH-3123-PABL
Movement: manually wound, Chronoswiss Caliber C.303; ø 32.8 mm; height 4.4 mm; 23 jewels; 28,800 vph; 1-minute flying tourbillon; plate and bridges with blue CVD coating; 60-hour power reserve
Functions: hours (off-center), minutes
Case: stainless steel, ø 44 mm, height 13.1 mm; sapphire crystal; transparent case back; water-resistant to 10 atm
Band: reptile skin, folding clasp
Remarks: hand-guillochéed dial
Price: $44,400; limited to 15 pieces

Open Gear Flying Tourbillon Meteorit

Reference number: CH-3123-BKBL
Movement: manually wound, Chronoswiss Caliber C.303; ø 32.8 mm; height 4.4 mm; 23 jewels; 28,800 vph; 1-minute flying tourbillon; plate and bridges with blue CVD coating; 60-hour power reserve
Functions: hours (off-center), minutes
Case: stainless steel, ø 44 mm, height 13.1 mm; sapphire crystal; transparent case back; water-resistant to 10 atm
Band: reptile skin, folding clasp
Remarks: hand-guillochéed dial
Price: $44,400; limited to 15 pieces

CLAUDE MEYLAN

Claude Meylan
Route de l'Hôtel de Ville 2
CH-1344 L'Abbaye
Switzerland

Tel.:
+41-21-841-1457

E-mail:
info@claudemeylan.ch

Website:
www.claudemeylan.ch

Founded:
originally mid-18th century; revived in mid-20th century and purchased in 2011

Number of employees:
7

Annual production:
approx. 1,000 pieces

Most important collections/price range:
Tortue, Lac, Lionne, Abbaye / $4,500 to $6,850; Légendes series / up to $33,000

In the quest for recognition, many companies, especially the smaller ones, look for a niche in which they can excel. The Swiss brand Claude Meylan, located in L'Abbaye near Joux Lake in the heart of watch country, specializes in skeletonization, which is the art of removing as much material as possible from bridges, plates, the dial, even the hands. The exercise is not just for fun. First, it transforms a watch, making it transparent and allowing a view of the mechanical innards. Second, it allows for imaginative designs using what's left of the material, notably the bridges. These can be either abstract or representative.

Skeletonization has become popular in recent years, but it is not as simple as it might sound. As the various metal components are hollowed out and properly finished with chamfering and sanding, the tensions within the material change. This can then have a deleterious effect on the functioning of the mechanism, since the bridges and plates are in fact used to hold and stabilize the movement.

In 1988, Claude Meylan founded his company. It was taken over soon after by another watchmaker, Henri Berney, who kept up the old tradition. In 2011, the next CEO, Philippe Belais, took charge. He also heads Vaudaux, a maker of high-end boxes and cases in Geneva.

Claude Meylan's products, which show many different aspects of the art of skeletonization, live up to the brand's tagline: "Sculptors of time." The company has five main collections, all relating in some way to the region: Lac, for Joux Lake; l'Abbaye; Légendes, exploring local tales; Lionne, the river that flows by the workshops; and, finally, Tortue, whose tonneau case is reminiscent of a turtle. It now comes in a beautiful version for smaller wrists. Remarkably, it was born in the mind of the company's communication officer, Pia de Chefdebien, who was asked to design the watch she would want, and of course, it pushes certain limits, discreetly, by boldly combining ornamental motifs, while perfectly exposing the delicate mechanism of the modified ETA automatic driving the hands.

Tortue Rainbow

Reference number: 6047-NO
Movement: manually wound, Claude Meylan Caliber 165CM14; ø 40 mm, height 4.5 mm; 17 jewels; 18,000 vph; open-worked dial, black and orange scheme, orange cathedral hands; 42-hour power reserve
Functions: hours, minutes
Case: stainless steel with black PVD, ø 40 x 40 mm, height 11 mm; sapphire crystal; transparent case back; water-resistant to 3 atm
Band: rubber, buckle
Price: $5,980
Variations: comes with different colors: yellow, green, blue, purple, indigo, and red

Tortue Lady

Reference number: 6080-DIA
Movement: automatic, Caliber 7.75CM17; ø 26.5 mm, height 5 mm; 25 jewels; 28,800 vph; 38-hour power reserve; microrotor with 68 pavé diamonds
Functions: hours, minutes, seconds
Case: stainless steel, ø 31 x 31 mm, height 11 mm; sapphire crystal; transparent case back; water-resistant to 3 atm
Band: technical satin, buckle
Price: $6,980

Lac

Reference number: 6144-NR
Movement: manually wound, modified Unitas 6497; ø 36.6 mm, height 4.5 mm; 17 jewels; 18,800 vph; skeletonized movement, red grid dial; 44-hour power reserve
Functions: hours (hand-cut into rotating dial), minutes
Case: stainless steel with PVD, ø 42 mm, height 11 mm; sapphire crystal; transparent case back; water-resistant to 3 atm
Band: leather, buckle
Price: $3,500
Variations: various bridge colors

Montres Corum Sàrl
Rue du Petit-Château 1
Case postale 374
CH-2301 La Chaux-de-Fonds
Switzerland

Tel.:
+41-32-967-0670

E-mail:
info@corum.ch

Website:
www.corum-watches.com

Founded:
1955

Number of employees:
50 worldwide

Annual production:
5,000 watches

U.S. distributor:
Montres Corum USA
CWJ BRANDS
1551 Sawgrass Corporate Parkway
Suite 109
Sunrise, FL 33323
954-279-1220
www.corum.ch

Most important collections/price range:
Admiral's Cup, Golden Bridge, Lab, Bubble, Coin, Heritage, Romvlvs and Artisan, $4,400 to over $1,000,000

CORUM

Founded in 1955, Switzerland's youngest luxury watch brand, Corum, celebrated sixty years of unusual—and sometimes outlandish—case and dial designs in 2015. The brand has had quite a busy history, but still by and large remains true to the collections launched by founders Gaston Ries and his nephew René Bannwart: the Admiral's Cup, Bridges, and Heritage. Among Corum's most iconic pieces is the legendary Golden Bridge baguette, or stick, movement, which has received a complete makeover in recent years with the use of modern materials and complicated mechanisms. It is built around the idea of concentrating all parts along a straight axis in the middle of a rectangular dial. The development of these extraordinary movements required great watchmaking craftsmanship.

The Bridges collection has always been an eye-catcher. It was originally the brainchild of the great watchmaker Vincent Calabrese, though these types of movements trace back further in time. Its introduction was a milestone in watchmaking history. And the Golden Bridge recently acquired a new highlight in the Golden Bridge Tourbillon Panoramique, with all components appearing to float in thin air. But Corum also has more classical watches, like the sporty Admiral's Cup collection, which is divided into the staid Legend and the more athletic AC-One 45.

In 2013, the Chinese Citychamp Group became a shareholder and added much needed development cash and an extensive distribution network in China. The Group has since also acquired the Rotary and Eterna brands, thus creating a strong manufacturing pool in Switzerland. Corum's vision is expressed in its logo: a key facing the sky, which symbolizes both the mysteries to be discovered as well as openness to the new. For a more popular experience of watch-wearing, the company revived the remarkable Bubble, which earned its moniker from the domed shape of the crystal, allowing room for all sorts of dial decoration. And in the midst of the pandemic, Corum to release a stunning concept watch, a skeleton timepiece, the Lab 2, which seems to do away with bridges altogether.

Admiral 38 Automatic

Reference number: A082/04243
Movement: automatic, Caliber CO 082 (Base ETA 2892-A2); ø 25.9 mm, height 3.6 mm; 25 jewels; 28,800 vph; 42-hour power reserve
Functions: hours, minutes, sweep seconds; date
Case: titanium, ø 38 mm, height 8.95 mm; sapphire crystal; transparent case back; water-resistant to 10 atm
Band: titanium, triple folding clasp
Price: $4,800

Admiral 42 Automatic

Reference number: A395/04240
Movement: automatic, Caliber CO 395 (Base ETA 2895-2); ø 25.9 mm, height 4.35 mm; 27 jewels; 28,800 vph; 42-hour power reserve
Functions: hours, minutes, subsidiary seconds; date
Case: stainless steel, ø 42 mm, height 10.3 mm; sapphire crystal; transparent case back; water-resistant to 10 atm
Band: stainless steel, triple folding clasp
Price: $4,500

Admiral 42 Automatic

Reference number: A395/04249
Movement: automatic, Caliber CO 395 (Base ETA 2895-2); ø 25.9 mm, height 4.35 mm; 27 jewels; 28,800 vph; 42-hour power reserve
Functions: hours, minutes, subsidiary seconds; date
Case: stainless steel, ø 42 mm, height 10.3 mm; rose gold bezel and crown; sapphire crystal; transparent case back; water-resistant to 10 atm
Band: stainless steel with rose gold elements, triple folding clasp
Price: $8,800; limited to 50 pieces

Admiral 42 Automatic

Reference number: A395/04319
Movement: automatic, Caliber CO 395 (Base ETA 2895-2); ø 25.9 mm, height 4.35 mm; 27 jewels; 28,800 vph; 42-hour power reserve
Functions: hours, minutes, subsidiary seconds; date
Case: bronze, ø 42 mm, height 9.5 mm; sapphire crystal; transparent case back; water-resistant to 10 atm
Band: calf leather, triple folding clasp
Price: $5,100; limited to 100 pieces

Admiral 45 Chronograph

Reference number: A132/04275
Movement: automatic, Caliber CO 132; ø 25.6 mm, height 6.1 mm; 39 jewels; 28,800 vph; rotor with black PVD; 42-hour power reserve
Functions: hours, minutes, subsidiary seconds; chronograph; date
Case: titanium, ø 45 mm, height 14.4 mm; sapphire crystal; transparent case back; water-resistant to 30 atm
Band: rubber, triple folding clasp
Price: $9,900; limited to 100 pieces

Admiral 45 Openworked

Reference number: A297/04290
Movement: automatic, Caliber CO 297; ø 25.6 mm, 37 jewels; 28,800 vph; skeletonized movement; 42-hour power reserve
Functions: hours, minutes, subsidiary seconds; power reserve indicator; chronograph, with 3-minute totalizer
Case: carbon fiber with Super-LumiNova inserts, ø 45 mm, height 14.4 mm; carbon and Super-LumiNova bezel; sapphire crystal; transparent case back; water-resistant to 10 atm
Band: rubber with textile overlay, triple folding clasp
Remarks: skeletonized dial
Price: $41,500; limited to 25 pieces

Golden Bridge Classic

Reference number: B113/01043
Movement: manually wound, Caliber CO 113; ø 25.6 mm, height 3 mm; 19 jewels; 28,800 vph; baguette movement, hand-engraved bridges and mainplate in gold; 40-hour power reserve
Functions: hours, minutes
Case: rose gold, 34 mm x 51 mm, height 10.9 mm; sapphire crystal; transparent case back; water-resistant to 3 atm
Band: reptile skin, triple folding clasp
Price: $40,900

Golden Bridge Automatic

Reference number: B313/04278
Movement: automatic, Caliber CO 313; ø 11.25 x 33.18 mm, 26 jewels; 28,800 vph; balance wheel with variable inertia, baguette work with gold bridges and plates, linear winding with platinum sliding weight; 40-hour power reserve
Functions: hours, minutes
Case: titanium with black DLC, 37.2 mm x 51.8 mm, height 13.7 mm; sapphire crystal; transparent case back; water-resistant to 3 atm
Band: reptile skin, triple folding clasp
Price: $35,900; limited to 50 pieces

Bubble 47 X-Ray II

Reference number: L082/04330
Movement: automatic, Caliber CO 082; ø 25.6 mm; 25 jewels; 28,800 vph; 42-hour power reserve
Functions: hours, minutes, sweep seconds
Case: stainless steel with black PVD; ø 47 mm, height 18.5 mm; sapphire crystal; transparent case back; water-resistant to 10 atm
Band: rubber with nylon overlay, buckle
Remarks: vaulted sapphire crystal
Price: $4,400; limited to 666 pieces

CUERVO Y SOBRINOS

Many brands have been going vintage to surf a wave of nostalgia in an age of techno-frigidity. Cuervo y Sobrinos, however, has vintage, nostalgia, romance, and a touch of derring-do as a genome set. The brand originated with Ramón Fernandos Cuervo, who emigrated from Spain to Cuba in 1862 and opened a jewelry business. Twenty years later, he recruited his sister's sons to help out with the booming business (that would be his nephews, the *sobrinos* of the brand name). Don Ràmon died in 1907, but the company continued to expand, adding wristwatches made in La Chauds de Fonds.

The advent of Communist rule on the island ended the streak of successes. But in 2002, an Italian watch enthusiast, Marzio Villa, resuscitated the brand. The tagline "Latin heritage, Swiss manufacture" says it all. These timepieces epitomize—or even romanticize—the island's heyday. The lines are at times elegant and sober, or blatantly vintage with fissured dial effect (the Historiador line), or radiate the ease of those who still have time on their hands, as it were. The color codes recall tobacco, coffee, the faded elegance of the age of steamships. The Pirata line even honors the buccaneer tradition of the region.

Modern ideas have recently begun creeping into the brand's look. The Buceador Caribe, reaches beyond the faded charm of Cuba as a modern diver's watch able to go down to 20 atm. Its broad, white hands contrast sharply with the sea- or sand-colored dials. And the Espléndidos line, whose tonneau dial and sepia color coding epitomizes the halcyon days for the well-to-do of the 1930s, now has an eye-popping version decorated by Scott Jacobs, an artist known for painting Harley Davidsons.

CyS SA
Via Carlo Maderno 54
CH-6825
Switzerland

Tel.:
+41-21-552-18-82

E-mail:
contact@cuervoysobrinos.com

Website:
www.cuervoysobrinos.com

Founded:
1882

Annual production:
3,500 watches

Distributor:
Provenance Gems LLC
ines@provenancegems.com
800-305-3869

Most important collections/price range:
Historiador, Prominente, Torpedo, Robusto / $2,000 to $20,000; higher for perpetual calendars and tourbillon models

Buceador Pipin

Reference number: 2860.1P
Movement: automatic, CYS 5104 (based Peseux 224); ø 25.6 mm, height: 4.6 mm, 28 jewels, 28,800 vph, oscillating weight with côtes de Genève and logo; 38-hour power reserve
Functions: hours, minutes, sweep seconds; date
Case: stainless steel, ø 43 mm, height 15.8mm; bezel locking function; sapphire crystal; water-resistant to 20 atm
Band: leather, folding clasp
Remarks: comes with additional orange rubber strap with green lining
Price: $3,750; limited to 100 pieces

Robusto Churchill "Sir Winston"

Reference number: 2180.1SW
Movement: automatic, CYS 5105 (based on STP 4-13); ø 29 mm, height 5.15 mm; 26 jewels; 28,800 vph; oscillating weight with logo; 44-hour power reserve
Functions: hours, minutes, sweep seconds; date
Case: stainless steel, ø 43 mm, height 12.45 mm; sapphire crystal; transparent case back; water-resistant to 10 atm
Band: reptile skin, folding clasp
Remarks: dial with blue clous de Paris guilloché
Price: $4,750; limited to 100 pieces
Variations: with various dial colors

Prominente Solo Tiempo

Reference number: 1012.1RM
Movement: automatic, Caliber CYS 5103 (base Soprod M100); ø 25.6 mm, height 3.6 mm; 25 jewels; 28,800 vph; oscillating weight with CyS logo; 42-hour power reserve
Functions: hours, minutes, sweep seconds; date
Case: stainless steel, 52 x 33.75 mm, height 10 mm; sapphire crystal; integrated and protected key winding crown; water-resistant to 5 atm
Band: leather, folding clasp
Remarks: vintage look inspired from 1950s Cuervo y Sobrinos timepieces
Price: $4,200

Historiador Asturias

Reference number: 30101.ASR
Movement: automatic, CYS 5121 (based on Sellita SW 200); ø 25.6 mm, height: 4.6 mm, 26 jewels, 28,800 vph, finished oscillating weight with engraving; 38-hour power reserve
Functions: hours, minutes, sweep seconds; date
Case: stainless steel, ø 40 mm, height 9.9 mm; sapphire crystal; screw-down transparent case back; water-resistant to 5 atm
Band: leather, folding clasp
Price: $2,400

Historiador Tradición "San Rafael"

Reference number: 3195.1SR.CH
Movement: automatic, Caliber CYS 5203 (base Sellita SW 240-1); ø 29 mm, height 5.05 mm; 26 jewels; 28,800 vph; rose gold-plated "frappage" grid decoration on dial; engraved oscillating weight; 38-hour power reserve
Functions: hours, minutes, sweep seconds; date
Case: stainless steel, ø 40 mm, height 10.7 mm; bubble-style sapphire crystal; screwed-down transparent case back with watch number printed on the sapphire crystal; water-resistant to 3 atm
Band: calf leather, buckle
Price: $3,250

Historiador 1519

Reference number: 3195.1AB
Movement: automatic, CYS 5104 (based Peseux 224); ø 25.6 mm, height: 4.6 mm, 28 jewels, 28,800 vph, oscillating weight with côtes de Genève and logo; 38-hour power reserve
Functions: hours, minutes, sweep seconds; date
Case: stainless steel, ø 40 mm, height 9.9 mm; sapphire crystal; screwed-down transparent case back; water-resistant to 3 atm
Band: reptile skin, buckle
Price: $2,950

Vuelo GMT

Reference number: 3204.1C
Movement: automatic, Caliber CYS 5123 (base Sellita 330); ø 25.6 mm, height 4.1 mm; 21 jewels; 28,800 vph; rotor with fan decoration and CyS engraving; 42-hour power reserve
Functions: hours, minutes, sweep seconds; 24-hour display (2nd time zone); date
Case: stainless steel, ø 44, height 11.4 mm; sapphire crystal; screw-down transparent case back; water-resistant to 3 atm
Band: stainless steel, folding clasp
Price: $5,050
Variation: blue dial

Espléndidos Vitola

Reference number: 2414.1CC
Movement: automatic, Caliber CYS 5103 (base Soprod M100); ø 25.6 mm, height 3.6 mm; 25 jewels; 28,800 vph; oscillating weight with CyS logo; 42-hour power reserve
Functions: hours, minutes, sweep seconds; date
Case: stainless steel, 47 x 35 mm, height 10 mm; sapphire crystal; screw-down transparent case back; water-resistant to 3 atm
Band: reptile skin, folding clasp
Price: $3,050
Variations: various dial colors

Espléndidos Scott Jacobs

Reference number: 2451.1S
Movement: automatic, Caliber CYS 5085 (base STP 1-11) 330); ø 25.6 mm, height 4.6 mm; 26 jewels; 28,800 vph; 44-hour power reserve; oscillating weight with CyS logo
Functions: hours, minutes, sweep seconds
Case: stainless steel, ø 47 x 36 mm, height 13.6 mm; sapphire crystal; screw-down transparent case back; water-resistant to 3 atm
Band: alcantara, buckle
Remarks: dial features section of prewar Harley Davidson EL Knucklehead, painted by Scott Jacobs
Price: $3,300; limited to 100 pieces

CVSTOS

Cvstos
3-5, rue Voltaire
CH-1201 Geneva
Switzerland

Tel.:
+41-22-989-1010

Fax:
+41-22-989-1019

E-mail:
info@cvstos.com

Website:
www.cvstos.com

Founded:
2005

U.S. distributor:
Mr. Dean Ross
954-892-6168
d.ross@cvstos.com

Most important collections/price range:
Challenge, Sealiner, Jetliner, Re-Belle, Metropolitan / $10,000 to $280,000

Dials in a conventional sense are something that one can search for in vain at Cvstos (Latin for guardian); technology rules the roost at the brand, and thus these extroverted, stately timepieces show what they're made of, quite literally. The look is cultivated throughout the collection, which veers sharply from the appearance of traditional *haute horlogerie*, targeting a clientele that does not necessarily search for standard elements such as côtes de Genève, gold, and guilloché in their aesthetic ideals, even if these elements are used at Cvstos, though sparingly.

Although it may not seem so at first sight, a great deal of watchmaking know-how goes into the making of a Cvstos, and that is no surprise for a brand that is the spiritual child of Sassoun Sirmakes, son of Vartan Sirmakes, the man who led Genevan watchmaker Franck Muller to world fame. Under the tutelage of his father, the cofounder of the Watchland *manufacture* in Genthod, young Sassoun was introduced to the hands-on side of watchmaking. In 2005, fate brought him together with designer and watchmaker Antonio Terranova, who had made a name for himself in the Swiss watch industry with the timepieces he designed and produced for leading brands. He had freelanced for some of the more staid brands, but Terranova had the heart of a genuine innovator, an avant-gardist willing to break free of the constraints of traditional forms—he collaborated on some of the early Richard Mille pieces, for example. A Cvstos will therefore have some thrilling complications, but expect some technoid materials and a few surprises. The recent crop includes the use of sapphire for the casings, a difficult material to work with and one that requires subtlety, namely that it should not be used just for its own sake. The Metropolitan line, for instance, demands a transparent case to highlight the remarkable skeletonizing work inside. Also of recent vintage is the Re-Belle, classified as a ladies' watch but actually adapted to anyone with a bold, i.e., rebellious, spirit.

Metropolitan PS Sapphire SQLT Green

Reference number: F00103.4287001
Movement: automatic, Cvstos Caliber CVS410; height 4.5 mm. 21 jewels; 28,800 vph; skeletonized movement, green PVD on bridges; skeletonized disc; 50-hour power reserve
Functions: hours, minutes, subsidiary seconds; date
Case: stainless steel, 51 x 42 mm, height 12.4 5mm; sapphire crystal; screw-in crown; transparent case back; water-resistant to 5 atm
Band: reptile skin, folding clasp
Remarks: sapphire case, dial integrated into the skeletonized movement
Price: $41,500; limited to 50 pieces
Variations: comes with closed movement, gold, or titanium

Re-Belle Moon Steel

Reference number: D00109.3603002
Movement: automatic, Cvstos Caliber CVS882; 26 jewels; 28,800 vph; 38-hour power reserve
Functions: hours, minutes; moon phase; date.
Case: stainless steel with snow-set with 327 colored sapphires, 36 X 47.2 mm, height 13.4 mm; sapphire crystal; transparent case back; screwed-in crown with red gold or steel insert, set with diamonds or colored sapphires; water-resistant to 10 atm
Band: reptile skin, pin buckle
Remarks: diamond markers on aventurine dial
Price: $35,400; limited to 50 pieces
Variations: rose gold or set with diamonds

Sea Liner PS Skyblue / Steel

Reference number: C00103.4106003
Movement: automatic, Cvstos Caliber CVS410; 4.5 mm; 21 jewels; 28,800 vph; skeletonized movement; skeletonized disc; 50-hour power reserve
Functions: hours, minutes, subsidiary seconds; date (on skeletonized disc); power reserve indicator
Case: stainless steel with blue PVD, 53.7 x 41 mm, height 16.65 mm; sapphire crystal; transparent case back; screw-in crown in titanium or red gold with rubber insert; water-resistant to 10 atm
Band: reptile skin, folding clasp
Remarks: teak base dial with gold/rhodium plating
Price: $17,700

Czapek & Cie.
18 Rue de la Corraterie
CH-1204 Geneva
Switzerland

Tel.:
+41-22-557-41-41

E-mail:
info@czapek.com

Website:
www.czapek.com

Founded:
2012

U.S. distributor:
Horology Works
11 Flagg Road
West Hartford, CT 06117
860-986-9676
info@horologyworks.com

Most important collections/price range:
Quai des Bergues men's and ladies' watches / from $12,000 to $55,000; Place Vendôme / up to $226,000; Faubourg de Cracovie / up to $26,800

CZAPEK & CIE.

Born in Bohemia (Czech Republic today) in 1811, watchmaker Frantiszek Czapek fought in the failed Polish insurrection of 1832 against Russia and then fled to Geneva. In 1839, he joined another Pole, Antoine de Patek, in a business venture. When the contract expired in 1845, Patek decided on a partnership with Jean Philippe, inventor of the keyless watch. Czapek went on to become purveyor of watches to Emperor Napoleon III and author of a book on watches. Then he vanished without a trace sometime in the late 1860s.

His "resurrection" is due to entrepreneur, art specialist, and occasional watch collector Harry Guhl, who registered the name and set up a management team that included Xavier de Roquemaurel and Sébastien Follonier. They chose Czapek's model No. 3430 as a model upon which to build up a new brand. It is an intriguing piece with elongated Roman numerals, elegant fleur-de-lis hands, and two oddly placed subdials at 7:30 and 4:30, one for small seconds, the other featuring a clever double hand for the seven-day power reserve and days of the week.

The team's claim to fame is collaborating with friends of the brand to create new models, which are always implemented by outstanding Swiss suppliers like Donzé for the grand-feu dials with the secret signature, and Aurélien Bouchet for the fine fleur-de-lis hands.

Over the years, Czapek has gradually diversified, producing classically stylish watches, like the Place Vendôme and the Faubourg de Cracovie. Recently, the company has even moved into some serious complications, with a split-seconds chronograph coupled with some impressive skeletonizing to show off, legitimately, the mechanism on the dial side. Czapek's name is old, but the brand is beginning to show some very modern, technical qualities.

Antarctique Passage de Drake

Reference number: Salmon S
Movement: automatic, Czapek Caliber SXH5; ø 30 mm, height 4.2 mm; 28 jewels; 28,800 vph; recycled platinum micro-rotor; balance with gold inertia-blocks; finely finished movement; 56-hour power reserve
Functions: hours, minutes, sweep seconds; date
Case: stainless steel, ø 38.5 mm, height 10.6 mm; sapphire crystal; transparent case back; water-resistant to 12 atm
Band: stainless steel, folding clasp
Price: $22,000
Variations: with blue dial; with 12 or double index at 12 o'clock; with additional leather or rubber strap

Quai des Bergues

Reference number: Sapphire Blue S
Movement: manually wound, Czapek Caliber SXH1; ø 32 mm, height 4.75 mm; 31 jewels; 21,600 vph; finely finished movement; 168-hour power reserve
Functions: hours, minutes, subsidiary seconds; power reserve indicator; weekday
Case: stainless steel, ø 38.5 mm, height 11.8 mm; sapphire crystal; transparent case back; water-resistant to 5 atm
Band: reptile skin, buckle
Remarks: hand-guillochéed flinqué enamel dial
Price: $20,300

Antarctique Rattrapante

Reference number: Ice Blue
Movement: automatic, Czapek Caliber SXH6; ø 34 mm, height 7.4 mm; 49 jewels; 21,600 vph; split-seconds-chronograph module positioned on the dial side; two column wheels
Functions: hours, minutes, subsidiary seconds; split-seconds-chronograph
Case: stainless steel, ø 42.5 mm, height 15.3 mm; sapphire crystal; transparent case back; water-resistant to 12 atm
Band: stainless steel, folding clasp
Price: $56,400; limited to 99 pieces
Variations: with additional rubber of leather strap

DAMASKO

Damasko GmbH
Unterheising 17c
93092 Barbing

Tel.:
+49-9401-80481

E-mail:
sales@damasko-watches.com

Website:
www.damasko-watches.com

Founded:
1994

Number of employees:
30

Distribution:
U.S. Sales
Island Watch
273 Walt Whitman Road, Suite 217
Huntington Station, NY 11746
631-470-0762
sales@longislandwatch.com

Price range:
$1,000 to $4,000

When it comes to sheer toughness, Damasko has built up quite a track record ever since its founding in 1994, in Germany. But it's not visible at first glance.

These unadorned watches with clean, sharp lines are almost archetypical watches. They are robust, indestructible even, and will not need much servicing.

The company's claim to fame lies in its choice of materials, such as polycrystalline silicon hairsprings and components made of a special ice-hardened steel. This special patent involves adding nitrogen and carbon to the molten stainless steel and then cooling it quickly. The resulting material, which has been used in machines like space shuttles, is extremely hard and does not corrode easily, so these are watches that will keep their look for a long time.

In fact, the research done by this small brand, located near Regensburg in southern Germany, has generated over one hundred patents for the brand, as well as registered samples and designs. The "German" look means well-groomed dials and an immediate view of the time, thanks to contrasting hues.

These watches boast outstanding technical quality, which combines with a very clear stylistic concept. The collection includes a range of model families ranging from very classical-functional pilot watches, to a line of timeless sportive chronographs, and some very elegant watches for daily use, like the Black Beauty.

Almost all parts are in fact made in-house, which testifies to the company's commitment to quality. Many of the models run on ETA movements, but Damasko also assembles its own caliber, the A35, which allows for a manufacturing depth of ninety percent. Parts made in the small factory include plates, bridges, pinions, balance, spring barrel, and rotors. Despite the strong focus on research, development, and use of new materials and processes, the watches produced manage to stay in the affordable range.

DC 76/2

Movement: automatic, Damasko Caliber C51-6 (base ETA 7750); ø 30.4 mm, height 7.9 mm; 27 jewels; 28,800 vph; central seconds and minute counters; shock-resistant and antimagnetic according to the German Industrial Norm (DIN); 50-hour power reserve
Functions: hours, minutes, subsidiary seconds; additional 24-hour display (2nd time zone); chronograph; date
Case: stainless steel, ø 41 mm, height 14.6 mm; sapphire crystal; screw-in crown; water-resistant to 10 atm
Band: calfskin, buckle
Price: $3,275
Variations: with rubber strap ($3,320)

DC 86/2

Movement: automatic, Damasko Caliber C51-6 (base ETA 7750); ø 30.4 mm, height 7.9 mm; 27 jewels; 28,800 vph; central seconds and minute counters; shock-resistant and antimagnetic according to the German Industrial Norm (DIN); 50-hour power reserve
Functions: hours, minutes, subsidiary seconds; additional 24-hour display (2nd time zone); chronograph; date
Case: ice-hardened stainless steel, ø 42 mm, height 14.4 mm; bidirectional bezel, with 0-12 scale; sapphire crystal; screw-in crown; water-resistant to 10 atm
Band: calfskin, buckle
Price: $3,469
Variations: stainless steel band ($4,072); rubber strap ($3,611)

DK 30

Movement: automatic, Damasko Caliber A26-1; ø 25.6 mm, height 4.6 mm; 20 jewels; 28,800 vph; shock-resistant and antimagnetic according to the German Industrial Norm (DIN); 42-hour power reserve
Functions: hours, minutes, sweep seconds
Case: stainless steel (submarine steel), ø 39 mm, height 9.95 mm; sapphire crystal; screw-in crown; water-resistant to 20 atm
Band: stainless steel, folding clasp
Price: $1,916
Variations: with calfskin strap ($1,419)

DK 32 Ocean

Movement: automatic, Damasko Caliber A26-2; ø 25.6 mm, height 4.6 mm; 20 jewels; 28,800 vph; shock-resistant and antimagnetic according to the German Industrial Norm (DIN); 42-hour power reserve
Functions: hours, minutes, sweep seconds; date
Case: stainless steel (submarine steel), ø 39 mm, height 9.95 mm; sapphire crystal; screw-in crown; water-resistant to 20 atm
Band: rubber, buckle
Price: $1,613
Variations: with stainless steel bracelet ($2,065)

DS 30 Yellow

Movement: automatic, ETA Caliber 2824-2; ø 25.6 mm, height 4.6 mm; 25 jewels; 28,800 vph; shockproof and antimagnetic according to the German Industrial Norm (DIN); 42-hour power reserve
Functions: hours, minutes, sweep seconds; date
Case: stainless steel (submarine steel), ø 39 mm, height 9.9 mm; sapphire crystal; screw-in crown; water-resistant to 20 atm
Band: calfskin, buckle
Price: $1,042
Variations: various colored hands

DS 30 Grey

Movement: automatic, ETA Caliber 2824-2; ø 25.6 mm, height 4.6 mm; 25 jewels; 28,800 vph; shockproof and antimagnetic according to the German Industrial Norm (DIN); 42-hour power reserve
Functions: hours, minutes, sweep seconds; date
Case: stainless steel (submarine steel), ø 39 mm, height 9.9 mm; sapphire crystal; screw-in crown; water-resistant to 20 atm
Band: stainless steel, folding clasp
Price: $1,540
Variations: with leather strap and black or brown dial

DSub50

Movement: automatic, Damasko Caliber A26-2; ø 25.6 mm, height 4.6 mm; 20 jewels; 28,800 vph; shock-resistant and antimagnetic according to the German Industrial Norm (DIN); 42-hour power reserve
Functions: hours, minutes, sweep seconds; date
Case: stainless steel (submarine steel) with black coating, ø 43 mm, height 12.6 mm; unidirectional bezel, with 0-60 scale; sapphire crystal; screw-in crown; water-resistant to 30 atm
Band: rubber with rubber overlay, folding clasp
Price: $2,190 on rubber

DC 72 Green

Movement: automatic, Damasko Caliber C51-2 (base ETA 7750); ø 30.4 mm, height 7.9 mm; 27 jewels; 28,800 vph; sweep seconds and minute counter; shock-resistant and antimagnetic according to the German Industrial Norm (DIN); 50-hour power reserve
Functions: hours, minutes; chronograph; date
Case: ice-hardened stainless steel, ø 41 mm, height 13.9 mm; sapphire crystal; screw-in crown; water-resistant to 10 atm
Band: calfskin, buckle
Price: $2,595
Variations: with folding clasp ($2,641)

DC 82

Movement: automatic, Damasko Caliber C51-2 (base ETA 7750); ø 30.4 mm, height 7.9 mm; 27 jewels; 28,800 vph; central seconds and minute counters; shock-resistant and antimagnetic according to the German Industrial Norm (DIN); 50-hour power reserve
Functions: hours, minutes; chronograph; date
Case: ice-hardened stainless steel, ø 42 mm, height 13.9 mm; bidirectional bezel, with 0-60 scale; sapphire crystal; screw-in crown; water-resistant to 10 atm
Band: stainless steel, folding clasp
Price: $3,393
Variations: calfskin strap and buckle ($2,789); rubber strap and buckle ($2,835)

DAVOSA

DAVOSA Swiss
Bohle GmbH
Bunsenstrasse 1a
32052 Herford
Germany

Tel.:
+49 (0)5221 9942400

E-mail:
info@davosa.com

Website:
www.davosa.com

Founded:
1881

U.S. distributor:
Davosa U.S.A
200 S. Biscayne Blvd
Miami, FL 33131
877-DAVOSA1
info@davosa-usa.com
www.davosa-usa.com

Most important collections/price range:
Apnea Diver, Argonautic, Classic, Gentleman, Military, Newton, Pilot, Ternos, Titanium / $600 to $2,400

One of the more important brands occupying the lower segment of the market is Davosa, which manufactures a wide range of watches with all the complications one might want but in an affordable segment: pilot watches, quality divers (with helium valve), dress watches, and ladies' watches. The brand has even come out with an apnea training watch that can be removed from its case. These timepieces use solid Swiss movements (Sellita and ETA), which are occasionally modified to fit the watches' specific designs, or they are given special coatings like the "gun" PVD coating on the latest Argonautics, which is dark green. The most recent series is dedicated to Isaac Newton. Among these dressy in a sporty sort of way timepieces, one finds a limited-edition automatic chronograph with a moon phase, at under $2,400.

To create a broad portfolio requires experience, and that is something Davosa has in spades. The company was founded in 1891 and therefore celebrated its 140th anniversary in 2021. Back then, farmer Abel Frédéric Hasler from Tramelan, in Switzerland's Jura mountains, spent the winter months making silver pocket watch cases. Later, two of his brothers ventured out to the city of Geneva and opened a watch factory. The third brother also opted to engage with the watch industry and moved to Biel. The entire next generation of Haslers went into watchmaking as well.

The name Hasler & Co. appeared on the occasional package mailed in Switzerland or overseas. Playing the role of unassuming private-label watchmakers, the Haslers remained in the background and let their customers in Europe and the United States run away with the show. It wasn't until after World War II that brothers Paul and David Hasler dared produce their own timepieces.

The long experience with watchmaking and watches culminated in 1987 with the brothers developing their own line of watches under the brand name Davosa. The Haslers then signed a partnership with the German distributor Bohle. In Germany, mechanical watches were experiencing a boom, so the brand was able to evolve quickly. In 2000, Corinna Bohle took over as manager of strategic development. Davosa now reaches well beyond Switzerland's borders and has become an integral part of the world of mechanical watches.

Argonautic BG Automatic

Reference number: 161.528.70
Movement: automatic, Davosa Caliber DAV3021 (base Sellita SW200-1); ø 25.6 mm, height 4.6 mm; 26 jewels; 28,800 vph; 38-hour power reserve
Functions: hours, minutes, sweep seconds; date
Case: stainless steel, ø 43 mm, height 13.5 mm; unidirectional bezel with ceramic insert, with 0-60 scale; sapphire crystal; screw-in crown, helium valve; water-resistant to 30 atm
Band: stainless steel, folding clasp with safety lock and extension link
Price: $899
Variations: various colors

Argonautic BGBS Automatic

Reference number: 161.528.10
Movement: automatic, Davosa Caliber DAV3021 (base Sellita SW200-1); ø 25.6 mm, height 4.6 mm; 26 jewels; 28,800 vph; 38-hour power reserve
Functions: hours, minutes, sweep seconds; date
Case: stainless steel, ø 43 mm, height 13.5 mm; unidirectional bezel with ceramic insert, with 0-60 scale; sapphire crystal; screw-in crown, helium valve; water-resistant to 30 atm
Band: stainless steel, folding clasp with safety lock and extension link
Price: $939

Argonautic Coral Limited Edition

Reference number: 161.527.40
Movement: automatic, Davosa Caliber DAV3021 (base Sellita SW200-1); ø 25.6 mm, height 4.6 mm; 26 jewels; 28,800 vph; 38-hour power reserve
Functions: hours, minutes, sweep seconds; date
Case: stainless steel, ø 43 mm, height 13.5 mm; unidirectional bezel with ceramic insert, with 0-60 scale; sapphire crystal; screw-in crown, helium valve; water-resistant to 30 atm
Band: stainless steel, folding clasp with safety lock and extension link
Price: $1,158
Variations: various colors

Ternos Medium

Reference number: 166.197.02
Movement: automatic, Davosa Caliber DAV3021 (base Sellita SW200-1); ø 25.6 mm, height 4.6 mm; 26 jewels; 28,800 vph; 38-hour power reserve
Functions: hours, minutes, sweep seconds; date
Case: stainless steel, ø 36.5 mm, height 11.8 mm; unidirectional rose gold-plated bezel with ceramic insert, with 60-minute division; sapphire crystal; screw-in crown; water-resistant to 20 atm
Band: stainless steel with rose-gold PVD coating, folding clasp with safety lock
Price: $949

Ternos Sixties

Reference number: 161.525.60S
Movement: automatic, Sellita Caliber SW200-1; ø 25.6 mm, height 4.6 mm; 26 jewels; 28,800 vph; 38-hour power reserve
Functions: hours, minutes, sweep seconds
Case: stainless steel, ø 40 mm, height 12 mm; unidirectional bezel with ceramic insert and 0-60 scale; sapphire crystal; screw-in crown; water-resistant to 10 atm
Band: stainless steel, folding clasp
Price: $899

Ternos Ceramic GMT Automatic

Reference number: 161.590.06
Movement: automatic, Davosa Caliber DAV3032 (base Sellita SW330-2); ø 25.6 mm, height 4.1 mm; 21 jewels; 28,800 vph; 50-hour power reserve
Functions: hours, minutes, sweep seconds; additional 24-hour display (second time zone); date
Case: stainless steel, ø 40 mm, height 12.2 mm; unidirectional bezel with ceramic insert, with 0-24 scale; sapphire crystal; screw-in crown; water-resistant to 20 atm
Band: stainless steel, folding clasp with safety lock and extension link
Remarks: comes with additional nylon strap
Price: $1,399
Variations: various colors

Newton Lady Diamond Automatic

Reference number: 166.191.10
Movement: automatic, Davosa Caliber DAV3021 (base Sellita SW200-1); ø 25.6 mm, height 4.6 mm; 26 jewels; 28,800 vph; 38-hour power reserve
Functions: hours, minutes, sweep seconds; date
Case: stainless steel, ø 34 mm, height 10.5 mm; bezel with set with diamonds; sapphire crystal; water-resistant to 5 atm
Band: stainless steel, folding clasp
Remarks: mother-of-pearl dial
Price: $1,998
Variations: various colors

Newton Pilot Speedometer Automatic

Reference number: 161.587.25
Movement: automatic, Davosa Caliber DAV3023 (base Sellita SW240-1); ø 29 mm, height 5.05 mm; 25 jewels; 28,800 vph; 38-hour power reserve
Functions: hours (digital, sliding, in an aperture), minutes, sweep seconds (disc)
Case: stainless steel, ø 44 mm, height 12.8 mm; sapphire crystal; transparent case back; water-resistant to 5 atm
Band: calfskin, buckle
Price: $998

Newton Pilot Moonphase Chronograph Limited Edition

Reference number: 161.586.45
Movement: automatic, ETA Caliber 7751; ø 30 mm, height 7.9 mm; 25 jewels; 28,800 vph; 42-hour power reserve
Functions: hours, minutes, subsidiary seconds; additional 24-hour display; chronograph; full calendar with date, weekday, month, moon phase
Case: stainless steel, ø 44 mm, height 14 mm; sapphire crystal; transparent case back; water-resistant to 5 atm
Band: calfskin, buckle
Price: $2,398

DEEP BLUE

As far as anyone can tell, the fish do not care what you are wearing on your wrist. For the diver, it has to be accurate, genuinely water-resistant, and readable in less-than-ideal conditions. Those are the basics—or should be— of any real diver's watch. The rest is in the eye of the beholder. And it seems that New York-based Deep Blue does not wander too far off home plate, as it were. The company was founded by Stan Betesh with the idea of providing divers with an array of tough watches that do the job and have the look and feel of a professional-quality diver's watch at a fraction of what you might expect to pay.

Little did he know in 2007 that his watches would achieve cult status among divers. Deep Blue watches are accurate, robust, and ready for life in the open and underwater. There's no need to hide them in a safe, and getting banged up a little does them no harm—it's called patina, and it gives these timepieces the look and feel of a real tool watch... which is what they are.

The collection includes all sorts of models for every type of diving. The power is supplied by an array of ETA, Sellita, Miyota, and Seiko/Time calibers, and occasionally quartz movements. Some have special features like ceramic bezels; some are water-resistant to as much as 3,000 meters, like the Depthmaster, whose dimensions (ø 49 mm, height 19.5) and weight (300 g) will certainly contribute to the speed of the diver's descent. Lots of care has been given to lighting the dial, with generous application of Superluminova and the occasional use of autoluminescent tritium tubes, which may well attract some interesting fish.

Deep Blue Watches
1716 Coney Island Avenue
Suite 3r
Brooklyn, NY 11230

Tel.:
718-484-7717

Website:
www.deepbluewatches.com

E-mail:
info@deepbluewatches.com

Founded:
2007

Number of employees:
70

Annual output:
n/a

Distribution:
Retail and online

Most important collections/price range:
Master 1000, Diver 1000, Defender / $300 to $500; Pro Sea Diver / $500 to $900; Daynight / $600 to $1,000; Alpha, Marine, Ocean / $700 to $1,500; Blue Water / $600 to $1,400

Deep Star 1000 Vintage Swiss Automatic

Reference number: DSTAREXPEDBLKWHITEBRC
Movement: automatic, Sellita Caliber SW-200-01; ø 25.6 mm, height 4.6 mm; 26 jewels; 28,800 vph; 38-hour power reserve
Functions: hours, minutes, sweep seconds; date
Case: stainless steel, ø 45 mm, height 15 mm; unidirectional ceramic bezel with 120 clicks; screw-down crown; helium release valve; transparent case back; sapphire crystal; water-resistant to 33 atm
Band: stainless steel mesh, folding clasp with wetsuit extension; **Remarks:** tritium gas-filled tube illumination on hands and hour markers
Price: $799
Variations: silicon or rubber strap

Daynight Alpha Marine 500 Tritium T-100 Swiss Automatic

Reference number: AM500TRITWHITBLUE
Movement: automatic, Sellita Caliber SW-200-1; ø 25.6 mm, height 4.6 mm; 26 jewels; 28,800 vph; 38-hour power reserve; **Functions:** hours, minutes, sweep seconds; date; **Case:** stainless steel, ø 45 mm, height 15 mm; unidirectional ceramic bezel with 0-60 scale and 120 clicks; screw-down crown and case back; transparent case back; helium release valve; sapphire crystal; water-resistant to 33 atm
Band: stainless steel, folding clasp with wetsuit extension; **Remarks:** tritium gas-filled tube illumination on hands and hour markers; full-lume blue dial; **Price:** $1,299
Variations: green lume dial; leather strap ($1,149)

Daynight Scuba 500 Tritium T-100 Swiss Automatic

Reference number: DNSCUBASW200BLACK
Movement: automatic, Sellita SW-200-1; ø 25.6 mm, height 4.6 mm; 26 jewels; 28,800 vph
Functions: hours, minutes, sweep seconds; 2nd time zone; date; **Case:** stainless steel, ø 45 mm, height 15 mm; unidirectional bezel with ceramic insert and 0-60 scale; transparent case back; sapphire crystal; water-resistant to 50 atm
Band: stainless steel, folding clasp with wetsuit extension
Remarks: tritium gas-filled tube illumination on hands and hour markers
Price: $1,299
Variations: with rubber strap ($1,149)

DELMA

Industries all have their major players and their minor ones. The major brands attract attention thanks, oftentimes, to lots of clamorous advertising plus name recognition. In the watch business, as in many others, there are smaller, less noisy brands that also produce quality watches.

Delma began as one of four brands produced by a company founded in 1924 by two brothers, Alfred and Adolf Gilomen. For several decades, they manufactured a number of different models, from classic pocket watches and dress watches to a fine chronograph marketed under the name Midland, in 1946, which made a bit of a splash.

In 1966, after Gilomen's passing, the brand was sold to Ulrich Wütrich. He decided to use a single name, Delma, and focus production on diver's watches, without, however, losing the customers in search of a nice watch that could be used every day. In 1969, they came out with the Periscope, an automatic diver's able to go down to 50 atm (500 meters). It established a new style for the brand, one it has remained faithful to ever since. A few years later, it released the Shell Star, a professional diver's watch.

Today, the company is run by Wütrich's son, Fred Leibundgut and his son Andreas. The brand still produces casual watches, but its claim to fame is still its diver's. The Periscope and Shell Star, which were rereleased in 2021, have been revived with a modernized look and more pertinent technology. The Shell Star features a special table to help divers optimize their gas mixtures in dives up to 70 atm. Another line, the Blue Shark, was launched in 2011. It could survive a 3,000-meter (9,900-foot) plunge. To prove they could improve even on that, in 2019 Delma came out with the Blue Shark III, which can go to 4,000 meters. It has a 6.8-millimeter sapphire crystal, and a thick steel back, so you may not survive the plunge, but the watch will.

Delma Watch Limited
Solothurnstrasse 47
2543 Lengnau
Switzerland

Tel.:
+41 32 654 22 11

E-mail:
info@delma.ch

Website:
www.delma.ch

Founded:
1924

Number of employees:
15

Annual production:
25,000 watches

Distribution:
Contact headquarters in Switzerland

Most important collections/price range:
Racing and Diver collections / up to $4,000

Quattro

Reference number: 41701.744.6.158
Movement: automatic, Sellita Caliber SW 200; ø 25.6 mm, height 4.6 mm; 25 jewels; 28,800 vph; custom rotor; 38-hour power reserve
Functions: hours, minutes, sweep seconds; date
Case: stainless steel, ø 44 mm, height 13.7 mm; helium safety valve; unidirectional bezel with black DLC; sapphire crystal; transparent case back (mineral glass); water-resistant to 50 atm
Band: stainless steel, folding clasp with security fold-over
Remarks: bracelet rapid-exchange system
Price: $2,390; limited to 999 pieces
Variations: comes with black rubber strap

Montego

Reference number: 41601.732.6.141
Movement: automatic, Valjoux 7750; ø 30 mm, height 7.9 mm; 29 jewels; 28,800 vph; custom rotor; 48-hour power reserve
Functions: hours, minutes, subsidiary seconds; chronograph; day, date; tachymeter
Case: stainless steel, ø 42 mm at bezel, height 16.2 mm; screw-down crown; sapphire crystal; transparent case back; water-resistant to 20 atm
Band: Cordura rubber, buckle
Price: $2,650
Variations: blue, white dials; with stainless steel bracelet and folding clasp

Commander

Reference number: 41702.580.6.049
Movement: automatic, Valjoux 7750; ø 30 mm, height 7.9 mm; 29 jewels; 28,800 vph; custom rotor; 48-hour power reserve
Functions: hours, minutes, subsidiary seconds; chronograph; weekday, date
Case: stainless steel, ø 45 mm at bezel, height 14.7 mm; screw-down crown; sapphire crystal; transparent case back; water-resistant to 10 atm
Band: stainless steel, folding clasp
Price: $2,990
Variations: with blue or black dial

Oceanmaster Antarctica

Reference number: 41701.670.6.049
Movement: automatic, Sellita Caliber SW 200; ø 25.6 mm, height 4.6 mm; 25 jewels; 28,800 vph; custom rotor; 38-hour power reserve
Functions: hours, minutes, sweep seconds; date
Case: stainless steel case, crown, and pushers, ø 44 mm at bezel, height 13.8 mm; unidirectional bezel; points of sail on dial, tactical planner and compass; Antarctica map on back; water-resistant to 50 atm
Band: stainless steel, folding clasp
Price: $1,450
Variations: blue dial

Blue Shark III Black Edition

Reference number: 41701.700.6.154
Movement: manually wound, Sellita SW-200; ø 25.6 mm, height 4.6 mm; 26 jewels; 28,800 vph; decorated rotor; 38-hour power reserve
Functions: hours, minutes, seconds; date
Case: stainless steel black DLC, ø 47 mm, height 18.5 mm; sapphire crystal; unidirectional bezel with DLC coating; helium valve; screw-down crown and case back; water-resistant to 400 atm (4,000 m)
Band: stainless steel black DLC, folding clasp
Price: $2,950; limited to 500 pieces
Variations: various dials ($2,950)

Heritage Chronograph LE

Reference number: 41601.730.6.032
Movement: automatic, Sellita Caliber SW510; ø 30 mm, height 7.9 mm; 27 jewels; 28,800 vph; 48-hour power reserve
Functions: hours, minutes, subsidiary seconds; chronograph; date
Case: stainless steel, ø 43 mm at bezel, height 15.7 mm; screw-down crown; sapphire crystal; transparent case back; water-resistant to 10 atm
Band: calfskin, folding clasp
Price: $2,990
Variations: with black, blue, green; yellow gold bezel and bicolor bracelet ($2,950)

Cayman Bronze

Reference number: 31601.726.6.044
Movement: automatic, Sellita Caliber SW 200; ø 25.6 mm, height 4.6 mm; 25 jewels; 28,800 vph; custom rotor; 38-hour power reserve
Functions: hours, minutes, sweep seconds; date
Case: stainless steel, ø 42 mm, height 13.3 mm; screw-in crown unidirectional bronze bezel; sapphire crystal; transparent case back (mineral glass); water-resistant to 50 atm
Band: cordura rubber, folding clasp
Price: $1,650; limited to 999 pieces
Variations: with blue or black dial

Cayman Field Automatic

Reference number: 41601.706.6.034
Movement: automatic, Sellita Caliber SW 200; ø 25.6 mm, height 4.6 mm; 25 jewels; 28,800 vph; custom rotor; 38-hour power reserve
Functions: hours, minutes, sweep seconds; date
Case: stainless steel, ø 42 mm, height 13.3 mm; unidirectional black anodized aluminum bezel; sapphire crystal; transparent case back (mineral glass); water-resistant to 50 atm
Band: canvas, folding clasp
Price: $1,225

Rimini

Reference number: 41711.625.1.046
Movement: quartz, Ronda 785; 42-month battery power
Functions: hours, minutes, sweep seconds; date
Case: stainless steel, ø 31 mm, height 8.4 mm; bezel set with 50 diamonds; water-resistant to 10 atm
Band: stainless steel, folding clasp
Price: $1,000
Variations: various dial colors

DETROIT WATCH COMPANY

Detroit Watch Company, LLC
P.O. Box 60
Birmingham, MI 48012

Tel:
248-321-5601

E-mail:
info@detroitwatchco.com

Founded:
2013

Number of employees:
3

Annual production:
500 watches

Distribution:
direct sales only

Most important collections/price range:
M1 Woodward Moonphase; 1701 Pontchartrain GMT; 1701 L'Horloge; B24 Liberator / $998 to $2,650

Patrick Ayoub and Amy Ayoub launched Detroit Watch Company in 2013 with the first and only mechanical timepieces designed and assembled in Detroit, Michigan. Patrick, a car designer, and Amy, an interior designer, share a passion for original design and timepieces and have worked hard to develop their brand, which draws inspiration from, and celebrates, the city of "Détroit."

Detroit means a lot of things to different people. Because the history of the people and places have shaped the city, Detroit's stories are also part of the Detroit Watch Company's collective story. The 1701, for instance, commemorates Antoine de la Mothe Cadillac, Knight of St. Louis, who, with his company of colonists, arrived at Détroit on July 24, 1701. On that day, under the patronage of Louis XIV and protected by the flag of France, the city, then called Fort Pontchartrain, was founded. These watches, while modern and chic, do recall the fairly clear-cut lines of an old church clock (*horloge*).

People phoning Detroit will understand why the company came out with a watch named 313. It's the area code of the city that brought not only cars, but also Motown (*motor + town*) music to the world. Needless to say, the dial looks like an old-fashioned phone dial. And where did Detroit's cars ride and race informally? On Woodward Avenue, the first mile of concrete highway in the USA, where carriages once rolled. It's the name for a collection of sporty chronographs. Finally, the city supplied the war effort against the Axis with many vital vehicles, including the B-24 Liberator bomber. No wonder the brand's line of watches includes an aviator collection.

The Detroit Watch Company timepieces are beautifully designed and hand-assembled in-house, and they may be purchased directly through the Detroit Watch Company website. The company also offers a wide range of straps and has a transparent and affordable servicing program.

Pontchartrain Watch Co. 1st Edition

Movement: automatic, Caliber ETA 2892-A2, ø 25.6 mm, height 3.6 mm; 28,800 vph, decorated movement with blued screws, perlage, côtes de Genève; 42-hour power reserve
Functions: hours, minutes, sweep seconds
Case: stainless steel, ø 42 mm, height 9.7 mm; sapphire crystal, transparent case back, screw-down crown; water-resistant to 5 atm
Band: calf leather, buckle
Price: $1,295
Variations: with stainless steel bracelet and folding clasp; black dial

1701 Pontchartrain GMT-Great Lakes Edition

Reference number: DWC-1701GMTGLE-S1
Movement: automatic, ETA Caliber 2893-2, ø 26.6 mm, height 4.1 mm; 21 jewels; 28,800 vph; 42-hour power reserve
Functions: hours, minutes, subsidiary seconds; second time zone, date
Case: stainless steel, ø 42 mm, height 13 mm; sapphire crystal, unidirectional bezel, screw-down crown; helium valve; water resistant to 300 atm
Band: calfskin, buckle
Price: $1,495
Variations: 1701 Pontchartrain ($1,395)

Louis XIV Moonphase

Movement: automatic, Caliber Sellita SW280-1; ø 25.6, height 5.4 mm, 26 jewels, 28,800 vph; decorated movement with blued screws, perlage, côtes de Genève; 38-hour power reserve
Functions: hours, minutes, sweep seconds; date with quick corrector; moon phase
Case: stainless steel, ø 42 mm, height 9.7 mm; sapphire crystal, transparent case back, screw-down crown; water-resistant to 5 atm
Band: calf leather, folding clasp
Price: $1,295
Variations: with stainless steel bracelet

M1 Woodward Sport chrono

Reference number: DWC M1W-EXH
Movement: automatic, Caliber Valjoux 7750; ø 30 mm, height 8.4 mm; 25 jewels; 28,800 vph; custom M1 rotor; 48-hour power reserve
Functions: hours, minutes, subsidiary seconds; chronograph; day, date
Case: stainless steel, ø 42 mm, 14.5 mm; transparent case back; screw-down crown; water-resistant to 5 atm
Band: calf leather, buckle
Price: $2,200
Variations: blue, white and black subsidiary dial at 9 o'clock

M1 24hr Legends

Reference number: DWC M1W-EXH
Movement: automatic, Caliber Valjoux 7750; ø 30 mm, height 8.4 mm; 25 jewels; 28,800 vph; custom M1 rotor; 48-hour power reserve
Functions: hours, minutes, subsidiary seconds; chronograph; day, date
Case: stainless steel, ø 42 mm, height 14.5 mm; transparent case back, screw-down crown; water-resistant to 5 atm
Band: calf leather, buckle
Variations: race number 6, 20
Price: $2,200

1701 Moonphase Chronograph

Reference number: PCT-Moon-Chrono
Movement: automatic, ETA Caliber 7751; ø 30 mm, height 7.9 mm; 25 jewels; 28,800 vph; 48-hour power reserve
Functions: hours, minutes, subsidiary seconds; chronograph; date, day, month; moon phase
Case: stainless steel, ø 42 mm, height 14.5 mm, sapphire crystal with anti-reflective coating, screw-down exhibition case back with engraving; water resistant to 5 atm
Band: calfskin
Price: $2,750

City collection 313

Reference number: DWC-CITY-313
Movement: automatic, ETA Caliber 2824-2, ø 26.6 mm, height 4.6 mm; 26 jewels; 28,800 vph; 38-hour power reserve
Functions: hours, minutes, subsidiary seconds
Case: stainless steel, ø 42 mm, height 9.4 mm, sapphire crystal with anti-reflective coating, Exhibition caseback; water resistant to 5 atm
Band: calfskin, buckle
Price: $1,150
Variations: Available in area codes: 202, 212, 305, 312, 415, 416, 504, 512, 713, 818, 310.

1701 Pontchartrain Power reserve

Reference number: DWC-1701-PW
Movement: automatic, Sellita SW279-1; ø 25.6, height 5.6 mm, 26 jewels; 28,800 vph; decorated movement with blued screws, perlage, côtes de Genève; 38-hour power reserve
Functions: hours, minutes, subsidiary seconds; power reserve indicator; date with quick corrector
Case: stainless steel, ø 42 mm, height 9.7; mm; sapphire crystal, transparent case back, screw-in crown; water-resistant to 5 atm
Band: calf leather, buckle
Price: $1,495

Aviator Power Reserve

Reference number: DWC-A-PW
Movement: automatic (or manual winding), Sellita SW279-1; ø 25.6, height 5.6 mm, 26 jewels (manual winding: height 4.35 mm, 24 jewels); 28,800 vph; decorated movement with blued screws, perlage, côtes de Genève; 38-hour power reserve
Functions: hours, minutes, subsidiary seconds; power reserve indicator; date with quick corrector
Case: stainless steel, ø 42 mm, height 9.7 mm; sapphire crystal, transparent case back, screw-in crown; water-resistant to 5 atm
Band: calf leather, buckle
Price: $1,495
Variations: graphite dial, green dial

DOXA

Watch aficionados who have visited the world-famous museum in Le Locle will know that the little castle in which it is housed once belonged to Georges Ducommun, the founder of Doxa. The *manufacture* was launched as a backyard operation in 1889 and originally produced pocket watches. Quality products and good salesmanship quickly put Doxa on the map, but the company's real game-changer came in 1967 with the uncompromising SUB 300, a heavy, bold diver's watch. It featured a unidirectional bezel with the official U.S. dive table engraved on it. The bright orange dial might seem quite ostentatious, but, in fact, it offers the best legibility under water. It also marked the beginning of a trend for colorful dials.

The popularity of Doxa watches was boosted early on by the commercialization of diving in the 1970s. Thriller writer Clive Cussler, chairman and founder of the National Underwater and Marine Agency (NUMA), even chose a Doxa as gear for his action hero Dirk Pitt.

The enduring vintage trend has shaped the recent development of the brand. Focus is on fewer lines with greater variations, with almost every model coming in different colors besides the striking orange: brilliant white, dreamy turquoise, bright yellow, and more.

Doxa has maintained its diving profile and, mostly, the cushion case and avoided too many fancy complications. The watches are usually three-handers with a date. The SUB 200 C-GRAPH is an automatic chronograph, however, and the SUB 300 Carbon Aqua Lung US Diver is, as the name says, made of a modern material. It's a revived and improved watch created in a collaboration with Aqua Lung, the company that essentially launched scuba diving with the creation of a demand regulator in 1943. The carbon case is light and robust and a good background for the non-compression dive table—devised originally by the U.S. Navy— made up of an orange depth scale on the outer bezel and an inner scale for the dive timing.

Montres DOXA SA
Rue de Zurich 23A
P.O. Box 6031
2500 Bienne 6, Switzerland

Tel.:
+41 32 344 42 72

E-mail:
contact@doxawatches.com

Website:
https://doxawatches.com

Founded:
1889

Number of employees:
40

Distribution:
DOXA USA
+1 520 369 2872
contact.usa@doxawatches.com

Most important collections/price range:
DOXA SUB dive watch collection / $950 to $4,900

DOXA Army

Reference number: 785.10.031.10
Movement: automatic, ETA Caliber 2824; ø 25.6 mm, height 4.6 mm; 25 jewels; 28,800 vph; 38-hour power reserve
Functions: hours, minutes, seconds; date
Case: stainless steel, ø 42.5 X 44.5 mm, height 11.95 mm; unidirectional rotating bezel in stainless steel with black ceramic inlay; sapphire crystal; screw-down crown; water-resistant to 30 atm
Band: stainless steel, folding clasp with wetsuit extension
Price: $2,090.00

DOXA Army

Reference number: 785.60.031.26
Movement: automatic, ETA Caliber 2824; ø 25.6 mm, height 4.6 mm; 25 jewels; 28,800 vph; 38-hour power reserve
Functions: hours, minutes, seconds; date
Case: stainless steel, ø 42.5 X 44.5 mm, height 11.95 mm; unidirectional rotating bezel in bronze with green ceramic inlay; sapphire crystal; screw-down crown; water-resistant to 30 atm
Band: FKM rubber, folding clasp with adjustable wetsuit extension
Price: $2,250.00

SUB 300 Professional

Reference number: 821.10.351.10
Movement: automatic, Sellita SW 200-1; ø 25.6 mm, height 4.6 mm; 26 jewels; 28,800 vph; COSC-certified chronometer; 38-hour power reserve
Functions: hours, minutes, seconds; date
Case: stainless steel, ø 42.5 X 45 mm, height 13.4 mm; unidirectional rotating bezel with depth and time scales; sapphire crystal; screw down crown; water-resistant to 30 atm
Band: stainless steel, folding clasp with dive suit extension
Price: $2,490

SUB 300 Carbon Aqua Lung US Divers Sharkhunter

Reference number: 822.70.101AQL.20
Movement: Sellita SW 200-1; ø 25.6 mm, height 4.6 mm; 26 jewels; 28,800 vph; COSC-certified chronometer; 38-hour power reserve
Functions: hours, minutes, seconds; date
Case: forged carbon, ø 42.5 X 45 mm, height 13.4 mm; unidirectional bezel with depth and time scales; sapphire crystal; titanium chamber; screw down case back; water-resistant to 30 atm
Band: rubber, folding clasp with black PVD coating, with ratcheting dive suit extension
Remarks: forged carbon dial; limited to 300 pieces
Price: $4,790

SUB 300 Carbon Whitepearl

Reference number: 822.70.011.20
Movement: Sellita SW 200-1; ø 25.6 mm, height 4.6 mm; 26 jewels; 28,800 vph; COSC-certified chronometer; 38-hour power reserve
Functions: hours, minutes, seconds; date
Case: forged carbon, ø 42.5 X 45 mm, height 13.4 mm; unidirectional bezel with depth and time scales; sapphire crystal; titanium chamber; screw-in case back; water-resistant to 30 atm
Band: rubber strap, folding clasp with black PVD coating, with ratcheting dive suit extension
Remarks: dial fully coated with white Super-LumiNova
Price: $3,990

SUB 300T Searambler

Reference number: 840.10.021.10
Movement: automatic, Sellita SW 200-1; ø 25.6 mm, height 4.6 mm; 26 jewels; 28,800 vph; 38-hour power reserve
Functions: hours, minutes, seconds; date
Case: stainless steel, ø 42.5 X 44.5 mm, height 13.65 mm; unidirectional rotating bezel with depth and time scales; helium release valve; sapphire crystal; screw down crown; water-resistant to 120 atm
Band: stainless steel, folding clasp with dive suit extension
Price: $1,890

SUB 200 Whitepearl

Reference number: 799.10.011.10
Movement: automatic, Sellita SW 200-1; ø 25.6 mm, height 4.6 mm; 26 jewels; 28,800 vph; 38-hour power reserve
Functions: hours, minutes, seconds; date
Case: stainless steel, ø 42 X 46 mm, height 13.8 mm; unidirectional bezel; sapphire crystal; screw-down crown; water-resistant to 20 atm
Band: stainless steel, folding clasp with dive suit extension
Price: $990

SUB 200 T.GRAPH Professional

Reference number: 805.10.351.10
Movement: mechanical, Valjoux 7734; ø 31 mm, height 6.65 mm; 17 jewels; 18,000 vph; 45-hour power reserve
Functions: hours, minutes, seconds; chronograph, 12-hour and 30-minute counters chronograph; date
Case: stainless steel, ø 45.5 x 43 mm, height 15.15 mm; unidirectional bezel with engraved decompression scale; sapphire crystal; screw-down crown; screw-down case back with sailboat engraving; water-resistant to 20 atm
Band: stainless steel, folding clasp with ratcheting dive suit extension
Price: $4,900; limited to 300 pieces

SUB 600T Aquamarine

Reference number: 862.10.241.10
Movement: automatic, Sellita SW200-1; ø 25.6 mm, height 4.6 mm; 26 jewels; 28,800 vph; 38-hour power reserve
Functions: hours, minutes, sweep seconds; date
Case: stainless steel, ø 47.6 x 40 mm, height 14.15 mm; unidirectional bezel; sapphire crystal; screw-in crown; screw-down case back; water-resistant to 60 atm
Band: stainless steel, folding clasp with dive suit extension
Price: $1,490

EBERHARD & CO.

Eberhard & Co.
73, Ave. Léopold-Robert
CH-2300 La Chaux-de-Fonds
Switzerland

Tel.:
+41-32-342-5141

E-mail:
info@eberhard1887.com

Website:
www.eberhard1887.com

Founded:
1887

Distribution:
Contact main office for information on U.S. distribution.

Official Agent for North America
Beaugeste Inc.
Mr. Thierry Chaunu
132 East 43rd Street #341, The Chrysler Building
New York, NY 10017
212-847-1371
tchaunu@beaugesteluxury.com

Most important collections:
Chrono 4; 8 Jours; Tazio Nuvolari; Extra-fort; Gilda; Scafograf

Chronographs weren't always the main focus of the Eberhard & Co. brand. In 1887, Georges-Emile Eberhard rented a workshop in La Chaux-de-Fonds to produce a small series of pocket watches, but it was the unstoppable advancement of the automotive industry that gave the young company its inevitable direction. By the 1920s, Eberhard was producing timekeepers for the first auto races. In Italy, Eberhard & Co. functioned well into the 1930s as the official timekeeper for all important events relating to motor sports. And the Italian air force later commissioned some split-second chronographs from the company, one of which went for 56,000 euros at auction.

Eberhard & Co. is still doing well, thanks to the late Massimo Monti. In the 1990s, he associated the brand with legendary racer Tazio Nuvolari. The company dedicated a chronograph collection to Nuvolari and sponsored the annual Gran Premio Nuvolari vintage car rally in his hometown of Mantua.

With the launch of its four-counter chronograph, this most Italian of Swiss watchmakers underscored its expertise and ambitions where short time/sports time measurement is concerned. Indeed, Eberhard & Co.'s Chrono 4 chronograph, featuring four little counters all in a row, has brought new life to the chronograph in general. CEO Mario Peserico has continued to develop it, putting out versions with new colors and slightly altered looks.

The brand is pure vintage, so it will come as no surprise that it regularly reissues and updates some of its older, popular models, and its Caliber EB 140, a beautifully simple, 28,800-vph movement that can be admired through the case back of its 1887 Hand-Wound model. The latest model to be revived for a contemporary audience is the Scientigraf, which was first issued in 1961. Besides being shielded from magnetism, its modernized cathedral hands come in an orange or "radium" Superluminova.

Chrono 4 "21-42"

Reference number: 31073.03 CN CU
Movement: automatic, Eberhard Caliber EB 250-12 1/2 (base ETA 2894-2); ø 33 mm, height 7.5 mm; 53 jewels; 28,800 vph; 4 totalizers in a row; 42-hour power reserve
Functions: hours, minutes, subsidiary seconds; additional 24-hour display; chronograph; date Case: stainless steel, ø 42 mm, height 13.3 mm; ceramic bezel; sapphire crystal; screw-in crown; water-resistant to 5 atm
Band: rubber, buckle
Remarks: the "21-42" collection stands for the launch year of the anniversary edition, 2021 (20 years Chrono 4) and the case diameter of 42 mm
Price: $6,850

Chrono 4 "21-42"

Reference number: 31073.12 CP
Movement: automatic, Eberhard Caliber EB 250-12 1/2 (base ETA 2894-2); ø 33 mm, height 7.5 mm; 53 jewels; 28,800 vph; 4 totalizers in a row; 42-hour power reserve
Functions: hours, minutes, subsidiary seconds; additional 12-hour display; chronograph; date Case: stainless steel, ø 42 mm, height 13.3 mm; sapphire crystal; screw-in crown; water-resistant to 5 atm
Band: reptile skin, buckle
Remarks: the "21-42" collection stands for the launch year of the anniversary edition, 2021, (20 years Chrono 4) and the case diameter of 42 mm
Price: $6,280

Scientigraf

Reference number: 41043.02 CAPS
Movement: automatic, Sellita Caliber SW300-1; ø 25.6 mm, height 3.6 mm; 25 jewels; 28,800 vph; 42-hour power reserve
Functions: hours, minutes, sweep seconds
Case: stainless steel, ø 41 mm, height 11.2 mm; sapphire crystal; screw-in crown; water-resistant to 10 atm
Band: stainless steel, folding clasp
Price: $3,430

Scafograf 300 MCMLIX

Reference number: 41034V.08 MCMLIX
Movement: automatic, ETA Caliber 2824-2; ø 25.6 mm, height 4.6 mm; 25 jewels; 28,800 vph; 42-hour power reserve
Functions: hours, minutes, sweep seconds; date
Case: stainless steel, ø 43 mm, height 12.6 mm; unidirectional bezel with ceramic insert, with 0-60 scale; sapphire crystal; screw-in crown, helium valve; water-resistant to 30 atm
Band: vintage calfskin, buckle
Remarks: inspired from a 1959 model
Price: $3,120
Variations: folding clasp

1887 Remontage Manuel

Reference number: 21028.03 CP (blue)
Movement: manually wound, Eberhard Caliber EB 140; ø 31.6 mm; 18 jewels; 28,800 vph; finely finished movement; 40-hour power reserve
Functions: hours, minutes, sweep seconds; date
Case: stainless steel, ø 41.8 mm, height 9.6 mm; sapphire crystal; transparent case back; water-resistant to 3 atm
Band: Jacquard satin, buckle
Price: $4,120
Variations: reptile skin band

Extra-fort Automatic

Reference number: 41029.9 CP
Movement: automatic, Sellita Caliber SW200-1; ø 35.6 mm, height 4.6 mm; 26 jewels; 28,800 vph; 42-hour power reserve
Functions: hours, minutes, sweep seconds; date
Case: stainless steel, ø 40 mm, height 10.07 mm; sapphire crystal; screw-in crown; water-resistant to 5 atm
Band: reptile skin, buckle
Price: $3,010
Variations: various bands and dials

Extra-fort Grande Taille "Roue à Colonnes"

Reference number: 31956 CP
Movement: automatic, ETA Caliber 2894-2; ø 28.6 mm, height 6.3 mm; 42 jewels; 28,800 vph; column-wheel control of chronograph functions; 42-hour power reserve
Functions: hours, minutes, subsidiary seconds; chronograph; date
Case: stainless steel, ø 41 mm, height 13.9 mm; sapphire crystal; screw-in crown; water-resistant to 5 atm
Band: reptile skin, buckle
Price: $4,710
Variations: folding clasp

Nuvolari Legend

Reference number: 31138.2 CP
Movement: automatic, ETA Caliber 7750; ø 30 mm, height 7.9 mm; 25 jewels; 28,800 vph; 48-hour power reserve
Functions: hours, minutes; chronograph
Case: stainless steel, ø 43 mm, height 13.5 mm; sapphire crystal; transparent case back; screw-in crown; water-resistant to 3 atm
Band: calfskin, buckle
Remarks: stylized gold Alfa Romeo on rotor
Price: $5,280
Variations: 39.5-mm case

8 Jours Grande Taille

Reference number: 21027.5 CP
Movement: manually wound, Eberhard Caliber EB 896.1 (base ETA 7001); ø 34 mm, height 5 mm; 25 jewels; 21,600 vph; 2 spring barrels, 192-hour power reserve
Functions: hours, minutes, subsidiary seconds; power reserve indicator
Case: stainless steel, ø 41 mm, height 10.85 mm; sapphire crystal; transparent case back; water-resistant to 3 atm
Band: reptile skin, buckle
Price: $4,950
Variations: white dial

ERNST BENZ

Ernst Benz, the man himself, was an accomplished Swiss inventor and engineer by trade who worked in numerous technologies. He was first known for his Benz Micro factory's production of timepiece and industrial jewels for watch movement manufacturers and his legendary namesake Benz Micro turntable styluses. As a passionate aviator and engineer, he developed aircraft instruments, including altimeters, timing devices for military applications, and the Benz Micro aircraft gauge, which became a standard in many small aircraft. Ernst soon realized the need for a large format, stable, reliable, and readable wristwatch that would be ideal for personal use in small aircraft and gliders' cockpits. Making ultimately readable watches was the next step.

He produced the first Great Circle ChronoScope for his own use and then gradually slipped into making timepieces based on the demand he received. Size and clarity were determining factors. Thus followed his clean vintage-inspired dials and 47mm diameters, as well as reliability, which was guaranteed by the no-nonsense Valjoux 7750. The approval of fellow pilots led him to increase production.

In 2002, the company's now-signature model, the ChronoLunar, made with the participation of Leonid Khankin, made a splash in the watch world. Three years later, Ernst asked the Khankins, a watchmaking family with two generations of experience in complicated horology, to take the company's helm. Leonid, who has spent a lifetime in the business's hands-on side, expanded the brand geographically while creating exciting new models and collaborations for which the brand is now known. The Chronoscope, ChronoLunar, and Chronosport models were updated and received many versions, along with the development of new models, including the ChronoFlite GMT, the WorldTimer, and the ChronoDiver inspired by Ernst's aviation instrument production.

Inspired by the history of horology and the spirit of travel, Khankin uses the broad dial of these distinct timepieces as a platform for adding design elements to tell the story of the founder, the company, and watchmaking.

Ernst Benz
7 Route de Crassier
CH-1262 Eysins
Switzerland

E-Mail:
info@ernstbenz.com

Website:
www.ernstbenz.com

Founded:
early 1960s

U.S. distributor:
Ernst Benz North America
177 S. Old Woodward
Birmingham, MI 48009
248-203-2323

Most important collections:
ChronoLunar, ChronoScope, ChronoSport, ChronoDiver, ChronoFlite

ChronoLunar Officer in Blue Metallic

Reference number: GC10386
Movement: automatic, Valjoux Caliber 7751; ø 30 mm, height 7.9 mm; 25 jewels; 28,800 vph
Functions: hours, minutes, subsidiary seconds; day, date, month, moon phase; 24-hour display; chronograph
Case: stainless steel, ø 47 mm, height 16 mm; sapphire crystal; screw-down transparent case back; double O-ring sealed crown; water-resistant to 5 atm
Band: leather, buckle
Price: $7,675
Variations: 44-millimeter ($7,075)

ChronoLunar Officer in Anthracite Grey

Reference number: GC10385
Movement: automatic, Valjoux Caliber 7751; ø 30 mm, height 7.9 mm; 25 jewels; 28,800 vph
Functions: hours, minutes, subsidiary seconds; day, date, month, moon phase; chronograph
Case: stainless steel, ø 47 mm, height 16 mm; sapphire crystal; screwed-down transparent case back; double O-ring sealed crown; water-resistant to 5 atm
Band: reptile skin, buckle
Price: $7,975
Variations: 44-millimeter case ($7,375)

ChronoLunar Officer

Reference number: GC10384
Movement: automatic, Valjoux Caliber 7751; ø 30 mm, height 7.9 mm; 25 jewels; 28,800 vph
Functions: hours, minutes, subsidiary seconds; day, date, month, moon phase; chronograph with hours, minutes sweep seconds
Case: stainless steel, ø 47 mm, height 16 mm; sapphire crystal; screw-down transparent case back; double O-ring sealed crown; water-resistant to 5 atm
Band: reptile skin
Price: $7,975
Variations: 44-millimeter case ($7,375)

Model: ChronoLunar Traditional

Reference number: GC10311
Movement: automatic, Valjoux Caliber 7751; ø 30 mm, height 7.9 mm; 25 jewels; 28,800 vph
Functions: hours, minutes, subsidiary seconds; day, date, month, moon phase; chronograph with hours, minutes sweep seconds
Case: stainless steel, ø 47 mm, height 16 mm; sapphire crystal; screw-down transparent case back; double O-ring sealed crown; water-resistant to 5 atm
Band: reptile skin, buckle
Price: $7,575
Variations: 44-millimeter ($6,975); 40-millimeter ($6,675)

Model: ChronoDiver Instrument

Reference number: GC10726
Movement: automatic, Valjoux Caliber 7750; ø 30 mm, height 7.9 mm; 25 jewels; 28,800 vph
Functions: hours, minutes, subsidiary seconds; day, date; chronograph with hours, minutes sweep seconds
Case: stainless steel, ø 47 mm, height 15.8 mm; unidirectionally rotating bezel with 60-minute divisions; sapphire crystal; screw-down transparent case back; screwed-in-crown; water-resistant to 20 atm
Band: reptile skin, buckle
Price: $5,825

Model: ChronoSport Officer

Reference number: GC10285
Movement: automatic, ETA Caliber 2836-2; ø 30 mm, height 5.5 mm; 25 jewels; 28,800 vph
Functions: hours, minutes, sweep seconds; day, date
Case: stainless steel, ø 47 mm, height 14 mm; sapphire crystal; screw-down transparent case back; double O-ring sealed crown; water-resistant to 5 atm
Band: reptile skin, buckle
Price: $3,675
Variations: 44-millimeter ($3,075)

Model: ChronoScope Traditional

Reference number: GC10112
Movement: automatic, Valjoux Caliber 7750; ø 30 mm, height 7.9 mm; 25 jewels; 28,800 vph
Functions: hours, minutes, subsidiary seconds; day, date; chronograph with hours, minutes sweep seconds
Case: stainless steel, ø 47 mm, height 16 mm; sapphire crystal; screw-down transparent case back; double O-ring sealed crown; water-resistant to 5 atm
Band: reptile skin, buckle
Price: $5,425
Variations: 44-millimeter ($4,825); 40-millimeter ($4,475)

ChronoScope Traditional DLC

Reference number: GC10119-DLC
Movement: automatic, Valjoux Caliber 7750; ø 30 mm, height 7.9 mm; 25 jewels; 28,800 vph
Functions: hours, minutes, subsidiary seconds; day, date; chronograph with hours, minutes sweep seconds
Case: stainless steel with black DLC, ø 47 mm, height 16 mm; sapphire crystal; screw-down transparent case back; double O-ring sealed crown; water-resistant to 5 atm
Band: reptile skin, buckle
Price: $6,225
Variations: 44-millimeter ($5,625)

ChronoScope Traditional DLC

Reference number: GC10115-DLC
Movement: automatic, Valjoux Caliber 7750; ø 30 mm, height 7.9 mm; 25 jewels; 28,800 vph
Functions: hours, minutes, subsidiary seconds; day, date; chronograph with hours, minutes sweep seconds
Case: black DLC coated brushed stainless, ø 47 mm, height 16 mm; sapphire crystal; screw-down transparent case back; double O-ring sealed crown; water-resistant to 5 atm
Band: bison, buckle
Price: $5,925
Variations: 44-millimeter ($5,325)

FERDINAND BERTHOUD

Chronométrie Ferdinand Berthoud SA
20, rue des Moulins
CH-2114 Fleurier
Switzerland

E-Mail:
contact@ferdinandberthoud.ch

Website:
www.ferdinandberthoud.ch

Founded:
2013

Distributor:
Cellini Jewelers
430 Park Avenue at 56th Street
New York, NY 10022
212-888-0505
www.cellinijewelers.com

Collections / price range:
Exclusively built chronometers: $150,000 to $260,000

The old saying "nomen est omen" could be the slogan for many brands in the watch industry, whose strategy and style is all in the name they choose. Karl-Friedrich Scheufele, himself vice president of a brand named after a Swiss watchmaker, Louis-Ulyssse Chopard, stumbled upon another historical personality when he founded his manufactory in the Jura in 1996: Ferdinand Berthoud. Berthoud (1727-1807) was one of the most important watchmakers of his era, a contemporary of Abraham-Louis Breguet and Thomas Mudge, a master watchmaker at the French court and supplier to the Royal Navy. He was also the author of numerous books and writings on the theory of watchmaking. Finally, he was not French, but Swiss, born in Val-de-Travers near Fleurier.

Reviving that eighteenth-century DNA seemed worthwhile. In 2015, the first Berthoud watch of the modern era was presented in Paris, a chronometer, of course. The movement of the FB 1 was a scaled-down version, but like its historical predecessors, it was equipped with a constant force mechanism using a traditional chain and fusee. It also features an interesting power reserve display (53 hours) and a rather large tourbillon under a filigree one-armed cock. Despite its historical inspiration, many aspects of the movement were technically modernized. Four patents are pending, including for the flying bearing of the fusee, barrel and power reserve cone, and the seconds wheel driven directly by the tourbillon sunwheel, visible in a large dial cutout at the "6."

The FB 1R model presented in 2016 has a special regulator dial with a discreet time display, and the FB 1L iteration that followed a little later shows the moon phase and moon age in an unusual way. In 2020, Ferdinand Berthoud launched a completely new collection with the FB 2RE, which is conspicuously inspired by Berthoud's marine chronometer No. 6 and combines the sophisticated mechanism of chain and fusee with a constant force escapement (*remontoir d'égalité*) and a jumping seconds display.

Chronomètre FB RSM

Reference number: FB 2RSM.1
Movement: manually wound, Ferdinand Berthoud Caliber FB-T.FC.RSM; ø 37.3 mm, height 9.89 mm; 60 jewels; 21,600 vph; 1-minute tourbillon; balance with 4 weight screws; torque regulator with a chain and worm screw; 53-hour power reserve; COSC-certified chronometer
Functions: hours (off-center), minutes (off-center), sweep seconds (jumping); power reserve on the rear
Case: white gold, ø 44 mm, height 14.3 mm; sapphire crystal; transparent case back; crown with torque limiter; water-resistant to 3 atm
Band: reptile skin, buckle
Price: on request; very limited edition of 20 movements, regardless of the model

Chronomètre FB RSM

Reference number: FB-2RSM.2
Movement: manually wound, Ferdinand Berthoud Caliber FB-T.FC.RSM; ø 37.3 mm, height 9.89 mm; 60 jewels; 21,600 vph; 1-minute tourbillon; balance with 4 weight screws; torque regulator with a chain and worm screw; 53-hour power reserve; COSC-certified chronometer
Functions: hours (off-center), minutes (off-center), sweep seconds (jumping); power reserve on the rear
Case: rose gold, ø 44 mm, height 14.3 mm; sapphire crystal; transparent case back; crown with torque limiter; water-resistant to 3 atm
Band: reptile skin, buckle
Price: on request; very limited edition of 20 movements, regardless of the model

Chronomètre FB RSM

Reference number: FB-2RSM.2-1
Movement: manually wound, Ferdinand Berthoud Caliber FB-T.FC.RSM; ø 37.3 mm, height 9.89 mm; 60 jewels; 21,600 vph; 1-minute tourbillon; balance with 4 weight screws; torque regulator with a chain and worm screw; 53-hour power reserve; COSC-certified chronometer
Functions: hours (off-center), minutes (off-center), sweep seconds (jumping); power reserve on the rear
Case: rose gold, ø 44 mm, height 14.3 mm; sapphire crystal; transparent case back; crown with torque limiter; water-resistant to 3 atm
Band: reptile skin, buckle
Price: on request; very limited edition of 20 movements, regardless of the model

Montres Journe SA
17 rue de l'Arquebuse
CH-1204 Geneva
Switzerland

Tel.:
+41-22-322-09-09

E-mail:
info@fpjourne.com

Website:
www.fpjourne.com

Founded:
1999

Number of employees:
135

Annual production:
around 1,000 watches

U.S. distributor:
Montres Journe America
Epic Hotel
270 Biscayne Boulevard Way
Miami, FL 33131
305-572-9802
america@fpjourne.com

Most important collections:
Classique, LineSport, Elégante
(Prices are in Swiss francs. Use daily exchange rate for calculations.)

F.P.JOURNE

Born in Marseilles in 1957, François-Paul Journe might have become something else had he concentrated in school. He was kicked out and went to Paris, where he completed watchmaking school before going to work for his watchmaking uncle. And he has never looked back. By the age of twenty-six he had made his first tourbillon and soon was producing watches for connoisseurs.

He then moved to Switzerland, where he started out with handmade creations for a limited clientele and developed the most creative and complicated timekeepers for other brands before taking the plunge and founding his own in the heart of Geneva. The timepieces he basically single-handedly and certainly single-mindedly—hence his tagline *invenit et fecit*—conceives and produces are of such extreme complexity that it is no wonder they leave his workshop in relatively small quantities. Journe has won numerous top awards, some several times over. He particularly values the Prix de la Fondation de la Vocation Bleustein-Blanchet, since it came from his peers.

The family of Journe watches is divided into four collections: the automatic Octa collection, with classic complications based on a very powerful caliber, the 1300.3, which offers 120 hours of power; the LineSport, focusing on contemporary sportive aesthetics; and the Elégante collection, an electromechanical watch providing 8 to 18 years of autonomy, depending on whether it is in daily use or in sleeping mode. The third is the Classique, featuring a minute repeater, a constant force tourbillon with dead-beat seconds, and a unique Chronomètre à Résonance with two escapements beating in resonance and providing chronometer precise timekeeping, especially in its most recent version, where it is equipped with a remontoir system to even out the mainspring's torque. A notorious piece is the Répétition Sounveraine, which manages to pack an outstanding repeater into a very discreet and thin case, of steel for better sound.

Chronomètre Bleu

Movement: manually wound, F.P.Journe Caliber 1304 in 18K rose gold; ø 30.4 mm, height 4.0 mm; 22 jewels; 21,600 vph; movement in 18K rose gold; 2 parallel barrel springs; free-sprung balance; finely finished movement; 56-hour power reserve
Functions: hours, minutes, subsidiary seconds
Case: tantalum, ø 39 mm, height 8.3 mm; sapphire crystal; transparent case back; water-resistant to 3 atm
Band: reptile skin, pin buckle
Remarks: blue chrome dial
Price: CHF 35,800

LineSport Chronomètre Rattrapante

Movement: manually wound, F.P.Journe Caliber 1518 in aluminum alloy; ø 33.6 mm, height 6.80 mm; 29 jewels; 21,600 vph; aluminum alloy plate and bridges; 80-hour power reserve without chronograph
Functions: hours, minutes, seconds; monopusher split-seconds chronograph; large date
Case: titanium, ø 44 mm, height 12.1 mm; tachymetric bezel with ceramic inlay; sapphire crystal; transparent case back; water-resistant to 3 atm
Remarks: aluminum alloy dial with engraved sapphire counters
Band: titanium bracelet and folding clasp
Price: CHF 68,100
Variations: 6N gold (CHF 86,000), platinum (CHF 116,600); both with Caliber 1518 in rose gold

Chronomètre à Résonance

Movement: manually wound, F.P.Journe Caliber 1520 in 18K rose gold; ø 34.6 mm, height 6.9 mm; 62 jewels; 21,600 vph; 2 balances mutually influence and stabilize each other via resonance; rose gold plate and bridges; 42-hour power reserve
Functions: hours, minutes, subsidiary seconds; 2nd time zone; power reserve indicator
Case: platinum, ø 40 or 42 mm, height 10.8 mm; sapphire crystal; transparent case back; water-resistant to 3 atm
Band: reptile skin, platinum pin buckle
Remarks: 2 constant force mechanisms, one single barrel, one differential, 2 secondary gear trains
Price: CHF 136,000
Variations: 6N gold (CHF 133,000)

Automatique Lune Havana

Movement: automatic F.P.Journe Caliber 1300.3 in rose gold; ø 34.6 mm, height 5.9 mm; 36 jewels; 21,600 vph; up to 160-hour power reserve of which 120 hours are chronometry-certified; 22K gold rotor; rose gold plate and bridges
Functions: hours, minutes, subsidiary seconds; moonphase; large date; power reserve indicator
Case: 18K 6N gold, ø 40 or 42 mm, height 10.7 mm; sapphire crystal; transparent case back; water-resistant to 3 atm
Band: reptile skin, pin buckle
Remarks: "Havana" color (combination of gold and ruthenium) on guilloché silver dial
Price: CHF 46,000
Variations: platinum (CHF 49,000)

Elégante 48 mm

Movement: electromechanical, F.P.Journe Caliber 1210; 28.5 x 28.3 mm, height 3.13 mm; 18 jewels; quartz frequency 32,768 Hz; autonomy: daily use up to 10 years, 18 years in standby mode
Functions: hours, minutes, subsidiary seconds; motion detector with inertia weight at 4:30
Case: titalyt, 48 x 40 mm, height 10.2 mm; sapphire crystal; transparent case back; water-resistant to 3 atm
Band: rubber, folding clasp
Remarks: goes into standby mode after 35 minutes without motion, microprocessor keeps time, restarts automatically, sets time when watch put back on; comes with straps in colored rubber, luminescent dial
Price: CHF 16,000
Variations: in titanium or titalyt set with diamonds (CHF 26,000); various strap colors

Elégante 40 mm Diamonds

Movement: electromechanical, F.P.Journe Caliber 1210; 28.5 x 28.3 mm, height 3.13 mm; 18 jewels; quartz frequency 32,768 Hz; autonomy: daily use up to10 years, 18 years in standby mode
Functions: hours, minutes, subsidiary seconds; motion detector with inertia weight at 4:30
Case: titalyt, 40 x 35 mm, height 8.35 mm; set with 222 diamonds 1.56 carat; sapphire crystal; transparent case back; water-resistant to 3 atm
Band: rubber, folding clasp
Remarks: goes into standby mode after 35 minutes without motion, microprocessor keeps time, restarts automatically, sets time when watch put back on; comes with straps in colored rubber
Price: CHF 20,300
Variations: in titanium with white dial; various strap colors

Répétition Souveraine

Movement: manually wound, F.P.Journe Caliber 1408 in rose gold; ø 32.2 mm, height 4.5 mm; 33 jewels; 21,600 vph; two parallel-mounted spring barrels; free-sprung balance; rose gold plate and bridges with perlage; blued steel hands; 56-hour power reserve
Functions: hours, minutes, subsidiary seconds; power reserve indicator; minute, quarter-hour and hour repeater on demand
Case: stainless steel, ø 40 mm, height 8.5 mm; sapphire crystal; screw-in crown and pusher; transparent case back; water-resistant to 3 atm
Remarks: gong mounted under the dial for greater sound; same hour and minute chime with brief separation
Band: reptile skin, double folding clasp
Price: CHF 280,000
Variations: with whitened silver guilloché dial (CHF 240,000)

Astronomic Souveraine: dial side

Movement: manually wound, F.P.Journe Caliber 1619 in rose gold; ø 37 mm, height 9.3 mm; 68 jewels; 21,600 vph; tourbillon; free-sprung balance with variable inertia; rose gold plate and bridges; 40-hour power reserve
Functions: dial side: hours, minutes, subsidiary seconds (on separate disk); 2nd time zone; sidereal hours and minutes indicator at 9 o'clock; sunrise and sunset; day and night; moon phase; power reserve indicator

Astronomic Souveraine: movement side

Functions: equation of time in the center of the dial (sun time); annual calendar surrounded by disc with astrological signs; tourbillon with constant force mechanism; minute, quarter-hour, and hour repetition
Case: stainless steel, ø 44 mm, height 13.7 mm; sapphire crystal; transparent case back; water-resistant to 3 atm
Band: reptile skin, pin buckle; double folding clasp; steel bracelet and folding clasp
Remarks: the watch began as a prototype for the 2019 Only Watch auction; white gold dial; subsidiary dials with clous de Paris decoration; double barrel; all settings by the crown
Price: CHF 950,000

Groupe Franck Muller Watchland SA
22, route de Malagny
CH-1294 Genthod
Switzerland

Tel.:
+41-22-959-88-88

E-mail:
contact@franckmuller.ch

Website:
www.franckmuller.com

Founded:
1991

Number of employees:
approx. 500 (estimated)

U.S. distributor:
Franck Muller USA, Inc.
207 W. 25th Street, 8th Floor
New York, NY 10001
212-463-8898
www.franckmuller-usa.com

Most important collections:
Giga Tourbillon, Aeternitas, Revolution, Evolution 3-1, Vanguard, Cintrée Curvex

FRANCK MULLER

Francesco "Franck" Muller has been considered one of the great creative minds in the industry ever since he designed and built his first tourbillon watch back in 1986. In fact, he never ceased amazing his colleagues and competition ever since, with his astounding timepieces that combined complications in a new and imaginative manner.

But a while ago the "master of complications" stepped away from the daily business of the brand, leaving space for the person who had paved young Muller's way to fame, Vartan Sirmakes. It was Sirmakes, previously a specialist in watch cases, who had contributed to the development of the double-domed, tonneau-shaped Cintrée Curvex case, with its elegant, 1920s retro look. The complications never stop, either. Muller created the Gigatourbillons, which are 20 millimeters across, and the Revolution series has a tourbillon that rises toward the crystal.

Even a brand that prides itself on a traditional look must make some concessions to modern aesthetics. The more recent Vanguards and pieces like the Skafander reveal an edginess that generates attractive tensions in that traditional Art-Deco tonneau-shaped case that is so typical of the brand. Lately, the brand has turned its attention to vivacious colors and playful dials, which in the somewhat stringent days of a pandemic seem to suggest fun lights at the end of the tunnel.

Muller and Sirmakes founded the Franck Muller Group Watchland in 1997. The Group now holds the majority interest in thirteen other companies, ten of which are watch brands. During the 2009 economic crisis, the company downsized a bit, but it was only a glitch in an otherwise well-planned-out strategy to focus on developing complicated watches, like the Vanguard series, which has gone through numerous iterations, including being skeletonized. The far-reaching synergies within the Group mean that the success of the leader is indeed trickling laterally to the other participants, like Backes & Strauss, Martin Braun, and Pierre Kunz.

Vanguard Krypton Racing

Reference number: V45 RCG SC DT KRY2 CAR-VE CAR VE NR (VE)
Movement: automatic, FM Caliber 2536-SCDT; ø 26.2 mm, height 5.35 mm; 25 jewels; 28,800 vph; finely finished movement; 42-hour power reserve
Functions: hours, minutes, sweep seconds; date
Case: carbon fiber, 44 x 53.7 mm, height 12.7 mm; sapphire crystal; transparent case back; water-resistant to 3 atm
Band: reptile skin with textile overlay, folding clasp
Price: $17,500
Variations: various case, bands, and dials

Vanguard Sapphire

Reference number: (BL)-V 45 T SQT COL DRM SAPH
Movement: manually wound, FM Caliber 1740-VS; 37.05 x 40.2 mm, height 6 mm; 21 jewels; 18,000 vph; triple-axis 1-minute tourbillon; 2 spring barrels; movement bridges coated in PVD of various colors, skeletonized movement; 192-hour power reserve
Functions: hours, minutes
Case: sapphire crystal with titanium body, 44 x 53.7 mm, height 12.7 mm; sapphire crystal; transparent case back; water-resistant to 3 atm
Band: reptile skin, folding clasp
Price: $286,700

Vanguard Mariner

Reference number: V45 YT SCDT MAR CRMR-CR BL-BLC-BLC
Movement: automatic, FM Caliber 800-DT; ø 25.6 mm, height 3.75 mm; 21 jewels; 28,800 vph; finely finished movement; 42-hour power reserve
Functions: hours, minutes, sweep seconds; date
Case: ceramic, 44 x 53.7 mm, height 12.7 mm; sapphire crystal; transparent case back; water-resistant to 3 atm
Band: rubber with reptile skin overlay, folding clasp
Price: $14,200
Variations: with white dial and band

FRÉDÉRIQUE CONSTANT

Peter and Aletta Stas, the Dutch couple who founded Frédérique Constant, have always sought to make high-end watches for consumers without deep pockets. So high-end, in fact, that in 2004 they went public with their first movement produced entirely in-house and equipped with silicon components. The company now has twenty-nine calibers to choose from.

The brand was founded in the late 1980s and named for Aletta's great-grandmother Frédérique Schreiner and Peter's great-grandfather Constant Stas. The couple parlayed affordable watches with very classic—i.e., not boat-rocking—design into a modern four-floor factory in Geneva's industrial Plan-les-Ouates, with ample room for manufacturing, administrative offices, conference rooms, a fitness area, and a cafeteria. Being in touch with the zeitgeist remained a key strateg., In 2015, Frederique Constant introduced the first Swiss-made "Horological Smartwatch" running on an MMT SwissConnect solution and with analog dial, launching a whole new watch category in the Swiss watch industry.

In 2016, Frédérique Constant and sister brand Alpina were sold to the Japanese brand Citizen. The factory in Geneva was expanded in 2019 to almost double its original size. This permitted a production projection of 250,000 watches per year by 2025. The highlight in the new building is the "Manufacture Experience," which takes up almost the entire first floor of and will be open to visitors in the future. Visitors can find out all they need to know about Frédérique Constant.

In 2021, Frederique Constant achieved a mechanical breakthrough, with a compact silicon escapement rather than a normal escapement with balance. The oscillator vibrates at a frequency of 288,000 vibrations per hour. The Slimline Monolithic Manufacture ticks ten times faster than most mechanical watches and appears to achieve far better chronometric results as well. A genuine horological innovation, the new escapement can be viewed through an opening at 6 o'clock.

Frédérique Constant SA
Chemin du Champ des Filles 32
CH-1228 Plan-les-Ouates (Geneva)
Switzerland

Tel.:
+41-22-860-0440

E-mail:
info@frederique-constant.com

Website:
www.frederique-constant.com

Founded:
1988

Number of employees:
100

Annual production:
approx. 130,000 watches

U.S. distributor:
Alpina Frederique Constant USA
350 5th Avenue, 29th Floor
New York, NY 10118
646-438-8124
lmellor@usa.frederique-constant.com

Most important collections/price range:
Tourbillon Perpetual Calendar Manufacture/ from approx. $21,995 to $32,995; Hybrid Manufacture / from approx. $3,695 to $3,895; Worldtimer Manufacture / from approx. $4,195 to 4,395; Vintage Rally Healey Chronograph / from approx. $2,795 to $3,095; Ladies' Automatic Double Heart Beat / from approx. $1,995

Highlife Monolithic Manufacture

Reference number: FC-810CDGG4NH6
Movement: automatic, Caliber FC-810; ø 30 mm, height 6.2 mm; 19 jewels; 288,000 vph; silicon Monolith escapement with pallet fork, balance and hairspring as a single component; 80-hour power reserve
Functions: hours, minutes, sweep seconds; date
Case: stainless steel, ø 40 mm, height 11.3 mm; sapphire crystal; transparent case back; water-resistant to 3 atm
Band: calfskin, folding clasp
Price: $6,795
Variations: in yellow gold, limited to 81 pieces ($15,000)

Highlife Perpetual Calendar

Reference number: FC-775BL4NH6B
Movement: automatic, Caliber UN-775; ø 30 mm, height 6.2 mm; 26 jewels; 28,800 vph; 38-hour power reserve
Functions: hours, minutes; perpetual calendar with date, weekday, months, moon phase, leap year
Case: stainless steel, ø 41 mm, height 12.15 mm; sapphire crystal; transparent case back; water-resistant to 5 atm
Band: stainless steel, folding clasp
Price: Price: $9,895

Classic Worldtimer Manufacture

Reference number: FC-718NWWM4H6
Movement: automatic, Caliber FC-718; ø 30 mm, height 6.2 mm; 26 jewels; 28,800 vph; 42-hour power reserve
Functions: hours, minutes, sweep seconds; world-time display (second time zone); date
Case: stainless steel, ø 42 mm, height 12.4 mm; crown-activated inner bezel with 0-24 scale and reference city names; sapphire crystal; transparent case back; water-resistant to 3 atm
Band: reptile skin, folding clasp
Price: $4,495

Highlife Ladies Automatic

Reference number: FC-303VD2NH5B
Movement: automatic, Caliber FC-310 (base Sellita SW200-1); ø 25.6 mm, height 4.6 mm; 26 jewels; 28,800 vph; skeletonized mainplate under the escapement section; 38-hour power reserve
Functions: hours, minutes, sweep seconds; date
Case: stainless steel with rose gold PVD coating, ø 34 mm, height 9.67 mm; sapphire crystal; transparent case back; water-resistant to 5 atm
Band: stainless steel with rose-gold colored PVD coating, folding clasp
Remarks: dial set with 8 diamonds
Price: $3,795

Highlife Chronograph Automatic

Reference number: FC-391WN4NH6
Movement: automatic, Caliber FC-391 (base Sellita SW510); ø 30 mm, height 7.9 mm; 26 jewels; 28,800 vph; 65-hour power reserve
Functions: hours, minutes, subsidiary seconds; chronograph; date
Case: stainless steel, ø 42 mm, height 14.45 mm; sapphire crystal; transparent case back; water-resistant to 10 atm
Band: calfskin, folding clasp
Price: $3,795

Vintage Rally Healey Chronograph

Reference number: FC-397HDGR5B6
Movement: automatic, Caliber FC-397 (base Sellita SW500); ø 30 mm, height 7.9 mm; 25 jewels; 28,800 vph; 46-hour power reserve
Functions: hours, minutes, subsidiary seconds; chronograph
Case: stainless steel, ø 42 mm, height 14.45 mm; sapphire crystal; transparent case back; water-resistant to 5 atm
Band: calfskin, buckle
Price: $3,195

Classics Heartbeat Automatic

Reference number: FC-310MC5B6
Movement: automatic, Caliber FC-310 (base Sellita SW200-1); ø 25.6 mm, height 4.6 mm; 26 jewels; 28,800 vph; skeletonized mainplate under the escapement; 38-hour power reserve
Functions: hours, minutes, sweep seconds
Case: stainless steel, ø 40 mm, height 10.5 mm; sapphire crystal; transparent case back; water-resistant to 5 atm
Band: calfskin, buckle
Remarks: opening in the dial
Price: $1,495

Highlife Automatic COSC

Reference number: FC-303DGR4NH6
Movement: automatic, Caliber FC-303 (base Sellita SW200-1); ø 25.6 mm, height 4.6 mm; 26 jewels; 28,800 vph; 38-hour power reserve; COSC-certified chronometer
Functions: hours, minutes, sweep seconds; date
Case: stainless steel, ø 41 mm, height 11.15 mm; sapphire crystal; transparent case back; water-resistant to 5 atm
Band: stainless steel, folding clasp
Price: $2,195

Highlife Tourbillon Perpetual Calendar Manufacture

Reference number: FC-975G4NH6B
Movement: automatic, Caliber FC-975; ø 30 mm, height 6.7 mm; 33 jewels; 28,800 vph; 1-minute tourbillon; 38-hour power reserve
Functions: hours, minutes; perpetual calendar with date, weekday, month, leap year
Case: stainless steel, ø 41 mm, height 12.65 mm; sapphire crystal; transparent case back; water-resistant to 3 atm
Band: stainless steel, folding clasp
Price: $22,995

Slimline Ladies Moonphase

Reference number: FC-206SW1S6
Movement: quartz
Functions: hours, minutes, moon phase
Case: stainless steel, ø 30 mm, height 7.7 mm; sapphire crystal; water-resistant to 3 atm
Band: calfskin, buckle
Price: $795

Runabout Automatic

Reference number: FC-303RMS5B4
Movement: automatic, Caliber FC-303 (base Sellita SW200-1); ø 25.6 mm, height 4.6 mm; 26 jewels; 28,800 vph; 38-hour power reserve
Functions: hours, minutes, sweep seconds; date
Case: stainless steel, rose gold-plated, ø 42 mm, height 11.5 mm; sapphire crystal; transparent case back; water-resistant to 5 atm
Band: calfskin, folding clasp
Price: $1,850

Classics Index Automatic

Reference number: FC-303MC5B4
Movement: automatic, Caliber FC-303 (base Sellita SW200-1); ø 25.6 mm, height 4.6 mm; 26 jewels; 28,800 vph; 38-hour power reserve; COSC-certified chronometer
Functions: hours, minutes, sweep seconds; date
Case: stainless steel with rose-gold PVD coating, ø 40 mm, height 10.3 mm; sapphire crystal; transparent case back; water-resistant to 5 atm
Band: calfskin, buckle
Price: $1,095

Caliber FC-718

Automatic; single spring barrel, 42-hour power reserve
Functions: hours, minutes, sweep seconds; 2nd time zone (world time display); date
Diameter: 30 mm
Height: 6.2 mm
Jewels: 26
Frequency: 28,800 vph
Hairspring: flat hairspring with fine adjustment
Shock protection: Incabloc
Remarks: crown-controlled functions

Caliber FC-810

Automatic; single spring barrel, 80-hour power reserve
Functions: hours, minutes, sweep seconds; date
Diameter: 30 mm
Height: 6.2 mm
Jewels: 19
Frequency: 28,000 vph
Hairspring: silicon Monolith escapement with pallet fork, balance and hairspring as a single component

Caliber FC-775

Automatic, single spring barrel, 38-hour power reserve
Functions: hours, minutes, perpetual calendar with date, weekday, month, moon phase and leap year
Diameter: 30.5 mm
Height: 6.67 mm
Jewels: 26
Frequency: 28,800 vph
Hairspring: flat hairspring with fine adjustment
Shock Protection: Incabloc II
Remarks: 191 parts

Garrick Watchmakers
Unit 2, Fletcher Way, Norwich, Norfolk
NR3 3ST
England

Tel.:
+44 (0)1603-327272

E-mail:
info@garrick.co.uk

Website:
www.garrick.co.uk

Founded:
2013

Employees:
9

Annual production:
70 watches maximum

Distribution:
direct sales

Most important collections/price range:
Regulator and S2 / £2,500 to £30,000
Prices only in pounds sterling

GARRICK

Britain has contributed enormously to the development of watchmaking, so it's hardly astonishing to find that the country is home to a growing number of brands vying on the international markets. Garrick Watchmakers is one of them. It was founded in 2013 in Devon by David Brailsford together with Simon Michlmayr, one of the top English watchmakers. The aim of these two men was to revive the old tradition of English watchmaking and to achieve the greatest possible vertical integration in the construction of their watches.

Wherever possible, Garrick either manufactures in its own workshop in Norwich in Norfolk or purchases from English suppliers. The company goes so far as to make its own hands, which is rare in the industry, since hands are very time-consuming to manufacture. The elaborately designed dials, too, are also entirely made in-house. Even cases are produced in England.

In the beginning Garrick had to go new ways and regain the necessary knowledge together with English precision mechanics. While the first models were still based on a Unitas caliber, the Portsmouth was presented in 2016, the first of what are now four of the company's own *manufacture* calibers. The same year saw the appearance of the Regulator, that uses its 42-millimeter case for three subdials and an opening on the free-sprung balance designed and built by the company. It was reinterpreted slightly for 2023. The so-called Trinity balance is made of a nonmagnetic alloy, Sircumet. To adjust the rate, the balance wheel is equipped with rim screws. The hairspring's position can be changed as well. In addition to genuine enamel dials, Garrick specializes in guilloché and finely engraved dials.

Garrick Watchmakers build no more than seventy watches every year. Thanks to its vertical manufacturing and the fact that each Garrick is built to order, Garrick can in fact build watches according to the wishes of its customers, including unique pieces, if need be, which is what attracts collectors.

Regulator MK II

Movement: manually wound, Garrick Caliber UT-G02; 19 jewels; 18,000 vph; free-sprung; 48-hour power reserve
Functions: hours, minutes, sweep seconds
Case: stainless steel, ø 42 mm, height 14 mm; sapphire crystal; water-resistant to 3 atm
Band: calfskin, buckle
Remarks: finely structured metal dial, applied chapter rings
Price: £10,995
Variations: engine turned dials

S5

Movement: manually wound, Garrick Caliber UT-G05; 20 jewels; 21,600 vph; heat-blued cheater ring; gold or silver frosted finish; screw-mounted, hand-polished chatons; 60-hour power reserve
Functions: hours, minutes, sweep seconds
Case: stainless steel, ø 39 mm, height 8 mm; sapphire crystal; transparent case back; water-resistant to 10 atm
Band: reptile skin or calfskin; buckle
Remarks: heat-blued or Breguet style chapter ring and hands
Price: £16,000

S6

Movement: manually wound, Garrick Caliber BF03 (modified ETA 6498); ø 36.6 mm, height 4.5 mm; 19 jewels; 18,000 vph; skeletonized balance cock with swan neck regulator, hand-matted, rhodium-plated, beveled parts; engraved barrel and crown wheel cover, hand-polished chatons; 53-hour power reserve
Functions: hours, minutes, subsidiary seconds
Case: stainless steel, ø 42 mm, height 11 mm; sapphire crystal; transparent case back; water-resistant to 10 atm
Band: reptile skin, buckle
Remarks: engine turned or frosted dial with applied ink-filled chapter ring
Price: £6,245
Variations: engine turned dials

GIRARD-PERREGAUX

Girard-Perregaux
1, Place Girardet
CH-2300 La Chaux-de-Fonds
Switzerland

Tel.:
+41-32-911-3333

Website:
www.girard-perregaux.com

Founded:
1791

U.S. distributor:
Girard-Perregaux
Tradema of America, Inc.
7900 Glades Road, Suite 200
Boca Raton, FL 33434
833-GPWATCH
www.girard-perregaux.com

Most important collections/price range:
Laureato / Vintage 1945 / approx. $7,500 to $625,000; ww.tc / $12,300 to $23,800; GP 1966 / $7,500 to $291,000

This venerable watch *manufacture* headquartered in La Chaux-de-Fonds is one of those with a very long history. It all began in 1791, though the genuinely successful part of the story is concentrated in the second half of the nineteenth century, 1867 to be precise, when Girard-Perregaux contributed a piece of watchmaking history with the aesthetically and technically sophisticated "Tourbillon with three golden bridges." Girard-Perregaux maintained its position at the forefront of Swiss watchmaking in the twentieth century with one of the first wrist-worn men's watches, as well as several pioneering achievements in mechanical watchmaking.

Italian entrepreneur Luigi ("Gino") Macaluso helped the brand achieve new greatness after 1992. In the wake of the renaissance of the mechanical watch, Girard-Perregaux managed to establish itself as a luxury manufacturer around the turn of the millennium. Following Macaluso's death in 2010, the company was purchased by the international Kering Group until it was taken over by its own management team led by CEO Patrick Pruniaux in the spring of 2022.

The tourbillon—in increasingly modern guises—remains the brand's focus, but along with the vintage trend and, no doubt, some nostalgia for the rational, elegant watches of older days, Girard-Perregaux decided to modernize the Laureato, a collection that was first introduced in 1975. It is considered one of the icons of the 1970s thanks to its sporty, striking aesthetics, octagonal bezel over a round base circle, and metal bracelet seamlessly integrated into the case. The recently rebuilt and modernized *manufacture* in La Chaux-de-Fonds quickly produced a number of remarkable creations based on the distinctive sports watch.

In 2021, Girard-Perregaux announced its long-term partnership with the British sports car manufacturer Aston Martin, which goes hand in hand with a commitment to the Formula 1 team and has already produced its first special edition watches.

Laureato 42mm Automatic

Reference number: 81010-11-431-11A
Movement: automatic, GP Caliber 01800-0013; ø 30 mm, height 3.97 mm; 28 jewels; 28,800 vph; 54-hour power reserve
Functions: hours, minutes, sweep seconds; date
Case: stainless steel, ø 42 mm, height 10.88 mm; sapphire crystal; transparent case back; water-resistant to 10 atm
Band: stainless steel, double folding clasp
Price: $14,300

Laureato 42mm Automatic Skeleton

Reference number: 81015-11-001-11A
Movement: automatic, GP Caliber 01800-0006; ø 30 mm, height 4.16 mm; 25 jewels; 28,800 vph; variable inertia balance; rotor in rose gold; fully skeletonized movement; 54-hour power reserve
Functions: hours, minutes, subsidiary seconds
Case: stainless steel, ø 42 mm, height 10.68 mm; sapphire crystal; transparent case back; water-resistant to 10 atm
Case: stainless steel, triple folding clasp
Remarks: skeletonized dial
Price: $43,600

Laureato Chronograph 42mm

Reference number: 81020-11-131-11A
Movement: automatic, GP Caliber 03300-0137/0138/0141; ø 25.95 mm, height 6.5 mm; 63 jewels; 28,800 vph; 46-hour power reserve
Functions: hours, minutes, subsidiary seconds; chronograph; date
Case: stainless steel, ø 42 mm, height 12.01 mm; sapphire crystal; water-resistant to 10 atm
Band: stainless steel, triple folding clasp
Price: $18,600

Laureato Absolute Chronograph 44mm

Reference number: 81060-21-491-FH6A
Movement: automatic, GP Caliber 03300-1058; ø 25.95 mm, height 6.5 mm; 63 jewels; 28,800 vph; 46-hour power reserve
Functions: hours, minutes, subsidiary seconds; chronograph; date
Case: titanium with black PVD coating, ø 44 mm, height 14.65 mm; sapphire crystal; transparent case back; water-resistant to 30 atm
Band: rubber, triple folding clasp
Price: $12,900

Free Bridge

Reference number: 82000-11-631-FA6A
Movement: automatic, GP Caliber 01800-1170; ø 36,2 mm, height 5,94 mm; 23 jewels; 28,800 vph; 54-hour power reserve
Functions: hours, minutes
Case: stainless steel with black DLC, ø 36.2 mm, height 5.94 mm; sapphire crystal; transparent case back; water-resistant to 3 atm
Band: calfskin, triple folding clasp
Price: $21,600

Tourbillon with Three Flying Bridges

Reference number: 99296-52-001-BA6A
Movement: automatic, GP Kaliber 09400-1273; ø 42 mm, height 9.45 mm; 27 jewels; 21,600 vph; 1-minute tourbillon under three titanium bridges; white gold microrotor; Balance with variable inertia and gold regulating screws, balance spring with Philips terminal curve; fully skeletonized movement; 60-hour power reserve
Functions: hours, minutes, subsidiary seconds, (on tourbillon cage)
Case: rose gold, ø 44 mm, height 15.52 mm; sapphire crystal; transparent case back; water-resistant to 3 atm
Band: reptile skin, triple folding clasp
Price: $172,000

GP 1966 40mm

Reference number: 49555-11-231-BB60
Movement: automatic, GP Caliber 03300-0130; ø 25.6 mm, height 3,36 mm; 27 jewels; 28,800 vph; 46-hour power reserve
Functions: hours, minutes, sweep seconds; date
Case: stainless steel, ø 40 mm, height 8.9 mm; sapphire crystal; transparent case back; water-resistant to 3 atm
Band: reptile skin, buckle
Price: $9,100
Variations: various dials

GP 1966 Blue Moon

Reference number: 49545-11-432-BH6A
Movement: automatic, GP Caliber 03300-0115; ø 25.6 mm, height 4.8 mm; 27 jewels; 28,800 vph; 46-hour power reserve
Functions: hours, minutes, sweep seconds; date, moon phase
Case: stainless steel with black PVD, ø 40 mm; height 10.8 mm; sapphire crystal; transparent case back; water-resistant to 3 atm
Band: reptile skin, buckle
Price: $11,100

Casquette 2.0

Reference number: 39800-32-001-32A
Movement: quartz, GP caliber 03980 with LED display
Functions: hours and minutes (digital); additional 24-hour indicator (second time zone); full calendar with date, month, year
Case: ceramic with titanium elements, 33.6 mm x 42.4 mm, height 14.64 mm; sapphire crystal
Band: ceramic with rubber inlay, folding clasp
Price: $4,700; limited to 820 pieces

GLASHÜTTE ORIGINAL

Is there a little nostalgia creeping into the designers at Glashütte Original? Or is it just understated ecstasy for older looks? The retro touches that started appearing again a few years ago with the Sixties Square Tourbillon are still in vogue as the company delves into its own past for inspiration, such as the use of a special silver treatment on dials.

Glashütte Original *manufacture* roots go back to the mid-nineteenth century, though the name itself came later. The company, which had a sterling reputation for precision watches, became subsumed in the VEB Glashütter Uhrenbetriebe, a group of Glashütte watchmakers and suppliers who were collectivized as part of the former East German system. After reunification, the company took up its old moniker of Glashütte Original, and in 1995, the *manufacture* released an entirely new collection. Later, it purchased Union Glashütte. In 2000, the Swiss Swatch Group acquired the whole company and invested in expanding the production space at Glashütte Original headquarters. The company decided to separate out Union Glashütte, whose models are not distributed in the USA, by the way.

Manufacturing depth has reached 95 percent. All movements are designed by a team of experienced in-house engineers, while the components they comprise, such as plates, screws, pinions, wheels, levers, spring barrels, balance wheels, and tourbillon cages, are manufactured in the upgraded production areas. These parts are lavishly finished by hand before assembly by a group of talented watchmakers. Even dials are in-house. Among the highlights of its catalogue are the Senator Chronometer, which boasts second and minute hands that automatically jump to zero when the crown is pulled, allowing for extremely accurate time setting; and the Spezialist, a diver's watch that is modeled on a design from 1969, which was developed especially for frogmen and sports divers and is not only precise but particularly resistant to shocks. Its SeaQ line comes in a wide range of iterations.

Glashütter Uhrenbetrieb GmbH
Altenberger Strasse 1
D-01768 Glashütte
Germany

Tel.:
+49-350-53-46-0

E-mail:
info@glashuette-original.com

Website:
www.glashuette-original.com

Founded:
1951 foundation as VEB Glashütter Uhrenbetriebe
1990 privatization and registration as Glashütter Uhrenbetrieb GmbH;

Annual production:
N/A

U.S. distributor:
Glashütte Original
The Swatch Group (U.S.), Inc.
1200 Harbor Boulevard
Weehawken, NJ 07087
201-271-1400

Most important collections/price range:
Senator, Pano, Spezialist, Vintage, Ladies / $4,900 to $152,300

Alfred Helwig Tourbillon 1920 – Limited Edition

Reference number: 1-54-01-01-01-01
Movement: manually wound, Glashütte Original Caliber 54-01; ø 30.2 mm, height 6 mm; 20 jewels; 21,600 vph; flying 1-minute tourbillon; Glashütte three-quarter plate with stripe finish, screw balance wheel with 10 weighted screws and 8 regulating screws, 2 diamond endstones; hand-engraved balance cock, blued screws, finely finished movement; 100-hour power reserve
Functions: hours, minutes, subsidiary seconds
Case: rose gold, ø 40 mm, height 11.6 mm; sapphire crystal; transparent case back; water-resistant to 3 atm
Band: reptile skin, folding clasp
Remarks: gold dial
Price: $121,800; limited to 25 pieces

PanoLunarTourbillon

Reference number: 1-93-02-05-05-05
Movement: automatic, Glashütte Original Caliber 93-02; ø 32.2 mm, height 7.65 mm; 48 jewels; 21,600 vph; flying 1-minute tourbillon, screw balance wheel with 10 weight and 8 regulating screws, 2 diamond capstones, blued screws, Glashütte three-quarter plate with stripe finish, skeletonized rotor with gold oscillating mass, finely finished movement; 48-hour power reserve
Functions: hours and minutes (off-center), subsidiary seconds (on the tourbillon cage); panorama date, moon phase
Case: red gold, ø 40 mm, height 13.1 mm; sapphire crystal; transparent case back; water-resistant to 5 atm
Band: reptile skin, folding clasp
Price: $132,000

PanoMaticLunar

Reference number: 1-90-02-23-35-30
Movement: automatic, Glashütte Original Caliber 90-02; ø 32.6 mm, height 7 mm; 47 jewels; 28,800 vph; screw balance, 18 weighted screws, duplex swan-neck fine adjustment; hand-engraved balance cock, Glashütte three-quarter plate with stripe finish, blued screws, skeletonized rotor with gold oscillating mass, finely finished movement; 42-hour power reserve
Functions: hours and minutes (off-center), subsidiary seconds; panorama date, moon phase
Case: red gold, ø 40 mm, height 12.7 mm; sapphire crystal; transparent case back; water-resistant to 5 atm
Band: reptile skin, folding clasp
Price: $20,500
Variations: in stainless steel ($9,900)

PanoMaticInverse

Reference number: 1-91-02-02-02-30
Movement: automatic, Glashütte Original Caliber 91-02; ø 38.2 mm, height 7.1 mm; 49 jewels; 28,800 vph; Glashütte three-quarter plate with stripe finish, screw balance with 18 weighted screws, duplex swan-neck fine adjustment; inverted movement architecture, hand-engraved balance cock, skeletonized rotor with gold oscillating mass, finely finished movement; 42-hour power reserve
Functions: hours and minutes (off-center), subsidiary seconds; panorama date
Case: stainless steel, ø 42 mm, height 12.3 mm; sapphire crystal; transparent case back; water-resistant to 5 atm
Band: reptile skin, folding clasp
Price: $12,700
Variations: with stainless steel bracelet ($13,900)

PanoReserve

Reference number: 1-65-01-23-12-04
Movement: manually wound, Glashütte Original Caliber 65-01; ø 32.2 mm, height 6.1 mm; 48 jewels; 28,800 vph; Glashütte three-quarter plate with stripe finish, screw balance with 18 weighted screws, duplex swan-neck fine adjustment, screw-mounted gold chatons, balance and seconds wheel cock, finely finished movement; 42-hour power reserve
Functions: hours and minutes (off-center), subsidiary seconds; power reserve display; panorama date
Case: stainless steel, ø 40 mm, height 11.7 mm; sapphire crystal; transparent case back; water-resistant to 5 atm
Band: reptile skin, folding clasp
Price: $9,900
Variations: in red gold ($20,500)

Senator Excellence Perpetual Calendar

Reference number: 1-36-02-02-05-61
Movement: automatic, Glashütte Original Caliber 36-02; ø 32.2 mm, height 7.35 mm; 49 jewels; 28,800 vph; silicon hairspring, screw balance wheel with 4 regulating screws, swan-neck fine adjustment, Glashütte three-quarter plate with stripe finish, blued screws, skeletonized rotor with gold oscillating mass, finely finished movement; 100-hour power reserve
Functions: hours, minutes, sweep second; perpetual calendar with panorama date, weekday, month, moon phase, leap year
Case: red gold, ø 42 mm, height 12.8 mm; sapphire crystal; transparent case back; water-resistant to 5 atm
Band: reptile skin, folding clasp
Price: $33,300
Variations: in stainless steel ($21,300)

Senator Chronometer

Reference number: 1-58-01-02-05-30
Movement: manually wound, Glashütte Original Caliber 58-01; ø 35 mm, height 6.47 mm; 58 jewels; 28,800 vph; Glashütte three-quarter plate with stripe finish, screw balance with 18 weighted screws, swan-neck fine adjustment; hand-engraved balance cock, finely finished movement; 45 hours power reserve; certified (DIN) chronometer
Functions: hours, minutes, subsidiary seconds; day/night indicator, power reserve indicator; panorama date
Case: red gold, ø 42 mm, height 12.47 mm; sapphire crystal; transparent case back; water-resistant to 5 atm
Band: reptile skin, folding clasp
Price: $26,100
Variations: in white gold ($30,000)

Senator Cosmopolite

Reference number: 1-89-02-05-02-70
Movement: automatic, Glashütte Original Caliber 89-02; ø 39.2 mm, height 8 mm; 63 jewels; 28.800 vph; Glashütte three-quarter plate, screw balance with 4 regulating screws, swan-neck fine adjustment, hand-engraved balance cock, blued screws, finely finished movement; 72-hour power reserve
Functions: hours, minutes, subsidiary seconds; additional 12-Std display (second time zone); world time display with 35 time zones, day/night indicator, power reserve indicator; panorama date
Case: stainless steel, ø 4 mm, height 14 mm; sapphire crystal; transparent case back, water-resistant to 5 atm
Band: stainless steel, folding clasp
Price: $22,700
Variations: with reptile skin band ($21,700); in red gold ($37,600); in white gold ($38,600)

Senator Excellence Panorama Date Moon Phase

Reference number: 1-36-04-04-02-30
Movement: automatic, Glashütte Original Caliber 36-04; ø 32.2 mm, height 6.7 mm; 43 jewels; 28,800 vph; silicon hairspring, swan neck fine adjustment, Glashütte three-quarter plate with stripe finish, blued screws, skeletonized rotor with gold oscillating mass, finely finished movement; 100-hour power reserve
Functions: hours, minutes, sweep seconds; panorama date, moon phase
Case: stainless steel, ø 42 mm, height 12.2 mm; sapphire crystal; transparent case back; water-resistant to 5 atm
Band: reptile skin, folding clasp
Price: $10,700
Variations: with buckle ($10,700); in red gold ($21,400); with stainless steel bracelet ($11,900)

SeaQ

Reference number: 1-39-11-10-90-34
Movement: automatic, Glashütte Original Caliber 39-11; ø 26 mm, height 4.3 mm; 25 jewels; 28,800 vph; swan neck fine regulation, Glashütte three-quarter plate with stripe, skeletonized rotor with heavy metal oscillating mass, finely finished movement; 40-hour power reserve
Functions: hours, minutes, sweep seconds; date
Case: stainless steel, ø 39.5 mm, height 12.15 mm; unidirectional bezel in yellow gold with ceramic insert, with 0-60 scale; sapphire crystal; screw-in crown, in yellow gold; water-resistant to 20 atm
Band: textile, folding clasp
Price: $12,500

SeaQ

Reference number: 1-39-11-09-82-70
Movement: automatic, Glashütte Original Caliber 39-11; ø 26 mm, height 4.3 mm; 25 jewels; 28,800 vph; swan neck fine adjustment, Glashütte three-quarter plate with stripe finish, skeletonized rotor with heavy metal oscillating mass, finely finished movement; 40-hour power reserve
Functions: hours, minutes, sweep seconds; date
Case: stainless steel, ø 39.5 mm, height 12.15 mm; unidirectional rotating bezel set with 47 diamonds; sapphire crystal; screw-in yellow-gold crown; water-resistant to 20 atm
Band: stainless steel, folding clasp
Price: $17,300
Variations: with textile strap ($16,400)

SeaQ

Reference number: 1-39-11-06-80-33
Movement: automatic, Glashütte Original Caliber 58-01; ø 26 mm, height 4.3 mm; 25 jewels; 28,800 vph; swan-neck fine adjustment, Glashütte three-quarter plate with stripe finish, skeletonized rotor with heavy metal oscillating mass, finely finished movement; 40-hour power reserve
Functions: hours, minutes, sweep seconds; date
Case: stainless steel, ø 39.5 mm, height 12.15 mm; unidirectional bezel with 60-minute scale; sapphire crystal; screw-in crown; water-resistant to 20 atm
Band: rubber, folding clasp
Price: $9,000
Variations: with synthetic strap ($9,000); with stainless steel bracelet ($9,900)

SeaQ Panorama Date

Reference number: 1-36-13-03-90-33
Movement: automatic, Glashütte Original Caliber 36-13; ø 32.2 mm, height 6.7 mm; 39 jewels; 28,800 vph; silicon hairspring, swan-neck fine adjustment for the rate, skeletonized rotor with gold oscillating mass; 100-hour power reserve
Functions: hours, minutes, sweep seconds; panorama date
Case: red gold, ø 43.2 mm, height 15.65 mm; unidirectional rotating bezel in with ceramic insert, with 0-60 scale; sapphire crystal; transparent case back; screw-in red gold crown; water-resistant to 30 atm
Band: textile, folding clasp
Price: $15,100
Variations: with textile Band

SeaQ Panorama Date

Reference number: 1-36-13-04-91-34
Movement: automatic, Glashütte Original Caliber 36-13; ø 32.2 mm, height 6.7 mm; 39 jewels; 28,800 vph; silicon hairspring, swan neck fine adjustment, skeletonized rotor with gold oscillating mass; 100-hour power reserve
Functions: hours, minutes, sweep seconds; panorama date
Case: stainless steel, ø 43.2 mm, height 15.65 mm; unidirectional bezel in pink gold with ceramic insert, with 0-60 scale; sapphire crystal; transparent case back; screw-in pink gold crown; water-resistant to 30 atm
Band: textile, folding clasp
Price: $15,100
Variations: rubber strap with folding clasp ($15,100)

SeaQ Panorama Date

Reference number: 1-36-13-07-83-33
Movement: automatic, Glashütte Original Caliber 36-13; ø 32.2 mm, height 6.7 mm; 39 jewels; 28,800 vph; silicon hairspring, swan-neck fine adjustment, screw balance wheel with 4 regulating screws, Glashütte three-quarter plate with stripe finish, blued screws, finely finished movement, skeletonized rotor with gold oscillating mass; 100-hour power reserve
Functions: hours, minutes, sweep seconds; panorama date
Case: stainless steel, ø 43.2 mm, height 15.65 mm; unidirectional bezel in with ceramic insert, with 0-60 scale; sapphire crystal; transparent case back; screw-in crown; water-resistant to 30 atm
Band: rubber, folding clasp
Price: $11,500
Variations: with stainless steel bracelet ($12,400)

Seventies Chronograph Panorama Date

Reference number: 1-37-02-08-02-70
Movement: automatic, Glashütte Original Caliber 37-02; ø 31.6 mm, height 8 mm; 65 jewels; 28,800 vph; screw balance with 4 regulating screws, swan-neck fine adjustment; Glashütte three-quarter plate with stripe finish, blued screws, skeletonized rotor with gold oscillating mass, finely finished movement; 70-hour power reserve
Functions: hours, minutes, subsidiary seconds; power reserve indicator; flyback chronograph; panorama date
Case: stainless steel, 40 mm x 40 mm, height 14.1 mm; sapphire crystal; transparent case back; screw-in crown; water-resistant to 10 atm
Band: stainless steel, folding clasp
Price: $14,600

Sixties Chronograph

Reference number: 1-39-34-03-22-04
Movement: automatic, Glashütte Original Caliber 39-34; ø 30.04 mm, height 7.2 mm; 51 jewels; 28,800 vph; swan-neck fine adjustment, skeletonized rotor with gold oscillating mass, finely finished movement; 40-hour power reserve
Functions: hours, minutes, subsidiary seconds; chronograph
Case: stainless steel, ø 42 mm, height 12.4 mm; sapphire crystal; transparent case back; water-resistant to 3 atm
Band: reptile skin, buckle
Price: $8,000

Sixties Panorama Date

Reference number: 2-39-47-06-02-04
Movement: automatic, Glashütte Original Caliber 39-47; ø 30.95 mm, height 5.9 mm; 39 jewels; 28,800 vph; swan-neck fine adjustment, Glashütte three-quarter plate with stripe finish, skeletonized rotor with gold oscillating mass, finely finished movement; 40-hour power reserve
Functions: hours, minutes, sweep seconds; panorama date
Case: stainless steel, ø 42 mm, height 12.4 mm; sapphire crystal; transparent case back; water-resistant to 3 atm
Band: reptile skin, buckle
Price: $8,000
Variations: with silver, black, or red dial ($8,000)

Sixties

Reference number: 1-39-52-01-01-04
Movement: automatic, Glashütte Original Caliber 39-52; ø 26 mm, height 4.3 mm; 25 jewels; 28,800 vph; swan-neck fine adjustment, Glashütte three-quarter plate with stripe finish, skeletonized rotor with gold oscillating mass, finely finished movement; 40-hour power reserve
Functions: hours, minutes, sweep seconds
Case: rose gold, ø 39 mm, height 9.4 mm; sapphire crystal; transparent case back; water-resistant to 3 atm
Band: reptile skin, buckle
Price: $12,800
Variations: with a black dial ($12,800); in stainless steel ($6,400)

PanoMatic Luna

Reference number: 1-90-12-03-12-02
Movement: automatic, Glashütte Original Caliber 90-12; ø 32.6 mm, height 7 mm; 47 jewels; 28,800 vph; screw balance with 18 weighted screws, duplex swan-neck fine adjustment, Glashütte three-quarter plate with stripe finish, hand-engraved balance cock, blued screws, skeletonized rotor with gold oscillating mass, finely finished movement; 42-hour power reserve
Functions: hours, minutes, subsidiary seconds; panorama date, moon phase
Case: stainless steel, ø 39.4 mm, height 12 mm; bezel set with 64 diamonds; sapphire crystal; transparent case back; crown with diamond; water-resistant to 3 atm
Band: reptile skin, folding clasp
Remarks: mother-of-pearl dial
Price: $17,500

Lady Serenade

Reference number: 1-39-22-09-16-04
Movement: automatic, Glashütte Original Caliber, 39-22; ø 26 mm, height 4.3 mm; 25 jewels; 28,800 vph; swan-neck fine adjustment, Glashütte three-quarter plate with stripe finish, skeletonized rotor with heavy metal oscillating weight; finely finished movement; 40-hour power reserve
Functions: hours, minutes, sweep seconds; date
Case: stainless steel, ø 36 mm, height 10.2 mm; rose gold bezel, set with 52 diamonds; sapphire crystal; transparent case back; rose gold crown with diamond; water-resistant to 5 atm
Band: reptile skin, folding clasp
Remarks: mother-of- pearl dial
Price: $14,100
Variations: buckle ($13,700); various dials, case materials, and bands

Caliber 36

Automatic; single spring barrel, 100-hour power reserve
Functions: hours, minutes, sweep seconds; **Diameter:** 32.2 mm; **Height:** 4.45 mm; **Jewels:** 27
Balance: screw balance with 4 regulating screws
Frequency: 28,800 vph; **Balance spring:** silicon, swan-neck spring to regulate rate symmetry; **Shock protection:** Incabloc
Remarks: very finely finished movement, three-quarter plate with Glashütte stripe finish, skeletonized rotor with gold oscillating mass
Related caliber: 36-02 (perpetual calendar), 36-03 (panorama date), 36-04 (panorama date and moon phase)

Caliber 37

Automatic; single spring barrel, 70-hour power reserve
Functions: hours, minutes, subsidiary seconds; power reserve indicator; flyback chronograph; panorama date; **Diameter:** 31.6 mm; **Height:** 8 mm;
Jewels: 65; **Balance:** screw balance with 4 gold regulating screws; **Frequency:** 28,800 vph
Balance spring: flat hairspring, swan-neck spring to regulate rate symmetry
Remarks: finely finished movement, beveled edges, polished steel parts, blued screws, three-quarter plate with Glashütte stripe finish, skeletonized rotor with 21-kt gold oscillating mass

Caliber 39

Automatic; single spring barrel, 40-hour power reserve
Functions: hours, minutes, sweep seconds (base caliber); **Diameter:** 26.2 mm; **Height:** 4.3 mm
Jewels: 25; **Balance:** glucydur;
Frequency: 28,800 vph; **Balance spring:** flat hairspring, swan-neck fine adjustment
Shock protection: Incabloc
Related caliber: 39-55 (GMT, 40 jewels), 38-52 (automatic, 25 jewels), 39-50 (perpetual calendar, 48 jewels), 38-41/39-42 (panorama date, 44 jewels), 39-31 (chronograph, 51 jewels), 39-21/39-22 (date, 25 jewels)

Caliber 54-01

Manually wound; 1-minute flying tourbillon; 2 diamond endstones; single spring barrel, 100-hour power reserve
Functions: hours, minutes, subsidiary seconds
Diameter: 30.2 mm
Height: 6 mm
Jewels: 20
Balance: screw balance with 10 weighted screws and 8 regulating screws
Frequency: 21,600 vph
Hairspring: flat spring
Remarks: finely finished movement, beveled edges, polished steel parts, screw-mounted gold chatons, blued screws; three-quarter plate with Glashütte stripe; hand-engraved balance cock

Caliber 58-05

Manually wound; flying 1-minute tourbillon; single spring barrel, 70-hour power reserve
Functions: hours, minutes (off-center), subsidiary seconds (on tourbillon cage); power reserve indicator
Diameter: 36.6 mm
Height: 8.48 mm
Jewels: 85
Balance: screw balance with 18 weighted screws
Frequency: 21,600 vph
Balance spring: silicon
Remarks: finely finished movement, beveled edges, polished steel parts, three-quarter plate with Glashütte stripe finish, blued screws, ratchet wheel with double sunburst brushing, hand-polished structural parts

Caliber 61

Manually wound; single spring barrel, 42-hour power reserve
Functions: hours, minutes (off-center), subsidiary seconds; flyback chronograph; panorama date
Diameter: 32.2 mm
Height: 7.2 mm
Jewels: 41
Balance: screw balance with 18 weighted screws
Frequency: 28,800 vph
Balance spring: flat hairspring, swan-neck fine adjustment
Remarks: finely finished movement, beveled edges, polished steel parts, screw-mounted gold chatons, blued screws, bridges and balance cock with Glashütte stripe finish, hand-engraved balance cock

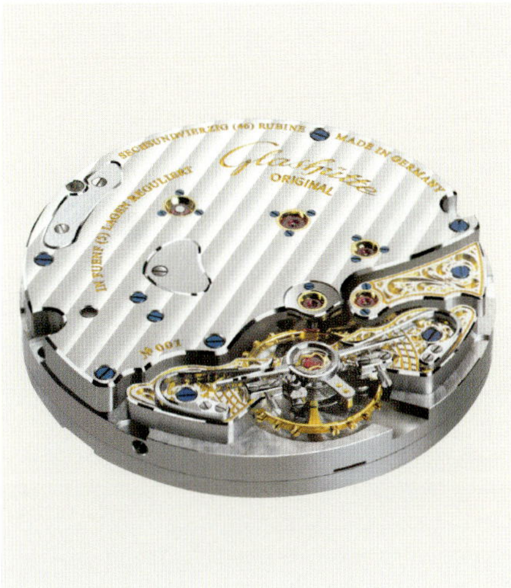

Caliber 65

Manually wound; single spring barrel, 42-hour power reserve
Functions: hours, minutes (off-center), subsidiary seconds; power reserve indicator; panorama date
Diameter: 32.2 mm
Height: 6.1 mm
Jewels: 48
Balance: screw balance with 18 weighted screws
Frequency: 28,800 vph
Balance spring: flat hairspring, duplex swan-neck fine adjustment for rate symmetry
Shock protection: Incabloc
Remarks: finely finished movement, three-quarter plate with Glashütte stripe finish, hand-engraved balance bridge

Caliber 89-02

Automatic; single spring barrel, 72-hour power reserve
Functions: hours, minutes, subsidiary seconds; 2nd time zone, world time with 37 time zones, day/night indicator, power reserve indicator; panorama date
Diameter: 39.2 mm; **Height:** 8 mm; **Jewels:** 63
Balance: screw balance with 4 gold regulating screws
Frequency: 28,800 vph
Balance spring: flat hairspring, duplex swan-neck fine adjustment for rate symmetry
Shock protection: Incabloc
Remarks: winding gears with double sun brushing, three-quarter plate with Glashütte stripe finish, hand-engraved balance bridge

Caliber 90

Automatic; single spring barrel, 42-hour power reserve
Functions: hours, minutes (off-center), subsidiary seconds; panorama date, moon phase
Diameter: 32.6 mm
Height: 5.4 mm
Jewels: 28
Balance: screw balance with 18 weighted screws
Frequency: 28,800 vph
Balance spring: flat hairspring, duplex swan-neck fine adjustment for rate symmetry
Shock protection: Incabloc
Remarks: eccentric, skeletonized, 21-kt gold oscillating weight, hand-engraved balance bridge

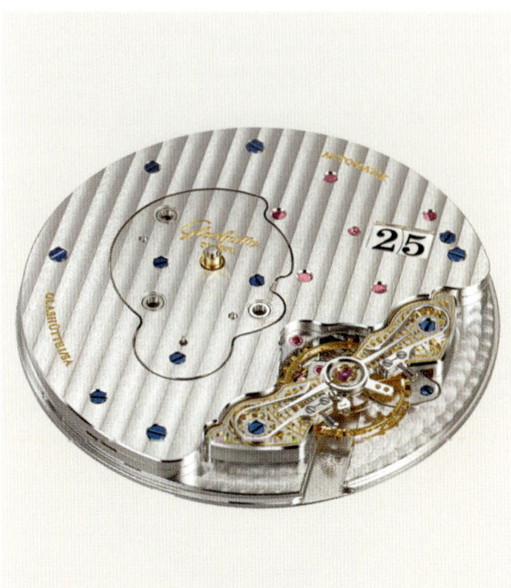

Caliber 91-02

Automatic; inverted movement with rate regulator on dial side; single spring barrel, 42-hour power reserve
Functions: hours, minutes (off-center), subsidiary seconds; panorama date
Diameter: 38.2 mm
Height: 7.1 mm
Jewels: 49
Balance: screw balance with 18 weighted screws
Frequency: 28,800 vph
Balance spring: flat hairspring, duplex swan-neck fine adjustment for rate symmetry
Shock protection: Incabloc
Remarks: finely finished movement, three-quarter plate with Glashütte stripe finish

Caliber 93-02

Automatic; flying tourbillon, single spring barrel, 48-hour power reserve
Functions: hours, minutes (off-center), subsidiary seconds (on tourbillon cage); panorama date, moon phase
Diameter: 32.2 mm
Height: 7.65 mm
Jewels: 48, plus 2 diamond end stones
Balance: screw balance with 18 weighted screws in rotating frame
Frequency: 21,600 vph
Balance spring: flat hairspring
Remarks: finely finished movement, off-center skeletonized rotor, with 21-kt gold oscillating mass

Caliber 96-01

Automatic; twin spring barrel, bidirectional winding in 2 speeds via stepped reduction gear; 42-hour power reserve
Functions: hours, minutes (off-center), subsidiary seconds; 2-digit counter (pusher-controlled, forward and backward); flyback chronograph; panorama date
Diameter: 32.2 mm
Height: 8.9 mm
Jewels: 72
Balance: screw balance with 18 weighted screws
Frequency: 28,800 vph
Balance spring: flat hairspring, swan-neck fine adjustment
Remarks: separate wheel bridges for winding and chronograph, finely finished movement

GRAND SEIKO

In 2017, Shinji Hattori, president of the Seiko Watch Company, announced that the Grand Seiko line had become a separate *manufacture* brand. In the years since, these watches have developed their own identity.

One must say, however, that this separate path had been taking shape for a while already. The Grand Seiko watches always existed in a segment of their own and had become something of a focus for collectors. For the brand's fiftieth anniversary in 2010, the Grand Seiko collection was given a host of new models and started being sold in the European market.

What makes the Grand Seiko collection special is the "Spring Drive" technology invented by a Seiko engineer that took twenty-eight years to perfect and, according to the company, six hundred prototypes. Essentially, it consists of a complex combination of mostly mechanical parts with a small but crucial electronic regulating element to tame the energy from the mainspring. The basic platform for all movements is the 9S mechanical caliber, introduced in 1998. It has been continuously improved over time, notably with the use of a special alloy called SPRON, used for the mainspring and the hairspring. Grand Seiko also draws on micromechanical systems (MEMS) technology to make parts boasting tolerances of a thousandth of a millimeter. Recent models include the Spring Drive Chronograph with the automatic caliber 9R86 with ratchet wheel control and vertical chronograph clutch. The caliber 9S86 Hi-Beat vibrates at 36,000 vph.

It's no surprise then that classic watch fans have welcomed the Grand Seikos into their midst. In the spring of 2022, Grand Seiko presented the first wristwatch with a major mechanical complication: a constant-force tourbillon that was skeletonized to reveal a fine movement. The name of the watch is Kodo, which means "heartbeat" in Japanese. Indeed, its carefully tuned escapement sounds like a beating heart. 2022 also saw the upgrade of the Evolution 9 collection, which now includes five sports watches with spring-drive movements: two GMT watches, two chronographs with GMT function, and a diver's watch water-resistant to 200 meters.

Seiko Holdings
Ginza, Chuo, Tokyo
Japan

Website:
www.grand-seiko.com

Founded:
1960

Number of employees:
90,000 (for the entire holding)

U.S. distributor:
Grand Seiko Corporation of America
1111 MacArthur Boulevard
Mahwah, NJ 07430
201-529-5730
info@grand-seiko.us.com
www.grand-seiko.us.com

Most important collections/price range:
Elegance, Sport, Heritage / approx. $5,000 to $59,000

Evolution 9 Hi-Beat 36,000 "White Birch"

Reference number: SLGH005
Movement: automatic, Grand Seiko Caliber 9SA5; ø 31.6 mm, height 5.18 mm; 47 jewels; 36,000 vph; antimagnetic to 4,800 A/m; 80-hour power reserve
Functions: hours, minutes, sweep seconds; date
Case: stainless steel, ø 40 mm, height 11.7 mm; sapphire crystal; transparent case back; screw-in crown; water-resistant to 10 atm
Band: stainless steel, folding clasp
Price: $9,100

Evolution 9 Spring Drive 5 Days "White Birch"

Reference number: SLGA009
Movement: automatic, Grand Seiko Caliber 9RA5; ø 31.6 mm, height 5.18 mm; 47 jewels; electromagnetic tri-synchro regulator escapement with sliding wheel; antimagnetic to 4,800 A/m; 120-hour power reserve
Functions: hours, minutes, sweep seconds; power reserve indicator (on the movement side); date
Case: stainless steel, ø 40 mm, height 11.8 mm; sapphire crystal; transparent case back; screw-in crown; water-resistant to 10 atm
Band: stainless steel, folding clasp
Price: $9,100

Evolution 9 Spring Drive 5 Days "Ushio"

Reference number: SLGA015
Movement: automatic, Grand Seiko Caliber 9RA5; ø 31.6 mm, height 5.18 mm; 47 jewels; electromagnetic tri-synchro regulator escapement with sliding wheel; antimagnetic to 4,800 A/m; 120-hour power reserve
Functions: hours, minutes, sweep seconds; power reserve indicator; date
Case: titanium, ø 43.8 mm, height 13.8 mm; unidirectional bezel with 0-60 scale; sapphire crystal; transparent case back; screw-in crown; water-resistant to 20 atm
Band: titanium, folding clasp with extension link
Price: $11,600

Constant Force Tourbillon "Kodo"

Reference number: SLGT003
Movement: manually wound, Grand Seiko Caliber 9ST1; ø 35 mm, height 7.98 mm; 44 jewels; 28,800 vph; 1-minute tourbillon; constant force escapement; skeletonized movement; 72-hour power reserve
Functions: hours and minutes (off-center), subsidiary seconds (on the tourbillon cage); power reserve indicator
Case: platinum, ø 43.8 mm, height 12.9 mm; sapphire crystal; transparent case back; water-resistant to 10 atm
Band: calfskin, triple folding clasp
Price: $350,000; limited to 20 pieces

Heritage Spring Drive "Snowflake"

Reference number: SBGA211
Movement: automatic, Grand Seiko Caliber 9R65; ø 30 mm, height 5.1 mm; 30 jewels; electromagnetic Tri-Synchro regulator escapement system with sliding wheel; antimagnetic to 4,800 A/m; 72-hour power reserve
Functions: hours, minutes, sweep seconds; power reserve indicator; date
Case: titanium (with hard coating), ø 41 mm, height 12.5 mm; sapphire crystal; transparent case back; screw-in crown; water-resistant to 10 atm
Band: titanium (with hard coating), folding clasp
Price: $6,200

Heritage Spring Drive 24 Sekki "Shunbun"

Reference number: SBGA413
Movement: automatic, Grand Seiko Caliber 9R65; ø 30 mm, height 5.1 mm; 30 jewels; electromagnetic tri-synchro regulator escapement with sliding wheel; antimagnetic to 4,800 A/m; 72-hour power reserve
Functions: hours, minutes, sweep seconds; power reserve indicator; date
Case: titanium, ø 40 mm, height 12.8 mm; sapphire crystal; transparent case back; screw-in crown; water-resistant to 10 atm
Band: titanium, folding clasp
Price: $6,600

Elegance Hi-Beat 36.000 GMT 24 Sekki "Shōsho"

Reference number: SBGJ249
Movement: automatic, Grand Seiko Caliber 9S86; ø 28.4 mm; 37 jewels; 36,000 vph; antimagnetic to 4800 A/m; 55-hour power reserve
Functions: hours, minutes, sweep seconds; additional 24-hour display (second time zone); date
Case: stainless steel, ø 39.5 mm, height 14.1 mm; sapphire crystal; water-resistant to 3 atm
Band: stainless steel, folding clasp
Price: $6,800

Elegance Mechanic With Manual Winding "Asakage"

Reference number: SBGW267
Movement: manually wound, Grand Seiko Caliber 9S64; ø 28.4 mm; 24 jewels; 28,800 vph; antimagnetic to 4,800 A/m; 72-hour power reserve
Functions: hours, minutes, sweep seconds
Case: stainless steel, ø 37.3 mm, height 11.6 mm; sapphire crystal; transparent case back; water-resistant to 3 atm
Band: calfskin, buckle
Price: $4,900 (not available in the USA)

Sport Quartz GMT

Reference number: SBGN021
Movement: quartz, Seiko Caliber 9F86; antimagnetic to 4,800 A/m
Functions: hours, minutes, sweep seconds; additional 24-hour indicator (second time zone); date
Case: stainless steel, ø 40 mm, height 13.1 mm; bezel with ceramic insert and 0-24 scale; sapphire crystal; water-resistant to 20 atm
Band: stainless steel, folding clasp
Price: $4,550

HABRING²

The name Habring² stands for Maria Kristina Habring and her husband, Richard. This very gifted, fun, and creative couple have been manufacturing fine mechanical works of art in a small workshop in Austria's Völkermarkt. "You get two for one," Richard jokes with the ease of someone whose name, when uttered, triggers sage nodding. Before setting off on his own, he had a very distinguished career at IWC developing a split-seconds chronograph.

The couple's first watch labeled with their own name came out in 2004: a simple three-handed watch based on a refined and unostentatiously decorated ETA pocket watch movement, the Unitas 6498-1. The exceptional quality visible in every detail made Habring² an instant success among connoisseurs.

Since then, they have worked on a wide range of products, notably their movements, like the Caliber A09, which is available in both a manual and a bidirectionally wound automatic version, or the versatile A11, which appears in numerous models with a few iterations. All the little details that differentiate this caliber are either especially commissioned or are made in-house. Its sporty version drives a pilot's watch.

Also more or less in-house are the components of Habring²'s Seconde Foudroyante, with the foudroyante mechanism fed by a separate spring barrel. For the twentieth anniversary of the IWC double chronograph, Habring² built a limited, improved edition. The movement, based on the ETA 7750 "Valjoux," was conceived in 1991-1992 with an additional module between the chronograph and automatic winder.

Suffice to say, the four-member team's technical sophistication is remarkable. They do not shy away from modern materials like silicon, or technologies, or ion etching. But they also keep their feet on the ground, using classic materials like steel. And whatever they can't do in- house, they will purchase to ensure quality, like the perpetual calendar module that goes into the brand's flagship model, the Perpetual Doppel.

Habring² Uhrentechnik OG
Hauptplatz 16
A-9100 Völkermarkt
Austria

Tel.:
+43-4232-51-300

E-mail:
info@habring.com

Website:
www.habring2.com

Founded:
1997

Number of employees:
5

Annual production:
300 watches

U.S. retailers:
Martin Pulli (USA-East)
215-508-4610
www.martinpulli.com
Passion Fine Jewelry (USA-West)
858-794-8000
www.passionfinejewelry.com

Most important collections/price range:
Felix / from $5,800; Erwin / from $ 7,200; Doppel Felix / from $9,800; COS Felix / from $8,900

Felix

Reference number: Felix
Movement: manually wound, Habring² Caliber A11B; ø 30 mm, height 4.2 mm; 18 jewels; 28,800 vph; Triovis fine adjustment, finely finished movement; 48-hour power reserve
Functions: hours, minutes, subsidiary seconds
Case: stainless steel, ø 38.5 mm, height 7 mm; sapphire crystal; transparent case back; water-resistant to 3 atm
Band: calfskin, buckle
Price: $5,400

Erwin

Reference number: Erwin
Movement: manually wound, Habring² Caliber A11S; ø 30 mm, height 5.7 mm; 21 jewels; 28,800 vph; antimagnetic escapement with Carl Haas hairspring, finely finished movement; 48-hour power reserve
Functions: hours, minutes, sweep seconds (jumping)
Case: stainless steel, ø 38.5 mm, height 9 mm; sapphire crystal; transparent case back; water-resistant to 3 atm
Band: calfskin, buckle
Price: $6,800
Variations: various dials

Foudroyante Felix

Reference number: Foudroyante Felix
Movement: manually wound, Habring² Caliber A11F; ø 30 mm, height 7.9 mm; 23 jewels; 28,800 vph; antimagnetic escapement with Carl-Haas balance hairspring, finely finished movement; 45-hour power reserve
Functions: hours, minutes, sweep seconds (jumping); foudroyante display of 1/8th of a second ("seconde foudroyante")
Case: stainless steel, ø 38.5 mm, height 11 mm; sapphire crystal; transparent case back; water-resistant to 3 atm
Band: calfskin, buckle
Price: $7,800
Variations: various dials

Chrono-Felix Sport

Reference number: Chrono-Felix Panda
Movement: automatic, Habring² Caliber A11C-H1; ø 30 mm, height 6.5 mm; 25 jewels; 28,800 vph; tangential screw fine adjustment, antimagnetic escapement with Carl-Haas balance hairspring; monopusher control of chronograph functions; 48-hour power reserve
Functions: hours, minutes, subsidiary seconds; chronograph
Case: stainless steel, ø 42 mm, height 11 mm; sapphire crystal; transparent case back; water-resistant to 5 atm
Band: calfskin, buckle
Price: $7,800
Variations: various dials

Erwin Globetrotter

Movement: automatic, Habring² Caliber A11S-24h; ø 30 mm, height 6.6 mm; 21 jewels; 28,800 vph; antimagnetic escapement with Carl-Haas balance hairspring, finely finished movement; 48-hour power reserve
Functions: hours, minutes, sweep seconds; additional 24-hour display (second time zone)
Case: stainless steel, ø 38.5 mm, height 11 mm; sapphire crystal; transparent case back; water-resistant to 3 atm
Band: calfskin, buckle
Price: $8,000

Chrono-Felix Globetrotter

Reference number: Chrono-Felix Globetrotter
Movement: automatic, Habring² Caliber A11C-24H; ø 30 mm, height 6.5 mm; 25 jewels; 28,800 vph; tangential screw fine adjustment, antimagnetic escapement with Carl-Haas balance hairspring; monopusher control of chronograph functions; 48-hour power reserve
Functions: hours, minutes, subsidiary seconds; additional 24-hour display (second time zone); chronograph
Case: stainless steel, ø 38.5 mm, height 11.5 mm; sapphire crystal; transparent case back; water-resistant to 5 atm
Band: calfskin, buckle
Price: $8,700
Variations: various dials

Chrono-Felix Date

Reference number: Chrono-Felix Date
Movement: automatic, Habring² Caliber A11CD; ø 30 mm, height 6.5 mm; 25 jewels; 28,800 vph; tangential screw fine adjustment, antimagnetic escapement with Carl-Haas balance hairspring; monopusher control of chronograph functions; 48-hour power reserve
Functions: hours, minutes, subsidiary seconds; chronograph; date
Case: stainless steel, ø 42 mm, height 11.5 mm; sapphire crystal; transparent case back; water-resistant to 5 atm
Band: calfskin, buckle
Price: $8,700
Variations: various dials

COS Felix

Reference number: COS Felix
Movement: automatic, Habring² Caliber A11COS; ø 30 mm, height 6.5 mm; 25 jewels; 28,800 vph; Triovis fine adjustment, crown operated control of chronograph functions; 48-hour power reserve
Functions: hours, minutes, subsidiary seconds; chronograph; date
Case: stainless steel, ø 42 mm, height 13 mm; sapphire crystal; transparent case back; water-resistant to 5 atm
Band: calfskin, buckle
Price: $8,400

Foudroyante Felix Date

Reference number: Foudroyante Felix Date
Movement: manually wound, Habring² Caliber A11MFD; ø 30 mm, height 7.9 mm; 23 jewels; 28,800 vph; tangential screw fine adjustment, antimagnetic escapement with Carl-Haas balance hairspring, finely finished movement; 48-hour power reserve
Functions: hours, minutes, sweep seconds (jumping); foudroyante display of 1/8th of a second ("seconde foudroyante"); date
Case: stainless steel, ø 42 mm, height 13 mm; sapphire crystal; transparent case back; water-resistant to 5 atm
Band: calfskin, buckle
Price: $8,700

HAGER

Keeping it simple is the best way to get things going. Hager, owned and operated by American service veteran Pierre "Pete" Brown, is simply named after Hagerstown, where the company was started in 2009. The business model was equally streamlined: create high-quality and affordable automatic watches accessible to those who have never experienced the joy of owning a mechanical watch. The look: rugged and refined, for individuals with a sense of adventure in their bones.

It began with sports watches, classic divers. They were designed by Brown and his small team in Hagerstown. All the cues are there for the watch connoisseur, the brushed and polished cases with beveled edges, two-tiered stadium dial, with brass markers and hands outlined in black and coated with Superluminova. The domed sapphire crystal, 120-click ceramic bezel, and 24 click GMT ceramic bezels are also enhanced with Superluminova. The cases are rated at 20 atm, meaning they are good for more than just washing the dishes. Inside them beats one of a variety of automatic winding Swiss and Japanese mechanical movements that are both installed and regulated in the USA.

Since its modest beginnings, Hager has expanded its line of watches and styles without, however, abandoning the sportive touch. For the elegant, yet casual dresser needing an everyday time-telling tool, there is the Pheon (an arrowhead), with a sandwich dial, or the square Interceptor. Brown has even produced a pocket watch with a tourbillon for under $3,000. Affordable luxury, one might say. "We aren't just selling watches," he says, "we are selling the experience of owning a luxury timepiece."

The company has also boldly sought to make its own movements by using trusty ETA calibers as a basis. And it has ventured into innovative dial design with fume enamels, a technique that gives dials a clear sheen.

Hager Watches
36 South Potomac Street
Suite 204
Hagerstown, MD 21740

Tel.:
240-232-2172

E-mail:
info@hagerwatches.com

Website:
www.hagerwatches.com

Founded:
2009

Number of employees:
2

Annual production:
1,000–1,500 watches

Most important collections/price range:
Commando, GMT Aquamariner, U2, Interceptor, Pheon, $550 to $3,000

Hager Interceptor Blue Fumé

Reference Number: 20035
Movement: automatic, Caliber MD7081 (base ETA 2824 clone stamped and assembled in the USA); ø 26 mm, height 4.6 mm, 25 jewels; 28,800 vph; 40-hour power reserve
Functions: hours, minutes, sweep seconds; date
Case: stainless steel, ø 38 mm x 38 mm, height 11 mm; screw-in crown; sapphire crystal; custom imprinted case back; water resistant to 10 atm
Band: rubber, buckle
Price: $865
Variations: black dial

Hager P01 Skeleton Pocket Watch

Reference Number: P01
Movement: manually wound automatic, Caliber MDI-40, ø 33 mm, height 5.7 mm, 20 jewels; 28,800 vph; 1-minute flying tourbillon; 65-hour power reserve
Functions: hours, minutes
Case: stainless steel skeletonized structure ø 42 mm x 42 mm; height 12.87 mm; sapphire crystal; transparent case back; water resistant to 3 atm.
Band: with brown leather fob
Price: $2,800
Variations: full dial with clous de Paris, stamped guilloché hobnail grain decoration

Hager Glacier Blue Fumé

Reference number: D0529G
Movement: automatic, Soprod C125; ø 25.6 mm, height 5.67 mm; 25 jewels; 28,800 vph; 40-hour power reserve
Functions: hours, minutes, seconds; sweep 2nd time zone
Case: stainless steel, ø 42 mm, height 10.5 mm; sapphire crystal; screw-down case back; water-resistant to 20 atm
Band: stainless steel, stitching, folding clasp with slidelock extension
Price: $1,050
Variations: stainless steel with seconds at 6 o'clock ($800) and 3-hand ($950)

Hamilton International Ltd.
Mattenstrasse 149
CH-2503 Biel/Bienne
Switzerland

Tel.:
+41-32-343-4004

E-mail:
info@hamiltonwatch.com

Website:
www.hamiltonwatch.com
shop.hamiltonwatch.com

Founded:
1892

U.S. distributor:
Hamilton
Swatch Group (US), Inc.
703 Waterford Way, Suite 450
Miami, FL 33126
800-234-8463
Hamilton.US@swatchgroup.com

Price range:
between approx. $500 and $2,500

HAMILTON

The Hamilton Watch Co. was founded in 1892 in Lancaster, Pennsylvania, and, within a very brief period, grew into one of the world's largest *manufactures*. Around the turn of the twentieth century, every second railway employee in the United States was carrying a Hamilton watch in his pocket, not only to make sure the trains were running punctually, but also to assist in coordinating them and organizing schedules. And during World War II, the American army officers' kits included a service Hamilton.

Hamilton is the sole survivor of the large U.S. watchmakers—though only as a brand within the Swiss Swatch Group. At one time, Hamilton had itself owned a piece of the Swiss watchmaking industry in the form of the Büren brand in the 1960s and 1970s. As part of a joint venture with Heuer-Leonidas, Breitling, and Dubois Dépraz, Hamilton-Büren also made a significant contribution to the development of the automatic chronograph. Just prior in its history, the tuning fork watch pioneer was all the rage when it took the new movement technology and housed it in a modern case created by renowned industrial designer Richard Arbib. The triangular Ventura took the watch world by storm in 1957, in what was truly a frenzy of innovation that benefited the brand especially in the U.S. market. The American spirit of freedom and belief in progress this model evokes, something reflected in Hamilton's current marketing, are taken quite seriously by its designers—even those working in Biel, Switzerland. Today's collections are more focused on adventure and aviator watches. But the brand also continues to create revamped versions of its classics, like the PSR, which boldly and loudly whoops up the glorious days of the digital watch. As for the Ventura, it can now be worn as a skeleton now, albeit without the tuning fork movement inside.

Khaki Field Titanium

Reference number: H70545560
Movement: automatic, Hamilton Caliber H-10 (Basis ETA C07.611); ø 25.6 mm, height 4.6 mm; 25 jewels; 21,600 vph; 80-hour power reserve
Functions: hours, minutes, sweep seconds
Case: titanium, ø 38 mm, height 11.68 mm; sapphire crystal; water-resistant to 10 atm
Band: calf leather, buckle
Price: $945

Ventura XXL Skeleton

Reference number: H24625330
Movement: automatic, Hamilton Caliber H-10-S (Basis ETA C07.811); ø 25.6 mm, height 4.6 mm; 25 jewels; 21,600 vph; skeletonized movement; 80-hour power reserve
Functions: hours, minutes, sweep seconds
Case: stainless steel, 45.5 x 46 mm, height 11.25 mm; sapphire crystal; transparent case back; water-resistant to 5 atm
Band: rubber, buckle
Remarks: skeletonized dial
Price: $1,795

Khaki Field Titanium

Reference number: H70215880
Movement: automatic, Hamilton Caliber H-10 (Basis ETA C07.611); ø 25.6 mm, height 4.6 mm; 25 jewels; 21,600 vph; 80-hour power reserve
Functions: hours, minutes, sweep seconds
Case: titanium with black PVD, ø 38 mm, height 11.68 mm; sapphire crystal; water-resistant to 10 atm
Band: calf leather, buckle
Price: $1,945
Variations: without PVD, with green or black dial ($895)

HANHART

The reputation of this rather special company really goes back to the twenties and thirties. At the time, the brand manufactured affordable and robust stopwatches, pocket watches, and chronograph wristwatches. These core timepieces were what the fans of instrument watches wanted, and so they were thrilled as the company slowly abandoned its quartz dabbling of the eighties and reset its sights on the brand's rich and honorable tradition. A new collection was in the wings, raising expectations of great things to come. Support by the shareholding Gaydoul Group provided the financial backbone to get things moving.

Hanhart managed to rebuild a name for itself with a foot in Switzerland and the other in Gütenbach in southern Germany, but it began to drift after the 2009 recession. Following bankruptcy, the company reorganized under the name Hanhart 1822 GmbH and moved everything to its German hometown. It has also returned to its stylistic roots: the characteristic red start/stop pusher grace the new collections, even on the bi-compax chronos of the Racemasters, which come with a smooth bezel. Pilots' chronographs have never lost any of their charm, either, and Hanhart was already making them in the 1930s, notably the Caliber 41 and the Tachy Tele, with asymmetrical pushers and the typical red pusher. These timepieces have to survive extreme conditions, like shocks and severe temperature fluctuations. Hanhart's long tradition and expertise with flyers' chronographs struck a chord with the Austrian Army. It ordered a special edition of the Primus series decorated with the coat-of-arms of the Austrian Airforce on the dial and certified by the military.

Hanhart 1882 GmbH
Hauptstrasse 33
D-78148 Gütenbach
Germany

Tel.:
+49-7723-93-44-0

Fax:
+49-7723-93-44-40

E-mail:
info@hanhart.com

Website:
www.hanhart.com

Founded:
1882 in Diessenhofen, Switzerland; in Germany since 1902

Number of employees:
22

Annual production:
approx. 1,000 chronographs and 30,000 stopwatches

U.S. distributor:
WatchBuys
888-333-4895
www.watchbuys.com

Most important collections/price range:
Mechanical stopwatches / from approx. $600; Pioneer / from approx. $1,070; Primus / from approx. $2,300

417 ES 1954

Reference number: H701.210-7010
Movement: manually wound, Sellita Caliber SW510; ø 30 mm, height 7.9 mm; 23 jewels; 28,800 vph; amagnetic to 16,000 A/m; 58-hour power reserve
Functions: hours, minutes, subsidiary seconds; chronograph
Case: stainless steel ø 39 mm, height 13.3 mm; bidirectional bezel with reference markings, sapphire crystal; water-resistant to 10 atm
Band: calf leather, buckle
Price: $2,240

Primus Desert Pilot Dark

Reference number: 740.550-3720
Movement: automatic, modified Sellita Caliber SW510; ø 30 mm, height 7.9 mm; 27 jewels; 28,800 vph; 48-hour power reserve
Functions: hours, minutes, subsidiary seconds; chronograph; date
Case: stainless steel with black DLC, ø 44 mm, height 16 mm; sapphire crystal; transparent case back; screw-in crown; water-resistant to 10 atm
Band: textile with calfskin overlay, folding clasp
Remarks: movable lugs
Price: $3,370; limited to 100 pieces

Pioneer Mk II 80 Jahre Jubiläum

Reference number: 716L.490-0110
Movement: automatic, ETA Caliber 7753; ø 30 mm, height 7.9 mm; 27 jewels; 28,800 vph; 42-hour power reserve
Functions: hours, minutes, subsidiary seconds; chronograph
Case: stainless steel, ø 40 mm, height 14.8 mm; bidirectional bezel with reference marking; sapphire crystal; transparent case back; water-resistant to 10 atm
Band: textile, buckle
Remarks: special model to celebrate the 80th anniversary of Hanhart pilot chronographs equipped with the Caliber 41
Price: $2,380; limited to 200 pieces

Hautlence
Rundbuckstrasse 10
CH - 8212 Neuhausen am Rheinfall
Switzerland

Tel.:
+41-32-924-00-60

E-Mail:
info@hautlence.com

Website:
www.hautlence.com

Founded:
2004

Number of employees:
10

Annual production:
150-200 watches

U.S. distributor:
Westime
8569 Westime Sunset Boulevard
West Hollywood, CA 90069
310-289-0808
info@westime.com
www.westime.com

Most important collections:
Concepts d'Exception, Vagabonde Series 4, Linear Series 1

HAUTLENCE

Time can be read in so many ways. Back in 2004, after spending years in the Swiss watch industry, Guillaume Tetu and Renaud de Retz decided that their idea for tracking it was new and unique. They were not watchmakers, but they knew whom to bring on board for the genesis of Hautlence, an anagram of Neuchâtel, the town where their small company made its debut. And soon, the first HL model was produced: a fairly large, rectangular timepiece with the ratios of a television set and a lively and visible mechanical life. All good things in watchmaking being small, the big innovation was a "connecting rod," as Tetu calls it, to propel the hour disk. When the retrograde minute hand reaches the end of its arc, it triggers the rod, which advances the hour.

Being unique in terms of design and mechanical hijinks, however, is not a recipe for immediate success, as many high-tech brands know. The road to finding that ideal balance between engineering and design and public perception is often rocky.

In 2012, Hautlence, after surviving the Great Recession, became the first member of the brand-new MELB Holding, headed by Georges-Henri Meylan (formerly of Audemars Piguet) and former Breguet CFO Bill Muirhead. The industrial look with the "television" proportions was maintained, but prices were lowered by using trusty Soprod or Dubois Dépraz calibers.

The next chapter of this uncommon brand began in 2019 with the Sphere, with jumping hours on a sphere and retrograde minutes. The case was given a more distinctive shape. And in 2022 came the Linear Series 1, with a flying tourbillon and a special module made in collaboration with the specialist company Aghenor and, and the fourth Vagabonde series. Both models run on in-house movements (the D50 and the B30 respectively). The new cases are thinner, more elegant, and come on a sportive blue rubber strap. Immediately noticeable are the more orderly dials.

Linear Series 1

Movement: automatic, in-house D50 caliber; 37.4 x 33.0 mm, height 8.2 mm; 21,600 vph; 39 jewels; 239 components decorated and finished by hand; 1-minute flying tourbillon; 72-hour power reserve
Functions: retrograde linear jumping hours
Case: satin-finished and polished steel; 43 x 50.8 mm, height 11.9 mm; crown with rubber ring; 3D beveled sapphire crystal; water-resistant to 10 atm
Band: rubber, steel clasp
Remarks: complex dial construction, rhodium-plated base dial, intermediate sapphire dial with engraved minute track
Price: $64,900; limited to 28 pieces

Vagabonde Series 4

Movement: automatic, in-house B30 caliber; 39.4 x 32.6 mm, height 7.7 mm; 21,600 vph; 34 jewels; 197 components decorated and finished by hand; 72-hour power reserve
Functions: "wandering" hours and minutes
Case: satin-finished and polished steel; 43 x 50.8 mm, height 11.9 mm; crown with rubber ring; 3D beveled sapphire crystal; water-resistant to 10 atm
Band: rubber, steel clasp
Remarks: complex dial construction, rhodium-plated base dial, intermediate sapphire dial with engraved minute track
Price: $33,000; limited to 28 pieces

HL Sphere 02

Movement: manually wound, HTL 501-1; ø 32.00 mm, height 5.5 mm; 38 jewels; 21,600 vph; components decorated and finished by hand; 72-hour power reserve
Functions: spherical hour, retrograde minutes
Case: satin-finished and polished white gold, 39 x 46 mm, height 12 mm, with 3.75 mm dome; polished white gold crown; transparent case back; water-resistant to 3 atm
Band: reptile skin, folding clasp
Remarks: spherical hour, with braked retrograde minute system
Price: $108,900; limited to 28 pieces

HERMÈS

La Montre Hermès SA
Erlenstrasse 31A
CH-2555 Brügg
Switzerland

Tel.:
+41-32-545-0400

E-mail:
info@hermes.com

Website:
www.hermes.com

Founded:
1978

Number of employees:
362

Annual production:
not specified

U.S. distributor:
Hermès of Paris, Inc.
55 East 59th Street
New York, NY 10022
800-441-4488
www.hermes.com

Most important collections/price range:
Arceau, Cape Cod, Clipper, Faubourg, Galop d'Hermès, Heure H, H08, Klikti, Kelly, Medor, Slim d'Hermès / $2,400 to $500,000

Thierry Hermès's timing was just right. When he founded his saddlery in Paris in 1837, France's middle class was up and coming and spending money on beautiful things and activities like horseback riding. Hermès became a household name and a symbol of good taste—not too flashy, not trendy, but quite useful. The advent of the automobile gave rise to luggage, bags, headgear, and soon Hermès, still in family hands today, diversified its range of products—foulards, fashion, porcelain, glass, perfume, and gold jewelry.

Watches were a natural, especially with the advent of the wristwatch in the years prior to World War I. Hermès even had a timepiece that could be worn on a belt. But some time passed before the company engaged in "real" watchmaking. In 1978, La Montre Hermès opened its watch manufactory in Biel.

Hermès went all in to acquire genuine expertise on watchmaking. "Our philosophy is all about the quality of time," says CEO Laurent Dordet. "It's about imagination; we want people to dream." The way there was through "poetic" complications that allowed the company to navigate between classy but plain watches and muscular tool timepieces bristling with complications. On the one hand there was the aesthetics: the lively leaning numerals of the Arceau series or the bridoon recalling the company's equine roots at 12 o'clock for holding the strap. The Cape Cod and Nantucket series recall some of the grand old days of Art Deco, with streamlined forms and orderly dials. As for in-house complications, they are produced in collaboration with external designers, notably Agenhor, one of the industry's top engineering firms. The Slim line includes a perpetual calendar with modern numerals that raise it above the standard retro watch. The clever "Temps Suspendu" lets the wearer stop time for a moment. There are also fascinating moon phase displays and charming countdowns that will add a little romantic pizzazz to the last hour before a rendezvous. For the 2022 Arceau Le temps voyageur (time as traveler), Hermès turned to Chronode in Le Locle for a special module that has the home time on a small dial traveling around watch's face. This remarkable complication won two prizes at the 2022 Grand Prix d'Horlogerie in Geneva

Arceau "Le Temps Voyageur"

Reference number: 057198WW00
Movement: automatic, Hermès Caliber H1837 (with "Le Temps Voyageur") module; ø 32.7 mm, height 4.4 mm; 35 jewels; 28,800 vph; 40-hour power reserve
Functions: hours and minutes (off-center, peripheral); world-time display (second time zone);
Case: platinum, ø 41 mm, titanium bezel with black DLC; sapphire crystal; transparent case back; water-resistant to 3 atm
Band: reptile skin, double folding clasp
Remarks: the "continents" on the world map on the dial are fictitious and named after key terms from the world of Hermès
Price: $28,825
Variations: in stainless steel in a 38-mm case

Slim d'Hermès Perpetual Calendar

Reference number: 053255WW00/MO-CA3.842.331/MM88
Movement: automatic, Hermès Caliber H1950 with Agenhor module; ø 30 mm, height 4 mm; 32 jewels; 21,600 vph; micro-rotor; finely finished movement; 42-hour power reserve
Functions: hours, minutes; additional 12-hour display (second time zone), day/night indication; perpetual calendar with date, month, moon phase, leap year
Case: titanium, ø 39.5 mm, height 9.48 mm; bezel in platinum; sapphire crystal; transparent case back; white gold crown and pushers; water-resistant to 3 atm
Band: reptile skin, buckle
Price: $38,825
Variations: in titanium with rose gold bezel ($38,625)

H08

Reference number: 049433WW00/MO-SP1.742.332/1C1
Movement: automatic, Hermès Caliber H1837; ø 25.6 mm, height 3.7 mm; 28 jewels; 28,800 vph; 50-hour power reserve
Functions: hours, minutes, sweep seconds; date
Case: composite material with graphene, 39 x 39 mm; bezel in ceramic; sapphire crystal; transparent case back; ceramic crown; water-resistant to 10 atm
Band: rubber with textile inserts, double folding clasp
Price: $8,100

Arceau Grande Lune

Reference number: 053222WW00/MO-AR8.810.630/MM7K
Movement: automatic, Hermès Caliber H1837 with "Grande Lune" module; ø 38 mm, height 7.9 mm; 42 jewels; 28,800 vph; finely finished movement; 42-hour power reserve
Functions: hours, minutes, sweep seconds; full calendar with date, weekday, month, moon phase
Case: stainless steel, ø 43 mm; sapphire crystal; transparent case back; water-resistant to 3 atm
Band: reptile skin, folding clasp
Price: $6,350

Slim d'Hermès "L'heure impatiente"

Reference number: 044960WW00/CA4.870.220/MM7K
Movement: automatic, Hermès Caliber H1912 (base with "L'heure impatiente" module); ø 31.96 mm, height 5.9 mm; 36 jewels; 28,800 vph; mainplate and bridges with snail and côtes de Genève decoration; 50-hour power reserve
Functions: hours, minutes; "Heure impatiente" alarm with 60-minute countdown
Case: rose gold, ø 40.5 mm, height 10.67 mm; sapphire crystal; transparent case back; water-resistant to 3 atm
Band: reptile skin, buckle
Price: $39,450

Arceau "Le Temps Suspendu"

Reference number: 036873WW00/AR8.910.220/MM41
Movement: automatic, modified ETA Caliber 2892; ø 26 mm, height 5.6 mm; 28,800 vph; hands can be parked at 12:30, then started again at current time with pusher; double spring barrel; 42-hour power reserve
Functions: hours, minutes; date (retrograde)
Case: stainless steel, ø 43 mm; sapphire crystal; transparent case back; water-resistant to 3 atm
Band: reptile skin, folding clasp
Price: $20,300
Variations: in rose gold ($41,825)

Arceau Hermès Story

Reference number: 059378WW00
Movement: automatic, Hermès Caliber H1912; ø 23.3 mm, height 3.9 mm; 28 jewels; 28,800 vph; perlage and snailing on mainplate; 2 spring barrels; 50-hour power reserve
Functions: hours, minutes
Case: rose gold, ø 43 mm; sapphire crystal; transparent case back; water-resistant to 3 atm
Band: reptile skin, pin buckle
Remarks: dial image uses marquetry, engraving and miniature painting
Price: $63,200; limited to 12 pieces in two editions
Variations: dial images

Kelly

Reference number: 056306WW00
Movement: quartz
Functions: hours, minutes
Case: stainless steel set with 24 diamonds, 20 x 20 mm; sapphire crystal; transparent case back; water-resistant to 3 atm
Band: stainless steel, folding clasp
Remarks: case as a detachable "padlock" on a stainless-steel bracelet
Price: $5,975
Variations: with stainless steel bracelet set with diamonds; without diamonds; in rose gold set with diamonds

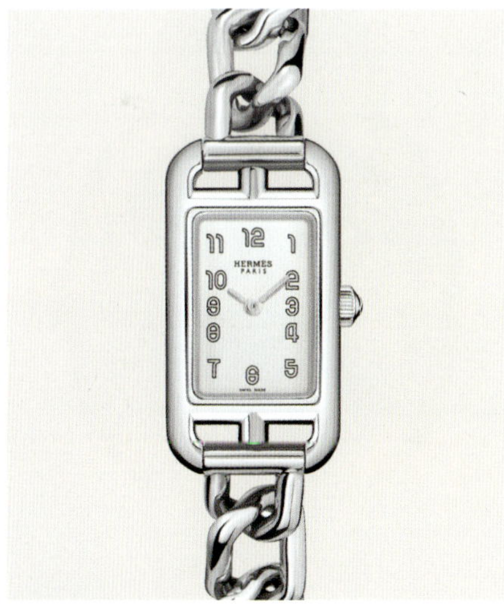

Nantucket

Reference number: 049592WW00/MO-NA2.110.220/4608
Movement: quartz
Functions: hours, minutes
Case: stainless steel, 17 x 23 mm, height 6 mm; sapphire crystal; water-resistant to 3 atm
Band: stainless steel, folding clasp
Price: $3,575
Variations: set with diamonds; in rose gold; in rose gold set with diamonds

H. MOSER & CIE.

H. Moser & Cie.
Rundbuckstrasse 10
CH-8212 Neuhausen am Rheinfall
Switzerland

Tel.:
+41-52-674-0050

E-mail:
info@h-moser.com

Website:
www.h-moser.com

Founded:
1828

Number of employees:
70

Annual production:
approx. 2,000 watches

U.S. distributor:
MELB AMERICAS
info@melb-americas.com
917-974-8245

Most important collections/price range:
Endeavour / approx. $17,500 to $352,000;
Pioneer / approx. $14,200 to $86,900;
Streamliner / approx. $21,900 to $175,000;
Heritage / approx. $15,300 to $275,000

H. Moser & Cie has been making a name for itself in the industry as a serious watchmaker, though not averse to flashes of humor, like the Swiss Mad (sic) Watch made of Vacherin Mont d'Or cheese it presented in 2017 (the cheese for the case is mixed with a hardening resin). And there's the Swiss Alp watch, made to look like an Apple Watch, but with all the essential Moser codes: streamlined design, top-notch technical implementation.

The company was originally founded in Le Locle in 1825 by one Heinrich Moser (1805–1874), from Schaffhausen, at the tender age of twenty-one. Soon after, he moved to Saint Petersburg, Russia, where ambitious watchmakers were enjoying a good market. In 1828, H. Moser & Cie. was brought to life—a brand resuscitated in modern times by a group of investors and watch experts together with Moser's great-grandson, Roger Nicholas Balsiger.

With the support of a host of Swiss and German specialists, the company returned to quality fundamentals. Its claim to fame is movements that contain a separate, removable escapement module supporting the pallet lever, escape wheel, and balance. The latter is fitted with the Straumann spring, made by Precision Engineering, another one of the Moser Group companies.

This small company has considerable technical know-how, which is probably what attracted MELB Holding, owners of Hautlence, and now majority owners of H. Moser shares. Under a new CEO, the brand redefined its style: understatement, soft tones, and subtle technicity. The three core collections— Endeavour, Venturer, and Pioneer—feature "clean" dials in solid colors, including the blackest black, called Vantablack. The month hand on the Endeavour is a mere arrowhead in the center of the dial that points to the hours, which double as the months. The minimalism extends to watches that would otherwise clamor for more complexity. In 2020, the company launched the Streamliner collection with a chronograph that uses the Aghenor mechanism to drive sweep second and minute hands inside a very flowing case. The collection has grown by several models, including a perpetual calendar, and in 2022, a tourbillon in a gold case with a Vantablack dial. It was followed by another symbiotic cooperation, with MB&F, which produced the Cylindrical Tourbillon, "side-cycling" of MB&F's remarkable Flying T.

Streamliner Tourbillon Vantablack

Reference number: 6804-0400
Movement: automatic, Moser Caliber HMC 804; ø 32 mm, height 5.5 mm; 27 jewels; 21,600 vph; escapement with Straumann double hairspring; bidirectional pawl winding; one-minute flying tourbillon; 72-hour power reserve
Functions: hours, minutes
Case: red gold, ø 40 mm, height 12.1 mm; sapphire crystal; transparent case back; screw-in crown; water-resistant to 12 atm
Band: red gold, triple folding clasp
Remarks: Vantablack dial
Price: $119,900

Streamliner Perpetual Calendar

Reference number: 6812-1200
Movement: manually wound, Moser Caliber HMC 812; ø 34 mm, height 6.3 mm; 33 jewels; 18,000 vph; exchangeable escapement with Straumann hairspring, "flash calendar" functions correctable forward and backward; twin spring barrels; fine finishing on movement; 168-hour power reserve
Functions: hours, minutes, sweep seconds; power reserve indicator; perpetual calendar with date, sweep months, leap year indicator on movement side
Case: stainless steel, ø 42.3 mm, height 11 mm; sapphire crystal; transparent case back; screw-in crown; water-resistant to 12 atm
Band: stainless steel, folding clasp
Price: $54,900

Pioneer Cylindrical Tourbillon Skeleton

RReference number: 3811-1200
Movement: automatic, Moser Caliber HMC 811; ø 34 mm, height 5.5 mm; 28 jewels; 21,600 vph; 1-minute flying tourbillon with cylindrical hairspring; skeletonized bridges, pink gold oscillating mass; 74-hour power reserve
Functions: hours and minutes (off-center)
Case: stainless steel, ø 42.8 mm, height 15.3 mm; sapphire crystal; transparent case back; screw-in crown; water-resistant to 12 atm
Band: reptile skin, folding clasp
Price: $86,900

Endeavour Centre Seconds Concept Lime Green

Reference number: 1200-1233
Movement: automatic, Moser Caliber HMC 200; ø 32 mm, height 5.5 mm; 27 jewels; 21,600 vph; escapement with Straumann double hairspring; 72-hour power reserve
Functions: hours, minutes, sweep seconds
Case: stainless steel, ø 40 mm, height 11.2 mm; sapphire crystal; transparent case back
Band: reptile skin, buckle
Remarks: enamel dial with hammered texture
Price: $27,600

Endeavour Small Seconds Total Eclipse

Reference number: 1327-1201
Movement: manually wound, Moser Caliber HMC 327; ø 32 mm, height 4.5 mm; 29 jewels; 18,000 vph; escapement with Straumann hairspring; 72-hour power reserve
Functions: hours, minutes, subsidiary seconds; power reserve display, (on the movement side)
Case: stainless steel, ø 38 mm, height 9.9 mm; 5N red gold flange; sapphire crystal; transparent case back
Band: calfskin, buckle
Price: Price: $25,900
Variations: in white gold, limited to 28 pieces

Endeavour Perpetual Calendar Funky Blue

Reference number: 1800-0204
Movement: manually wound, Moser Caliber HMC 800; ø 34 mm, height 6.3 mm; 32 jewels; 18,000 vph; exchangeable escapement with Straumann hairspring, "flash calendar" functions correctable forward and backward; twin spring barrels; fine finishing on movement; 168-hour power reserve
Functions: hours, minutes, subsidiary seconds; power reserve indicator; perpetual calendar with large date and small sweep month display; leap year display (movement side)
Case: white gold, ø 42 mm, height 11.9 mm; sapphire crystal; transparent case back; water-resistant to 3 atm
Band: kudu leather, folding clasp
Price: $60,000

Heritage Dual Time

Reference number: 8809-1200
Movement: automatic, Moser Caliber HMC 809; ø 32 mm, height 6 mm; 27 jewels; 21,600 vph; 72 hours power reserve
Functions: hours, minutes, sweep seconds; additional 12-hour display (second time zone); date
Case: stainless steel, ø 42 mm, height 11.6 mm; sapphire crystal; transparent case back
Band: kudu leather, buckle
Price: $21,900

Caliber HMC 812

Manually wound; exchangeable escapement with gold pallet lever and escape wheel; "flash calendar" functions correctable forward and backward; twin spring barrel, 168-hour power reserve
Functions: hours, minutes, sweep seconds; power reserve indicator; perpetual calendar with date, sweep month, leap year indicator on movement side
Diameter: 34 mm
Height: 6.3 mm
Jewels: 33
Balance: glucydur
Frequency: 18,000 vph
Hairspring: Straumann
Shock protection: Incabloc

Caliber HMC 902

Automatic; column-wheel control of chronograph functions; horizontal clutch with friction wheel to avoid intermeshing of gears and to minimize accidental jumps when chronograph is activated; inverted movement with tungsten winding rotor under the dial; double spring barrel; 54-hour power reserve
Functions: hours, minutes; flyback chronograph
Diameter: 34.4 mm
Height: 7.3 mm
Jewels: 55
Frequency: 21,600 vph
Remarks: developed with Agenhor for H. Moser & Cie.; 434 parts

HUBLOT

Ever since Hublot moved into a new, modern, spacious factory building in Nyon, near Geneva, the brand has evolved with stunning speed. The growth has been such that Hublot has even built a second factory, which is even bigger than the first. The ground-breaking ceremony took place on March 3, 2014, and the man holding the spade was then-Hublot chairman Jean-Claude Biver, who now also heads LVMH Group's Watch Division.

Hublot grew and continues to grow thanks to a combination of innovative watchmaking and vigorous communication. It was together with current CEO Ricardo Guadalupe that Biver developed the idea of fusing different and at times incompatible materials in a watch: carbon composite and gold, ceramic and steel, denim and diamonds. In 2011, the brand introduced the first scratchproof precious metal, an alloy of gold and ceramic named "Magic Gold." In 2014, Hublot came out with a watch whose dial is made of osmium, one of the world's rarest metals. Using a new patented process, Hublot has also implemented a unique concept of cutting wafer-thin bits of glass that are set in the open spaces of a skeletonized movement plate.

The "art of fusion" tagline drove the brand into all sorts of technical and scientific partnerships and created a buzz that is ongoing, apparently, regardless of the economic environment. Hublot's concept is based on the idea of "being the first, different and unique." To achieve that goal, it has associated its name with major sports events and brands.

The current trend in the industry is to integrate bracelets, an idea that was already floated, even implemented, in the 1970s. And even though Hublot did not exist back then, the new Big Bang Integral does have the feeling of déjà vu. But oddly, a careful look reveals the strap to be a veritable bracelet rather than a strap made of rubber, silicone, patent leather, Kevlar, or jeans. The links are polished in the same way the cases of these watches are and so the Big Bangs look as if they had always come on bracelets. That, however, is not the case.

Hublot SA
Chemin de la Vuarpillière 33
CH-1260 Nyon
Switzerland

Tel.:
+41-22-990-9000

E-mail:
info@hublot.ch

Website:
www.hublot.com

Founded:
1980

Number of employees:
approx. 700

Annual production:
approx. 50,000 watches

U.S. distributor:
Hublot of America, Inc.
100 N. Biscayne Blvd., Suite 1900
Miami, FL 33132
786-405-8677

Most important collections/price range:
Big Bang / $11,000 to $1,053,000;
Classic Fusion / $5,200 to $474,000;
Manufacture Piece (MP) / $82,000 to $579,000

Big Bang Integrated Time Only All Black

Reference number: 456.CX.0140.CX
Movement: automatic, Caliber HUB 1710 (base ETA 670); ø 26.2 mm, height 3.7 mm; 27 jewels; 28,800 vph; 50-hour power reserve
Functions: hours, minutes, sweep seconds; date
Case: ceramic, ø 40 mm, height 9.25 mm; bezel screwed to case back with 6 titanium screws; sapphire crystal; transparent case back; water-resistant to 10 atm
Band: ceramic, folding clasp
Price: $19,900
Variations: various colors

Classic Fusion Chronograph Yellow Gold

Reference number: 541.VX.1130.RX
Movement: automatic, Caliber HUB 1143; ø 30 mm, height 6.9 mm; 59 jewels; 28,800 vph; 42-hour power reserve
Functions: hours, minutes, subsidiary seconds; chronograph; date
Case: yellow gold, ø 42 mm, height 11.9 mm; bezel screwed to case back with 6 titanium screws; sapphire crystal; transparent case back; water-resistant to 5 atm
Band: rubber, folding clasp
Price: $28,300

Big Bang Sang Bleu II Green Ceramic

Reference number: 418.GX.5207.RX.MXM22
Movement: automatic, Caliber HUB 1240.MXM "Unico"; ø 34 mm, height 8.05 mm; 38 jewels; 28,800 vph; 72-hour power reserve
Functions: hours, minutes, subsidiary seconds, (disk display with index corners); chronograph; date
Case: ceramic, ø 45 mm, height 16.5 mm; bezel screwed to case back with 6 titanium screws; sapphire crystal; transparent case back; water-resistant to 10 atm
Band: rubber, folding clasp
Price: $27,300; limited to 200 pieces

Big Bang One Click Steel Pavé

Reference number: 485.SX.1270.RX.1604
Movement: automatic, Caliber HUB 1120; ø 25.6 mm, height 3.6 mm; 25 jewels; 28,800 vph; 40-hour power reserve
Functions: hours, minutes, sweep seconds; date
Case: stainless steel, ø 33 mm, height 10.55 mm; screwed to case back with 6 titanium screws; sapphire crystal; transparent case back; water-resistant to 10 atm
Band: rubber, folding clasp
Remarks: dial set with 11 diamonds; patented quick-change strap system
Price: $19,900
Variations: stainless steel with diamond bezel ($14,600); with full diamond dial ($32,500)

Big Bang Unico Golf Orange Carbon

Reference number: 416.YO.1120.VR
Movement: automatic, Caliber HUB 1580 "Unico"; ø 34 mm, height 10.4 mm; 43 jewels; 28,800 vph; 72-hour power reserve
Functions: hours, minutes, mechanical golf counter for strokes per hole, stroke and hole totalizer
Case: carbon fiber and texalium, ø 45 mm, height 18.1 mm; bezel, screwed to case back with 6 titanium screws; sapphire crystal; transparent case back; water-resistant to 10 atm
Band: rubber with leather overlay folding clasp
Price: $32,500; limited to 100 pieces
Variations: various colors

Square Bang Unico King Gold

Reference number: 821.OX.0180.RX
Movement: automatic, Caliber HUB 1280 "Unico 2"; ø 30 mm, height 6.75 mm; 43 jewels; 28,800 vph; mainplate and bridges with grey coating; 72-hour power reserve
Functions: hours, minutes, subsidiary seconds; flyback chronograph; date
Case: rose gold, 43 mm x 43 mm, height 14.5 mm; bezel screwed to case back with 6 titanium screws; sapphire crystal; screw-in crown; water-resistant to 10 atm
Band: rubber, folding clasp
Price: $43,100
Variations: in all-black ceramic ($26,200, limited to 250 pieces); in titanium with ceramic bezel ($24,100)

Classic Fusion Orlinski Bracelet Titanium White

Reference number: 550.NS.2200.NS.ORL22
Movement: automatic, Caliber HUB 1100; ø 25.6 mm, height 3.6 mm; 25 jewels; 28,800 vph; personalized Hublot rotor; 42-hour power reserve
Functions: hours, minutes, sweep seconds
Case: titanium, ø 40 mm, height 11.1 mm; bezel screwed to case back with 6 titanium screws; sapphire crystal; transparent case back; water-resistant to 5 atm
Band: titanium, folding clasp
Price: $15,700
Variations: with a black dial; set with diamonds ($45,200)

Big Bang Tourbillon Automatic Purple Sapphire

Reference number: 429.JM.0120.RT
Movement: manually wound, Caliber HUB 6035; ø 34 mm, height 5.7 mm; 26 jewels; 21,600 vph; 1-minute tourbillon; micro-rotor, skeletonized movement; 72-hour power reserve
Functions: hours, minutes
Case: sapphire crystal, ø 44 mm, height 14.5 mm; bezel screwed to case back with 6 titanium screws; sapphire crystal; transparent case back; screw-in crown; water-resistant to 3 atm
Band: transparent purple lined rubber, folding clasp
Price: $200,000; limited to 50 pieces

Big Bang Integrated Sky Blue Ceramic

Reference number: 451.EX.5120.EX
Movement: automatic, Caliber HUB 1280 "Unico 2"; ø 30 mm, height 6.75 mm; 43 jewels; 28,800 vph; mainplate and bridges with grey coating; 72-hour power reserve
Functions: hours, minutes, subsidiary seconds; flyback chronograph; date
Case: ceramic, ø 42 mm, height 13.45 mm; bezel mounted onto the case with 6 titanium screws; sapphire crystal; transparent case back; water-resistant to 10 atm
Band: ceramic, titanium folding clasp
Price: $24,100
Variations: various colors

Big Bang Integrated Beige Ceramic

Reference number: 451.CZ.4620.CZ
Movement: automatic, Caliber HUB 1280 "Unico 2"; ø 30 mm, height 6.75 mm; 43 jewels; 28,800 vph; mainplate and bridges with grey coating; 72-hour power reserve
Functions: hours, minutes, subsidiary seconds; flyback chronograph; date
Case: ceramic, ø 42 mm, height 13.45 mm; bezel screwed to case back with 6 titanium screws; sapphire crystal; transparent case back; water-resistant to 10 atm
Band: ceramic, titanium folding clasp
Price: $24,100
Variations: various colors

Big Bang Integrated Green Ceramic

Reference number: 451.GX.5220.GX
Movement: automatic, Caliber HUB 1280 "Unico 2"; ø 30 mm, height 6.75 mm; 43 jewels; 28,800 vph; mainplate and bridges with grey coating; 72-hour power reserve
Functions: hours, minutes, subsidiary seconds; flyback chronograph; date
Case: ceramic, ø 42 mm, height 13.45 mm; bezel screwed to case back with 6 titanium screws; sapphire crystal; transparent case back; water-resistant to 10 atm
Band: ceramic, titanium folding clasp
Price: $24,100
Variations: various colors

Spirit of Big Bang Tourbillon 5-Day Power Reserve Orange Sapphire

Reference number: 645.JO.0120.RT
Movement: manually wound, Caliber HUB 6020; ø 31.65 mm, height 5.7 mm; 25 jewels; 21,600 vph; 1-minute tourbillon; skeletonized movement; 115-hour power reserve
Functions: hours and minutes (off-center); power reserve indicator
Case: sapphire crystal; 42 mm x 51 mm, height 15.3 mm; bezel screwed to case back with 6 titanium screws; sapphire crystal; transparent case back; water-resistant to 3 atm
Band: rubber, folding clasp
Price: $185,000; limited to 50 pieces

Spirit of Big Bang Magic Sapphire

Reference number: 642.JX.0170.RX
Movement: automatic, Caliber HUB 4700 (based on the Zenith El Primero); ø 30 mm, height 6.6 mm; 31 jewels; 36,000 vph; 115-hour power reserve
Functions: hours, minutes, subsidiary seconds; chronograph; date
Case: sapphire crystal; 42 mm x 51 mm, height 14.1 mm; bezel screwed to case back with 6 titanium screws; sapphire crystal; transparent case back; water-resistant to 5 atm
Band: rubber, folding clasp
Price: $90,000; limited to 200 pieces

Caliber HUB 1201

Manually wound skeletonized movement; silicon pallet lever and escape wheel; double mainspring barrel, 240-hour power reserve
Functions: hours, minutes, subsidiary seconds; power reserve indicator; date
Diameter: 34.80 mm
height: 6.8 mm
Jewels: 24
Balance: CuBe
Frequency: 21,600 vph
Balance spring: flat hairspring with fine adjustment
Shock protection: Incabloc
Remarks: 223 parts

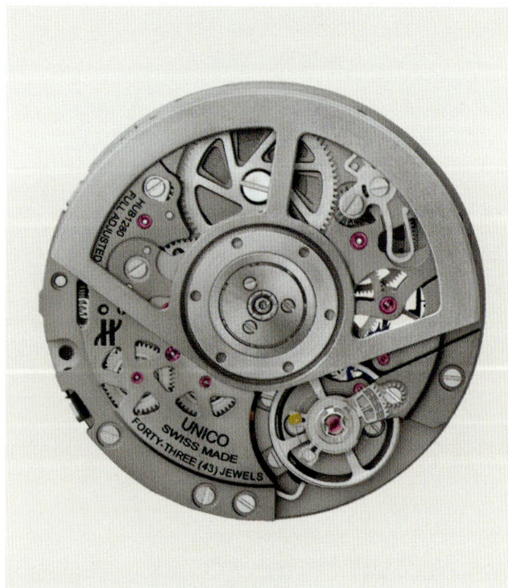

Caliber HUB 6035

Automatic; flying 1-minute tourbillon; decentral microrotor, skeletonized movement; single spring barrel, 72-hour power reserve
Functions: hours, minutes,
Diameter: 34 mm
Height: 5.7 mm
Jewels: 26
Balance: glucydur
Frequency: 21,600 vph
Balance spring: flat hairspring with fine adjustment
shock protection: Incabloc
Remarks: 282 parts

HYT

HYT SA
Rue de Prébarreau 17
CH-2000 Neuchâtel
Switzerland

Tel.:
+41-32-323-2770

E-mail:
contact@hytwatches.com

Website:
www.hytwatches.com

Founded:
2012

Number of employees:
45 (including the sister company Preciflex)

Annual production:
approx. 350 wristwatches

U.S. retailers:
Contact main office in Neuchâtel for information on U.S. retailers

Most important collections/price range:
Various models with a liquid time display / $39,000-$320,000

The earliest timekeepers were water clocks, known as clepsydras. The ancient Greeks had already devised a system by which water was guided from one vessel into another through an orifice of a predetermined diameter. Time was read on a calibrated scale on the second vessel. The three founders of HYT loved this idea of displaying the passage of time with moving fluids, and so they set out to solve the many problems generated if one were to introduce a liquid into a watch.

They developed a closed system made up of a capillary tube that would serve as a time track. It had a special pump-tank at either end that could either receive or pump out liquid. The two tanks had their dedicated space at 6 o'clock. These were based on sensors used by NASA. The piston-driven bellows are made of ultrathin but robust material that bends easily and offers a stable surface. This allows very exact amounts of liquid to be pumped from one tank into the other.

HYT attracted a lot of attention with its unique way of showing time, but the investment costs were very high. In 2021, the company was taken over by Kairos Technology Switzerland (KTS), and an experienced CEO, Davide Cerrato, was hired to relaunch the brand. The new collections were developed by Eric Coudray and Paul Clementi, two top-notch watchmakers who work with TEC Group. The models, the Moon Runner and the Hastroid series, are complicated watches, with a moon phase or a power reserve indicator. They come in a variety of strong colors.

Hastroid Green Nebula

Reference number: H02698-A
Movement: manually wound, HYT Caliber 501-CM; 41 jewels; 28,800 vph; module with two bellows and a capillary tube containing two immiscible fluids, the meeting between the two liquids is the hour pointer; 72-hour power reserve
Functions: hours (retrograde fluidic), minutes; subsidiary seconds; power reserve indication
Case: carbon and black-coated titanium, 52.30 x 48 mm, height 17.20 mm; sapphire crystal; water-resistant to 5 atm
Band: rubber, folding clasp
Price: $70,000; limited to 27 pieces

Hastroid Supernova Blue

Reference number: H02754-A
Movement: manually wound, HYT Caliber 501-CM; 41 jewels; 28,800 vph; module with two bellows and a capillary tube containing two immiscible fluids, the meeting between the two liquids is the hour pointer; 72-hour power reserve
Functions: hours (retrograde fluidic), minutes; subsidiary seconds; power reserve indication
Case: black-coated brass, 52.30 x 48 mm, height 17.20 mm; sapphire crystal; water-resistant to 5 atm
Band: rubber, folding clasp
Price: $70,000; limited to 27 pieces

Moon Runner Red Magma

Reference number: H02757-A
Movement: manually wound, HYT Caliber 601-MO; 42 jewels; 28,800 vph; module with two bellows and a capillary tube containing two immiscible fluids; black-coated movement; 72-hour power reserve
Functions: hours (retrograde fluidic), minutes; day, month, 3D central moon phase, subsidiary seconds; power reserve indicator
Case: carbon and red-coated titanium, 52.30 x 48 mm, height 21.80 mm; sapphire crystal; black-coated titanium crown; water-resistant to 5 atm
Band: rubber, folding clasp
Price: $120,000; limited to 27 pieces

ITAY NOY

Our relationship to precious objects is complex and ultimately reveals as much about ourselves as about the object. Furthermore, the relationship we build up with precious objects is special. Itay Noy's watches, each unique in its look and feel, seem made to foster this conversation and, in many ways, keep it going. Noy, who hails from and lives in Israel, produces watches that immediately fire up the imagination. They are each a talking piece for the public, a touchstone for the owner.

His journey began with the City Squares model, which shows time on the backdrop of a map of the owner's favorite or native city. In 2013, Noy showcased a square watch run on a Technotime automatic movement with a face-like dial that changes with the movement of the hands, a tongue-in-cheek reminder of our daily communication with our phones and the meaning of the frame.

Exploring this intimacy between the watch and the owner is an endless source of inspiration for Noy, a jeweler by trade who, with time, as it were, has begun reaching into the engineer's magic box. He has even worked on a bespoke movement with a Swiss firm. In 2016, he created the Chrono Gears, which essentially runs on a large, invisible circular gear that drives a.m. and p.m. indicators and more. A year later, Time Tone, another "dynamic dial," to use his term, gave the owner the choice of a colored hour disk that only he or she will know, while the minute hand does its work in the center of the dial. The Full Month shows the date or the moon appearing through a circle of digits carved into the dial. The 2019 object is a subtle reminder that hours are almost irrelevant, but every minute counts: ReOrder has the hours digitally flashing on a sandwich dial, haphazardly it would seem. And with the recent Time Quarters, Noy has managed once again to rearrange time on the dial, now into four independent quadrants.

ITAY NOY
19 Mazal Arieh
Old Jaffa
Israel

Tel. (for customer questions):
+972-352-473-80

Fax:
+972-352-473-81

E-mail:
studio@itay-noy.com

Website:
www.itay-noy.com

Founded:
2000

Number of employees:
4

Annual production:
150

U.S distribution:
Please contact Studio ITAY NOY for information.
www.itay-noy.com

Most important collections/price range:
Time Quarters, ReOrder, Full Month, Chrono Gears, Part Time and Night Flight / $2,400 to $16,800

Time Quarters

Reference number: TT.4C
Movement: manually wound IN.AR; ø 36.6mm, Height 5.5mm; 20 jewels; 18,000 vph; 46-hour power reserve
Functions: dynamic dial with 4 time-display windows indicating, hours, minutes, and central seconds
Case: stainless steel, ø 44 mm, height 12 mm; sapphire crystal; transparent case back; water-resistant to 5 atm
Band: hand-made leather band, double folding clasp
Price: $6,800; limited and numbered edition of 24 pieces
Variations: yellow, red, green or four-color time displays

Night Flight Jerusalem

Reference number: NF.Jerusalem
Movement: manually wound skeleton 6497-1; ø 36.6 mm, height 4.5 mm; 17 jewels; 18,000 vph; 38-hour power reserve
Functions: hours, minutes, subsidiary seconds
Case: stainless steel with black PVD, ø 44 mm, height 12 mm; sapphire crystal; transparent case back; water-resistant to 5 atm
Remarks: dial made of layers of lacquer combined with gold
Band: hand-made leather band, double folding clasp
Price: $16,800
Variations: different cities around the world

Chrono Gears

Reference number: CG.BK
Movement: manually wound IN.IP13; ø 36.6 mm, height 5.5 mm; 20 jewels; 21,600 vph; 42-hour power reserve
Functions: chronogear hand indicator for a.m./p.m., chronogear hand indicator for 8 time situations, central hours, minutes, seconds
Case: stainless steel, ø 44 mm, height 12 mm; sapphire crystal; transparent case back; water-resistant to 5 atm
Band: leather, double folding clasp
Price: $6,800; limited and numbered edition of 24 pieces
Variations: blue or black

ReOrder

Reference number: RO.WT
Movement: manually wound, Caliber IN.IP13; ø 36.6 mm, height 5.5 mm; 20 jewels; 21,600 vph; 42-hour power reserve
Functions: dynamic dial with 12 digit-shaped windows indicating the hours, minutes, and central seconds
Case: stainless steel, ø 44 mm, height 12 mm; sapphire crystal; transparent case back; water-resistant to 5 atm
Band: hand-made leather band, double folding clasp
Price: $6,800; limited and numbered edition of 24 pieces
Variations: blue, white and gold plated

Full Month

Reference number: FM-NUM.WT
Movements: automatic, Caliber IN.VMF5400; ø 30 mm, height 3 mm; 29 jewels; 21,600 vph; extra-thin micro-rotor; 48-hour power reserve
Functions: hours, minutes, sweep seconds; full date window
Case: stainless steel, 7.36 mm; sapphire crystal; transparent case back; water-resistant to 5 atm
Band: hand-made leather band, double folding clasp
Remarks: date projected through digit-shaped slits in dial
Price: $9,800; limited and numbered edition of 18 pieces

Identity Hebrew

Reference number: ID-HEB.BL
Movement: automatic, ETA Caliber 2824-2; ø 25.6 mm, height 4.6 mm; 25 jewels; 28,800 vph; 38-hour power reserve
Functions: hours, minutes, sweep seconds; quick-set date window
Case: stainless steel, ø 42.4 mm, height 10 mm; sapphire crystal; screw-down case back; water-resistant to 5 atm
Band: hand-made leather band, folding clasp
Price: $2,800; limited and numbered edition of 99 pieces
Variations: black or brown leather band

Open Mind

Reference number: OM-S.GB
Movement: manually wound, ETA Caliber 6497-1; ø 36.6 mm, height 4.5 mm; 17 jewels; 21,600 vph; openworked dial reveals escapement; 38-hour power reserve
Functions: hours, minutes, subsidiary seconds
Case: stainless steel, ø 44 mm, height 12 mm; sapphire crystal; transparent case back; water-resistant to 5 atm
Band: leather, double folding clasp
Price: $4,400; limited to 99 numbered pieces
Variations: blue or black dial; black or brown leather band

Rally

Reference number: RALLY.BPVD
Movement: manually wound skeleton 6498; ø 36.6 mm, height 4.5 mm; 17 jewels; 18,000 vph, 46-hour power reserve
Functions: hours, minutes, subsidiary seconds
Case: stainless steel with black PVD, ø 44 mm, height 12 mm; sapphire crystal; transparent case back; water-resistant to 5 atm
Band: hand-made leather band, double folding clasp
Price: $5,150; limited and numbered edition of 99 pieces
Variations: stainless steel

X-Ray

Reference number: XRAY6498.INV
Movement: manually wound, ETA Caliber 6498-1; ø 36.6 mm, height 4.5 mm; 17 jewels; 18,000 vph; 46-hour power reserve
Functions: hours, minutes, subsidiary seconds
Case: stainless steel, 41.6 x 44.6 mm, height 10 mm; sapphire crystal; screw-down case back; water-resistant to 5 atm
Band: hand-made leather band, double folding clasp
Price: $3,900; limited and numbered edition of 99 pieces
Variations: black or gold-plated dial; black or brown leather band

IWC

It was an American who laid the cornerstone for an industrial watch factory in Schaffhausen—now environmentally state-of-the-art facilities. In 1868, Florentine Ariosto Jones, watchmaker and engineer from Boston, crossed the Atlantic to the then low-wage venue of Switzerland to open the International Watch Company Schaffhausen.

Jones was a talented designer as well, who had a significant influence on the development of watch movements. Soon, he gave IWC its own seal of approval, the *Ingenieursmarke* (Engineer's Brand), a standard it still maintains today. The company has never deviated from that course, in spite of many different owners. The portfolio includes the rugged and sportive Pilot and Big Pilot watches, the refined Da Vincis, elegant Portofinos, and complicated Portuguese.

IWC movements include the Jones caliber, named for the IWC founder, and the pocket watch caliber 89, introduced in 1946 as the creation of then technical director Albert Pellaton. Four years later, Pellaton created the first IWC automatic movement. In 2020, IWC decided to equip all the Portuguese models with in-house calibers, including the automatic 52000 and 82000 caliber families, which use Pellaton or double-pawl winding mechanisms.

Pilot's watches nowadays play an important role in IWC's portfolio. The company has expanded the Top Gun line in the Pilot's Watches collection to include new models with ceramic cases. Already in 2019, the first models in sand-colored ceramic appeared. The recent models are in green and white, colors developed by IWC that have their own names: "IWC Woodland," for example, is the name of the green ceramic case and dial, which is also named after IWC in the official Pantone color system. Not only was choosing the right shade a challenge, according to IWC, but so was perfectly matching the colors of the other components - from the dial to the rubber straps with textile inlay. Only the pushers and crown are different. The case backs are made of matte black Ceratanium, a titanium-based material.

International Watch Co.
Baumgartenstrasse 15
CH-8201 Schaffhausen
Switzerland

Tel.:
+41-52-635-6565

E-mail:
info@iwc.com

Website:
www.iwc.com

Founded:
1868

Number of employees:
approx. 750

U.S. distributor:
IWC North America
645 Fifth Avenue, 5th Floor
New York, NY 10022
800-432-9330

Most important collections/price range:
Da Vinci, Pilot's, Portuguese, Ingenieur, Aquatimer, Pallweber / approx. $4,000 to $260,000

Pilot's Watch chronograph 41

Reference number: IW388102
Movement: automatic, IWC Caliber 69385; ø 30 mm, height 7.9 mm; 33 jewels; 28,800 vph; 46-hour power reserve
Functions: hours, minutes, subsidiary seconds; chronograph; date and weekday
Case: stainless steel, ø 41.1 mm, height 14.5 mm; sapphire crystal; transparent case back; screw-in crown; water-resistant to 10 atm
Band: stainless steel, folding clasp
Price: $8,500
Variations: with calfskin strap ($7,600)

Pilot's Watch Chronograph 41

Reference number: IW388109
Movement: automatic, IWC Caliber 69385; ø 30 mm, height 7.9 mm; 33 jewels; 28,800 vph; 46-hour power reserve
Functions: hours, minutes, subsidiary seconds; chronograph; date and weekday
Case: bronze, ø 41.1 mm, height 14.5 mm; sapphire crystal; transparent case back; screw-in crown; water-resistant to 10 atm
Band: textile, folding clasp
Price: $8,250

Pilot's Watch Automatic Top Gun

Reference number: IW326901
Movement: automatic, IWC Caliber 32110; ø 28.2 mm, height 4.2 mm; 21 jewels; 28,800 vph; soft iron cap for antimagnetic protection; 72-hour power reserve
Functions: hours, minutes, sweep seconds; date
Case: ceramic, ø 41 mm, height 11.4 mm; sapphire crystal; screw-in crown; water-resistant to 6 atm
Band: textile, buckle
Price: $6,350

Pilot's Watch Chronograph 41 Top Gun Ceratanium

Reference number: IW388106
Movement: automatic, IWC Caliber 69385; ø 30 mm, height 7.9 mm; 33 jewels; 28,800 vph; 46-hour power reserve
Functions: hours, minutes, subsidiary seconds; chronograph; date and weekday
Case: special alloy based on ceramic and titanium (Ceratanium), ø 41.1 mm, height 14.5 mm; sapphire crystal; transparent case back; screw-in crown; water-resistant to 10 atm
Band: rubber with textile overlay, buckle
Price: $12,600

Pilot's Watch Chronograph 41 "Mercedes-AMG Petronas Formula One Team"

Reference number: IW388108
Movement: automatic, IWC Caliber 69385; ø 30 mm, height 7.9 mm; 33 jewels; 28,800 vph; 46-hour power reserve
Functions: hours, minutes, subsidiary seconds; chronograph; date and weekday
Case: titanium, ø 41.1 mm, height 14.5 mm; sapphire crystal; transparent case back; screw-in crown; water-resistant to 10 atm
Band: rubber, buckle
Remarks: special edition for the years of cooperation with the Mercedes-AMG Petronas Formula One Team
Price: $7,850
Variations: with leather strap

Big Pilot's Watch 43

Reference number: IW329306
Movement: automatic, IWC Caliber 82100; ø 30 mm; 22 jewels; 28,800 vph; 60-hour power reserve
Functions: hours, minutes, sweep seconds
Case: stainless steel, ø 43 mm, height 13.6 mm; sapphire crystal; transparent case back; screw-in crown; water-resistant to 10 atm
Band: rubber, folding clasp
Price: $8,950
Variations: various bands and dials

Big Pilot's Watch

Reference number: IW501015
Movement: automatic, IWC Caliber 52110; ø 38.2 mm, height 7.6 mm; 31 jewels; 28,800 vph; 2 spring barrels, Breguet hairspring; Pellaton winding system; antimagnetic soft iron core; 168-hour power reserve
Functions: hours, minutes, sweep seconds; power reserve display; date
Case: stainless steel, ø 46.2 mm, height 15.5 mm; sapphire crystal; screw-in crown; water-resistant to 6 atm
Band: calfskin, folding clasp
Price: $13,200

Big Pilot's Watch Perpetual Calendar Top Gun Ceratanium

Reference number: IW503604
Movement: automatic, IWC Caliber 52615; ø 37.8 mm, height 9 mm; 54 jewels; 28,800 vph; Breguet hairspring, gold oscillating mass; 168-hour power reserve
Functions: hours, minutes, subsidiary seconds; power reserve display; perpetual calendar with date, weekday, month, moon phase, year (4 digits)
Case: special alloy based on ceramic and titanium (Ceratanium), ø 46.2 mm, height 15.4 mm; sapphire crystal; transparent case back; screw-in crown; water-resistant to 6 atm
Band: special alloy based on ceramic and titanium (Ceratanium), folding clasp
Price: $56,700

Big Pilot's Watch 43 Top Gun

Reference number: IW329801
Movement: automatic, IWC Caliber 82100; ø 30 mm; 22 jewels; 28,800 vph; 60-hour power reserve
Functions: hours, minutes, sweep seconds
Case: ceramic, ø 43 mm, height 13.6 mm; sapphire crystal; transparent case back; screw-in crown; water-resistant to 10 atm
Band: textile, folding clasp
Price: $10,500

Portuguese Automatic

Reference number: IW500701
Movement: automatic, IWC Caliber 52010; ø 37.8 mm, height 7.5 mm; 31 jewels; 28,800 vph; Pellaton winding; 168-hour power reserve
Functions: hours, minutes, subsidiary seconds; power reserve indicator; date
Case: pink gold, ø 42.3 mm, height 14.1 mm; sapphire crystal; transparent case back; water-resistant to 3 atm
Band: reptile skin, buckle
Price: $25,600

Portuguese Perpetual Calendar

Reference number: IW503302
Movement: automatic, IWC Caliber 52615; ø 37.8 mm, height 9 mm; 54 jewels; 28,800 vph; Breguet hairspring, gold oscillating mass; 168-hour power reserve
Functions: hours, minutes, subsidiary seconds; power reserve display; perpetual calendar with date, weekday, month, moon phase, year (4 digits)
Case: red gold, ø 44.2 mm, height 14.9 mm; sapphire crystal; transparent case back; water-resistant to 3 atm
Band: reptile skin, folding clasp
Price: $43,400

Portuguese Chronograph

Reference number: IW371611
Movement: automatic, IWC Caliber 69355; ø 30 mm, height 7.9 mm; 27 jewels; 28,800 vph; column-wheel control; finely finished with côtes de Genève and perlage; 46-hour power reserve
Functions: hours, minutes, subsidiary seconds; chronograph
Case: pink gold, ø 41 mm, height 13 mm; sapphire crystal; transparent case back; water-resistant to 3 atm
Band: reptile skin, buckle
Price: $19,200
Variations: with white dial; in stainless steel ($8,400)

Portofino Automatic

Reference number: IW356527
Movement: automatic, IWC Caliber 35111 (base Sellita SW300-1); ø 35.6 mm, height 3.75 mm; 25 jewels; 28,800 vph; finely finished with côtes de Genève; 42-hour power reserve
Functions: hours, minutes, sweep seconds; date
Case: stainless steel, ø 40 mm, height 9.3 mm; sapphire crystal, water-resistant to 3 atm
Band: reptile skin, buckle
Price: $5,050
Variations: in pink gold ($13,400)

Portofino Chronograph

Reference number: IW391037
Movement: automatic, IWC Caliber 75320 (base ETA 7750); ø 30 mm, height 7.9 mm; 25 jewels; 28,800 vph; finely finished with côtes de Genève; 44-hour power reserve
Functions: hours, minutes, subsidiary seconds; chronograph; date and weekday
Case: stainless steel, ø 42 mm, height 13.6 mm; sapphire crystal, water-resistant to 3 atm
Band: reptile skin, buckle
Price: $6,700
Variations: in pink gold ($17,300); various dials and bands

Portofino Hand-Wound Moon Phase

Reference number: IW516401
Movement: manually wound, IWC Caliber 59800; ø 37.8 mm; 30 jewels; 28,800 vph; Breguet hairspring; finely finished with côtes de Genève; 192-hour power reserve
Functions: hours, minutes, subsidiary seconds; power reserve display; date, moon phase
Case: stainless steel, ø 45 mm, height 13.2 mm; sapphire crystal; transparent case back; water-resistant to 3 atm
Band: reptile skin, buckle
Price: $13,900
Variations: in pink gold ($24,800)

Caliber 82200

Automatic; double-pawl winding (Pellaton system); single spring barrel, 60-hour power reserve
Functions: hours, minutes, subsidiary seconds
Diameter: 30 mm
height: 6.6 mm
Jewels: 31
Frequency: 28,800 vph
Hairspring: flat hairspring
Remarks: movement with perlage and finely finished with côtes de Genève

Caliber 69355

Automatic; column-wheel control of chronograph functions; single spring barrel, 46-hour power reserve
Functions: hours, minutes, subsidiary seconds; chronograph
Diameter: 30 mm
height: 7.9 mm
Jewels: 27
Balance: glucydur
Frequency: 28,800 vph
Hairspring: flat hairspring
Remarks: movement with perlage and finely finished with côtes de Genève

Caliber 82650

Automatic; double-pawl winding (Pellaton system); single spring barrel, 60-hour power reserve
Functions: hours, minutes, sweep seconds; perpetual calendar with date, weekday, month, moon phase
Diameter: 30 mm
height: 7.8 mm
Jewels: 46
Frequency: 28,800 vph
Hairspring: flat hairspring
Remarks: movement with perlage and finely finished with côtes de Genève; 326 parts

Caliber 52615

Automatic; double-pawl winding (Pellaton system) with ceramic wheels; double spring barrel, 168-hour power reserve
Functions: hours, minutes, subsidiary seconds; power reserve indicator; perpetual calendar with month, weekday, date, double moon phase (for northern and southern hemispheres), 4-digit year display
Diameter: 37.8 mm
height: 9 mm
Jewels: 54
Balance: with variable inertia
Frequency: 28,800 vph
Hairspring: Breguet
Shock protection: Incabloc

Caliber 89361

Automatic; double-pawl winding (Pellaton system), column-wheel control of chronograph functions; single spring barrel, 68-hour power reserve
Base caliber: 89000
Functions: hours, minutes, subsidiary seconds; flyback chronograph; date
Diameter: 30 mm
height: 7.46 mm
Jewels: 38
Balance: glucydur with variable inertia
Frequency: 28,800 vph
Hairspring: flat hairspring
Shock protection: Incabloc
Remarks: concentric chronograph totalizer for minutes and hours

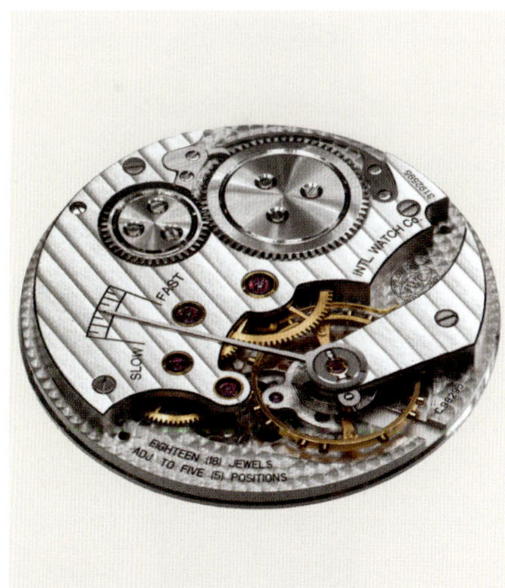

Caliber 98295 "Jones"

Manually wound; single spring barrel, 46-hour power reserve
Base caliber: 98000
Functions: hours, minutes, subsidiary seconds
Diameter: 38.2 mm
height: 5.3 mm
Jewels: 18
Balance: screw balance with fine adjustment cams
Frequency: 18,000 vph
Balance spring: Breguet
Shock protection: Incabloc
Remarks: exceptionally long regulator index; three-quarter plate of German silver, hand-engraved balance cock

JAEGER-LECOULTRE

The Jaeger-LeCoultre *manufacture* has had a long and tumultuous history. In 1833, Antoine LeCoultre opened his own workshop for the production of gearwheels. Having made his fortune, he then did what many other artisans did; in 1866, he had a large house built and brought together all the craftspeople needed to produce timepieces, from the watchmakers to the turners and polishers. He outfitted the workshop with the most modern machinery of the day, all powered by a steam engine. "La Grande Maison" was the first watch *manufacture* in the Vallée de Joux.

At the start of the twentieth century, the grandson of the company founder, Jacques-David LeCoultre, built slender, complicated watches for the Paris manufacturer Edmond Jaeger. The Frenchman was so impressed with these that, after a few years of fruitful cooperation, he engineered a merger of the two companies.

In the 1970s, the German VDO Group (later Mannesmann) took over the company and helped it weather the quartz crisis.

Thanks to its inclusion in the Richemont stable, Jaeger-LeCoultre continued to grow. A vast array of calibers (around 1,200), including minute repeaters, tourbillons, and other *grandes complications*, a lubricant-free movement, and more than 400 patents, tell their own story. Today, it is the largest employer in the Vallée de Joux—just as it was back in the 1860s. The most enduring collection produced by the brand is probably the Reverso, which can swivel around to show a second watch face on the back. Jaeger-LeCoultre boasts other iconic collections, like the Master, the Polaris, and the Atmos.

The brand has always managed to unify technical wizardry with a very fine sense of aesthetics, which is expressed in many models illustrating the many métiers d'art from the watch world. The Master Grande Tradition Grande Complication, for example, displays sidereal time combined with a minute repeater that rings on sapphire crystal gongs soldered to the sapphire crystal itself for a more penetrating sound. As for the Rendez-Vous line, in 2022 it featured a poetic shooting star that crosses the dial apparently randomly.

Manufacture Jaeger-LeCoultre
Rue de la Golisse, 8
CH-1347 Le Sentier
Switzerland

Tel.:
+41-21-852-0202

E-mail:
info@jaeger-lecoultre.com
client.relations.us@jaeger-lecoultre.com

Website:
www.jaeger-lecoultre.com

Founded:
1833

Number of employees:
over 1,000

Annual production:
approx. 50,000 watches

U.S. distributor:
Jaeger-LeCoultre
645 Fifth Avenue
New York, NY 10022
877-552-1833
www.jaeger-lecoultre.com

Most important collections/price range:
Atmos / starting at $7,100; Duomètre / starting at $41,700; Master / starting at $7,250; Polaris / starting at $7,250; Rendez-Vous / starting at $7,850; Reverso / starting at $4,750

Master Hybris Artistica Calibre 945 Atomium

Reference number: Q5263481
Movement: manually wound, JLC Caliber 945; ø 34.7 mm, height 12.56 mm; 52 jewels; 28,800 vph; flying one-minute tourbillon, 40-hour power reserve
Functions: hours, minutes, sidereal time (on the tourbillon cage) with star chart; minute repeater, with crystal gongs affixed on the sapphire crystal
Case: white gold, ø 45 mm, height 16.05 mm; sapphire crystal; water-resistant to 5 atm
Band: reptile skin, double folding clasp
Price: $535,000; limited to 5 pieces

Master Hybris Artistica Calibre 945 Galaxia

Reference number: Q5262470
Movement: manually wound, JLC Caliber 945; ø 34.7 mm, height 12.56 mm; 52 jewels; 28,800 vph; flying one-minute tourbillon, 40-hour power reserve
Functions: hours, minutes, sidereal time (on the tourbillon cage) with star chart; minute repeater, with crystal gongs affixed on the sapphire crystal
Case: red gold, ø 45 mm, height 16.05 mm; sapphire crystal; water-resistant to 5 atm
Band: reptile skin, double folding clasp
Price: $515,000; limited to 5 pieces

Master Grande Tradition Calibre 948

Reference number: Q52834E1
Movement: manually wound, JLC Caliber 948; ø 43 mm, height 11.24 mm; 42 jewels; 28,800 vph; flying one-minute tourbillon, 48-hour power reserve
Functions: hours, minutes, subsidiary seconds; world time display (second time zone)
Case: white gold, ø 43 mm, height 14.13 mm; sapphire crystal; transparent case back; water-resistant to 5 atm
Band: reptile skin, double folding clasp
Price: on request; limited to 20 pieces

Master Control Memovox Timer

Reference number: Q410257J
Movement: automatic, JLC Caliber 956AA; ø 28 mm, height 7.47 mm; 24 jewels; 28,800 vph; 45-hour power reserve
Functions: hours, minutes, sweep seconds; alarm clock; (set to the minute); date
Case: red gold, ø 40 mm, height 12.39 mm; crown-adjustable wake-up times in the dial center; sapphire crystal; transparent case back; water-resistant to 5 atm
Band: reptile skin, double folding clasp
Price: $33,600

Master Control Calendar

Reference number: Q4148480
Movement: automatic, JLC Caliber 866AA; ø 26 mm, height 6.15 mm; 34 jewels; 28,800 vph; 70-hour power reserve
Functions: hours, minutes, subsidiary seconds; full calendar with date, weekday, month, moon phase
Case: stainless steel, ø 40 mm, height 10.95 mm; sapphire crystal; transparent case back; water-resistant to 5 atm
Band: calfskin, double folding clasp
Price: $13,100

Master Control Date

Reference number: Q4018480
Movement: automatic, JLC Caliber 866AA; ø 26 mm, height 6.15 mm; 34 jewels; 28,800 vph; 70-hour power reserve
Functions: hours, minutes, sweep seconds; date
Case: stainless steel, ø 40 mm, height 8.78 mm; sapphire crystal; transparent case back; water-resistant to 5 atm
Band: calfskin, double folding clasp
Price: $8,700

Master Control Chronograph Calendar

Reference number: Q413812J
Movement: automatic, JLC Caliber 759; ø 25.6 mm, 41 jewels; 28,800 vph; silicon escapement, column wheel control of chronograph functions, gold rotor; 65-hour power reserve
Functions: hours, minutes, subsidiary seconds; chronograph; full calendar with date, weekday, month, moon phase
Case: stainless steel, ø 40 mm, height 12.05 mm; sapphire crystal; transparent case back; water-resistant to 5 atm
Band: stainless steel, double folding clasp
Price: $17,500

Master Control Calendar

Reference number: Q4148120
Movement: automatic, JLC Caliber 866AA; ø 26 mm, height 6.15 mm; 34 jewels; 28,800 vph; 70-hour power reserve
Functions: hours, minutes, subsidiary seconds; full calendar with date, weekday, month, moon phase
Case: stainless steel, ø 40 mm, height 10.95 mm; sapphire crystal; transparent case back; water-resistant to 5 atm
Band: calfskin, double folding clasp
Price: $14,500

Master Ultra Thin Moon

Reference number: Q1368480
Movement: automatic, JLC Caliber 925AA; ø 26 mm, height 4.9 mm; 30 jewels; 28,800 vph; 70-hour power reserve
Functions: hours, minutes, sweep seconds; date, moon phase
Case: stainless steel, ø 39 mm, height 10.04 mm; sapphire crystal; transparent case back; water-resistant to 5 atm
Band: reptile skin, buckle
Price: $11,000

Master Ultra Thin Moon

Reference number: Q1368471
Movement: automatic, JLC Caliber 925AA; ø 26 mm, height 4.9 mm; 30 jewels; 28,800 vph; 70-hour power reserve
Functions: hours, minutes, sweep seconds; date, moon phase
Case: stainless steel, ø 39 mm, height 10.04 mm; sapphire crystal; transparent case back; water-resistant to 5 atm
Band: reptile skin, buckle
Price: $11,000

Master Ultra Thin Moon

Reference number: Q1368430
Movement: automatic, JLC Caliber 925/2; ø 26 mm, height 4.9 mm; 30 jewels; 28,800 vph; 70-hour power reserve
Functions: hours, minutes, sweep seconds; date, moon phase
Case: stainless steel, ø 39 mm, height 10.04 mm; sapphire crystal; transparent case back; water-resistant to 5 atm
Band: reptile skin, buckle
Price: $11,000
Variations: in pink gold ($21,700)

Master Ultra Thin Moon

Reference number: Q1362510
Movement: automatic, JLC Caliber 925AA; ø 26 mm, height 4.9 mm; 30 jewels; 28,800 vph; 70-hour power reserve
Functions: hours, minutes, sweep seconds; date, moon phase
Case: pink gold, ø 39 mm, height 10.04 mm; sapphire crystal; transparent case back; water-resistant to 5 atm
Band: reptile skin, buckle
Price: $21,700
Variations: in stainless steel ($11,000)

Master Ultra Thin Moon

Reference number: Q1362502
Movement: automatic, JLC Caliber 925AA; ø 26 mm, height 4.9 mm; 30 jewels; 28,800 vph; 70-hour power reserve
Functions: hours, minutes, sweep seconds; date, moon phase
Case: red gold, ø 39 mm, height 10.04 mm; bezel set with 60 diamonds; sapphire crystal; transparent case back; water-resistant to 5 atm
Band: reptile skin, buckle
Price: $28,200
Variations: in stainless steel ($11,000)

Polaris Perpetual Calendar

Reference number: Q9082680
Movement: automatic, JLC Caliber 868AA; ø 26 mm, height 4.72 mm; 46 jewels; 28,800 vph; 70-hour power reserve
Functions: hours, minutes, sweep seconds; perpetual calendar with date, weekday, month, moon phase, year display (four digits)
Case: pink gold, ø 42 mm, height 11.97 mm; sapphire crystal; transparent case back; water-resistant to 5 atm
Band: rubber, buckle
Price: $48,100

Polaris Perpetual Calendar

Reference number: Q9088180
Movement: automatic, JLC Caliber 868AA; ø 26 mm, height 4.72 mm; 46 jewels; 28,800 vph; 70-hour power reserve
Functions: hours, minutes, sweep seconds; perpetual calendar with date, weekday, month, moon phase, year display (four digits)
Case: stainless steel, ø 42 mm, height 11.97 mm; sapphire crystal; transparent case back; water-resistant to 5 atm
Band: stainless steel, folding clasp
Price: $32,800

Polaris Date Green

Reference number: Q906863J
Movement: automatic, JLC Caliber 899AB; ø 26 mm, height 4.6 mm; 32 jewels; 28,800 vph; 70-hour power reserve
Functions: hours, minutes, sweep seconds; date
Case: stainless steel, ø 42 mm, height 13.1 mm; crown-adjustable inner bezel with 0-60 scale;sapphire crystal; water-resistant to 20 atm
Band: rubber, double folding clasp
Price: $9,450; limited to 800 pieces

Polaris Mariner Memovox

Reference number: Q9038180
Movement: automatic, JLC Caliber 956AA; ø 28 mm, height 7.47 mm; 24 jewels; 28,800 vph; 45-hour power reserve
Functions: hours, minutes, sweep seconds; alarm clock; date
Case: stainless steel, ø 42 mm, height 15.63 mm; crown-activated scale ring with 0-60 scale and waking time disk in the dial middle; sapphire crystal; transparent case back; water-resistant to 30 atm
Band: stainless steel, double folding clasp
Price: $18,100

Shooting Star

Reference number: Q364247J
Movement: automatic, JLC Caliber 734; height 5.66 mm; 52 jewels; 28,800 vph; 70-hour power reserve
Functions: hours, minutes, shooting star (on demand)
Case: pink gold, ø 36 mm, height 11.11 mm; scale; bezel set with 181 diamonds; sapphire crystal; water-resistant to 5 atm
Band: leather, double folding clasp
Remarks: blue aventurine dial; a shooting star crosses the dial 4 to 6 times an hour when the watch is worn
Price: $84,500

Polaris Chronograph

Reference number: Q9028471
Movement: automatic, JLC Caliber 751H; ø 25.6 mm, height 5.7 mm; 37 jewels; 28,800 vph; skeletonized rotor; 65-hour power reserve
Functions: hours, minutes; chronograph
Case: stainless steel, ø 42 mm, height 11.9 mm; sapphire crystal; transparent case back; water-resistant to 10 atm
Band: calfskin strap, double folding clasp
Price: $12,200
Variations: with stainless steel bracelet ($10,700)

Reverso Quadriptyque

Reference number: Q7103420
Movement: manually wound, JLC Caliber 185; 97 jewels; 28,800 vph; 1-minute tourbillon; 50-hour power reserve
Functions: 1st dial: hours, minutes, subsidiary seconds (on the tourbillon cage); perpetual calendar with large date, weekday, month, leap year, day/night display; 2nd dial: hours (digital, jumping), minutes; minute repeater; 3rd dial: eternal (synodic, draconic and anomalistic) moon calendar, month, year (4-digits); 4th dial: moon phases of the southern hemisphere
Case: white gold, 31 x 51.2 mm, height 15.15 mm; sapphire crystal; transparent case back
Band: reptile skin, double folding clasp
Remarks: first wristwatch with four dials, two in the base case
Price: $1,350,000; limited to 10 pieces

Reverso Tribute Small Seconds

Reference number: Q3978430
Movement: manually wound, JLC Caliber 822/2; 17.2 x 22 mm, height 2.94 mm; 19 jewels; 21,600 vph; 42-hour power reserve
Functions: hours, minutes, subsidiary seconds
Case: stainless steel, 27.4 mm x 45.6 mm, height 8.5 mm; sapphire crystal; water-resistant to 3 atm
Band: calfskin, double folding clasp
Remarks: case turns and swivels 180°
Price: $8,850

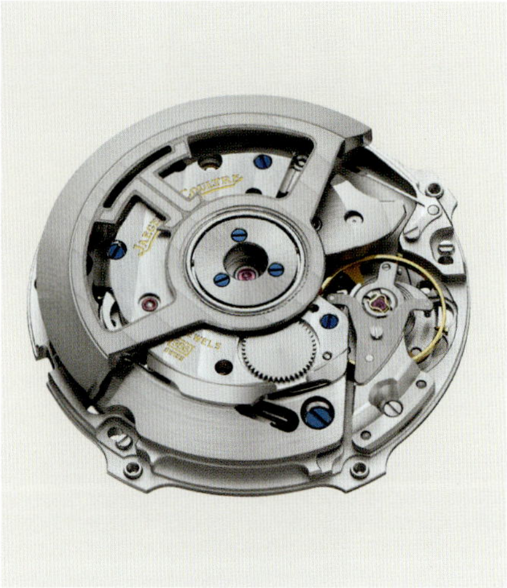

Caliber 956AA

Automatic; automatic winding for time and alarm mechanisms; single spring barrel, 44-hour power reserve
Functions: hours, minutes, sweep seconds; date; alarm
Diameter: 28 mm
Height: 7.47 mm
Jewels: 24
Balance: glucydur
Frequency: 28,800 vph
Balance spring: flat hairspring
Remarks: perlage on mainplate, bridges with côtes de Genève, element for sounding board; 271 parts

Caliber 899AC

Automatic; silicon escapement; gold rotor; single spring barrel, 70-hour power reserve
Functions: hours, minutes, sweep seconds; date
Diameter: 26 mm
Height: 3.7 mm
Jewels: 32
Frequency: 28,800 vph
Remarks: mainplate with perlage, bridges with côtes de Genève; 218 parts

Caliber 866AA

Automatic; silicon escapement; gold rotor; single spring barrel, 70-hour power reserve
Functions: hours, minutes, subsidiary seconds; full calendar with date, weekday, month, moon phase
Diameter: 26 mm
Height: 5.65 mm
Jewels: 34
Balance: glucydur
Frequency: 28,800 vph
Remarks: mainplate with perlage, bridges with côtes de Genève

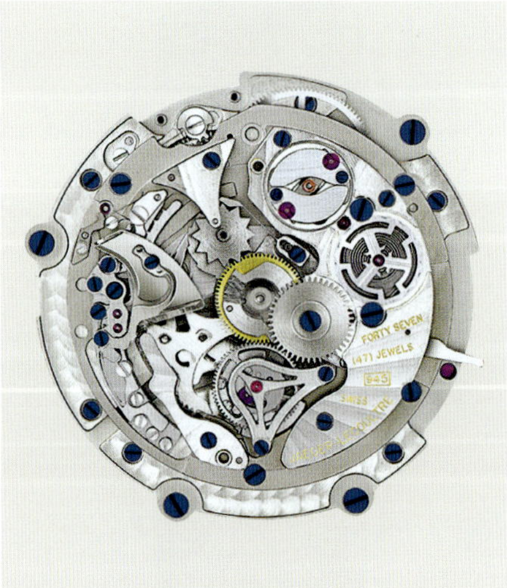

Caliber 945

Manually wound; silicon anchor with integrated pallets, flying tourbillon rotates with dial in 56 minutes (sidereal time, star time); single spring barrel, 48-hour power reserve
Functions: hours, minutes, hours, quarter hour and minute repeater; perpetual calendar with, date, month, celestial map with zodiac signs
Diameter: 34.7 mm
Height: 12.62 mm
Jewels: 49
Balance: screw balance
Frequency: 28,800 vph
Hairspring: flat hairspring
Remarks: repetition with "trebuchet" hammers to strengthen the impulses; 527 parts

Caliber 925AA

Automatic; single spring barrel, 70-hour power reserve
Functions: hours, minutes, sweep seconds; date, moon phase
Diameter: 26 mm
Height: 4.9 mm
Jewels: 30
Frequency: 28,800 vph
Remarks: mainplate with perlage, bridges with côtes de Genève; 245 parts

Caliber 759

Automatic; silicon escapement, column-wheel control of chronograph functions, gold rotor; single spring barrel, 65-hour power reserve
Functions: hours, minutes, subsidiary seconds; chronograph; full calendar with date, weekday, month, moon phase
Diameter: 25.6 mm
Jewels: 41
Frequency: 28,800 vph

Caliber 751

Automatic; column wheel control of chronograph functions; double spring barrel, 65-hour power reserve
Functions: hours, minutes, subsidiary seconds; chronograph
Diameter: 26.2 mm
Height: 5.7 mm
Jewels: 37
Balance: screw balance with 4 weights
Frequency: 28,800 vph
Balance spring: flat hairspring
Shock protection: Kif
Remarks: 262 parts

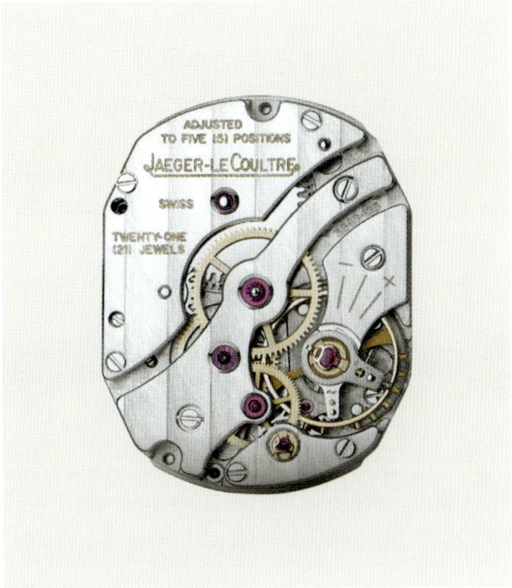

Caliber 822/2

Manually wound; single spring barrel, 42-hour power reserve
Functions: hours, minutes, subsidiary seconds
Dimensions: 17.2 x 22 mm
Height: 2.94 mm
Jewels: 19
Balance: screw balance
Frequency: 21,600 vph
Hairspring: flat hairspring

Caliber 925/2

Automatic; single spring barrel, 70-hour power reserve
Functions: hours, minutes, sweep seconds; date, moon phase
Diameter: 26 mm
Height: 4.9 mm
Jewels: 30
Frequency: 28,800 vph
Remarks: 245 parts

Caliber 978F

Automatic; 1-minute tourbillon; gold rotor; single spring barrel, 45-hour power reserve
Functions: hours, minutes, subsidiary seconds (on the tourbillon cage); hand date (jumping from the 15th to the 16th of the month)
Diameter: 30 mm
Height: 7.2 mm
Jewels: 33
Balance: glucydur with weighted screws
Frequency: 28,800 vph
Hairspring: Breguet-Hairspring
Shock protection: Kif
Remarks: mainplate with perlage, bridges with côtes de Genève; 302 parts

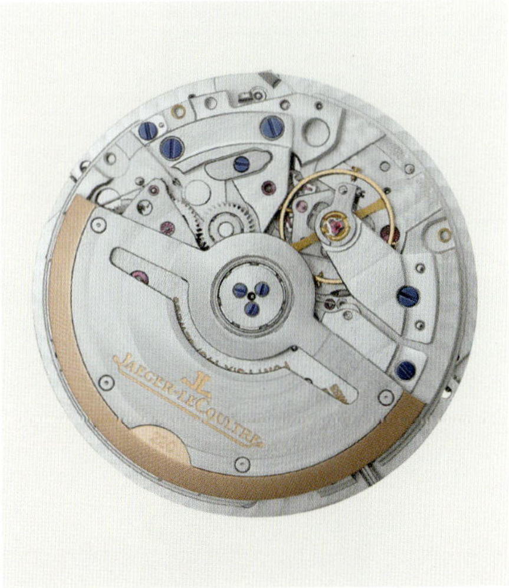

Caliber 868/A2

Automatic; single spring barrel, 70-hour power reserve
Functions: hours, minutes, sweep seconds; perpetual calendar with date, weekday, month, moon phase, 4-digit year display
Diameter: 26 mm
Height: 4.72 mm
Jewels: 46
Balance: glucydur
Frequency: 28,800 vph
Remarks: 332 parts

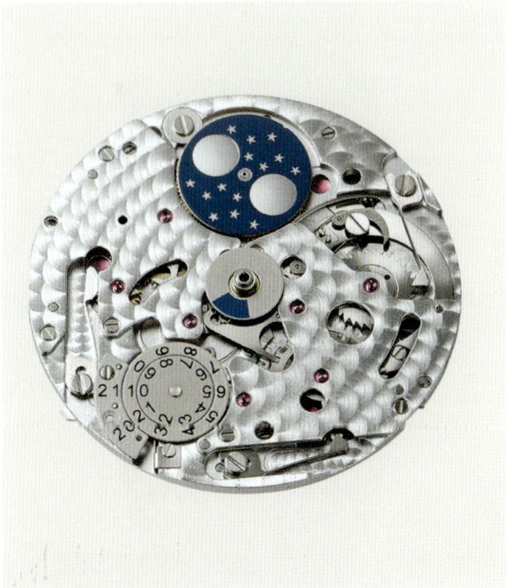

Caliber 868/1

Automatic; single spring barrel, 38-hour power reserve
Functions: hours, minutes, sweep seconds; perpetual calendar with date, weekday, month, moon phase, 4-digit year display
Diameter: 27.8 mm
Height: 4.72 mm
Jewels: 46
Balance: glucydur
Frequency: 28,800 vph
Remarks: 336 parts

JAQUET DROZ

Though this watch brand first gained real notice when it was bought by the Swatch Group in 2001, Jaquet Droz looks back on a long, 280-year-old tradition. Pierre Jaquet-Droz (1721–1790) was actually supposed to be a pastor, but instead followed the call to become a mechanic and a watchmaker. In the mid-eighteenth century, he began to push the limits of micromechanics, and his enthusiasm for it quickly led him to work on watch mechanisms and more complicated movements, which he attempted to operate through purely mechanical means.

Jaquet-Droz became famous in Europe for his automatons. More than once, he had to answer to religious institutions, whose guardians of public morals suspected there might be some devil's work and witchcraft behind his mechanical children, scribes, and organists. He even designed prostheses. A small enterprise in La Chaux-de-Fonds still produces items of this applied art, proof that the name Jaquet-Droz is still alive and well in the Jura mountains, and its watches combined with automatons continue to thrill collectors and enthusiasts alike.

The Swatch Group has developed an aesthetically and technically sophisticated collection based on outstanding wristwatch movements from Le Brassus (the former Frédéric Piguet movement factory, now serving as the exclusive extended workbench for the top-of-the-line brands in the Swatch Group portfolio). In recent years, the classically beautiful watch dials have taken on a slightly modern look without losing any of their identity. The brand has also amazed the watch world with a number of beautiful and clever automatons for the wrist, the most recent being a tribute to the Rolling Stones!

Montres Jaquet Droz SA
CH-2300 La Chaux-de-Fonds
Switzerland

Tel.:
+41-32-924-2888

E-mail:
info@jaquet-droz.com

Website:
www.jaquet-droz.com

Founded:
1738

U.S. Distribution:
The Swatch Group (U.S.), Inc.
1200 Harbor Boulevard
Weehawken, NJ 07086
201-271-1400
www.swatchgroup.com

Most important collections:
Les Ateliers d'Art, Grande Seconde, Grande Seconde SW, Astrale Collection, Petite Heure Minute, Lady 8

Grande Seconde "Skelet-One" Plasma Ceramic

Reference number: J003525542
Movement: automatic, Jaquet Droz Caliber 2663 SQ; ø 26.2 mm, height 3.8 mm; 30 jewels; 28,800 vph; double barrel spring, silicon anchor horns and hairspring; skeletonized movement, oscillating weight in pink gold; 68-hour power reserve
Functions: hours, minutes (off-center), subsidiary seconds
Case: plasma-treated ceramic, ø 41.5 mm, height 12.48 mm; sapphire crystal; transparent case back; water-resistant to 3 atm
Band: textile, folding clasp
Remarks: sapphire crystal dial
Price: $26,300

Grande Seconde Quantième Dark Blue Enamel

Reference number: J007023201
Movement: automatic, Jaquet Droz Caliber 2660Q2; ø 26.2 mm; 30 jewels; 28,800 vph; double barrel spring, silicon anchor horns and hairspring; oscillating weight in pink gold; 68-hour power reserve
Functions: hours, minutes (off-center), subsidiary seconds; date
Case: pink gold, ø 41 mm, height 12.1 mm; sapphire crystal; water-resistant to 3 atm
Band: reptile skin, buckle
Remarks: enamel dial
Price: $20,000

The Rolling Stones Automaton

Reference number: J0328330011
Movement: automatic, Jaquet Droz Caliber 2653AT2; ø 26.2 mm, height 4.95 mm; 56 jewels; 28,800 vph; double spring barrel; silicon pallet levers and hairspring; gold oscillating weight with "Sticky Fingers 1971 RSM" engraved; 68-hour power reserve
Functions: hours and minutes (off-center)
Case: stainless steel, ø 43 mm, height 16.96 mm; bezel in ceramic; sapphire crystal; water-resistant to 3 atm
Band: textile, folding clasp
Remarks: automaton with record and logo, manually wound with crown pusher activation
Price: $17,200

Jörg Schauer
Durowe GmbH
Jörg Schauer
Pforzheimer Straße 41
75331 Engelsbrand
Germany

Tel.:
+49-(0)7235-975-87 45

E-mail:
info@durowe.com

Website:
www.durowe.com

Founded:
1990

Number of employees:
2

Annual production:
approx. 50 watches

Distribution:
direct sales; online shop; please contact the address in Germany

JÖRG SCHAUER

Jörg Schauer's watches are first and foremost cool. The cases have been carefully worked, and the look is planned to draw the eye. After all, he is a perfectionist and leaves nothing to chance. He works on every single case himself, polishing and performing his own brand of magic for as long as it takes to display his personal touch. This time-consuming process is one that Schauer believes is absolutely necessary. "I do this because I place a great deal of value on the fact that my cases are absolutely perfect," he explains. "I can do it better than anyone, and I would never let anyone else do it for me."

Schauer, a goldsmith by training, has been making watches since 1990. He began by doing one-off pieces in precious metals for collectors and then opened his business and simultaneously moved to stainless steel. His style is to produce functional, angular cases with visibly screwed-down bezels and straightforward dials in plain black or white. Forget finding any watch close to current trends in his collection; Schauer only builds timepieces that he genuinely likes.

Purchasing a Schauer is not that easy. He has chosen a strategy of genuine quality over quantity and only produces about 50 watches annually. This includes special watches like the One-Hand Durowe, running on a modified Unitas made by the movement manufacturer Durowe, which Schauer acquired in 2002. It has been revived as the One-Hand 44. His production structure is a vital part of his success and includes prototyping, movement modification, finishing, case production, dial painting and printing—all done in Schauer's own workshop in Engelsbrand. Any support he needs from the outside he prefers to find among regional specialists.

Chronograph Kulisse Edition 10 Jubiläum

Movement: automatic, ETA Caliber 7753; ø 30 mm, height 7.9 mm; 25 jewels; 28,800 vph; with decorative ribbing and blued screws; 48-hour power reserve
Functions: hours, minutes, subsidiary seconds; chronograph; date
Case: stainless steel, ø 42 mm, height 14.9 mm; bezel fixed with 12 screws; sapphire crystal; transparent case back; water-resistant to 5 atm
Band: reptile skin, folding clasp
Price: $4,500; limited to 130 pieces
Variations: with metal link bracelet ($4,800); with manual winding ($4,900)

One-Hand Jubiläum

Movement: automatic, ETA Caliber 2824-2; ø 25.6 mm, height 4.6 mm; 25 jewels; 28,800 vph; fine finishing, special engraved rotor; 38-hour power reserve
Functions: hours (each line stands for five minutes)
Case: stainless steel, ø 42 mm, height 10.2 mm; bezel fixed with 12 screws; sapphire crystal; transparent case back; water-resistant to 5 atm
Band: rubber, folding clasp
Price: $2,200; limited to 100 pieces
Variations: with metal link bracelet ($2,500)

Chronograph Kulisse Edition 15

Movement: automatic, ETA Caliber 7753; ø 30 mm, height 7.9 mm; 25 jewels; 28,800 vph; with decorative ribbing and blued screws, exclusive engraved "Schauer" rotor; 48-hour power reserve
Functions: hours, minutes, subsidiary seconds; chronograph; date
Case: stainless steel, ø 44 mm, height 15 mm; bezel fixed with 12 screws; sapphire crystal; transparent case back; water-resistant to 5 atm
Band: calfskin, folding clasp
Remarks: chronograph hands colors on request
Price: $4,700
Variations: with manual winding ($5,100); various bands; with carbon fiber dial

JS WATCH CO.

JS Watch Co. Reykjavik
Laugavegur 62
101 Reykjavik
Iceland

Tel.:
+354-551-05-00

E-mail:
info@jswatch.com

Website:
www.jswatch.com

Founded:
2003

Number of employees:
5

Annual production:
500 pieces

Distribution:
Retail and direct sales
info@jswatch.com
+354-551-41-00

Price range:
$1,978 to $14,147

When they weren't pillaging Europe and terrorizing populations from the British Isles to Russia, the Vikings were in fact a very hardworking and talented bunch, and when not roaming about, they tended their fields, herds, and houses and, as a number of exhibitions in the past twenty years have shown, made jewelry. Their work in this field was remarkable and fed their commercial supply chains, to use a modern term.

Iceland is where many descendants of the Norsemen live—a rugged and stark landscape, with over three hundred volcanoes and long winter nights. The ability to design and create fine jewelry lives on, and since 2003, the tiny country with a population of 330,000 has been producing watches as well, thanks to four friends, designer Grimkell Sigurþórsson, watchmakers Sigurður Gilbertsson and Gilbert Guðjónsson, and Júliús Heiðarsson.

Their first launch in 2005 of one hundred watches sold out within half a year, and so they persisted, using Swiss or German parts and movements (ETA, Sellita) but creating watches with some unique features paying tribute to their small but very intriguing country. The "execution top" movements provide solid chronometric performance and standard decoration, meaning lower prices but good quality. The timepieces are inspired and named after an event, place, or year in Iceland or Icelandic history. "We made the Sif N.A.R.T., which was named for the first helicopter of Iceland's Coast Guard rescue teams and the North Atlantic Rescue Timer," says Sigurþórsson, now the Director of Design and Marketing of the tiny company. In 2018, when Iceland qualified for the Football World Cup, JS Watch Co. was ready with a limited series.

Other ways of tying their product to their country are the use of volcanic ash from the Eyjafjallajökull on the dial and carving head letters (Höfðaletur) or Viking motifs into the case, as with the Frisland Goð Special Edition. The Gilbert collection pays tribute to the company's own watchmaker, Gilbert Guðjónsson, and is in the sober, one could say self-effacing, style the brand cultivates.

Vínland GMT

Reference number: Vin-41-1
Movement: automatic, Eterna Caliber 3914A; 30.0 mm, height 5.6 mm; 29 jewels; 28,800 vph; 65-hour power reserve
Function: small seconds counter; date display; second time-zone
Case: stainless steel, 0 41 mm, height 11.6 mm; sapphire crystal; transparent case back; water-resistant to 5 atm
Band: Milanese mesh, folding clasp
Price: $6,209
Variations: silver, blue or black dial

Islandus Dakota 44 mm

Reference number: Dak-44-1
Movement: automatic, Soprod Caliber M100; 25.60 mm, height 3.60 mm; 25 jewels; 28,800 vph; 42-hour power reserve
Functions: central hours, minutes, subsidiary seconds; date
Case: stainless steel, 44 mm, height 11.5 mm; sapphire crystal; transparent case back; water-resistant to 5 atm
Band: calf leather, buckle
Price: $2,631
Variations: black or white dials; with roman numerals

Gilbert Vintage Dictator 38.5 mm

Reference number: GIL-DI-1
Movement: automatic, Soprod Caliber M100; 25.60 mm, height 3.60 mm; 25 jewels; 28,800 vph; 42-hour power reserve
Functions: central hours, minutes, subsidiary seconds; date
Case: stainless steel, 38.5 mm, height 10.3 mm; sapphire crystal; transparent case back; water-resistant to 5 atm
Band: calf leather, buckle
Price: $2,393
Variations: black or white dials, roman numerals

JUNGHANS

Uhrenfabrik Junghans GmbH & Co. KG
Geisshaldenstrasse 49
D-78713 Schramberg

Tel.:
+49-742-218-0

E-mail:
info@junghans.de

Website:
www.junghans.de

Founded:
1861

Number of employees:
127

Annual production:
approx. 60,000 watches

U.S. distributor:
DKSH Luxury & Lifestyle North America Inc.
9-D Princess Road
Lawrenceville, NJ 08648
609-750-8800

Most important collections/price range:
Meister; Max Bill by Junghans; MEGA; 1972 Competition; Form / from approx. $395 to $2,500; special pieces up to $16,000

The town of Glashütte in Saxony was already a watchmaking name to be reckoned with when Erhard Junghans founded his factory in 1861 in Schramberg, a small town in the Black Forest . His son Arthur then developed it into a large-scale production site on the American industrial model. At the height of its success, the factory employed nearly three thousand men and women making nine thousand wall clocks and alarm clocks daily.

In the boom years after World War II, the company, with its logo featuring a star, produced mainly wristwatches. It went on to ring in modern times with its own solar and radio-controlled watches. Junghans was twice the official timekeeper at the Olympic Games.

In 2009, Dr. Hans-Jochem Steim, a successful entrepreneur and political figure from Schramberg, purchased the company, which had gone bankrupt. An infusion of cash allowed it to set up a new production and distribution schedule. Today, the brand boasts an extensive collection of high-quality wristwatches, ranging from genuine icons of design to major classics, all the way to sporty chronographs. In 2018, the company opened a watch- and clockmaking museum in the restored Terrassenbau, a century-old, terraced construction that allowed Junghans employees to work with strong natural lighting. In the same year, Junghans came out with a brand-new radio-controlled movement, the Caliber J101, designed to mix high-tech with a classic look. To satisfy a broad market, Junghans manufactures quartz and mechanical watches, all in a sober Bauhaus idiom. The latest products include the Meister S, a sporty, masculine watch, and a series of watches that combine the radio-controlled Caliber J101 with the latest in solar technology, all packaged in the traditional Junghans look. A brand-new time signal enables rapid synchronization with a smartphone thanks to a specially developed app.

In 2022, Junghans released two limited, revised editions of its 1972 Competition watch, a bullhead, as bicompax and tri-compax chronographs with striking orange subdials. They celebrate the Olympic year 1972, an era when the name Junghans was identified as an official timekeeper of major sporting events.

1972 Competition Edition

Reference number: 27/9204.00
Movement: automatic, Caliber J880.1 (base ETA 7750); ø 30 mm, height 7.9 mm; 25 jewels; 28,800 vph; rhodium-plated movement; blue screws, rotor with côtes de Genève; 48-hour power reserve
Functions: hours, minutes, subsidiary seconds; chronograph; date
Case: white gold, ø 45.5 mm, height 14.5 mm; sapphire crystal; screw-in crown; water-resistant to 10 atm
Band: calfskin, buckle
Remarks: homage to Junghans' activities in historic sports time measurement
Price: $17,900; limited to 50 pieces

1972 Competition

Reference number: 27/4203.00
Movement: automatic, Caliber J880.5 (base ETA 7750); ø 30 mm, height 7.9 mm; 25 jewels; 28,800 vph; rhodium-plated movement; blue screws, rotor with côtes de Genève; 48-hour power reserve
Functions: hours, minutes, subsidiary seconds; chronograph; date
Case: stainless steel, ø 45.5 mm, height 14.5 mm; sapphire crystal; screw-in crown; water-resistant to 10 atm
Band: calfskin, buckle
Remarks: homage to Junghans' historic involvement in sports measurement
Price: $2,600; limited to 1972 pieces

Meister S Chronoscope

Reference number: 027/4023.44
Movement: automatic, Caliber J880.1 (base ETA 7750); ø 30 mm, height 7.9 mm; 25 jewels; 28,800 vph; rhodium-plated movement, blued screws; rotor with côtes de Genève; 48-hour power reserve
Functions: hours, minutes, subsidiary seconds; chronograph; date and weekday
Case: stainless steel, ø 45 mm, height 15.9 mm; sapphire crystal; screw-in crown; water-resistant to 20 atm
Band: stainless steel, double folding clasp
Price: $2,650
Variations: with a gray dial

Meister Fein Automatic

Reference number: 27/4154.00
Movement: automatic, Caliber J800.1 (base ETA 2824-2 or Sellita SW200-1); ø 25.6 mm, height 4.6 mm; 25 or 26 jewels; 28,800 vph; 38-hour power reserve
Functions: hours, minutes, sweep seconds; date
Case: stainless steel, ø 39.5 mm, height 10.3 mm; sapphire crystal; transparent case back; water-resistant to 5 atm
Band: calfskin, buckle
Price: $1,450
Variations: with white dial and dark-brown strap

Meister Fein Automatic

Reference number: 27/4153.44
Movement: automatic, Caliber J800.1 (base ETA 2824-2 or Sellita SW200-1); ø 25.6 mm, height 4.6 mm; 25 or 26 jewels; 28,800 vph; 38-hour power reserve
Functions: hours, minutes, sweep seconds; date
Case: stainless steel, ø 39.5 mm, height 10.3 mm; sapphire crystal; transparent case back; water-resistant to 5 atm
Band: stainless steel Milanese mesh, folding clasp
Price: $1,550

Meister Fein Automatic

Reference number: 27/7150.00
Movement: automatic, Caliber J800.1 (base ETA 2824-2 or base ETA SW200-1); ø 25.6 mm, height 4.6 mm; 25 or 26 jewels; 28,800 vph; rhodium-plated movement, blued screws, rotor with côtes de Genève; 38-hour power reserve
Functions: hours, minutes, sweep seconds; date
Case: stainless steel with yellow-gold colored PVD coating, ø 39.5 mm, height 10.3 mm; sapphire crystal; transparent case back; water-resistant to 5 atm
Band: calfskin, buckle
Price: $1,450

Meister Telemeter

Reference number: 027/3380.00
Movement: automatic, Caliber J880.3 (base ETA 2892-2 with Dubois Dépraz module); ø 30 mm, height 6.5 mm; 45 jewels; 28,800 vph; rhodium-plated movement, blued screws, rotor with côtes de Genève; 42-hour power reserve
Functions: hours, minutes, subsidiary seconds; chronograph
Case: stainless steel, ø 40.8 mm, height 12.6 mm; plexiglass; transparent case back; water-resistant to 3 atm
Band: calfskin, buckle
Remarks: hard plexiglas, with scratch-resistant coating
Price: $1,450

Meister Worldtimer

Reference number: 27/3011.46
Movement: automatic, Caliber J820.5 (base ETA 2893-1); ø 25.6 mm, height 4.1 mm; 21 jewels; 28,800 vph; rhodium-plated movement, blued screws, rotor with côtes de Genève; 42-hour power reserve
Functions: hours, minutes, sweep seconds; world time display (second time zone)
Case: stainless steel, ø 40.4 mm, height 10.4 mm; sapphire crystal; transparent case back; water-resistant to 5 atm
Band: stainless steel, folding clasp
Price: $2,150

Meister Chronoscope

Reference number: 27/4222.02
Movement: automatic, Caliber J880.1 (base ETA 7750 or base ETA SW500); ø 30 mm, height 7.9 mm; 25 jewels; 28,800 vph; rhodium-plated movement, blued screws, rotor with côtes de Genève; 48-hour power reserve
Functions: hours, minutes, subsidiary seconds; chronograph; date and weekday
Case: stainless steel, ø 40.7 mm, height 13.9 mm; sapphire crystal; transparent case back; water-resistant to 5 atm
Band: ostrich leather, buckle
Price: $2,300

Max Bill Regulator Edition

Reference number: 27/3190.02
Movement: automatic, Caliber J800.5 (base Sellita SW266-1); ø 25.6 mm, height 4.6 mm; 25 jewels; 28,800 vph; 42-hour power reserve
Functions: hours (off-center), minutes, subsidiary seconds
Case: stainless steel with anthracite PVD, ø 38 mm, height 10.5 mm; sapphire crystal; water-resistant to 3 atm
Band: calfskin, buckle
Remarks: only available as the "Max Bill Edition Set 60" with two additional watches (Automatic and MEGA Small Seconds); set limited to 1060 pieces
Price: $4,900 (part of a three-watch set "Max Bill Edition Set 60" with the Small Seconds and the Automatic)

Max Bill Automatic Edition

Reference number: 27/4108.02
Movement: automatic, Caliber J800.1 (base Sellita SW200-1); ø 25.6 mm, height 4.6 mm; 26 jewels; 28,800 vph; 38-hour power reserve
Functions: hours, minutes, sweep seconds; date
Case: stainless steel with anthracite PVD, ø 38 mm, height 10 mm; sapphire crystal; water-resistant to 3 atm
Band: calfskin, buckle
Remarks: only available as the "Max Bill Edition Set 60" with two additional watches (Regulator and MEGA Small Seconds); set limited to 1,060 pieces
Price: $4,900 (part of a three-watch set "Max Bill Edition Set 60" with the Regulator and the Small Seconds)

Form A

Reference number: 27/4239.00
Movement: automatic, Caliber J800.2 (base ETA 2824-2 or base SW200-1); ø 25.6 mm, height 4.6 mm; 25 or 26 jewels; 28,800 vph; 38-hour power reserve
Functions: hours, minutes, sweep seconds; date
Case: stainless steel, ø 39.2 mm, height 9.5 mm; sapphire crystal; transparent case back; water-resistant to 5 atm
Band: calfskin, buckle
Price: $1,000
Variations: various bands and dials

Max Bill Chronoscope

Reference number: 27/4600.02
Movement: automatic, Caliber J880.2 (base ETA 7750 or Sellita SW500); ø 30 mm, height 7.9 mm; 25 jewels; 28,800 vph; 48-hour power reserve
Functions: hours, minutes; chronograph; date
Case: stainless steel, ø 40 mm, height 14.4 mm; sapphire crystal; water-resistant to 3 atm
Band: calfskin, buckle
Price: $2,350

Max Bill Automatic

Reference number: 27/4700.02
Movement: automatic, Caliber J800.1 (base ETA 2824-2 or base SW200-1); ø 25.6 mm, height 4.6 mm; 25 or 26 jewels; 28,800 vph; 38-hour power reserve
Functions: hours, minutes, sweep seconds; date
Case: stainless steel, ø 38 mm, height 10 mm; sapphire crystal; water-resistant to 5 atm
Band: calfskin, buckle
Price: $1,300

Max Bill MEGA Solar

Reference number: 059/2022.48
Movement: quartz, multifrequency radio-controlled Caliber J101.85; time-zone recognition and setting to the second, app for time-setting; "perpetual" date (in quartz mode as well), solar cell charging
Functions: hours, minutes, sweep seconds; date
Case: titanium, ø 38 mm, height 9 mm; plexiglass; water-resistant to 3 atm
Band: titanium Milanaise mesh, folding clasp
Remarks: hard plexiglas, with scratch-resistant coating
Price: $1,350
Variations: with leather strap

KLEYNOD

Watches were a common gift in the former Soviet Union, so it may not come as a great surprise that millions of timepieces of all types were manufactured during that period. Today, many swamp the online auction markets, much appreciated for their rugged look, the very identifiable symbols (like the red star), and their robust construction. There were several big names, of course: Vostok, Sturmanskie, and Raketa, among others. Most are still with us these days as new post-Soviet brands in their own right and with distinctive looks.

Among the more recent enterprises is the Kyiv Ukranian Watch Factory, founded in 1997 in the Ukrainian capital. It was a manufacturer for the Russian brand Poljot, among others. Perhaps more notorious in Ukraine at least was the making of a watch for Ukrainian astronaut Leonid Kadeniuk, who was on the international STS-87 mission carried out by the space shuttle Columbia. In 2002, the company decided to create a distinct brand of its own. They chose the name Kleynod, which derives from the German *Kleinod*, or Polish *klejnot*, an old word for "gem."

The output is divided up into six main collections. For the sake of affordability, the movements used are mostly quartz, but a fair number of the watches do come equipped with Swiss-made Ronda movements. Still, they are all under the $1,000 mark. Perhaps more interesting though are the motifs on the dials that reflect a pride in the country's long history. The 3, 6, 9, and 12 that appear on the dial of the Kleynods of Independence collection may hardly be recognizable at first because they have been stylized to look like the *tryzub*, the distinctive Ukrainian trident, on a guilloché background, which originates back in the mists of the nation's history.

The numerals of the Classic model also mirror the style of the *tryzub*, though the dial is far simpler. As for the Embroidery collection, its geometrical decorative pattern suggests an ancient craft from certain regions of the country—other regions, notably in the east, lean towards floral patterns.

Kleynod Ukrainian Watches
Kyrylivska Street 69
Kyiv, 04080 Ukraine

Tel.:
+38-067-223-1085

E-mail:
trade@kleynod.ua

Website:
www.kleynodwatches.com

Founded:
2002

Number of employees:
100

Annual production:
approx. 90,000 watches

U. S. Distributor:
V2Com Commerce LLC
775 Bloomfield Ave,
Suite 1B
Clifton, New Jersey 07012
973-272-8251
kleynodusa@gmail.com

Most important collections/price range
Mechanical and quartz: Antonov (quartz) / Classic / Embroidery / Kleynods of Independence / Football Collection / Kleynod Forces; up to $785

Classic Collection

Reference number: K 348-523
Movement: automatic, Caliber Ronda R-150; ø 25.6 mm, height 4.4 mm; 25 jewels; 28,800 vph; 40-hour power reserve
Functions: hours, minutes, sweep seconds; date
Case: stainless steel, 42 mm, height 10.6 mm; sapphire crystal; water-resistant to 5 atm
Band: leather, folding clasp
Remarks: guilloché in the center of the dial
Price: $570

Kleynods of Independence

Reference number: K 25-606
Movement: automatic, Caliber Ronda R-150; ø 25.6 mm, height 4.4 mm; 25 jewels; 28,800 vph; 40-hour power reserve
Functions: hours, minutes, sweep seconds; date
Case: stainless steel with gold plating (IPG), ø 44 mm, height 11.2 mm; sapphire crystal; water-resistant to 5 atm
Band: leather, folding clasp
Remarks: guilloché on the dial
Price: $715; limited to 2,500 pieces
Variations: comes in stainless steel, with white dial; also in tonneau version

Embroidery by Kleynod

Reference number: K 308-511 B
Movement: automatic, Caliber Ronda R-150; ø 25.6 mm, height 4.4 mm; 25 jewels; 28,800 vph; 40-hour power reserve
Functions: hours, minutes, sweep seconds; date
Case: stainless steel, ø 37 mm, height 10.4 mm; sapphire crystal; water-resistant to 5 atm
Band: natural leather with sateen on the top, buckle
Remarks: geometric pattern on the dial inspired by Ukrainian embroidery.
Price: $520

Kobold Time GmbH
Willibald-Alexis-Strasse 18
D-10965 Berlin
Germany

Tel.:
+49-151-105-500-10
1-877-SOARWAY

E-mail:
info@koboldwatch.com

Website:
www.koboldwatch.com

Founded:
1998

Number of employees:
8

Annual production:
maximum 2,500 watches

Distribution:
factory-direct, select retailers
1-877-SOARWAY

Most important collection/price range:
Soarway, Phantom, SMG / $2,650 to $48,000

KOBOLD

Like many others in the field, Michael Kobold had already developed an interest in the watch industry in childhood. As a young man, he found a mentor in Chronoswiss founder Gerd-Rüdiger Lang, who encouraged him to start his own brand. This he did in 1998—at the age of nineteen while he was still a student at Carnegie Mellon University. Today, after changes occasioned by the COVID-19 crisis, Kobold Watch Company stretches across three continents. Part is in Pittsburgh, where it manufactures cases and movement components; some components are also manufactured in Nepal, while the founder himself lives in his native Germany.

It is not surprising for a company whose motto is "Embrace Adventure." Explorers such as Sir Ranulph Fiennes, whom Guinness Book of World Records describes as "the world's greatest living explorer, have worn these tough mechanical instruments. The brand's centerpiece is the Soarway collection and the fabled Soarway case, which was originally created in 1999 by Sir Ranulph, master watchmaker; Chronoswiss founder Lang; and company founder Kobold, himself an avid mountain climber. Advice and funding came in part from the late James Gandolfini, better known to TV audiences as Tony Soprano.

Kobold's love of the Himalayas has driven his commitment to the people of Nepal. He produces leather accessories and straps there and uses the operation to offer women vocational training. In 2015, he launched the Soarway Foundation to help Nepal in the event of earthquakes. His love of that country is also behind the Fire Truck Expedition as a way to supply the mountain-clad country with key firefighting equipment.

Kobold has contributed to the renaissance of American watchmaking and originally set its sights even higher, namely on an in-house U.S.-made movement. Things have changed, though. "We make tough, rugged watches and so the case plays a more important role than the movement," says Kobold. "So for now, we're concentrating on making the toughest cases possible.

Seal Ceramic James Gandolfini—Meteorite dial

Reference number: KD 842121C
Movement: automatic, ETA 2892-A2; ø 36 mm, height 3.6 mm; 21 jewels; 28,800 vph; 46-hour power reserve
Functions: hours, minutes, sweep seconds
Case: ceramic, ø 44 mm, height 17.0 mm; unidirectional rotating bezel with 60-minute divisions; Antireflective sapphire crystal; screwed-in crown; screwed-down case back; water-resistant to 100 atm
Band: rubber, signed buckle
Price: $8,500; limited to 51 pieces
Variations: varied dials, including Mount Everest summit rock, malachite, turquoise

SMG-2

Reference number: KD 5546142
Movement: automatic, Caliber ETA 2893-A2; ø 26.2 mm, height 4.1 mm; 21 jewels; 28,800 vph; 40-hour power reserve
Functions: hours, minutes, sweep seconds; 2nd time zone; date
Case: stainless steel, ø 43 mm, height 12.75 mm; unidirectional bezel with 0-60 scale; antireflective sapphire crystal; screwed-down case back; screwed-in crown; water-resistant to 20 atm
Band: rubber, buckle
Price: $6,450

Phantom SL Chronograph

Reference number: KD 7934552
Movement: automatic, ETA 7750; ø 25.6 mm, height 7.9 mm; 25 jewels; 28,800 vph; côtes de Genève, perlage, engraved and skeletonized gold-plated rotor; 38-hour power reserve
Functions: hours, minutes, subsidiary seconds; date, day; chronograph
Case: titanium, ø 40.5 mm, height 17 mm; bezel with tachymeter scale (blank bezel optional); screwed-in crown; sapphire crystal; screwed-down back; water-resistant to 20 atm
Band: reptile skin, buckle
Price: $3,450

Arctic Diver

Reference number: KD 9652155
Movement: automatic, ETA 2824; ø 25.6 mm, height 4.6 mm; 25 jewels; 28,800 vph; côtes de Genève, perlage, engraved gold-plated rotor; soft iron core; 38-hour power reserve
Functions: hours, minutes, sweep seconds; date (optional)
Case: DLC-coated titanium, ø 44.5 mm, height 15 mm; unidirectional bezel with 60-minute divisions (blank bezel optional); screwed-in crown; sapphire crystal; screwed-down back; water-resistant to 50 atm
Band: rubber, buckle
Price: $5,650

Soarway Diver

Reference number: KD 1113145
Movement: automatic, ETA 2892; ø 25.6 mm, height 3.6 mm; 25 jewels; 28,800 vph; côtes de Genève, perlage, engraved and skeletonized gold-plated rotor; 38-hour power reserve
Functions: hours, minutes, sweep seconds; date (optional)
Case: DLC-coated stainless steel, ø 40.5 mm, height 10 mm; unidirectional bezel with 60-minute divisions; screwed-in crown; antireflective sapphire crystal; screwed-down back; water-resistant to 30 atm
Band: canvas, buckle
Price: $5,950

Phantom Safari Chronograph

Reference number: KD 7935455
Movement: automatic, ETA 7750; ø 25.6 mm, height 7.9 mm; 25 jewels; 28,800 vph; with côtes de Genève, perlage, engraved and skeletonized gold-plated rotor; 38-hour power reserve
Functions: hours, minutes, subsidiary seconds; date, day; chronograph
Case: titanium with DLC coating, ø 40.5 mm, height 17 mm; unidirectional bezel with 0-60 scale; screwed-in crown; screw-locked push buttons; sapphire crystal; screwed-down case back; water-resistant to 30 atm
Band: canvas, buckle
Price: $7,950

Seal

Reference number: KD 842121
Movement: automatic, ETA 2892-A2; ø 36 mm, height 3.6 mm; 21 jewels; 28,800 vph; 46-hour power reserve
Functions: hours, minutes, sweep seconds
Case: stainless steel, ø 44 mm, height 15 mm; unidirectional rotating bezel with 0-60 scale; sapphire crystal; screwed-down case back; screw ed-in crown; water-resistant to 100 atm
Band: Calfskin, buckle
Price: $5,650

Polar Surveyor Chronograph

Reference number: KD 9266452
Movement: automatic, ETA 7750; ø 25.6 mm, height 7.9 mm; 25 jewels; 28,800 vph; côtes de Genève, perlage, engraved and skeletonized gold-plated rotor; 38-hour power reserve
Functions: hours, minutes, subsidiary seconds; date, day; chronograph; second time zone
Case: titanium, ø 40.5 mm, height 17 mm; unidirectional bezel with 60-minute divisions; screwed-in crown; screw-locked push buttons; sapphire crystal; screwed-down back; water-resistant to 30 atm
Band: stainless steel, buckle
Price: $9,450

Himalaya Everest Edition

Reference number: KD 2143211
Movement: automatic, ETA 2892-A2; ø 36 mm, height 3.6 mm; 21 jewels; 28,800 vph; 46-hour power reserve
Functions: hours, minutes, sweep seconds
Case: stainless steel, ø 44 mm, height 14.0 mm; sapphire crystal; screwed-down case back; water-resistant to 10 atm
Band: calfskin, buckle
Remarks: dial made from Mount Everest summit rock
Price: $24,500

Kudoke Uhren
Tannenweg 5
D-15236 Frankfurt (Oder)
Germany

Tel.:
+49-335-280-0409

E-mail:
info@kudoke.eu

Website:
www.kudoke.eu

Founded:
2007

Number of employees:
4

Annual production:
150 watches

Distribution:
Contact the brand directly for information

Price range:
between approx. $4,500 and $32,000

KUDOKE

Stefan Kudoke, a watchmaker from Frankfurt an der Oder, has made a name for himself as an extremely skilled and imaginative creator of timepieces. He apprenticed with two experienced watchmakers and graduated as the number one trainee in the state of Brandenburg. This earned him a stipend from a federal program promoting gifted individuals. He then moved on to one of the large *manufactures* in Glashütte, where he refined his skills in its workshop for complications and prototyping. At the age of twenty-two, with a master's diploma in his pocket, he decided to get an MBA and then devote himself to building his own company.

His guiding principle is individuality, and that is not possible to find in a serial product. So Kudoke began building unique pieces. By realizing the special wishes of customers, he manages to reflect each person's uniqueness in each watch. And he has produced some genuinely outstanding timepieces, like the ExCentro1 and 2 or more recently a watch with an octopus that seems to be climbing out of the case. Even his more minimalistic pieces, like the Kudoke 1 and 2 are deeply thought-out. They come in carefully chosen, yet toned-down colors like anthracite, that interact subtly with the shapes.

Kudoke has divided his output into two clear categories: HANDwerk, meaning crafts, and referring to straight watchmaking, and KUNSTwerk, which means artwork or art movement. The latter category gives him the opportunity to work his specialties, like engraving and goldsmithing. Under his creative hand, ridges might be turned into graceful bodies, or a plate fragment might be turned into figures and garlands. His recent creations include a skull watch done with characteristic care, and the White Flower, a 38-millimeter gem, which, although it is in the ladies' watch category, could easily fit a man's wrist.

Kudoke 1 Anthracite

Movement: manually wound, Kudoke Caliber 1; ø 30 mm, height 4.3 mm; 18 jewels; 28,800 vph; hand-engraved and finished movement; 46-hour power reserve
Functions: hours, minutes, subsidiary seconds
Case: stainless steel, ø 39 mm, height 9.5 mm; sapphire crystal; transparent case back
Band: reptile skin, buckle
Price: $8,360

Kudoke 2 Black

Movement: manually wound, Kudoke Caliber 1 - Version 24h; ø 30 mm, height 5.05 mm; 18 jewels; 28,800 vph; hand-engraved and finished movement; 46-hour power reserve
Functions: hours, minutes; additional 24-hour display
Case: stainless steel, ø 39 mm, height 10.7 mm; sapphire crystal; transparent case back
Band: reptile skin, buckle
Remarks: hand-engraved celestial disk with three-color galvanic treatment
Price: $10,690

White Flower

Movement: automatic, ETA Caliber 2824-2; ø 25.6 mm, height 4.6 mm; 25 jewels; 28,800 vph; rhodium-plated and hand-engraved rotor; 38-hour power reserve
Functions: hours, minutes, sweep seconds
Case: stainless steel, ø 38 mm, height 10 mm; sapphire crystal; transparent case back
Band: reptile skin, buckle
Remarks: silver dial with relief engraving and set with 8 diamonds
Price: $6,600

LONGINES

The Longines winged hourglass logo is the world's oldest trademark, according to the World Intellectual Property Organization (WIPO). Since its founding in 1832, the brand has manufactured somewhere in the region of 35 million watches, making it one of the genuine heavyweights of the Swiss watch world. In 1983, Nicolas G. Hayek merged the two major Swiss watch manufacturing groups ASUAG and SIHH into what would later become the Swatch Group. Longines, the leading ASUAG brand, barely missed capturing the same position in the new concern; that honor went to Omega, the SIHH frontrunner. However, from a historical and technical point of view, this brand has what it takes to be at the helm of any group. Was it not Longines that equipped polar explorer Roald Amundsen and air pioneer Charles Lindbergh with their watches? It has also been the timekeeper at many Olympic Games and, since 2007, the official timekeeper for the French Open at Roland Garros. In fact, this brand is a major sponsor at many sports events, from riding to archery.

It is not surprising then to find that this venerable Jura company also has an impressive portfolio of in-house calibers in stock, from simple manual winders to complicated chronographs. Thanks to this stock, it can supply Swatch Group with anything from cheap, thin quartz watches to heavy gold chronographs and calendars with quadruple retrograde displays. In addition to elegant ladies' watches and modern sports watches, the remakes of great classics from the company's own history are a particular specialty of the house. Thanks to its many years of experience as a timekeeper at world championships and as a partner of international federations, Longines has also been able to forge close and lasting relationships with the world of sports, which is evidenced with great regularity in limited special editions. The brand is represented in over 150 countries worldwide.

Longines Watch Co.
Rue des Longines 8
CH-2610 St-Imier
Switzerland

Tel.:
+41-32-942-5425

E-mail:
info@longines.com

Website:
www.longines.com

Founded:
1832

Number of employees:
worldwide approx. 2,000

U.S. distributor:
Longines
The Swatch Group (U.S.), Inc.
Longines Division
703 Waterford Way, Ste. 450
Miami, FL 33126
786-725-5393
www.longines.com

Most important collections/price range:
The Longines Master Collection, Longines DolceVita, HydroConquest, Heritage Collection / from approx. $1,000 to $6,500

Spirit Zulu Time

Reference number: L3.812.4.63.6
Movement: automatic, Longines Caliber L844 (base ETA A31.411); ø 25.6 mm, height 3.85 mm; 21 jewels; 25,200 vph; silicon hairspring; 72-hour power reserve; COSC-certified chronometer
Functions: hours, minutes, sweep seconds; additional 24-hour display (second time zone); date
Case: stainless steel, ø 42 mm, height 13.9 mm; bidirectional rotating bezel with ceramic inlay, with 0-24 scale; sapphire crystal; screw-in crown; water-resistant to 10 atm
Band: stainless steel, double folding clasp
Price: $3,050
Variations: various bands and dials

Spirit Zulu Time

Reference number: L3.812.4.93.2
Movement: automatic, Longines Caliber L844 (base ETA A31.411); ø 25.6 mm, height 3.85 mm; 21 jewels; 25,200 vph; silicon hairspring; 72-hour power reserve; COSC-certified chronometer
Functions: hours, minutes, sweep seconds; additional 24-hour display (second time zone); date
Case: stainless steel, ø 42 mm, height 13.9 mm; bidirectional bezel with ceramic insert; with 0-24 scale; sapphire crystal; screw-in crown; water-resistant to 10 atm
Band: calfskin, double folding clasp
Price: $2,950
Variations: various bands and dials

Spirit

Reference number: L3.410.4.63.6
Movement: automatic, Longines Caliber L888 (base ETA A31. L11); ø 25.6 mm, height 3.85 mm; 21 jewels; 25,200 vph; silicon hairspring; 72-hour power reserve; COSC-certified chronometer
Functions: hours, minutes, sweep seconds; date
Case: stainless steel, ø 37 mm, height 12.2 mm; sapphire crystal; screw-in crown; water-resistant to 10 atm
Band: stainless steel, triple folding clasp
Price: $2,400

Spirit

Reference number: L3.410.4.93.0
Movement: automatic, Longines Caliber L888.4 (base ETA A31. L11); ø 25.6 mm, height 3.85 mm; 21 jewels; 25,200 vph; silicon hairspring; 72-hour power reserve; COSC-certified chronometer
Functions: hours, minutes, sweep seconds; date
Case: stainless steel, ø 37 mm, height 12.2 mm; sapphire crystal; screw-in crown; water-resistant to 10 atm
Band: calfskin, buckle
Price: $2,150

HydroConquest

Reference number: L3.780.4.96.6
Movement: automatic, Longines Caliber L888 (base ETA A31. L01); ø 25.6 mm, height 3.85 mm; 21 jewels; 25,200 vph; silicon hairspring; 72-hour power reserve; COSC-certified chronometer
Functions: hours, minutes, sweep seconds; date
Case: stainless steel, ø 39 mm, height 12.7 mm; unidirectional bezel with ceramic inlay, with 0-60 scale; sapphire crystal; screw-in crown; water-resistant to 30 atm
Band: stainless steel, double folding clasp, with safety lock and diving extension
Price: $1,700
Variations: various bands and dials

HydroConquest

Reference number: L3.780.3.78.6
Movement: automatic, Longines Caliber L888.5 (base ETA A31. L01); ø 25.6 mm, height 3.85 mm; 21 jewels; 25,200 vph; silicon hairspring; 72-hour power reserve
Functions: hours, minutes, sweep seconds; date
Case: stainless steel, ø 39 mm, height 12.7 mm; crown with rose gold-colored PVD coating with ceramic insert, unidirectional bezel with 60-minute scale; sapphire crystal; screw-in crown; water-resistant to 30 atm
Band: stainless steel, double folding clasp, with safety lock and diving extension
Price: $1,950
Variations: various bands and dials

Ultra-Chron

Reference number: L2.836.4.52.6
Movement: automatic, Longines Caliber L836 (base ETA C07.L11); ø 25.6 mm, 25 jewels; 36,000 vph; silicon hairspring; Timelab-certified chronometer, 52-hour power reserve
Functions: hours, minutes, sweep seconds
Case: stainless steel, ø 43 mm, height 13.6 mm; unidirectional bezel with sapphire crystal insert; sapphire crystal; transparent case back; water-resistant to 30 atm
Band: stainless steel, folding clasp
Price: $3,450
Variations: in a Prestige box with additional textile strap $3,700

Legend Diver Watch

Reference number: L3.774.4.70.2
Movement: automatic, Longines Caliber L888.5 (base ETA A31. L11); ø 25.6 mm, height 3.85 mm; 21 jewels; 25,200 vph; silicon hairspring; 72-hour power reserve
Functions: hours, minutes, sweep seconds; date
Case: stainless steel, ø 42 mm, height 12.7 mm; crown-controlled inner scale ring, with 0-60 scale; sapphire crystal; screw-in crown; water-resistant to 30 atm
Band: textile, buckle
Price: $2,400

Legend Diver Watch

Reference number: L3.374.4.40.2
Movement: automatic, Longines Caliber L592 (base ETA C20.L11); ø 19.4 mm, height 4.1 mm; 22 jewels; 28,800 vph; silicon hairspring; 45-hour power reserve
Functions: hours, minutes, sweep seconds; date
Case: stainless steel, ø 36 mm, height 11.9 mm; crown-controlled inner scale ring, with 0-60 scale; sapphire crystal; screw-in crown; water-resistant to 30 atm
Band: textile, buckle
Price: $2,400

Evidenza

Reference number: L2.142.4.56.2
Movement: automatic, Longines Caliber L592 (base ETA C20.L11); ø 19.4 mm, height 4.1 mm; 22 jewels; 28,800 vph; silicon hairspring; 45-hour power reserve
Functions: hours, minutes, sweep seconds; date
Case: stainless steel, 26 mm x 30.6 mm, height 8.7 mm; sapphire crystal; water-resistant to 3 atm
Band: reptile skin, buckle
Price: $2,100

Master Collection Moonphase

Reference number: L2.409.4.87.6
Movement: automatic, Longines Caliber L899 (base ETA C31.L91); ø 25.6 mm, height 5.55 mm; 21 jewels; 25,200 vph; silicon hairspring; 72-hour power reserve
Functions: hours, minutes, sweep seconds; date, moon phase
Case: stainless steel, ø 34 mm, height 11 mm; sapphire crystal; water-resistant to 3 atm
Band: stainless steel, triple folding clasp
Remarks: mother-of-pearl dial set with 12 diamonds
Price: $2,850

Master Collection Automatic

Reference number: L2.357.4.07.2
Movement: automatic, Longines Caliber L888 (base ETA A31. L01); ø 25.6 mm, height 3.85 mm; 21 jewels; 25,200 vph; silicon hairspring; 72-hour power reserve
Functions: hours, minutes, sweep seconds; date
Case: stainless steel, ø 34 mm, height 9.2 mm; sapphire crystal; water-resistant to 3 atm
Band: reptile skin, triple folding clasp
Remarks: dial set with 12 diamonds
Price: $2,500

Master Collection Automatic

Reference number: L2.793.4.73.2
Movement: automatic, Longines Caliber L888 (base ETA A31. L01); ø 25.6 mm, height 3.85 mm; 21 jewels; 25,200 vph; silicon hairspring; 72-hour power reserve
Functions: hours, minutes, sweep seconds
Case: stainless steel, ø 40 mm, height 9.2 mm; sapphire crystal; water-resistant to 3 atm
Band: reptile skin, buckle
Remarks: jubilee model for the brand's 190th anniversary
Price: $2,400

Master Collection Automatic

Reference number: L2.793.6.73.2
Movement: automatic, Longines Caliber L888 (base ETA A31. L01); ø 25.6 mm, height 3.85 mm; 21 jewels; 25,200 vph; silicon hairspring; 72-hour power reserve
Functions: hours, minutes, sweep seconds
Case: yellow gold, ø 40 mm, height 9.35 mm; sapphire crystal; water-resistant to 3 atm
Band: reptile skin, buckle
Remarks: jubilee model for the brand's 190th anniversary
Price: $12,000; limited to 190 pieces

Master Collection Automatic

Reference number: L2.793.8.73.2
Movement: automatic, Longines Caliber L888 (base ETA A31. L01); ø 25.6 mm, height 3.85 mm; 21 jewels; 25,200 vph; silicon hairspring; 72-hour power reserve
Functions: hours, minutes, sweep seconds
Case: rose gold ø 40 mm, height 9.35 mm; sapphire crystal; water-resistant to 3 atm
Band: reptile skin, buckle
Remarks: jubilee model for the brand's 190th anniversary
Price: $12,000; limited to 190 pieces

Louis Erard SA
Ouest 2
CH-2340 Le Noirmont
Switzerland

Tel.:
+41-32-957-65-30

E-mail:
info@louiserard.com

Website:
www.louiserard.com

Founded:
1929

Number of employees:
15

Annual production:
not specified

Distribution/sales:
Contact the company in Switzerland.
In the USA:
Exquisite Timepieces
4380 Gulfshore Blvd., N. Suite 800
Naples, Fl 34103
239-666-8163
exquisitetimepieces.com

Cellini Jewelers
430 Park Ave
New York, NY 10022
212-888-0505
cellinijewelers.com

Most important collections/price range:
Excellence, La Sportive, Heritage, / $1,000 to $ 5,000

LOUIS ERARD

Once upon a time in the watchmaking workshops, there was a large clock that gave the minutes as the main time increment and the hours on a separate dial. This allowed the watchmakers to set and test the accuracy of the piece they were assembling. Over time, so-called regulator dials became popular with the public. It is said that train conductors preferred them because they needed accuracy to the minute.

Among the rare brands that have made regulator watches an important part of their output is Louis Erard. The company namesake (1893-1964), a watchmaker by trade, founded a watchmaking school in his native La Chauds-de-Fonds, and later a casing business for the thriving industry, and then a watchmaking company under his own name.

Erard's business acumen was as good as his technical skill. In the 1930s, he worked on the legendary Valjoux 72 chronograph movement, and in 1956, his company received the coveted right to manufacture movements. In fact, Louis Erard, the company, managed to weather the quartz crisis thanks to a careful modernization program in the 1970s launched by Erard's grandson.

The company changed hands in 1992, moved to Le Noirmont farther up the Jura mountains for a restructuring. In 2003, it was purchased again. The new CEO, Alain Spinedi, understood the need for a distinct look with affordable pricing. The regulator dial thus became the hallmark of the brand and one that well represents its origins in the hands-on, salt-of-the-earth world of watchmaking in the Jura Mountains.

Louis Erard has four distinct lines. The regulators are found under the heading Excellence and they tend to stand out thanks to collaborations with the likes of Label Noir, a top-tier customization specialist, and guilloché wizards Fehr & Cie SA, which boldly finds new ways to create unique dials with this traditional form of horological decoration.

Le Régulateur Louis Erard x Label Noir

Reference number: 85237NN57
Movement: automatic, Sellita SW266-1; ø 25.6 mm, height 5.6 mm; 31 jewels; 28,800 vph; carefully decorated with open-worked oscillating weight; 38-hour power reserve
Functions: off-center hours, minutes, subsidiary seconds
Case: stainless steel with black PVD, ø 42 mm, height 12.25 mm; sapphire crystal; green transparent case back; water-resistant to 5 atm
Collaboration: watch developed in association with Label Noir, a company specializing in personalizing watches
Band: black nylon, calfskin lining, buckle, quick strap change system
Price: $3,850; limited to 178 pieces

Excellence Petite Seconde Malachite

Reference number: 34238AA39
Movement: automatic, Sellita SW261-1; ø 25.60 mm, height 5.60 mm; 31 jewels; 28,800 vph; open-worked oscillating weight with Louis Erard logo, 38-hour power reserve
Functions: hours, minutes, subsidiary seconds
Case: stainless steel, ø 39 mm, height 12.25 mm; sapphire crystal; transparent case back; water-resistant to 5 atm
Band: calfskin, buckle, quick strap change system
Remarks: dial of natural malachite; limited to 99 pieces
Price: $2,750
Variations: with lapis lazuli or aventurine dial

Excellence Guilloché Main II

Reference number: 34237AA95
Movement: automatic, Sellita SW261-1; ø 25.60 mm, height 5.60 mm; 31 jewels; 28,800 vph; open-worked oscillating weight with Louis Erard logo, 38-hour power reserve
Functions: hours, minutes
Case: stainless steel, ø 42 mm, height 12.25 mm; sapphire crystal; transparent case back; water-resistant to 5 atm
Band: calfskin with blue-grained lining, buckle, quick strap change system
Remarks: hand-guilloché square pattern on dial; limited to 99 pieces
Price: $4,290

LOUIS MOINET

There's always something happening at Louis Moinet. What may have given the brand a boost was a rather special historic discovery: in the race to be the first to invent something new, Louis Moinet (1768–1853), it seems, has emerged as the first maker of a chronograph. His *Compteur de tierces*, dating to 1816, was revealed to the public in 2013. This special chronograph counted one-sixtieth of a second with a frequency of 216,000 vph.

The original Louis Moinet was a professor at the Academy of Fine Arts in Paris and president of the Société Chronométrique and was without a doubt one of the most inventive, multitalented men of his time. He worked with such eminent watchmakers as Breguet, Berthoud, Winnerl, Janvier, and Perrelet. Among his accomplishments is an extensive two-volume treatise on horology.

Following in such footsteps is hardly an easy task, but Jean-Marie Schaller and Micaela Bertolucci decided that their idiosyncratic creations were indeed imbued with the spirit of the great Frenchman. They work with a team of independent designers, watchmakers, movement specialists, and suppliers to produce the most unusual wristwatches filled with clever functions and surprising details. The Jules Verne chronographs have hinged levers, for example, and the second hand on the Tempograph changes direction every ten seconds.

Increasingly, this independent-minded brand is exploring the space-time continuum and the worlds of astronomy, space travel, science fiction, and even ancient spirituality. The Mars Mission recalls the earliest snapshot of the planet and has a bit of Martian meteorite inside. The Maya Eclipse features a sculptural version of Chichén Itzá with two tourbillons balanced by the sun and moon revolving around the dial and crossing paths every now and then. As for the Time to Race, the customer can pick his or her number, and that watch will then be unique.

Les Ateliers Louis Moinet SA
Rue du Temple 1
CH-2072 Saint-Blaise
Switzerland

Tel.:
+41-32-753-6814

E-mail:
info@louismoinet.com

Website:
www.louismoinet.com

Founded:
2005

U.S. distributor:
Fitzhenry Consulting
1029 Peachtree Parkway, #346
Peachtree City, GA 30269
561-212-6812
Don@fitzhenry.com

Most important collections:
Memoris, Sideralis, Tempograph Chrome, Spacewalker, Ultravox; numerous unique pieces

Time to Race

Reference number: LM-96.20.8R | LM-96.20.8B | LM-96.20.8VF
Movement: automatic, Louis Moinet Caliber LM 96; ø 30.40 mm, height 10.69 mm; 30 jewels; 28,800 vph; column-wheel control, monopusher chronograph; screw balance; oscillating mass with clous de Paris; mainplate with côtes de Genève on movement side; 48-hour power reserve
Functions: hours, minutes, seconds, chronograph
Case: titanium, ø 40.7 mm, height 17.92 mm; sapphire crystal; screw-in transparent back; water-resistant to 5 atm
Band: rubber, folding clasp
Remarks: customers can choose their "lucky number," so each piece is unique and will never be made again
Price: $36,000; unique timepieces
Variations: in red (Rosso Corsa), blue (Bleu de France), and green (Racing Green)

Mars Mission

Reference number: LM-75.10.MA-B
Movement: automatic, Louis Moinet Caliber LM45; ø 30.4 mm, height 6.7 mm; 22 jewels; 28,800 vph; côtes de Genève, circular-grained wheels, clous de Paris on rotor; 48-hour power reserve
Functions: hours, minutes, secondary seconds
Case: stainless steel, ø 45.40 mm, height 14.95 mm; transparent case back; water-resistant to 5 atm
Band: reptile skin, folding clasp
Remarks: a genuine meteorite fragment from Mars is in a frame at 3 o'clock; dial fashioned after the first ever photograph of Mars, taken by the Mariner 4 in 1965
Price: $22,500; limited to 100 pieces

Maya Eclipse

Reference number: LM-105.50.MA
Movement: manually wound, Louis Moinet Caliber LM105; ø 38.50 mm, height 13.6 mm; 56 jewels; 21,600 vph; 2 spring barrels for the 2 tourbillons rotating in opposite directions crossing paths 18 times per hour; each tourbillon with counterweights to ensure smooth rotation; 48-hour power reserve
Functions: hours, minutes
Case: rose gold, ø 43.5 mm, height 18.3 mm; sapphire crystal; transparent case back; water-resistant to 1 atm
Band: reptile skin, folding clasp
Remarks: sculpture of Chichen Itza on the dial
Price: $465,000; unique piece

Luminox Watches (Lumondi)
27 W. 24th Street
Suite 804
New York, NY 10010

Tel.:
917-522-3600

E-mail:
info@luminoxusa.com

Website:
www.luminox.com
shop.luminox.com

Founded:
1989

Most important collections:
Navy Seal 3500, Leatherback Sea, Atacama Field, Turtle Giant, XCOR Aerospace

LUMINOX

Watches, as the old industry axiom goes, are jewelry for men. And many men do tend to like watches that express their masculinity in no uncertain terms, or that feel like tools or cockpits of fast-moving vehicles. So when Barry Cohen came across mb-microtech's tiny tritium gas-filled tubes in the late eighties, he immediately spotted an opportunity. Here was a way to give sports watches the kind of illumination that would make them dependable and practical time-givers at night. The radioactive tritium, which has a half-life of 12.4 years, makes a coating on the inside of the tubes glow for up to twenty-five years.

Cohen and his business partner Richard Timbo called their brand Luminox, derived from the Latin words for light and night. They created a collection of rugged-looking sports timepieces and set about convincing watch fans of their product. In 1992 came the first big breakthrough, when a Luminox prevailed in a tough competition to become a mission watch for Navy SEALS. The brand now had a reputation, and other law enforcement agencies and organizations began ordering watches, notably F-117 Nighthawk and Stealth pilots.

As the brand grew and expanded beyond American borders, it continued developing its product. It introduced a new lightweight carbon case with a matte finish that regulates temperature on the wrist better. A special mineral crystal was also developed that is highly scratch resistant. To manufacture watches in Switzerland, Luminox partnered with Mondaine (see page 216), famous for its Railroad Watch. In 2016, that partnership became a full takeover, as the co-heads of Mondaine sought to further grow the brand. Besides its line of military style watches, Luminox now has some elegant collections, like the Atacama Field automatics, which run on mechanical movements and retain the sportive quality of being water-resistant to 20 atm. The price points are also attractive, thanks to Mondaine's impressive industrial production facilities.

XCOR Aerospace Automatic Valjoux Chronograph

Reference number: 5261
Movement: automatic, ETA Caliber 7750 Valjoux; ø 30 mm, height 7.9; 25 jewels; 28,800 vph; 42-hour power reserve
Functions: hours, minutes, chronograph; date
Case: titanium and black PVD, ø 45.5 mm, height 18 mm; sapphire crystal; titanium screw-down case back; water-resistant to 20 atm
Band: calfskin, titanium buckle
Remarks: constant glow for up to 25 years in any light condition
Price: $3,000

Atacama Field Automatic

Reference number: XL.1907.NF
Movement: automatic, Sellita Caliber SW220-1 HH5; ø 25.6 mm, height 6.2 mm; 26 jewels; 28,800 vph; 38-hour power reserve
Functions: hours, minutes, sweep seconds; day, date
Case: stainless steel, ø 44 mm, height 15 mm; sapphire crystal with anti-reflective coating; screw-in crown; screw-down case back; water resistant to 20 atm
Band: textile NATO-style, buckle
Remarks: constant glow in orange and green for up to 25 years in any light condition.
Price: $975
Variations: with blue NATO strap; stainless steel bracelet ($1,075)

Sport Timer Automatic

Reference number: 0927
Movement: automatic, Sellita Caliber SW220-1; ø 25.6 mm, height 6.2 mm; 26 jewels; 28,800 vph; 38-hour power reserve
Functions: hours, minutes; date; 2nd time zone
Case: bronze, ø 42 mm, height 13 mm; unidirectional bezel; sapphire crystal; water-resistant to 20 atm
Band: leather, buckle
Remark: constant glow for up to 25 years in any light condition
Price: $1,695; limited to 500 pieces

MAURICE LACROIX

The roots of the brand Maurice Lacroix run deep, all the way to the late nineteenth century, in fact. The name Maurice Lacroix, however, was chosen in 1975 and carried the brand to respectable international success. In 2011, DKSH (Diethelm Keller & SiberHegner), a Swiss holding company that specializes in international market expansions, became the majority shareholder. This has ensured Maurice Lacroix a strong position in all major markets, with flagship stores and its own boutiques.

Nevertheless, the heart of the company remains the production facilities in the highlands of the Jura, in Saignelégier and Montfaucon, where the brand built La Manufacture des Franches-Montagnes SA (MFM) outfitted with state-of-the-art technology for the production of very specific individual parts and movement components.

The watchmaker can thank the clever interpretations of "classic" pocket watch characteristics for its steep ascent in the 1990s. Since then, the *manufacture* has redesigned the complete collection, banning every lick of Breguet-like bliss from its watch designs. In the upper segment, *manufacture* models such as the chronograph and the retrograde variations on Unitas calibers set the tone. In the lower segment, modern "little" complications outfitted with module movements based on ETA and Sellita are the kings. The brand is mainly associated with the hypnotically turning square wheel, the "roue carrée." The idea was used for the latest ladies' watch, the Power of Love, which has three turning hearts forming the word "love" at regular intervals.

The Aikon collection has been gaining in popularity ever since its introduction in 2016. It has a sort of back-to-the-roots quality: precise timekeeping, high readability, and exceptionally comfortable wear. And like all other Maurice Lacroix watches, the Aikon offers a lot of perceived value. The latest creation in the Aikon family is a collaboration with Tide Ocean SA, a company with the mission of recycling and upcycling plastic collected from the oceans. The Aikon #tide comes in a variety of bright colors. The design is genuinely cool, and many parts are made of environmentally friendly material made from upcycled ocean plastic!

Maurice Lacroix SA
Rüschlistrasse 6
CH-2502 Biel/Bienne
Switzerland

Tel.:
+41-44-209-1111

E-mail:
info@mauricelacroix.com

Website:
www.mauricelacroix.com

Founded:
1975

Number of employees:
about 250 worldwide

Annual production:
approx. 90,000 watches

U.S. distributor:
DKSH Premium Brand Distribution
31 NE 17TH St
Miami, FL 33132
609-750-8800

Most important collections/price range:
Aikon / $890 to $2,900; Les Classiques / $950 to $4,300; Eliros / $690 to $1,390; Fiaba (ladies') / $980 to $2,900; Pontos / $1,750 to $7,900; Masterpiece manufacture models / $6,800 to $14,900

Masterpiece Gravity

Reference number: MP6118-SS001-115-1
Movement: automatic, Caliber ML 230; ø 37.2 mm, height 9.05 mm; 35 jewels; 18,000 vph; inverted movement design with dial-side escapement; silicon pallet lever and escape wheel; 50-hour power reserve
Functions: hours and minutes (off-center), subsidiary seconds
Case: stainless steel, ø 43 mm, height 16 mm; sapphire crystal; transparent case back; water-resistant to 5 atm
Band: calfskin, folding clasp
Price: $10,500

Masterpiece Embrace

Reference number: MP6068-SS001-160-1
Movement: automatic, Caliber ML 258; ø 34 mm, height 8.6 mm; 37 jewels; 28,800 vph; finely finished movement; 36-hour power reserve
Functions: hours, minutes, subsidiary seconds (heart-shaped discs rotating into each other); date (retrograde, with quote instead of numerals)
Case: stainless steel, ø 40 mm, height 14 mm; sapphire crystal; transparent case back; water-resistant to 10 atm
Band: calf leather, folding clasp
Price: $7,650

Aikon Master Grand Date

Reference number: AI6118-SS00E-430-C
Movement: automatic, Caliber ML 331; ø 37.2 mm, height 8.4 mm; 43 jewels; 18,000 vph; 50-hour power reserve
Functions: hours and minutes (off-center), subsidiary seconds; large date
Case: stainless steel, ø 45 mm, height 15 mm; sapphire crystal; water-resistant to 10 atm
Band: textile, double folding clasp
Price: $8,150
Variations: various bands

Pontos Day Date

Reference number: PT6358-BRZ01-63E-3
Movement: automatic, automatic, Caliber 143 (base Sellita SW220); ø 25.6 mm, height 4.6 mm; 26 jewels; 28,800 vph; 38-hour power reserve
Functions: hours, minutes, sweep seconds; date and weekday
Case: bronze, ø 41 mm, height 11.1 mm; sapphire crystal; transparent case back; screw-in crown; water resistant to 10 atm
Band: calf leather, double folding clasp
Price: $2,200

Pontos Chronograph

Reference number: PT6388-SS001-120-4
Movement: automatic, Caliber ML 112 (base Sellita SW500); ø 30 mm, height 7.9 mm; 21 jewels; 28,800 vph; 42-hour power reserve
Functions: hours, minutes, subsidiary seconds; chronograph; date
Case: stainless steel, ø 43 mm, height 15 mm; sapphire crystal; water-resistant to 10 atm
Band: calf leather, double folding clasp
Price: $2,990
Variations: various band and dial colors

Aikon Automatic Chronograph Sprint

Reference number: AI6038-DLB01-330-4
Movement: automatic, Caliber ML 112 (Base ETA 7750); ø 30 mm, height 7.9 mm; 25 jewels; 28,800 vph; 48-hour power reserve
Functions: hours, minutes, subsidiary seconds; chronograph; date and weekday
Case: stainless steel with black DLC; ø 44 mm, height 15 mm; sapphire crystal; transparent case back; screw-in crown; water resistant to 20 atm
Band: rubber, double folding clasp
Price: $3,300

Aikon Automatic Chronograph

Reference number: AI6038-SS000-430-4
Movement: automatic, Caliber ML 112 (Base ETA 7750); ø 30 mm, height 7.9 mm; 25 jewels; 28,800 vph; 48-hour power reserve
Functions: hours, minutes, subsidiary seconds; chronograph; date and weekday
Case: stainless steel, ø 44 mm, height 15 mm; sapphire crystal; transparent case back; screw-in crown; water resistant to 20 atm
Band: rubber, double folding clasp
Price: $2,950

Aikon Automatic 42mm

Reference number: AI6008-SS002-230-1
Movement: automatic, Caliber ML 115 (base Sellita SW200-1); ø 25.6 mm, height 4.6 mm; 26 jewels; 28,800 vph; 38-hour power reserve
Functions: hours, minutes, sweep seconds; date
Case: stainless steel, ø 42 mm, height 11 mm; sapphire crystal; transparent case back; screw-in crown; water resistant to 20 atm
Band: stainless steel, double folding clasp
Price: $2,000

Aikon Venturer

Reference number:AI6057-SSL50-630-5
Movement: automatic, Caliber ML 115 (base Sellita SW200-1); ø 25.6 mm, height 4.6 mm; 26 jewels; 28,800 vph; 38-hour power reserve
Functions: hours, minutes, sweep seconds; date
Case: stainless steel, ø 38 mm, height 12 mm; unidirectional bezel with 0-60 scale; sapphire crystal; screw-in crown; water-resistant to 30 atm
Band: rubber, buckle
Price: $2,100

AIKON Automatic Skeleton

Reference number: AI6007-SS002-030-1
Movement: automatic, Caliber ML 115 (base Sellita SW200-1); ø 25.6 mm, height 4.6 mm; 26 jewels; 28,800 vph; skeletonized movement; 38-hour power reserve
Functions: hours, minutes, sweep seconds; date
Case: stainless steel, ø 39 mm, height 11 mm; sapphire crystal; transparent case back; screw-in crown; water resistant to 20 atm
Band: stainless steel, double folding clasp
Remarks: skeletonized dial
Price: $3,450

Aikon Automatic Bicolor

Reference number: AI6007-SP012-130-1
Movement: automatic, Caliber ML 115 (base Sellita SW200-1); ø 25.6 mm, height 4.6 mm; 26 jewels; 28,800 vph; 38-hour power reserve
Functions: hours, minutes, sweep seconds; date
Case: stainless steel, ø 42 mm, height 11 mm; bezel with rose-gold layered elements; sapphire crystal; transparent case back; screw-in crown; water resistant to 20 atm
Band: stainless steel with rose-gold layered elements, double folding clasp
Price: $2,550

Aikon Quartz

Reference number: AI1108-SS002-430-1
Movement: quartz
Functions: hours, minutes, sweep seconds; date
Case: stainless steel, ø 40 mm, height 9 mm; sapphire crystal; water-resistant to 10 atm
Band: stainless steel, double folding clasp
Price: $1,000

Eliros Date

Reference number: EL1118-SS001-620-5
Movement: quartz
Functions: hours, minutes, sweep seconds; date
Case: stainless steel, ø 40 mm, height 8 mm; sapphire crystal; water-resistant to 5 atm
Band: calf leather, folding clasp
Price: $750
Variations: various band and dial colors

Aikon #tide

Reference number: AI2008-00000-300-0
Movement: quartz,
Functions: hours, minutes, sweep seconds; date
Case: acrylic, ø 40 mm, height 11 mm; sapphire crystal; water-resistant to 10 atm
Band: silicone, buckle
Remarks: case and buckle of recycled ocean plastic
Price: $750

Aikon #tide

Reference number: AI2008-CCCC1-3A0-0
Movement: quartz
Functions: hours, minutes, sweep seconds; date
Case: plastic, ø 40 mm, height 11 mm; sapphire crystal; water-resistant to 10 atm
Band: silicone, buckle
Remarks: case and buckle of recycled ocean plastic, dial set with 44 artificial diamonds
Price: $925

MB&F
Route de Drize, 2
CH-1227 Carouge
Switzerland

Tel.:
+41-22-786-3618

E-mail:
info@mbandf.com

Website:
www.mbandf.com

Founded:
2005

Number of employees:
40

Annual production:
approx. 350 watches

U.S. distributors:
Westime Los Angeles and Miami
310-470-1388 (Los Angeles)
786-347-5353 (Miami)
info@westime.com
Provident Jewelry, Florida
561-747-4449; nick@providentjewelry.com
Stephen Silver, Redwood City (California)
650-325-9500; www.shsilver.com
Cellini, New York
212-888-0505; contact@cellinijewelers.com
Watches of Switzerland Las Vegas
702-792-0183, www.watchesofswitzerland.com

Most important collections/price range:
Horological Machines / from $90,000; Legacy Machines / from $64,000

MB&F

In the world of alternative time-tellers, there is one prophet: Maximilian Büsser. After breaking away from brand constraints at Harry Winston, where he launched the Opus line, Büsser founded MB&F (that is, and friends) with the mission of setting creators free. He acts as initiator and coordinator. His Horological Machines are developed and realized in cooperation with highly specialized watchmakers, inventors, and designers in an "idea collective" creating unheard-of mechanical timepieces of great inventiveness, complication, and exclusivity. The composition of this collective varies as much as each machine. Number 5 ("On the Road Again") is an homage to the 1970s, when streamlining rather than brawn represented true strength. The display in the lateral window is reflected by a prism. HM10 is engineering imitating nature, as the watch turns into a bulldog, with bulging, conical "eyes" that tell the time and jaws that open and close to tell you the power reserve.

Contrasting sharply with the modern productions are the Legacy Machines, which reach into horological history and reinterpret past mechanical feats. Even these, of late, have been showing some futuristic chromosomes, as it were. The incredibly complicated Sequential Evo, a collaboration with supreme watch wizard Stephen McDonnell, features two chronographs and a special switch, the "Twinverter," allowing for multiple time computations.

MB&F machines have won awards, several in different categories at the Grand Prix d'Horlogerie, but this year the company clinched the Aiguille d'Or, an award that no one in the great hall could begrudge Büsser, whose work and brand has tirelessly promoted the highest level of watchmaking. And though he is not himself a watchmaker, his spirit, his deep knowledge of engineering, and his sense of aesthetics are always present in each new watch. They are also vented freely in the M.A.D. Galleries the world round, where one finds "mechanical art objects" that are beautiful, intriguing, technically impeccable, and sometimes perfectly useless. They have their own muse and serve as worthy companions to the sci-fi-inspired table clocks that MB&F produces with L'épée 1938.

Legacy Machine Sequential EVO

Reference number: LM Sequential EVO
Movement: manually wound, MB&F Caliber LM Sequential; ø 36.6 mm, height 12.6 mm; 59 jewels; 21,600 vph; dual spring barrel, inverted movement design with balance wheel hovering over the dial; dual chronograph mechanism with twin pushers to switch between modes; finely finished with côtes de Genève; 72-hour power reserve
Functions: hours and minutes (decentral); power reserve indicator; double chronograph with independent measurement
Case: zirconium, ø 44 mm, height 18.2 mm; sapphire crystal; transparent case back; water-resistant to 8 atm
Band: rubber, folding clasp
Price: $180,000
Variations: with black dial

Horological Machine No. 10 "Bulldog"

Reference number: HM10
Movement: manually wound, MB&F Caliber HM10; 34 jewels;18,000 vph; inverted movement design with balance wheel hovering over the dial; 45-hour power reserve
Functions: hours (left display cone), minutes (right display cone); power reserve display (shaped like an opening and closing mouth of a dog)
Case: red gold with titanium elements, 45 x 54 mm, height 24 mm; sapphire crystal; transparent case back; screw-in crown; water resistant to 5 atm
Band: calf leather, folding clasp
Price: $120,000; limited to 8 pieces
Variations: in titanium or in blackened stainless steel with blue "eyes" ($105,000)

Legacy Machine Perpetual EVO

Reference number: Perpetual LMP EVO
Movement: manually wound, MB&F Caliber LM Perpetual; ø 36.6 mm. height 12.6 mm; 41 jewels; 18,000 vph; dual spring barrel, inverted movement design with balance wheel hovering over the dial; finely finished with côtes de Genève; 72-hour power reserve
Functions: hours and minutes (decentral); power reserve indicator; perpetual calendar with date, weekday, month, leap year (reverse counting)
Case: titanium, ø 44 mm. height 17.5 mm; sapphire crystal; transparent case back; water-resistant to 8 atm
Band: rubber, folding clasp
Price: $167,000
Variations: with zirconium case

MEISTERSINGER

MeisterSinger, headquartered in Münster, Germany, has made minimalism a genuine hallmark of this brand, which was launched in 2001. Founder Manfred Brassler chose a look that, in many ways, returns to the very beginnings of watchmaking. Notably, watch hands have different functions. The seconds hand is essentially there to tell that the watch is working, and the hour hand is essentially a slower minute hand, so all three can be pressed into service for a single function, thereby making space on the dial for the eye to wander on their one-handed watches.

MeisterSinger customers are looking for that combination of technical and cultural tradition of early watchmaking with Swiss-made quality and a uniquely reduced design. The quality of the design has been indicated by almost three dozen awards received to date.

Looking at these ultimately simplified dials does tempt one to classify the one-hand watch as an archetype. The single hand simply cannot be reduced any further, and the 144 minutes for 12 hours around the dial do have a normative function of sorts. In one model, the hour jumps very precisely in a window under 12 o'clock—hence its Italian name *Salthora*, or "jumping hour."

With the series novelty Singularis, MeisterSinger has released the second generation of watches with the in-house automatic caliber MSA01. The movement boasts two barrels and 120 hours of power reserve coupled with a unique design and finish. The brand has also been introducing more complications quietly, one watch at a time. There is the particularly large moon phase of the Stratoscope or the almost forgotten complication of the hour strike reserved for the Bell Hora. The Astroscope combines a day and date function with a look at heavenly bodies.

This year, the new Primatic features a power reserve display and comes in no less than four colors. As for the Unimat, it is the brand's first amagnetic watch.

MeisterSinger GmbH & Co. KG
Hafenweg 46
D-48155 Münster
Germany

Tel.:
+49-251-133-4860

E-mail:
info@meistersinger.de

Website:
www.meistersinger.de

Founded:
2001

Number of employees:
13

Annual production:
approx. 10,000 watches

U.S. distributor:
Duber Time
1115 4th Street North, Unit #B
Saint Petersburg, FL 33701
727-896-4278
damir@dubertime.com

Price range:
from approx. $995 to $5,900

Singularis

Reference number: SIN908
Movement: automatic, MeisterSinger Caliber MSA01; ø 32.7 mm, height 6.4 mm; 29 jewels; 28,800 vph; 2 spring barrels; finely finished movement; 120-hour power reserve
Functions: hours (each line stands for 5 minutes); date
Case: stainless steel, ø 43 mm, height 13.5 mm; sapphire crystal; transparent case back; water-resistant to 5 atm
Band: calfskin, folding clasp
Price: $5,399

Primatic Green

Reference number: PR919
Movement: automatic, Sellita Caliber SW270; ø 25.6 mm, height 5.6 mm; 26 jewels; 28,800 vph; 38-hour power reserve
Functions: hours (each line stands for 5 minutes); power reserve indicator; date
Case: stainless steel, ø 41.5 mm, height 13 mm; sapphire crystal; transparent case back; water-resistant to 30 atm
Band: calfskin, buckle
Price: $2,499
Variations: various dial colors

Bell Hora Black

Reference number: BHO902G
Movement: automatic, MeisterSinger Caliber MS-Bell (Basis Sellita SW200-1 with hour-striking module); ø 25.6 mm, height 6.9 mm; 26 jewels; 28,800 vph; 38-hour power reserve
Functions: hours (each line stands for 5 minutes), passing hour chime (can be silenced)
Case: stainless steel, ø 43 mm, height 13 mm; sapphire crystal; transparent case back
Band: calfskin, folding clasp
Price: $4,249
Variations: with blue or ivory-colored dial

N° 01

Reference number: AM3303
Movement: manually wound, Sellita Caliber SW210; ø 25.6 mm, height 3.4 mm; 19 jewels; 28,800 vph; 42-hour power reserve
Functions: hours (each scale line indicates 5 minutes)
Case: stainless steel, ø 43 mm, height 11.5 mm; sapphire crystal; water-resistant to 5 atm
Band: calfskin, buckle
Price: $1,649
Variations: with a blue dial

Perigraph Petrol

Reference number: AM1002P
Movement: automatic, Sellita Caliber SW200-1; ø 25.6 mm, height 4.6 mm; 26 jewels; 28,800 vph; 38-hour power reserve
Functions: hours (each scale line indicates 5 minutes); date (disc display)
Case: stainless steel, ø 43 mm, height 11.5 mm; sapphire crystal; transparent case back; water-resistant to 5 atm
Band: calfskin, buckle
Price: $2,099
Variations: various dial colors

Neo Plus Grün

Reference number: NE419D
Movement: automatic, Sellita Caliber SW200-1; ø 25.6 mm, height 4.6 mm; 26 jewels; 28,800 vph; 38-hour power reserve
Functions: hours (each scale line indicates 5 minutes); date
Case: stainless steel, ø 40 mm, height 9.7 mm; acryl; water-resistant to 3 atm
Band: horse leather, buckle
Price: $1,399
Variations: various dial colors

Stratoscope

Reference number: ST982
Movement: automatic, MeisterSinger Caliber MS-Luna (base Sellita SW220-1); ø 25.6 mm, height 5.05 mm; 26 jewels; 28,800 vph; 38-hour power reserve
Functions: hours (each scale line indicates 5 minutes); date, moon phase
Case: stainless steel, ø 43 mm, height 12.4 mm; sapphire crystal; transparent case back; water-resistant to 5 atm
Band: calfskin, buckle
Price: $4,449

Astroscope

Reference number: AS902B
Movement: automatic, Sellita Caliber SW220-1; ø 25.6 mm, height 5.1 mm; 26 jewels; 28,800 vph; 38-hour power reserve
Functions: hours (each scale line indicates 5 minutes); date and weekday
Case: stainless steel, ø 40 mm, height 10.5 mm; sapphire crystal; transparent case back; water-resistant to 5 atm
Band: calfskin, buckle
Remarks: weekdays are represented by the moon, Mars, Mercury, Jupiter, Venus, Saturn and the sun. The indication is a white dot that seems to jump around erratically across the dial
Price: $2,399

Unomat Blue

Reference number: UN918
Movement: automatic, Sellita Caliber SW400-1; ø 31 mm, height 4.67 mm; 26 jewels; 28,800 vph; antimagnetic; 38-hour power reserve
Functions: hours (each scale line indicates 5 minutes); date
Case: stainless steel, ø 43 mm, height 13.2 mm; sapphire crystal; screw-in crown; water-resistant to 30 atm
Band: stainless steel, folding clasp
Price: $2,399
Variations: various dial colors

MIDO

Among the legacies of World War I was the popularization of the wristwatch, which had freed up soldiers' and aviators' hands to fight and steer, respectively, and permitted artillery officers to coordinate barrages. And, not surprisingly, this led to a kind of reindustrialization of the watch industry. Among the earliest companies to appear on the scene was Mido, which was founded on November 11, 1918—Armistice Day—by Georges Schaeren in Solothurn, Switzerland. The name means "I measure" in Spanish.

At first, the brand produced colorful and imaginative watches that were well suited to the Roaring Twenties. But in the 1930s Mido began making more serious, robust, sportive timepieces better suited for everyday use. For the watch fan of today, water resistance and self-winding are normal. Mido, however, was already offering this functionality in the 1930s with the introduction of the Multifort, which really put the company on the map. This Swiss manufacturer was equally innovative with its movements. It developed a number of very practical novelties like the Radiotime model (1939) and the Multicenterchrono (1941), which today have become genuine collectors' items.

In 1971 the Schaeren family sold the company to the General Watch Co. Ltd., a holding company belonging to ASUAG, which, in turn became the SMH and, ultimately, Swatch Group. Mido continues to produce mostly mechanical watches with about one-quarter of its production devoted to quartz movements. In 1998, Mido decided to revive some of its older watchmaking values. The Multifort, Commander, Battalion, and Baroncelli collections are each in their own way expressions of that mission. Nothing in-your-face, just affordable timepieces with the basic hallmarks of a good Swiss watch, like côtes de Genève on the rotors and, in some cases, even COSC certification. In the meantime, the brand has extended its sales potential to about 2,700 retailers in seventy countries.

Mido SA
Chemin des Tourelles 17
CH-2400 Le Locle
Switzerland

Tel.:
+41-32-933-35-11

Website:
www.mido.ch

Founded:
1918

Number of employees:
50 (estimated)

Annual production:
over 100,000

U.S. distributor:
Mido, division of The Swatch Group (U.S.) Inc.
703 Waterford Way, Suite 450
Miami, FL 33126
www.midowatches.com

Most important collections/price ranges:
Baroncelli / $460 to $1,450; Commander / $710 to $2,000; Multifort / $620 to $2,230; Ocean Star / $890 to $1,700

Ocean Star 200C

Reference number: M042.430.11.091.00
Movement: automatic, Mido Caliber 80.621 (base ETA C07.621); ø 25.6 mm, height 5.22 mm; 25 jewels; 21,600 vph; rotor with côtes de Genève; 80-hour power reserve
Functions: hours, minutes, sweep seconds; date, weekday
Case: stainless steel, ø 42.5 mm, height 12.25 mm; unidirectional bezel with ceramic inlay, with 0-60 scale; sapphire crystal; screw-in crown; water-resistant to 20 atm
Band: stainless steel, folding clasp with extension link
Price: $1,150

Ocean Star GMT

Reference number: M026.629.17.051.00
Movement: automatic, Mido Caliber 80.661 (base ETA C07.661); ø 25.6 mm, height 5.22 mm; 25 jewels; 21,600 vph; with côtes de Genève; 80-hour power reserve
Functions: hours, minutes, sweep seconds; additional 24-hour display (second time zone); date
Case: stainless steel, ø 44 mm, height 13.28 mm; unidirectional bezel with ceramic inlay, with 0-60 scale; sapphire crystal; screw-in crown; water-resistant to 20 atm
Band: textile, buckle
Price: $1,190

Ocean Star 600 Chronometer

Reference number: M026.608.11.041.01
Movement: automatic, Mido Caliber 80.821 (base ETA C07.821); ø 25.6 mm, height 5.22 mm; 25 jewels; 21,600 vph; silicon hairspring; rotor with côtes de Genève; 80-hour power reserve; COSC-certified chronometer
Functions: hours, minutes, sweep seconds; date
Case: stainless steel, ø 43.5 mm, height 14.05 mm; unidirectional bezel with 0-60 scale; sapphire crystal; screw-in crown, helium valve; water-resistant to 60 atm
Band: stainless steel, folding clasp with extension link
Remarks: European diving certified
Price: $1,700

Multifort Patrimony

Reference number: M040.427.36.042.00
Movement: automatic, Mido Caliber 60.A05H31 (base ETA C05.H31); ø 30 mm, height 7.9 mm; 27 jewels; 28,800 vph; rotor with côtes de Genève, 60-hour power reserve
Functions: hours, minutes, subsidiary seconds; chronograph; date
Case: stainless steel with rose gold colored PVD coating, ø 42 mm, height 15.2 mm; sapphire crystal; transparent case back; water-resistant to 5 atm
Band: calfskin, buckle
Price: $1,000

Multifort Skeleton Vertigo

Reference number: M038.436.36.042.00
Movement: automatic, Mido Caliber 80.631 (base ETA C07.631); ø 25.6 mm, height 4.74 mm; 25 jewels; 21,600 vph; partially skeletonized mainplate; 80-hour power reserve
Functions: hours, minutes, sweep seconds
Case: stainless steel with black PVD coating, ø 42 mm, height 10.63 mm; sapphire crystal; transparent case back; water-resistant to 10 atm
Band: calfskin with textile overlay, buckle
Remarks: skeletonized dial
Price: $1,160

Commander Icône

Reference number: M031.631.11.091.00
Movement: automatic, Mido Caliber 80.821 COSC (base ETA C07.821); ø 25.6 mm, height 5.22 mm; 25 jewels; 21,600 vph; silicon hairspring; 80-hour power reserve; COSC-certified chronometer
Functions: hours, minutes, sweep seconds; date and weekday
Case: stainless steel, ø 42 mm, height 11.42 mm; sapphire crystal; transparent case back; water-resistant to 5 atm
Band: stainless steel, folding clasp
Remarks: comes with additional leather band
Price: $1,240

Baroncelli Lady 25

Reference number: M039.007.11.046.00
Movement: automatic, Mido Caliber 48.111 (Basis ETA Caliber 2671); ø 17.5 mm, height 4.8 mm; 25 jewels; 28,800 vph; rotor with côtes de Genève, 48-hour power reserve
Functions: hours, minutes, sweep seconds; date
Case: stainless steel, ø 25 mm, height 9.1 mm; sapphire crystal; transparent case back; water-resistant to 5 atm
Band: stainless steel, folding clasp
Remarks: dial set with 12 diamonds
Price: $930

Baroncelli Signature Gent

Reference number: M037.407.11.041.00
Movement: automatic, Mido Caliber 80.611 (base ETA C07.611); ø 25.6 mm, height 4.4 mm; 25 jewels; 21,600 vph; rotor with côtes de Genève, 80-hour power reserve
Functions: hours, minutes, sweep seconds; date
Case: stainless steel, ø 39 mm, height 9.93 mm; sapphire crystal; transparent case back; water-resistant to 5 atm
Band: stainless steel, folding clasp
Price: $930

Baroncelli Signature Gent

Reference number: M037.407.16.031.00
Movement: automatic, Mido Caliber 80.611 (base ETA C07.611); ø 25.6 mm, height 4.74 mm; 25 jewels; 21,600 vph; rotor with côtes de Genève, 80-hour power reserve
Functions: hours, minutes, sweep seconds; date
Case: stainless steel, ø 39 mm, height 9.93 mm; sapphire crystal; transparent case back; water-resistant to 5 atm
Band: calfskin, folding clasp
Price: $860

MILUS

Milus is one of those brands that has had quite a journey in recent times. It was founded by Paul William Junod in Biel/Bienne and remained in family hands until the year 2002. A new era began then with the founding of Milus International SA under Jan Edöcs and with investments from the giant Peace Mark Group from Hong Kong.

Within a few years, the brand had made a new name for itself with a triple retrograde seconds indicator, which was developed together with the specialists at Agenhor in Geneva. And that made all the difference to the Milus image. In the 1970s, the brand had a considerable reputation for jewelry. Now, however, it has become a genuine and respected watchmaker, one producing top-drawer horological complications. The TriRetrograde function is a Milus trademark and could be found in a host of models all named after constellations (Tirion, Merea, Zetios).

After the Peace Mark Group collapsed in 2008, Milus quickly found another investor in the Chow Tai Fook Group owned by Dr. Cheng Yu-tung. In 2011, Cyril Dubois took over at the head of the company. Quietly, but surely, the brand expanded on several fronts with the triretrogrades in the lead. Unfortunately, it had no staying power. And in 2017, a family named Tissot bought up the brand and started working on streamlining the portfolio, putting out three attractive collections, including a vigorous diver, the Archimèdes, with an inner bezel that can be turned using a separate crown. The simple LAB 01 features a modern fiberglass dial. And the third, the Snow Star, is all that's left from the old collections. It dates originally from the 1940s and was rebuilt and modernized.

Milus International SA
Rue de Reuchenette 19
CH-2502 Biel/Bienne
Switzerland

Tel.:
+41-32-344-3939

E-mail:
info@milus.com

Website:
www.milus.com

Founded:
1919

Distribution:
Contact company in Switzerland

Most important collections/price range:
Milus Snow Star / from approx. $1,763; Archimèdes by Milus / from approx. $2,000; Milus LAB 01 / from approx. $1,000

Snow Star

Reference number: MIH.02.001.IB
Movement: automatic, ETA 2892-A2; ø 25.6 mm, height 3.6 mm; 21 jewels; 28,800 vph; 42-hour power reserve
Functions: hours, minutes, sweep seconds; date
Case: stainless steel, ø 39 mm; sapphire glass; water-resistant to 10 atm
Band: calf leather, buckle
Remarks: Polished 904L steel
Price: $1,763
Variations: ADLC-coated

Archimèdes

Reference number: MIH.01.001.WG
Movement: automatic, ETA 2892-A2; ø 25.6 mm, height 3.6 mm; 21 jewels; 28,800 vph; 42-hour power reserve
Functions: hours, minutes, sweep seconds; date
Case: stainless steel, ø 41 mm; bidirectional inner bezel, screw-in crowns, helium valve; sapphire crystal; water-resistant to 30 atm
Band: rubber, buckle
Price: $2,002

LAB 01

Reference number: MIL.01.001
Movement: automatic, Sellita SW200; ø 26 mm, height 4.6 mm; 26 jewels; 28,800 vph; 38-hour power reserve
Functions: hours, minutes, sweep seconds
Case: stainless steel, ø 40 mm; sapphire glass; water-resistant to 3 atm
Band: Milanese mesh bracelet, folding clasp
Remarks: fiberglass dial
Price: $1,022

Minase
Company representation
H-Development Sarl
Ch. du Long-Champ 99
CH-2504 Biel-Bienne
Switzerland

Tel.:
+41 32 521 06 13

E-mail:
info@h-development.ch

Website:
www.minasewatches.ch
www.h-development.ch

Founded:
2005

Distribution:
Contact the representation in Switzerland

Annual production:
approx. 500 pieces

Most important collections/price range:
Five Windows, Seven Windows, Horizon, Divido; $3,800 to $5,000; special editions

MINASE

Successful companies frequently like to build a monument to their achievements. It might be a real structure, like the Chrysler Building in New York, or something more ephemeral, like an arts endowment. In 2005, Kyowa, a toolmaking enterprise founded in Japan in 1963, paid homage to its own skills in working on watch components by launching a watch brand. Its logo, appearing at 12 o'clock on some models, was inspired from a step drill.

Minase Watches was named after a small village some 250 miles north of Tokyo that was absorbed in that same year 2005 into the neighboring city of Yuzawa. Until recently, it produced no more than three hundred watches a year for the Japanese market, but lately it has begun widening its horizons internationally.

The brand has three basic collections, each of which expresses the company's dedication to traditional hand-finishing. The Five Windows features multiple sapphire crystals integrated into the cases to reveal each watch's complex case-in-case structure, the intricate dial, and the mechanism inside. The date aperture is oversized, emphasizing the feeling of spaciousness on the dial. A subcollection with two extra openings, the Seven Windows, occasionally becomes a canvas for limited editions decorated by select Japanese artists. Lacquerware specialist Junichi Hakose, for example, used the *maki-e urushi* technique—sap from the urushi tree, with gold sprinklings—to create a riveting pattern on one of the dials.

The Horizon line is more sportive, with an elegantly curved sapphire crystal covering an arched dial on a tonneau case. The Divido is far more classical, with a round dial in a slightly angular case. The latest version features the *shibo urushi* technique, lacquer with egg white, which produces a smooth malleable surface that can be sprinkled with inserts.

The physical appearance of a product in Japan is of utmost importance because it suggests extreme care at all levels of design and production. Minase watches are all made according to this *monozukuri* philosophy, which essentially means excellent manufacturing practices. One technique used is *sallaz,* or block polishing, which gives a particularly sparkling polish. Even the stainless-steel bracelets have been inspired by complex Japanese wooden puzzles.

Divido Sky of Shells

Reference number: VM14-M01KA4
Movement: automatic, KT7002 (base ETA 2892); ø 25.6 mm, height 3.6 mm; 28,800 vph; 21 jewels; 50-hour power reserve
Functions: hours, minutes, sweep seconds
Case: stainless steel, ø 40.6 mm, height 11 mm; sapphire crystal, transparent case back; water-resistant to 3 atm
Band: stainless steel, folding clasp
Remarks: dial features shibo urushi technique, a mix of urushi laquer and egg white
Price: $8,200

Seven Windows

Reference number: 15-CDBNGY-SSD
Movement: automatic, KT7002 (base ETA 2892); ø 25.6 mm, height 3.6 mm; 28,800 vph; 21 jewels; 50-hour power reserve
Functions: hours, minutes and central second hands; date
Case: stainless steel, ø 38 x 47 mm, height 13 mm; domed box sapphire crystal (non-reflective coating) on top; transparent case back; 5 sapphire crystals at 12, 6 and 9 o'clock, and 2 sapphire crystals at 3 o'clock; water-resistant to 3 atm
Band: leather, folding clasp
Price: $4,300

Makie Urushi by Hakose - Komon

Reference number: 15-CBKMA2-SSD
Movement: automatic, KT7002 (base ETA 2892); ø 25.6 mm, height 3.6 mm; 28,800 vph; 21 jewels; 50-hour power reserve
Functions: hours, minutes and central second hands
Case: stainless steel, ø 38 x 47 mm, height 13 mm; domed box sapphire crystal (non-reflective coating) on top, see-through sapphire case back and 5 sapphire crystals at 12, 6 and 9 o'clock, and 2 at 3 o'clock; transparent case back; water-resistant to 3 atm
Band: calfskin, folding clasp
Price: $14,500

MING

Horologer Ming Sdn Bhd
B-3A-3, Sunway Palazzio
1 Jalan Sri Hartamas 3
50480 Kuala Lumpur
Malaysia

E-mail:
hello@ming.watch

Website:
www.ming.watch

Founded:
August 2017

Number of employees:
6

Distribution:
online, direct to customer

Annual production:
3000+ pieces

Most important collections/price range:
20 series, 37 series; Special Projects /
CHF 2,500 - CHF 60,000

It takes a certain courage to launch a new watch brand in a crowded market that is subject to emotional swings. Ming, however, is no ordinary brand. It is a cooperative enterprise made up of six watchmaking enthusiasts from around the world. Leading the team is Ming Thein, a well-known photographer, designer, corporate strategist, and watch fan. He hails from Malaysia. Added up, the Ming team computes to a total of eighty solid years' experience collecting watches of all sorts, from vintage pieces to avant-garde works of kinetic art, from robust ground-level timepieces to custom-made products in the six-figure range.

Each of their purchases always gave them a genuine feeling of value and happiness. The mission of the six brand founders was therefore to reconnect with that feeling of emotional excitement that comes from discovering an authentic diamond in the rough. Their strategy was to create a series of watches that are conscientiously finished and stand out thanks to some subtle details in the finishing and the design. These are not flashy pieces but rather subtle seducers by dint of the details, like the carefully worked lugs or the modified ETA 7001 caliber, turning a fairly square assembly into a delicate and colorful ballet of gearwheels and bridges.

The company is not a classical *manufacture*. Rather, they cooperate with partners that are compatible with the brand's aesthetic goals and price points. All Ming watches are assembled, adjusted, and tested in Switzerland. The final quality control is then done in Kuala Lumpur by Ming Thein in person. The technical wizardry of the brand extends to the look: the Mosaic series explores the possibilities of sapphire, which is used for the hands and on the dial. The tesserae are not pasted on, of course, but rather burnt in at different layers using laser busts. And this year, to celebrate its fifth anniversary, the company came out with a new mosaic at a lower price (thanks in part to the use of a robust Sellita movement). They also released a very special monopusher chronograph with a single totalizer for the minutes.

37.04 Monopusher

Reference number: 37.04
Movement: manually wound, LJP 5000.M1; ø 34 mm, height 5.35 mm; 22 jewels; 21,600 vph; skeletonized rose gold-plated bridges; 38-hour power reserve
Functions: hours, minutes; monopusher chronograph, 30-minute totalizer
Case: titanium, ø 38 mm, height 10.9 mm; domed sapphire crystal front and rear; water-resistant to 5 atm
Band: calfskin, buckle
Remarks: guilloché dial with tachymeter and pulsometer scale
Price: $29,500; limited to 100 pieces

37.07 Mosaic For All

Reference number: 37.07
Movement: automatic, modified Sellita SW210.M1, ø 25.6 mm, height 3.35 mm; 19 jewels; 28,800 vph; tungsten micro-rotor; partially skeletonized movement with bicolour bridges; 40-hour power reserve
Functions: hours, minutes
Case: stainless steel, ø 38 mm, height 14 mm; sapphire crystal; transparent case back; water-resistant to 10 atm
Band: calfskin, buckle
Remarks: composite metal and laser-etched sapphire dial with inlaid HyCeram ceramic SuperLumiNova
Price: $3,250

37.05 Moonphase

Reference number: 37.05
Movement: manually wound, Sellita for MING Cal. 288. M1; ø 25.6 mm, height 5.65 mm; 18 jewels; 28,800 vph; anthracite skeletonized bridges with contrast rhodium circular brushing; 38-hour power reserve
Functions: hours, minutes, central moon phase indication and date with quick-set mechanism
Case: stainless steel, ø 38 mm, height 11.9 mm; water-resistant to 10 atm
Band: leather, buckle with micro adjustment
Remarks: luminous moon indication; composite metal and laser-etched sapphire dial with inlaid HyCeram ceramic SuperLumiNova
Price: $5,400

Mk II Corporation
303 W. Lancaster Avenue, #283
Wayne, PA 19087

E-mail:
info@mkiiwatches.com

Website:
www.mkiiwatches.com
tornek-rayville.us

Founded:
2002

Number of employees:
3

Annual production:
1,200 watches

Distribution:
Direct sales

Most important collections/price range:
Ready-to-Wear Collection / $500 to $995;
Benchcrafted collection / $1,000 to $2,000

MK II

If vintage and unserviceable watches had their say, they would probably be naturally attracted to Mk II for the name alone, which is a military designation for the second generation of equipment. The company, which was founded by watch enthusiast and maker Bill Yao in 2002, not only puts retired designs back into service, but also modernizes and customizes them. Before the screwed-down crown, diving watches were not nearly as reliably sealed, for example. And some beautiful old pieces were made with plated brass cases or featured Bakelite components, which are either easily damaged or have aged poorly. The company substitutes not only proven modern materials, but also modern manufacturing methods and techniques to ensure a better outcome.

These are material issues that the team at Mk II handles with great care. They will not, metaphorically speaking, airbrush a Model-T. As genuine watch lovers themselves, they make sure that the final design is in the spirit of the watch itself, which still leaves a great deal of leeway for many iterations, given a sufficient number of parts. In the company's output, vintage style and modern functionality are key. The watches are assembled by hand at the company's workshop in Pennsylvania—and subjected to a rigorous regimen of testing. The components are individually inspected, the cases tested at least three times for water resistance, and at the end the whole watch is regulated in six positions. The ready-to-wear collection is made in Japan and finished in the USA. These watches are robust, timeless and, for the collector of lesser means, affordable. In this era of vintage adulation, Yao intends to develop the clean vintage-style watches of the brand into classics in their own right.

Paradive

Reference number: CD04.1-2004AmK
Movement: automatic (hack setting), TMI Caliber NE15; ø 27.40 mm, height 5.32 mm; 24 jewels; 21,600 vph; rotor decorated with côtes de Genève; 50-hour power reserve
Functions: hours, minutes, sweep seconds, date
Case: stainless steel, ø 41.2 mm, height 15.50 mm; unidirectional bezel with 0-120 scale; high-domed sapphire crystal with antireflective coating; screw-down case back; screw-in crown; water-resistant to 20 atm
Band: nylon
Price: $895
Variations: bezel with 0-12 scale, rubber strap

Stingray

Reference number: CD02.2-K-1002AmK
Movement: automatic (hack setting), TMI Caliber NE15 (made in Japan); ø 27.40 mm, height 5.32 mm; 24 jewels; 21,600 vph; rotor decorated with côtes de Genève; 50-hour power reserve
Functions: hours, minutes, sweep seconds, date
Case: stainless steel; ø 40 mm, height 14.72 mm; unidirectional bezel with 0-120 scale; high-domed sapphire crystal with antireflective coating; screw-down case back; screw-in crown; water-resistant to 20 atm
Band: nylon
Price: $895
Variations: rubber strap, luminous acrylic inlay

TR-660

Reference number: CD02.2-TR660-1002AmK
Movement: automatic (hack setting), TMI Caliber NE15 (made in Japan); ø 27.40 mm, height 5.32 mm; 24 jewels; 21,600 vph; rotor decorated with côtes de Genève; 50-hour power reserve
Functions: hours, minutes, sweep seconds, date
Case: stainless steel, ø 40 mm, height 14.72 mm; unidirectional bezel with 0-120 scale; high-domed sapphire crystal with antireflective coating; screw-down case back; screw-in crown; water-resistant to 20 atm
Band: nylon
Price: $949
Variations: rubber strap, luminous acrylic inlay

MONDAINE

Mondaine Watch Ltd.
Etzelstrasse 27
CH-8808 Pfäffikon SZ
Switzerland

Tel.:
+41-58-666-88-00

E-mail:
info@mondaine.com

Website:
www.mondaine.com

Founded:
1951

Number of employees:
120

Distributor:
Mondaine USA
Lumondi Inc.
27 W. 24th St., Suite 700B
New York, NY 10010
www.mondaine-usa.com
917-522-3421

Most important collections/price range:
Quartz and mechanical versions of the Swiss Railways Watch / $195 to $1,150

On February 23, 1983, Switzerland's Migros supermarket chain presented its annual report to the business press. In addition to the reams of paper, each reporter present received a watch. The day after, all the papers in Switzerland were talking not about groceries but rather about the birth of the M-Watch, the *Volksuhr*, the "people's watch." It was a week before the coming-out of Swatch...

Few have ever realized that the "M" stood not for Migros but for Mondaine Watch, a company founded in the early 1950s by Erwin Bernheim, who parlayed a side job dealing in watches into a sizable company carrying several brands. The Migros cooperation was a major coup. But then Bernheim, now joined by his sons Ronnie and André, decided to make something quintessentially Swiss. After some intense brainstorming, they locked onto the Swiss Railways (SBB) clock, originally designed by the Bauhaus engineer Hans Hilfiker (1901–1993).

Like its model, which hangs in every Swiss railway station, this watch features a simple dial with the characteristic red second hand with its round end, recalling the stationmaster's signaling pan. It became a sensation and has appeared in dozens of iterations, including wall clocks and dashboard watches. A special series was even made that replicates the characteristic 58.5-second journey of the second hand that travelers always see. Before hitting the 12, the second hand pauses to let all clocks in Swiss railway stations be synchronized.

A new Swiss icon, the Helvetica, was released in 2014. It was the first watch to pay tribute to a font. It is in some ways a contradiction, a watch that attracts attention by being as unobtrusive as possible. Helvetica's only character with a serif, the number 1, was cleverly worked into the lugs. The series, however, has since reached the end of its journey.

Swiss Railways Evo2 Automatic

Reference number: MST.4161B.SJ
Movement: automatic, Sellita Caliber SW200-1; ø 25.6 mm, height 4.6 mm; 26 jewels; 28,800 vph; 38-hour power reserve
Functions: hours, minutes, sweep seconds; date
Case: stainless steel, ø 41 mm, height 11 mm; sapphire crystal; transparent case back; water-resistant to 3 atm
Band: stainless steel, folding clasp
Price: $665
Variations: different diameters and dials; quartz

Swiss Railways Evo2 Automatic

Reference number: MSE.40610.LC
Movement: automatic, Sellita Caliber SW200-1; ø 25.6 mm, height 4.6 mm; 26 jewels; 28,800 vph; 38-hour power reserve
Functions: hours, minutes, sweep seconds; date
Case: stainless steel, ø 40 mm, height 7.5 mm; sapphire crystal; transparent case back; water-resistant to 3 atm
Band: leather, buckle
Price: $665
Variations: different diameters and dials; quartz

Classic Forest Green

Reference number: A660.30360.60SBJ
Movement: quartz, Caliber Ronda 513 RL
Functions: hours, minutes, sweep seconds
Case: stainless steel, ø 40 mm, height 10 mm; crown with hardened mineral glass; water-resistant to 3 atm
Band: Milanese mesh, folding clasp
Price: $250

Montblanc Montre SA
10, chemin des Tourelles
CH-2400 Le Locle
Switzerland

Tel.:
+41-32-933-8888

E-mail:
service@montblanc.com

Website:
www.montblanc.com

Founded:
1997 (1906 in Hamburg)

Number of employees:
worldwide approx. 3,000

U.S. distributor:
Montblanc North America
645 Fifth Avenue, 7th Floor
New York, NY 10022
800-995-4810
www.montblanc.com

Most important collections:
Heritage Chronométrie, Heritage Spirit, Meisterstück, Minerva, Nicolas Rieussec, 4810, TimeWalker, Collection Villeret, 1858 Collection, Iced Sea

MONTBLANC

It was with great skill and cleverness that Nicolas Rieussec (1781–1866) used the invention of a special chronograph—the "Time Writer," a device that released droplets of ink onto a rotating sheet of paper—to make a name for himself. Montblanc, once famous only for its exclusive writing implements, borrowed that name on its way to becoming a distinguished watch brand. Within a few years, it had created an impressive range of chronographs driven by in-house calibers: from simple automatic stopwatches to flagship pieces with two independent spring barrels for time and "time-writing."

The Richemont Group, owner of Montblanc, has placed great trust in its "daughter" company, having put the little *manufacture* Minerva, which it purchased at the beginning of 2007, at the disposal of Montblanc. Minerva, which was founded in Villeret in 1858, was already building keyless pocket watches in the 1880s, and by the early twentieth century was producing monopusher chronographs with a reputation for precision. Today, the Minerva Institute serves as a kind of think tank for the future, a place where young watchmakers can absorb the old traditions and skills, as well as the wealth of experience and mindset of the masters.

Montblanc is maintaining the over 160-year Minerva tradition with four leading collections. The 1858 and the Heritage clearly draw inspiration from the company's genomes, with quotations from the 1920s and 1930s, like those salmon-colored dials. The Star Legacy and the TimeWalker lines allow Montblanc to explore some more complex complications packaged in more modern forms.

1858 Iced Sea Automatic Date

Reference number: 129765
Movement: automatic, Montblanc Caliber MB 24.17 (base ETA 2824-2); ø 25.6 mm, height 4.6 mm; 25 jewels; 28,800 vph; 38-hour power reserve
Functions: hours, minutes, sweep seconds; date
Case: stainless steel, ø 41 mm, height 12.9 mm; unidirectional bezel with ceramic insert, with 0-60 scale; sapphire crystal; water-resistant to 30 atm
Band: rubber, double folding clasp
Price: $2,975
Variations: with stainless steel band ($3,190)

1858 Geosphere Chronograph "Zero Oxygen"

Reference number: 129624
Movement: automatic, Caliber MB 29.27; 33 jewels; 28,800 vph; 46-hour power reserve
Functions: hours, minutes; additional 12-hour display (second time zone); synchronously counter-rotating world time indicators for northern and southern hemispheres; chronograph; date
Case: titanium, ø 44 mm, height 17.1 mm; bezel with ceramic insert; sapphire crystal; water-resistant to 10 atm
Band: calfskin, folding clasp
Remarks: case filled with 100% nitrogen; limited to 290 pieces as homage to mountain climber Nimsdai Purja, who wants to climb Mount Everest (29,000 feet high) alone and without oxygen
Price: $8,600

1858 Minerva Monopusher Chronograph "Red Arrow"

Reference number: 129614
Movement: manually wound, Caliber MB M13.21; ø 29.5 mm, height 6.4 mm; 22 jewels; 18,000 vph; single pusher for chronograph functions; screw balance, balance spring with Philips terminal curve; 60-hour power reserve
Functions: hours, minutes, subsidiary seconds; chronograph
Case: stainless steel, ø 42 mm, height 13.15 mm; white gold bezel; bidirectional bezel with reference marker; sapphire crystal; transparent case back; water-resistant to 3 atm
Band: reptile skin, triple folding clasp
Price: $29,500; limited to 88 pieces

The Unveiled Secret Minerva Monopusher Chronograph

Reference number: 129622
Movement: manually wound, Caliber MB M16.26; ø 37.5 mm, height 7.05 mm; 26 jewels; 18,000 vph; inverted movement design with chronograph mechanism on dial-side; column wheel control of chronograph functions using a single pusher; screw balance; 50-hour power reserve
Functions: hours, minutes, subsidiary seconds; chronograph
Case: rose gold, ø 43 mm, height 14.18 mm; sapphire crystal; water-resistant to 3 atm
Band: reptile skin, buckle
Remarks: skeletonized dial
Price: $46,500; limited to 18 pieces

1858 GMT Automatic Date

Reference number: 129615
Movement: automatic, Caliber ML 24.33 (Sellita SW330); ø 25.6 mm, height 3.6 mm; 25 jewels; 28,800 vph; 42-hour power reserve
Functions: hours, minutes, sweep seconds; additional 24-hour display (second time zone); date
Case: stainless steel, ø 42 mm, height 12.25 mm; rotating bezel with aluminum insert; sapphire crystal; water-resistant to 10 atm
Band: stainless steel, double folding clasp
Price: $3,730
Variations: with a blue bezel, dial, and rubber strap

Star Legacy Moonphase

Reference number: 129631
Movement: automatic, Montblanc Caliber ML 24.31 (Sellita SW380); ø 25.6 mm, height 4.1 mm; 25 jewels; 28,800 vph; 50-hour power reserve
Functions: hours, minutes, sweep seconds; date, moon phase
Case: stainless steel, ø 42 mm, height 11.38 mm; sapphire crystal; transparent case back; water-resistant to 5 atm
Band: stainless steel, triple folding clasp
Price: $4,600; limited to 1786 pieces
Variations: with reptile skin strap ($4,300)

1858 Geosphere Ultra-Black

Reference number: 128257
Movement: automatic, Caliber MB 29.25 (Sellita SW300 with Montblanc manufacture complication); ø 25.6 mm; 26 jewels; 28,800 vph; 42-hour power reserve
Functions: hours, minutes; additional12-hour display (second time zone), synchronously counter-rotating world time indicators for northern and southern hemispheres; date
Case: stainless steel, ø 42 mm, height 12.8 mm; bidirectional bezel with ceramic insert; sapphire crystal; water-resistant to 10 atm
Band: calfskin, triple folding clasp
Price: $6,800; limited to 858 pieces

1858 Automatic 24H

Reference number: 126007
Movement: automatic, Caliber MB 24.20 (base Sellita SW330); ø 25.6 mm; height 4.1 mm; 25 jewels; 28,800 vph; 42-hour power reserve
Functions: 24-hour display (each line on dial indicates 15 minutes)
Case: stainless steel, ø 42 mm, height 11.2 mm; bezel in bronze; sapphire crystal; water-resistant to 10 atm
Band: textile, buckle
Price: $3,235

Heritage Pythagore Small Second LE148

Reference number: 128667
Movement: manually wound, Caliber MB M14.08; ø 31.6 mm, height 4.07 mm; 19 jewels; 18,000 vph; screw balance, German silver plates and bridges, finely finished movement; 80-hour power reserve
Functions: hours, minutes, subsidiary seconds
Case: rose gold, ø 39 mm, height 9.5 mm; sapphire crystal; transparent case back; water-resistant to 5 atm
Band: reptile skin, buckle
Price: $20,500; limited to 148 pieces
Variations: in white gold

Caliber MB R200

Automatic; monopusher column-wheel control, vertical chronograph clutch, stop-seconds mechanism; double spring barrel, 72-hour power reserve
Functions: hours, minutes, subsidiary seconds; additional 12-hour display (2nd time zone); chronograph; date
Diameter: 31 mm
Height: 8.46 mm
Jewels: 40
Balance: screw balance
Frequency: 28,800 vph
Balance spring: flat hairspring
Remarks: rhodium-plated mainplate with perlage, bridges with côtes de Genève

Caliber MB M62.00

Manually wound; swan-neck fine adjustment; single spring barrel, 50-hour power reserve
Functions: hours, minutes, subsidiary seconds
Diameter: 23.6 mm
Height: 3.9 mm
Jewels: 20
Frequency: 18,000 vph
Remarks: replica of a historical Minerva caliber, finely finished

Caliber MB M13.21

Manually wound; column-wheel control of chronograph functions; single spring barrel, 60-hour power reserve
Functions: hours, minutes, subsidiary seconds; chronograph
Diameter: 29.5 mm
Height: 6.4 mm
Jewels: 22
Balance: screw balance with weights
Frequency: 18,000 vph
Balance spring: with Phillips end curve
Shock protection: Incabloc
Remarks: German silver plates and bridges, rhodium-plated, partially with perlage, hand-beveled

Caliber MB 29.22

Automatic; single spring barrel, 48-hour power reserve
Base caliber: Cartier 1904-PS MC
Functions: hours, minutes, sweep seconds; additional 12-hour display (2nd time zone); perpetual calendar with date, weekday, month, moon phase, leap year
Diameter: 28.2 mm
Height: 4.95 mm
Jewels: 77
Frequency: 28,800 vph
Balance spring: flat hairspring
Remarks: 378 parts

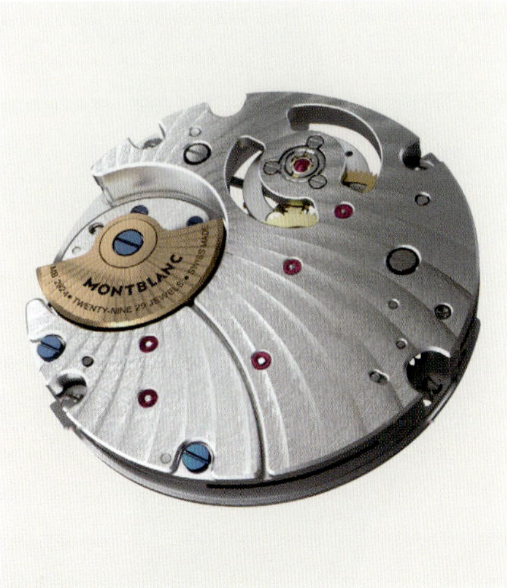

Caliber MB M29.24

Automatic; 1-minute tourbillon with external hairspring; 2 spring barrels, 48-hour power reserve
Functions: hours, minutes
Diameter: 30.6 mm
Height: 4.5 mm
Jewels: 27
Balance: screw balance with 18 weighted screws
Frequency: 21,600 vph
Hairspring: flat hairspring
Remarks: gold micro rotor, bridges with côtes de Genève

Caliber MB M16.31

Manually wound; monopusher for column-wheel control of chronograph functions, swan-neck fine adjustment; single spring barrel, 50-hour power reserve
Functions: hours, minutes, subsidiary seconds; split-second chronograph
Diameter: 38.4 mm
Height: 8.13 mm
Jewels: 22
Balance: screw balance with Breguet hairspring
Frequency: 18,000 vph
Balance spring: with Phillips end curve
Remarks: rhodium-plated mainplate with perlage, bridges with côtes de Genève, gold-plated wheelworks; 262 parts

MONTRES CHOISI

Montres Choisi
Rue des Draizes n° 5
CH-2000 Neuchâtel
Switzerland

Tel.:
+41-79-765-1466

E-mail:
askme@choisiwatch.com

Website:
www.choisiwatch.com

Founded:
1929

Number of employees:
4

Distribution:
Montres Choisi deals directly with customers.

Most important collections/price range:
1929 Collection / from $800; Heritage Collection / from $800

Sometimes even the most forward-thinking and forward-conceiving artists may feel, for whatever reason, the need to express their art in a more conventional style. One might think of Arnold Schoenberg transcribing Strauss waltzes. Similarly, watch brands engaging in some very creative, avant-garde watchmaking or, as some might call it, kinetic art, may feel the impulse to just make a watch with a wide appeal that can be worn every day without necessarily attracting undue attention. It was one reason why Azimuth (see page 74), according to its CEO, Chris Long, purchased in 2013 a venerable Swiss brand that had sunk into obscurity.

Montres Choisi is a member of that coterie of companies that boosted the reputation of Swiss watchmaking during the twentieth century. It traces its roots to 1924 but became a full-fledged brand in 1929, manufacturing and distributing a host of attractive and fashionable watches. During World War II, it branched out into robust military timepieces that were purchased by both sides of the conflict. It managed to stay above water during the 1950s but then went dormant.

When reviving the brand, the new owners decided to focus on two clear lines that are unabashedly vintage but include modern touches like brushed surfaces and a more honed look. This is particularly true for the 1929 line, whose cushion cases give it a timeless vintage demeanor, anywhere between the 1920s and early 1970s. Of note is the 2019 Diver, celebrating Choisi's ninetieth anniversary with its a minimalist bezel providing minute markers only for the last critical fifteen minutes of a dive.

Another noteworthy watch is the Docteurgraph, a chronograph with a pulsometer on a racy black dial and striking gold hands. The pushers for this left-handed watch are all on the left side of the case to avoid their pressing into the wearer's hand in the event he or she must perform CPR.

The second line is called Heritage and is distinguished by its round, 42-millimeter cases and dials that are elegant and discrete. All watches run on robust ETA, Unitas, or vintage movements, like the FHF 96.

Heritage Pilot

Movement: manually wound, FHF96; ø 25.6 mm, height 4.5 mm; 17 jewels; 18,000 vph; 48-hour power reserve
Functions: hours, minutes, sweep seconds
Case: stainless steel, ø 42 mm, height 11.8 mm; transparent case back; water-resistant to 5 atm
Band: calfskin, folding clasp
Remarks: available with silver dial
Price: $900

1929 Diver 90th Anniversary Model

Movement: manually wound, AS1950/51; ø 25.6 mm, height 4.50 mm; 17 jewels; 21,600 vph; 46-hour power reserve
Functions: hours, minutes, sweep seconds; date
Case: stainless steel, ø 41 mm, height 12.5 mm; unidirectional bezel; water-resistant to 20 atm
Band: textile, folding clasp
Remarks: special 90th anniversary edition
Price: $900; limited to 90 pieces

Military Original

Movement: manually wound, Unitas 6498-1; ø 36.60 mm, height 4.50 mm; 17 jewels; 53-hour power reserve
Functions: hours, minutes, subsidiary seconds
Case: stainless steel, ø 42 mm, height 11.8 mm; water-resistant to 5 atm
Band: calfskin, folding clasp
Remarks: 1950s vintage movement
Price: $950

1929 Tachygraph

Movement: automatic, Valjoux 7750; ø 30 mm, height 7.9 mm; 29 jewels; 28,800 vph; 48-hour power reserve
Functions: hours, minutes, chronograph with minute totalizer; tachymeter
Case: stainless steel, 44 mm, height 16.5 mm; water-resistant to 5 atm
Band: calfskin, folding clasp
Price: $1,800

Heritage Tachygraph

Movement: automatic, Valjoux 7750; ø 30 mm, height 7.9 mm; 29 jewels; 28,800 vph; 48-hour power reserve
Functions: hours, minutes, chronograph, subsidiary seconds; tachymeter
Case: stainless steel, ø 42 mm, height 15.5 mm; water-resistant to 5 atm
Band: calfskin, folding clasp
Price: $1,800

1929 Docteurgraph

Movement: automatic, Valjoux 7750; ø 30 mm, height 7.9 mm; 29 jewels; 28,800 vph; 48-hour power reserve
Functions: hours, minutes, chronograph with minute totalizer; 30-pulsation graph
Case: stainless steel, 44 mm, height 16.5 mm; water-resistant to 5 atm
Band: calfskin, folding clasp
Price: $1,800
Variations: black dial

1929 Bienne

Movement: manually wound, FHF96; ø 25.6 mm, height 4.5 mm; 17 jewels; 18,000 vph; 48-hour power reserve
Functions: hours, minutes, sweep seconds
Case: stainless steel, 44 mm, height 12.2 mm; water-resistant to 5 atm
Band: calfskin, folding clasp
Remarks: 1960s vintage movement
Price: $800

Heritage GT FHF96

Movement: manually wound, FHF96; ø 25.6 mm, height 4.5 mm; 17 jewels; 18,000 vph; 48-hour power reserve
Functions: hours, minutes, sweep seconds
Case: stainless steel, ø 42 mm, height 11.8 mm; water-resistant to 5 atm
Band: calf strap, folding clasp
Remarks: 1960s vintage movement
Price: $800

1929 GT FHF96

Movement: manually wound, FHF96; ø 25.6 mm, height 4.5 mm; 17 jewels; 18,000 vph; 48-hour power reserve
Functions: hours, minutes, sweep seconds
Case: stainless steel, ø 44 mm, height 12.2 mm; water-resistant to 5 atm
Band: calfskin strap, folding clasp
Remarks: 1960s vintage movement
Price: $800

MÜHLE GLASHÜTTE

Mühle Glashütte GmbH
Nautische Instrumente und Feinmechanik
Altenberger Strasse 35
D-01768 Glashütte
Germany

Tel.:
+49-35053-3203-0

E-mail:
info@muehle-glashuette.de

Website:
www.muehle-glashutte.de

Founded:
first founding 1869; second founding 1993

Number of employees:
47

U.S. distributor:
Mühle Glashütte USA
920 Dr. MLK Jr. Street North
St. Petersburg, FL 33704
727-896-4278
www.muehleglashuetteusa.com

Most important collections/price range:
mechanical wristwatches / approx. $1,399 to $5,400

Family-run businesses are notoriously successful, especially as each generation must balance tradition with managing the challenges that time brings. Rob. Mühle & Sohn has been doing just this for over 150 years. It started as a manufacturer of precision measuring instruments and managed to survive the ups and downs of German history. Originally, this was for the local watch industry and the German School of Watchmaking. By the early 1920s, the firm was supplying the automobile industry, making speedometers, automobile clocks, tachometers, and other measurement instruments.

As a supplier for the Wehrmacht, it drew Soviet bombers during World War II, and was then nationalized. After the fall of the Iron Curtain, Hans-Jürgen Mühle took the helm, followed, in 2007, by his son, Thilo Mühle.

The wristwatch line was launched as a sideline of sorts in mid-1994 but has now overtaken the nautical instruments for which Mühle was famous. Its collection comprises mechanical wristwatches at entry- and mid-level prices. For these, the company uses Swiss base movements that are equipped with such in-house developments as a patented woodpecker-neck regulation and the Mühle rotor. The modifications are so extensive that they have led to the calibers having their own names. The traditional line named "R. Mühle & Sohn," introduced in 2014, is equipped with the RMK 1 and RMK 2 calibers. And there are other, somewhat less nautically inspired timepieces, like the Lunova series or the 29ers, which are simply elegant in an unspectacular way. While the watches are by and large in the sportive-elegant segment, the company has shown some boldness in the color of the dials and straps.

S.A.R. Rescue-Timer Lumen

Reference number: M1-41-08-KB
Movement: automatic, Sellita Caliber SW200-1; ø 25.6 mm, height 4.6 mm; 26 jewels; 28,800 vph; with woodpecker-neck adjustment, Mühle rotor, carefully reworked with special Mühle finish; 38-hour power reserve
Functions: hours, minutes, sweep seconds; date
Case: stainless steel, ø 42 mm, height 13.5 mm; bezel with rubber ring; sapphire crystal; screw-in crown; water-resistant to 100 atm
Band: rubber, folding clasp, with extension link
Remarks: dial completely covered with luminescent mass
Price: $2,399
Variations: with textile strap ($2,399); with stainless steel bracelet ($2,499)

S.A.R. Flieger-Chronograph

Reference number: M1-41-33-KB
Movement: automatic, Caliber MU 9413 (base Sellita SW500); ø 30 mm, height 7.9 mm; 25 jewels; 28,800 vph; woodpecker-neck adjustment, three-quarter plate, Mühle rotor, carefully reworked with special Mühle finish; 48-hour power reserve
Functions: hours, minutes, subsidiary seconds; chronograph; date
Case: stainless steel, ø 45 mm, height 16.2 mm; bidirectional bezel with 0-60 scale; sapphire crystal; transparent case back; screw-in crown; water-resistant to 10 atm
Band: rubber, folding clasp, with extension link
Price: $4,149
Variations: with stainless steel bracelet ($4,299)

Sea-Timer BlackMotion

Reference number: M1-41-83-NB
Movement: automatic, Sellita Caliber SW200-1; ø 25.6 mm, height 4.6 mm; 26 jewels; 28,800 vph; woodpecker-neck adjustment, Mühle rotor, carefully reworked with special Mühle finish; 38-hour power reserve
Functions: hours, minutes, sweep seconds; date
Case: stainless steel with black titanium carbide coating, ø 44 mm, height 12.5 mm; bidirectional bezel with 0-60 scale; sapphire crystal; transparent case back; screw-in crown; water-resistant to 30 atm
Band: textile, buckle
Price: $2,599

Panova Blau

Reference number: M1-40-72-NB
Movement: automatic, Sellita Caliber SW200-1; ø 25.6 mm, height 4.6 mm; 26 jewels; 28,800 vph; woodpecker-neck adjustment, Mühle rotor, carefully reworked with special Mühle finish; 38-hour power reserve
Functions: hours, minutes, sweep seconds
Case: stainless steel, ø 40 mm, height 10.4 mm; sapphire crystal; screw-in crown; water-resistant to 10 atm
Band: textile, buckle
Price: $999
Variations: with calfskin strap ($999)

29er Big

Reference number: M1-25-37-CB
Movement: automatic, Sellita Caliber SW200-1; ø 25.6 mm, height 4.6 mm; 26 jewels; 28,800 vph; woodpecker-neck adjustment, Mühle rotor, carefully reworked with special Mühle finish; 38-hour power reserve
Functions: hours, minutes, sweep seconds; date
Case: stainless steel, ø 42.4 mm, height 11.3 mm; sapphire crystal; transparent case back; screw-in crown; water-resistant to 10 atm
Band: textile, buckle
Price: $1,899
Variations: with stainless steel bracelet ($1,999)

29er Casual

Reference number: M1-25-72-NB
Movement: automatic, Sellita Caliber SW300-1; ø 25.6 mm, height 3,6 mm; 25 jewels; 28,800 vph; woodpecker-neck adjustment, Mühle rotor, carefully reworked with special Mühle finish; 42-hour power reserve
Functions: hours, minutes, sweep seconds; date
Case: stainless steel, ø 42.4 mm, height 9.75 mm; sapphire crystal; transparent case back; screw-in crown; water-resistant to 10 atm
Band: textile, buckle
Price: $1,999
Variations: with calfskin strap ($2,199)

Lunova Day/Date

Reference number: M1- 43- 26- LB
Movement: automatic, Sellita Caliber SW220-1; ø 25.6 mm, height 5.05 mm; 26 jewels; 28,800 vph; woodpecker-neck adjustment, Mühle rotor, carefully reworked with special Mühle finish; 38-hour power reserve
Functions: hours, minutes, sweep seconds; date, weekday
Case: titanium, ø 42.3 mm, height 11 mm; sapphire crystal; transparent case back; screw-in crown; water-resistant to 10 atm
Band: reptile skin, buckle
Price: $2,349

Teutonia Sport II "Racing Green"

Reference number: M1-29-74-LB
Movement: automatic, Sellita Caliber SW290-1; ø 25.6 mm, height 5.6 mm; 31 jewels; 28,800 vph; woodpecker-neck adjustment, Mühle rotor, carefully reworked with special Mühle finish; 38-hour power reserve
Functions: hours, minutes, subsidiary seconds; date
Case: stainless steel, ø 41.6 mm, height 12.8 mm; sapphire crystal; transparent case back; screw-in crown; water-resistant to 10 atm
Band: calfskin, buckle
Price: $2,799

Teutonia IV Lady

Reference number: M1-44-51-LB-V-VII
Movement: automatic, Sellita Caliber SW200-1; ø 25.6 mm, height 4.6 mm; 26 jewels; 28,800 vph; woodpecker-neck fine adjustment, Mühle rotor, carefully reworked with Mühle special finishing; 38-hour power reserve
Functions: hours, minutes, sweep seconds; date
Case: stainless steel, ø 33.5 mm, height 10.2 mm; yellow-gold bezel sapphire crystal; transparent case back; screw-in crown; water-resistant to 30 atm
Band: calf leather, buckle
Price: $2,199

NOMOS

Who says Germans have no sense of humor? The best of it is simply subtle enough to be accessible to the poets and thinkers (*Dichter und Denker*) with command of the language and its many dialects. At its apex, humor pays tribute to the joke-tellers themselves, by being self-deprecatory and deadpan. This may be the reason for Nomos's global success. Ever since its founding in 1990 by Roland Schwertner and his associate Uwe Ahrendt, the company's marketing measures have harmonized with the product in a subtly playful and humorous manner.

Their emphasis on design meant that the brand needed its own calibers, and these are wisely distributed throughout the eleven model families with about eighty variations that grace the company's portfolio. The first one was the manually wound Alpha. The one that made a loud splash, however, was undoubtedly the DUW 4401 (Deutsche Uhrenwerke Nomos Glashütte), equipped with an in-house escapement with a spring "made in Germany." This regulating component was presented to the watch world in 2014 and has gradually been integrated into all the brand's movements, including the new, automatic, ultrathin DUW 3001. The key to Nomos is streamlining, so complications are introduced with the movements in homeopathic doses. For example, the DUW 6101 features a safe and easy date correction, and it is a mere 3.6 millimeters high including the date, which fits well in the company's design efforts.

Speaking of design, of the two hundred or so people who work at Nomos, about twenty are members of the Berlin-based company Berlinerblau and are spread out across the world, from New York to Lake Como in Italy. This aesthetic-philosophical scrim, as it were, has produced the swimmer's watch Ahoi (as in "ship ahoy!"), with an optional synthetic strap like those that carry locker keys at Germany's public swimming pools. The Autobahn is a panegyric to Germany's favorite playground, the highway. Worthy of note: Nomos has won over 160 prizes for design and quality since its launch.

Nomos Glashütte/SA
Roland Schwertner KG
Ferdinand-Adolph-Lange-Platz 2
01768 Glashütte
Germany

Tel.:
+49-35053-404-0

E-mail:
nomos@glashuette.com

Website:
nomos-glashuette.com

Founded:
1990

Number of employees:
approx. 200

U.S. distributor:
For the U.S. market, please contact:
NOMOS Glashuette USA Inc.
347 W. 36th St.
New York, NY 10018
212-929-2575
contact@nomos-watches.com

Most important collections/price range:
Ahoi / $4,020 to $4,660; Autobahn / $4,800; Club / $1,500 to $4,060; Lambda / $17,000 to $20,000; Ludwig / $1,380 to $4,000; Lux / $19,500 to $21,500; Metro / $2,860 to $9,700; Orion / $1,600 to $4,350; Tangente / $1,440 to $4,980; Tangomat / $3,280 to $4,920; Tetra / $1,660 to $3,980; Zürich / $4,480 to $6,100

Tangente Neomatik 39 Platinum Gray

Reference number: 143
Movement: automatic, Nomos Caliber DUW 3001; ø 28.8 mm, height 3.2 mm; 27 jewels; 21,600 vph; three-quarter plate, fine finishing on movement; 43-hour power reserve
Functions: hours, minutes, subsidiary seconds
Case: stainless steel, ø 38.5 mm, height 6.9 mm; sapphire crystal; water-resistant to 5 atm
Band: horse leather, winged clasp
Price: $3,070

Tangente Neomatik 41 Update

Reference number: 180
Movement: automatic, Nomos Caliber DUW 6101; ø 35.2 mm, height 3.6 mm; 27 jewels; 21,600 vph; three-quarter plate, finely finished movement; 42-hour power reserve
Functions: hours, minutes, subsidiary seconds; date
Case: stainless steel, ø 40.5 mm, height 7.8 mm; sapphire crystal; transparent case back; water-resistant to 5 atm
Band: horse leather, buckle
Price: $4,100

Club Neomatik 42 Date Blue

Reference number: 782
Movement: automatic, Nomos Caliber DUW 6101; ø 35.2 mm, height 3.6 mm; 27 jewels; 21,600 vph; three-quarter plate, finely finished movement; 42-hour power reserve
Functions: hours, minutes, subsidiary seconds; date
Case: stainless steel, ø 42 mm, height 10.2 mm; sapphire crystal; transparent case back; screw-in crown; water-resistant to 30 atm
Band: stainless steel, folding clasp
Price: $3,960

Tangente 38 Date

Reference number: 130
Movement: automatic, Nomos Caliber DUW 4101; ø 32.1 mm, height 2.8 mm; 23 jewels; 21,600 vph; three-quarter plate, fine finishing on movement; 42-hour power reserve
Functions: hours, minutes, subsidiary seconds; date
Case: stainless steel, ø 37.5 mm, height 6.8 mm; sapphire crystal; transparent case back; water-resistant to 3 atm
Band: horse leather, buckle
Price: $2,780

Tangente Neomatik 41 Update Midnight Blue

Reference number: 182
Movement: automatic, Nomos Caliber DUW 6101; ø 35.2 mm, height 3.6 mm; 27 jewels; 21,600 vph; three-quarter plate, finely finished movement; 42-hour power reserve
Functions: hours, minutes, subsidiary seconds; date
Case: stainless steel, ø 40.5 mm, height 7.8 mm; sapphire crystal; transparent case back; water-resistant to 5 atm
Band: horse leather, buckle
Price: $4,100

Ludwig 38 Enamel White

Reference number: 236
Movement: manually wound, Nomos Caliber Alpha; ø 23.3 mm, height 2.6 mm; 17 jewels; 21,600 vph; three-quarter plate, finely finished movement; 43-hour power reserve
Functions: hours, minutes, subsidiary seconds
Case: stainless steel, ø 37.5 mm, height 6.7 mm; sapphire crystal; water-resistant to 3 atm
Band: horse leather, buckle
Price: $1,960

Orion 38 Silver

Reference number: 378
Movement: manually wound, Nomos Caliber Alpha; ø 23.3 mm, height 2.6 mm; 17 jewels; 21,600 vph; three-quarter plate, finely finished movement; 43-hour power reserve
Functions: hours, minutes, subsidiary seconds
Case: stainless steel, ø 38 mm, height 8.9 mm; sapphire crystal; transparent case back; water-resistant to 3 atm
Band: suede, buckle
Price: $2,260

Metro Neomatik 41 Update

Reference number: 1165
Movement: automatic, Nomos Caliber DUW 6101; ø 35.2 mm, height 3.6 mm; 27 jewels; 21,600 vph; three-quarter plate, finely finished movement; 42-hour power reserve
Functions: hours, minutes, subsidiary seconds; date
Case: stainless steel, ø 40.5 mm, height 9.1 mm; sapphire crystal; transparent case back; water-resistant to 5 atm
Band: textile, winged clasp
Price: $4,660

Metro Date Power Reserve

Reference number: 1101
Movement: manually wound, Nomos Caliber DUW 4401; ø 32.1 mm, height 2.8 mm; 23 jewels; 21,600 vph; three-quarter plate, finely finished movement; 42-hour power reserve
Functions: hours, minutes, subsidiary seconds; power reserve display; date
Case: stainless steel, ø 37 mm, height 7.7 mm; sapphire crystal; transparent case back; water-resistant to 3 atm
Band: horse leather, buckle
Price: $3,780

Ahoi Neomatik

Reference number: 560
Movement: automatic, Nomos Caliber DUW 3001; ø 28.8 mm, height 3.2 mm; 27 jewels; 21,600 vph; three-quarter plate, fine finishing on movement; 43-hour power reserve
Functions: hours, minutes, subsidiary seconds
Case: stainless steel, ø 36.3 mm, height 9.6 mm; sapphire crystal; screw-in crown; water-resistant to 20 atm
Band: textile, winged clasp
Price: $4,020

Tangente Sport Neomatik 42 Date Marine Black

Reference number: 581
Movement: automatic, Nomos Caliber DUW 6101; ø 35.2 mm, height 3.6 mm; 27 jewels; 21,600 vph; three-quarter plate, fine finishing on movement; 42-hour power reserve
Functions: hours, minutes, subsidiary seconds; date
Case: stainless steel, ø 42 mm, height 10.9 mm; sapphire crystal; transparent case back; screw-in crown; water-resistant to 30 atm
Band: stainless steel, folding clasp
Price: $4,980

Autobahn Neomatik 41 Date Sports Gray

Reference number: 1303
Movement: automatic, Nomos Caliber DUW 6101; ø 35.2 mm, height 3.6 mm; 27 jewels; 21,600 vph; three-quarter plate, finely finished movement; 42-hour power reserve
Functions: hours, minutes, subsidiary seconds; date
Case: stainless steel, ø 41 mm, height 10.5 mm; sapphire crystal; transparent case back; water-resistant to 10 atm
Band: textile, winged clasp
Price: $4,800

Club Sport Neomatik 42 Date Black

Reference number: 781
Movement: automatic, Nomos Caliber DUW 6101; ø 35.2 mm, height 3.6 mm; 27 jewels; 21,600 vph; three-quarter plate, finely finished movement; 42-hour power reserve
Functions: hours, minutes, subsidiary seconds; date
Case: stainless steel, ø 42 mm, height 10.2 mm; sapphire crystal; transparent case back; screw-in crown; water-resistant to 30 atm
Band: stainless steel, folding clasp
Price: $3,960

Club Campus 38 Blue Purple

Reference number: 730
Movement: manually wound, Nomos Caliber Alpha; ø 23.3 mm, height 2.6 mm; 17 jewels; 21,600 vph; three-quarter plate, finely finished movement; 43-hour power reserve
Functions: hours, minutes, subsidiary seconds
Case: stainless steel, ø 38.5 mm, height 8.5 mm; sapphire crystal; water-resistant to 10 atm
Band: suede, buckle
Price: $1,650

Club Campus Deep Pink

RReference number: 711
Movement: manually wound, Nomos Caliber Alpha; ø 23.3 mm, height 2.6 mm; 17 jewels; 21,600 vph; three-quarter plate, finely finished movement; 43-hour power reserve
Functions: hours, minutes, subsidiary seconds
Case: stainless steel, ø 36 mm, height 8.2 mm; sapphire crystal; water-resistant to 10 atm
Band: suede, buckle
Price: $1,500

Ludwig Gold 33

Reference number: 240
Reference number: 210
Movement: manually wound, Nomos Caliber Alpha; ø 23.3 mm, height 2.6 mm; 17 jewels; 21,600 vph; three-quarter plate, finely finished movement; 43-hour power reserve
Functions: hours, minutes, subsidiary seconds
Case: rose gold ø 32.8 mm, height 6.6 mm; sapphire crystal; transparent case back; water-resistant to 3 atm
Band: horse leather, buckle
Price: $10,140

Tetra 27 Duo

Reference number: 405
Movement: manually wound, Nomos Caliber Alpha.2; ø 23.3 mm, height 2.6 mm; 17 jewels; 21,600 vph; three-quarter plate, finely finished movement; 43-hour power reserve
Functions: hours, minutes
Case: stainless steel, 27.5 x 27.5 mm, height 6.1 mm; sapphire crystal; water-resistant to 3 atm
Band: suede, buckle
Price: $1,660

Orion 33 Gold

Reference number: 358
Movement: manually wound, Nomos Caliber Alpha; ø 23.3 mm, height 2.6 mm; 17 jewels; 21,600 vph; three-quarter plate, finely finished movement; 43-hour power reserve
Functions: hours, minutes, subsidiary seconds
Case: stainless steel, ø 32.8 mm, height 7.6 mm; sapphire crystal; water-resistant to 3 atm
Band: suede, buckle
Price: $1,920

Caliber DUW 1001

Manually wound; swan-neck fine adjustment; double spring barrel, 84-hour power reserve
Functions: hours, minutes, subsidiary seconds; power reserve indicator
Diameter: 32 mm
height: 3.6 mm
Jewels: 29, including 5 in screw-mounted gold chatons
Balance: screw balance
Frequency: 21,600 vph
Hairspring: Nivarox 1A
Shock protection: Incabloc
Remarks: hand-engraved balance cock, beveled and polished edges, rhodium-plated movement with Glashütte sun-burst ribbing and perlage

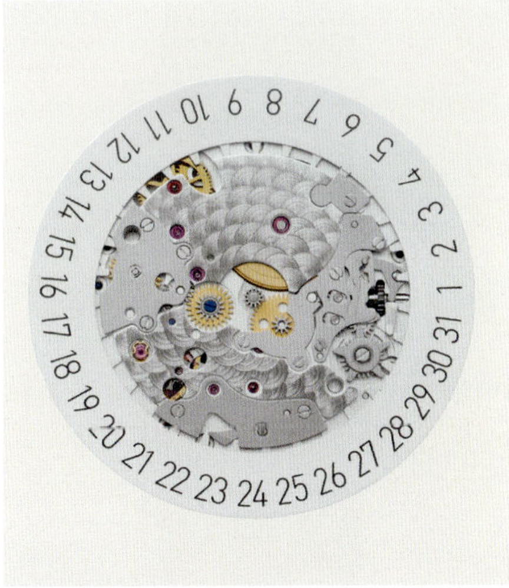

Caliber DUW 6101

Automatic; single spring barrel, 43-hour power reserve
Functions: hours, minutes, subsidiary seconds; date
Diameter: 35.2 mm
height: 3.6 mm
Jewels: 27
Balance: in-house
Frequency: 21,600 vph
Hairspring: made in-house, heat-blued
Shock protection: Incabloc
Remarks: three-quarter plate, rhodium-plated movement with Glashütte ribbing and perlage, gold-plated engravings

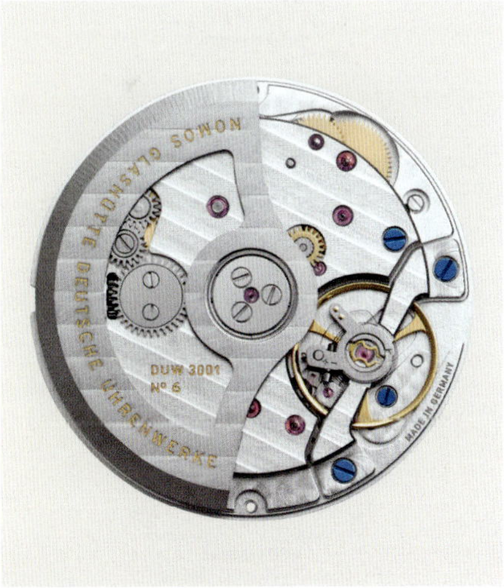

Caliber DUW 3001

Automatic; single spring barrel, 43-hour power reserve
Functions: hours, minutes, subsidiary seconds
Diameter: 28.8 mm
height: 3.2 mm
Jewels: 27
Balance: made in-house
Frequency: 21,600 vph
Balance spring: made in-house, tempered-blue
Shock protection: Incabloc
Remarks: three-quarter plate, rhodium-plated movement with Glashütte ribbing and Nomos perlage

OMEGA

As the largest brand in the SSIH Group, Omega had an important role to play during the quartz crisis that hit the Swiss watch industry in the 1970s. The Société Suisse de l'Industrie Horlogère and the Allgemeine Schweizerische Uhrenindustrie AG (ASUAG) merged to form the founding company of the Swatch Group. It became the flagship brand of the entire group and therefore had a leading position in terms of design, technology, and functionality.

With 20/20 hindsight, we can say that the industrializing of the special and complex escapement, which includes components requiring ultimate precision, is among the main achievements of the Group's various competence centers. Omega became quite naturally the first company to try out new materials like titanium and ceramic for the cases, the central tourbillon, or the coaxial escapement designed originally by George Daniels. In the new Central Tourbillon, the two technologies are used side by side.

Technology and design are very much responsible for Omega's success. The 15,000-gauss amagnetic movement introduced a few years ago has also been used in many of the new products. And there is a plethora of new "Master Chronometer" movements, which not only meet the stringent requirements set out by the COSC but also must pass the tests developed by Switzerland's Federal Institute of Metrology (METAS). The testing and certification process is performed in the new production building at the entirely renovated Swatch Group premises in Bienne/Biel. After promulgating the benefits of decentralization for years, Omega appears to be returning to the good old *manufacture* system of all crafts under a single roof. Swatch Group subsidiary Nivarox-FAR has finally mastered the production of the difficult, oil-free parts of the system designed by Englishman George Daniels, although the escapement continues to include lubrication, as the long-term results of "dry" coaxial movements are less than satisfactory. Thus, the most important plus for this escapement design remains a high rate stability after careful regulation. True to its sports associations, Omega has also produced a Seamaster—the Planet Ocean 6000M—that can take a plunge to around 18,000 feet under the sea.

Omega SA
Jakob-Stämpfli-Strasse 96
CH-2502 Biel/Bienne
Switzerland

Tel.:
+41-32-343-9211

E-mail:
info@omegawatches.com

Website:
www.omegawatches.com

Founded:
1848

U.S. distributor:
Omega
703 Waterford Way, Suite 920
Miami, FL 33126
800-766-6342
www.omegawatches.com

Most important collections:
Seamaster, Constellation, Speedmaster; as of $3,200

Speedmaster Moonwatch Caliber 321

Reference number: 311.30.40.30.01.001
Movement: manually wound, Omega Caliber 321B; ø 27 mm, height 6.87 mm; 17 jewels; 18,000 vph; re-edition of a historic movement used in the first Speedmaster models; Breguet hairspring; column-wheel control of chronograph functions; finely finished movement; 55-hour power reserve
Functions: hours, minutes, subsidiary seconds; chronograph
Case: stainless steel, ø 39.7 mm, height 13.71 mm; sapphire crystal; transparent case back; water-resistant to 5 atm
Band: stainless steel, folding clasp
Price: $14,100

De Ville Trésor Power Reserve

Reference number: 435.53.40.22.02.001
Movement: manually wound, Omega Caliber 8935; ø 29 mm, height 5.5 mm; 30 jewels; 25,200 vph; 2 spring barrels, co-axial escapement, silicon hairspring, antimagnetic to 15,000 gauss; METAS-certified chronometer; 72-hour power reserve
Functions: hours, minutes, subsidiary seconds; power reserve display
Case: yellow gold, ø 40 mm, height 10.07 mm; sapphire crystal; transparent case back; screw-in crown; water-resistant to 3 atm
Band: reptile skin, folding clasp
Price: $18,400

Seamaster Aqua Terra Master Chronometer

Reference number: 220.10.38.20.09.001
Movement: automatic, Omega Caliber 8800; ø 26 mm, height 4.6 mm; 35 jewels; 25,200 vph; 2 spring barrels, coaxial escapement, silicon hairspring, antimagnetic to 15,000 gauss; METAS-certified chronometer; 60-hour power reserve
Functions: hours, minutes, sweep seconds; date
Case: stainless steel, ø 38 mm, height 13.2 mm; sapphire crystal; transparent case back; screw-in crown; water-resistant to 15 atm
Band: stainless steel, folding clasp
Price: $6,000
Variations: various dial colors; calfskin or reptile skin strap; rubber strap

Seamaster 300

Reference number: 234.92.41.21.10.001
Movement: automatic, Omega Caliber 8912; ø 29 mm, height 5.5 mm; 38 jewels; 25.200 vph; 2 spring barrels, coaxial escapement, silicon hairspring, antimagnetic to 15,000 gauss; METAS-certified chronometer; 60-hour power reserve
Functions: hours, minutes, sweep seconds
Case: bronze-gold alloy ø 41 mm, height 14.4 mm; unidirectional bezel with ceramic insert, with 0-60 scale; sapphire crystal; transparent case back; screw-in crown; helium valve; water-resistant to 30 atm
Band: calfskin, folding clasp
Price: $12,100
Variations: in stainless steel ($6,500 and $7,000)

Seamaster Diver 300M

Reference number: 210.30.42.20.01.001
Movement: automatic, Omega Caliber 8800; ø 26 mm, height 4.6 mm; 35 jewels; 25,200 vph; 2 spring barrels, coaxial escapement, silicon balance and hairspring, antimagnetic to 15,000 gauss; METAS-certified chronometer; 55-hour power reserve
Functions: hours, minutes, sweep seconds; date
Case: stainless steel, ø 42 mm, height 13.56 mm; unidirectional bezel with ceramic insert, with 0-60 scale; sapphire crystal; transparent case back; screw-in crown, helium valve; water-resistant to 30 atm
Band: rubber, folding clasp
Price: $5,400
Variations: various cases, straps, and dial types

Seamaster Diver "Black Black"

Reference number: 210.92.44.20.01.003
Movement: automatic, Omega Caliber 8806; ø 26 mm, height 4.6 mm; 35 jewels; 25.200 vph; 2 spring barrels, coaxial escapement, silicon balance and hairspring, antimagnetic to 15,000 gauss; METAS-certified chronometer; 55-hour power reserve
Functions: hours, minutes, sweep seconds
Case: ceramic, ø 43.5 mm, height 14.47 mm; unidirectional bezel with 0-60 scale; sapphire crystal; screw-in crown, helium valve; water-resistant to 30 atm
Band: rubber, buckle
Price: $8,650

Seamaster Diver 300M Chronograph

Reference number: 210.30.44.51.03.001
Movement: automatic, Omega Caliber 9900; ø 32.5 mm, height 7.6 mm; 54 jewels; 28,800 vph; 2 spring barrels, coaxial escapement, silicon balance and hairspring, antimagnetic to 15,000 gauss; METAS-certified chronometer; 60-hour power reserve
Functions: hours, minutes, subsidiary seconds; chronograph; date
Case: stainless steel, ø 44 mm, height 17.2 mm; unidirectional bezel with ceramic insert, with 0-60 scale; sapphire crystal; screw-in crown and pushers, ceramic pushers, helium valve; water-resistant to 30 atm
Band: stainless steel, folding clasp
Price: $7,800

Seamaster Diver Professional

RReference number: 210.30.42.20.10.001
Movement: automatic, Omega Caliber 8800; ø 26 mm, height 4.6 mm; 35 jewels; 25,200 vph; co-axial escapement, silicon balance and balance spring, antimagnetic to 15,000 gauss, METAS-certified chronometer; 55-hour power reserve
Functions: hours, minutes, sweep seconds; date
Case: stainless steel, ø 42 mm, height 13.56 mm; unidirectional bezel with ceramic insert, with 0-60 scale; sapphire crystal; transparent case back; screw-in crown, helium valve; water-resistant to 30 atm
Band: stainless steel, folding clasp
Price: $5,400
Variations: various cases, bands, and dials

Seamaster Aqua Terra Worldtimer

Reference number: 220.12.43.22.03.001
Movement: automatic, Omega Caliber 8938; ø 29 mm, height 6.5 mm; 39 jewels; 25,200 vph; coaxial escapement, silicon balance and hairspring; antimagnetic to 15,000 gauss; METAS-certified chronometer; 60-hour power reserve
Functions: hours, minutes, sweep seconds; world time display (2nd time zone); date
Case: stainless steel, ø 43 mm, height 14.3 mm; sapphire crystal; transparent case back; screw-in crown; water-resistant to 15 atm
Band: rubber, buckle
Price: $8,900
Variations: stainless steel band

Seamaster Planet Ocean Ultra Deep

Reference number: 215.30.46.21.06.001
Movement: automatic, Omega Caliber 8912; ø 29 mm, height 5.5 mm; 38 jewels; 25,200 vph; 2 spring barrels; co-axial escapement, silicon balance and balance spring, antimagnetic to 15,000 gauss; METAS-certified chronometer; 60-hour power reserve
Functions: hours, minutes, sweep seconds
Case: stainless steel, ø 45.5 mm, height 6.5 mm; unidirectional bezel with ceramic insert, with 0-60 scale; sapphire crystal; screw-in crown; water-resistant to 600 atm
Band: stainless steel, folding clasp
Price: $11,600
Variations: titanium with textile strap ($12,300)

Seamaster Planet Ocean Deep Black Master Chronometer

Reference number: 215.92.46.22.01.001
Movement: automatic, Omega Caliber 8906; ø 29 mm, height 6 mm; 38 jewels; 25,200 vph; 2 spring barrels, coaxial escapement, silicon balance and hairspring, antimagnetic to 15,000 gauss; METAS-certified chronometer; 60-hour power reserve
Functions: hours, minutes, sweep seconds; additional 24-hour display (2nd time zone); date
Case: ceramic, ø 43.5 mm, height 17.04 mm; unidirectional bezel with 0-60 scale; sapphire crystal; screw-in crown, helium valve; water-resistant to 60 atm
Band: rubber with textile layer, folding clasp
Price: $11,700

Seamaster Planet Ocean Ultra Deep

Reference number: 215.92.46.21.01.001
Movement: automatic, Omega Caliber 8912; ø 29 mm, height 5.5 mm; 38 jewels; 25,200 vph; 2 spring barrels, co-axial escapement, silicon balance and balance spring, antimagnetic until 15,000 gauss; METAS-certified chronometer; 60-hour power reserve
Functions: hours, minutes, sweep seconds
Case: titanium, ø 45.5 mm, height 18.2 mm; unidirectional bezel with ceramic insert, with 0-60 scale; sapphire crystal; screw-in crown; water-resistant to 600 atm
Band: textile, buckle
Price: $ 12,300
Variations: in stainless steel with stainless steel bracelet ($11,600)

Constellation Master Chronometer

Reference number: 131.33.41.21.04.001
Movement: automatic, Omega Caliber 8800; ø 26 mm, height 4.6 mm; 35 jewels; 25,200 vph; co-axial escapement, silicon balance and balance spring, antimagnetic to 15,000 gauss; METAS-certified chronometer; 55-hour power reserve
Functions: hours, minutes, sweep seconds; date
Case: stainless steel, ø 39 mm, height 12.43 mm; sapphire crystal; transparent case back; water-resistant to 5 atm
Band: reptile skin, folding clasp
Price: $6,500
Variations: various dials

Seamaster Aqua Terra Railmaster

Reference number: 220.10.40.20.01.001
Movement: automatic, Omega Caliber 8806; ø 26 mm, height 4.6 mm; 35 jewels; 25,200 vph; coaxial escapement, silicon balance and hairspring, antimagnetic to 15,000 gauss; METAS-certified chronometer; 55-hour power reserve
Functions: hours, minutes, sweep seconds
Case: stainless steel, ø 40 mm, height 12.65 mm; sapphire crystal; water-resistant to 15 atm
Band: stainless steel, folding clasp
Price: $5,200
Variations: various dials; calfskin strap; textile strap

Speedmaster Moonwatch Professional

Reference number: 310.62.42.50.99.001
Movement: manually wound, Omega Caliber 3861; ø 27 mm, height 6.9 mm; 26 jewels; 21,600 vph; co-axial escapement, silicon balance and balance spring; antimagnetic to 15,000 gauss; METAS-certified chronometer; 50-hour power reserve
Functions: hours, minutes, subsidiary seconds; chronograph
Case: yellow gold ("Moonshine Gold"), ø 42 mm, height 14 mm; unidirectional rotating bezel with aluminum insert; sapphire crystal; transparent case back; water-resistant to 5 atm
Band: rubber, folding clasp
Price: $28,700

Speedmaster Dark Side of the Moon "Apollo 8"

Reference number: 311.92.44.30.01.001
Movement: manually wound, Omega Caliber 1869; ø 27 mm, height 6.87 mm; 19 jewels; 21,600 vph; 48-hour power reserve
Functions: hours, minutes, subsidiary seconds; chronograph
Case: ceramic, ø 44.25 mm, height 13.8 mm; sapphire crystal; transparent case back; water-resistant to 5 atm
Band: calfskin, buckle
Remarks: mainplate and bridges with carefully replicated moon surface
Price: $9,750

Speedmaster Moonwatch Master Chronometer

Reference number: 310.30.42.50.01.001
Movement: manually wound, Omega Caliber 3861; ø 27 mm, height 6.9 mm; 26 jewels; 21,600 vph; coaxial escapement, silicon balance and hairspring, antimagnetic to 15,000 gauss; METAS-certified chronometer; 50-hour power reserve
Functions: hours, minutes, subsidiary seconds; chronograph
Case: stainless steel, ø 42 mm, height 14 mm; bezel with aluminum insert; sapphire crystal; water-resistant to 5 atm
Band: stainless steel, folding clasp
Price: $6,400

Speedmaster Moonphase

Reference number: 304.33.44.52.03.001
Movement: automatic, Omega Caliber 9904; ø 32.5 mm, height 8.35 mm; 54 jewels; 28,800 vph; 2 spring barrels, coaxial escapement, silicon balance and hairspring, antimagnetic to 15,000 gauss; METAS-certified chronometer; 60-hour power reserve
Functions: hours, minutes, subsidiary seconds; chronograph; date, moon phase
Case: stainless steel, ø 44.25 mm, height 16.85 mm; bezel with ceramic insert; sapphire crystal; water-resistant to 10 atm
Band: reptile skin, folding clasp
Price: $10,600

De Ville Trésor Small Seconds

Reference number: 435.53.40.21.11.002
Movement: manually wound, Omega Caliber 8927; ø 29 mm, height 5.5 mm; 29 jewels; 25,200 vph; 2 spring barrels, coaxial escapement, silicon balance and hairspring, antimagnetic to 15,000 gauss; METAS-certified chronometer; 72-hour power reserve
Functions: hours, minutes, subsidiary seconds
Case: rose gold ("Sednagold"), ø 40 mm, height 10.07 mm; sapphire crystal; water-resistant to 3 atm
Band: reptile skin, folding clasp
Price: $17,700

Seamaster Diver James Bond Edition

Reference number: 210.90.42.20.01.001
Movement: automatic, Omega Caliber 8806; ø 26 mm, height 4.6 mm; 35 jewels; 25,200 vph; coaxial escapement, silicon balance and hairspring, antimagnetic to 15,000 gauss; METAS-certified chronometer; 55-hour power reserve
Functions: hours, minutes, sweep seconds
Case: titanium, ø 42 mm, height 13.3 mm; unidirectional bezel with ceramic insert, with 0-60 scale; sapphire crystal; screw-in crown, helium valve; water-resistant to 30 atm
Band: titanium Milanese mesh, folding clasp
Price: $9,200

Speedmaster '57

Reference number: 332.12.41.51.03.001
Movement: automatic, Omega Caliber 9906; ø 32.5 mm, height 7.6 mm; 54 jewels; 28,800 vph; coaxial escapement, silicon balance and hairspring; METAS-certified chronometer; 60-hour power reserve
Functions: hours, minutes, subsidiary seconds; chronograph; date
Case: stainless steel, ø 41.5 mm, height 16.17 mm; sapphire crystal; water-resistant to 10 atm
Band: calfskin, buckle
Price: $8,300
Variations: various dials; stainless steel band

Caliber 8800

Automatic; coaxial escapement; amagnetic up to 15,000 gauss; METAS-certified chronometer; single spring barrel, 55-hour power reserve
Functions: hours, minutes, sweep seconds; date
Diameter: 26 mm
Height: 4.6 mm
Jewels: 35
Balance: silicon, without regulator
Frequency: 25,200 vph
Balance spring: silicon
Shock protection: Nivachoc
Remarks: blackened screws

Caliber 321B

Manually wound; Breguet hairspring; column-wheel control of chronograph functions; single spring barrel, 55-hour power reserve
Base caliber: Lémania 2310
Functions: hours, minutes, subsidiary seconds; chronograph
Diameter: 27 mm
Height: 6.87 mm
Jewels: 17
Frequency: 18,000 vph
Remarks: re-edition of historic movement used in first Speedmaster models; red-gold plated, finely finished

Caliber 8900

Automatic; coaxial escapement; amagnetic up to 15,000 gauss; METAS-certified chronometer; double spring barrel, 60-hour power reserve
Functions: hours, minutes, sweep seconds; date
Diameter: 29 mm
Height: 5.5 mm
Jewels: 39
Balance: silicon, without regulator
Frequency: 25,200 vph
Balance spring: silicon
Shock protection: Nivachoc
Remarks: mainplate, bridges, and rotor with "arabesque" côtes de Genève, rhodium-plated, spring barrels, blackened balance wheel and screws

Caliber 9900

Automatic; coaxial escapement; column-wheel control of chronograph functions; amagnetic up to 15,000 gauss; METAS-certified chronometer; double spring barrel, 60-hour power reserve
Functions: hours, minutes, subsidiary seconds; chronograph; date
Diameter: 32.5 mm
Height: 7.6 mm
Jewels: 5.4
Balance: silicon, without regulator
Frequency: 28,800 vph
Balance spring: silicon
Shock protection: Nivachoc
Remarks: mainplate, bridges, and rotor with "arabesque" côtes de Genève

Caliber 8935

Manually wound; co-axial escapement, amagnetic to 15,000 gauss; METAS-certified chronometer; 2 spring barrels, 72-hour power reserve
Functions: hours, minutes, subsidiary seconds; power reserve display
Diameter: 29 mm
Height: 5.5 mm
Jewels: 30
Balance: silicon, indexless
Frequency: 25,200 vph
Balance: silicon, indexless
Shock protection: Nivachoc
Remarks: mainplate and bridges with côtes de Genève, "Sednagold" balance bridge; blackened spring barrels, balance wheel and screws

Caliber 3861

Manually wound; coaxial escapement, amagnetic protection to 15,000 gauss; METAS-certified chronometer; single spring barrel, 50-hour power reserve
Functions: hours, minutes, subsidiary seconds; chronograph
Diameter: 27 mm
Height: 6.87 mm
Jewels: 26
Frequency: 21,600 vph
Balance spring: silicon
Remarks: gold-plated movement ("Moonshine Gold"); 240 parts

TORNEK - RAYVILLE
U.S.
AUTOMATIC
200 m
15
30
45

ORIS

Oris SA
Ribigasse 1
CH-4434 Hölstein
Switzerland

Tel.:
+41-61-956-1111

E-mail:
MyOris@oris.ch

Website:
www.oris.ch

Founded:
1904

Number of employees:
210

U.S. distributor:
Oris Watches USA
50 Washington Street, Suite 302
Norwalk, CT 06854
203-857-4769

Most important collections/price range:
Divers Sixty-Five, Big Crown, Artelier, Aquis, ProPilot / approx. $1,300 to $10,300

Oris, located near Basel, Switzerland, since its founding in 1904, has stuck to its strategic guns for as long as it has existed: affordable quality. The result has been growing international success, now with a portfolio divided up into four "product worlds," each with its own distinct identity: aviation, motor sports, diving, and culture. In utilizing specific materials—a tungsten bezel for the divers, for example—and functions based on these types, Oris makes certain that each will fit perfectly into the world for which it was designed. Yet the heart of every watch houses a small, high-quality "high-mech" movement identifiable by the brand's standard red rotor.

A bold step came in 2014 with the in-house Caliber 110, a plain, but technically efficient, manually wound movement. It was made together with the engineers from the Technical College of Le Locle and features a massive 6-foot (1.8-meter) mainspring. Almost as regular as clockwork, the brand has produced further calibers, numbered 111, 112 (with GMT function), and 113.

In October 2020, the first wristwatches with the new Caliber 400 were launched. One goal in creating the movement was to eliminate problems even before they occur. Beat Fischli and his team needed five years to meet the established and defined criteria: five-day power reserve, special resistance to magnetic fields, chronometer rate accuracy, and high serviceability with long maintenance intervals of ten years.

The next logical step was the further development to the Caliber 401 and 403, which differ from the Caliber 400 by a subsidiary seconds dial at 6 o'clock and a date hand. The Caliber 400 family debuted in the Aquis series, but has already been used in various editions of the Big Crown and Divers Sixty-Five series.

Aquis Date Calibre 400

Reference number: 01 400 7763 4135
Movement: automatic, Oris Caliber 400; ø 30 mm, height 4.75 mm; 21 jewels; 28,800 vph; 120-hour power reserve
Functions: hours, minutes, sweep seconds; date
Case: stainless steel, ø 43.5 mm, height 13.5 mm; unidirectional bezel with ceramic insert, with 0-60 scale; sapphire crystal; screw-in crown; water-resistant to 30 atm
Band: stainless steel, folding clasp, with safety lock, with extension link
Price: $4,400

Aquis Date 41.5mm Calibre 400

Reference number: 01 400 7769 4154
Movement: automatic, Oris Caliber 400; ø 30 mm, height 4.75 mm; 21 jewels; 28,800 vph; 120-hour power reserve
Functions: hours, minutes, sweep seconds; date
Case: stainless steel, ø 41.5 mm, height 13.1 mm; unidirectional bezel with ceramic insert, with 0-60 scale; sapphire crystal; screw-in crown; water-resistant to 30 atm
Band: stainless steel, folding clasp, with safety lock, with extension link
Price: $4,400
Variations: with green or blue dial; with rubber strap ($4,100)

Aquis Pro Date Calibre 400

Reference number: 01 400 7767 7754
Movement: automatic, Oris Caliber 400; ø 30 mm, height 4.75 mm; 21 jewels; 28,800 vph; 120-hour power reserve
Functions: hours, minutes, sweep seconds; date
Case: titanium with black DLC, ø 49.5 mm, height 17.5 mm; unidirectional bezel with ceramic insert, with 0-60 scale; sapphire crystal; screw-in crown; water-resistant to 100 atm
Band: rubber, folding clasp, with safety lock and extension link
Price: $4,600

Aquis Date 41.5 mm Calibre 400

Reference number: 01 400 7769 6357-07 4 22 77FC
Movement: automatic, Oris Caliber 400; ø 30 mm, height 4.75 mm; 21 jewels; 28,800 vph; 120-hour power reserve
Functions: hours, minutes, sweep seconds; date
Case: stainless steel, ø 41.5 mm, height 13.1 mm; unidirectional yellow gold bezel with ceramic inlay and 0-60 scale; sapphire crystal; screw-in crown; water-resistant to 30 atm
Band: rubber, folding clasp with safety lock and extension link
Price: $4,400
Variations: with blue dial; with a stainless-steel bracelet ($4,600)

Aquis Date 41.5

Reference number: 01 733 7766 4158
Movement: automatic, Oris Caliber 733 (base Sellita SW200-1); ø 25.6 mm, height 4.6 mm; 26 jewels; 28,800 vph; 38-hour power reserve
Functions: hours, minutes, sweep seconds; date
Case: stainless steel, ø 41.5 mm, height 12.7 mm; unidirectional bezel with 0-60 scale; sapphire crystal; screw-in crown; water-resistant to 30 atm
Band: stainless steel, folding clasp, with extension link
Price: $2,300
Variations: with rubber strap ($2,100)

Aquis Date Upcycle

Reference number: 01 733 7766 4150-Set
Movement: automatic, Oris Caliber 733 (base Sellita SW200); ø 25.6 mm, height 4.6 mm; 26 jewels; 28,800 vph; 38-hour power reserve
Functions: hours, minutes, sweep seconds; date
Case: stainless steel, ø 41.5 mm, height 12.7 mm; unidirectional bezel with 0-60 scale; sapphire crystal; screw-in crown; water-resistant to 30 atm
Band: stainless steel, folding clasp with extension link
Remarks: unique dial of recycled plastic refuse recovered from the sea
Price: $2,300
Variations: with 36.5 mm case ($2,300)

ProPilot X Calibre 400

Reference number: 01 400 7778 7155-07 7 20 01TLC
Movement: automatic, Oris Caliber 400; ø 30 mm, height 4.75 mm; 21 jewels; 28,800 vph; 120-hour power reserve
Functions: hours, minutes, sweep seconds; date
Case: titanium, ø 39 mm, height 12 mm; sapphire crystal; water-resistant to 10 atm
Band: titanium, folding clasp
Price: $4,300

Divers Sixty-Five Cotton Candy

Reference number: 01 733 7771 3155
Movement: automatic, Oris Caliber 733 (base Sellita SW200-1); ø 25.6 mm, height 4.6 mm; 26 jewels; 28,800 vph; 38-hour power reserve
Functions: hours, minutes, sweep seconds; date
Case: bronze, ø 38 mm, height 12.8 mm; unidirectional bezel with 0-60 scale; sapphire crystal; screw-in crown; water-resistant to 10 atm
Band: bronze, folding clasp
Price: $2,750
Variations: with pink dial; with calfskin strap ($2,450)

Divers Sixty-Five Glow

Reference number: 01 733 7707 4053-07 5 20 89
Movement: automatic, Oris Caliber 733 (base Sellita SW200-1); ø 25.6 mm, height 4.6 mm; 26 jewels; 28,800 vph; 38-hour power reserve
Functions: hours, minutes, sweep seconds
Case: stainless steel, ø 40 mm, height 13 mm; unidirectional bezel with 0-60 scale; sapphire crystal; screw-in crown; water-resistant to 10 atm
Band: calfskin, folding clasp with extension link
Price: $2,200
Variations: with stainless steel bracelet ($2,400)

Big Crown ProPilot Big Date Bronze

Reference number: 01 751 7761 3164-07 3 2003BRLC
Movement: automatic, Oris Caliber 751 (base Sellita SW200); ø 32.2 mm, height 5.05 mm; 26 jewels; 28,800 vph; 38-hour power reserve
Functions: hours, minutes, sweep seconds; date
Case: bronze, ø 41 mm, height 12 mm; sapphire crystal; transparent case back; screw-in crown; water-resistant to 10 atm
Band: textile, folding clasp
Price: $2,200

Divers Sixty-Five

Reference number: 01 733 7707 4356
Movement: automatic, Oris Caliber 733 (base Sellita SW200-1); ø 25.6 mm, height 4.6 mm; 26 jewels; 28,800 vph; 38-hour power reserve
Functions: hours, minutes, sweep seconds; date
Case: stainless steel, ø 40 mm, height 12.8 mm; unidirectional bronze bezel with 0-60 scale; sapphire crystal; screw-in crown; water-resistant to 10 atm
Band: calfskin, folding clasp
Price: $2,400
Variations: with bronze bracelet ($2,600)

Big Crown ProPilot Big Day Date

Reference number: 01 752 7760 4164
Movement: automatic, Oris Caliber 752 (base Sellita SW220-1); ø 25.6 mm, height 5.05 mm; 26 jewels; 28,800 vph; 38-hour power reserve
Functions: hours, minutes, sweep seconds; date and weekday
Case: stainless steel, ø 44 mm, height 12.5 mm; sapphire crystal; water-resistant to 10 atm
Band: textile, folding clasp
Price: $1,900
Variations: with blue or anthracite dial; with calfskin strap ($1,900); with stainless steel bracelet ($2,100)

Big Crown Pointer Date Calibre 403

Reference number: 01 403 7776 4065-07 5 19 11
Movement: automatic, Oris Caliber 403; ø 30 mm, height 4.75 mm; 24 jewels; 28,800 vph; 120-hour power reserve
Functions: hours, minutes, subsidiary seconds; date
Case: stainless steel, ø 38 mm, height 11.8 mm; sapphire crystal; transparent case back; water-resistant to 30 atm
Band: calfskin, buckle
Price: $3,400

Big Crown ProPilot X Calibre 115

Reference number: 01 115 7759 7153
Movement: manually wound, Oris Caliber 115; ø 34 mm, height 6 mm; 38 jewels; 21,600 vph; skeletonized movement; central, open spring barrel, 240-hour power reserve
Functions: hours, minutes, subsidiary seconds; power reserve display
Case: titanium, ø 44 mm, height 12.5 mm; sapphire crystal; transparent case back; screw-in crown; water-resistant to 10 atm
Band: titanium, folding clasp
Remarks: skeletonized dial
Price: $7,600
Variations: with calfskin strap ($7,200)

Oris X Cervo Volante

Reference number: 01 754 7779 4065-Set
Movement: automatic, Oris Caliber 754 (base Sellita SW200); ø25.6 mm, height 4.6 mm; 26 jewels; 28,800 vph; 38-hour power reserve
Functions: hours, minutes, sweep seconds; date
Case: stainless steel, ø 38 mm, height 12.8 mm; sapphire crystal; transparent case back; water-resistant to 5 atm
Band: deer leather, buckle
Price: $2,000
Variations: with green or grey dial

CLAUDE MEYLAN
VALLÉE DE JOUX
CLAUDE MEYLAN
VALLÉE DE JOUX
Tortue de Joux
With its pure and timeless curves associated with a proven mechanical, "Tortue de Joux" introduces a new sculpture of time.

PANERAI

Officine Panerai (in English: Panerai Workshops) joined the Richemont Group in 1997. Since then, it has made an unprecedented rise from an insider niche brand to a lifestyle phenomenon. The company, founded in 1860 by Giovanni Panerai, supplied the Italian navy with precision instruments. In the 1930s, the Florentine engineers developed a series of waterproof wristwatches that could be used by commandos under especially extreme and risky conditions. After 1997, under the leadership of Angelo Bonati, the company came out with a collection of oversize wristwatches, both stylistically and technically based on those historical models.

In 2002, Panerai opened a *manufacture* in Neuchâtel, and by 2005 it was already producing its own movements (caliber family P.2000). In 2009, the new "little" Panerai *manufacture* movements (caliber family P.9000) were released. From the start, the idea behind them was to provide a competitive alternative to the base movements available until a couple of years ago. In 2014, a new *manufacture* was inaugurated in Neuchâtel to bring development, manufacturing, assembly, and quality control under one roof.

Parallel to consolidating, the brand has been steadily expanding its portfolio of new calibers. Fairly early on, it came out with an automatic chronograph with a flyback function, the P.9100. This was followed by a string of new calibers, almost one per year, to gradually replace "foreign" movements. Notorious is the P.4000, with an off-center winding rotor. At 3.95 millimeters, it is very thin for Panerai, but then again, it was developed for a new set of models.

The idea of sustainability is continuing to spread among watch manufacturers. Panerai's new eLAB-ID concept watch bears the tagline "Do you want to be part of the solution?" It is made of over ninety-eight percent recycled materials: titanium for the case, sapphire for the glass, silicon for the escapement, PET bottles for the strap, SuperLumiNova for the dial. Only thirty pieces were produced, but Panerai has another solution, too: it uses recycled steel scrap for the case of the new Luminor Marina eSteel.

Officine Panerai
Viale Monza, 259
I-20126 Milan
Italy

Tel.:
+39-02-363-138

Website:
www.panerai.com

Founded:
1860 in Florence, Italy

Number of employees:
Around 1,000 employees

U.S. distributor:
Panerai
645 Fifth Avenue
New York, NY 10022
877-PANERAI
concierge.usa@panerai.com;
www.panerai.com

Most important collections/price range:
Luminor / \$5,000 to \$25,000; Luminor / \$8,000 to \$30,000; Radiomir / \$8,000 to \$133,000; special editions / \$10,000 to \$125,000; clocks and instruments / \$20,000 to \$250,000

Submersible QuarantaQuattro

Reference number: PAM01229
Movement: automatic, Panerai Caliber P.900; ø 28.19 mm, height 4.2 mm; 23 jewels; 28,800 vph; 72-hour power reserve
Functions: hours, minutes, subsidiary seconds; date
Case: stainless steel, ø 44 mm, height 13.35 mm; unidirectionally rotating bezel, with 0-60 scale; sapphire crystal; crown with crown guard and hinged lever; water-resistant to 30 atm
Band: rubber, buckle
Price: \$9,400

Submersible QuarantaQuattro Carbotech Blu Abisso

Reference number: PAM01232
Movement: automatic, Panerai Caliber P.900; ø 28.19 mm, height 4.2 mm; 23 jewels; 28,800 vph; 72-hour power reserve
Functions: hours, minutes, subsidiary seconds; date
Case: composite material, ("Carbotech"), ø 44 mm, height 14.25 mm; unidirectionally rotating bezel, with 0-60 scale; sapphire crystal; crown with crown guard and hinged lever; water-resistant to 30 atm
Band: rubber, buckle
Price: \$18,000

Submersible QuarantaQuattro Bianco

Reference number: PAM01226
Movement: automatic, Panerai Caliber P.900; ø 28.19 mm, height 4.2 mm; 23 jewels; 28,800 vph; 72-hour power reserve
Functions: hours, minutes, subsidiary seconds; date
Case: stainless steel, ø 44 mm, height 13.35 mm; unidirectionally rotating bezel, with 0-60 scale; sapphire crystal; crown with crown guard and hinged lever; water-resistant to 30 atm
Band: rubber, buckle
Price: \$9,400

Luminor Calendario Perpetuo Experience

Reference number: PAM01269
Movement: automatic, Panerai Caliber P.4100; ø 35.1 mm, height 7 mm; 55 jewels; 28,800 vph; 2 spring barrels; 72-hour power reserve
Functions: hours, minutes, subsidiary seconds; additional 24-hour indicator (second time zone); perpetual calendar with date, weekday
Case: rose gold ("Goldtech"), ø 44 mm, height 15.25 mm; sapphire crystal; transparent case back; crown with crown guard and hinged lever; water-resistant to 5 atm
Band: reptile skin, buckle
Remarks: dial with blackened sapphire crystal
Price: $83,700

Luminor Chrono Monopulsante 8 Giorni GMT Blu Notte

Reference number: PAM01135
Movement: manually wound, Panerai Caliber P.2004; ø 31 mm, height 8.2 mm; 30 jewels; 28,800 vph; 3 spring barrels; column wheel control of chronograph functions using a single pusher; 192-hour power reserve
Functions: hours, minutes, subsidiary seconds; 12-hour display (second time zone), power reserve indicator; chronograph
Case: black ceramic, ø 44 mm, height 19.55 mm; sapphire crystal; transparent case back; crown with crown guard and hinged lever; water-resistant to 10 atm
Band: calf dark blue, buckle
Remarks: comes with additional rubber strap
Price: $22,500

Luminor Chrono

Reference number: PAM01109
Movement: automatic, Panerai Caliber MB P.9200 (based on Sellita SW200 with module); ø 31 mm, height 6.9 mm; 41 jewels; 28,800 vph; 42-hour power reserve
Functions: hours, minutes, subsidiary seconds; chronograph
Case: stainless steel, ø 44 mm, height 15.65 mm; sapphire crystal; crown with crown guard and hinged lever; water-resistant to 10 atm
Band: reptile skin, buckle
Remarks: comes with additional rubber strap
Price: $9,400

Luminor Luna Rossa

Reference number: PAM01342
Movement: manually wound, Panerai Caliber P.6000; ø 25.6 mm, height 4.5 mm; 19 jewels; 21,600 vph; 72-hour power reserve
Functions: hours, minutes, subsidiary seconds
Case: stainless steel, ø 44 mm, height 13.05 mm; sapphire crystal; crown with crown guard and hinged lever; water-resistant to 10 atm
Band: rubber with textile overlay, buckle
Price: $6,000

Submersible Chrono Mike Horn Edition

Reference number: PAM01291
Movement: automatic, Panerai Caliber P.9100; ø 31 mm, height 8.15 mm; 37 jewels; 28,800 vph; 2 spring barrels; 72-hour power reserve
Functions: hours, minutes, subsidiary seconds; flyback chronograph
Case: titanium, ø 47 mm; unidirectional bezel with ceramic insert with 0-60 scale; sapphire crystal; crown with crown guard and hinged lever; water-resistant to 30 atm
Band: rubber, buckle
Price: $ 20,500

Luminor Piccolo Due Goldtech Madreperla

Reference number: PAM01280
Movement: automatic, Panerai Caliber P.900; ø 28.19 mm, height 4.2 mm; 23 jewels; 28,800 vph; 72-hour power reserve
Functions: hours, minutes, subsidiary seconds; date
Case: rose gold ("Goldtech"), ø 38 mm, height 11.2 mm; sapphire crystal; transparent case back; crown with crown guard and hinged lever; water-resistant to 3 atm
Band: reptile skin, buckle
Remarks: mother-of-pearl dial
Price: $17,400

Luminor Quaranta

Reference number: PAM01270
Movement: automatic, Panerai Caliber P.900; ø 28.19 mm, height 4.2 mm; 23 jewels; 28,800 vph; 72-hour power reserve
Functions: hours, minutes, subsidiary seconds; date
Case: stainless steel, ø 40 mm, height 12.45 mm; sapphire crystal; crown with crown guard and hinged lever; water-resistant to 10 atm
Band: reptile skin, buckle
Price: $7,400

Luminor Quaranta

Reference number: PAM01272
Movement: automatic, Panerai Caliber P.900; ø 28.19 mm, height 4.2 mm; 23 jewels; 28,800 vph; 72-hour power reserve
Functions: hours, minutes, subsidiary seconds; date
Case: stainless steel, ø 40 mm, height 12.45 mm; sapphire crystal; crown with crown guard and hinged lever; water-resistant to 10 atm
Band: reptile skin, buckle
Price: $7,400

Submersible QuarantaQuattro eSteel Verde Smeraldo

Reference number: PAM01287
Movement: automatic, Panerai Caliber P.900; ø 28.19 mm, height 4.2 mm; 23 jewels; 28,800 vph; 72-hour power reserve
Functions: hours, minutes, subsidiary seconds; date
Case: recycled stainless steel, ø 44 mm, height 13.35 mm; unidirectional bezel with ceramic insert and 0-60 scale; sapphire crystal; crown with crown guard and hinged lever; water-resistant to 30 atm
Band: recycled textile, buckle
Price: $11,000

Submersible QuarantaQuattro eSteel Grigio Roccia

Reference number: PAM01288
Movement: automatic, Panerai Caliber P.900; ø 28.19 mm, height 4.2 mm; 23 jewels; 28,800 vph; 72-hour power reserve
Functions: hours, minutes, subsidiary seconds; date
Case: recycled stainless steel, ø 44 mm, height 13.35 mm; unidirectional bezel with ceramic insert and 0-60 scale; sapphire crystal; crown with crown guard and hinged lever; water-resistant to 30 atm
Band: recycled textile, buckle
Price: $11,000

Luminor Marina eSteel Verde Smeraldo

Reference number: PAM01356
Movement: automatic, Panerai Caliber P.9010; ø 31 mm, height 6 mm; 31 jewels; 28,800 vph; 2 spring barrels, 72-hour power reserve
Functions: hours, minutes, subsidiary seconds; date
Case: recycled stainless steel, ø 44 mm, height 15.45 mm; sapphire crystal; crown with crown guard and hinged lever; water-resistant to 30 atm
Band: recycled textile, folding clasp
Price: $9,200
Variations: with blue or gray strap or dial

Luminor Marina eSteel Blu Profondo

Reference number: PAM01157
Movement: automatic, Panerai Caliber P.9010; ø 31 mm, height 6 mm; 31 jewels; 28,800 vph; 2 spring barrels, 72-hour power reserve
Functions: hours, minutes, subsidiary seconds; date
Case: recycled stainless steel, ø 44 mm, height 15.45 mm; sapphire crystal; crown with crown guard and hinged lever; water-resistant to 30 atm
Band: recycled textile, folding clasp
Price: $ 9,200
Variations: with green or gray strap or dial

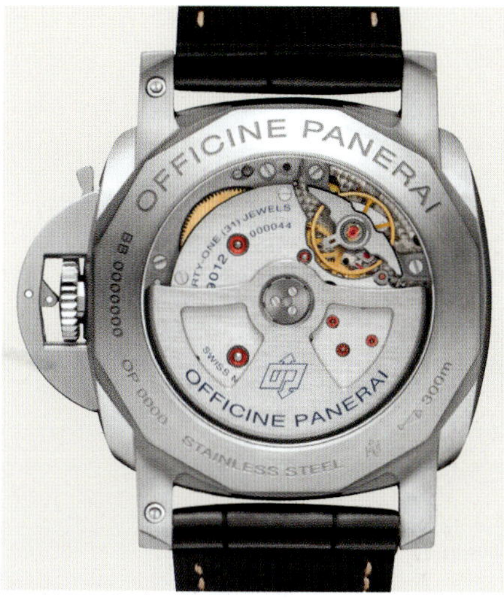

Caliber P.9012

Automatic; serially arranged double spring barrel, 72-hour power reserve
Functions: hours, minutes, subsidiary seconds; additional 12-hour display (2nd time zone); power reserve display; date
Diameter: 31 mm
Height: 6 mm
Jewels: 31
Balance: glucydur
Frequency: 28,800 vph
Shock protection: Incabloc
Remarks: 231 parts

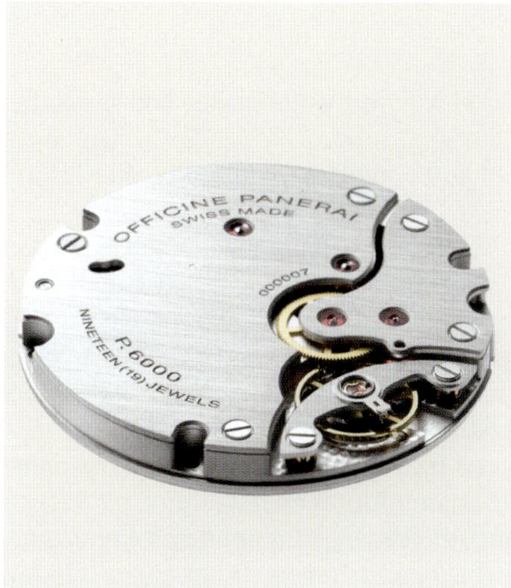

Caliber P.6000

Manually wound; single spring barrel; 72-hour power reserve
Functions: hours, minutes, subsidiary seconds
Diameter: 34.9 mm
Height: 4.5 mm
Jewels: 19
Balance: glucydur
Frequency: 21,600 vph
Shock protection: Incabloc
Remarks: 110 parts

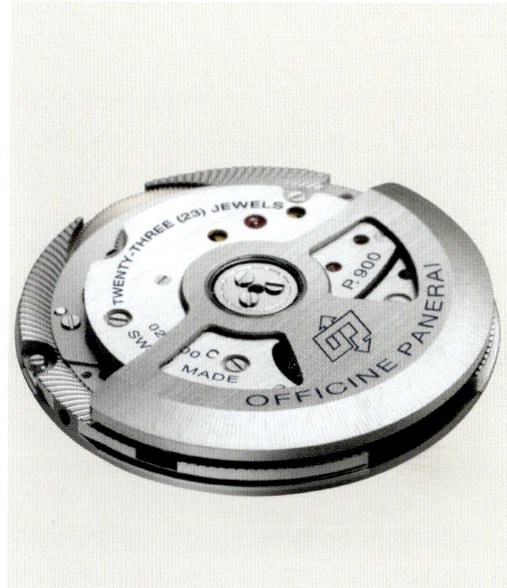

Caliber P.900

Automatic; single spring barrel, 72-hour power reserve
Functions: hours, minutes, subsidiary seconds; date
Diameter: 28.19 mm
Height: 4.2 mm
Jewels: 23
Balance: glucydur
Frequency: 28,800 vph
Shock protection: Incabloc
Remarks: 171 parts

Caliber P.9010

Automatic; double, serially arranged spring barrel, 72-hour power reserve
Functions: hours, minutes, subsidiary seconds; date
Diameter: 31 mm
Height: 6 mm
Jewels: 31
Balance: Glucydur
Frequency: 28,800 vph
Remarks: 200 parts

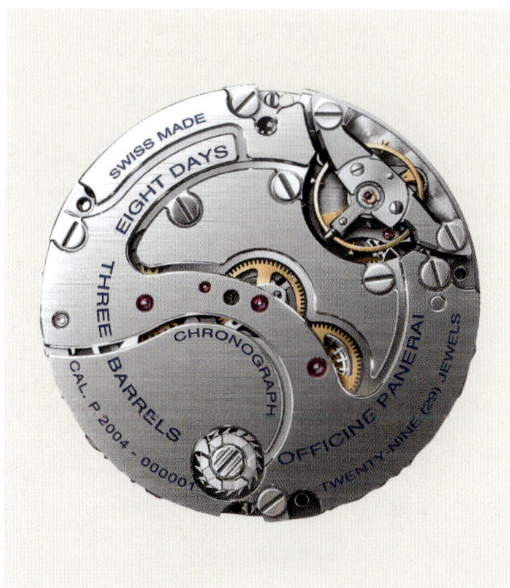

Caliber P.2004

Manually wound; column wheel control of the chronograph-functions, single pusher; 3 serially connected barrel springs, 192-hour power reserve
Functions: hours, minutes, subsidiary seconds; additional 12-hour indication (second time zone), day/night indication, power reserve indication; chronograph
Diameter: 34.9 mm
Height: 8.2 mm
Stones: 29
Balance: glucydur, with variable inertia
Frequency: 28.800 A/h
Remarks: zero position of the second hand when pulling the crown ("Zero Reset" function); 333 parts

Caliber P.4001

Automatic; microrotor; crown-activated stop-seconds mechanism and zero-reset; double spring barrel, 72-hour power reserve
Functions: hours, minutes, subsidiary seconds; additional 24-hour display (2nd time zone), power reserve indicator (on back); date
Diameter: 30 mm
Height: 5.04 mm
Jewels: 31
Balance: glucydur
Frequency: 28,800 vph
Hairspring: flat hairspring
Shock protection: Kif
Remarks: 278 parts

PARMIGIANI

What began as the undertaking of a single man—a gifted watchmaker and reputable restorer of complicated vintage timepieces—in the small town of Fleurier in Switzerland's Val de Travers has now grown into an empire of sorts comprising several factories and more than 400 employees.

Michel Parmigiani is in fact just doing what he has done since 1976, when he began restoring vintage works. An exceptional talent, his output soon attracted the attention of the Sandoz Family Foundation, an organization established by a member of one of Switzerland's most famous families in 1964. The foundation bought 51 percent of Parmigiani Mesure et Art du Temps SA in 1996, turning what was practically a one-man show into a full-fledged and fully financed watch *manufacture*.

After the merger, Swiss suppliers were acquired by the partners, furthering the quest for horological autonomy. Atokalpa SA in Alle (Canton of Jura) manufactures parts such as pinions, wheels, and micro components. Bruno Affolter SA in La Chaux-de-Fonds produces precious metal cases, dials, and other specialty parts. Les Artisans Boitiers (LAB) and Quadrance et Habillage (Q&H) in La Chaux-de-Fonds manufacture cases out of precious metals and dials as well. Elwin SA in Moutier specializes in turned parts. In 2003, the movement development and production department officially separated from the rest as Vaucher Manufacture, now an autonomous entity with a sterling reputation.

Montre Hermès has also held a stake in Vaucher Manufacture, securing the supply of custom watchmaking technology and leather straps for its ambitious model policy.

Parmigiani has enjoyed great independence and was growing strongly for a while, notably in the United States. The old partnership with Bugatti was terminated and more emphasis placed on watches that can be used daily and are not quite what the rest of the industry considers "sportive." Under CEO Guido Terreni, the Tonda PF collection was redesigned, for instance, and given new complications, including a time zone watch with rattrapante mechanism for rapidly resetting the second local time.

Parmigiani Fleurier SA
Rue du Temple 11
CH-2114 Fleurier
Switzerland

Tel.:
+41-32-862-6630

E-mail:
info@parmigiani.ch

Website:
www.parmigiani.ch

Founded:
1996

Number of employees:
425

Annual production:
approx. 6,000 watches

U.S. distributor:
Parmigiani Fleurier Distribution Americas LLC
2655 S. Le Jeune Road
Penthouse 1G
Coral Gables, FL 33134
305-260-7770; 305-269-7770
americas@parmigiani.com

Most important collections/price range:
Chronor, Kalpa, Tonda, Toric / approx. $15,000 to $80,000 for core collections, $300,000+ for *haute horlogerie* watches; no limit for unique models

Tonda PF Flying Tourbillon

Reference number: PFH921-2020001-200182
Movement: automatic, Parmigiani Caliber PF517; ø 32 mm, height 3.4 mm; 29 jewels; 21,600 vph; flying one-minute tourbillon; platinum micro-rotor, finely finished movement; 48-hour power reserve
Functions: hours, minutes
Case: platinum, ø 42 mm, height 8.6 mm; sapphire crystal; transparent case back; water-resistant to 10 atm
Band: platinum, white gold folding clasp
Price: $155,000; limited to 25 pieces

Tonda PF GMT Rattrapante

Reference number: PFC905-1020001-100182
Movement: automatic, Parmigiani Caliber PF051; ø 30 mm, height 4.9 mm; 31 jewels; 21,600 vph; rose gold micro-rotor, finely finished movement; 48-hour power reserve
Functions: hours, minutes; additional 12-hour display (second time zone) pusher for reset (rattrapante function)
Case: stainless steel, ø 40 mm, height 10.7 mm; platinum bezel; sapphire crystal; transparent case back; rose gold pusher; water-resistant to 6 atm
Band: stainless steel, folding clasp
Price: $28,700

Tonda PF Skeleton Steel

Reference number: PFC912-1020001-100182
Movement: automatic, Parmigiani Caliber PF777; ø 30 mm, height 3.9 mm; 29 jewels; 28,800 vph; movement entirely skeletonized and blackened rose gold skeletonized rotor; 60-hour power reserve
Functions: hours, minutes
Case: stainless steel, ø 40 mm, height 8.4 mm; platinum bezel; sapphire crystal; transparent case back; water-resistant to 10 atm
Band: stainless steel, folding clasp
Price: $65,300
Variations: in rose gold ($97,400)

Tonda PF Skeleton Rose Gold

Reference number: PFC912-2020001-200182
Movement: automatic, Parmigiani Caliber PF777; ø 30 mm, height 3.9 mm; 29 jewels; 28,800 vph; movement entirely skeletonized and blackened rose gold skeletonized rotor; 60-hour power reserve
Functions: hours, minutes,
Case: rose gold, ø 40 mm, height 8.4 mm; sapphire crystal; transparent case back; water-resistant to 10 atm
Band: rose gold, folding clasp
Price: $97,400
Variations: in stainless steel ($65,300)

Tonda PF Microrotor Steel

Reference number: PFC914-1020001-100182
Movement: automatic, Parmigiani Caliber PF703; ø 30 mm, height 3 mm; 29 jewels; 21,600 vph; platinum micro-rotor; 48-hour power reserve
Functions: hours, minutes; date
Case: stainless steel, ø 40 mm, height 7.8 mm; platinum bezel; sapphire crystal; transparent case back; water-resistant to 10 atm
Band: stainless steel, folding clasp
Price: $22,900
Variations: in rose gold ($53,900)

Tonda PF Microrotor Rose Gold

Reference number: PFC914-2020001-200182
Movement: automatic, Parmigiani Caliber PF703; ø 30 mm, height 3 mm; 29 jewels; 21,600 vph; platinum micro-rotor; 48-hour power reserve
Functions: hours, minutes; date
Case: rose gold, ø 40 mm, height 7.8 mm; sapphire crystal; transparent case back; water-resistant to 10 atm
Band: rose gold, folding clasp
Price: $53,900
Variations: in stainless steel ($22,900)

Tonda PF Annual Calendar Rose Gold

Reference number: PFC907-2020001-200182
Movement: automatic, Parmigiani Caliber PF339; ø 27.1 mm, height 5.5 mm; 32 jewels; 28,800 vph; rose gold skeletonized rotor; 50-hour power reserve
Functions: hours, minutes, sweep seconds; annual calendar with date, weekday, months, moon phase
Case: rose gold, ø 42 mm, height 11.1 mm; sapphire crystal; transparent case back; water-resistant to 10 atm
Band: rose gold, folding clasp
Price: $77,500

Tonda PF Chronograph Steel

Reference number: PFC915-1020001-100182
Movement: automatic, Parmigiani Caliber PF070; ø 30.6 mm, height 6.95 mm; 42 jewels; 36,000 vph; skeletonized bridges, rose gold skeletonized rotor; 65-hour power reserve COSC-certified chronometer
Functions: hours, minutes, subsidiary seconds; chronograph; date
Case: stainless steel, ø 42 mm, height 12.4 mm; sapphire crystal; transparent case back; water-resistant to 10 atm
Band: stainless steel, folding clasp
Price: $31,000

Tonda GT Chronograph Rose Gold Big Date Granata

Reference number: PFC903-2020002-400181
Movement: automatic, Parmigiani Caliber PF701; ø 30.6 mm, height 8 mm; 42 jewels; 36,000 vph; rose gold skeletonized rotor; finely finished movement; 65-hour power reserve; COSC-certified chronometer
Functions: hours, minutes, subsidiary seconds; chronograph; large date
Case: rose gold, ø 42 mm, height 14.3 mm; sapphire crystal; transparent case back; water-resistant to 10 atm
Band: rubber, folding clasp
Price: $47,700

Tonda GT Chronograph Steel Big Date Quantum Grey

Reference number: PFC906-1020001-400181
Movement: automatic, Parmigiani Caliber PF043; ø 30 mm, height 7.4 mm; 56 jewels; 28,800 vph; rose gold skeletonized rotor; finely finished movement; 45-hour power reserve
Functions: hours, minutes, subsidiary seconds; chronograph; full calendar with large date, month
Case: stainless steel, ø 42 mm, height 13.7 mm; sapphire crystal; transparent case back; water-resistant to 10 atm
Band: rubber, folding clasp
Price: $21,400
Variations: with stainless steel bracelet

Tonda GT Chronograph Steel Silver Black

Reference number: PFC906-0000140-B00182
Movement: automatic, Parmigiani Caliber PF043; ø 30 mm, height 7.4 mm; 56 jewels; 28,800 vph; rose gold skeletonized rotor, finely finished movement; 45-hour power reserve
Functions: hours, minutes, subsidiary seconds; chronograph; full calendar with large date, month
Case: stainless steel, ø 42 mm, height 13.7 mm; sapphire crystal; transparent case back; water-resistant to 10 atm
Band: stainless steel, folding clasp
Price: $22,600
Variations: with rubber strap ($21,400)

Tonda GT Steel Silver Black

Reference number: PFC910-0000141-X01482
Movement: automatic, Parmigiani Caliber PF044; ø 30 mm, height 5.3 mm; 33 jewels; 28,800 vph; rose gold skeletonized rotor, finely finished movement; 45-hour power reserve
Functions: hours, minutes, subsidiary seconds; large date
Case: stainless steel, ø 42 mm, height 11.2 mm sapphire crystal; transparent case back; water-resistant to 10 atm
Band: rubber, folding clasp
Price: $15,700
Variations: with stainless steel bracelet

Tonda GT Steel Silver Black

Reference number: PFC910-0000141-B00182
Movement: automatic, Parmigiani Caliber PF044; ø 30 mm, height 5.3 mm; 33 jewels; 28,800 vph; rose gold skeletonized rotor, finely finished movement; 45-hour power reserve
Functions: hours, minutes, subsidiary seconds; large date
Case: stainless steel, ø 42 mm, height 11.2 mm; sapphire crystal; transparent case back; water-resistant to 10 atm
Band: stainless steel, folding clasp
Price: $16,800
Variations: with rubber strap ($15,700)

Tonda GT Rose Gold Silver Black

Reference number: PFC910-1500140-X01482
Movement: automatic, Parmigiani Caliber PF044; ø 30 mm, height 5.3 mm; 33 jewels; 28,800 vph; rose gold skeletonized rotor, finely finished movement; 45-hour power reserve
Functions: hours, minutes, subsidiary seconds; large date
Case: rose gold, ø 42 mm, height 11.2 mm; sapphire crystal; transparent case back; water-resistant to 10 atm
Band: rubber, folding clasp
Price: $28,800
Variations: with a rose gold bracelet ($57,500)

Tonda GT Rose Gold Silver Black

Reference number: PFC910-1500140-X10082
Movement: automatic, Parmigiani Caliber PF044; ø 30 mm, height 5.3 mm; 33 jewels; 28,800 vph; rose gold skeletonized rotor, finely finished movement; 45-hour power reserve
Functions: hours, minutes, subsidiary seconds; large date
Case: rose gold, ø 42 mm, height 11.2 mm; sapphire crystal; transparent case back; water-resistant to 10 atm
Band: rose gold, folding clasp
Price: $57,500
Variations: with rubber strap ($28,800)

Caliber PF043

Automatic; skeletonized rotor; single spring barrel, 45-hour power reserve
Functions: hours, minutes, subsidiary seconds; chronograph; annual calendar with large date, month
Diameter: 30 mm
Height: 7.4 mm
Jewels: 56
Frequency: 28,800 vph
Remarks: 443 parts

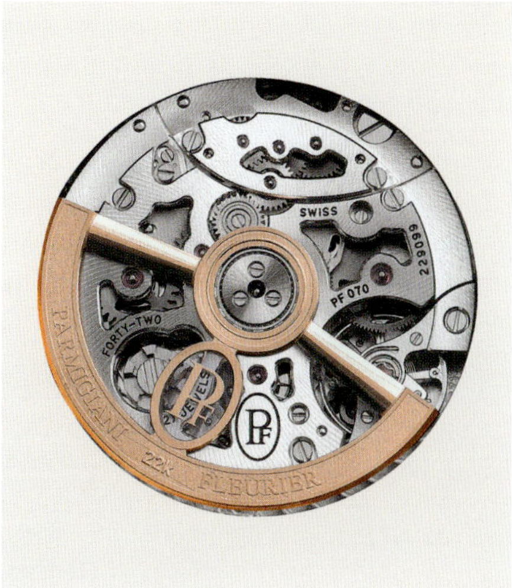

Caliber PF070

Automatic; skeletonized bridges, rose gold skeletonized rotor; single spring barrel, 65-hour power reserve, COSC-certified chronometer
Functions: hours, minutes, subsidiary seconds; chronograph; date
Diameter: 30.6 mm
Height: 6.95 mm
Jewels: 42
Frequency: 36,000 vph

Caliber PF517

Automatic; flying 1-minute tourbillon, platinum microrotor; single spring barrel, 48-hour power reserve
Functions: hours, minutes, subsidiary seconds; (on tourbillon cage)
Diameter: 32 mm
Height: 3.4 mm
Jewels: 29
Frequency: 21,600 vph
Remarks: 205 parts

Caliber PF777

Automatic; movement entirely skeletonized and blackened rose-gold skeletonized rotor; single spring barrel, 60-hour power reserve
Functions: hours, minutes,
Diameter: 30 mm
Height: 3.9 mm
Jewels: 29
Frequency: 28,800 vph
Remarks: 187 parts

Caliber PF051

Automatic; platinum microrotor; single spring barrel, 48-hour power reserve
Functions: hours, minutes; additional 12-hour display (second time zone); pusher activated zero-reset (split seconds function)
Diameter: 30 mm
Height: 4.9 mm
Jewels: 31
Frequency: 21,600 vph
Remarks: 207 parts

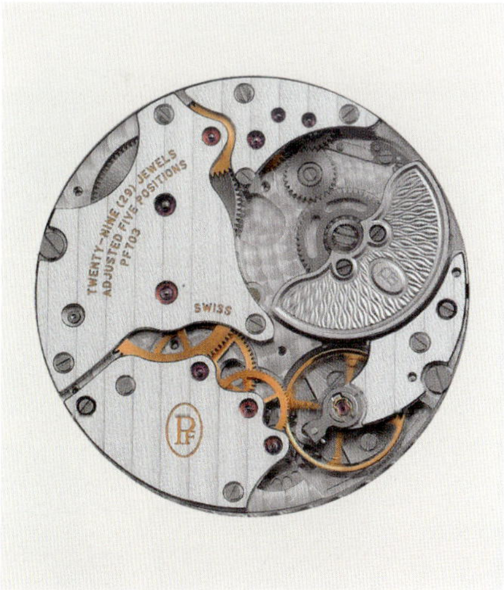

Caliber PF703

Automatic; platinum microrotor; single spring barrel, 48-hour power reserve
Functions: hours, minutes, date
Diameter: 30 mm
Height: 3 mm
Jewels: 29
Frequency: 21,600 vph
Remarks: 176 parts

PATEK PHILIPPE

In the Swiss watchmaking landscape, Patek Philippe has a special status as the last independent family-owned business. The company originated in 1839 with two Polish émigrés to Switzerland, Count Norbert Antoine de Patek and Franciszek Czapek. In 1845, following the natural end of their contract, Patek sought another partner in the master watchmaker Jean Adrien Philippe, who had developed a keyless winding and time-setting mechanism. Ever since, Patek Philippe has been known for creating high-quality mechanical watches, some with extremely sophisticated complications. Even among its competition, the *manufacture* enjoys the greatest respect.

In 1932, Charles-Henri Stern took over the manufacture. His son Henri and grandson Philippe continued the tradition of solid leadership, steering the company through the notorious quartz crisis without ever compromising quality. The next in line, also Henri, heads the enterprise these days.

Producing an impressive 66,000-plus watches yearly demands ultramodern facilities. The year 2019 closed with the opening of large, new, ultramodern premises in Geneva, where various manufacturing activities can be performed under a single roof with an optimized workflow. The site is a complement to another industrial hub between La Chaux-de-Fonds and Le Locle, where case components are manufactured, cases are polished, and gem setting is done.

While Patek Philippe's main headquarters remains in Geneva, the manufacture no longer really has a need for that city's famed quality seal: all of its mechanical watches now feature the "Patek Philippe Seal," the criteria for which far exceed the requirements of the Poinçon de Genève and include specifications for the entire watch, not just the movement. Among the most recent creations to make that grade is the World Time Chronograph, a masterful extension of the company's large range of chronographs. To make space, there is no second hand and only a thirty-minute counter. A moving city ring and twenty-four-hour ring have a place on the dial as well, and the whole piece is just over 12 millimeters high.

Patek Philippe SA
Chemin du pont-du-centenaire 141
CH-1228 Plan-les-Ouates
Switzerland

Tel.:
+41-22-884-20-20

Website:
www.patek.com

Founded:
1839

Number of employees:
approx. 2,000 (estimated)

Annual production:
approx. 60,000 watches worldwide per year

U.S. distributor:
Patek Philippe USA
45 Rockefeller Center, Suite 401
New York, NY 10111
212-218-1240

Most important collections
Aquanaut, Calatrava, Ellipse, Gondolo / ladies' timepieces

Perpetual Calendar

Reference number: 5320G-011
Movement: automatic, Patek Philippe Caliber 324 S Q; ø 32 mm, height 4.97 mm; 29 jewels; 28,800 vph; silicon Spiromax hairspring; gold rotor; 35-hour power reserve
Functions: hours, minutes, sweep seconds; day/night indication; perpetual calendar with date, weekday, month, moon phase, leap year
Case: white gold, ø 40 mm, height 11.13 mm; sapphire crystal; transparent case back; water-resistant to 3 atm
Band: reptile skin, folding clasp
Remarks: comes with additional white-gold case back
Price: $82,800

Chronograph Perpetual Calendar

Reference number: 5270P-014
Movement: manually wound, Patek Philippe Caliber CH 29-535 PS Q; ø 32 mm, height 7 mm; 33 jewels; 28,800 vph; 55-hour power reserve
Functions: hours, minutes, subsidiary seconds; day/night indication; chronograph; perpetual calendar with date, weekday, month, moon phase, leap year
Case: platinum, ø 41 mm, height 12.4 mm; sapphire crystal; transparent case back; water-resistant to 3 atm
Band: reptile skin, folding clasp
Price: $211,720

Chronograph Perpetual Calendar

Reference number: 5270J-001
Movement: manually wound, Patek Philippe Caliber CHR 29-535 PS Q; ø 32 mm, height 7 mm; 33 jewels; 28,800 vph; 55-hour power reserve
Functions: hours, minutes, subsidiary seconds; day/night indicator; chronograph; perpetual calendar with date, weekday, month, moon phase, leap year
Case: yellow gold, ø 41 mm, height 12.4 mm; sapphire crystal; transparent case back; water-resistant to 3 atm
Band: reptile skin, folding clasp
Price: $182,150
Variations: in rose gold ($218,820)

Perpetual Calendar

Reference number: 5236P-001
Movement: automatic, Patek Philippe Caliber 31-260 PS QL; ø 34 mm, height 5.8 mm; 55 jewels; 28,800 vph; Gyromax balance and Spiromax hairspring: platinum micro-rotor; 38-hour power reserve
Functions: hours, minutes, subsidiary seconds; day/night indication; perpetual calendar with date, weekday, month, moon phase, leap year
Case: platinum, ø 41.3 mm, height 11.07 mm; sapphire crystal; transparent case back; water-resistant to 3 atm
Band: reptile skin, folding clasp
Remarks: comes with additional platinum case back
Price: $136,020

Perpetual Calendar with Split-Seconds Chronograph

Reference number: 5204R-011
Movement: manually wound, Patek Philippe Caliber CHR 29-535 PS Q; ø 32 mm, height 8.7 mm; 34 jewels; 28,800 vph; Breguet hairspring; 55-hour power reserve
Functions: hours, minutes, subsidiary seconds; split-seconds chronograph; perpetual calendar with date, weekday, month, moon phase, leap year, day/night indication
Case: rose gold, ø 40 mm, height 14.3 mm; sapphire crystal; transparent case back; water-resistant to 3 atm
Band: calfskin, folding clasp
Remarks: comes with additional rose gold case back
Price: $315,810

Monopusher Chronograph 1/10 Second

Reference number: 5470P-001
Movement: manually wound, Patek Philippe Caliber CH 29-535 PS 1/10; ø 29.6 mm, height 6.96 mm; 38 jewels; 36,000 vph; silicon hairspring (Spiromax), pallet lever and escape wheel (Pulsomax), monopusher control of chronograph functions; 48-hour power reserve
Functions: hours, minutes, subsidiary seconds; chronograph with 1/10th-second measurement
Case: platinum, ø 41 mm, height 13.68 mm; sapphire crystal; transparent case back; water-resistant to 3 atm
Band: calf leather, folding clasp
Remarks: comes with additional platinum case back
Price: on request

Annual Calendar Travel Time

Reference number: 5326G-001
Movement: automatic, Patek Philippe Caliber 31-260 PS QA LU FUS 24H; ø 33 mm, height 5,6 mm; 31 jewels; 28.800 vph; platinum micro-rotor; 38-hour power reserve
Functions: hours, minutes, subsidiary seconds; additional 12-hour display (second time zone), day/night indication, (for local and home time); annual calendar with date, weekday, month, moon phase
Case: white gold, ø 41 mm, height 11.07 mm; sapphire crystal; transparent case back; water-resistant to 3 atm
Band: calf leather, folding clasp
Price: $76,880

Chronograph

Reference number: 5172G-010
Movement: manually wound, Patek Philippe Caliber CH 29-535 PS; ø 29.6 mm, height 5.35 mm; 33 jewels; 28,800 vph; Breguet hairspring, column-wheel control of chronograph functions; 65-hour power reserve
Functions: hours, minutes, subsidiary seconds; chronograph
Case: white gold, ø 41 mm, height 11.45 mm; sapphire crystal; transparent case back; water-resistant to 3 atm
Band: reptile skin, folding clasp
Price: $80,430

Annual Calendar Moon Phase

Reference number: 5205R-011
Movement: automatic, Patek Philippe Caliber 324 S QA LU 24H; ø 32.6 mm, height 5.78 mm; 34 jewels; 28,800 vph; 35-hour power reserve
Functions: hours, minutes, sweep seconds; additional 24-hour display; annual calendar with date, weekday, month, moon phase
Case: rose gold, ø 40 mm, height 11.36 mm; sapphire crystal; transparent case back; water-resistant to 3 atm
Band: reptile skin, buckle
Price: $55,590

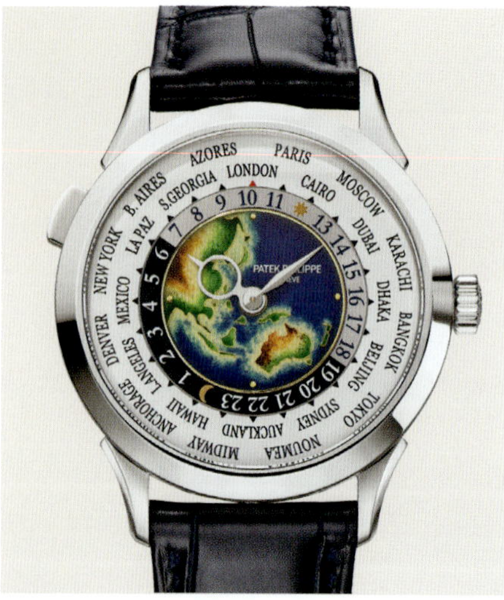

World Time Watch

Reference number: 5231G-001
Movement: automatic, Patek Philippe Caliber 240 HU; ø 27.5 mm, height 3.88 mm; 33 jewels; 21,600 vph; silicon Spiromax hairspring; gold microrotor; 48-hour power reserve
Functions: hours, minutes; world time display (second time zone)
Case: white gold, ø 38.5 mm, height 10.23 mm; pusher-activated inner bezel with city references; sapphire crystal; transparent case back; water-resistant to 3 atm
Band: reptile skin, folding clasp
Remarks: enamel dial
Price: $79,500

World Time Watch

Reference number: 5230P-001
Movement: automatic, Patek Philippe Caliber 240 HU; ø 27.5 mm, height 3.88 mm; 33 jewels; 21,600 vph; silicon Spiromax hairspring; gold microrotor; 48-hour power reserve
Functions: hours, minutes; world time display (second time zone)
Case: platinum, ø 38.5 mm, height 10.23 mm; pusher-activated inner bezel with city references; sapphire crystal; transparent case back; water-resistant to 3 atm
Band: calfskin, folding clasp
Price: $70,970

World Time Watch

Reference number: 7130R-014
Movement: automatic, Patek Philippe Caliber 240 HU; ø 27.5 mm, height 3.88 mm; 33 jewels; 21,600 vph; silicon Spiromax hairspring; gold microrotor; 48-hour power reserve
Functions: hours, minutes; world-time display (second time zone)
Case: rose gold, ø 36 mm, height 8.83 mm; bezel set with 62 diamonds; pusher-activated inner bezel with city references; sapphire crystal; transparent case back; water-resistant to 3 atm
Band: calfskin, buckle set with 27 diamonds
Price: $57,960

Moon Phase Watch

Reference number: 7121/200G-001
Movement: manually wound, Patek Philippe Caliber 215 PS LU; ø 21.9 mm, height 3 mm; 18 jewels; 28,800 vph; silicon Spiromax hairspring; 39-hour power reserve
Functions: hours, minutes, subsidiary seconds; moon phase
Case: white gold, ø 33 mm, height 8.35 mm; bezel set with 132 diamonds, sapphire crystal; transparent case back; water-resistant to 3 atm
Band: reptile skin, buckle
Price: $42,580

Flyback Chronograph Annual Calendar

Reference number: 5905/1 A-001
Movement: automatic, Patek Philippe Caliber CH 28-520 QA 24H; ø 33 mm, height 7.68 mm; 37 jewels; 28,800 vph; silicon Spiromax hairspring, gold rotor, 45-hour power reserve
Functions: hours, minutes; flyback chronograph; annual calendar with date, weekday, month
Case: stainless steel, ø 42 mm, height 14.3 mm; sapphire crystal; transparent case back; water-resistant to 3 atm
Band: stainless steel, folding clasp
Price: $61,510

Annual Calendar Moon Phase

Reference number: 5396/R-015
Movement: automatic, Patek Philippe Caliber 324 S QA LU 24H/303; ø 33.3 mm, height 5.78 mm; 34 jewels, 28,800 vph; silicon Spiromax hairspring; 35-hour power reserve
Functions: hours, minutes, sweep seconds; additional 24-hour display; annual calendar with date, weekday, month, moon phase
Case: rose gold, ø 38.5 mm, height 11.2 mm; sapphire crystal; transparent case back; water-resistant to 3 atm
Band: reptile skin, folding clasp
Remarks: dial set with 12 baguette-cut diamonds
Price: $55,590
Variations: in white gold ($55,590)

World Time Watch Flyback Chronograph

Reference number: 5230P-001
Movement: automatic, Patek Philippe Caliber 240 HU; ø 27.5, height 3.88 mm; 33 jewels; 21,600 vph, silicon Spiromax hairspring; 48-hour power reserve
Functions: hours, minutes; world-time display (second time zone); day/night indication; flyback chronograph
Case: platinum, ø 38.5 mm, height 10.23 mm; pusher-activated inner bezel with city references; sapphire crystal; transparent case back; water-resistant to 3 atm
Band: reptile skin, folding clasp
Price: $70,970

Annual Calendar Moon Phase

Reference number: 4947/1A-001
Movement: automatic, Patek Philippe Caliber 324 S QA LU; ø 30 mm, height 5,32 mm; 34 jewels; 28,800 vph; silicon Spiromax hairspring, gold rotor; 35-hour power reserve
Functions: hours, minutes, sweep seconds; annual calendar with date, weekday, month, moon phase
Case: stainless steel, ø 38 mm, height 11 mm; sapphire crystal; transparent case back; water-resistant to 3 atm
Band: stainless steel, folding clasp
Price: $49,680

Calatrava

Reference number: 5226G-001
Movement: automatic, Patek Philippe Caliber 26-330 S C; ø 27 mm, height 3.3 mm; 30 jewels; 28,800 vph; silicon Spiromax hairspring, gold rotor; 35-hour power reserve
Functions: hours, minutes, sweep seconds; date
Case: white gold, ø 40 mm, height 8.53 mm; sapphire crystal; transparent case back; water-resistant to 3 atm
Band: calfskin, buckle
Price: $39,030

Calatrava

Reference number: 6119R-001
Movement: manually wound, Patek Philippe Caliber 30-255 PS; ø 31 mm, height 2.55 mm; 27 jewels; 28,800 vph; Gyromax balance wheel and Spiromax hairspring; 65-hour power reserve
Functions: hours, minutes, subsidiary seconds
Case: rose gold, ø 39 mm, height 8.1 mm; sapphire crystal; transparent case back
Band: reptile skin, buckle
Price: $30,750

Calatrava Weekly Calendar

Reference number: 5212A-001
Movement: automatic, Patek Philippe Caliber 26-330 S C J SE; ø 27 mm, height 4.82 mm; 50 jewels; 28,800 vph; silicon Spiromax hairspring, gold rotor, 35-hour power reserve
Functions: hours, minutes, sweep seconds date, weekday, calendar week
Case: stainless steel, ø 40 mm, height 10.79 mm; sapphire crystal; transparent case back; water-resistant to 3 atm
Band: calfskin, buckle
Price: $37,260

Twenty-4

Reference number: 4910/1200A-011
Movement: quartz
Functions: hours, minutes
Case: stainless steel, set with 36 diamonds, 25.1 mm x 30 mm, height 6.8 mm; sapphire crystal; water-resistant to 3 atm
Band: stainless steel, folding clasp
Price: $15,380

Caliber 324 S Q

Automatic; gold rotor; single spring barrel, 35-hour power reserve
Functions: hours, minutes, sweep seconds; sweep secdonds; perpetual calendar with date
Diameter: 32 mm
Height: 4.97 mm
Jewels: 29
Balance: Gyromax
Frequency: 28,800 vph

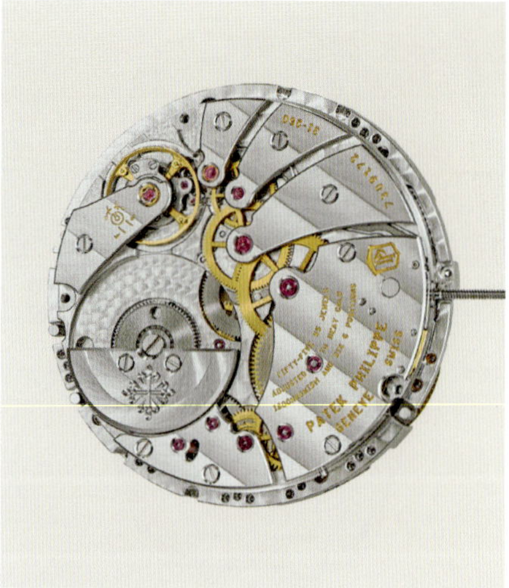

Caliber 31-260 PS QL

Automatic; platinum microrotor; single spring barrel, 38-hour power reserve
Functions: hours, minutes, subsidiary seconds; day/night indication; perpetual calendar with date , weekday, month, moon phase, leap year
Diameter: 34 mm
Height: 5.8 mm
Jewels: 55
Balance: Gyromax
Frequency: 28,800 vph
Balance spring: silicon Spiromax

Caliber 31-260 PS QA LU FUS 24H

Automatic; platinum microrotor; single spring barrel, 38-hour power reserve
Functions: hours, minutes, subsidiary seconds; additional 12-hour display (second time zone), day/night indication for local and home time); annual calendar with date, weekday, months moon phase
Diameter: 33 mm
Height: 5.6 mm
Jewels: 47
Balance: Gyromax
Frequency: 28,800 vph
Balance spring: Spiromax silicon spring
Remarks: 409 parts

Caliber CH 29-535 PS

Manually wound; column-wheel control of chronograph functions, precisely jumping 30-minute totalizer; single spring barrel, 65-hour power reserve
Functions: hours, minutes, subsidiary seconds; flyback chronograph
Diameter: 29.6 mm
Height: 7.1 mm
Jewels: 34
Balance: Gyromax, 4-armed, with 4 regulating weights
Frequency: 28,800 vph
Balance spring: Breguet
Shock protection: Incabloc
Remarks: 312 parts

Caliber CHR 29-535 PS Q

Manually wound; two column wheels to control chronograph functions, flyback mechanism with isolator; single spring barrel, 65-hour power reserve
Functions: hours, minutes, subsidiary seconds; day/night indicator; flyback chronograph; perpetual calendar with date, weekday, month, moon phase, leap year
Diameter: 32 mm
Height: 8.7 mm
Jewels: 34
Balance: Gyromax, 4-armed, with 4 regulating weights
Frequency: 28,800 vph
Hairspring: Breguet
Remarks: 496 parts, including 182 for perpetual calendar and 42 for flyback mechanism with isolator

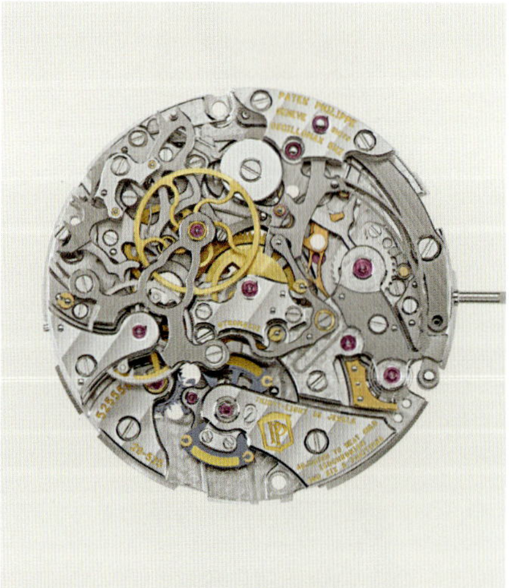

Caliber CH 29-535 PS 1/10

Manually wound; silicon anchor and escape wheel (Pulsomax), single pusher for chronograph functions; single spring barrel, 48-hour power reserve
Functions: hours, minutes, subsidiary seconds; chronograph with 1/10th second measurement
Diameter: 29.6 mm
Height: 6.96 mm
Jewels: 38
Balance: Gyromax
Frequency: 36,000 vph
Balance spring: Spiromax silicon spring
Shock protection: Incabloc
Remarks: 396 parts

Caliber 240 Q

Automatic; gold microrotor; single spring barrel, 48-hour power reserve
Functions: hours, minutes; additional 24-hour power reserve display (second time zone); perpetual calendar with date, weekday, month, moon phase, leap year
Diameter: 30 mm
Height: 3.75 mm
Jewels: 27
Balance: Gyromax, with 8 "masselotte" regulating weights
Frequency: 21,600 vph
Balance: flat spring
Shock protection: Kif

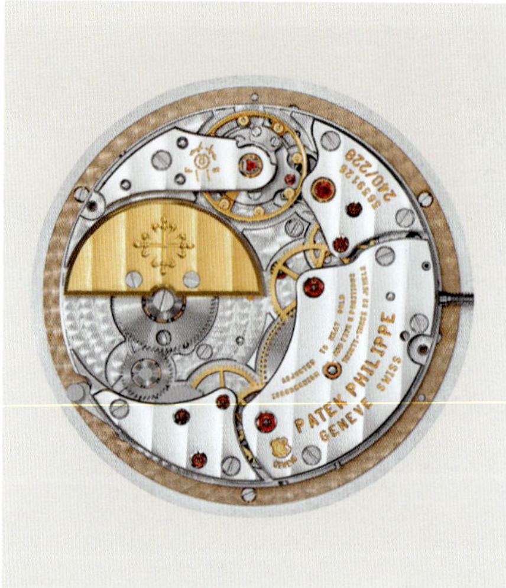

Caliber 240 HU

Automatic; 22-kt gold unidirectional off-center winding microrotor on ball-bearings; single spring barrel, 48-hour power reserve
Functions: hours, minutes; world-time display (second time zone)
Diameter: 27.5 mm
Height: 3.88 mm
Jewels: 33
Balance: Gyromax
Frequency: 21,600 vph
Remarks: 239 parts

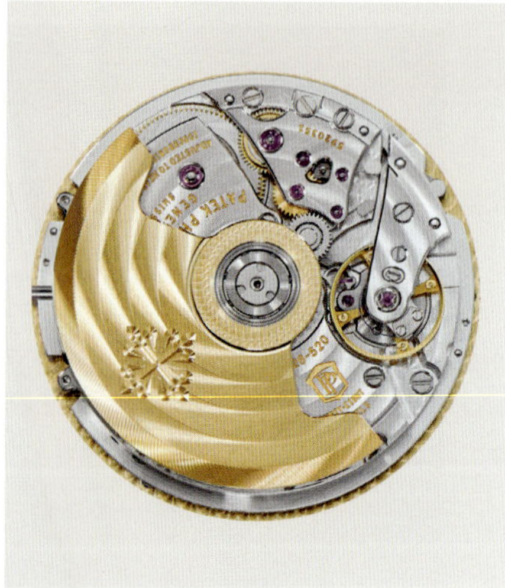

Caliber CH 28-520 HU

Automatic; single barrel spring, 50-hour power reserve
Functions: hours, minutes, world time indicator (second time zone); flyback chronograph
Diameter: 33 mm
Height: 7.97 mm
Jewels: 38
Balance: Gyromax
Frequency: 28,800 vph
Balance spring: Spiromax silicon spring
Remarks: 343 parts very fine movement finishing

Caliber 26-330 S C J SE

Automatic; gold rotor; single spring barrel, 35-hour power reserve
Functions: hours, minutes, sweep seconds; date, weekday, weeks of the year
Diameter: 27 mm
Height: 4.82 mm
Jewels: 50
Frequency: 28,800 vph
Balance spring: Spiromax silicon spring

Caliber 26-330 S C

Automatic; gold rotor; single spring barrel, 35-hour power reserve
Functions: hours, minutes, sweep seconds; date
Diameter: 27 mm
Height: 3.3 mm
Jewels: 30
Balance: Gyromax
Frequency: 28,800 vph
Balance spring: Spiromax silicon spring
Remarks: 212 parts

Caliber 30-255 PS

Manually wound; single spring barrel, 65-hour power reserve
Functions: hours, minutes, subsidiary seconds
Diameter: 31 mm
Height: 2.55 mm
Jewels: 27
Balance: Gyromax
Frequency: 28,800 vph
Balance spring: Spiromax with silicon escapement

Montres Péquignet
1, rue du Bief
F-25503 Morteau
France

Tel:
+33 381 67 30 66

E-mail:
contact@pequignet.com

Website:
www.pequignet.com

Founded:
1973

Number of employees:
50

U.S. distributor:
About Time Luxury Group
210 Bellevue Avenue
Newport, RI 02840
401-846-0598

Most important collections / price range:
Men's and women's watches from $1,700 to $5,500

PEQUIGNET

The Jura mountains, which saddle Switzerland and France are not only home to inventive and dogged craftspeople, notably watchmakers, on the Swiss side. In 1973, in Morteau, a small town close to the border, one Emile Pequignet founded a watch and jewelry company producing contemporary pieces that caught the spirit of the age and enjoyed a fair success. In 2004, Pequignet himself retired and sold the brand to one Didier Leibundgut. This whole industry was bursting with energy, creating bigger and crazier watches. Pequignet decided to maintain its classic look and develop its own *manufacture* movement, investing millions into the Calibre Royal.

The elaborate automatic movement is subject to eight patents. It can drive various functions, like a full calendar with moon phase or a power reserve indicator to tell the wearer how many of the 100 hours the large spring barrel delivers have been used up. Since it does not need any modules, the movement is quite thin and can be configured for other functions quite easily.

The Calibre Royal reinvigorated the company, but it also cost inordinate amounts of money. The decade following its development was spent under the threat of liquidation. Finally, in December 2021, it was announced that a family fund had purchased the brand and the majority shareholder, Hugues Souparis, was now the new CEO. Morteau (pop. around 6,900) breathed a sigh of relief: maintaining the last independent French watch brand is a matter of honor in the region.

Pequignet still has quite a wide range of collections, but the focus has been on the calibers inside. In 2021, the *manufacture* developed a second one called "Initial." It was initially used in a limited gold edition of the Attitude line and is now also available in stainless steel. A limited-edition watch is scheduled for the brand's fiftieth anniversary.

Attitude Acier

Reference number: 9060343 AN
Movement: automatic, Caliber Initial EPM03; ø 25.6 mm, height 4.2 mm; 21 jewels; 28,800 vph; skeletonized winding rotor; 65-hour power reserve
Functions: hours, minutes, sweep seconds; date
Case: stainless steel, ø 39 mm, height 9.05 mm; sapphire crystal; transparent case back; water-resistant to 5 atm
Band: reptile skin, folding clasp
Price: $2,970

Royale Saphir

Reference number: 9010883 CB
Movement: automatic, Caliber Royal EPM01; ø 30 mm, height 5.88 mm; 39 jewels; 21,600 vph; large spring barrel, finely finished with chamfered edges and perlage; 72-hour power reserve
Functions: hours, minutes, subsidiary seconds; power reserve indicator; date and weekday; moon phase
Case: stainless steel, ø 42 mm, height 12.3 mm; sapphire crystal; transparent case back; water-resistant to 5 atm
Band: reptile skin, double folding clasp
Remarks: multipart translucent sapphire crystal dial
Price: $10,890

Royale Manuelle

Reference number: 9080413 CB
Movement: manually wound, Caliber Royal EPM02; ø 30 mm, height 5.88 mm; 21 jewels; 21,600 vph; finely finished, chamfered edges and perlage; 100-hour power reserve
Functions: hours, minutes, subsidiary seconds
Case: stainless steel, ø 42 mm, height 12.3 mm; sapphire crystal; transparent case back; water-resistant to 10 atm
Band: calfskin, double folding clasp
Price: $3,685

PERRELET

The Perrelet story will sound familiar to anyone who has read about Swiss watchmaking. Abraham-Louis Perrelet (1729–1826) was the son of a middle-class farmer from Le Locle who developed an interest in watchmaking early on in life. He was the first watchmaker in Le Locle to work on cylinder and duplex escapements, and there is a persistent rumor that he was responsible for a repeater that could be heard echoing in the mountains.

Many watchmakers later to become famous were at one time Perrelet's apprentices, and some historians even suggest that Abraham-Louis Breguet was in this illustrious group. Suffice to say, Perrelet invented a great deal, including the "perpetual" watch from around 1770, a pocket watch that wound itself using the motion of the wearer.

When the brand hit the market in 1995, it came out with a double rotor and a movement, the P-181, which made waves in the industry. The Turbine soon followed, featuring a kind of jet engine fan that decoratively turns over the dial, creating all sorts of effects and giving lots of potential for creative designing. It was all creative and successful enough to attract the attention of Festina Group, which purchased the brand in 2004.

After a few years of silence, during which the company reorganized its distribution network, Perrelet returned to the watch world, having also made improvements to its automatic movements to ensure that their precision was at COSC level. The revised automatic P-411 still drives the LAB, cleverly designed to show the rotor just under a transparent dial. The turbines are back, with that attractive hallmark animation on the dial of Turbine EVO, driven by the caliber P-331-MH with COSC certificate. The fan-shaped wheel on the upper part of the dial, which rotates at full speed depending on the movements of the wrist, creates fascinating and original visual effects depending on the decoration of the dial below.

Perrelet SA
Rue Bubenberg 7
CH-2502 Biel/Bienne
Switzerland

Tel.:
+41-32-346-2626

Fax:
+41-32-346-2627

E-mail:
perrelet@perrelet.com

Website:
www.perrelet.com

Founded:
brand founded in 1777, acquired by Festina Group in 2004

U.S. distributor:
Perrelet USA
2937 SW 27th Avenue Suite 102
Miami, FL 33133
305-588-3628
info@perreletusa.com

Most important collections:
LAB, Turbine, First Class, Diamond Flower

Turbine Carbon Racing

Reference number: A4065/3
Movement: automatic, Perrelet Caliber P-331-MH (on Soprod base); ø 26.2 mm, height 3.6 mm; 25 jewels; 28,800 vph; 42-hour power reserve; COSC-certified chronometer
Functions: hours, minutes, sweep seconds
Case: carbon fiber, black PVD-coated, ø 44 mm, height 13.8 mm; sapphire crystal; transparent case back; water-resistant to 10 atm
Band: leather with rubber lining, folding clasp
Remarks: "turbine" animation of anodized aluminum on the dial (no winding function)
Price: $4,750
Variations: various dial colors; polished stainless steel; with stainless-steel link bracelet

LAB Peripheral Dual Time Big Date

Reference number: A1101/4
Movement: automatic, Perrelet Caliber P-421; ø 34.8 mm, height 6.32 mm; 30 jewels; 28,800 vph; peripheral rotor visible on the dial side; 42-hour power reserve
Functions: hours, minutes, sweep seconds; day/night indication (second time zone); large date
Case: stainless steel, ø 42 mm, height 13.5 mm; sapphire crystal; transparent case back; water-resistant to 5 atm
Band: leather, folding clasp
Price: $4,980
Variations: with a silver-white, black, or green dial

Weekend GMT

Reference number: A1304/3
Movement: automatic, Perrelet Caliber P-401 (on Soprod base); ø 26.2 mm, height 4.25 mm; 25 jewels; 28,800 vph; 42-hour power reserve
Functions: hours, minutes, sweep seconds; additional 24-hour display (second time zone); date
Case: stainless steel, ø 39 mm, height 9.5 mm; sapphire crystal; transparent case back; water-resistant to 5 atm
Band: calfskin, folding clasp
Price: $1,680
Variations: with a silver-white, black, or green dial

Piaget SA
CH-1228 Plan-les-Ouates
Switzerland

Tel.:
+41-32-867-21-21

E-mail:
info@piaget.com

Website:
www.piaget.com

Founded:
1874

Number of employees:
900

Annual production:
about 25,000 watches

U.S. distributor:
Piaget North America
645 5th Avenue, 6th Floor
New York, NY 10022
212-909-4362
www.piaget.com

Most important collections:
Altiplano, Polo S, Limelight, Possession

PIAGET

Piaget began making watch movements in the secluded Jura village of La Côte-aux-Fées in 1874. For decades, those movements were delivered to other watch brands. The *manufacture* itself, strangely enough, remained in the background. It wasn't until the 1940s that the Piaget family began to offer complete watches under their own name. Even today, Piaget, which long ago moved the business side of things to Geneva, still makes its watch movements at its main facility high in the Jura mountains.

In the late fifties, Piaget began investing in the design and manufacturing of ultrathin movements. This lends these watches the kind of understated elegance that became the company's hallmark. In 1957, Valentin Piaget presented the first ultrathin men's watch, the Altiplano, with the manual caliber 9P, which was 2 millimeters high. Shortly after, it came out with the 12P, an automatic caliber that clocked in at 2.3 millimeters.

The Altiplano has faithfully accompanied the brand for sixty years now. The movement has evolved over time. The recent 900P measures just 3.65 millimeters and is inverted to enable repairs, making the case back the mainplate with the dial set on the upper side.

Piaget is continuing to strive for thinner watches, even in the third millennium. In 2018, it came out with the Altiplano Ultimate Concept, which, in all its beauty, even briefly set a world record: the thinnest mechanical watch with manual winding of only two millimeters total height. It was not an easy task to make, having taken four years of research and development. In the meantime, the miniaturized work of art, which was planned purely as a study, is also available for regular purchase. It is handmade in tiny batches and, in view of the steep price, probably only for the most solvent among us.

Altiplano Ultimate Automatic

Reference number: G0A45123
Movement: automatic, Piaget Caliber 910P; ø 41 mm, height 4.3 mm (case and movement); 30 jewels; 21,600 vph; inverted movement construction in a single construction unit with the case, hubless peripheral rotor; 50-hour power reserve
Functions: hours and minutes (off-center)
Case: white gold, ø 41 mm, height 4.3 mm; sapphire crystal
Band: reptile skin, buckle
Price: $31,900

Altiplano Ultimate Automatic

Reference number: G0A47124
Movement: automatic, Piaget Caliber 910P; ø 41 mm, height 4.3 mm (case and movement); 30 jewels; 21,600 vph; inverted movement construction in a single construction unit with the case, hubless peripheral rotor; 50-hour power reserve; mainplate and bridges with blue PVD; 50-hour power reserve
Functions: hours and minutes (off-center)
Case: rose gold ø 41 mm, height 4.3 mm; bezel set with diamonds; sapphire crystal;
Band: reptile skin, buckle
Price: $42,500

Altiplano Ultimate Concept

Reference number: G0A47505
Movement: manually wound, Piaget Caliber 900P-UC; ø 41 mm, height ø 2 mm (case and movement); 13 jewels; 28,800 vph; inverted movement construction in a single construction unit with the case, flying (one-sided) mounting of wheels; 44-hour power reserve
Functions: hours and minutes (off-center)
Case: cobalt-based composite material, ø 41 mm, height 2 mm; sapphire crystal
Band: reptile skin, buckle
Remarks: manufactured in minimal batches as a concept watch for high-end collectors
Price: $451,000

Polo Date

Reference number: G0A47010
Movement: automatic, Piaget Caliber 1110P; ø 25.58 mm, height 4 mm; 25 jewels; 28,800 vph; perlage on mainplate, blued screws, fine finishing with côtes de Genève; 50-hour power reserve
Functions: hours, minutes, sweep seconds
Case: rose gold ø 42 mm, height 9.4 mm; sapphire crystal; transparent case back; water-resistant to 10 atm
Band: reptile skin, folding clasp
Price: $30,000

Polo Date

Reference number: G0A47014
Movement: automatic, Piaget Caliber 1110P; ø 25.58 mm, height 4 mm; 25 jewels; 28,800 vph; perlage on mainplate, blued screws, fine finishing with côtes de Genève; 50-hour power reserve
Functions: hours, minutes, sweep seconds; date
Case: stainless steel, ø 42 mm, height 9.4 mm; sapphire crystal; transparent case back; water-resistant to 10 atm
Band: rubber, folding clasp
Price: $11,600

Polo Skeleton Diamond Paved

Reference number: G0A47005
Movement: automatic, Piaget Caliber 1200S1; ø 29.9 mm, height 2.4 mm; 25 jewels; 21,600 vph; fully skeletonized movement, mainplate and bridges with blue PVD; 44-hour power reserve
Functions: hours, minutes
Case: white gold, set with 268 diamonds, ø 42 mm, height 7.35 mm; sapphire crystal; transparent case back
Band: white-gold bezel set with 1,278 diamonds, folding clasp
Price: $226,000

Polo Skeleton

Reference number: G0A45004
Movement: automatic, Piaget Caliber 1200S1; ø 29.9 mm, height 2.4 mm; 25 jewels; 21,600 vph; fully skeletonized movement, mainplate and bridges with blue PVD; 44-hour power reserve
Functions: hours, minutes
Case: stainless steel, ø 42 mm, height 6.5 mm; sapphire crystal; transparent case back
Band: stainless steel, folding clasp
Price: $30,900
Variations: in rose or white gold ($47,100)

Polo Skeleton Gold

Reference number: G0A46009
Movement: automatic, Piaget Caliber 1200S1; ø 29.9 mm, height 2.4 mm; 25 jewels; 21,600 vph; fully skeletonized movement, mainplate and bridges with blue PVD; 44-hour power reserve
Functions: hours, minutes
Case: rose gold ø 42 mm, height 6.5 mm; sapphire crystal; transparent case back
Band: reptile skin, folding clasp
Price: $47,100
Variations: in white gold ($47,100)

Polo Date 36mm

Reference number: G0A46019
Movement: automatic, Piaget Caliber 500P1; ø 20.5 mm, height 3.4 mm; 26 jewels; 21,600 vph; fine finishing on movement; 40-hour power reserve
Functions: hours, minutes, sweep seconds; date
Case: stainless steel, ø 36 mm, height 8.8 mm; bezel set with 60 diamonds; sapphire crystal; transparent case back; water-resistant to 5 atm
Band: stainless steel, folding clasp
Remarks: indices set with 36 diamonds
Price: $21,400
Variations: various cases, bands, and dials

Polo Date 36mm

Reference number: G0A46023
Movement: automatic, Piaget Caliber 500P1; ø 20.5 mm, height 3.4 mm; 26 jewels; 21,600 vph; fine finishing on movement; 40-hour power reserve
Functions: hours, minutes, sweep seconds; date
Case: rose gold ø 36 mm, height 8.8 mm; bezel set with 60 diamonds; sapphire crystal; transparent case back; water-resistant to 5 atm
Band: reptile skin, buckle
Remarks: indices set with 36 diamonds
Price: $38,500
Variations: various cases, bands, and dials

Possession 34mm

Reference number: G0A45072
Movement: quartz
Functions: hours, minutes
Case: rose gold ø 34 mm, height 7.47 mm; bezel set with 9 diamonds; sapphire crystal; water-resistant to 3 atm
Band: reptile skin, buckle
Remarks: mother-of-pearl dial set with 11 diamonds
Price: $15,100

Possession 34mm

Reference number: G0A44292
Movement: quartz
Functions: hours, minutes
Case: rose gold ø 34 mm, height 7.47 mm; bezel set with 46 diamonds; sapphire crystal; water-resistant to 3 atm
Case: reptile skin, buckle
Remarks: mother-of-pearl dial set with 11 diamonds
Price: $19,500

Caliber 1200S1

Automatic; micro-rotor in platinum; single spring barrel, 44-hour power reserve; Geneva Seal
Functions: hours, minutes
Diameter: 29.9 mm
Height: 2.4 mm
Jewels: 25
Balance: Glucydur
Frequency: 21,600 vph
Hairspring: flat hairspring
Remarks: completely skeletonized movement; blue PVD on bridges and plates; 189 parts

Caliber 1160P

Automatic; single spring barrel, 50-hour power reserve
Functions: hours, minutes; chronograph; date
Diameter: 25.58 mm
Height: 5.72 mm
Jewels: 35
Frequency: 28,800 vph
Remarks: perlage on mainplate, blued screws, finely finished with côtes de Genève; 262 parts

Caliber 910P

Automatic; inverted construction in a single assembly with the case; hubless peripheral rotor; single spring barrel, 50-hour power reserve
Functions: hours, minutes (off-center)
Diameter: 41 mm
Height: 4.3 mm
Jewels: 30
Balance: Glucydur
Frequency: 21,600 vph
Hairspring: flat hairspring
Remarks: finely finished movement; 238 parts

PILO WATCHES

Brimming bank accounts held by mysterious and at times shady characters may not be Geneva's best-kept secrets anymore, not in the age of leaks to the media. That is more like the cliché generated by countless spy movies and thrillers and due no doubt to the high concentration of international organizations in the city. Far less known is the fact that Geneva is a veritable hub of all sorts of crafts, notably those associated with watch-making, and they were at one time concentrated in the district of St. Gervais and referred to as "Les Cabinotiers." Among them are little watch companies that continue to produce excellent watches and survive in the shadow of the big brands and groups that have also made the city their home.

One of these independent companies, Pilo & Co., celebrated its twentieth anniversary in 2021 with a get-together in St. Gervais, where it keeps one of two shops. It was founded by Amarildo Pilo, who, while not of Swiss origin, has a very Genevan story. His father was an Albanian diplomat who was called back when the government changed in his native country at the end of the 1980s. His two sons stayed to continue their studies. Amarildo decided on an internship with a watch distributor and ended up traveling a great deal, making numerous contacts, and falling in love with the watch world. One thing led to another, and in 2001 he opened his own brand, Pilo & Co.

Twenty years later, his brand is represented throughout Switzerland and has found faithful customers in Europe and in Asia. They manufacture quartz watches but have increasingly been using mechanical movements, which are modified and reworked. The dials, if not in brilliant ceramic colors, are often open-worked or fully skeletonized. Pilo has also been very fond of tonneau dials, which offer a special kind of elegance. The portfolio has now grown to fifteen collections of affordable watches that combine good looks with outstanding workmanship.

PILO & CO SA
11 Faubourg-de-Cruseilles
CH-1227 Carouge
Switzerland

Tel.:
+41-22-328-0112

E-mail:
contact@pilo-watches.com

Website:
www.pilo-watches.com

Founded:
2001

Number of employees:
7

Distribution:
Contact main office in Geneva
contact@pilo-watches.com

Most important collections/price range:
Mechanical and quartz watches: Allegra, Corleone, Doppio Orario, Illusione, Invidia, Montecristo, Tempo and Exceptional Pieces / $300 to $5,000

Série Limitée

Reference number: P0517HAB
Movement: automatic, modified Caliber ETA 2824-2; ø 25.60 mm, height 4.6 mm; 23 jewels; 28,800 vph; skeletonized movement; 38-hour power reserve
Functions: hours, minutes, sweep seconds
Case: stainless steel black PVD, ø 43 mm, height 10mm; sapphire crystal; transparent case back; water-resistant to 3 atm
Band: calfskin, folding clasp
Remarks: black ceramic dial
Price: $1,860

Tempo

Reference number: P0527DAS
Movement: automatic, modified ETA 2824/2; ø 25.60 mm, height 4.6 mm; 23 jewels; 28,800 vph; skeletonized movement; 38-hour power reserve
Functions: hours, minutes, sweep seconds
Case: stainless steel, ø 36 mm, height 9 mm; sapphire crystal; bezel set with Swarowski crystal stones; transparent case back; water-resistant to 3 atm
Band: calfskin, folding clasp
Remarks: mother-of-pearl dial
Price: $1,620

Epoca

Reference number: P0700HMS
Movement: manually wound, vintage Unitas 6498 caliber; ø 36.6 mm, height 4.55 mm; 21 jewels; 18,000 vph; skeletonized movement; 36-hour power reserve
Functions: hours, minutes
Case: stainless steel, ø 41 mm, height 10.7 mm; sapphire crystal; transparent case back; water-resistant to 5 atm
Band: calfskin, folding clasp
Price: $2,860

PORSCHE DESIGN

Porsche Design Group
Groenerstrasse 5
D-71636 Ludwigsburg
Germany

Tel.:
+49-711-911-0

E-mail:
contact@porsche-design.us

Website:
www.porsche-design.com

Founded:
1972

U.S. distributor:
Porsche Design of America, Inc.
Plaza Tower
600 Anton Blvd., Suite 1280
Costa Mesa, CA 92626
770-290-7500
timepieces@porsche-design.us
www.porsche-design.com

Most important collections:
1919 Collection, Chronotimer Flyback, Monobloc Actuator, custom-built timepieces

Porsche Design always made sure it was partnering with companies, like IWC and later Eterna, to manufacture its products. But since 2014, all Porsche Design watches have been developed by the company subsidiary Porsche Design Timepieces in Solothurn, Switzerland, in collaboration with the well-established design studio in Zell-am-See, Austria.

Porsche Design was founded in 1972 by Professor Ferdinand Alexander Porsche, who died in April 2012. He created a string of classic objects at his "Studio," but sports car fans will always remember him for the Porsche 911.

In 2003, the Professor—a title bestowed by the Austrian government—founded a separate company to explore designs and different materials, notably for watches. In the 1970s already, it was using black PVD-coated aluminum and titanium for its watches and cases. The Chronotimer collection harked back to this very avant-garde esthetic statement.

Porsche Design engineers inspire themselves from the automobile industry when it comes to materials and functionality. The innovative rocker arm that activates the chronograph of the new Monobloc Actuator was inspired from the valve control of high-powered race cars using tappets. It improves ease of use and increases the mechanism's durability.

At the heart of the development of the timepieces is the cooperation with Porsche Motorsport. The cooperation allows the latest technologies and findings from the world of racing to be incorporated into the development of the watches. In keeping with this tradition, Porsche Design dedicated itself to the further development of engines, as it were, and has been relying on exclusive COSC-certified movements since 2017.

In collaboration with the engineers at the Porsche Development Center in Weissach (Germany), the company has produced technical masterpieces and unique calibers that impose Porsche's high quality to the "sports cars on your wrist."

Their calibers include Caliber 01.200, with a complex flyback mechanism; Caliber 04.110, with a very clever GMT switching mechanism; and two new in-house calibers, 01.100 and 03.100. Among the newer collections is the Chronograph I, a boldly sportive line with special models, such as the Chronograph 1 - All Black Numbered Edition.

Sport Chrono Subsecond 39 Titanium & Black

Reference number: 6023.3.71.001.07.2
Movement: automatic, Porsche Design Caliber WERK 03.200 (base Sellita SW260-1); ø 25.6 mm, height 5.6 mm; 31 jewels; 28,800 vph; COSC-certified chronometer; 38-hour power reserve
Functions: hours, minutes, subsidiary seconds; date
Case: titanium, ø 39 mm, height 12.25 mm; sapphire crystal; screw-in crown; water-resistant to 10 atm
Band: calfskin, folding clasp
Price: $5,350

Sport Chrono Subsecond 39 Titanium & Blue

Reference number: 6023.3.71.002.07.2
Movement: automatic, Porsche Design Caliber WERK 03.200 (base Sellita SW260-1); ø 25.6 mm, height 5.6 mm; 31 jewels; 28,800 vph; COSC-certified chronometer; 38-hour power reserve
Functions: hours, minutes, subsidiary seconds; date
Case: titanium, ø 39 mm, height 12.25 mm; sapphire crystal; screw-in crown; water-resistant to 10 atm
Band: calfskin, folding clasp
Price: $5,350

Sport Chrono Subsecond 39 Titanium & Brown

Reference number: 6023.3.71.003.07.2
Movement: automatic, Porsche Design Caliber WERK 03.200 (base Sellita SW260-1); ø 25.6 mm, height 5.6 mm; 31 jewels; 28,800 vph; COSC-certified chronometer; 38-hour power reserve
Functions: hours, minutes, subsidiary seconds; date
Case: titanium, ø 39 mm, height 12.25 mm; sapphire crystal; screw-in crown; water-resistant to 10 atm
Band: calfskin, folding clasp
Price: $5,350

1919 Globetimer UTC Titanium & Black

Reference number: 6023.4.05.001.07.2
Movement: automatic, Porsche Design Caliber WERK 04.110; ø 28.5 mm, height 6.94 mm; 26 jewels; 28,800 vph; COSC-certified chronometer; 38-hour power reserve
Functions: hours, minutes, sweep seconds; additional 24-hour display (2nd time zone), day/night indicator; date
Case: titanium, ø 42 mm, height 14.9 mm; sapphire crystal; screw-in crown; water-resistant to 10 atm
Band: calfskin, folding clasp with pusher
Price: $6,350

1919 Globetimer UTC All titanium Blue

Reference number: 6023.4.05.002.05.5
Movement: automatic, Porsche Design Caliber WERK 04.110; ø 28.5 mm, height 6.94 mm; 26 jewels; 28,800 vph; COSC-certified chronometer; 38-hour power reserve
Functions: hours, minutes, sweep seconds; additional 24-hour display (second time zone), day/night indication; date
Case: titanium, ø 42 mm, height 14.9 mm; sapphire crystal; screw-in crown; water-resistant to 10 atm
Band: titanium, folding clasp
Price: $6,900

Monobloc Actuator 24H-Chronotimer Black & Rubber

Reference number: 6030.6.01.007.05.2
Movement: automatic, ETA Caliber 7754; ø 30 mm, height 7.9 mm; 25 jewels; 28,800 vph; 48-hour power reserve
Functions: hours, minutes; rate control; additional 24-hour display (second time zone); chronograph; date
Case: titanium with black titanium carbide coating, ø 45.5 mm, height 15.6 mm; sapphire crystal; transparent case back screw-in crown; water-resistant to 10 atm
Band: rubber, folding clasp
Remarks: rocker switch integrated into the right side of the case
Price: $6,700

Chronograph 1 – All Black

Reference number: 6043.7.01.001.01.5
Movement: automatic, Porsche Design Caliber WERK 01.140 (based on Concepto 2000); ø 30 mm, height 7.9 mm; 25 jewels; 28,800 vph; COSC-certified chronometer; 48-hour power reserve
Functions: hours, minutes, subsidiary seconds; chronograph; date and weekday
Case: stainless steel bezel with black titanium carbide coating; ø 40.8 mm, height 14.15 mm; sapphire crystal; transparent case back, screw-in crown; water-resistant to 10 atm
Band: stainless steel, folding clasp
Price: $9,650; limited to 1,000 pieces per year

Sport Chrono Black & Leather

Reference number: 6023.1.02.001.07.2
Movement: automatic, Porsche Design Caliber WERK 01.100 (base ETA 7750); ø 30 mm, height 7.9 mm; 25 jewels; 28,800 vph; COSC-certified chronometer; 48-hour power reserve
Functions: hours, minutes; rate control; chronograph; date
Case: titanium, ø 42 mm, height 14.9 mm; sapphire crystal; transparent case back; screw-in crown; water-resistant to 10 atm
Band: calfskin, folding clasp
Price: $5,350

Chronotimer Flyback

Reference number: 6013.6.04.001.08.2
Movement: automatic, Porsche Design Caliber WERK 01.200; ø 30 mm, height 7.9 mm; 25 jewels; 28,800 vph; COSC-certified chronometer; 48-hour power reserve
Functions: hours, minutes; rate control; flyback chronograph; date
Case: titanium with black titanium carbide coating, ø 42 mm, height 14.62 mm; sapphire crystal; screwed-in case back; black-tinted sapphire crystal opening; screw-in crown; water-resistant to 5 atm
Band: calfskin, titanium folding clasp
Price: $6,700

Pramzius Watches
31 Halls Hill Road
Colchester, CT 06415

Website:
www.pramzius.com

E-mail:
info@pramzius.com

Founded:
2017

Number of employees:
4

Annual production:
2,500

Distribution:
direct sales

Most important collections/price range:
Trans-Siberian Railroad / $479;
Berlin Wall Watch / $649 to $949;
Military Iron Wolf Watch / $699;
Master Gauge / $1,299

PRAMZIUS

Whatever their political affiliations or leanings, no one can deny that Eastern Europe, the Baltic states, and Russia, in particular, exert a considerable fascination on people. It may be the extreme quality of everything that comes from that part of the world that appeals to our need for drama—the long and troubled history; the brutal leaders; the staggeringly talented people, from musicians to chess players; the brooding novels about adultery, complex love, suicide, war, dark morality; the antics of modern-day Russians caught on smartphones and dashcams. This may explain the success of Détente Group and its boisterous watches celebrating Big Mechanics—not for the limp-wristed, by any stretch.

In 2017, Craig Hester, distributor of Vostok-Europe, Sturmanskie, and other brands, parlayed over 20 years' experience in the watch business into the launch of a series of watches that would pay tribute to this wild, dangerous, creative, and at times sincerely eccentric part of the world. The name Pramzius is a reference to the Baltic ruler of time—an ancient and, appropriately, pagan god. Funding for the project came from a Kickstarter campaign.

The first series of Pramzius was inspired by the renowned Trans-Siberian Railway and correspondingly themed pocket watch from back in the day. The Berlin Wall (2019) celebrated the fall of the infamous border: its dial features graffiti from the last stretch of the Wall and a crown housing a bit of real Wall cement. The Iron Wolf was named after the legend behind the founding of the Lithuanian capital, Vilnius. It has become the official watch of a Lithuanian NATO brigade and its vehicle. Their insignia, a wolf's head, appears on the dial with the word vilkas, wolf. The Gauge Master (2020) is a replica of a gauge originally made in Switzerland but installed on a vintage steam locomotive from Germany, whose trains also plied the Baltic coast. Train fans will enjoy the industrial look and the plate on the dial made from iron from a real hog.

Gauge Master

Movement: automatic, Miyota Caliber 82S5; ø 26 mm, height 5.67 mm; 21 jewels; 21,600 vph; bidirectional rotor; 42-hour power reserve
Functions: hours, minutes, subsidiary disk seconds; 24-hour indicator
Case: stainless steel, ø 53 x 45 mm, height 15 mm; water-resistant to 10 atm
Band: calfskin, buckle
Remarks: made partly of original steel from a vintage German locomotive
Price: $1,299

Military Iron Wolf Chronograph

Reference number: P715303
Movement: quartz, 6S21 Miyota Caliber; ø 34.6 mm, height 4.9 mm
Functions: hours, minutes, subsidiary seconds; 24-hour indicator
Case: stainless steel, ø 44 mm, height 14 mm; bezel with 0-120 scale; sapphire crystal; screw-down crown; water-resistant to 10 atm
Band: stainless steel, clasp
Remarks: full lume sandwich dial; bezel with "wolf teeth" indicators; comes with NATO nylon strap and bund strap
Price: $699

Berlin Wall Watch

Movement: automatic, Seiko Caliber NH35; ø 27.4 mm, height 5.32 mm; 24 jewels; 21,600 vph; bidirectional rotor; 41-hour power reserve
Functions: hours, minutes, sweep seconds; date
Case: stainless steel, ø 42 mm, height 14 mm; K1 mineral glass; screw-down crown; 3D rendering of Brandenburg Gate on case back; water-resistant to 10 atm
Band: calfskin strap, buckle
Remarks: genuine marble dial featuring original graffiti from Berlin Wall; bits of Berlin Wall in crown; comes with extra leather-nylon strap
Price: $649 leather; with stainless steel bracelet ($699)
Variations: ETA 2824 movement ($899–$949); 48-millimeter case ($649–$699)

RADO

Rado Uhren AG
Bielstrasse 45
CH-2543 Lengnau
Switzerland

Tel.:
+41-32-655-6111

E-mail:
info@rado.com

Website:
www.rado.com
www.store.us.rado.com

Founded:
1957

Number of employees:
approx. 470

U.S. distributor:
Rado
The Swatch Group (U.S.), Inc.
703 Waterford Way, Suite 450
Miami, FL 33126
786-725-5393

Most important collections/price range:
Hyperchrome / from approx $1,100;
Diamaster / from approx. $1,500;
Integral / from approx. $2,000;
True Square / from approx. $1,400;
Centrix / from approx. $800;
Coupole Classic / from approx. $1,000;
Tradition / from approx. $2,000

Rado is a relatively young brand, especially for a Swiss one. The company, which grew out of the Schlup clockwork factory, launched its first watches in 1957, but it achieved international fame only five years later, in 1962, when it surprised the world with a revolutionary invention. Rado's oval DiaStar was the first truly scratch-resistant watch ever, sporting a case made of the impervious alloy hardmetal. In 1985, its parent company, the Swatch Group, decided to put Rado's know-how and extensive experience in developing materials to good use, and from then on the brand intensified its research activities at its home in Lengnau, Switzerland, and continued to produce only watches with extremely hard cases. A record of sorts was even set in 2004, when they managed to create a 10,000-Vickers material, which is as hard as natural diamond.

Rado also made jewel watches, but over time it was the high-tech watches and pioneering spirit of the brand's ceramic researchers and engineers that won out. The company already holds more than thirty patents arising from research and production of new case materials. In 2011, for example, they produced the ultra-light Ceramos, which went into the D-Star collection.

A special material is worth nothing without a strict design code. The True Square collection is a comfortably wearable design watch with a 38-millimeter edge length. It is available in black or in metallic shiny plasma ceramic and now, in a collaboration with British industrial designer Tej Chauhan, in a bright yellow that has a redolence of the 1970s.

The reborn diving watch classic Captain Cook also serves as a presentation surface for this modern ceramic development from the alchemist's kitchen of Comadur, a sister company within the Swatch Group. The high-tech plasma ceramic is available either in deep black or with a shimmering metallic plasma coating. With the latter, the watch case and bracelet links are heated once again to 20,000 °C until the surface melts into a glass-hard layer.

Captain Cook High-Tech Ceramic Diver

Reference number: R32144202
Movement: automatic, ETA Caliber R763; ø 25.6 mm, height 4.74 mm; 25 jewels; 21,600 vph; 80-hour power reserve
Functions: hours, minutes, sweep seconds; date
Case: plasma-treated ceramic, ø 43 mm, height 14.6 mm; unidirectional bezel with ceramic insert, with 0-60 scale; sapphire crystal; screw-in crown; water-resistant to 30 atm
Band: plasma-treated ceramic, folding clasp
Price: $3,500
Variations: various case, bands, and dials

Captain Cook High-Tech Ceramic Diver

Reference number: R32129158
Movement: automatic, ETA Caliber R763; ø 25.6 mm, height 4.74 mm; 25 jewels; 21,600 vph; 80-hour power reserve
Functions: hours, minutes, sweep seconds; date
Case: ceramic, ø 43 mm, height 14.6 mm; unidirectional bezel with ceramic insert, with 0-60 scale; sapphire crystal; screw-in crown; water-resistant to 30 atm
Band: rubber, folding clasp
Price: $3,000
Variations: various case, bands, and dials

Captain Cook High-Tech Ceramic Diver

Reference number: R32130318
Movement: automatic, ETA Caliber R763; ø 25.6 mm, height 4.74 mm; 25 jewels; 21,600 vph; 80-hour power reserve
Functions: hours, minutes, sweep seconds; date
Case: ceramic, ø 43 mm, height 14.6 mm; unidirectional bezel with ceramic insert, with 0-60 scale; sapphire crystal; screw-in crown; water-resistant to 30 atm
Band: rubber, folding clasp
Price: $3,000
Variations: various case, bands, and dials

Captain Cook Chronograph

Reference number: R32146208
Movement: automatic, ETA Caliber R801; ø 28 mm, height 6.36 mm; 37 jewels; 28,800 vph; 59-hour power reserve
Functions: hours, minutes, subsidiary seconds; chronograph; date
Case: bronze, ø 43 mm, height 14.8 mm; unidirectional bezel with ceramic insert, with 0-60 scale; sapphire crystal; screw-in crown; water-resistant to 30 atm
Band: textile, buckle
Remarks: comes with additional calfskin and textile strap
Price: $4,410

Captain Cook Chronograph

Reference number: R32145208
Movement: automatic, ETA Caliber R801; ø 28 mm, height 6.36 mm; 37 jewels; 28,800 vph; 59-hour power reserve
Functions: hours, minutes, subsidiary seconds; chronograph; date
Case: stainless steel, ø 43 mm, height 14.8 mm; unidirectional bezel with ceramic inlay, with 0-60 scale; sapphire crystal; screw-in crown; water-resistant to 30 atm
Band: stainless steel, buckle
Remarks: comes with additional leather and textile strap
Price: $3,710

Captain Cook Over-Pole

Reference number: R32116158
Movement: manually wound, ETA Caliber R862; ø 25.6 mm, height 3.37 mm; 17 jewels; 21,600 vph; 80-hour power reserve
Functions: hours, minutes, sweep seconds; date
Case: stainless steel, ø 37 mm; bidirectional bezel with city references; sapphire crystal; transparent case back; water-resistant to 10 atm
Band: calfskin, buckle
Remarks: comes with extra stainless-steel bracelet; limited to 1962 pieces
Price: $2,400

True Square Automatic Open Heart

Reference number: R27086162
Movement: automatic, ETA Kaliber C07.631; ø 25.6 mm, height 5.2 mm; 23 jewels; 21,600 vph; partially skeletonized dial; 80-hour power reserve
Functions: hours, minutes, sweep seconds
Case: ceramic, 38 x 44.2 mm, height 9.7 mm; sapphire crystal; water-resistant to 5 atm
Band: ceramic, triple folding clasp
Price: $2,350
Variations: with silver hands and indexes; in white or plasma-colored ceramic with blue dial

True Square Automatic Open Heart

Reference number: R27073702
Movement: automatic, ETA Kaliber C07.631; ø 25.6 mm, height 5.2 mm; 23 jewels; 21,600 vph; partially skeletonized dial; 80-hour power reserve
Functions: hours, minutes, sweep seconds
Case: ceramic, 38 x 44.2 mm, height 9.7 mm; sapphire crystal; water-resistant to 5 atm
Band: ceramic, triple folding clasp
Remarks: dial set with 12 diamonds
Price: $2,350

Coupole Classic Power Reserve

Reference number: R22879215
Movement: automatic, ETA Caliber R772; ø 25.6 mm, height 5.77 mm; 25 jewels; 21,600 vph; 80-hour power reserve
Functions: hours, minutes, sweep seconds; power reserve indicator; date
Case: stainless steel with rose gold PVD, ø 41 mm, height 11.7 mm; sapphire crystal; transparent case back; water-resistant to 5 atm
Band: calfskin, folding clasp
Price: $1,700

RAKETA WATCHES

The city of Saint Petersburg, known as Russia's cultural capital, is not that old. Its founding goes back to Czar Peter I, later known as "the Great," who was intent on modernizing his country and decided to have a city built that would face the West and reflect Western values. It was a costly enterprise, especially in lives, since the builders were serfs and the swampy area was rife with disease, but in the end, he got his city. He had a fleet built as well and, in 1721, opened a lapidary known as Petrodvorets (or Peter's Palace), which would later prepare precious stones for the czars.

That factory has had many lives in its three-hundred-year history. Since 1949, after restoration following destruction during World War II, it has been producing watches, first under the name Pobeda (Victory) and Zvezda (Star). On April 12, 1961, Yuri Gagarin orbited Earth once in the Vostok 1 spacecraft, opening the way to human space exploration. The following year saw the launch of the Raketa (rocket) brand at the Petrodvorets factory, which had quite a success with Soviet citizenry.

When David Henderson-Stewart, a young English businessman, visited the factory in 2010, the shine had gone under the onslaught of the free market. A few stalwart employees kept the home fires burning, but everything was run down. Though not from the watch world —an innocence he credits for his spontaneous decision and commitment— he saw the potential. Investors were found, experts brought in, and Raketa was put back into business with several rich collections all made totally in-house and visually unique. Soviet-era or Russian iconography are the main themes. There are military style 24-hour watches from the world of submariners, seamen, soldiers, and cosmonauts, as well as models honoring some of the artistic movements of the revolutionary era, like the Big Zero Malevich, named after a work by Kazimir Malevich, a founder of the Supremacists. The Avant-Garde has hands borrowed from the "Beat the Whites with the Red Wedge" propaganda poster by Constructivist artist El (Lazar) Lissitzky.

Raketa Watch Factory LTD
Sankt-Peterburgskiy prospekt, 60
198516 St. Petersburg, Peterhof
Russia

Tel.:
+7-926-304-0591

E-mail:
info@raketa.com

Website:
www.raketa.com

Founded:
1721 /1961

U.S. distributor:
-

Most important collections/price range:
Avant-Garde, Space Launcher, Copernicus, Baikonur, Russian Code / $ 800 to $3,750

Sputnik-1

Reference number: W-06-17-30-0290 / W-06-17-40-0291
Movement: automatic, Raketa 2624; ø 26 mm, height 6.8 mm; 24 jewels; 18,000 vph; decoration: rotor with hand-made Neva waves + Print; 40-hour power reserve
Functions: 24 hours, minutes, sweep seconds
Case: stainless steel, ø 40.5 mm, height 16.55 mm; sapphire crystal; transparent mineral glass case back; water-resistant to 5 atm
Band: stainless steel
Remarks: dial made of the special alloy AMg6, identical to that used for part of the world's first artificial Earth satellite Sputnik-1
Price: $1,800; limited to 500 pieces (250 with bracelet; 250 with canvas strap at $1,700)
Variations: various straps

Big Zero

Reference number: W-11-16-10-0283
Movement: automatic, Raketa 2615; ø 26 mm, height 6.8 mm; 24 jewels; 18,000 vph; decoration: Laser engraving, Neva waves, Red rotor; 40-hour power reserve
Functions: hours, minutes, sweep seconds
Case: stainless steel, ø 40 mm, height 14.05 mm; sapphire crystal; transparent case back (mineral glass); water-resistant to 10 atm
Band: leather, buckle
Remarks: "0" instead of "12" on the dial
Price: $1,400
Variations: various strap colors

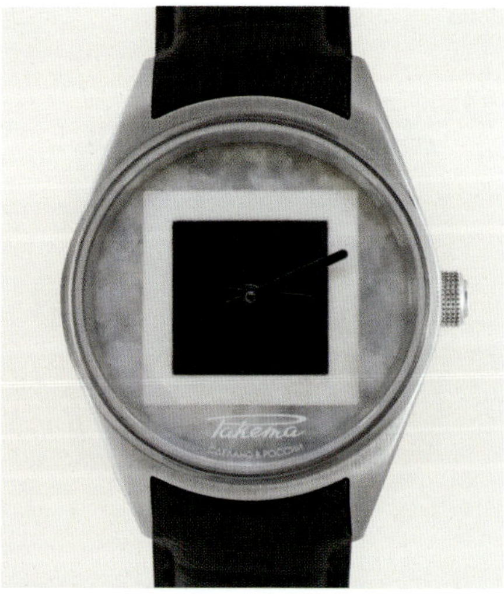

Big Zero Malevich 0273

Reference number: W-20-16-10-0273
Movement: automatic, Raketa 2615; ø 26 mm, height 6.8 mm; 24 jewels; 18,000 vph; decoration: rotor with hand-made Neva waves + Print; 40-hour power reserve
Functions: hours, minutes, sweep seconds
Case: stainless steel, ø 38.8 mm, height 12.65 mm; sapphire crystal; transparent case back (mineral glass); water-resistant to 10 atm
Band: leather, buckle
Remarks: tribute to avant-garde artist Kazimir Malevich (1879-1935) and his "Black Square" exhibited at the Tretyakov Gallery; Malevich's comment engraved on the back: *"... all the phenomena of the world are reduced to a big Zero—or Zero contains all the phenomena of the world."*
Price: $1,600; limited to 300 pieces

Avant-Garde

Reference number: W-06-16-10-0279
Movement: automatic, Raketa 2615; ø 26 mm, height 6.8 mm; 24 jewels; 18,000 vph; rotor with print decoration; 40-hour power reserve
Functions: hours, minutes, sweep seconds
Case: stainless steel with black PVD, ø 40.5 mm, height 16.55 mm; sapphire crystal; transparent case back (mineral glass); water-resistant to 5 atm
Band: leather, buckle
Remarks: 3 geometric shapes for hands recall Constructivist art of the revolutionary period
Price: $1,500; limited to 300 pieces
Variations: various strap colors

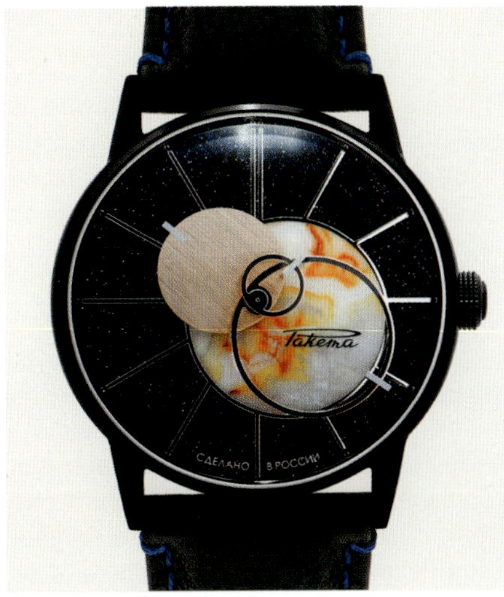

Copernicus 0280

Reference number: W-05-16-10-0280
Movement: automatic, Raketa 2615; ø 26 mm, height 6.8 mm; 24 jewels; 18,000 vph, decoration: Gold Plating, engraving, printing, hand-made Neva waves; 40-hour power reserve
Functions: hours, minutes, sweep seconds
Case: stainless steel with black PVD, ø 40.5 mm, height 16.55 mm; sapphire crystal; transparent case back (mineral glass); water-resistant to 5 atm
Band: leather, buckle
Remarks: 3 circular "hands" for 3 planets in the starry sky (aventurine) revolving around the sun (a yellow agate): Earth (minutes); Jupiter (hour hand, orbits the sun in 12 Earth years)
Price: $1,600; limited to 300 pieces
Variations: various dial colors

Space Launcher 0281

Reference number: W-30-19-40-0281
Movement: automatic, Raketa Caliber 2624☒; ø 26mm, height 6.8 mm; 24 jewels; 18,000 vph; decoration: hand-made Neva waves + Print; 40-hour power reserve
Functions: hours, minutes, sweep seconds (on central globe; compass function on bezel) **Case:** stainless steel, metal piece of the "Soyuz-2.1a" launcher, ø 43 mm, height 13.15 mm; screw-in crown; sapphire crystal; transparent case back (mineral glass); water-resistant to 20 atm
Band: fabric from "Sokol" space suit with extra leather strap, buckle **Remarks:** the gift set with two watches, one with white dial, the other with aventurine dial; bezel made of metal from the Soyuz-2.1a launcher; strap made from Sokol space suit; quick-change mechanism, comes with an extra leather strap **Price:** $1,900; limited to 300 pieces

Leopard 24 0274

Reference number: W-45-17-10-0274
Movement: automatic, Raketa Caliber 2624 a; ø 26 mm, height 6.8 mm; 24 jewels; 18,000 vph; decoration: red screws and rotor with hand-made Onega wave; 40-hour power reserve
Functions: hours, minutes; 24-hour dial to distinguish day and night
Case: stainless steel from the submarine Leopard K-328, ø 44 mm, height 14.25 mm; screw-in crown; sapphire crystal; transparent case back (mineral glass); water-resistant to 20 atm
Band: rubber, buckle
Remarks: bezel made of metal from Leopard K-328 submarine; replication of submarine hands
Price: $1,700; limited to 300 pieces

Russian Code 0275

Reference number: W-07-20-10-0275
Movement: automatic, Raketa 2615R (modified to turn counterclockwise); ø 26 mm, height 6.8 mm; 24 jewels; 18,000 vph; decoration: rotor with hand-made Neva waves + Print; 40-hour power reserve
Functions: hours, minutes, central seconds
Case: stainless steel with gold, ø 40.5 mm, height 16.55 mm; sapphire crystal; transparent case back (mineral glass); water-resistant to 5 atm
Band: leather, buckle
Remarks: replicates the counterclockwise movement of the Earth around the sun.
Price: $1,500; limited to 300 pieces

Baikonur 0247

Reference number: W-30-19-30-0247
Movement: automatic, Raketa 2624A; ø 26 mm, height 6.8; 24 jewels; 18,000 vph; rotor with print decoration; 40-hour power reserve
Functions: hours, minutes, central seconds; 24-hour dial to distinguish day and night
Case: stainless steel, ø 43 mm, height 13.15 mm; titanium bezel; sapphire crystal; transparent case back (mineral glass); screw-in crown; water-resistant to 20 atm
Band: rubber, buckle
Price: $1,500

RESSENCE

Belgian Benoit Mintiens had the luck of the newcomer at Baselworld 2010. He showed up at the last minute and found some space to show a strange watch with an almost two-dimensional dial. . . . He returned in 2011 with the Type 1001. It consisted of a large rotating dial carrying a hand that pointed to a minute track on the bezel. Hours, small second, and a day/night indication rotated on dedicated subsidiary dials. The ballet on the dial mesmerized those who saw it, so he sold all fifty of his models off the bat.

The mechanics behind the Ressence watches—the name is a compounding of Renaissance of the Essential—are basically simple: a stripped-down and rebuilt ETA 2824 leaves the minute wheel as the main driver of the other wheels.

In a bid to improve readability, he immersed the dial section in oil, giving the displays a very contemporary two-dimensional look, much like an electronic watch. The movement had to be kept separate from the oil and was connected to the dial using magnets and a set of superconductors and a Faraday cage to protect the movement from magnetism. Baffles compensate for the expanding and contracting of the oil due to temperature shifts. The Type 3 also lost the crown, the only obstacle to making a perfectly smooth watch, in favor of a clever setting and winding mechanism controlled by the case back. The watch was an automatic, of course.

The variations on the theme have been emerging from the Ressence studio at a regular pace. Several watches came with slightly different design. One was a diver's watch chic enough to wear for any occasion. The latest innovation is the e-Crown, which allows the wearer to reset the time electronically by discreetly tapping twice on the watch's crystal. Mintiens always makes sure that each model preserves the special charm that comes from their rounded, gently curved shape on all sides without a glass holder rim. The curvature of the surface has a radius of 12.5 centimeters, which is approximately the half-diameter of a bowling ball. In 2022, Ressence came out with a much simpler version, maybe a sign of more austere times to come?.

Ressence Watches
Meirbrug 1
2000 Antwerp
Belgium

Tel.:
+32-3-446-0060

E-mail:
hello@ressence.be

Website:
www.ressencewatches.com

Founded:
2010

U.S. distributor:
Totally Worth It (TWI2, Inc.)
76 Division Avenue
Summit, NJ 07901-2309
201-894-4710
724-263-2286
info@totallyworthit.com

Collection prices:
Type 1: $20,600; Type 2: $48,800; Type 3: $42,200; Type 5: $35,800; Type 8: $15,000

Type 3B Black

Movement: automatic, ROCS 3.5 (Modul, base ETA 2824-2); ø 32 mm; 47 jewels; 28,800 vph; case back for winding and time setting; 36-hour power reserve
Functions: minutes, hours and 180-second "runner;" Ressence Orbital Convex System (ROCS): rotating minute dial with rotating satellites; oil temperature; date and day of week
Case: titanium, ø 44 mm, height 15 mm; sapphire crystal; splash-resistant to 1 atm
Band: premium leather, Ardillon buckle
Remarks: 2 separately sealed case chambers; dial-side chamber filled with oil; ROCS module propelled by magnetic drive
Price: $42,200 including taxes
Variations: white dial

Type 8C - Cobalt Blue

Movement: automatic, ROCS 8.1 (Modul, base ETA 2892/2); ø 32 mm; 31 jewels; 28,800 vph; case back for winding and time setting; gear train with 20 gearwheels; 36-hour power reserve
Functions: hours, minutes; Ressence Orbital Convex System (ROCS) rotating minute dial with 1 rotating satellite
Case: titanium, ø 42.9 mm, height 11 mm; sapphire crystal; splash-resistant to 1 atm
Band: leather, buckle
Price: $15,000 including taxes

Type 2G - Grey

Movement: automatic, ROCS 2.1 (Modul, base ETA 2892A); ø 32 mm; 45 jewels; 28,800 vph; case back for winding and time setting; gear train with 37 gearwheels; eCrown® module activated by double-tapping the sapphire crystal; 36-hour power reserve
Functions: hours, minutes, seconds (Ressence Orbital Convex System: rotating minute dial with rotating satellites); eCrown® functions (2nd time zone, energy saving, automatic time setting)
Case: titanium, ø 45 mm, height 12 mm; sapphire crystal
Band: leather, buckle
Remarks: up to 3 months dark power reserve
Price: $49,500 including taxes
Variations: blue or anthracite dial

RGM Watch Company
801 W. Main Street
Mount Joy, PA 17552

Tel.:
717-653-9799

E-mail:
sales@rgmwatches.com

Web:
www.rgmwatches.com

Founded:
1992

Number of employees:
12

Annual production:
200–300 watches

Distribution:
RGM deals directly with customers
sales@rgmwatches.com

Most important collection/price range:
Pennsylvania Series (completely made in the U.S.) / $2,500 to $125,000

RGM

The traditional values of hard work and persistence are alive and well in Roland Murphy, founder of RGM, one of the U.S.'s most famous and exclusive watch companies. Murphy, born in Maryland, went through the watchmaker's drill, studying at the Bowman Technical School, then in Switzerland, and finally working with Swatch before launching his own business in 1992 in Pennsylvania, which could be considered a kind of "watch valley."

The secret to his success, however, has been always to stay in touch with fundamental American values and icons. His first watch, the Signature, resurrected vintage pocket watch movements developed by Hamilton. The Railroad series today is run on restored Hamilton movements. His second big project was the Caliber 801, the first "high-grade mechanical movement made in series in America since Hamilton stopped production of the 992 B in 1969," Murphy shares with a grin. This was followed by an all-American-made watch, the Pennsylvania Tourbillon.

And so, model by model, Murphy continues to expand his "Made in U.S.A." portfolio. Lately, he has added American-made cases for the Model 151 series, chic pilot watches, that at times escape the definition by simply being elegant. "You cannot compare us to the big brands," says Murphy. "We are small and specialized, the needs are different. We work directly with the customer." This may account for the brand's diversity. There are retro-themed watches, sports-themed watches (honoring baseball or chess, notably Paul Morphy), a diver water-resistant to 70 atm, and the series 400 chronograph with a pulsometer and extra-large subdials for visibility.

Of late, Murphy has turned to the many crafts associated with watchmaking, notably engine-turned guilloche. He has also produced a series of dials with cloisonné enamel motifs or hand-painted images on mother of pearl. In 2020, he came out with a spectacular homage to Robert Falcon Scott's dramatic 1910–1913 expedition to Antarctica on the ship *Terra Nova*.

Chronograph 600

Movement: automatic, Valjoux Caliber 7753; ø 30 mm, height 7.60 mm; 27 jewels; 28,800 vph; rhodium-plated and decorated with Côtes de Genève; 48-hour power reserve
Functions: hours, minutes, subsidiary seconds; chronograph; date
Case: stainless steel, ø 42 mm, height 14 mm; sapphire crystal; solid case back; water-resistant to 10 atm
Band: leather, buckle
Remarks: date at 3 o'clock, 6 o'clock, or no date
Price: $4,250

151-PR "Professional Pilot"

Movement: automatic, RGM/ETA Caliber 2892-A2; ø 25.6 mm; 21 jewels; 28,800 vph; rhodium finish with perlage and côtes de Genève
Functions: hours, minutes, sweep seconds; date
Case: stainless steel, ø 38.5 mm, height 9.9 mm; sapphire crystal; transparent case back; water-resistant to 5 atm
Band: rubber or reptile skin, buckle
Remarks: date at 4.30, at 3 o'clock, or no date
Price: $3,250
Variations: without date; with black dial; titanium case ($4,250)

Type II Montgomery Marginal Minutes

Reference number: 222 RR
Movement: manually wound, restored Hamilton 921 or 923; ø 38.1 mm; 21 or 23 jewels; 18,000 vph; lever escapement; screw balance; U.S.-made bridges, mainplate, settings, 7-tooth winding click; circular côtes de Genève; 42-hour power reserve
Functions: hours, minutes, subsidiary seconds
Case: stainless steel, ø 41 mm, height 12 mm; sapphire crystal; transparent case back; water-resistant to 5 atm; **Band:** leather, buckle
Remarks: grand-feu white glass enamel "boxcar" dial; blued hands
Price: $7,950 for the 923 movement; $5,950 for the 921

RICHARD MILLE

Mille never stops delivering the wow to the watch world with what he calls his "race cars for the wrist." He is not an engineer, however, but rather a marketing expert who earned his first paychecks in the watch division of the French defense, automobile, and aerospace concern Matra in the early 1980s. "I have no historical relationship with watchmaking whatsoever," says Mille, "and so I have no obligations either. The mechanics of my watches are geared towards technical feasibility."

His early work was with the wizards at Audemars Piguet Renaud & Papi (APRP) in Le Locle, who would take on the Mille challenge. Audemars Piguet even tested some of those scandalous innovations—materials, technologies, functions—in a Richard Mille watch before daring to use them in its own collections (Tradition d'Excellence).

In 2007, Audemars Piguet finally became a shareholder in Richard Mille, and so the three firms are now closely bound. The assembly of the watches is done in the Franches-Montagnes region in the Jura, where Richard Mille opened the firm Horométrie. These days, the watch business is in the hands of daughter Amanda and son Alexandre, so that the father has more time for his racing cars has more time for his racing cars.

To keep its fans happy, the brand enjoys exploring the lunatic fringe of the technically possible. A collaboration with Airbus Corporate Jets gave rise to a case made of a lightweight titanium-aluminum alloy used in turbines. The superlight and tough material called graphene, developed at the University of Manchester, also found its way to Horometrie and McLaren as well. Richard Mille timepieces have survived on wrists of elite athletes, like tennis star Rafael Nadal and sprinter Yohan Blake. And if anyone thought Mille was ignoring the race to the thinnest watch being run by several big brands, 2022 has proven them wrong. In a collaboration with Ferrari, the company has reengineered the whole idea of the watch to produce a 1.75-millimeter miracle that is even fairly shock-resistant.

Richard Mille
c/o Horométrie SA
11, rue du Jura
CH-2345 Les Breuleux
Switzerland

Tel.:
+41-32-959-4353

E-mail:
info@richardmille.ch

Website:
www.richardmille.com

Founded:
2000

Annual production:
approx. 4,600 watches

U.S. distributor:
Richard Mille Americas
8701 Wilshire Blvd.
Beverly Hills, CA 90211
310-205-5555

Richard Mille watches are priced in Swiss francs.

RM UP-01 Ferrari

Reference number: RM UP-01
Movement: manually wound, Richard Mille Caliber RMUP-01; 41.45 x 28.85 mm, height 1.18 mm; 23 jewels; 28,800 vph; modified lever escapement; titanium main-plate and bridges; 45-hour power reserve
Functions: hours, minutes,
Case: titanium, 51 x 39 mm, height 1.75 mm; sapphire crystal (2 crystals 0.2 and 0.4 mm thick)
Band: rubber, buckle
Remarks: winding crown and selector (winding, hand-setting) placed between the back and top plate; currently the world's thinnest mechanical wristwatch
Price: $1,888,000; limited to 150 pieces

RM 72-01 Lifestyle Chronograph Automatic

Reference number: RM 72-01
Movement: automatic, Caliber RMAC1; 29.10 x 31.25 mm, height 6.05 mm; 39 jewels; 28,800 vph; fully skeletonized titanium main-plate and bridges; free-sprung balance with variable inertia; 50-hour power reserve
Functions: hours, minutes, subsidiary seconds; crown position display; flyback chronograph; large date
Case: white gold, 38.4 x 47.34 mm, height 11.68 mm; bezel set with diamonds; sapphire crystal; transparent case back; crown with selector function; water-resistant to 5 atm
Band: rubber, buckle
Price: $185,000
Variations: with baguette diamonds; in red gold or titanium; in black or white ceramic

RM 032 VDSB

Reference number: RM 032
Movement: automatic, Richard Mille Caliber RMAC2; ø 39.15 mm, height 9 mm; 62 jewels; 28,800 vph; monodirectional winding rotor with variable geometry; 50-hour power reserve Functions: hours, minutes, subsidiary seconds (function control); flyback chronograph; full calendar with large date, month
Case: ceramic (TPT quartz), ø 50 mm, height 17.8 mm; unidirectional bezel of TPT quartz; sapphire crystal; transparent case back; crown and pushers can be locked using central ring on the crown; water-resistant to 30 atm
Band: rubber, folding clasp
Remarks: special limited edition of 120 pieces for the "Voiles de St. Barth" regatta
Price: $145,000

ROBOT Watch
Bohematic s.r.o.
Maiselova 2
101 00 Prag
Czech Republic

Tel.:
+420-722-977-256

E-mail:
info@bohematic.cz

Website:
www.robot-watch.com

Founded:
2018

Number of employees:
16

Annual production:
approx. 200 watches

Distribution:
direct sales; online shop; please contact the company directly

Collections and price range:
Various models, $4,000 to $10,000

ROBOT

When brainstorming a name for a new line of watches to be produced by his company, Bohematic, entrepreneur Josef Zajíček Bohematic decided to tap the Czech Republic's long and rich literary culture and call the line Robot. Few probably know that the word is originally Czech and refers to hard work. As such, it is related to the German word, which in older German actually meant burdensome work, tedium, if you will.

Be that as it may, the name for Czechs (and those who know the nation's literature) will immediately recall the science fiction play *R.U.R* (it stands for Rossum's Universal Robots) by the famous writer Karel Čapek, written in 1920. In it, Čapek describes androids created by humans to serve them.

The watches are manufactured at Nové Město nad Metují, a center of the Czech precision engineering and watchmaking industry. The tradition of precision manufacturing is not only continued here but constantly developed.

The manufacture was founded in 2018 by Zajíček, the Olgoj Chorchoj design studio, and a team of experienced watchmakers, designers, and craftsmen. They are all in tune with the rich history

of the Czech industrial culture and are intent on implementing their plans for mechanical wristwatches with an independent design and thus contributing to traditional watchmaking on the highest European level. This translates as watches created by dint of demanding handwork. The designers are inspired by great Czech stories that have left their mark on the world of design, industry, and motor sports. The Aerodynamic, for example, pays tribute to the Czechoslovak Tatra T77—the world's first aerodynamically shaped mass-produced car.

It is worth noting that Zajíček began his enterprise making parts, and as such became familiar with robots and their ability to relieve humans of tough and dangerous work. As for the watches' engines, they are usually from Swiss manufacturers, like Eterna and La Joux-Perret.

Graphic

Reference number: 1901ST04
Movement: automatic, Eterna Caliber 3909A; ø 30 mm, height 5.6 mm; 29 jewels; 28,800 vph; 65-hour power reserve
Functions: hours, minutes, sweep seconds; date
Case: stainless steel, ø 42 mm, height 12 mm; sapphire crystal; transparent case back; water-resistant to 5 atm
Band: hand-made calfskin, buckle
Remarks: galvanoplasty relief dial, perlage on crown
Price: $3,900
Variations: various dials

Minor "Emerson Fittipaldi" Limited Edition

Reference number: 2001LE03
Movement: automatic, La Joux-Perret Caliber 8120; ø 30.4 mm, height 7.9 mm; 26 jewels; 28,800 vph; 55-hour power reserve
Functions: hours, minutes, subsidiary seconds; chronograph; date
Case: titanium with black PVD coating, ø 44 mm, height 15 mm; bidirectional bezel with 0-12 scale; sapphire crystal; transparent case back; water-resistant to 10 atm
Band: hand-made calfskin, buckle
Remarks: with Formula-1 legend Emerson Fittipaldi's signature and initials on the seconds hand
Price: $6,690; limited to 100 pieces

Aerodynamic

Reference number: 2101ST05
Movement: automatic, La Joux-Perret Caliber LJP 7513; ø 33 mm, height 4.5 mm; 33 jewels; 28,800 vph; movement partially skeletonized, bridges with sunburst pattern, 60-hour power reserve
Functions: hours, minutes, subsidiary seconds; power reserve indicator; date
Case: titanium, ø 39 mm, height 12.2 mm; sapphire crystal; transparent case back; water-resistant to 5 atm
Band: hand-made calfskin, buckle
Price: $7,130
Variations: various dials

ROGER DUBUIS

Roger Dubuis has always been a *manufacture* committed to luxury and *"très haute horlogerie."* The brand makes some outstanding movement components—parts that, because of their quality and geographical origins, bear the coveted Seal of Geneva. Founder Roger Dubuis, who passed away in 2017, was steeped in watchmaking and the business. In 2008, he sold 60 percent of the company shares to Richemont Group, which benefited from the resulting synergies, especially Cartier, which gets its skeletonized movements from the Roger Dubuis *manufacture*. In early 2016, Richemont went all the way and acquired the remaining 40 percent of the Genevan brand.

Roger Dubuis was founded in 1995 as SOGEM SA (Société Genevoise des Montres) by name-giver Roger Dubuis and financier Carlos Dias, who came up with timepieces with unheard-of dimensions and incomparable complications. The meteoric development of this *manufacture* and the incredible frequency of its new introductions—even technical ones—continue to amaze colleagues and consumers alike. Today, Roger Dubuis develops all of its own movements, currently numbering more than thirty different mechanical calibers. In addition, it produces almost all components in-house, from base plates to escapements and balance springs. With this heavy-duty technological know-how in its quiver, the brand has been able to build some remarkable movements, like the massive RD101, with four balance springs and all manner of differentials and gear works to drive the Excalibur Quatuor, the equivalent in horology to a monster truck. The recent Monobalancier has made the striking star-shaped bridge a part of the complex open-worked dial.

The brand's most natural partners, though, are in motor sports. Over the years, Roger Dubuis has rubbed elbows with tire-maker Pirelli and with Lamborghini's motor sports division, Lamborghini Squadra Corse. The result has been models inspired by the design of such cars as the Aventador and the Huracàn.

Manufacture Roger Dubuis
2, rue André-De-Garrini - CP 149
CH-1217 Meyrin 2 (Geneva)
Switzerland

Tel.:
+41-22-783-2828

E-mail:
info@rogerdubuis.com

Website:
www.rogerdubuis.com

Founded:
1995

Annual production:
over 5,000 watches (estimated)

U.S. distributor:
Roger Dubuis New York
545 Madison Ave.
New York, NY 10022
212-651-3773

Roger Dubuis Beverly Hills
9490C Brighton Way
Beverly Hills, CA 90210
310-734-1855

Most important collections/price range:
Excalibur, Velvet / $12,000 to $1,100,000

Excalibur Monobalancier

Reference number: DBEX0953
Movement: automatic, Roger Dubuis Caliber RD720SQ; ø 36.1 mm, height 5.95 mm; 32 jewels; 28,800 vph; skeletonized movement, micro-rotor; 72-hour power reserve; Geneva Seal
Functions: hours, minutes
Case: rose gold ("Eon Gold"), ø 42 mm, height 11.9 mm; bezel set with 6 diamonds; sapphire crystal; transparent case back; water-resistant to 10 atm
Band: calfskin, triple folding clasp
Price: $84,000

Excalibur Monobalancier

Reference number: DBEX0954
Movement: automatic, Roger Dubuis Caliber RD720SQ; ø 36.1 mm, height 5.95 mm; 32 jewels; 28,800 vph; skeletonized movement, microrotor; 72-hour power reserve; Geneva Seal
Functions: hours, minutes
Case: rose gold ("Eon Gold"), ø 42 mm, height 11.9 mm; sapphire crystal; transparent case back; water-resistant to 10 atm
Band: calfskin, triple folding clasp
Price: $77,000

Excalibur Double Tourbillon

Reference number: DBEX0820
Movement: manually wound, Roger Dubuis Caliber RD108SQ; ø 37.8 mm, height 7.3 mm; 32 jewels; 21,600 vph; flying double tourbillon with differential gear, skeletonized movement; 72-hour power reserve; Geneva Seal
Functions: hours, minutes
Case: ceramic, ø 45 mm, height 13 mm; sapphire crystal; transparent case back; water-resistant to 5 atm
Band: calfskin, triple folding clasp
Price: $277,500; limited to 28 pieces

Excalibur Monotourbillon

Reference number: RDDBEX0889
Movement: manually wound, Roger Dubuis Caliber RD512SQ; ø 37.1 mm, height 6.9 mm; 19 jewels; 28,800 vph; flying 1-minute tourbillon; skeletonized movement; 72-hour power reserve; Geneva Seal
Functions: hours, minutes, subsidiary seconds (on the tourbillon cage)
Case: titanium with black DLC, ø 42 mm, height 12.7 mm; sapphire crystal; transparent case back; water-resistant to 10 atm
Band: calfskin, triple folding clasp
Price: $144,500; limited to 88 pieces

Excalibur Spider Huracàn

Reference number: DBEX0750
Movement: automatic, Roger Dubuis Caliber RD630; ø 36.1 mm, height 7.78 mm; 29 jewels; 28,800 vph; 2 spring barrels; 60-hour power reserve
Functions: hours, minutes, sweep seconds; date
Case: rose gold, ø 45 mm, height 13.3 mm; titanium bezel, case back and crown; sapphire crystal; water-resistant to 5 atm
Band: rubber, folding clasp
Price: $73,500
Variations: in titanium ($50,500)

Excalibur Spider Monotourbillon

Reference number: DBEX0816
Movement: manually wound, Roger Dubuis Caliber RD510SQ; ø 27.2 mm, height 5.13 mm; 17 jewels; 28,800 vph; flying 1-minute tourbillon; skeletonized movement; 60-hour power reserve; Geneva Seal
Functions: hours, minutes, subsidiary seconds, (on the tourbillon cage)
Case: rose gold, ø 39 mm, height 13.3 mm; sapphire crystal; transparent case back; water-resistant to 10 atm
Band: rubber, triple folding clasp
Price: $174,000; limited to 88 pieces

Caliber RD 103SQ

Manually wound; double sprung balance with angled balance wheels, 28,800 vph each; power transmission and synchronization via planetary gears; skeletonized movement; single spring barrel, 40-hour power reserve; Geneva Seal
Functions: hours, minutes, sweep seconds (jumping); power reserve indicator
Diameter: 36.1 mm
Height: 7.8 mm
Jewels: 48
Frequency: 57,600 vph

Caliber RD820SQ

Automatic; skeletonized movement; microrotor; single spring barrel, 60-hour power reserve; Geneva Seal
Functions: hours, minutes
Diameter: 36.1 mm
Height: 6.38 mm
Jewels: 35
Frequency: 28,800 vph
Remarks: rhodium-plated movement, finely finished with perlage; 167 parts

Caliber RD101

Manually wound; 4 radially assembled lever escapements, synchronized with 3 balancing differentials; additional planetary gears for winding and power reserve indicator; skeletonized movement; double spring barrel, 40-hour power reserve; Geneva Seal
Functions: hours, minutes; power reserve indicator
Diameter: 37.9 mm
Height: 10.6 mm
Jewels: 113
Balance: glucydur (4x)
Frequency: 28,800 vph
Balance spring: flat hairspring
Remarks: galvanic black movement, beveled and with perlage; 590 parts

ROLEX

Rolex SA
Rue François-Dussaud 3
CH-1211 Geneva 26
Switzerland

Website:
www.rolex.com

Founded:
1908

Number of employees:
over 2,000 (estimated)

Annual production:
approx. 1,000,000 watches (estimated)

U.S. distributor:
Rolex Watch U.S.A., Inc.
650 Fifth Avenue
New York, NY 10019
212-758-7700
www.rolex.com

Essentially, the Rolex formula for success has always been "what you see is what you get"—and plenty of it. For over a century now, the company has made wristwatch history without a need for *grandes complications*, perpetual calendars, tourbillons, or exotic materials. And its output in sheer quantity is phenomenal, at not quite a million watches per year. But make no mistake about it: the quality of these timepieces is legendary.

For as long as anyone can remember, this brand has held the top spot in the COSC's statistics, and year after year Rolex delivers just about half of all the official institute's successfully tested mechanical chronometer movements. The brand has also pioneered several fundamental innovations: Rolex founder Hans Wilsdorf invented the hermetically sealed Oyster case in the 1920s, which he later outfitted with a screwed-in crown and an automatic movement wound by rotor. Shock protection, water resistance, the amagnetic Parachrom hairspring, and automatic winding are some of the virtues that make wearing a Rolex timepiece much more comfortable and reliable. As for movements, the automatic caliber 3255 features new materials (nickel-phosphorus), special micromanufacturing technology (LIGA) to make the pallet fork and balance wheel of the Chronergy escapement, and a barrel spring that can store up more energy than ever. Roley also uses what it calls "Oyster" steel, an alloy of 904L steel, and puts some models on a "Jubilee" bracelet that is five links wide, giving it extra suppleness.

Rolex watches are produced in four different locations in Switzerland. Headquarters in Geneva handles final assembly and quality control and sales. All development, manufacturing, and quality control is done a few miles away in Plan-les-Ouates. Jewel-setting and dial-making are done in the Chêne-Bourg district of Geneva, and movements come from a factory in Biel/Bienne.

Meanwhile the company has built up representation in nearly one hundred countries in the world, with over thirty subsidiaries with customer service centers. The vast network also includes around four thousand watchmakers trained according to Rolex's own standards, who work in the branch offices or at the dealers themselves.

Oyster Perpetual GMT-Master II

Reference number: 126720VTNR
Movement: automatic, Rolex Caliber 3285; ø 28.5 mm, height 6.4 mm; 31 jewels; 28,800 vph; Parachrom hairspring, Paraflex shock absorber, Chronergy escapement; 70-hour power reserve; COSC-certified chronometer
Functions: hours (switched via crown), minutes, sweep seconds; additional 24-hour display (2nd time zone); date
Case: stainless steel, ø 40 mm, height 13 mm; bidirectional bezel with ceramic insert, with 0-24 scale; sapphire crystal; screw-in crown; water-resistant to 10 atm
Band: Jubilee stainless steel, folding clasp with safety lock and extension link
Price: $11,250

Oyster Perpetual GMT-Master II

Reference number: 126710BLNR
Movement: automatic, Rolex Caliber 3285; ø 28.5 mm, height 6.4 mm; 31 jewels; 28,800 vph; Parachrom hairspring, Paraflex shock absorber, Chronergy escapement; 70-hour power reserve; COSC-certified chronometer
Functions: hours (switched via crown), minutes, sweep seconds; additional 24-hour display (2nd time zone); date
Case: stainless steel, ø 40 mm, height 13 mm; bezel with ceramic inserts, bidirectional bezel with 24-minute scale; sapphire crystal; screw-in crown; water resistant to 10 atm
Band: Jubilee stainless steel, folding clasp with safety lock and extension link
Price: $10,750

Oyster Perpetual GMT-Master II

Reference number: 126711CHNR
Movement: automatic, Rolex Caliber 3285; ø 28.5 mm, height 6.4 mm; 31 jewels; 28,800 vph; Parachrom hairspring, Paraflex shock absorber, Chronergy escapement; 70-hour power reserve; COSC-certified chronometer
Functions: hours (switched via crown), minutes, sweep seconds; additional 24-hour display (2nd time zone); date
Case: stainless steel, ø 40 mm, height 13 mm; rose gold bezel with ceramic inserts, bidirectional bezel with 24-minute scale; sapphire crystal; screw-in crown; water resistant to 10 atm
Band: Oyster steel with rose gold elements, folding clasp with safety lock and extension link
Price: $15,250

Oyster Perpetual Submariner

Reference number: 124060
Movement: automatic, Rolex Caliber 3230; ø 29.1 mm, 31 jewels; 28,800 vph; Parachrom spring, Paraflex shock absorber, Chronergy escapement, glucydur balance with Microstella regulating bolts; 70-hour power reserve; COSC-certified chronometer
Functions: hours, minutes, sweep seconds
Case: stainless steel, ø 41 mm, height 12.5 mm; unidirectional bezel with ceramic insert, with 0-60 scale; sapphire crystal; screw-in crown; water-resistant to 30 atm
Band: Oyster stainless steel, folding clasp, with extension link
Price: $8,950

Oyster Perpetual Submariner Date

Reference number: 126610LV
Movement: automatic, Rolex Caliber 3230; ø 29.1 mm, 31 jewels; 28,800 vph; Parachrom spring, Paraflex shock absorber, Chronergy escapement, glucydur balance with Microstella regulating bolts; 70-hour power reserve; COSC-certified chronometer
Functions: hours, minutes, sweep seconds; date
Case: stainless steel, ø 41 mm, height 12.5 mm; unidirectional bezel with ceramic insert, with 0-60 scale; sapphire crystal; screw-in crown; water resistant to 30 atm
Band: Oyster stainless steel, folding clasp with extension link
Price: $10,600
Variations: in white gold ($40,650)

Oyster Perpetual Sea-Dweller

Reference number: 126603
Movement: automatic, Rolex Caliber 3235; ø 29.1 mm, 31 jewels; 28,800 vph; Parachrom hairspring, Paraflex shock absorber, Chronergy escapement, glucydur balance with Microstella regulating bolts; 70-hour power reserve; COSC-certified chronometer
Functions: hours, minutes, sweep seconds; date
Case: stainless steel, ø 43 mm, height 13.8 mm; yellow-gold bezel with ceramic inserts, unidirectional bezel with 0-60 scale; sapphire crystal; screw-in crown, helium valve; water-resistant to 122 atm
Band: Oyster steel with yellow gold elements, folding clasp with safety lock and extension link, with fine regulation
Price: $17,000
Variations: in stainless steel ($12,950)

Oyster Perpetual Sea-Dweller Deepsea

Reference number: 116660
Movement: automatic, Rolex Caliber 4130; ø 30.5 mm, height 6.5 mm; 44 jewels; 28,800 vph; Parachrom spring, glucydur balance with Microstella regulating bolts; 72-hour power reserve; COSC-certified chronometer
Functions: hours, minutes, subsidiary seconds; chronograph; date
Case: stainless steel, ø 44 mm, height 12.8 mm; Cerachrom bezel; sapphire crystal; screw-in crown and pusher; water-resistant to 10 atm
Band: Oyster steel, folding clasp with safety lock and extension link
Price: $14,150
Variations: with black dial $13,850

Oyster Perpetual Cosmograph Daytona

Reference number: 116500LN
Movement: automatic, Rolex Caliber 4130; ø 30.5 mm, height 6.5 mm; 44 jewels; 28,800 vph; Parachrom spring, glucydur balance with Microstella regulating bolts; 72-hour power reserve; COSC-certified chronometer
Functions: hours, minutes, subsidiary seconds; chronograph
Case: stainless steel, ø 40 mm, height 12.8 mm; Cerachrom bezel; sapphire crystal; screw-in crown and pusher; water-resistant to 10 atm
Band: Oyster steel, folding clasp with safety lock and extension link
Price: $14,550
Variations: with black dial

Oyster Perpetual Explorer II

Reference number: 226570
Movement: automatic, Rolex Caliber 3285; ø 28.5 mm, height 6.4 mm; 31 jewels; 28,800 vph; Parachrom hairspring, Paraflex shock absorber, Chronergy escapement; 70-hour power reserve; COSC-certified chronometer
Functions: hours (switched via crown), minutes, sweep seconds; additional 24-hour display (2nd time zone); date
Case: stainless steel, ø 42 mm; sapphire crystal; screw-in crown; water resistant to 10 atm
Band: Oyster steel, folding clasp with extension element
Price: $9,500
Variations: with black dial

Oyster Perpetual Explorer

Reference number: 124273
Movement: automatic, Rolex Caliber 3230; ø 29.1 mm, 31 jewels; 28,800 vph; Parachrom spring, Paraflex shock absorber, Chronergy escapement, glucydur balance with Microstella regulating bolts; 70-hour power reserve; COSC-certified chronometer
Functions: hours, minutes, sweep seconds
Case: stainless steel, ø 36 mm; yellow gold bezel; sapphire crystal; screw-in crown; water resistant to 10 atm
Band: Oyster steel with yellow gold elements, folding clasp with extension link
Price: $11,150
Variations: in stainless steel ($7,200)

Oyster Perpetual Air-King

Reference number: 126900
Movement: automatic, Rolex Caliber 3230; ø 28.5 mm; 31 jewels; 28,800 vph; Parachrom hairspring, glucydur balance with Microstella regulating bolts; soft iron cap for amagnetic protection; 70-hour power reserve; COSC-certified chronometer
Functions: hours, minutes, sweep seconds
Case: stainless steel, ø 40 mm, height 11.6 mm; sapphire crystal; screw-in crown; water-resistant to 10 atm
Band: Oyster steel, folding clasp, with safety lock and extension link
Price: $7,400

Oyster Perpetual Milgauss

Reference number: 116400GV
Movement: automatic, Rolex Caliber 3131; ø 28.5 mm, 31 jewels; 28,800 vph; Parachrom spring, glucydur balance with Microstella regulating bolts; soft iron cap for anti-magnetic protection; 48-hour power reserve; COSC-certified chronometer
Functions: hours, minutes, sweep seconds
Case: stainless steel, ø 40 mm; sapphire crystal; screw-in crown; water resistant to 10 atm
Band: Oyster stainless steel, folding clasp with safety lock and extension link
Price: $9,150
Variations: with a blue dial

Oyster Perpetual Sky-Dweller

Reference number: 326933
Movement: automatic, Rolex Caliber 9001; ø 33 mm, height 8 mm; 40 jewels; 28,800 vph; Parachrom spring, Paraflex shock absorber, glucydur balance with Microstella regulating bolts; 72-hour power reserve; COSC-certified chronometer
Functions: hours, minutes, sweep seconds; additional 24-hour display (second time zone); annual calendar with date, month
Case: Oyster steel, ø 42 mm, height 14.1 mm; yellow gold bezel, bidirectionally rotating bezel to control functions; sapphire crystal; screw-in crown; water resistant to 10 atm
Band: Oyster steel with yellow gold elements, folding clasp with extension link
Price: $18,200
Variations: in stainless steel/white gold ($15,200); in yellow gold ($46,750)

Oyster Perpetual Yacht-Master II

Reference number: 116681
Movement: automatic, Rolex Caliber 4161 (base Caliber 4130); ø 31.2 mm, height 8.05 mm; 42 jewels; 28,800 vph; Parachrom hairspring, glucydur balance with Microstella regulating bolts; 72-hour power reserve; COSC-certified chronometer
Functions: hours, minutes, subsidiary seconds; programmable regatta countdown with memory
Case: stainless steel, ø 44 mm, height 13.8 mm; bidirectional rose gold bezel with ceramic insert; sapphire crystal; screw-in crown; water-resistant to 10 atm
Band: Oyster steel with rose gold elements, folding clasp, with safety lock and extension link
Price: $25,350
Variations: yellow gold ($43,550); stainless steel ($18,750)

Oyster Perpetual Yacht-Master 42

Reference number: 226658
Movement: automatic, Rolex Caliber 3135; ø 28.5 mm, height 6 mm; 31 jewels; 28,800 vph; Parachrom hairspring, glucydur balance with Microstella regulating bolts; 48-hour power reserve; COSC-certified chronometer
Functions: hours, minutes, sweep seconds; date
Case: yellow gold, ø 42 mm, height 11.9 mm; bidirectional bezel with ceramic insert and 0-60 scale; sapphire crystal; screw-in crown; water-resistant to 10 atm
Band: elastomer with metal mesh inside, folding clasp
Price: $28,300
Variations: 40-mm or 37-mm case; in rose gold

Oyster Perpetual Datejust 41

Reference number: 126300
Movement: automatic, Rolex Caliber 3235; ø 29.1 mm; 31 jewels; 28,800 vph; Parachrom hairspring, Paraflex shock protection, Chronergy escapement, glucydur balance with Microstella regulating bolts; 70-hour power reserve; COSC-certified chronometer
Functions: hours, minutes, sweep seconds; date
Case: Oyster steel, ø 41 mm, height 11.6 mm; white gold bezel; sapphire crystal; screw-in crown; water-resistant to 10 atm
Band: Jubilee stainless steel, folding clasp, with extension link
Price: $8,150

Oyster Perpetual Datejust 41

Reference number: 126334
Movement: automatic, Rolex Caliber 3235; ø 29.1 mm; 31 jewels; 28,800 vph; Parachrom hairspring, Paraflex shock protection, Chronergy escapement, glucydur balance with Microstella regulating bolts; 70-hour power reserve; COSC-certified chronometer
Functions: hours, minutes, sweep seconds; date
Case: Oyster steel, ø 41 mm, height 11.6 mm; white gold bezel; sapphire crystal; screw-in crown; water-resistant to 10 atm
Band: Jubilee stainless steel, folding clasp, with extension link
Price: $10,250

Oyster Perpetual Datejust 41

Reference number: 126333
Movement: automatic, Rolex Caliber 3235; ø 29.1 mm; 31 jewels; 28,800 vph; Parachrom hairspring, Paraflex shock protection, Chronergy escapement, glucydur balance with Microstella regulating bolts; 70-hour power reserve; COSC-certified chronometer
Functions: hours, minutes, sweep seconds; date
Case: Oyster steel, ø 41 mm, height 11.6 mm; white gold bezel; sapphire crystal; screw-in crown; water-resistant to 10 atm
Band: Jubilee stainless steel with yellow-gold elements, folding clasp, with extension link
Price: $13,550

Oyster Perpetual Day-Date 40

Reference number: 228236
Movement: automatic, Rolex Caliber 3255; ø 29.1 mm, height 5.4 mm; 31 jewels; 28,800 vph; Parachrom hairspring, Paraflex shock absorption, Chronergy escapement, glucydur balance with Microstella regulating bolts; 70-hour power reserve; COSC-certified chronometer
Functions: hours, minutes, sweep seconds; date, weekday
Case: platinum, ø 40 mm, height 11.6 mm; sapphire crystal; screw-in crown; water-resistant to 10 atm
Band: President white gold, covered folding clasp
Price: $63,350
Variations: white gold ($40,350)

Oyster Perpetual Day-Date 40

Reference number: 228238
Movement: automatic, Rolex Caliber 3255; ø 29.1 mm, height 5.4 mm; 31 jewels; 28,800 vph; Parachrom hairspring, Paraflex shock absorption, Chronergy escapement, glucydur balance with Microstella regulating bolts; 70-hour power reserve; COSC-certified chronometer
Functions: hours, minutes, sweep seconds; date, weekday
Case: yellow gold, ø 40 mm, height 11.6 mm; sapphire crystal; screw-in crown; water-resistant to 10 atm
Band: President yellow gold, folding clasp
Price: $37,450
Variations: white or rose gold ($40,350)

Cellini Moonphase

Reference number: 50535
Movement: automatic, Rolex Caliber 3195; ø 28.5 mm; 31 jewels; 28,800 vph; Parachrom hairspring, Paraflex shock protection, Chronergy escapement; 48-hour power reserve; COSC-certified chronometer
Functions: hours, minutes, sweep seconds; date, moon phase
Case: rose gold, ø 39 mm; sapphire crystal; screw-in crown; water-resistant to 5 atm
Band: reptile skin, folding clasp
Remarks: blue enameled celestial disk with rhodium-plated meteorite as a moon
Price: $26,750

Caliber 3255

Automatic; optimized Chronergy escapement, nickel phosphorus pallet lever and escape wheel made using LIGA process; single spring barrel, 70-hour power reserve; COSC-certified chronometer
Functions: hours, minutes, sweep seconds; date, weekday
Diameter: 29.1 mm
Height: 5.4 mm
Jewels: 31
Balance: glucydur with Microstella regulating bolts
Frequency: 28,800 vph
Balance spring: Parachrom Breguet hairspring
Shock protection: Paraflex
Remarks: used in Day-Date 40

Caliber 3235

Automatic; optimized Chronergy escapement, nickel phosphorus pallet lever and escape wheel made using LIGA process; single spring barrel, 70-hour power reserve; COSC-certified chronometer
Functions: hours, minutes, sweep seconds; date
Diameter: 28.5 mm
Height: 6 mm
Jewels: 31
Balance: glucydur with Microstella regulating bolts
Frequency: 28,800 vph
Balance spring: Parachrom Breguet hairspring
Shock protection: Paraflex
Remarks: used in Datejust

Caliber 2236

Automatic; single spring barrel, 55-hour power reserve; COSC-certified chronometer
Functions: hours, minutes, sweep seconds; date
Diameter: 20 mm
Height: 5.95 mm
Jewels: 31
Balance: glucydur with Microstella regulating bolts
Frequency: 28,800 vph
Balance spring: Parachrom flat hairspring
Shock protection: Kif
Remarks: used in Lady Datejust

Caliber 4130

Automatic; single spring barrel, 72-hour power reserve; COSC-certified chronometer
Functions: hours, minutes, subsidiary seconds; chronograph
Diameter: 30.5 mm
Height: 6.5 mm
Jewels: 44
Balance: glucydur with Microstella regulating bolts
Frequency: 28,800 vph
Balance spring: Parachrom Breguet hairspring
Shock protection: Kif
Remarks: used in Daytona

Caliber 4161

Automatic; single spring barrel, 72-hour power reserve; COSC-certified chronometer
Base caliber: Caliber 4130
Functions: hours, minutes, subsidiary seconds; programmable regatta countdown with memory
Diameter: 31.2 mm
Height: 8.05 mm
Jewels: 42
Balance: glucydur with Microstella regulating bolts
Frequency: 28,800 vph
Balance spring: Parachrom Breguet hairspring
Shock protection: Kif
Remarks: used in Yacht-Master II

Caliber 9001

Automatic; single spring barrel, 72-hour power reserve; COSC-certified chronometer
Functions: hours, minutes, sweep seconds; additional 24-hour display (2nd time zone); annual calendar with date, month
Diameter: 33 mm
Height: 8 mm
Jewels: 40
Balance: glucydur with Microstella regulating bolts
Frequency: 28,800 vph
Balance spring: Parachrom Breguet hairspring
Shock protection: Kif
Remarks: used in Sky-Dweller

SCHAUMBURG WATCH

Schaumburg Watch
Kirchplatz 5 and 6
D-31737 Rinteln
Germany

Tel.:
+49-5751-923-351

E-mail:
info@schaumburgwatch.com

Website:
www.schaumburgwatch.com

Founded:
1998

Number of employees:
9

U.S. distributor:
Schaumburg Watch
About Time Luxury Group
210 Bellevue Avenue
Newport, RI 02840
401-846-0598
nicewatch@aol.com

Most important collections/price range:
mechanical wristwatches / approx. $1,500 to $13,000

If you are searching for a brand whose brand strategy is anti-brand, then Schaumburg is your brand. Frank Dilbakowski is the owner of this small watchmaking business in Rinteln, Westphalia, which has been producing very unusual yet affordable timepieces since 1998. The name Schaumburg comes from the surrounding region. The firm has gained a reputation for high-performance timepieces for rugged sports and professional use. But expect to be surprised. The portfolio includes such pieces as the chronometer line Aquamatic, with water resistance to 1,000 meters, and the Aquatitan models, secure to 2,000 meters (200 atm). If you are into the worn-down industrial look, there is the Steam Punk collection, which looks as if it had been buried in someone's garden and has now been unearthed, cleaned up, but not restored. It is a particular way to surf the vintage wave.

The watches work well, of course, because Dilbakowski has prioritized traditional watchmaking. The Rinteln workbenches produce the plates and bridges and provide all the finishing as well (perlage, engraving, skeletonizing). Some of the bracelets, cases, and dials are even manufactured here, but the base movements come from Switzerland. Besides unadorned one-hand watches like the recent Squarematic Unique, which mixes 1970s-style modernity with a little rusty steampunk, the current portfolio of timepieces includes such outstanding pieces as another of Schaumburg's special moon phases, with a "shadow" crossing over an immobile photo-like reproduction of the moon brightly lit with Superluminova. The Church Tower Clock is an homage to the old clocks out of which watches were ultimately born. As for the Wonderland, it is a riot of hand-engraved bridges and mainplate, all colored. Schaumburg is a courageous brand, and one that needs a bit of boldness on the part of the buyer. But it does produce genuinely unique pieces that will inevitably attract some amazed looks.

Church Tower Clock

Movement: manually wound, Caliber ML SW-07.1; ø 37.2 mm, height 4.5 mm; 17 jewels; 18,000 vph; screw balance: three-quarter plate; 38-hour power reserve
Functions: hours, minutes
Case: distressed stainless steel, ø 42 mm, height 13 mm; sapphire crystal; transparent case back; water-resistant to 3 atm
Band: calf leather, buckle
Remarks: sterling silver dial with patina
Price: $3,210; limited to 55 pieces

MooN Galilei

Reference number: SW-M-WE19
Movement: automatic, Caliber SW 11 (base MAB 88); ø 25.6 mm, height 3.6 mm; 25 jewels; 28,800 vph; astronomically precise moon phase; perlage on movement, côtes de Genève on the rotor; 42-hour power reserve
Functions: hours, minutes; moon phase
Case: stainless steel, ø 43 mm, height 12.4 mm; sapphire crystal; water-resistant to 5 atm
Band: textile with leather lining, buckle
Price: $5,370

Wonderland

Reference number: SW-U-W020
Movement: manually wound, Caliber SW 07.1 (base ETA 6497); ø 36.6 mm, height 4.5 mm; 17 jewels; 18,000 vph; screw balance; extensively and finely finished skeletonized movement; 38-hour power reserve
Functions: hours, minutes
Case: thermally-patinated stainless steel, ø 42 mm, height 11 mm; sapphire crystal; transparent case back
Band: leather, buckle
Remarks: extensively skeletonized and decorated dial and movement
Price: $3,950

Schwarz Etienne SA
Route de L'Orée-du-Bois 5
CH-2300 La Chaux-de-Fonds
Switzerland

Tel.:
+41-32-967-9420

E-mail:
info@schwarz-etienne.ch

Website:
www.schwarz-etienne.com

Founded:
1902

Number of employees:
22

Annual production:
300 to 500

Distribution:
Contact main office in Switzerland.

Most important collections:
La Chaux-de-Fonds, Roma, Roswell, Fiji, special editions

SCHWARZ ETIENNE

When Raffaello Radicchi, who hails from Perugia, Italy, talks about his business, you might think he was talking about a little shop he set up in Neuchâtel. Ask him why he went into watchmaking, he answers, "I was allergic to the metal and could only wear a gold watch." Subtext: He could not afford a gold watch, so he founded a watch company.

Radicchi is a genuine maverick and a lone figure in this somewhat hermetic industry. He arrived in Switzerland at eighteen, a mason. He retrained as a carpenter and started buying and renovating homes, and soon he was earning some serious money. In the early aughts, an acquaintance bought up a watch brand in La Chaux-de-Fonds and suggested that Radicchi buy the building that came with it. The brand, once a big name in the industry and a supplier of movements (to Chanel, among others), had originally been founded by Paul Schwarz and Olga Etienne.

By 2008, Radicchi owned the whole package. He understood that the company needed independence to survive. Having a number of outstanding suppliers locally to partner with was a good start. But Schwarz Etienne needed movements. By 2013, Radicchi had two, and a third came in 2015. These calibers drive a series of watches, including a tourbillon, that are classical in look, yet very modern-technical, thanks to the inverted movement construction that puts the off-center microrotor on the dial. They've recently started appearing in the watches of other brands as well.

For all its traditionalism, the brand still maintains a feeling of youthful creativity with a lot of good and bold humor rarely found in the industry. The Roswell's case, for example, is shaped like a comic-book UFO. The Ode To The 70's is a perfect reminder of those brave old days as the hippie movement became gentrified, and the Roma Synergy features a complex guilloché dial by Kari Voutilainen with a special galvanic treatment.

Roma Synergy

Reference number: WROVMA03SSCUBCLTD-A
Movement: automatic, Schwarz Etienne Caliber ASE 200.00 with micro-rotor; finely finished movement with guilloché and snailing; ø 30.40 mm, height 5.35 mm; 33 jewels; 21,600 vph; 86-hour power reserve
Functions: hours, minutes, subsidiary seconds
Case: stainless steel, ø 39 mm, height 11 mm; sapphire crystal; water-resistant to 5 atm
Band: calfskin, folding clasp
Remarks: royal blue dial; fish scale, wave, and sun guilloché on the dial by the Ateliers Kari Voutilainen
Price: $30,000; limited to 50 pieces
Variations: sand-grey dial

Ode To The 70's

Reference number: WCF09TSE70IESWG03AA-A
Movement: automatic, Schwarz Etienne Caliber TSE 121.00; ø 30.4 mm, height 5.35 mm; 34 jewels; 21,600 vph; with "irreversible" micro-rotor; 1-minute flying tourbillon; 86-hour power reserve
Functions: hours, minutes, seconds on tourbillon cage
Case: white gold, ø 44 mm, height 13.70 mm; sapphire crystal; transparent case back; water-resistant to 5 atm
Band: blue jean with hand-painted splashes and reptile skin lining, folding clasp
Remarks: cloisonné and champlevé grand feu enamel
Price: $135,000; limited edition of 23 pieces

Roswell 08

Reference number: WRW11TJ33SS21AA-A
Movement: automatic, Schwarz Etienne Caliber ISE-100.11; ø 30.40 mm, height 6.30 mm; 36 jewels; 21,600 vph; with "irreversible" micro-rotor; finely finished parts; 86-hour power reserve
Functions: hours, minutes, subsidiary seconds; date aperture at 2 o'clock
Case: stainless steel, ø 45 mm, height 12.24 mm; sapphire crystal; transparent case back; water-resistant to 5 atm
Remarks: tobacco-colored dial
Band: calfskin, folding clasp
Price: $17,300

SEIKO

The Japanese watch giant is a part of the Seiko Holding Company, whose story began one hundred and forty years ago, when twenty-two-year-old entrepreneur Kintaro Hattori opened a store in central Tokyo, repairing and selling wristwatches and wall clocks. Today, the company is one of the few watch manufacturers that can carry out all steps of watchmaking in-house, from developing movements to producing parts and assembling all components. Seiko makes every variety of portable timepiece and offers mechanical watches with both manual and automatic winding, quartz watches with battery and solar power or with the brand's own mechanical "kinetic" power generation, as well as the groundbreaking "Spring Drive" hybrid technology. This intelligent mix of mechanical energy generation and electronic regulation is reserved for Seiko's top models.

Classic Seikos are designed for tradition-conscious buyers. The Astron, however, with its automatic GPS-controlled time setting, is something of a trailblazer. In its second incarnation, the Astron is 30 percent more compact, and the energy to operate the GPS system inside is supplied by a high-tech solar cell on the dial. As for the new Prospex collection, released for the fiftieth anniversary of the first Seiko diver's watches, it has an unmistakably modern look.

Diving watches from Seiko have been around for over fifty years. They have featured many important innovations, like the first titanium case for a diving watch, or the invention of the "accordion" strap and the single-shell construction of the case with external protection.

The Japanese sense of aesthetics is combined with traditional craftsmanship and Seiko's skill in making mechanical watches in the Presage collection. Using a variety of dial materials such as Arita porcelain or enamel, watches are created here that express the passion and high perfection of watchmakers and craftsmen in every detail. This is also evident in the latest "Sharp Edged" series: the traditional shape of the round case is contoured by sharply angled surfaces, which are reflected in the design of the structured dial.

Seiko Holdings
Ginza, Chuo, Tokyo
Japan

Website:
www.seikowatches.com

Founded:
1881

U.S. distributor:
Seiko Corporation of America
1111 MacArthur Boulevard
Mahwah, NJ 07430
201-529-5730
custserv@seikousa.com
www.seikousa.com

Most important collections/price range:
Astron / approx. $1,850 to $3,400; Presage / approx. $425 to $4,500; Prospex / approx. $395 to $6,000

Prospex Save the Ocean Special Edition

Reference number: SPB297
Movement: automatic, Seiko Caliber 6R35; ø 27.4 mm, height 5.25 mm; 24 jewels; 21,600 vph; antimagnetic to 4,800 A/m; 70-hour power reserve
Functions: hours, minutes, sweep seconds; date
Case: stainless steel (hard coating), ø 40.5 mm, height 13.2 mm; unidirectional bezel with 0-60 scale; sapphire crystal; screw-in crown; water-resistant to 20 atm
Band: stainless steel (hard coating), folding clasp, with safety lock and extension link
Remarks: modern reinterpretation of the first Diver's from 1965
Price: $1,250

Prospex Save the Ocean Special Edition

Reference number: SPB301
Movement: automatic, Seiko Caliber 6R35; ø 27.4 mm, height 5.25 mm; 24 jewels; 21,600 vph; antimagnetic to 4,800 A/m; 70-hour power reserve
Functions: hours, minutes, sweep seconds; date
Case: stainless steel (hard coating), ø 44 mm, height 13 mm; unidirectional bezel with 0-60 scale; sapphire crystal; screw-in crown; water-resistant to 20 atm
Band: stainless steel (hard coating), folding clasp, with safety lock and extension link
Remarks: modern reinterpretation of the 1970 Diver's watch
Price: $1,350

Prospex Automatic "Alpinist"

Reference number: SPB245
Movement: automatic, Seiko Caliber 6R35; ø 27.4 mm, height 5.25mm; 24 jewels; 21,600 vph; antimagnetic to 4,800 A/m; 70-hour power reserve
Functions: hours, minutes, sweep seconds; date
Case: stainless steel, ø 38 mm, height 12.9 mm; sapphire crystal; transparent case back; screw-in crown; water-resistant to 20 atm
Band: cordovan, folding clasp
Remarks: modern reinterpretation of the 1959 Alpinist watch
Price: $725
Variations: with stainless steel bracelet

Prospex Speedtimer Automatic Chronograph

Reference number: SRQ037
Movement: automatic, Seiko Caliber 8R46; ø 28.6 mm, height 7.47 mm; 34 jewels; 28,800 vph; antimagnetic to 4,800 A/m; chronograph with column wheel and vertical clutch mechanism; 45-hour power reserve
Functions: hours, minutes, subsidiary seconds; chronograph; date
Case: stainless steel, ø 42.5 mm, height 15.1 mm; sapphire crystal; transparent case back; water-resistant to 10 atm
Band: stainless steel, folding clasp
Price: $3,000

Prospex Speedtimer Solar Chronograph

Reference number: SSC815
Movement: quartz, Seiko Caliber V192; independent energy generation using solar cells in the dial
Functions: hours, minutes, subsidiary seconds; additional 24-hour display; chronograph; date; power reserve display.
Case: stainless steel, ø 39 mm, height 13.3 mm; sapphire crystal; water-resistant to 10 atm
Band: stainless steel, folding clasp
Price: $675

Presage Automatic "Sharp-Edged" GMT

Reference number: SPB221
Movement: automatic, Seiko Caliber 6R64; ø 27.4 mm, height 6.3m; 29 jewels; 28,800 vph; antimagnetic to 4,800 A/m; 45-hour power reserve
Functions: hours, minutes, sweep seconds; additional 24-hour display (second time zone); power reserve indicator; date
Case: stainless steel (hard coating), ø 42.2 mm, height 13.7 mm; sapphire crystal; transparent case back; water-resistant to 10 atm
Band: stainless steel (hard coating), folding clasp
Price: $1,400

Presage "Sharp-Edged" Multifunction

Reference number: SPB305
Movement: automatic, Seiko Caliber 6R21; ø 27.4 mm, height 6.15 mm; 29 jewels; 28,800 vph; antimagnetic to 4,800 A/m; 45-hour power reserve
Functions: hours, minutes, sweep seconds; power reserve indicator; date and weekday
Case: stainless steel (hard coating), ø 40.2 mm, height 13.7 mm; sapphire crystal; transparent case back; water-resistant to 10 atm
Band: stainless steel (hard coating), folding clasp
Price: $1,100

Presage Style 60's

Reference number: SRPG03
Movement: automatic, Seiko Caliber 4R35; ø 27.4 mm, height 5.25 mm; 23 jewels; 21,600 vph; antimagnetic to 4,800 A/m; 41-hour power reserve
Functions: hours, minutes, sweep seconds; date
Case: stainless steel, ø 40.8 mm, height 12 mm; hardened mineral crystal; transparent case back; water-resistant to 5 atm
Band: stainless steel, folding clasp
Price: $525

Astron GPS Solar Dual Time

Reference number: SSH109
Movement: quartz, Seiko Caliber 5X53; autonomous energy from solar cells on dial
Functions: hours, minutes, sweep seconds; additional 12-hour display (2nd time zone), world time function (39 time zones), flight mode, signal reception indication, daylight saving time indication; perpetual calendar, date, weekday
Case: titanium (super hard coating), ø 42.7 mm, height 12.2 mm; sapphire crystal; water-resistant to 10 atm
Band: titanium (super hard coating), folding clasp
Price: $2,500

SINN

Sinn Spezialuhren GmbH
Wilhelm-Fay-Strasse 21
D-65936 Frankfurt/Main
Germany

Tel.:
+49-69-9784-14-200

E-mail:
info@sinn.de

Website:
www.sinn.de

Founded:
1961

Number of employees:
approx. 135

Annual production:
approx. 14,000 watches

U.S. distributor:
WatchBuys
888-333-4895
www.watchbuys.com

Most important collections/price range:
Financial District, U-Models, Diapal / from approx. $1,000 to $17,000

Pilot and flight instructor Helmut Sinn began manufacturing watches in Frankfurt am Main because he thought the pilot's watches on the market were too expensive. The resulting combination of top quality, functionality, and a good price-performance ratio turned out to be an excellent sales argument. Sinn Spezialuhren zu Frankfurt am Main is a brand with origins in technology. There is hardly another source that offers watch lovers such a sophisticated and reasonable collection of sporty watches, many conceived to survive in extreme conditions by conforming to German DIN industrial norms.

In 1994, Lothar Schmidt took over the brand, and his product developers began looking for inspiration in other industries and the sciences. They did so out of a practical technical impulse without any plan for launching a trend. Research and development are consistently aimed at improving the functionality of the watches. This includes application of special Sinn technology such as moisture-proofing cases by pumping in an inert gas like argon. Other Sinn innovations include the Diapal (a lubricant-free lever escapement), the Hydro (an oil-filled diver's watch), and tegiment processing (for hardened steel and titanium surfaces). Having noticed a lack of norms for aviator watches, Schmidt negotiated a partnership with the Aachen Technical University to create the *Technischer Standard Fliegeruhren* (TESTAF, or Technical Standard for Pilot's Watches), which is housed at the Eurocopter headquarters.

Sinn recently joined forces with two German watch companies, the Sächsische Uhrentechnologie Glashütte (SUG) and the Uhren-Werke-Dresden (UWD). The latter produced the outstanding UWD 33.1 caliber with Sinn as chaperone. That movement was then used to drive the Meisterbund I, which translates as "master alliance."

All these moves have brought the company enough wherewithal to open new headquarters in the Sossenheim district of Frankfurt. The building offers nearly 25,000 square feet of space, most of which is devoted to assembly and manufacturing. At the heart of the two-story construction is a grandiose atrium with a skylight offering lots of natural light. The roof was also turned into an open-air terrace.

6060 B

Reference number: 6060.013
Movement: automatic, Sellita Caliber SW330-1; ø 25.6 mm, height 4.1 mm; 25 jewels; 28,800 vph; fine finishing on the movement, 50-hour power reserve
Functions: hours, minutes, sweep seconds; additional 24-hour display (second time zone); date
Case: stainless steel, ø 38.5 mm, height 12 mm; crown-adjustable inner bezel with 0-12 scale; sapphire crystal; transparent case back; screw-in crown; water-resistant to 10 atm
Band: stainless steel, double folding clasp
Remarks: comes with calfskin band
Price: $2,880
Variations: with black dial

EZM 13.1

Reference number: 613.011
Movement: automatic, Caliber SZ02 (based on Concepto C99001); ø 30.4 mm, height 7.9 mm; 28 jewels; 28,800 vph; sweep stop second and minute hand; antimagnetic according to the German Industrial Norm (DIN); fine finishing on movement; 46-hour power reserve
Functions: hours, minutes, subsidiary seconds; chronograph; date
Case: stainless steel, ø 41 mm, height 15 mm; sapphire crystal; screw-in crown; water-resistant to 50 atm
Band: stainless steel, folding clasp with extension link
Remarks: dehumidifying technology (protective gas)
Price: $3,270
Variations: with silicone band ($3,400); with calf leather band ($3,400)

1800 S GG Damaszener

Reference number: 1800.050
Movement: automatic, Sellita Caliber SW300-1; ø 25.6 mm, height 3.6 mm; 25 jewels; 28,800 vph; 42-hour power reserve
Functions: hours, minutes, sweep seconds; date
Case: Damascus steel with black hard-coating, ø 43 mm, height 10.4 mm; sapphire crystal; transparent case back; screw-in crown; water-resistant to 10 atm
Band: calfskin, buckle
Remarks: Damascus steel dial; comes with calfskin band; limited to 100 pieces
Price: $8,940

103 Ti Ar

Reference number: 103.071
Movement: automatic, Caliber MU C99001; ø 30.4 mm, height 7.9 mm; 28 jewels; 28,800 vph; antimagnetic according to the German Industrial Norm (DIN); fine finishing on movement; 46-hour power reserve
Functions: hours, minutes, subsidiary seconds; chronograph; date and weekday
Case: titanium, ø 41 mm, height 17 mm; bidirectional bezel with 0-60 scale; sapphire crystal; screw-in crown; water-resistant to 20 atm
Band: textile, buckle
Remarks: dehumidifying technology (protective gas)
Price: $2,930
Variations: with Diapal escapement ($3,930)

717

Reference number: 717.010
Movement: automatic, Sinn Caliber SZ01 (base Concepto C99001); ø 30.4 mm, height 8.5 mm; 28 jewels; 28,800 vph; sweep stop seconds; 46-hour power reserve
Functions: hours, minutes, subsidiary seconds; chronograph; date
Case: tegimented stainless steel, with black hard coating, ø 45 mm, height 15.3 mm; sapphire crystal; screw-in crown; water-resistant to 20 atm
Band: calfskin, buckle
Remarks: dehumidifying technology (protective gas)
Price: $5,160
Variations: with silicone strap

358 Sa FLIEGER DS

Reference number: 358.065
Movement: automatic, Sellita Caliber SW500 (modified); ø 30 mm, height 7.9 mm; 25 jewels; 28,800 vph; antimagnetic according to German Industrial Norm (DIN); finely finished movement; 48-hour power reserve
Functions: hours, minutes, subsidiary seconds; chronograph; date und weekday
Case: stainless steel, ø 42 mm, height 15 mm; sapphire crystal; transparent case back; water-resistant to 10 atm
Band: textile, buckle
Remarks: dehumidifying technology (protective gas)
Price: $3.150
Variations: with blue dial; with Diapal technology

144 St S Jubiläum II

Reference number: 144.083
Movement: automatic, Concepto Caliber C99001; ø 30.4 mm, height 7.9 mm; 25 jewels; 28,800 vph; 46-hour power reserve
Functions: hours, minutes, subsidiary seconds; chronograph; date und weekday
Case: tegimented stainless steel, with black hard coating, ø 41 mm, height 14.5 mm; sapphire crystal; transparent case back; screw-in crown; water-resistant to 20 atm
Band: silicone, double folding clasp, with extension link
Remarks: dehumidifying technology (protective gas); comes with additional stainless steel bracelet; limited to 600 pieces
Price: $3,540

910 SRS

Reference number: 910.020
Movement: automatic, ETA Caliber 7750 (modified); ø 30 mm, height 8.4 mm; 25 jewels; 28,800 vph; column wheel control of chronograph functions; antimagnetic according to German Industrial Norm (DIN); finely finished movement; 46-hour power reserve
Functions: hours, minutes, subsidiary seconds; flyback-chronograph; date
Case: stainless steel, ø 41.5 mm, height 15.5 mm; sapphire crystal; transparent case back; water-resistant to 10 atm
Band: calfskin, buckle
Price: $4.360
Variations: with stainless steel bracelet ($4.660)

R500

Reference number: 500.010
Movement: automatic, ETA Caliber 7750 (base modified); ø 30.4 mm, height 7.9 mm; 25 jewels; 28,800 vph; finely finished movement; 46-hour power reserve
Functions: hours, minutes, subsidiary seconds; power reserve display; chronograph; date
Case: titanium, ø 42 mm, height 16 mm; sapphire crystal; screw-in crown; water-resistant to 30 atm
Band: calfskin, buckle
Remarks: so-called "bullhead chronograph"
Price: $4.480; limited to 300 pieces
Variations: with stainless steel bracelet

1739 Ag B

Reference number: 1739.021
Movement: automatic, Sellita Caliber SW300-1; ø 25.6 mm, height 3.6 mm; 25 jewels; 28,800 vph; 42-hour power reserve
Functions: hours, minutes
Case: stainless steel, with silver alloy, ø 39 mm, height 9.1 mm; sapphire crystal; transparent case back; screw-in crown; water-resistant to 10 atm
Band: calfskin, buckle
Price: $2,680
Variations: without silver alloy, with silver-plated dial; without silver alloy, with silver-plated dial

104 St Sa I A

Reference number: 104.014
Movement: automatic, Sellita Caliber SW220-1; ø 25.6 mm, height 4.6 mm; 26 jewels; 28,800 vph; fine finishing on movement; 38-hour power reserve
Functions: hours, minutes, sweep seconds; date and weekday
Case: stainless steel, ø 41 mm, height 11.9 mm; bidirectional bezel with 0-60 scale; sapphire crystal; transparent case back; screw-in crown; water-resistant to 20 atm
Band: calfskin, buckle
Price: $1,490
Variations: with stainless steel bracelet ($1,810)

105 St Sa UTC

Reference number: 105.020
Movement: automatic, Sellita Caliber SW330-2; ø 25.6 mm, height 4.1 mm; 25 jewels; 28,800 vph; finely finished movement; 42-hour power reserve
Functions: hours, minutes, sweep seconds; additional 24-hour display (second time zone); date
Case: stainless steel, ø 41 mm, height 11.9 mm; bidirectional bezel with 0-24 scale; sapphire crystal; transparent case back; screw-in crown; water-resistant to 20 atm
Band: stainless steel, folding clasp with safety lock
Price: $2,150
Variations: with a white dial

105 St Sa W

Reference number: 105.011
Movement: automatic, Sellita Caliber SW220-1; ø 25.6 mm, height 5.05 mm; 26 jewels; 28,800 vph; 38-hour power reserve
Functions: hours, minutes, sweep seconds; date and weekday
Case: stainless steel, ø 41 mm, height 11.9 mm; bidirectional bezel with 0-12 scale; sapphire crystal; transparent case back; screw-in crown; water-resistant to 20 atm
Band: silicon, buckle
Price: $1,630
Variations: with black dial

556 A RS

Reference number: 556.0141
Movement: automatic, Sellita Caliber SW200-1; ø 25.6 mm, height 4.6 mm; 26 jewels; 28,800 vph; antimagnetic according to German Industrial Norm (DIN); 38-hour power reserve
Functions: hours, minutes, sweep seconds; date
Case: stainless steel, ø 38.5 mm, height 11 mm; sapphire crystal; transparent case back; screw-in crown; water-resistant to 20 atm
Band: stainless steel, folding clasp, with safety catch
Price: $1.530
Variations: with Index-dial ($1,530); with mother-of-pearl dial ($1,490 with black second hand and leather strap, without date)

556 I Mother-of-Pearl S

Reference number: 556.0105
Movement: automatic, Sellita Caliber SW200-1; ø 25.6 mm, height 4.6 mm; 26 jewels; 28,800 vph; antimagnetic according to the German Industrial Norm (DIN); 38-hour power reserve
Functions: hours, minutes, sweep seconds
Case: stainless steel, ø 38.5 mm, height 11 mm; sapphire crystal; transparent case back; screw-in crown; water-resistant to 20 atm
Band: stainless steel, folding clasp with safety lock
Remarks: mother-of-pearl dial
Price: $1,720
Variations: various colors

3006 Hunting Watch

Reference number: 3006.010
Movement: automatic, Caliber MU C99002; ø 30.4 mm, height 7.9 mm; 25 jewels; 28,800 vph; antimagnetic according to the German Industrial Norm (DIN); 46-hour power reserve
Functions: hours, minutes, subsidiary seconds; additional 24-hour display; chronograph; date, weekday, months, moon phase
Case: tegimented stainless steel, ø 44 mm, height 15.5 mm; sapphire crystal; transparent case back; screw-in crown; water-resistant to 20 atm
Band: calfskin, buckle
Remarks: dehumidifying technology (protective gas)
Price: $4,480
Variations: with stainless steel bracelet ($4,910); with silicone band ($4,840)

U2 S

Reference number: 1020.020
Movement: automatic, Sellita Caliber SW330-1; ø 25.6 mm, height 4.6 mm; 25 jewels; 28,800 vph; 38-hour power reserve
Functions: hours, minutes, sweep seconds; additional 24-hour display (second time zone); date
Case: stainless steel, (U-Boot steel), tegimented, with black hard-coating, ø 44 mm, height 15.5 mm; unidirectional bezel with 60-minute scale; sapphire crystal; screw-in crown; water-resistant to 200 atm
Band: silicon, folding clasp
Remarks: EU diving certified
Price: $3,530
Variations: without hard covering ($2,980); bezel with black coating ($3,030)

U50

Reference number: 1050.010
Movement: automatic, Sellita Caliber SW300-1; ø 25.6 mm, height 3.6 mm; 25 jewels; 28,800 vph; 42-hour power reserve
Functions: hours, minutes, sweep seconds; date
Case: submarine steel, ø 41 mm, height 11.5 mm; unidirectional bezel with 0-60 scale; sapphire crystal; screw-in crown; water-resistant to 50 atm
Band: silicone, folding clasp
Remarks: EU diving certified
Price: $2,470
Variations: with black hard-coating ($3,260); with black hard-coating and blue-black dial ($3,310)

6012

Reference number: 6012.010
Movement: automatic, Caliber B LZ06 (base ETA 7751); ø 30.4 mm, height 7.9 mm; 25 jewels; 28,800 vph; antimagnetic according to German Industrial Norm (DIN); 42-hour power reserve
Functions: hours, minutes, subsidiary seconds; chronograph; full calendar with date, weekday, month, moon phase
Case: stainless steel, ø 41.5 mm, height 14.5 mm; sapphire crystal; transparent case back; water-resistant to 10 atm
Band: calfskin, buckle
Remarks: comes with additional stainless steel bracelet
Price: $5,240

434 St GG B

Reference number: 434.032
Movement: quartz, antimagnetic according to German Industrial Norm (DIN)
Functions: hours, minutes, sweep seconds
Case: stainless steel, ø 34 mm, height 8 mm; bezel in white gold, set with 68 diamonds; sapphire crystal; water-resistant to 10 atm
Band: stainless steel, double folding clasp
Remarks: Q-technology (reduction of electromagnetic pulse)
Price: $1,960
Variations: with black dial; with a stainless steel bezel ($910)

EZM 12

Reference number: 112.010
Movement: automatic, ETA Caliber 2836-2; ø 25.6 mm, height 5.05 mm; 25 jewels; 28,800 vph; antimagnetic to 84,000 A/m according to German Industrial Norm (DIN); 38-hour power reserve
Functions: hours, minutes, sweep seconds; date and weekday
Case: tegimented stainless steel, ø 44 mm, height 14 mm; bidirectional bezel with 60-minute division (counting down); crown-controlled inner bezel with 0-60 scale (upward counting); sapphire crystal, water-resistant to 20 atm
Band: silicone, folding clasp
Remarks: developed for medevac services; with pulse rotor scale; dehumidifying technology (protective gas)
Price: $3,930

STOWA

Stowa GmbH & Co. KG
Gewerbepark 16
D-75331 Engelsbrand
Germany

Tel.:
+49-7082-942630

E-mail:
info@stowa.com

Website:
www.stowa.com

Founded:
1927

Number of employees:
20

Annual production:
around 4,500 watches

Distribution:
Direct sales; please contact company in Germany; orders taken by phone Monday through Friday 9 a.m. to 5 p.m. European time. Note: Prices are determined according to daily exchange rate.

When a watch brand organizes a museum for itself, it is usually with good reason. The firm Stowa may not be the biggest fish in the horological pond, but it has been around for more than eighty years, and its products are well worth taking a look at as expressions of German watchmaking culture. Stowa began in Pforzheim, then moved to the little industrial town of Rheinfelden, and now operates in Engelsbrand, a "suburb" of Pforzheim.

Stowa is one of the few German brands to have operated without interruption since the start of the twentieth century, albeit with a new owner as of 1990. Besides all the political upheavals, it survived the quartz crisis of the 1970s, during which Europe was flooded with cheap watches from Asia and many traditional German watchmakers were put out of business. Founder Walter Storz managed to keep Stowa going, but even a quality fanatic has to pay a price during times of trouble: with huge input from his son, Werner, Storz restructured the company so that it was able to begin encasing reasonably priced quartz movements rather than being strictly an assembler of mechanical ones.

Another watchmaker, Jörg Schauer, took over the brand in 1996. Spurred on by the success of his own brand, he focused on mechanics from the very beginning. Collaboration with designer Hartmut Esslinger, the founder of Frog Design, resulted in a modern design language that is expressed above all in the Flieger collection. After 25 years, Schauer sold the Stowa watch brand to the Tempus Arte Group, which includes Lang & Heyne Dresden and the affiliated Uhren Werke Dresden (UWD) and Leinfelder Uhren in Munich. The group also holds a stake in customization specialist Blaken.

Flieger Verus 40

Reference number: FliegerVerus40
Movement: automatic, ETA Caliber 2824-2; ø 25.6 mm, height 4.6 mm; 25 jewels; 28,800 vph; 38-hour power reserve
Functions: hours, minutes, sweep seconds; date
Case: stainless steel, ø 40 mm, height 10.2 mm; sapphire crystal; water-resistant to 5 atm
Band: calfskin, buckle
Price: $840
Variations: with top-rated movement ($990)

Flieger Klassik 40

Reference number: FliegerKlassik40
Movement: automatic, ETA Caliber 2824-2; ø 25.6 mm, height 4.6 mm; 25 jewels; 28,800 vph; 38-hour power reserve
Functions: hours, minutes, sweep seconds
Case: stainless steel, ø 40 mm, height 10.2 mm; sapphire crystal; transparent case back; water-resistant to 5 atm
Band: calfskin, buckle
Price: $1,250
Variations: with manually wound movement ($1,270)

Flieger Bronze Vintage

Reference number: FliegerBronzeVintage
Movement: manually wound, ETA Caliber 2804-2; ø 25.6 mm, height 3.35 mm; 17 jewels; 28,800 vph; 42-hour power reserve
Functions: hours, minutes, sweep seconds
Case: bronze, ø 40 mm, height 9.2 mm; sapphire crystal; water-resistant to 5 atm
Band: calfskin, buckle
Price: $1,450

Marine Klassik 40 Roman White

Reference number: MarineKlassik40Römisch
Movement: automatic, ETA Caliber 2824-2; ø 25.6 mm, height 4.6 mm; 25 jewels; 28,800 vph; 40-hour power reserve
Functions: hours, minutes, sweep seconds
Case: stainless steel, ø 40 mm, height 10.2 mm; sapphire crystal; water-resistant to 5 atm
Band: calfskin, buckle
Price: $840
Variations: with top-rated movement ($1,010); with manually wound movement ($1,020)

Marine Original

Reference number: MarineOriginalpolweissarabisch
Movement: manually wound, ETA Caliber 6498-1; ø 36.6 mm, height 4.5 mm; 17 jewels; 18,000 vph; screw balance, swan-neck fine adjustment, côtes de Genève, blued screws; 46-hour power reserve
Functions: hours, minutes, subsidiary seconds
Case: stainless steel, ø 41 mm, height 12 mm; sapphire crystal; transparent case back; water-resistant to 5 atm
Band: calfskin, buckle
Price: $1,505
Variations: silver dial ($1,669)

Antea 390 with Date "Back to Bauhaus"

Reference number: Antea390b2bdatumweiss
Movement: automatic, ETA Caliber 2824-2; ø 25.6 mm, height 4.6 mm; 25 jewels; 28,800 vph; blued screws, handmade rotor; 40-hour power reserve
Functions: hours, minutes, sweep seconds; date
Case: stainless steel, ø 39 mm, height 9.2 mm; sapphire crystal; transparent case back; water-resistant to 5 atm
Band: calfskin, buckle
Price: $1,069

Chronograph 1938 Black

Reference number: chronograph1938schwarz
Movement: automatic, ETA Caliber 7753; ø 30 mm, height 7.9 mm; 27 jewels; 28,800 vph; 48-hour power reserve
Functions: hours, minutes, subsidiary seconds; chronograph
Case: stainless steel, ø 41 mm, height 13.7 mm; sapphire crystal; transparent case back; water-resistant to 5 atm
Band: calfskin, buckle
Price: $2,171
Variations: manually wound movement ($2,498)

Partitio Black Red Second

Reference number: PartitioschwarzroteSek
Movement: manually wound, ETA Caliber 2804-2; ø 25.6 mm. height 3.35 mm; 17 jewels; 28,800 vph; 42-hour power reserve
Functions: hours, minutes, sweep seconds
Case: stainless steel, ø 37 mm, height 9.8 mm; sapphire crystal; transparent case back; water-resistant to 5 atm
Band: calfskin, buckle
Price: $1,075
Variations: with white dial; with automatic movement ($910)

Prodiver Mauritius Limited

Reference number: Prodiverblackgreenkeramik
Movement: automatic, ETA Caliber 2824-2; ø 25.6 mm, height 4.6 mm; 25 jewels; 28,800 vph; 38-hour power reserve
Functions: hours, minutes, sweep seconds; date
Case: titanium, ø 42 mm, height 15.6 mm; unidirectional bezel with ceramic insert with 0-60 scale; sapphire crystal; screw-in crown; water-resistant to 100 atm
Band: rubber, folding clasp, with safety
Price: $1,800

TAG HEUER

TAG Heuer
Branch of LVMH SA
6a, rue L.-J.-Chevrolet
CH-2300 La Chaux-de-Fonds
Switzerland

Tel.:
+41-32-919-8164

E-mail:
info@tagheuer.com

Website:
www.tagheuer.com

Founded:
1860

Number of employees:
1,470 employees internationally

U.S. distributor:
TAG Heuer/LVMH Watch & Jewelry USA
966 South Springfield Avenue
Springfield, NJ 07081
973-467-1890

Most important collections/price range:
TAG Heuer Carrera, Monaco, Aquaracer, Formula 1, Link, Connected / from approx. $1,450 to $21,000

Measuring speed accurately in ever greater detail was always the goal of TAG Heuer, a company founded in 1860 in St. Imier, Switzerland, by Edouard Heuer. With this in mind, the brand strove for a number of technical milestones, including the first automatic chronograph caliber with a microrotor, created in 1969 with Hamilton-Büren, Breitling, and Dubois Dépraz. That was before Techniques d'Avant Garde (TAG), a high-tech firm, bought the company.

In 1999, TAG Heuer became part of LVMH Group and in addition to producing its own watches also, later, served as an extended workbench for companion brands Zenith and Hublot.

TAG Heuer has continued to break world speed records for mechanical escapements. For example, the Caliber 360 combined a standard movement with a 360,000-vph (50-Hz) chronograph mechanism able to measure hundredths of a second. And then there is the MikrotourbillonS, which features a separate chronograph escapement driven at a breakneck 360,000 vph.

TAG Heuer, now under CEO Frédéric Arnault, son of LVMH owner Bernard Arnault, is evolving along several lines. One is to re-release Heuer classics in more modern garb. The Heuer 02 manufacture caliber, for example, was a redeveloped chronograph movement, produced in a specially built, ultra-modern factory in Chevenez. In addition to cooperations with the sports car manufacturer Porsche and the unchanged strong commitment to Formula 1 (with Red Bull Racing), the relaunch of the successful diving watch line Aquaracer was on the agenda in 2021. The watch, with a distinctive dodecagonal rotating bezel, has been streamlined, becoming somewhat thinner and more colorful.

The company has also continued exploring contemporary technology, with a line of connected watches. By the same token, it has not abandoned its analog pursuits, like electromagnetic, hairspring-less pendulum watches, or new materials, like graphene. In April 2022, it presented its most expensive watch ever, the Carrera Plasma, featuring a dial covered in lab-grown diamonds.

Connected Calibre E4

Reference number: SBR8010.BT6255
Movement: quartz, Processor: ARM Cortex A53Smartwatch with Google's Wear operating system; 430mAh lithium-ion battery
Functions: hours, minutes, seconds (digital; Heart-rate sensors, compass, speed; Near-field communication (NFC), microphone; various installable micro-apps; date and weekday
Case: stainless steel, ø 42 mm; sapphire crystal; water-resistant to 5 atm
Band: rubber, folding clasp
Price: $ 1,800

Connected Calibre E4

Reference number: SBR8A10.BA0616
Movement: quartz, processor: ARM Cortex A53Smartwatch with Google's Wear operating system; 430mAh lithium ion battery
Functions: hours, minutes, seconds (digital; heart-rate sensors, compass, speed; near-field communication (NFC), microphone; various installable micro-apps; date
Case: stainless steel, ø 45 mm; bezel with ceramic insert; sapphire crystal; water-resistant to 5 atm
Band: stainless steel, folding clasp
Price: $ 2,250

Formula 1 Calibre 6

Reference number: WAZ2014.BA0842
Movement: automatic, TAG Heuer Caliber 6 (base Sellita SW260-1); ø 25.6 mm; height 4.35 mm; 27 jewels; 28,800 vph; 42-hour power reserve
Functions: hours, minutes, subsidiary seconds; date
Case: stainless steel, ø 43 mm, height 12 mm; unidirectional bezel with 60-minute scale; sapphire crystal; water-resistant to 20 atm
Band: stainless steel, folding clasp
Price: $ 2,050
Variations: with a white or black dial ($ 2,150)

TAG Heuer Aquaracer Calibre 5 Professional 200

Reference number: WBP2110.BA0627
Movement: automatic, TAG Heuer Caliber 5 (base ETA 2824-2); ø 26 mm, height 4.6 mm; 25 jewels; 28,800 vph
Functions: hours, minutes, sweep seconds; date
Case: Stainless steel, ø 40 mm; unidirectional bezel with 60-minute scale; sapphire crystal; screw-in crown; water-resistant to 20 atm
Band: stainless steel, folding clasp
Price: $2,850
Variations: various colors

Aquaracer Calibre 5 Professional 300 Orange Diver

Reference number: WBP201F.BA0632
Movement: automatic, TAG Heuer Caliber 5 (base ETA 2824-2); ø 26 mm, height 4.6 mm; 25 jewels; 28,800 vph
Functions: hours, minutes, sweep seconds; date
Case: stainless steel, ø 43 mm; unidirectional bezel with ceramic insert and 60-minute scale; sapphire crystal; screw-in crown; water-resistant to 30 atm
Band: stainless steel, folding clasp
Price: $3,400
Variations: various colors

Aquaracer Calibre 5 Professional 1000 Superdiver

Reference number: WBP5A8A.BF0619
Movement: automatic, TAG Heuer Caliber TH30-00 (base Kenissi); ø 26 mm, height 4.6 mm; 28 jewels; 28,800 vph; 38-hour power reserve; COSC-certified chronometer
Functions: hours, minutes, sweep seconds; date
Case: titanium, ø 45 mm, height 15.75 mm; unidirectional bezel with ceramic insert and 60-minute scale; sapphire crystal; screw-in crown, with crown guard; helium valve; water-resistant to 110 atm
Band: titanium, folding clasp
Price: $6,650

Link Calibre 5

Reference number: WBC2110.BA0603
Movement: automatic, TAG Heuer Caliber 5 (base ETA 2824-2); ø 26 mm, height 4.6 mm; 25 jewels; 28,800 vph; 38-hour power reserve
Functions: hours, minutes, sweep seconds; date
Case: stainless steel, ø 41 mm; sapphire crystal; water-resistant to 10 atm
Band: stainless steel, folding clasp
Price: $3,300
Variations: white dial

Carrera Calibre 7 Twin-Time

Reference number: WBN201A.BA0640
Movement: automatic, TAG Heuer Caliber 7 (base ETA 2893-2); ø 25.6 mm, height 4.1 mm; 21 jewels; 28,800 vph; 38-hour power reserve
Functions: hours, minutes, sweep seconds; additional 12-hour display (second time zone); date
Case: stainless steel, ø 41 mm; sapphire crystal; transparent case back; water-resistant to 10 atm
Band: stainless steel, folding clasp
Price: $3,650

Carrera Calibre 16

Reference number: CBM2110.BA0651
Movement: automatic, TAG Heuer Caliber 16 (base ETA 7750); ø 30.4 mm, height 7.9 mm; 25 jewels; 28,800 vph
Functions: hours, minutes, subsidiary seconds; chronograph; date
Case: stainless steel, ø 41 mm; ceramic bezel; sapphire crystal; screw-in crown; water-resistant to 10 atm
Band: stainless steel, folding clasp
Price: $4,700

Carrera Calibre Heuer 02

Reference number: CBN2011.BA0642
Movement: automatic, TAG Heuer Caliber Heuer 02; ø 31 mm, height 6.9 mm; 33 jewels; 28,800 vph; 80-hour power reserve
Functions: hours, minutes, subsidiary seconds; chronograph; date
Case: stainless steel, ø 42 mm; sapphire crystal; transparent case back; water-resistant to 10 atm
Band: stainless steel, folding clasp
Price: $5,750
Variations: various bands and dials

Carrera Calibre Heuer 02 Porsche Limited Edition

Reference number: CBN2A1H.FC6512
Movement: automatic, TAG Heuer Caliber Heuer 02; ø 31 mm, height 6.9 mm; 33 jewels; 28,800 vph; 80-hour power reserve
Functions: hours, minutes, subsidiary seconds; chronograph; date
Case: stainless steel with black DLC-coating, ø 44 mm; ceramic bezel; sapphire crystal; transparent case back; water-resistant to 10 atm
Band: rubber with leather overlay, folding clasp
Remarks: special edition in cooperation with the sports car manufacturer Porsche
Price: $7,050; limited to 1,500 pieces

Carrera Calibre Heuer 02T C.O.S.C.

Reference number: CAR5A8C.BF0707
Movement: automatic, TAG Heuer Caliber Heuer 02T COSC; ø 31 mm, height 6.9 mm; 33 jewels; 28,800 vph; 1-minute tourbillon; COSC-certified chronometer
Functions: hours, minutes, chronograph
Case: titanium, ø 45 mm; ceramic bezel; sapphire crystal; transparent case back; water-resistant to 10 atm
Band: titanium, folding clasp
Price: $23,150

Monaco Calibre 11

Reference number: CAW211P.FC6356
Movement: automatic, TAG Heuer Caliber 11 (base Sellita SW300 with Dubois Dépraz module 2006); ø 30 mm, height 7.3 mm; 59 jewels; 28,800 vph
Functions: hours, minutes, subsidiary seconds; chronograph; date
Case: stainless steel, 39 mm x 39 mm, height 14.5 mm; sapphire crystal; transparent case back; water-resistant to 10 atm
Band: calfskin, folding clasp
Price: $7,300

Autavia Calibre 7 GMT C.O.S.C.

Reference number: WBE511A.BA0650
Movement: automatic, TAG Heuer Caliber 7 (base ETA 2893-2); ø 25.6 mm, height 4.1 mm; 21 jewels; 28,800 vph; 38-hour power reserve; COSC-certified chronometer
Functions: hours, minutes, sweep seconds; additional 24-hour display (second time zone); date
Case: stainless steel, ø 42 mm; ceramic bezel, bidirectional bezel with 24-minute scale; sapphire crystal, water-resistant to 10 atm
Band: stainless steel, folding clasp
Price: $4,350

Autavia Calibre Heuer 02 Flyback COSC

Reference number: CBE511B.FC8279
Movement: automatic, TAG Heuer Caliber Heuer 02; ø 31 mm, height 6.9 mm; 33 jewels; 28,800 vph; 80-hour power reserve; COSC-certified chronometer
Functions: hours, minutes, subsidiary seconds; flyback chronograph; date
Case: stainless steel, ø 42 mm; ceramic bezel; sapphire crystal; transparent case back; screw-in crown and pushers; water-resistant to 10 atm
Band: reptile skin, folding clasp
Price: $6,750

Temption GmbH
Raistinger Str. 46
D-71083 Herrenberg
Germany

Tel.:
+49-7032-977-954

E-mail:
ftemption@aol.com

Website:
www.temption.info

Founded:
1997

Number of employees:
4

Annual production:
700 watches

U.S. distributor:
Debby Gordon
3306 Arrow Creek Dr.
Granbury, TX 76049
debby@temptionusa.com
Toll-free number: 1-888-400-4293

Most important collections/price range:
automatics (three-hand), GMT, chronographs, and chronographs with complications / approx. $1,900 to $4,200

TEMPTION

Temption has been operating under the leadership of Klaus Ulbrich since 1997. Ulbrich is an engineer with special training in the construction of watches and movements, and right from the start, he intended to develop timekeepers that were modern in their aesthetics but not subject to the whims of zeitgeist. Retro watches would have no place in his collections. The design behind all Temption models is inspired by two contrasting stylistic movements: the modernist design codes of the Irish architect Eileen Gray (1878-1976) and the fascinating Japanese concept of wabi-sabi, the aesthetics of passing time and its impact on the world we create.

Ulbrich sketches all the watches himself. The components are purchased from various sources, though some are made in-house. Assembly is done in the company facility in Herrenberg, a town just to the east of the Black Forest. The primary functions are always easy to read, even in low light. The company logo is discreetly included on the dial.

Ulbrich works according to a model he calls the "information pyramid." Hours and minutes are at the tip, with all other functions subordinated. To maintain this hierarchy and the calm aesthetics, the date windows are in the same hue as the dials, and the subdials are not framed in any way. The most unimportant information for reading time comes at the end of the "pyramid"; it is the logo, which appears as a shiny image on the dial and can only be identified in lateral light.

The Temption chronographs are perfect expressions of this vision of simplicity even with a naturally complex dial. With the CGK205, Ulbrich took the concept out of the case. Whether it be the leather strap or the stainless-steel bracelet, the watch's attachment is seamlessly integrated into the case, without any visible split. Of late, though, some models have also been given touches of color, notably red coral cabochons in the crown and pushers.

Formula

Reference number: FOR316LSST
Movement: automatic, Caliber T17.1 (base ETA 7750); ø 30 mm, height 7.8 mm; 25 jewels; 28,800 vph; finely finished movement; 42-hour power reserve
Functions: hours, minutes, subsidiary seconds; chronograph; date and weekday
Case: stainless steel, ø 43 mm, height 14.8 mm; sapphire crystal; transparent case back; screw-in crown and pushers, with coral cabochons; water-resistant to 10 atm
Band: calfskin, folding clasp
Price: $2,500
Variations: with rubber strap

Chronograph CGK204-White

Reference number: 204V2316BSST
Movement: automatic, Temption Caliber T18.1 (base ETA 7751); ø 30 mm, height 7.8 mm; 25 jewels; 28,800 vph; finely finished movement; 42-hour power reserve
Functions: hours, minutes, subsidiary seconds; additional 24-hour display (second time zone); chronograph; full calendar with date, weekday, month, moon phase
Case: stainless steel, ø 43 mm, height 14 mm; sapphire crystal; transparent case back; screw-in crown and pushers, with coral cabochons; water-resistant to 10 atm
Band: calfskin, folding clasp
Price: $2,700
Variations: with rubber strap

Chronograph CGK205-Blue V2

Reference number: 205V2316BSST
Movement: automatic, Temption Caliber T18.1 (base ETA 7751); ø 30 mm, height 7.8 mm; 25 jewels; 28,800 vph; finely finished movement; 42-hour power reserve
Functions: hours, minutes, subsidiary seconds; additional 24-hour power reserve display; chronograph; full calendar with date, weekday, month, moon phase
Case: stainless steel, ø 43 mm, height 14 mm; sapphire crystal; transparent case back; screw-in crown and pushers, with colored cabochons; water-resistant to 10 atm
Band: calfskin, folding clasp
Remarks: comes with additional stainless steel link bracelet
Price: $3,000

TISSOT

The Swiss watchmaker Tissot was founded in 1853 in the town of Le Locle in the Jura mountains. In the century that followed, it gained international recognition for its Savonnette pocket watch. And even when the wristwatch became popular in the early twentieth century, time and again Tissot managed to attract attention to its products. To this day, the Banana Watch of 1916 and its first watches in the art deco style (1919) remain design icons of that epoch. The watchmaker has always been at the top of its technical game as well: the first amagnetic watch (1930), the first mechanical plastic watch (Astrolon, 1971), and its touch-screen T-Touch (1999) all bear witness to Tissot's remarkable capacity for finding unusual and modern solutions.

Today, Tissot belongs to the Swatch Group and, with its wide selection of quartz and inexpensive mechanical watches, serves as the group's entry-level brand. Within this price segment, Tissot offers something special for the buyer who values traditional watchmaking but is not of limitless financial means. The brand has been cultivating a sportive image of late, expanding into everything from basketball to superbike racing, from ice hockey to fencing—and water sports, of course. Partnerships with several NBA teams have been signed, notably with the Houston Rockets, Chicago Bulls, and Washington Wizards in October 2018. The chronograph Couturier line is outfitted with the new ETA chronograph caliber C01.211. This caliber features a number of plastic parts: another step in simplifying, and lowering the cost of, mechanical movements.

Increasingly, in addition, a number of Tissot models are being equipped with the automatic caliber Powermatic 80, which boasts a silicon hairspring, which has outstanding isochronous oscillation and is impervious to magnetic fields and changes in temperature. And for the buyer, it means only a slight increase in price.

Tissot SA
Chemin des Tourelles, 17
CH-2400 Le Locle
Switzerland

Tel.:
+41-32-933-3111

E-mail:
info@tissot.ch

Website:
www.tissotwatches.com

Founded:
1853

U.S. distributor:
Tissot
The Swatch Group (U.S.), Inc.
703 Waterford Way, Suite 450
Miami, FL 33126
www.us.tissotshop.com

Most important collections/price range:
Ballade / from $925; T-Touch / from $850; NBA Collection / from $375; Chemin des Tourelles / from $795; Seastar from $495; Swissmatic from $395

PRX Powermatic 80

Reference number: T931.407.41.041.00
Movement: automatic, ETA Caliber Powermatic 80 (base ETA 2824-2); ø 25.6 mm, height 4.74 mm; 23 jewels; 21,600 vph; 80-hour power reserve
Functions: hours, minutes, sweep seconds; date
Case: stainless steel, ø 40 mm, height 10.93 mm; rose-gold bezel; sapphire crystal; transparent case back; water-resistant to 10 atm
Band: stainless steel, folding clasp
Price: $1,850

PRX Powermatic 80

Reference number: T137.407.11.091.00
Movement: automatic, ETA Caliber Powermatic 80 (base ETA 2824-2); ø 25.6 mm, height 4.74 mm; 23 jewels; 21,600 vph; 80-hour power reserve
Functions: hours, minutes, sweep seconds; date
Case: stainless steel, ø 40 mm, height 10.93 mm; sapphire crystal; transparent case back; water-resistant to 10 atm
Band: stainless steel, folding clasp
Price: $650

PRX Powermatic 80

Reference number: T137.407.16.041.00
Movement: automatic, ETA Caliber Powermatic 80 (base ETA 2824-2); ø 25.6 mm, height 4.74 mm; 23 jewels; 21,600 vph; 80-hour power reserve
Functions: hours, minutes, sweep seconds; date
Case: stainless steel, ø 40 mm, height 10.93 mm; sapphire crystal; transparent case back; water-resistant to 10 atm
Band: calfskin, folding clasp
Price: $625

Seastar 2000 Professional Powermatic 80

Reference number: T120.607.37.041.00
Movement: automatic, ETA Caliber Powermatic 80 (base ETA 2824-2); ø 25.6 mm, height 4.74 mm; 23 jewels; 21,600 vph; 80-hour power reserve
Functions: hours, minutes, sweep seconds; date
Case: stainless steel with black PVD coating, ø 46 mm, height 16.25 mm; unidirectional rotating bezel with ceramic inlay and 60-minute divisions; sapphire crystal; transparent case back; screw-in crown, helium valve; water-resistant to 60 atm
Band: rubber with textile overlay, buckle
Price: $1,075

PRX Automatic Chronograph

Reference number: T137.427.11.041.00
Movement: automatic, ETA Caliber A05.H31; ø 30 mm, height 7.9 mm; 27 jewels; 28,800 vph; 60-hour power reserve
Functions: hours, minutes, subsidiary seconds; chronograph; date
Case: stainless steel, ø 42 mm, height 14.54 mm; sapphire crystal; transparent case back; water-resistant to 10 atm
Band: stainless steel, double folding clasp
Price: $1,750

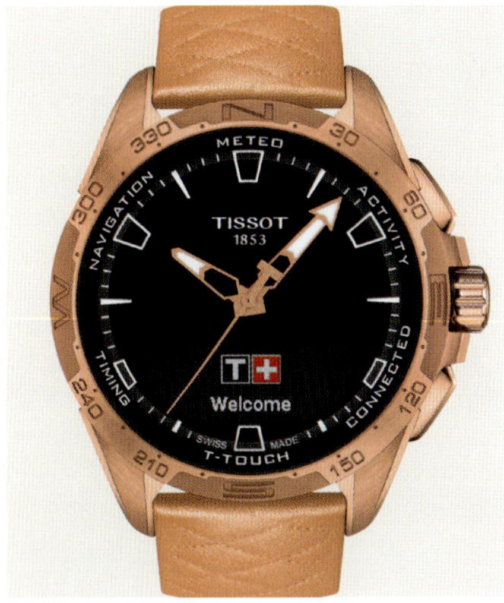

T-Touch Connect Solar

Reference number: T121.420.46.051.00
Movement: quartz, multifunctional movement with LCD-Display and power from a solar cell in the dial
Functions: hours, minutes; additional 12/24-hour power reserve display (second time zone), smartwatch functions (displays incoming calls and messages, activity tracker, barometer, altimeter, compass; chronograph with countdown function; perpetual calendar with date, weekday, calendar week
Case: titanium with rose-gold PVD, ø 47 mm, height 15.3 mm; sapphire crystal; water-resistant to 10 atm
Band: calf leather, folding clasp
Remarks: analog and digital display (hybrid); display and function control over the touch sapphire crystal
Price: $1,150

Seastar 2000 Professional Powermatic 80

Reference number: T120.607.17.441.01
Movement: automatic, ETA Caliber Powermatic 80 (base ETA 2824-2); ø 25.6 mm, height 4.74 mm; 23 jewels; 21,600 vph; 80-hour power reserve
Functions: hours, minutes, sweep seconds; date
Case: stainless steel, ø 46 mm, height 16.25 mm; unidirectional bezel with ceramic inlay, 0-60 scale; sapphire crystal; transparent case back; screw-in crown, helium valve; water-resistant to 60 atm
Band: rubber with textile overlay, buckle
Price: $995

PRX automatic Chronograph

Reference number: T137.427.11.011.00
Movement: automatic, ETA Caliber A05.H31; ø 30 mm, height 7.9 mm; 27 jewels; 28,800 vph; 60-hour power reserve
Functions: hours, minutes, subsidiary seconds; chronograph; date
Case: stainless steel, ø 42 mm, height 14.54 mm; sapphire crystal; transparent case back; water-resistant to 10 atm
Band: stainless steel, double folding clasp
Price: $1,750

T-Touch Connect Solar

Reference number: T121.420.47.051.06
Movement: quartz, multifunctional movement with LCD-Display and power from a solar cell in the dial
Functions: hours, minutes; additional 12/24-hour power reserve display (second time zone), smartwatch functions (displays incoming calls and messages, activity tracker, barometer, altimeter, compass; chronograph with countdown function; perpetual calendar with date, weekday, calendar week
Case: titanium, ø 47 mm, height 15.3 mm; sapphire crystal; water-resistant to 10 atm
Band: textile, folding clasp
Remarks: analog and digital display (hybrid); display and function control over the touch sapphire crystal
Price: $1,025

TOURBY WATCHES

In an industry and a world that tries hard to attract attention at times by fairly spectacular means, Tourby Watches is slowly but surely gathering a following and fan club by keeping it simple and elegant. The company, which is headquartered in the town of Wetter in Westphalia, Germany, manufactures mechanical wristwatches whose design is inspired by classic models. This little brand has already quite a following in the U.S., notably. A pilot's watch was made especially for the dangerous deployments of the Strike Fighters Weapons School Pacific, a U.S. Navy training school for fighter pilots.

The story began when Erdal Yildiz inherited a pocket watch from his grandfather. The Unitas movement inside was in need of serious revision. So, he looked around for a proper watchmaker and was soon enamored with the craft itself. The world of mechanical watches became a genuine passion during his studies. He then contacted a number of suppliers in Germany and Switzerland, and in 2007 founded his own brand. The name Tourby has nothing to do with tourbillons, which his company does not manufacture. Rather, it is his nickname; it is short and memorable, and the domain name was still available!

All raw materials are purchased from top-notch suppliers in Germany and Switzerland. Some of the parts are ready to use on delivery; others need to be reworked in the company's own workshops in the cities of Bochum and Hagen. The cases are finished by hand, for example, as are the movements—all Swiss ETA calibers—which are extensively decorated, and the dials, in part at least. The leather straps are stitched by hand. Final assembly, quality control, and after-sales service are all done by the company.

Tourby Watches produces series but also does made-to-order pieces. The customer can choose his or her case, dial, hands, strap, and even the movement with its decoration. Another option is skeletonization. It's a good way to get hold of a unique piece.

Tourby Watches
Königstrasse 78
D-58300 Wetter an der Ruhr
Hagen in Westfalen
Germany

Tel:
+49-176-8311-83-82

E-mail:
info@tourbywatches.com

Website:
www.tourbywatches.com

Founded:
2007

Number of employees:
5

Annual production:
500

Distribution:
Tourby deals directly with customers

Most important collections/price range:
Lawless Diver / from $1,400; Art Deco Classic / from $1,800; Ottoman / from $1,575; Planetarium / $9,000; special set

Art Deco Salmon Dial 40

Reference number: 2043
Movement: manually wound, ETA Caliber 6498-2; ø 37 mm, height 4.5 mm; 17 jewels; 21,600 vph; skeletonized movement with circular côtes de Genève; double sunburst wheels; blued screws; blued swan-neck fine adjustment; 60-hour power reserve
Functions: hours, minutes, subsidiary seconds
Case: stainless steel, 40.5 mm, height 10.6 mm; arched sapphire crystal; transparent case back; water-resistant to 5 atm
Band: reptile skin, buckle
Remarks: sterling silver dial
Price: $2,950
Variations: comes in different case diameters (40, 43 and 45 mm)

Planetarium 40

Reference number: 7000
Movement: manually wound, ETA Caliber 6498-2; ø 37 mm, height 4.5 mm; 17 jewels; 21,600 vph; skeletonized movement with circular côtes de Genève; double sunburst wheels; blued screws; 60-hour power reserve
Functions: hours, minutes
Case: stainless steel, 40.5 mm, height 10.6 mm; arched sapphire crystal; transparent case back; water-resistant to 5 atm
Band: reptile skin, buckle
Remarks: hand engraved and skeletonized silver dial
Price: $8,500
Variations: comes in different case diameters (40 and 43 mm)

Around The World America

Reference number: 7002
Movement: manually wound, ETA Caliber 6498-2; ø 37 mm, height 4.5 mm; 17 jewels; 21,600 vph; skeletonized movement with circular côtes de Genève; double sunburst wheels; blued screws; 60-hour power reserve
Functions: hours, minutes, subsidiary seconds
Case: stainless steel, 40.5 mm, height 10.6 mm; arched sapphire crystal; transparent case back; water-resistant to 5 atm
Band: reptile skin, buckle
Remarks: hand-painted dial
Price: $11,000

Lawless Skeleton 40

Reference number: 6240
Movement: automatic, ETA Caliber 2824-2; ø 25.6 mm, height 4.6 mm; 25 jewels; 28,800 vph; skeletonized movement; chronometer; 40-hour power reserve
Functions: hours, minutes, center seconds
Case: stainless steel, 40 mm, height 11.8 mm; sapphire crystal; transparent case back; water-resistant to 20 atm
Band: stainless steel, buckle
Remarks: sapphire bezel inlay
Price: $3,000

Aventurine 40

Reference number: 8000
Movement: manually wound, ETA Caliber 6498-2; ø 37 mm, height 4.5 mm; 17 jewels; 21,600 vph; skeletonized movement with circular côtes de Genève; double sunburst wheels; blued screws; 60-hour power reserve
Functions: hours, minutes, subsidiary seconds
Case: stainless steel, 40.5 mm, height 10.6 mm; arched sapphire crystal; transparent case back; water-resistant to 5 atm
Band: reptile skin, buckle
Remarks: aventurine gemstone dial
Price: $4,000
Variations: comes in different case diameters (37, 40 and 43 mm)

Lapis 43

Reference number: 8010
Movement: manually wound, ETA Caliber 6498-2; ø 37 mm, height 4.5 mm; 17 jewels; 21,600 vph; skeletonized movement with circular côtes de Genève; double sunburst wheels; blued screws; 60-hour power reserve
Functions: hours, minutes, subsidiary seconds
Case: stainless steel, 43 mm, height 10.4 mm; arched sapphire crystal; transparent case back; water-resistant to 5 atm
Band: reptile skin, buckle
Remarks: lapis dial
Price: $4,000
Variations: comes in different case diameters (37, 40 and 43 mm)

Turquoise 40

Reference number: 8020
Movement: manually wound, ETA Caliber 6498-2; ø 37 mm, height 4.5 mm; 17 jewels; 21,600 vph; skeletonized movement with côtes de Genève; double sunburst wheels; blued screws; 60-hour power reserve
Functions: hours, minutes, subsidiary seconds
Case: stainless steel, 40.5 mm, height 10.6 mm; arched sapphire crystal; transparent case back; water-resistant to 5 atm
Band: reptile skin, buckle
Remarks: turquoise dial
Price: $4,000
Variations: comes in different case diameters (37, 40 and 43 mm)

Old Military Vintage 45

Reference number: 1404
Movement: manually wound, ETA Caliber 6498-2; ø 37 mm, height 4.5 mm; 17 jewels; 21,600 vph; skeletonized movement with circular côtes de Genève; double sunburst wheels; blued screws; blued swan-neck fine adjustment; 60-hour power reserve
Functions: hours, minutes, subsidiary seconds
Case: stainless steel, 45 mm, height 13.35 mm; arched sapphire crystal; transparent case back; water-resistant to 5 atm
Band: leather, buckle
Price: $2,750
Variations: blue or enamel dial; comes in different case diameters (40, 43 or 45 mm)

Ottoman Enamel 40

Reference number: 2091
Movement: manually wound, ETA Caliber 6498-2; ø 37 mm, height 4.5 mm; 17 jewels; 21,600 vph; skeletonized movement with circular côtes de Genève; double sunburst wheels; blued screws; blued swan-neck fine adjustment; 60-hour power reserve
Functions: hours, minutes, subsidiary seconds
Case: stainless steel, 40.5 mm, height 10.6 mm; arched sapphire crystal; transparent case back; water-resistant to 5 atm
Band: leather, buckle
Price: $2,225
Remarks: old Ottoman numerals
Variations: comes in different case diameters (40, 43 and 45 mm)

TOWSON WATCH COMPANY

Spencer Shattuck was thirteen when he wrote an eighth-grade thesis on watchmaking. His key source was a week of hanging out with George Thomas and Hartwig Balke, two passionate and highly experienced watchmakers. While close to retirement, the two men founded Towson Watch Company in Baltimore, Maryland.

The two men had stories to tell. Thomas's first tourbillon pocket watches are displayed at the National Watch and Clock Museum in Columbia, Pennsylvania. In 1999, Balke made his first wrist chronograph, the STS-99 Mission, for a NASA astronaut and mission specialist. The two also restored one of the world's oldest watches, one belonging to Philip Melanchton. In 2009, Thomas was invited to open up a pocket watch belonging to President Lincoln, and revealed a secret message engraved by a servicing watchmaker and Union supporter working in Maryland: "Jonathan Dillon April 13- 1861 Fort Sumpter was attacked by the rebels on the above date. J Dillon."

Towson watches pay tribute to local sites in and around Baltimore, like the Choptank and Potomac rivers. The timepieces are imaginative, with a retro feel—not to mention affordable. The collection includes a number of chronographs and watches with moon phases. And the brand has also ventured into tonneau cases and one oddity, the Pride II, which pays tribute to Baltimore's own schooner. The case is shaped like the company logo and the crown is a miniature winch.

Their local commitment was also shared by entrepreneur and former University of Maryland football captain Kevin Plank, founder of the sports apparel company Under Armour, who purchased a 25 percent stake in Towson in 2016. In 2020, he sold it to a friend, Spencer Shattuck, who was in his last year at Johns Hopkins University. Shattuck is a watch fan who aims to refresh the brand, without losing any of its charm, and to make it better known to a broader public.

Towson Watch Company
101 W. Dickman St.
Baltimore, MD 21230

Tel.:
410-733-2991

Fax:
410-823-8581

E-Mail:
towsonwatchco@aol.com

Website:
www.twcwatches.com

Founded:
2000

Number of employees:
5

Annual production:
200 watches

Distribution:
retail

Most important collections/price range:
Skipjack GMT / approx. $2,950; Mission / approx. $2,500; Potomac / approx. $2,000; Choptank / approx. $4,500; Martin / approx. $3,950 / custom design / $10,000 to $35,000

Potomac S2

Reference number: P100-S2
Movement: manually wound, ETA/Unitas Caliber 6498; ø 36.6 mm; height 4.5 mm; 17 jewels; 18,000 vph; 46-hour power reserve
Functions: hours; minute; subsidiary second
Case: stainless steel; ø 42 mm; height 12.5 mm; domed sapphire crystal; screwed transparent case back; water-resistant to 5 atm
Band: calf leather, buckle
Price: $2,600
Variations: black dial with gold numerals and black calfskin leather band; with stainless steel mesh bracelet ($2,850)

Skipjack B2

Reference number: SKJ100-B2
Movement: automatic Caliber ETA 2893-2 Ø 25.6 mm; height 4.1mm; 21 jewels; 28,800 vph; fine finish with côtes de Genève
Functions: hour; minute sweep second; date; 24-hour adjustable hand
Case: stainless steel with cannelage; ø 41.5 mm; sapphire crystal; screwed transparent back with sapphire crystal; water-resistant to 5 atm
Band: calf leather, folding clasp.
Price: $2,500; limited to 100 pieces

Choptank C1

Reference number: E250-C1
Movement: automatic, ETA Caliber 7751 Valjoux; ø 30 mm; height 7.9 mm; 25 jewels; 28,800 vph; fine finishing with côtes de Genève
Functions: hours; minute; subsidiary second; weekday; month; date; moon phase; 24-h display; chronograph
Case: stainless steel; dimension 40 mm x 44 mm; height 13.5 mm; sapphire crystal at front; transparent screwed-down case back; water resistant to 5 atm
Band: reptile skin with folding clasp
Price: $4,750; limited to 100 pieces
Variations: mesh stainless steel bracelet ($8,850)

Mission Moon SB2

Reference number: MM250-SB2
Movement: automatic ETA Caliber 7750; ø 30 mm, height 7.6 mm; 25 jewels; 28,800 vph; fine finishing with côtes de Genève; 54-hour power reserve
Functions: hours, minutes, subsidiary seconds; chronograph; weekday, month, date; moon phase; 24-hour display
Case: stainless steel, 42 mm, height XX mm, sapphire crystal, screwed down back with engraving, water resistant to 5 atm
Band: calf leather, orange stitching, folding clasp.
Price: $3,950; limited to 100 pieces

Cockpit Chronograph

Reference number: C250-B
Movement: automatic, Caliber 7750 Valjoux; ø 30 mm, height 7.9 mm; 21 jewels; 28,800 vph; fine finish with côtes de Genève
Functions: hours, minutes, subsidiary seconds; chronograph; date
Case: stainless steel, ø 38 mm, height 13.5 mm; sapphire crystal; transparent screwed-down back; water-resistant to 5 atm
Band: reptile skin, folding clasp
Price: $2,970
Variations: black dial; reptile skin; stainless steel bracelet ($2,595)

Classic Chronograph

Movement: automatic, Caliber 7750 Valjoux; ø 30 mm, height 7.9 mm; 21 jewels; 28,800 vph; fine finish with côtes de Genève
Functions: hours, minutes, subsidiary seconds; chronograph; date
Case: stainless steel, ø 41 mm, height 14 mm; sapphire crystal; transparent screwed-down back; water-resistant to 5 atm
Remarks: solid silver hand-guillochéed dial
Band: reptile skin, folding clasp
Price: $6,900

Martin M-130

Reference number: CC100
Movement: automatic, ETA Caliber 7750 Valjoux, ø 30 mm; height 7.9 mm; 25 jewels; 28,800 vph; fine finishing with côtes de Genève; 48-hour power reserve
Functions: hours, minutes, subsidiary second, chronograph, date
Case: stainless steel, ø 42 mm, height 13.5 mm, sapphire crystal, screwed-down case back, water resistant to 5 atm
Band: leather, folding clasp
Remarks: case back with engraving of famous China Clipper flying boat from the 1930s built by the Glenn B. Miller company
Price: $4,200
Variations: mesh stainless steel bracelet ($4,250)

North.er

Reference number: NP250
Movement: automatic, ETA Caliber 2893-2; ø 25.6 mm, height 4.1 mm; 24 jewels; 28,800 vph; 48-hour power reserve
Functions: hours, minutes, sweep seconds; date; 2nd time zone hand
Case: stainless steel, 42 mm, height 13.5 mm; sapphire crystal, transparent case back, water-resistant to 5 atm
Band: calfskin, folding clasp
Price: $3,400

Pride II

Reference number: PR250-S
Movement: automatic, Caliber ETA 2892-A2; ø 25.6 mm, height 3.6 mm; 21 jewels; 28,800 vph; fine finish with côtes de Genève; 46-hour power reserve
Functions: hours, minutes, sweep seconds; date
Case: stainless steel shield shape, 39 mm × 44 mm; sapphire crystal; screwed-down back with engraving of Pride of Baltimore II schooner; water-resistant to 5 atm
Band: calf leather, folding clasp
Price: $4,100
Variations: black dial with rhodium-plated numerals

TUDOR

Montres Tudor SA
Rue François-Dussaud 3-5-7
1211 Geneva 26
Switzerland

Tel.:
+41-22-302-2200

Website:
www.tudorwatch.com

Founded:
1946

U.S. distributor:
Tudor Watch U.S.A., LLC
665 Fifth Avenue
New York, NY 10022
212-897-9900
www.tudorwatch.com

Most important collections/price range:
Black Bay / $2,475 to $6,800; Heritage / $2,675 to $6,175; Pelagos / $4,450; 1926 / $1,725 to $3,475

The Tudor brand came out of the shadow cast by its "big sister" Rolex in 2007 and worked hard to develop its own personality. The strategy focuses on distinctive models that draw inspiration from the brand's rich past but remain in the "affordable quality watch segment."

Rolex founder Hans Wilsdorf started Tudor in 1946 as a second brand to offer the legendary reliability of his watches at a more affordable price. To this day, Tudor still benefits from the same industrial platform as Rolex, especially in cases and bracelets, assembly, and quality assurance, not to mention distribution and after-sales. However, the movements themselves are usually delivered by ETA and "Tudorized" according to the company's own aesthetic and technical criteria.

The 1950s look being more popular today than ever, the company had an easy time registering with consumers with the Heritage Black Bay line about five years ago. The first edition of the model with a wine-red bezel was followed by numerous variants with and without a rotating bezel, and with a GMT function. The latter was the second new development by the Rolex sister brand after the three-hand manufacture calibers. In the summer of 2021, Tudor finally presented a brand-new surprise: the Black Bay Ceramic is the first model to feature a ceramic case and a completely magnetic field-resistant movement. As a result, the Black Bay Ceramic even passes the stringent Swiss METAS magnetism test, making Tudor the second brand (after Omega) with a Master Chronometer certificate.

As for movements, the MT-5621 made its debut in the simple North Flag and as the MT-5612 in the Pelagos models. The M5601/5602 calibers, with three hands and a date, were followed by an attractive automatic chronograph using Breitling's B01 Caliber. The Tudor calibers are produced by the movement manufacturer Kenissi, a joint venture with Breitling, among others. The movement of the automatic chronograph, which is basically a Breitling caliber B01, is also "shared" with this brand.

After launching various Black Bay models made of unusual case materials, Tudor invested in the development of the Pelagos special FXD model for professional use with integrated strap bars. Price-conscious Tudor fans will be delighted with the Ranger, which was presented in 2022, a basic three-hander but done with great attention to details.

Black Bay Pro

Reference number: 79470
Movement: automatic, Tudor Caliber MT5652, ø 31.8 mm, height 7.52 mm; 28 jewels; 28,800 vph; silicon hairspring; 70-hour power reserve; COSC-certified chronometer
Functions: hours (crown-switched in steps), minutes, sweep seconds; additional 24-hour display (second time zone); date
Case: stainless steel, ø 39 mm; with 24-hour divisions; sapphire crystal; screw-in crown; water-resistant to 20 atm
Band: stainless steel, folding clasp with safety lock
Price: $4,000
Variations: with calfskin/rubber or textile strap ($3,675)

Black Bay Ceramic

Reference number: 79210CNU
Movement: automatic, Tudor Caliber MT5602-1U; ø 31.8 mm, height 6.5 mm; 25 jewels; 28,800 vph; silicon hairspring, antimagnetic geartrain components; blackened movement; Master Chronometer certification (METAS); 70-hour power reserve; COSC-certified chronometer
Functions: hours, minutes, sweep seconds
Case: ceramic, ø 41 mm; unidirectional bezel in stainless steel with black PVD and 0-60 scale; sapphire crystal; transparent case back; screw-in crown; water-resistant to 20 atm
Band: textile, buckle
Remarks: comes with additional calfskin strap with rubber overlay
Price: $4,825

Black Bay P01

Reference number: 70150
Movement: automatic, Tudor Caliber MT5612; ø 31.8 mm, height 6.5 mm; 26 jewels; 28,800 vph; silicon hairspring, balance with variable inertia; 70-hour power reserve; COSC-certified chronometer
Functions: hours, minutes, sweep seconds; date
Case: stainless steel, ø 42 mm; bidirectional bezel, 0-12 scale, with stop system (hinged element on upper lug); sapphire crystal; screw-in crown; water-resistant to 20 atm
Band: calfskin with rubber coating, folding clasp with safety lock
Remarks: release of a 1960s prototype for the U.S. Navy that was never manufactured serially
Price: $4,100

Black Bay GMT

Reference number: 79833MN
Movement: automatic, Tudor Caliber MT5652, ø 31.8 mm, height 7.52 mm; 28 jewels; 28,800 vph; silicon hairspring; 70-hour power reserve; COSC-certified chronometer
Functions: hours (crown-switched in steps), minutes, sweep seconds; additional 24-hour display (second time zone); datum
Case: stainless steel, ø 41 mm; yellow gold bezel, bidirectional bezel with 0-24 hour scale; sapphire crystal; screw-in crown; water-resistant to 20 atm
Band: stainless steel with yellow gold elements, folding clasp with safety lock
Price: $5,550
Variations: with calfskin/rubber or textile strap ($4,300)

Black Bay Chrono

Reference number: 79363N
Movement: automatic, Tudor Caliber MT5813, ø 30.4 mm, height 7.23 mm; 41 jewels; 28,800 vph; silicon hairspring, balance with variable inertia; 70-hour power reserve; COSC-certified chronometer
Functions: hours, minutes, subsidiary seconds; chronograph; date
Case: stainless steel, ø 41 mm; sapphire crystal; yellow-gold screw-in crown and pushers; water-resistant to 20 atm
Band: stainless steel with yellow gold elements, folding clasp
Remarks: comes with additional textile band
Price: $7,250
Variations: with calfskin/rubber or textile strap ($6,000)

Black Bay 41 S&G

Reference number: 79683
Movement: automatic, Tudor Caliber MT5601, ø 33.8 mm, height 6.5 mm; 25 jewels; 28,800 vph; silicon hairspring; 70-hour power reserve; COSC-certified chronometer
Functions: hours, minutes, sweep seconds
Case: stainless steel, ø 41 mm; yellow gold bezel, sapphire crystal; screw-in crown; water-resistant to 10 atm
Band: stainless steel with yellow gold elements, folding clasp with safety lock
Price: $5,250
Variations: in 31-, 36- or 39-mm diameter

Black Bay Bronze

Reference number: 79250BA
Movement: automatic, Tudor Caliber MT5601, ø 33.8 mm, height 6.5 mm; 25 jewels; 28,800 vph; silicon hairspring; 70-hour power reserve; COSC-certified chronometer
Functions: hours, minutes, sweep seconds
Case: bronze, ø 43 mm; unidirectionally rotating bezel with aluminum inlay; sapphire crystal; screw-in crown; water-resistant to 20 atm
Band: textile, buckle
Price: $4,250
Variations: with leather strap ($4,250)

Black Bay Fifty-Eight

Reference number: 79030N
Movement: automatic, Tudor Caliber MT5402; ø 26 mm, height 4.99 mm; 27 jewels; 28,800 vph; silicon hairspring; 70-hour power reserve; COSC-certified chronometer
Functions: hours, minutes, sweep seconds
Case: stainless steel, ø 39 mm, height 11.9 mm; unidirectional bezel with aluminum insert, with 0-60 scale; sapphire crystal; screw-in crown; water-resistant to 20 atm
Band: stainless steel, buckle
Price: $3,800
Variations: with textile or leather strap ($3,475)

Black Bay

Reference number: 79230R
Movement: automatic, Tudor Caliber MT5602, ø 33.8 mm, height 6.5 mm; 25 jewels; 28,800 vph; silicon hairspring; 70-hour power reserve; COSC-certified chronometer
Functions: hours, minutes, sweep seconds
Case: stainless steel, ø 41 mm; unidirectional bezel with 0-60 scale; sapphire crystal; screw-in crown; water-resistant to 20 atm
Band: aged calfskin, buckle
Price: $3,575
Variations: with red or black textile strap ($3,575); with stainless-steel link band ($3,900)

Pelagos FXD

Reference number: 25707B
Movement: automatic, Tudor Caliber MT5602, ø 33.8 mm, height 6.5 mm; 25 jewels; 28,800 vph; silicon hairspring; 70-hour power reserve; COSC-certified chronometer
Functions: hours, minutes, sweep seconds
Case: titanium, ø 42 mm; bidirectional bezel with ceramic numeral disc, with 0-60 scale (countdown); sapphire crystal; screw-in crown; water-resistant to 20 atm
Band: looped-textured fabric, velcro fastener
Remarks: fixed lug screws (tear-protected)
Price: $3,900
Variations: with black dial; with titanium band ($4,575)

Pelagos LHD

Reference number: 25610TNL
Movement: automatic, Tudor Caliber MT5612LHD; ø 31.8 mm, height 6.5 mm; 25 jewels; 28,800 vph; silicon hairspring; 70-hour power reserve; COSC-certified chronometer
Functions: hours, minutes, sweep seconds; date
Case: titanium, ø 42 mm; unidirectional stainless-steel bezel with ceramic numeral disc, with 0-60 scale; sapphire crystal; screw-in crown, helium valve; water-resistant to 50 atm
Band: titanium, folding clasp with safety lock and extension link, with fine regulation
Remarks: comes with additional rubber strap
Price: $4,400

Ranger

Reference number: 79950
Movement: automatic, Tudor Caliber MT5402; ø 26 mm, height 4.99 mm; 27 jewels; 28,800 vph; silicon hairspring; 70-hour power reserve; COSC-certified chronometer
Functions: hours, minutes, sweep seconds
Case: stainless steel, ø 39 mm; sapphire crystal; screw-in crown; water-resistant to 10 atm
Band: rubber/leather, folding clasp with safety lock
Price: $2,725
Variations: with textile strap ($2,725); with stainless steel links bracelet ($3,050)

Caliber MT5601

Automatic; single spring barrel, 70-hour power reserve; COSC-certified chronometer
Functions: hours, minutes, sweep seconds
Diameter: 33.8 mm
Height: 6.5 mm
Jewels: 25
Balance: glucydur with weighted screws
Frequency: 28,800 vph
Hairspring: silicon
Related caliber: MT5612 (with smaller, 31.8 mm insertable diameter)

Caliber MT5402

Automatic; single spring barrel, 70-hour power reserve; COSC-certified chronometer
Functions: hours, minutes, sweep seconds
Diameter: 26 mm
Height: 4.99 mm
Jewels: 27
Balance: glucydur with weighted screws
Frequency: 28,800 vph
Hairspring: silicon

Caliber MT5813

Automatic; single spring barrel, 70-hour power reserve; COSC certified chronometer
Functions: hours, minutes, subsidiary seconds; chronograph; date
Diameter: 30.4 mm
Height: 7.23 mm
Jewels: 41
Balance: glucydur with weighted screws
Frequency: 28,800 vph
Hairspring: silicon

YVAN MONNET
GENÈVE
FIVE
The pentagon revisited
Exclusive design
Made in Geneva
Stainless steel
Waterproff 20 atm (200m)
Hour marker superluminova 3D
Sapphire glass
WWW.YMONNET.CH

TUTIMA

Tutima Uhrenfabrik GmbH Ndl. Glashütte
Altenberger Strasse 6
D-01768 Glashütte
Germany

Tel.:
+49-35053-320-20

E-mail:
info@tutima.com

Website:
www.tutima.com

Founded:
1927

Number of employees:
approx. 60

U.S. distributor:
Tutima USA, Inc.
P.O. Box 983
Torrance, CA 90508
1-TUTIMA-1927
info@tutimausa.com
www.tutima.com

Most important collections/price range:
Patria, Saxon One, M2, Grand Flieger, Hommage / approx. $1,650 to $29,500

The name Glashütte is synonymous with watches in Germany. The area, also known for precision engineering, already had quite a watchmaking industry going when World War I closed off markets, followed by the hyperinflation of the early twenties. To rebuild the local economy, a conglomerate was created to produce finished watches, under the leadership of jurist Dr. Ernst Kurtz, consisting of the movement manufacturer UROFA Glashütte AG and UFAG. The top watches were given the name Tutima, derived from the Latin *tutus*, meaning whole, sound. Among the brand's most famous timepieces was a pilot's watch that set standards in terms of aesthetics and functionality.

A few days before World War II ended, Kurtz left Glashütte and founded Uhrenfabrik Kurtz in southern Germany. A young businessman and former employee of Kurtz by the name of Dieter Delecate is credited with keeping the manufacturing facilities and the name Tutima going even as the company sailed through troubled waters. In founding Tutima Uhrenfabrik GmbH in Ganderkesee, this young, resolute entrepreneur prepared the company's strategy for the coming decades.

Delecate has had the joy of seeing Tutima return to its old home and vertically integrated operations, meaning it is once again a genuine *manufacture*. In 2013, Tutima proudly announced a genuine made-in-Glashütte movement (at least 50 percent must be produced in the town), Caliber 617. Tutima Glashütte has started reviving the great watchmaking crafts that have made the region world famous. Among these horological treats is the Hommage minute repeater and the three-hand Patria, which comes in a noble steel or gold case with a blue dial. For a genuine vintage feeling, the brand introduced the Tempostopp, a flyback chronograph run on the Caliber 659, a replica of the legendary Urofa Caliber 59 from the 1940s with a few necessary improvements in the details. More contemporary is the Saxon One line with a range of classic complications. And then there are the military-inspired models for everyday usage based on military watches, like the M2 Coastline, of lightweight titanium but with soft edges that will not ruin a silk shirt cuff.

M2 Chronograph

Reference number: 6450-04
Movement: automatic, Tutima Caliber 521 (base ETA 7750); ø 30 mm, height 7.9 mm; 25 jewels; 28,800 vph; sweep minute counter, rotor with gold seal; 48-hour power reserve
Functions: hours, minutes; chronograph; date
Case: titanium, ø 46 mm, height 15.5 mm; sapphire crystal; screw-in crown; water-resistant to 30 atm
Band: textile, folding clasp
Price: $4,900

M2 Seven Seas S

Reference number: 6156-04
Movement: automatic, Tutima Caliber 330 (base ETA 2836-2); ø 25.6 mm, height 5.05 mm; 25 jewels; 28,800 vph; rotor with gold seal; 38-hour power reserve
Functions: hours, minutes, sweep seconds; date
Case: titanium, ø 40 mm, height 12.5 mm; unidirectional bezel with 0-60 scale; sapphire crystal; screw-in crown; water-resistant to 50 atm
Band: stainless steel, folding clasp
Price: $2,350

M2 Seven Seas

Reference number: 6151-09
Movement: automatic, Tutima Caliber 330 (base ETA 2836-2); ø 25.6 mm, height 5.05 mm; 25 jewels; 28,800 vph; rotor with gold seal; 38-hour power reserve
Functions: hours, minutes, sweep seconds; date and weekday
Case: titanium, ø 44 mm, height 13 mm; unidirectional bezel with 0-60 scale; sapphire crystal; screw-in crown; water-resistant to 50 atm
Band: rubber with textile overlay, folding clasp
Remarks: various dials with fitting straps
Price: $1,980

Grand Flieger Classic Chronograph

Reference number: 6408-01
Movement: automatic, Tutima Caliber 310 (base ETA 7750); ø 30 mm, height 7.9 mm; 25 jewels; 28,800 vph; rotor with gold seal; 48-hour power reserve
Functions: hours, minutes, subsidiary seconds; chronograph; date
Case: stainless steel, ø 41 mm, height 16 mm; bidirectional bezel with reference marker; sapphire crystal; transparent case back; screw-in crown; water-resistant to 20 atm
Band: calfskin, folding clasp
Price: $3,900

Grand Flieger Airport Chronograph

Reference number: 6406-03
Movement: automatic, Tutima Caliber 310 (base ETA 7750); ø 30 mm, height 7.9 mm; 25 jewels; 28,800 vph; rotor with gold seal; 48-hour power reserve
Functions: hours, minutes, subsidiary seconds; chronograph; date, weekday
Case: stainless steel, ø 43 mm, height 16 mm; bezel with ceramic insert, bidirectional bezel with 0-60 scale; sapphire crystal; transparent case back; screw-in crown; water-resistant to 20 atm
Band: calfskin with textile overlay, folding clasp
Price: $2,500

Grand Flieger Airport Automatic

Reference number: 6107-06
Movement: automatic, Tutima Caliber 330 (base ETA 2836-2); ø 25.6 mm, height 5.05 mm; 25 jewels; 28,800 vph; rotor with gold seal; 38-hour power reserve
Functions: hours, minutes, sweep seconds; date and weekday
Case: stainless steel, ø 41 mm, height 13 mm; bidirectionally rotating bezel with ceramic inlay, with 0-60 scale; sapphire crystal; transparent case back; screw-in crown; water-resistant to 20 atm
Band: stainless steel, folding clasp
Price: $2,900

Sky

Reference number: 6105-22
Movement: automatic, Tutima Caliber 330 (base ETA 2836-2); ø 25.6 mm, height 5.05 mm; 25 jewels; 28,800 vph; rotor with gold seal; 38-hour power reserve
Functions: hours, minutes, sweep seconds; date and weekday
Case: stainless steel, ø 41 mm, height 13 mm; sapphire crystal; transparent case back; water-resistant to 10 atm
Band: stainless steel Milanese bracelet, folding clasp
Price: $1,750

Saxon One Chronograph Racing Red

Reference number: 6420-07
Movement: automatic, Tutima Caliber 521 (base ETA 7750); ø 30 mm, height 7.9 mm; 25 jewels; 28,800 vph; sweep minute counter; rotor with gold seal; 48-hour power reserve
Functions: hours, minutes, subsidiary seconds; additional 24-hour display; chronograph; date
Case: stainless steel, ø 43 mm, height 15.7 mm; bidirectional bezel with reference marker; sapphire crystal; transparent case back; screw-in crown; water-resistant to 20 atm
Band: stainless steel, folding clasp
Price: $6,500

Tempostopp

Reference number: 6650-01
Movement: manually wound, Tutima Caliber 659; ø 33.7 mm, height 6.6 mm; 28 jewels; 21,600 vph; screw balance with gold weight screws and Breguet hairspring; winding wheels with click; hand-engraved balance cock, gold-plated and finely finished movement; 65-hour power reserve
Functions: hours, minutes, subsidiary seconds; flyback chronograph
Case: rose gold, ø 43 mm, height 12.95 mm; sapphire crystal; transparent case back
Band: reptile skin, buckle
Remarks: runs on an optimized replica of legendary UROFA Caliber 59 from 1940s
Price: $42,500

Patria

Reference number: 6600-03
Movement: manually wound, Tutima Caliber 617; ø 31 mm, height 4.78 mm; 20 jewels; 21,600 vph; screw balance with weighted screws and Breguet hairspring; Glashütte three-quarter plate; winding wheels with click; gold-plated and finely finished movement; 65-hour power reserve
Functions: hours, minutes, subsidiary seconds
Case: rose gold, ø 43 mm, height 11.2 mm; sapphire crystal; transparent case back; water-resistant to 5 atm
Band: reptile skin, buckle
Price: $21,000

Patria

Reference number: 6610-02
Movement: manually wound, Tutima Caliber 617; ø 31 mm, height 4.78 mm; 20 jewels; 21,600 vph; screw balance with weight screws and Breguet hairspring; Glashütte three-quarter plate; winding wheels with click; gold-plated and finely finished movement; 65-hour power reserve
Functions: hours, minutes, subsidiary seconds
Case: stainless steel, ø 43 mm, height 11.2 mm; sapphire crystal; transparent case back; water-resistant to 5 atm
Band: reptile skin, buckle
Price: $8,900
Variations: comes in various colors

Hommage

Reference number: 6800-02
Movement: manually wound, Tutima Caliber 800; ø 32 mm, height 7.2 mm; 42 jewels; 21,600 vph; screw balance with gold weight screws and Breguet hairspring; Glashütte three-quarter plate; winding wheels with click; gold-plated and finely finished movement; hand-engraved balance cock; 65-hour power reserve
Functions: hours, minutes, subsidiary seconds; minute repeater
Case: rose gold, ø 43 mm, height 13.4 mm; sapphire crystal; transparent case back
Band: reptile skin, buckle
Price: on request

Caliber Tutima 618

Manually wound; 3 screw-mounted gold chatons, Glashütte three-quarter plate; winding wheels with click; single spring barrel, 65-hour power reserve
Functions: hours, minutes, subsidiary seconds; power reserve indicator
Diameter: 31 mm
Height: 4.78 mm
Jewels: 27
Balance: screw balance with gold weight screws
Frequency: 21,600 vph
Balance spring: Breguet hairspring
Remarks: gold-plated and finely finished movement

Caliber Tutima 659

Manually wound; column-wheel control of chronograph functions; single spring barrel, 65-hour power reserve
Functions: hours, minutes, subsidiary seconds; flyback chronograph
Diameter: 33.7 mm
Height: 6.6 mm
Jewels: 28
Balance: screw balance with gold weight screws
Frequency: 21,600 vph
Balance spring: Breguet hairspring
Remarks: optimized replica of the legendary UROFA Caliber 59; gold-plated and finely finished movement

Caliber Tutima 800

Manually wound; 4 screw-mounted gold chatons, Glashütte three-quarter plate, 2 gongs, winding wheels with click; single spring barrel, 65-hour power reserve
Functions: hours, minutes, subsidiary seconds; minute repeater
Diameter: 32 mm
Height: 7.2 mm
Jewels: 42
Balance: screw balance with gold weight screws
Frequency: 21,600 vph
Balance spring: Breguet hairspring
Remarks: gold-plated and finely finished movement

ULYSSE NARDIN

Ulysse Nardin SA
3, rue du Jardin
CH-2400 Le Locle
Switzerland

Tel.:
+41-32-930-7400

Website:
www.ulysse-nardin.com

Founded:
1846

U.S. distributor:
Ulysse Nardin Inc.
7900 Glades Rd., Suite 200
Boca Raton, FL 33434
646 500 8664
usa@ulysse-nardin.com

Most important collections:
FREAK Collection, Blast Collection, Marine Collection and Diver Collection; Dual Time (also ladies watches); complications and *métiers d'art* (alarm clocks, perpetual calendar, tourbillons, minute repeaters, jacquemarts, astronomical watches, enamel, micropainting)

Ulysse Nardin celebrated 175 years in 2021, though a few of those years were dormant. It was Rolf Schnyder who revived the venerable brand after the quartz crisis. At one time it had a reputation for marine chronometers and precision watches. Schnyder had the luck to meet the multitalented Dr. Ludwig Oechslin, who developed a host of innovations for Ulysse Nardin, from intelligent calendar movements to escapement systems. He was the first to use silicon and synthetic diamonds. In fact, just about every Ulysse Nardin has become famous for some spectacular technical innovation, be it the Moonstruck with its stunning moon phase accuracy or the outlandish Freak series that more or less does away with the dial.

After Schnyder's death in 2011, the brand developed a strategy of partnerships and acquisitions, notably of the enameler Donzé Cadrans SA, which gave rise to the Marine Chronometer Manufacture, powered by the Caliber UN-118.

In 2014, the French luxury group Kering, owner of Sowind (Girard-Perregaux), purchased Ulysse Nardin. The two companies were neighbors in La Chaux-de-Fonds, Switzerland, and this created synergies. Ulysse Nardin continued developing clever solutions such as a new blade-driven anchor escapement and the regatta countdown watch with a second hand that runs counterclockwise first before running clockwise like a conventional chronograph once the race has started.

A joint venture with Sigatec in Sion and its sister company, Mimotec, which specialize in lithogalvanics (LIGA) and processing silicon, allowed Ulysse Nardin to continue developing its advanced technologies. Specialties such as the dual Ulysse escapement in the Freak model and the Ulysse anchor escapement in the tourbillon caliber 178 with the flying bearing of the anchor made of silicon would not have been feasible without the new manufacturing possibilities and materials.

More changes are on the way, because Kering Group sold off Ulysse Nardin and Girard-Perregaux in a management buyout under the guidance of Patrick Pruniaux, CEO of both brands. It is likely to bring the two watch brands even closer together in the medium term. As both companies are based in La Chaux-de-Fonds, the exploitation of production synergies, for example, is obvious. At any rate, Pruniaux has promised loud and clear that the brands will keep on producing unconventional watches.

Marine Torpilleur

Reference number: 1182-310/42
Movement: automatic, Caliber UN-118; ø 31.6 mm, height 6.45 mm; 50 jewels; 28,800 vph; DIAMonSIL escapement, silicon hairspring; 60-hour power reserve; COSC-certified chronometer
Functions: hours, minutes, subsidiary seconds; power reserve indicator; date
Case: rose gold, ø 42 mm, height 11.73 mm; sapphire crystal; transparent case back; screw-in crown; water-resistant to 10 atm
Band: reptile skin, folding clasp
Price: $19,300

Marine Torpilleur Moon Phase

Reference number: 1192-310-0A/1A
Movement: automatic, Caliber UN-119; ø 31.6 mm, height 6.2 mm; 45 jewels; 28,800 vph; DIAMonSIL escapement, silicon hairspring; 60 hours power reserve; COSC-certified chronometer
Functions: hours, minutes, subsidiary seconds; power reserve indicator; moon phase
Case: rose gold, ø 42 mm, height 13 mm; sapphire crystal; transparent case back; screw-in crown; water-resistant to 5 atm
Band: reptile skin, folding clasp
Price: $22,600

Marine Torpilleur Tourbillon

Reference number: 1283-310-0AE/1A
Movement: automatic, Caliber UN-128; ø 31.6 mm, height 7.4 mm; 36 jewels; 28,800 vph; one-minute flying tourbillon; silicon escapement and hairspring; 60-hour power reserve
Functions: hours, minutes; power reserve indicator
Case: rose gold, ø 42 mm, height 11.93 mm; sapphire crystal; transparent case back; screw-in crown; water resistant to 5 atm
Band: reptile skin, folding clasp
Price: $39,600

Marine Torpilleur Dual Time

Reference number: 3343-320-3A/1A
Movement: automatic, Caliber UN-24; ø 25.6 mm, height 5.35 mm; 23 jewels; 28,800 vph; 42-hour power reserve
Functions: hours, minutes, subsidiary seconds; additional 24-hour indicator (second time zone); large date
Case: stainless steel, ø 42 mm, height 13 mm; bidirectional ceramic bezel; sapphire crystal; transparent case back; screw-in crown; water-resistant to 5 atm
Band: reptile skin, folding clasp
Price: $11,500

Diver

Reference number: 8163-175-7M/92
Movement: automatic, Caliber UN-816 (base Sellita SW300); ø 25.6 mm, height 3.6 mm; 25 jewels; 28,800 vph; 42-hour power reserve
Functions: hours, minutes, sweep seconds; date
Case: stainless steel, ø 42 mm, height 10.75 mm; unidirectional bezel with rubber inserts, with 0-60 scale; sapphire crystal; screw-in crown; water-resistant to 30 atm
Band: stainless steel, buckle
Price: $7,500

Diver Chronometer

Reference number: 1183-170-3/93
Movement: automatic, Caliber UN-118; ø 31.6 mm, height 6.45 mm; 50 jewels; 28,800 vph; DIAMonSIL balance, silicon hairspring; 60-hour power reserve; COSC-certified chronometer
Functions: hours, minutes, subsidiary seconds; power reserve indicator; date
Case: titanium, ø 44 mm, height 13.1 mm; unidirectional rose gold bezel with rubber inserts, with 0-60 scale; sapphire crystal; transparent case back; screw-in crown; water-resistant to 30 atm
Band: rubber, buckle
Price: $9,400
Variations: with black dial ($9,400); with stainless steel bracelet ($10,100) with textile strap ($9,400)

Diver Chronograph

Reference number: 1503-170-3/93
Movement: automatic, Caliber UN-150; ø 31 mm, height 6.75 mm; 25 jewels; 28,800 vph; silicon escapement; 48-hour power reserve
Functions: hours, minutes, subsidiary seconds; chronograph; date
Case: titanium, ø 44 mm; height 16.1 mm; unidirectionally rotating bezel with 60-minute divisions; sapphire crystal; transparent case back; water-resistant to 30 atm
Band: rubber, buckle
Price: $12,600

Marine Chronograph

Reference number: 1502-170-3/93
Movement: automatic, Caliber UN-150; ø 31 mm, height 6.75 mm; 25 jewels; 28,800 vph; silicon escapement; 48-hour power reserve
Functions: hours, minutes, subsidiary seconds; chronograph; date
Case: rose gold, ø 44 mm; height 16.1 mm; unidirectionally rotating bezel with 60-minute divisions; sapphire crystal; transparent case back; water-resistant to 30 atm
Band: rubber with rose-gold elements, buckle
Price: $40,600

Blast Dual Time

Reference number: 243-20-3/42
Movement: automatic, Caliber UN-24; ø 25.6 mm, height 5.6 mm; 23 jewels; 28,800 vph; 42-hour power reserve
Functions: hours, minutes, subsidiary seconds; additional 24-hour display (second time zone); large date
Case: stainless steel, ø 42 mm, height 12 mm; ceramic bezel; sapphire crystal; transparent case back; screw-in crown; water-resistant to 5 atm
Band: rubber, buckle
Price: $9,400
Variations: with leather

Skeleton X Titan

Reference number: 3713-260-3/03
Movement: manually wound, Caliber UN-371; ø 37 mm, height 5.86 mm; 23 jewels; 18,000 vph; skeletonized movement, double spring barrels; silicon escape wheel and hairspring; 96-hour power reserve
Functions: hours, minutes
Case: titanium, ø 42 mm, height 10.85 mm; bezel with blue PVD, sapphire crystal; transparent case back; water-resistant to 5 atm
Band: rubber, buckle
Price: $20,600
Variations: with reptile skin strap; in carbon; completely of titanium

Blast Tourbillon

Reference number: 1723-400-3A/03
Movement: automatic, Caliber UN-172; ø 37 mm, height 6.1 mm; 25 jewels; 1-minute tourbillon; platinum micro-rotor; 72-hour power reserve
Functions: hours, minutes
Case: titanium, ø 45 mm; ceramic bezel; sapphire crystal; transparent case back; water-resistant to 5 atm
Band: rubber, folding clasp
Price: $50,600
Variations: with leather strap ($50,600)

Blast Hourstriker

Reference number: 6215-400-3A/02
Movement: automatic, Caliber UN-621; ø 35.5 mm, height 10.8 mm; 46 jewels; 28,800 vph; flying 1-minute tourbillon, silicon escapement; platinum micro-rotor (manual winding for the chime), 60-hour power reserve
Functions: hours, minutes "au-passage" hour and half-hour striking on request
Case: rose gold, barrel section of DLC-coated titanium, ø 45 mm; sapphire crystal; transparent case back; water-resistant to 3 atm
Band: rubber, folding clasp
Price: $109,700
Variations: with reptile skin band ($109,700); with satin strap

Blast Moonstruck

Reference number: 1063-400-2A/3B
Movement: automatic, Caliber UN-106; 28,800 vph; silicon escapement; micro-rotor; 50-hour power reserve
Functions: hours, minutes, world time display, power reserve (second time zone), tide display, display of sun and moon position; date, moon phase and age
Case: titanium with black DLC, ø 45 mm, height 15.1 mm; sapphire crystal; transparent case back; water-resistant to 3 atm
Band: rubber with reptile skin overlay, folding clasp
Price: $79,100

Freak X

Reference number: 2303-270.1/03
Movement: automatic, Caliber UN-230; ø 34.5 mm, height 10.1 mm; 21 jewels; 28,800 vph; baguette movement on a rotating carousel, silicon balance, movement components are used as hands, crown-controlled conventional winding and hands-setting; 72-hour power reserve
Functions: hours, minutes,
Case: titanium, ø 43 mm, height 13.5 mm; sapphire crystal; transparent case back
Band: calfskin, folding clasp
Price: $24,800
Variations: with reptile skin strap; with black DLC coating

Freak S

Reference number: 2513-500LE-2A-BLACK-5N/1A
Movement: automatic, Caliber UN-251; ø 34.5 mm, height 10.1 mm; 21 jewels; 28,800 vph; baguette movement on a peripheral and flying carousel, double silicon escapement and hairspring, movement components are used as hands, crown-controlled conventional winding and hands-setting; 72-hour power reserve
Functions: hours, minutes
Case: titanium with black DLC, ø 45 mm, height 13.8 mm; bezel in rose gold; sapphire crystal; transparent case back; water-resistant to 5 atm
Band: calfskin, folding clasp
Price: $137,200

URWERK

Many watchmakers make unique pieces, but Felix Baumgartner and designer Martin Frei are in and of themselves unique. Their products are immediately recognizable, their ultra-technical style—never losing sight of the visual codes they laid down when they founded their company in 1997—has always been the source of eye-popping mechanisms. It's all in the name, a play on the words *Uhrwerk*, for movement, and *Urwerk*, meaning a sort of primal mechanism. Their specialty is inventing surprising time indicators featuring digital numerals that rotate like satellites and display the time in a relatively linear depiction on a small "dial" at the front of the flattened case, which could almost—but not quite—be described as oval. Their inspiration goes back to the so-called night clock of the eighteenth-century Campanus brothers, but the realization is purely 2001: A Space Odyssey.

Urwerk's debut was with the Harry Winston Opus 5. Later, they created the Black Cobra, which displays time using cylinders and other clever ways to recoup energy for driving rather heavy components. The Torpedo is another example of high-tech watchmaking, again based on the satellite system of revolving and turning hands. With each return to the drawing board, Baumgartner and Frei find new ways to explore what has now become an unmistakable form, using high-tech materials, like aluminum titanium nitride (AlTiN), or a gold-silver alloy known as electrum, or finding new functions for the owner to play with.

Urwerk is continually pushing the envelope, even by its own standards. The latest implemented idea is the continuation of the minute hand trajectory along a 20-minute scale representing the 555 kilometers (345 miles) you would travel if standing that long on the equator. A scale opposite tracks your 20-minute journey around the sun as 35,740 kilometers (22,216 miles). This concept was applied to the UR-100V "Ultra Violet," which comes in a violet hue at the edge of the visual spectrum. For this particular project, Urwerk even updated the 12.01 movement (to 12.02).

Urwerk SA
114, rue du Rhône
CH-1204 Geneva
Switzerland

Tel:
+41-22-900-2027

E-mail:
info@urwerk.com

Website:
www.urwerk.com

Founded:
1995

Annual production:
150 watches

U.S. distributor:
Ildico Inc.
8701 Wilshire Blvd.
Beverly Hills, CA 90211
310-205-5555

UR-120 aka Spock "Live Long and Prosper!"

Movement: automatic, Caliber UR 20.01; 28,800 vph; 32 jewels; beryllium-copper with grey and gold PVD, anodized aluminum, ARCAP, titanium; côtes de Genève; 48-hour power reserve
Functions: hours (on satellite), minutes (retrograde)
Case: sandblasted titanium and stainless steel, 44 x 47 mm, height 15.8 mm; sapphire crystal; water-resistant to 3 atm
Band: calfskin, buckle
Remarks: satellite hour on two studs that open (looking like a Vulcan greeting) and shut as they rotate to form the hour numeral
Price: $108,000; limited to 25 pieces

UR-220 SL Asimov

Movement: manually wound, Caliber UR-7.20; 59 jewels; winding system steered by 2 turbines; 28,800 vph; wandering aluminum satellites with titanium Geneva Cross control and planetary transmission, finely finished; 48-hour power reserve
Functions: hours (digital, rotating) on Super-LumiNova, retrograde minutes; double power reserve; oil change indicator showing running time of the movement in months
Case: carbon CTP, 43.8 x 53.7 mm, height 14.8 mm; sapphire crystal; DLC-coated caseback; water-resistant to 3 atm
Band: cured rubber, buckle and Velcro fastening
Price: $157,000

UR-100 Ultraviolet

Movement: automatic, Caliber UR 12.02; 28,800 vph; 40 jewels; aluminum carousel; carousel and baseplates in ARCAP alloy; finely finished movement with circular graining and shot-blasting; 48-hour power reserve
Functions: satellite hours (on beryllium bronze Geneva crosses), minutes; rotational distance at the equator in 20 minutes and orbital distance in 20 minutes
Case: titanium with violet DLC, 41 x 49.7 mm, height 14 mm; sapphire crystal; transparent case back; water-resistant to 3 atm
Band: rubber, buckle
Price: $59,000

UTS Watches, Inc.
P.O. Box 6293
Los Osos, CA 93412

Tel.:
877-887-0123 or 805-528-9800

E-mail:
info@utswatches.com

Website:
www.utswatches.com

Founded:
1999

Number of employees:
2

Annual production:
fewer than 500

Distribution:
direct sales only

Most important collections/price range:
sports and diver's watches, chronographs / from $2,500 to $7,000

UTS

UTS, or "Uhren Technik Spinner," was the natural outgrowth of a company based in Munich and manufacturing CNC tools and machines for the watch industry. Nicolaus Spinner, a mechanical engineer and aficionado in his own right, learned the nitty-gritty of watchmaking by the age-old system of taking watches apart. From there to making robust diver's watches was just a short step. The collection has grown considerably since he started production in 1999. The watches are built mainly around ETA calibers. Some, like the new 4000M, feature a unique locking bezel using a stem, a bolt, and a ceramic ball bearing system invented by Spinner. Another specialty is the 6-mm sapphire crystal, which guarantees significant water resistance. Spinner's longtime friend and business partner, Stephen Newman, is the owner of the UTS trademark in the United States. He not only has worked on product development, but has also contributed his own design ideas and handles sales and marketing for the small brand. A new watch released in 2014, the 4000M Diver, boasts an extreme depth rating even without the need for a helium escape valve and is available in a GMT version. The collection is small, but UTS has a faithful following in Germany and the United States. The key for the fan club is a unique appearance coupled with mastery of the technology. These are pure muscle watches with no steroids.

Diver 4000M GMT

Movement: automatic, ETA Caliber 2893-2; ø 25.6 mm, height 4.6 mm; 25 jewels; 28,800 vph; 42-hour power reserve
Functions: hours, minutes, sweep seconds; date; 2nd time zone
Case: stainless steel, ø 45 mm, height 17.5 mm; bidirectional bezel with 0-60 scale; 6-mm sapphire crystal, antireflective on back; screwed-down case back; screw-in crown and buttons; locking bezel; water-resistant to 400 atm
Band: stainless steel with diver's extension folding clasp or rubber or leather strap
Price: $6,800

2000M

Movement: automatic, ETA Caliber 2824-2; ø 25.6 mm, height 4.6 mm; 25 jewels; 28,800 vph; 42-hour power reserve
Functions: hours, minutes, sweep seconds; date
Case: stainless steel, ø 44 mm, height 16.5 mm; unidirectional bezel with 0-60 scale; automatic helium escape valve; sapphire crystal, antireflective on back; screwed-down case back; screw-in crown and buttons; water-resistant to 200 atm
Band: stainless steel with diver's extension folding clasp, comes with rubber leather strap
Price: $3,950

Adventure Manual Wind

Movement: manually wound, ETA Unitas Caliber 6497; ø 36.6 mm, height 5.4 mm; 18 jewels; 18,000 vph; 48-hour power reserve
Functions: hours, minutes, subsidiary seconds
Case: stainless steel, ø 46 mm, height 14 mm; screw-in crown; antireflective sapphire crystal; screwed-down sapphire crystal case back; water-resistant to 50 atm
Band: leather, buckle
Price: $3,400
Variations: rubber strap

VACHERON CONSTANTIN

Vacheron Constantin
Chemin du Tourbillon
CH-1228 Plan-les-Ouates
Switzerland

Tel.:
+41-22-930-2005

E-mail:
info@vacheron-constantin.com

Website:
www.vacheron-constantin.com

Founded:
1755

Number of employees:
approx. 800

U.S. distributor:
Vacheron Constantin
645 Fifth Avenue
New York, NY 10022
877-701-1755

Most important collections:
Patrimony, Traditionnelle, Métiers d'Art, Overseas, Fiftysix, Historiques and Égérie. As well as unique and bespoke timepieces from its Les Cabinotiers department

The origins of this oldest continuously operating watch *manufacture* can be traced back to 1755 when Jean-Marc Vacheron opened his workshop in Geneva. His highly complex watches were particularly appreciated by clients in Paris. The development of such an important outlet for horological works there had a lot to do with the emergence of a wealthy class around the powerful French court. The Revolution put an end to all the financial excesses of that market, however, and the Vacheron company suffered as well, until the arrival of marketing wizard François Constantin in 1819.

Fast-forward to the late twentieth century: the brand with the Maltese cross logo had evolved into a tradition-conscious keeper of *haute horlogerie* under the aegis, starting in the mid-1990s, of the Vendôme Luxury Group (today's Richemont SA).

Vacheron Constantin is one of the last luxury brands to have abandoned the traditional way of dividing up labor. Today, most of its basic movements are made in-house at the production facilities and headquarters in Plan-les-Ouates and the workshops in Le Brassus in Switzerland's Jura region.

Products range from the world's most complicated watch, like the 57260, and the finely crafted Les Cabinotiers and Traditionelle collections. For daily use, there are the elegant Overseas models and the entry-level collection, the Fiftysix, with a basic movement and no Geneva Seal. In 2019, the brand's competence in movements produced a genuine novelty: a perpetual calendar driven by the "Twin Beat" escapement. It runs at 36,000 vph on the wearer's arm, and can be switched to 8,640 vph when stored, giving it a 65-day power reserve.

2021 brought forth a revisited American 1921 model, now made from 100-year-old spare parts and components and manufactured with 100-year-old tools. This watchmaking icon with its boldly oblique dial differs from the current models in the 1921 collection in that the dial and crown are tilted to the left.

Les Cabinotiers Minute Repeater Tourbillon Split-Seconds Monopusher Chronograph

Reference number: 9750C/000R-002C
Movement: manually wound, Vacheron Constantin Caliber 2757; ø 33.3 mm, height 10.4 mm; 59 jewels; 18,000 vph; 1-minute tourbillon; 60-hour power reserve; Geneva Seal
Functions: hours and minutes (off-center), subsidiary seconds; minute repeater; split-seconds chronograph
Case: rose gold, ø 45 mm, height 16.4 mm; sapphire crystal; transparent case back
Band: reptile skin, folding clasp
Remarks: unique piece

Traditionelle Complete Calendar Openface

Reference number: 4020T/000G-B655
Movement: automatic, Vacheron Constantin Caliber 2460 QCL/2; ø 29 mm, height 5.45 mm; 27 jewels; 28,800 vph; 40-hour power reserve; Geneva Seal
Functions: hours, minutes; full calendar with date, weekday, months, moon phase
Case: white gold, ø 41 mm, height 10.7 mm; sapphire crystal; transparent case back; water-resistant to 3 atm
Band: reptile skin, folding clasp
Remarks: sapphire crystal dial
Price: $47,300
Variations: in rose gold

Overseas Tourbillon Skeleton

Reference number: 6000V/110T-B935
Movement: automatic, Vacheron Constantin Caliber 2160 SQ; ø 31 mm, height 5.65 mm; 30 jewels; 18,000 vph; 1-minute tourbillon; hubless, peripheral winding rotor; 80-hour power reserve; Geneva Seal
Functions: hours, minutes, subsidiary seconds, (on tourbillon cage)
Case: titanium, ø 42.5 mm, height 10.39 mm; sapphire crystal; transparent case back; water-resistant to 5 atm
Band: titanium, folding clasp
Remarks: sapphire crystal dial
Price: $164,000

Fiftysix Self-Winding

Reference number: 4600E/000A-B442
Movement: automatic, Vacheron Constantin Caliber 1326; ø 26.2 mm, height 4.3 mm; 25 jewels; 28,800 vph; 48-hour power reserve
Functions: hours, minutes, sweep seconds; date
Case: stainless steel, ø 40 mm, height 9.6 mm; sapphire crystal; transparent case back; water-resistant to 3 atm
Band: reptile skin, folding clasp
Price: $12,300
Variations: rose gold ($23,100)

Fiftysix Self-Winding

Reference number: 4600E/000R-B576
Movement: automatic, Vacheron Constantin Caliber 1326; ø 26.2 mm, height 4.3 mm; 25 jewels; 28,800 vph; 48-hour power reserve
Functions: hours, minutes, sweep seconds; date
Case: rose gold, ø 40 mm, height 9.6 mm; sapphire crystal; transparent case back; water-resistant to 3 atm
Band: calfskin, buckle
Price: $23,100

Fiftysix Complete Calendar

Reference number: 4000E/000R-B438
Movement: automatic, Vacheron Constantin Caliber 2460 QCL/1; ø 29 mm, height 5.4 mm; 27 jewels; 28,800 vph; 40-hour power reserve; Geneva Seal
Functions: hours, minutes, sweep seconds; full calendar with date, weekday, month
Case: rose gold, ø 40 mm, height 11.6 mm; sapphire crystal; transparent case back; water-resistant to 3 atm
Band: reptile skin, folding clasp
Price: $40,500
Variations: stainless steel ($26,400)

Historiques American 1921

Reference number: 82035/000G-B735
Movement: manually wound, Vacheron Constantin Caliber 4400AS; ø 28.6 mm, height 2.8 mm; 21 jewels; 28,800 vph; 65-hour power reserve; Geneva Seal
Functions: hours, minutes, subsidiary seconds
Case: platinum, ø 40 mm, height 8.06 mm; sapphire crystal; transparent case back; water-resistant to 3 atm
Band: reptile skin, buckle
Remarks: modeled after a vintage piece from 1921
Price: $36,800

Historiques 222

Reference number: 4200H/222J-B935
Movement: automatic, Vacheron Constantin Caliber 2455/2; ø 26.2 mm, height 3.6 mm; 27 jewels; 28,800 vph; 40-hour power reserve; Geneva Seal
Functions: hours, minutes; date
Case: yellow gold, ø 37 mm, height 7.95 mm; sapphire crystal; transparent case back; water-resistant to 5 atm
Band: yellow gold, triple folding clasp
Remarks: carefully modernized reedition for the 45th anniversary of the "222"
Price: $69,000

Overseas Perpetual Calendar Ultra-Thin Skeleton

Reference number: 4300V/120G-B945
Movement: automatic, Vacheron Constantin Caliber 1120 QP/1; ø 29.6 mm, height 4.05 mm; 36 jewels; 19,800 vph; skeletonized movement; 40-hour power reserve; Geneva Seal
Functions: hours, minutes; perpetual calendar with date, weekday, month, moon phase, leap year
Case: white gold, ø 41.5 mm, height 8.1 mm; sapphire crystal; transparent case back; water-resistant to 5 atm
Band: white gold, triple folding clasp
Remarks: soft-iron cage to protect from magnetism; comes with reptile skin and rubber strap.
Price: $102,000
Variations: in rose gold ($93,000)

Overseas Chronograph

Reference number: 5500V/110A-B481
Movement: automatic, Vacheron Constantin Caliber 5200; ø 30.6 mm, height 6.6 mm; 54 jewels; 28,800 vph; column-wheel control of chronograph functions; gold rotor; 52-hour power reserve; Geneva Seal
Functions: hours, minutes, subsidiary seconds; chronograph; date
Case: stainless steel, ø 42.5 mm, height 13.7 mm; sapphire crystal; transparent case back; screw-in crown and pushers; water-resistant to 15 atm
Band: rubber, double folding clasp
Price: $32,400
Variations: reptile skin band

Overseas Self-Winding

Reference number: 4500V/110A-B128
Movement: automatic, Vacheron Constantin Caliber 5100; ø 30.6 mm, height 4.7 mm; 37 jewels; 28,800 vph; gold rotor; 60-hour power reserve; Geneva Seal
Functions: hours, minutes, sweep seconds; date
Case: stainless steel, ø 41 mm, height 11 mm; sapphire crystal; transparent case back; water-resistant to 15 atm
Band: stainless steel, double folding clasp
Price: $22,500
Variations: reptile skin strap; rubber strap

Traditionnelle Chronograph Perpetual Calendar

Reference number: 5000T/000P-B975
Movement: manually wound, Vacheron Constantin Caliber 1142 QP; ø 27.5 mm, height 7.37 mm; 21 jewels; 21,600 vph; column wheel control of the chronograph functions; 48-hour power reserve; Geneva Seal
Functions: hours, minutes, subsidiary seconds; chronograph; perpetual calendar with date, weekday, months, moon phase, leap year
Case: platinum, ø 43 mm, height 12.94 mm; sapphire crystal; transparent case back; water-resistant to 3 atm
Band: reptile skin, folding clasp
Price: $164,000

Traditionnelle Complete Calendar

Reference number: 4010T/000R-B344
Movement: manually wound, Vacheron Constantin Caliber 2460 QCL; ø 29 mm, height 5.4 mm; 27 jewels; 28,800 vph; 40-hour power reserve; Geneva Seal
Functions: hours, minutes, sweep seconds; full calendar with date, weekday, month, moon phase
Case: rose gold, ø 41 mm, height 10.7 mm; sapphire crystal; transparent case back; water-resistant to 3 atm
Band: reptile skin, folding clasp
Price: $41,300

Patrimony Self-Winding

Reference number: 85180/000R-B515
Movement: automatic, Vacheron Constantin Caliber 2450 Q6; ø 26.2 mm, height 3.6 mm; 27 jewels; 28,800 vph; 40-hour power reserve; Geneva Seal
Functions: hours, minutes, sweep seconds; date
Case: rose gold, ø 40 mm, height 8.55 mm; sapphire crystal; water-resistant to 3 atm
Band: reptile skin, buckle
Price: $28,900

Patrimony Retrograde Day-Date

Reference number: 4000U/000R-B516
Movement: automatic, Vacheron Constantin Caliber 2460 R31R7/2; ø 27.2 mm, height 5.4 mm; 27 jewels; 28,800 vph; 40-hour power reserve; Geneva Seal
Functions: hours, minutes; date, weekday (retrograde)
Case: rose gold, ø 42.5 mm, height 9.7 mm; sapphire crystal; water-resistant to 3 atm
Band: reptile skin, folding clasp
Price: $44,800

Overseas Self-Winding

Reference number: 2305V-100R-B077
Movement: automatic, Vacheron Constantin Caliber 5300; ø 22.6 mm, height 4 mm; 31 jewels; 28,800 vph; gold rotor; 44-hour power reserve; Geneva Seal
Functions: hours, minutes, subsidiary seconds
Case: rose gold, ø 37 mm, 10.8 mm; dial set with 84 diamonds; sapphire crystal; transparent case back; water-resistant to 15 atm
Band: rose gold, double folding clasp
Price: $40,100
Variations: with reptile skin/rubber strap; in stainless steel

Égérie Self-Winding

Reference number: 4605F/110R-B496
Movement: automatic, Vacheron Constantin Caliber 1088; ø 20.8 mm, height 3.8 mm; 26 jewels; 28,800 vph; 40-hour power reserve
Functions: hours, minutes, sweep seconds; date
Case: rose gold, ø 35 mm, height 9.32 mm; bezel set with 58 diamonds; sapphire crystal; transparent case back; crown with moonstone cabochon; water-resistant to 3 atm
Band: rose gold, triple folding clasp
Remarks: dial set with 34 diamonds
Price: $43,100
Variations: white gold

Égérie Self-Winding

Reference number: 4605F/110A-B495
Movement: automatic, Vacheron Constantin Caliber 1088; ø 20.8 mm, height 3.8 mm; 26 jewels; 28,800 vph; 40-hour power reserve
Functions: hours, minutes, sweep seconds; date
Case: stainless steel, ø 35 mm, height 9.32 mm; bezel set with 58 diamonds; sapphire crystal; transparent case back; crown with moonstone cabochon; water-resistant to 3 atm
Band: stainless steel, triple folding clasp
Remarks: dial set with 34 diamonds
Price: $21,800
Variations: rose gold

Égérie Moon Phase

Reference number: 8005F/000R-B498
Movement: automatic, Vacheron Constantin Caliber 1088 L; ø 30 mm, height 5 mm; 26 jewels; 28,800 vph; 40-hour power reserve
Functions: hours, minutes, sweep seconds; moon phase
Case: rose gold, ø 37 mm, height 10.08 mm; bezel set with 58 diamonds; sapphire crystal; transparent case back; crown with moonstone cabochon; water-resistant to 3 atm
Band: reptile skin, buckle
Remarks: dial set with 36 diamonds; comes with 2 additional reptile skin straps
Price: $36,200
Variations: stainless steel

Patrimony Self-Winding

Reference number: 4115U/000R-B907
Movement: automatic, Vacheron Constantin Caliber 2450 Q6/3; ø 26.2 mm, height 3.6 mm; 27 jewels; 28,800 vph; 40-hour power reserve; Geneva Seal
Functions: hours, minutes, sweep seconds; date
Case: rose gold, ø 36.5 mm, height 8.45 mm; bezel set with 72 diamonds; sapphire crystal; transparent case back; water-resistant to 3 atm
Band: reptile skin, buckle
Price: $35,200

Traditionelle Perpetual Calendar Ultra-Thin

Reference number: 4305T/000G-B948
Movement: automatic, Vacheron Constantin Caliber 1120 QP; ø 29.6 mm, height 4.05 mm; 36 jewels; 19,800 vph; 40-hour power reserve; Geneva Seal
Functions: hours, minutes; perpetual calendar with date, weekday, months, moon phase, leap year
Case: white gold, ø 36.5 mm, height 8.43 mm; bezel and lugs set with 76 diamonds; sapphire crystal; transparent case back; crown with a diamond; water-resistant to 3 atm
Band: reptile skin, buckle
Price: $87,500

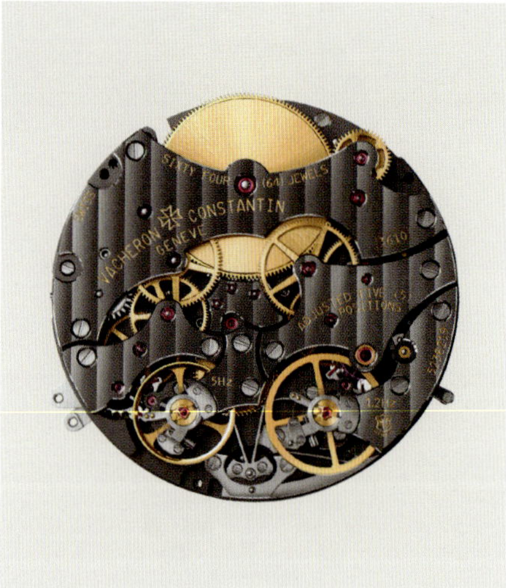

Caliber 3610

Manually wound, with two escapements "Twin-Beat-System", switchable between active and passive mode (for ex. when in a safe); single spring barrel, 65-day or 96-hour power reserve; Geneva Seal
Functions: hours, minutes; mode display: dual power reserve display for active and passive mode; perpetual calendar with date, month, leap year
Diameter: 32 mm
Height: 6 mm
Jewels: 64
Balance: glucydur
Frequency: 8,640 vph
Remarks: 480 parts

Caliber 2460 QCL/1

Automatic; stop-seconds mechanism; single spring barrel, 40-hour power reserve; Geneva Seal
Functions: hours, minutes, sweep seconds; full calendar with date, weekday, month
Diameter: 29 mm
Height: 5.4 mm
Jewels: 27
Balance: glucydur
Frequency: 28,800 vph
Remarks: gold rotor; 308 parts

Caliber 5110 DT

Automatic; single spring barrel, 60-hour power reserve; Geneva Seal
Functions: hours, minutes, sweep seconds; additional 12-hour display (second time zone), day/night indication; date
Diameter: 30.6 mm
Height: 6 mm
Jewels: 37
Balance: glucydur
Frequency: 28,800 vph
Remarks: gold rotor; 234 parts

Caliber 2160

Manually wound; 1-minute tourbillon; double spring barrel, 80-hour power reserve; Geneva Seal
Functions: hours, minutes, subsidiary seconds (on the tourbillon cage)
Diameter: 31 mm
Height: 5.65 mm
Jewels: 30
Balance: glucydur
Frequency: 18,000 vph
Remarks: 188 parts

Caliber 2460 G4/1

Automatic; single spring barrel, 40-hour power reserve; Geneva Seal
Functions: disk display for hours, minutes; disk display for date, weekday
Diameter: 31 mm
Height: 6.05 mm
Jewels: 27
Balance: glucydur
Frequency: 28,800 vph
Remarks: gold rotor; 237 parts

Caliber 3300

Manually wound; column-wheel control of chronograph functions, horizontal clutch; single spring barrel, 65-hour power reserve; Geneva Seal
Functions: hours, minutes, subsidiary seconds; power reserve indicator; chronograph with crown pusher
Diameter: 32.8 mm
Height: 6.7 mm
Jewels: 35
Balance: glucydur
Frequency: 21,600 vph
Remarks: 252 parts

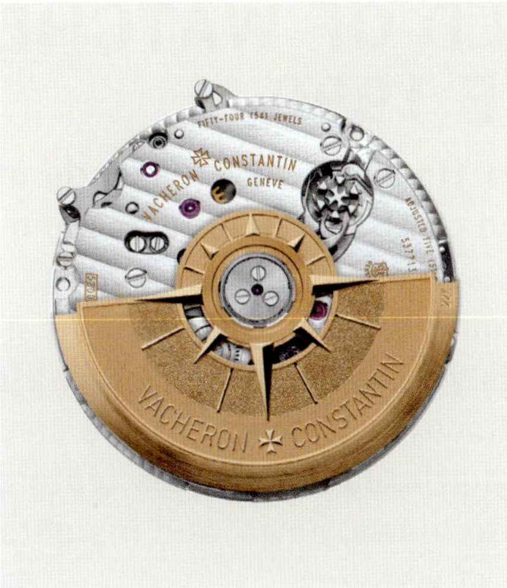

Caliber 5200

Automatic; column-wheel control of the chronograph functions; single spring barrel, 52-hour power reserve; Geneva Seal
Functions: hours, minutes, subsidiary seconds; chronograph; date
Diameter: 30.6 mm
Height: 6.6 mm
Jewels: 54
Balance: glucydur
Frequency: 28,800 vph
Remarks: gold rotor; 263 parts

Caliber 1120 QP

Automatic; extra-thin construction; winding rotor with supporting ring; single spring barrel, 40-hour power reserve; Geneva Seal
Functions: hours, minutes; perpetual calendar with date, weekday, month, moon phase, leap year
Diameter: 29.6 mm
Height: 4.05 mm
Jewels: 36
Balance: glucydur
Frequency: 19,800 vph
Remarks: skeletonized rotor with gold oscillating mass; 276 parts

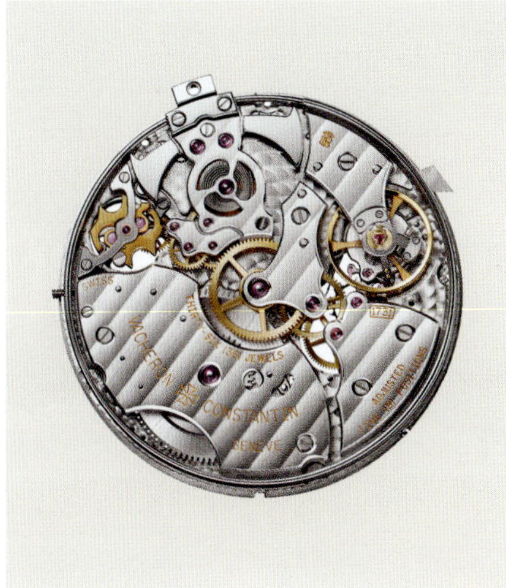

Caliber 1731

Manually wound; single spring barrel, 65-hour power reserve; Geneva Seal
Functions: hours, minutes, subsidiary seconds; hour, quarter-hour, and minute repeater
Diameter: 32.8 mm
Height: 3.9 mm
Jewels: 36
Balance: glucydur
Frequency: 21,600 vph
Remarks: perlage on mainplate, beveled edges, bridges with côtes de Genève

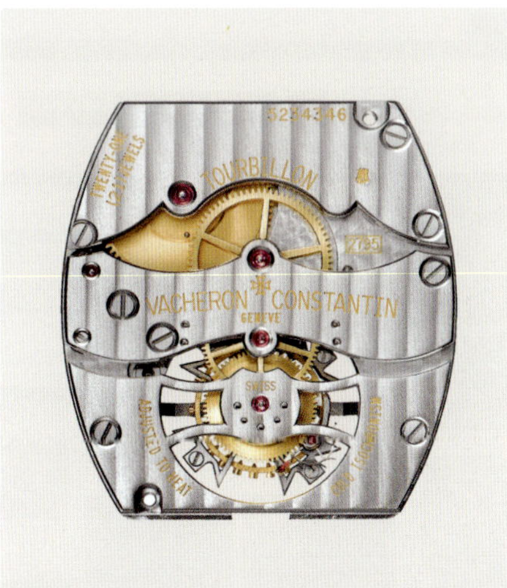

Caliber 2795

Automatic; 1-minute tourbillon; single spring barrel, 45-hour power reserve; Geneva Seal
Functions: hours, minutes, subsidiary seconds (on tourbillon cage)
Dimensions: 27.37 × 29.3 mm
Height: 6.1 mm
Jewels: 27
Balance: glucydur
Frequency: 18,000 vph
Remarks: tonneau- shaped

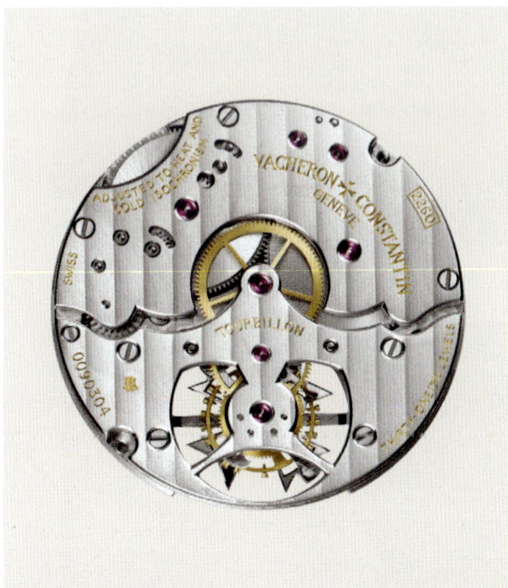

Caliber 2260

Manually wound; 1-minute tourbillon; quadruple spring barrel, 336-hour power reserve; Geneva Seal
Functions: hours, minutes, subsidiary seconds (on the tourbillon cage); power reserve display Diameter: 29.1 mm
Height: 6.8 mm
Jewels: 31
Balance: glucydur
Frequency: 18,000 vph
Remarks: 231 parts

Caliber 1003

Manually wound; single spring barrel, 31-hour power reserve; Geneva Seal
Functions: hours, minutes
Diameter: 21.1 mm
Height: 1.64 mm
Jewels: 18
Balance: glucydur
Frequency: 18,000 vph
Remarks: currently the thinnest industrially-produced mechanical caliber being produced

VAN CLEEF & ARPELS

Van Cleef & Arpels
2, rue du Quatre-Septembre
F-75002 Paris
France

Tel.:
+33-1-70-70-36-56

Website:
www.vancleefarpels.com

Founded:
1906

U.S. distributor:
1-877-VAN-CLEEF

Most important collections:
Charms; Pierre Arpels; Poetic Complications

In 1999, while shopping around for more companies to add to its roster of high-end jewelers, Richemont Group decided to purchase Van Cleef & Arpels. The venerable jewelry brand had a lot of name recognition, thanks in part to a host of internationally known customers, like Jacqueline Kennedy Onassis, whose two marriages each involved a Van Cleef & Arpels ring. It also had a reputation for the high quality of its workmanship. It was Van Cleef & Arpels that came up with the mystery setting using a special rail and cut totally hidden from the casual eye.

Van Cleef & Arpels was a family business that came to be when a young stonecutter, Alfred van Cleef, married Estelle Arpels in 1896, and ten years later opened a business on Place Vendôme in Paris with Estelle's brother Charles. More of Estelle's brothers joined the firm, which was soon booming and serving, quite literally, royalty.

Watches were always a part of the portfolio. But after joining Richemont, Van Cleef now had the support of a very complete industrial portfolio that would allow it to make stunning movements that could bring dials to life. Most models today run on the Valfleurier Q020 movement exclusively developed for the company. But it was a collaboration with Jean-Marc Wiederrecht and Agenhor on the Pont des Amoureux with its stunning retrograde complication that has become a standard for the brand. The idea has been replicated in the Ballerine Enchantée, whose tutu, on demand, suddenly becomes butterfly wings pointing to the hours and minutes. Among the most talked-about watches of 2022, though, was surely the Heures Florales, which replicates the concept garden of Swedish botanist and taxonomist Carl Linnaeus, where time could be read according to which flowers are open. This remarkable feat comes in a red pattern (Cerisier) as well.

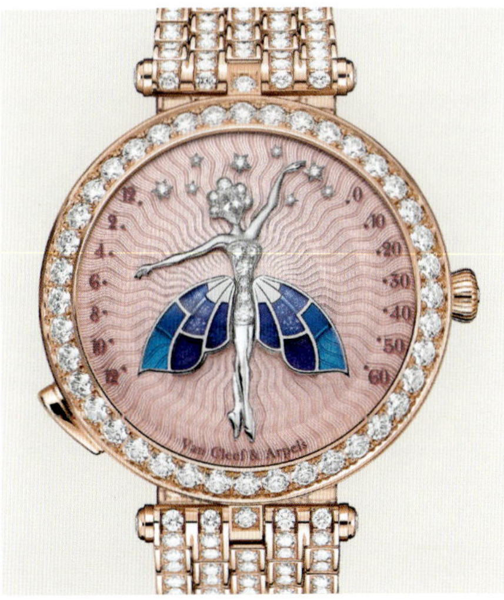

Lady Arpels Ballerine Enchantée

Reference number: VCARPBER00
Movement: manually wound, Valfleurier Q020; ø 36 mm, height 12.6 mm; 28,8000 vph; 58 jewels; 36-hour power reserve
Functions: retrograde hours and minutes with time-on-demand module
Case: rose gold, ø 41 mm, height 12.6 mm; bezel and crown in white gold set with 137 diamonds; water-resistant to 3 atm
Band: reptile skin; rose gold buckle set with diamonds
Remarks: guilloché rose enamel dial, rose-gold ballerina with butterfly wings made with plique-à-jour enamel and diamonds
Price: $127,000

Lady Arpels Heures Florales Cerisier

Reference number: VCARPBJM00
Movement: automatic, Valfleurier Q020, with special module to open the flowers; ø 36 mm, height 12.6 mm; 93 jewels; 28,8000 vph; 36-hour power reserve
Functions: count open flowers for the hour, minutes in side window
Case: rose gold, ø 38 mm, height 14.64 mm; round diamond on crown; water resistant up to 3 atm
Remarks: floral arrangement on the dial inspired by Linnaeus' flower clock; mother-of-pearl marquetry, miniature painting, sapphires and diamonds, and three colors of gold; 295 diamonds in all
Band: reptile skin, buckle
Price: $240,000

Pierre Arpels

Reference number: VCARO3GL00
Movement: manually wound, Caliber 830P; ø 26.80, height 19 mm; 19 jewels; 21,600 vph; 60-hour power reserve
Functions: hours, minutes
Case: rose gold, ø 38 mm, height 5.8 mm; rose gold bezel with 81 diamonds
Band: reptile skin, buckle
Remarks: honeycomb motif on lacquer dial
Price: $16,200
Variations: white gold ($32,000)

VOSTOK-EUROPE

Vostok-Europe is a young brand with old roots. In 2022, it is celebrating its eighteenth anniversary.

What started as a joint venture between the original Vostok company—a wholly separate entity—deep in the heart of Russia and a start-up in the newly minted European Union member nation of Lithuania has grown into something altogether different over the years. Originally, every Vostok model had a proprietary Russian engine, a 32-jewel automatic built by Vostok in Russia. Over the years, demand and the need for alternative complications expanded the portfolio of movements to include Swiss and Japanese ones. While the heritage of the eighty-year Russian watch industry is still evident in the inspirations and designs of Vostok-Europe, the watches built today have become favorites of extreme athletes the world over.

"Real people doing real things" is the mantra that Igor Zubovskij, managing director of the company, often repeats. "We don't use models to market our watches. Only real people test our watches in many different conditions."

That community of "real people" includes cross-country drivers in the Dakar Rally, one of the most famous aerobatic pilots in the world, a team of spelunkers who literally went to the bottom of the world in the Krubera Cave, and world free-diving champions. In 2020 the brand because the official watch of the SSN-571 Alumni Association and a part of the history of the world's first nuclear submarine.

Much of the Vostok-Europe line is of professional dive quality. For illumination, some models incorporate tritium tube technology, which offers about twenty-five years of constant lighting. The Lunokhod 2, the current flagship of the brand, incorporates vertical tubes in a "candleholder" design for full 360-degree illumination.

The watches are assembled in Vilnius, Lithuania, and Zubvoskij still personally oversees quality control operations.

Koliz Vostok Co. Ltd.
Naugarduko 41
LT-03227 Vilnius
Lithuania

Tel.:
+370-5-2106342

E-mail:
info@vostok-europe.com

Website:
www.vostok-europe.com

Founded:
2003

Number of employees:
24

Annual production:
30,000 watches

U.S. distributor:
Vostok-Europe
Détente Watch Group
244 Upton Road, Suite 4
Colchester, CT 06415
877-486-7865
www.detentewatches.com

Most important collections/price range:
Anchar / from $759; Lunokhod / from $899; Mriya / from $649

Space Race

Reference number: YN55325B664
Movement: automatic, Seiko Epson Caliber YN55A; ø 29.36 mm, height 5.37 mm; 22 jewels; 21,600 vph; bidirectional winding; 40-hour power reserve
Functions: hours, minutes, sweep seconds; date
Case: stainless steel, ø 47 mm, height 17 mm; hardened antireflective K1 mineral crystal; screw-in crown; transparent case back; water-resistant to 20 atm
Band: calfskin, buckle
Price: $479

Almaz

Reference number: YM8J-320D6567
Movement: quartz, Seiko Epson YM8J
Functions: hours, minutes, sweep seconds; world time with city references; weekday, date, 24-hour chronograph, 24-hour countdown, 24-hour sound alarm
Case: stainless steel, ø 47 mm, height 17.5 mm; unidirectional bezel with 0-60 scale, hardened antireflective K1 mineral glass; screw-in crown; water-resistant to 20 atm
Band: leather, buckle
Price: $759; limited and numbered edition of 3,000 pieces

Energia II

Reference number: NH35-575A650
Movement: automatic, Seiko SII NH35; ø 27.40 mm; height 5.32; 24 jewels; 21,600 vph ; 41-hour power reserve
Functions: hours, minutes, sweep seconds; date
Case: stainless steel, ø 49 mm, height 17.5 mm; unidirectional bezel with 0-60 scale, hardened antireflective K1 mineral glass; water-resistant to 30 atm, helium release valve
Band: calfskin, buckle
Remarks: with 2nd silicon strap, screwdriver, and dry box; "Trigalight" constant tritium illumination
Price: $899

Waldan Watches
600 5th Ave.
FLR 2
New York, NY 10020

Tel.:
212-308-5310

E-mail:
info@waldanwatches.com

Website:
www.waldanwatches.com

Founded:
1979

Number of employees:
6

Annual production:
approx. 6,000

Distribution:
See headquarters.

Most important collections/price range:
Waldan Heritage / $299 to $1,000; Waldan Classic / $8,000 to $18,000

WALDAN

Oscar Waldan, born in Poland, has a remarkable life story. He was already a watch fan by the time he ended up in Terezin concentration camp, where he befriended a fellow prisoner who was a watchmaker. After the war, he plunged headfirst into the industry, supplying various high-profile retailers in the United States with in-house-branded timepieces. He also worked with major brands like Omega. And then, Waldan decided he had the experience and the wherewithal and the ideas to produce his own timepieces. In 1979, he launched Waldan International. The quartz crisis was still weighing on the industry, but he designed a series of mechanical watches and built his cases and dials to reflect the quality Swiss engines within. These early Waldans included such counterintuitive pieces as a moon phase chronograph, and they remain collector's favorites, embodying what a fine luxury wristwatch should be: a mechanical complication with top-quality components inside and out and a design that will never go out of style.

The first generation of Waldan watches (now known as the Classic collection) are Swiss Made timepieces crafted in 18-kt gold or platinum. In 2018, Oscar's son Andrew took the reins and decided it was time to evolve by adding a new line that would take the classic look of the existing Waldans and build a high-quality watch priced to appeal to a much wider audience. The Heritage collection is crafted in steel, sapphire, and fine leather, and is now built in the USA. While the Classic collection remains available to high-end collectors, the new Heritage collection embraces a retail price segment under $500, with a goal of offering the timeless Waldan design(s) to a far wider audience.

World Time Chronometer

Movement: automatic, ETA 2893-3 Caliber; ø 25.6 mm, height 4.1 mm; 21 jewels; 28,800 vph; decorated movement and rotor; COSC-certified movement; 38-hour power reserve
Functions: hours, minutes, sweep seconds; world time indicator
Case: rose gold, ø 40 mm; sapphire crystal; transparent case back; water-resistant to 3 atm
Price: $18,000

Retro Alarm

Movement: manually wound, caliber AS 1931; ø 25.6 mm, height 6.9 mm; 17 jewels; 21,600 vph; dual spring barrels; 13-second alarm; 48-hour power reserve
Functions: hours, minutes, sweep seconds; date; mechanical alarm
Case: rose gold, ø 38 mm, height 12 mm; sapphire crystal; full case back; water-resistant to 3 atm
Band: reptile skin, buckle
Remarks: 1970–1974 Vintage NOS retro alarm movement; white porcelain enamel dial
Price: $8,000

Astronic Chronograph

Movement: automatic, 1969 Zenith "El Primero" Caliber 3019 PHF; ø 30 mm, height 6.5 mm; 31 jewels; 36,000 vph; 50-hour power reserve
Functions: hours, minutes, seconds on subdial, 12-hour chronograph, day of week, date, month, moon phase
Case: pink gold, ø 39.5mm, height 20 mm; sapphire crystal; transparent case back; water-resistant to 3 atm
Band: reptile skin, buckle
Remarks: enamel dial with applied gold Breguet numerals
Price: $16,000

WEMPE GLASHÜTTE I/SA

Ever since 2005, the global jewelry chain Gerhard D. Wempe KG has been putting out watches under its own name again. It was probably inevitable: Gerhard D. Wempe, who founded the company in the late nineteenth century in Oldenburg, was himself a watchmaker. And in the 1930s, the company also owned the Hamburg chronometer works that made watches for seafarers and pilots.

Today, while Wempe remains formally in Hamburg, its manufacturing is done in Glashütte. The move to the fully renovated and expanded Urania observatory in the hills above town was engineered by Eva-Kim Wempe, great-granddaughter of the founder. There, the company does all its after-sales service and tests watches using the strict German Industrial Norm (DIN 8319), with official blessings from the Saxon and Thuringian offices for measurement and calibration, and according to international norms paid out by the German Calibration Service.

The move to Glashütte coincided with a push to verticalize by creating a line of in-house movements for the exclusive Chronometerwerke models, like the very retro Chronometerwerke Power Reserve, or the eminently noticeable Tonneau Tourbillon. The calibers, bearing the initials CW, are made in partnership with companies like Nomos in Glashütte or the Swiss workshop MHVJ. In 2016, Wempe released the CW4, an automatic that had its first "outing" in a classic three-hander. It has a promising future ahead of it.

The second Wempe line is called Zeitmeister, or Master of Time. This collection uses more standard, but reworked, ETA or Sellita calibers. It meets all the requirements of the high art of watchmaking and, thanks to its accessible pricing, is attractive for budding collectors. All models are in the middle price range, which the luxury watch industry has long shunned. In 2020, Wempe joined a large community of brands with sportive-elegant timepieces. The Iron Walker series is supposed to be inspired by the workers who built the great skyscrapers of New York in the 1920s. The line is characterized by the elegant bracelet that integrates almost seamlessly into the case. The skyscrapers are hinted at in the shape of the hands.

Gerhard D. Wempe KG
Steinstrasse 23
D-20095 Hamburg
Germany

Tel.:
+49-40-334-480

E-mail:
info@wempe.de

Website:
www.wempe.com

Founded:
1878

Number of employees:
845 worldwide; 65 at Wempe Glashütte I/SA

Annual production:
5,000 watches

U.S. distributor:
Wempe
700 Fifth Avenue
New York, NY 10019
212-397-9000
www.wempe.com

Most important collections/price range:
Wempe Zeitmeister / approx. $1,000 to $4,500; Wempe Chronometerwerke / approx. $6,000 to $56,500; Wempe Iron Walker / $1,950 to $4,250

Iron Walker Automatic Men's Watch

Reference number: WI 100006
Movement: automatic, ETA Caliber 2892-A2; ø 25.6 mm, height 3.6 mm; 21 jewels; 28,800 vph; officially certified chronometer according to ISO 3159; 50-hour power reserve
Functions: hours, minutes, sweep seconds; date
Case: stainless steel, ø 40 mm, height 9.75 mm; sapphire crystal; water-resistant to 10 atm
Band: stainless steel, folding clasp, with safety catch
Price: $2,995
Variations: with white or black dial

Iron Walker Automatic Diver

Reference number: WI 200001
Movement: automatic, ETA Caliber 2892-A2; ø 25.6 mm, height 3.6 mm; 21 jewels; 28,800 vph; officially certified chronometer according to ISO 3159; 42-hour power reserve
Functions: hours, minutes, sweep seconds; date
Case: stainless steel, ø 42 mm, height 11.7 mm; crown-activated inner bezel with 0-60 scale; sapphire crystal; screw-in crown; water-resistant to 30 atm
Band: stainless steel, folding clasp, with safety catch, with extension link
Price: $3,785
Variations: with blue dial

Iron Walker Automatic Chronograph

Reference number: WI 300002
Movement: automatic, ETA Caliber 7753; ø 30 mm, height 7.9 mm; 27 jewels; 28,800 vph; officially certified chronometer according to ISO 3159; 48-hour power reserve
Functions: hours, minutes, subsidiary seconds; chronograph; date
Case: stainless steel, ø 42 mm, height 13.95 mm; sapphire crystal; screw-in crown; water-resistant to 10 atm
Band: stainless steel, folding clasp, with safety catch
Price: $4,615
Variations: with black dial

Iron Walker Automatic Ladies' Watch

Reference number: WI 100007
Movement: automatic, ETA Caliber 2892-A2; ø 25.6 mm, height 3.6 mm; 21 jewels; 28,800 vph; ISO 3159-certified chronometer; 42-hour power reserve
Functions: hours, minutes, sweep seconds; date
Case: stainless steel, ø 36 mm, height 9.75 mm; bezel set with 60 brilliant-cut diamonds; sapphire crystal; water-resistant to 10 atm
Band: stainless steel, folding clasp with safety lock
Price: $6,325
Variations: with a blue dial

Iron Walker Automatic GMT

Reference number: WI 250002
Movement: automatic, Sellita Caliber SW330; ø 25.6 mm, height 4.1 mm; 21 jewels; 28,800 vph; officially certified chronometer according to ISO 3159; 42-hour power reserve
Functions: hours, minutes, sweep seconds; additional 24-hour display (second time zone); date
Case: stainless steel, ø 42 mm, height 11.7 mm; crown-adjustable inner bezel with 0-24 scale; sapphire crystal; screw-in crown; water-resistant to 10 atm
Band: stainless steel, folding clasp with safety lock
Price: $4,035
Variations: with black-white scale ring

Iron Walker Automatic Chronograph XL

Reference number: WI 400001
Movement: automatic, Sellita Caliber SW500-1; ø 30 mm, height 7.9 mm; 25 jewels; 28,800 vph; officially certified chronometer according to ISO 3159; 48-hour power reserve
Functions: hours, minutes, subsidiary seconds; chronograph; date
Case: stainless steel, ø 44 mm, height 15.8 mm; bezel, rubber-covered crown and pushers; sapphire crystal; water-resistant to 10 atm
Band: rubber, folding clasp
Price: $5,075
Variations: with blue dial and band; with stainless steel band ($5,075); blue dial and stainless-steel band ($5,075)

Chronometerwerke Automatic

Reference number: WG 090007
Movement: automatic, Wempe Caliber CW4; ø 32.8 mm, height 6 mm; 35 jewels; 28,800 vph; 2 spring barrels; three-quarter plate, hand-engraved balance cock, 6 gold chatons, tungsten micro-rotor, finely finished, with Glashütte ribbing; officially certified chronometer according to ISO 3159; 90-hour power reserve
Functions: hours, minutes, sweep seconds; date
Case: stainless steel, ø 41 mm, height 11.7 mm; sapphire crystal; transparent case back; water-resistant to 3 atm
Band: stainless steel, folding clasp
Price: $7,100
Variations: with a white dial

Zeitmeister Aviator Chronograph XL Antique

Reference number: WM 690027
Movement: automatic, ETA Caliber A07.211; ø 36.6 mm, height 7.9 mm; 25 jewels; 28,800 vph; officially certified chronometer according to ISO 3159; 46-hour power reserve
Functions: hours, minutes, subsidiary seconds; chronograph; date
Case: stainless steel with black PVD coating, ø 45 mm, height 15.45 mm; sapphire crystal; water-resistant to 5 atm
Band: textile, folding clasp
Price: $3,200

Zeitmeister Aviator Watch Big Date Antique

Reference number: WM 690026
Movement: automatic, ETA Caliber 2892-A2 with TT651.00; ø26.2 mm, height 5.25 mm; 21 jewels; 28,800 vph; officially certified chronometer according to ISO 3159; 42-hour power reserve
Functions: hours, minutes, sweep seconds; additional 12-hour display (second time zone); large date
Case: stainless steel with black PVD coating, ø 42 mm, height 13.65 mm; sapphire crystal; water-resistant to 5 atm
Band: textile, folding clasp
Price: $3,200; limited to 100 pieces

YVAN MONNET

Yvan Monnet
Place Simon-Goulart, 2 38
CVH-1201 Genève
Switzerland

Tel:
+41-32-967-97-97

E-mail:
yvan@yvm2.ch

Website:
www.ymonnet.ch

Founded:
2016; Tzoumy in 2021

Number of employees:
5

Number of watches:
100 (Five), Tzoumy (750)

Distributor:
For all questions and orders, contact the company directly

Most important collections/price range:
Five, Mina, Tzoumy / $2,350 to $5,800

After two decades working with Patek Philippe and Vacheron Constantin, Valais-born Yvan Monnet faced a bit of a dilemma: either continue finding work in the beehives of large companies with security but little autonomy, or set sail on his own. He decided to tap into his extensive experience with what is known as *habillage*, all the jobs related to the complex art of finishing in watchmaking and conceive his own brand.

"For it to be relevant," says Monnet, "it had to be something that was never done before." He wanted a watch that would be essentially unisex, that would reflect his own positive personality traits: sports-loving, entertaining, sociable, communicative. "I wanted a watch I could take to work, to a concert, to a cocktail, and then go take a swim in the lake without having to leave a precious object in my shoes on the beach."

He began by simply brainstorming on paper. The design that stuck was a pentagonal bezel, not very attractive on paper, but after lots of tweaking and fine-tuning, he obtained what he had originally intended in his mind's eye. It is not an easy shape to fit onto a round dial and the barrel. He avoided gilding the lily with lots of decoration, opting for a great degree of coherence between the hands, the colors, and the numerals. The screw-in crown at 2:30 is also pentagonal and allows the watch to dive two-hundred meters. The colors are stark without being overbearing: black, blue, a pine green, and light chocolate. They come in a larger size, the Five, and a smaller size, the Mina. They are driven by a Selitta caliber.

In a bid to spread his pentagonal gospel to a larger market, Monnet then come up with the Tzoumy. This side brand is slightly thinner and runs on a robust Landeron caliber. It, too, comes in a variety of colors that are carefully chosen to stand out without being flamboyant. Yvan Monnet products hide complex design behind a look of simplicity.

Five Black

Reference number: 1001V2
Movement: automatic, Selitta SW400-1; ø 31 mm, height 7.9 mm; 26 jewels; 28,800 vph; custom rotor with black PVD; 38-hour power reserve
Functions: hours, minutes, sweep seconds
Case: stainless steel, ø 43 x 42.1 mm, height 10.80 mm; sapphire crystal; screw-in crown; water-resistant to 20 atm
Band: calfskin, folding clasp
Remarks: comes with additional "waterproof" strap on rubber padding with buckle
Price: $5,780
Variations: comes in different dial colors

Tzoumy Denim

Reference number: TZ01
Movement: automatic, Landeron 24 Caliber; ø 25.6 mm, height 4.6 mm; 25 jewels; 28,800 vph; Tzoumy special rotor, 36-hour power reserve
Functions: hours, minutes, sweep seconds
Case: stainless steel, ø 40.1 x 39.55 mm, height 9.5 mm; sapphire crystal; water-resistant to 5 atm
Band: calfskin, buckle
Remarks: sunburst finishing on the dial
Price: $2,350
Variations: comes in different dial colors

Mina Cacao

Reference number: 2103
Movement: manually wound, modified Sellita Caliber SW210-1; ø 25.6 mm, height 3.35 mm; 19 jewels; 28,800 vph; 42-hour power reserve
Functions: hours, minutes, sweep seconds
Case: stainless steel, ø 40.1 x 39.55 mm, height 9.5 mm; sapphire crystal; water-resistant to 5 atm
Band: calfskin, buckle
Remarks: comes with additional satin strap and buckle
Price: $3,100
Variations: white or blue lacquered dial; comes in automatic version with Selitta SW300-1 movement ($3,350)

Zeitwinkel Montres SA
Rue Pierre-Jolissaint 35
CH-2610 Saint-Imier
Switzerland

Tel.:
+41-32-940-17-71

E-mail:
info@zeitwinkel.ch

Website:
www.zeitwinkel.ch

Founded:
2006

Annual production:
less than 1,000 watches

U.S. distributor:
available directly from the manufacture, contact through Instagram, website, email or by phone

Most important collections/price range:
mechanical wristwatches / starting at around CHF 9,000

ZEITWINKEL

Zeitwinkel turned sixteen in 2022, but that is not really important for this small, independent company based in Saint-Imier, one of the hubs of the watch industry in Switzerland. The key attributes of the brand, ones that many watch manufacturers aspire to endow their creations with, are "timeless, simple, and sustainable." So time is, in essence, timeless. And because of that concept, the company feels no pressure to enter the rat race of producing new models like clockwork, but rather waits for the inspiration.

The models produced by Zeitwinkel (the name means "time angle") are deceptively classical. The simplest exemplar is a two-hand watch; the most complicated, the 273°, a three-hand timepiece with power reserve display and large date. The most decoration one will find on the dials is a spangling of stylized Ws, which is the inverted logo derived from the brand's proprietary typeface. The cases feature a delicate interplay of sandblasted and polished areas, but they are discreetly elegant, in a fairly "German" way, which comes as no surprise because Zeitwinkel's founders, Ivica Maksimovic and Peter Nikolaus, hail from there. Some details will catch the eye, notably the extra-large subsidiary seconds dial and the aperture for the patented large date, found beside the 11 o'clock marker.

The most valuable part of the watches is their veritable manufacture movements, plates and bridges made of German silver, which is fairly rare in the business. All components are made in-house or come courtesy of longtime independent suppliers not far from Zeitwinkel's workshop in Saint-Imier, where all movements as well as all watches are assembled and regulated by hand. The 273° Saphir Fumé comes with a smoked sapphire crystal dial. The enamel dial of the 082° Email Grand Feu is smaller, but the brilliance of the enamel is a perfect backdrop to the gentle blue numerals and indices that recall timepieces of a past era.

In keeping with the company's ideals, you won't find any alligator in Zeitwinkel watch straps. Choices here are exclusively rubber, calfskin, or calfskin with an alligator-like pattern.

082° Email Grand Feu

Reference number: 082-46023-00
Movement: automatic, Caliber ZW0102; ø 30.4 mm, height 5.7 mm; 30 jewels; 28,800 vph; German silver three-quarter plate with côtes de Genève and perlage; polished screws and edges; 72-hour power reserve, blued screws
Functions: hours, minutes, sweep seconds
Case: stainless steel, ø 39 mm, height 11.6 mm; sapphire crystal; transparent case back; water-resistant to 5 atm
Band: calfskin, folding clasp
Remarks: white enamel dial, grand feu
Price: $12,200
Variations: different bands

273° Saphir Bleu

Reference number: 273-45018-00
Movement: automatic, Caliber ZW0103; ø 30.4 mm, height 8 mm; 49 jewels; 28,800 vph; German silver three-quarter plate and bridges, côtes de Genève, polished screws and edges; perlage on dial side; 72-hour power reserve
Functions: hours, minutes, subsidiary seconds; power reserve indicator; patented big date mechanism
Case: stainless steel, ø 42.5 mm, height 13.8 mm; sapphire crystal; transparent case back; water-resistant to 5 atm; **Band:** calfskin, folding clasp
Remarks: blue sapphire crystal dial
Price: $17,500
Variations: smoked sapphire dial, various dial colors; different bands

188°

Reference number: 188-42023-00
Movement: automatic, Caliber ZW0102; ø 30.4 mm, height 5.7 mm; 28 jewels; 28,800 vph; German silver three-quarter plate and bridges, guilloché, polished screws and edges; 72-hour power reserve
Functions: hours, minutes, subsidiary seconds; date
Case: stainless steel, ø 39 mm, height 11.6 mm; sapphire crystal; transparent case back; water-resistant to 5 atm
Band: calfskin, folding clasp
Price: $10,200
Variations: various dial colors

ZENITH

Zenith, still housed in a tall, light-bathed industrial building in Le Locle, Switzerland, was founded in 1865 by Georges Favre-Jacot as a small watch reassembly workshop. It has produced all kinds of watches in its long history, but its claim to fame is the El Primero caliber, the first wristwatch chronograph movement boasting automatic winding and a frequency of 36,000 vph, allowing for measurements of a tenth of a second. It was 1969, and only a few manufacturers had risked such a high oscillation frequency—and none of them with such complexity as the integrated chronograph mechanism and bilaterally winding rotor of the El Primero.

LVMH Group bought the brand in 1999, boosting its technical possibilities. Zenith was dusted off and modernized. The historic complex in Le Locle, which was put on UNESCO's World Heritage list in 2009, was thoroughly renovated. Over eighty different crafts are now practiced here, from watchmaking to design, from art to prototyping. Synergies with the Group companions Hublot and TAG Heuer produced the Defy 21, a complex chronograph movement based on the 36,000-vph El Primero. It features two separate gear trains and escapements for time and chronograph functions, respectively. The chronograph movement beats at 360,000 vph, allowing the hundredths of a second to be displayed. The other technical feat is the Zero G that keeps the escapement system in the horizontal position.

The vintage movement has also produced nostalgic pilot's watches chez Zenith, and more recently a re-edition of several historic models housed in identifiably classic cases. This has led the company to promote a circular economy, whereby older models can be perfectly restored and remain in circulation. The original El Primero is often used to drive the hands, so in 2020, Zenith released the El Primero 3600 caliber, a technically modernized version of the original one with a little more power reserve but still running at 36,000 vph. And finally, there is the new Chronomaster Sport, a 41-millimeter gem with a ceramic bezel in three colors, a feat much more complex to achieve than one might think.

Zenith SA
34, rue des Billodes
CH-2400 Le Locle
Switzerland

Tel.:
+41-32-930-6262

Website:
www.zenith-watches.com

Founded:
1865

Number of employees:
over 330 employees worldwide

U.S. distributor:
Zenith Watches
966 South Springfield Avenue
Springfield, NJ 07081
866-675-2079
contact.zenith@lvmhwatchjewelry.com

Most important collections/price range:
Academy / from $80,900; Elite / from $4,700; Chronomaster / from $6,700; Pilot / from $5,700; Defy / from $5,900

Defy Skyline

Reference number: 03.9300.3620/51.I001
Movement: automatic, Zenith Caliber 3620 "El Primero"; ø 30 mm, height 6.6 mm; 26 jewels; 36,000 vph; 60-hour power reserve
Functions: hours, minutes, subsidiary seconds; date
Case: stainless steel, ø 41 mm, height 11.6 mm; sapphire crystal; transparent case back; screw-in crown; water-resistant to 10 atm
Band: stainless steel, folding clasp
Price: $8,400

Defy Skyline

Reference number: 03.9300.3620/21.I001
Movement: automatic, Zenith Caliber 3620 "El Primero"; ø 30 mm, height 6.6 mm; 26 jewels; 36,000 vph; 60-hour power reserve
Functions: hours, minutes, subsidiary seconds; date
Case: stainless steel, ø 41 mm, height 11.6 mm; sapphire crystal; transparent case back; screw-in crown; water-resistant to 10 atm
Band: stainless steel, folding clasp
Price: $8,400

Defy Skyline

Reference number: 03.9300.3620/01.I001
Movement: automatic, Zenith Caliber 3620 "El Primero"; ø 30 mm, height 6.6 mm; 26 jewels; 36,000 vph; 60-hour power reserve
Functions: hours, minutes, subsidiary seconds; date
Case: stainless steel, ø 41 mm, height 11.6 mm; sapphire crystal; transparent case back; screw-in crown; water-resistant to 10 atm
Band: rubber, folding clasp
Price: $8,400

Defy Midnight Borealis

Reference number: 16.9200.670/33.MI001
Movement: automatic, Zenith Caliber 670 SK "Elite"; ø 25.6 mm, height 3.88 mm; 27 jewels; 28,800 vph; skeletonized movement; 48-hour power reserve
Functions: hours, minutes, sweep seconds; date
Case: stainless steel, ø 36 mm; bezel set with 44 diamonds; sapphire crystal; transparent case back; water-resistant to 10 atm
Band: stainless steel, folding clasp
Remarks: dial set with 11 diamonds; comes with 3 additional reptile skin straps
Price: $11,400

Defy Midnight Borealis

Reference number: 16.9200.670/34.MI001
Movement: automatic, Zenith Caliber 670 SK "Elite"; ø 25.6 mm, height 3.88 mm; 27 jewels; 28,800 vph; skeletonized movement; 48-hour power reserve
Functions: hours, minutes, sweep seconds; date
Case: stainless steel, ø 36 mm; bezel set with 44 diamonds; sapphire crystal; transparent case back; water-resistant to 10 atm
Band: stainless steel, folding clasp
Remarks: dial set with 11 diamonds; comes with 3 additional reptile skin straps
Price: $11,400

Defy El Primero 21

Reference number: 95.9002.9004/78.M9000
Movement: automatic, Zenith Caliber 9004 "El Primero"; ø 32 mm, height 7.9 mm; 53 jewels; 36,000 vph; independent chronograph mechanism with separate escapement system (360,000 vph) and its own power management; Timelab-certified chronometer, 50-hour power reserve
Functions: hours, minutes, subsidiary seconds; power reserve display (for chronograph functions) chronograph (display of the 100th of seconds)
Case: titanium, ø 44 mm, height 14.5 mm; sapphire crystal; transparent case back; water-resistant to 10 atm
Band: titanium, double folding clasp
Price: $14,000

Defy Classic Black Carbon

Reference number: 10.9000.670/80.R795
Movement: automatic, Zenith Caliber 670 SK "Elite"; ø 25.6 mm, height 3.88 mm; 27 jewels; 28,800 vph; skeletonized movement; 48-hour power reserve
Functions: hours, minutes, sweep seconds; date
Case: carbon fiber, ø 36 mm, height 10.75 mm; sapphire crystal; transparent case back; water-resistant to 10 atm
Band: rubber with textile overlay, folding clasp
Remarks: skeletonized dial
Price: $11,900

Defy Extreme Carbon

Reference number: 10.9100.9004/22.I200
Movement: automatic, Zenith Caliber 9004 "El Primero"; ø 32 mm, height 7.9 mm; 53 jewels; 36,000 vph; independent chronograph mechanism with separate escapement system (360,000 vph) and its own power management; Timelab-certified chronometer, 50-hour power reserve
Functions: hours, minutes, subsidiary seconds; power reserve display (for chronograph functions); chronograph (display of the 100th of seconds)
Case: carbon fiber, ø 45 mm, height 15.4 mm; sapphire crystal; transparent case back; water-resistant to 20 atm
Band: textile, double folding clasp
Price: $25,100

Defy Extreme

Reference number: 97.9100.9004/02.I001
Movement: automatic, Zenith Caliber 9004 "El Primero"; ø 32 mm, height 7.9 mm; 53 jewels; 36,000 vph; independent chronograph mechanism with separate escapement system (360,000 vph) and its own power management; Timelab-certified chronometer, 50-hour power reserve
Functions: hours, minutes, subsidiary seconds; power reserve display (for chronograph functions); chronograph (display of the 100th of seconds)
Case: titanium (sand-blasted), ø 45 mm, height 15.4 mm; sapphire crystal; transparent case back; water-resistant to 20 atm
Band: titanium (sand-blasted), double folding clasp
Price: $18,000

Chronomaster Sport

Reference number: 18.3101.3600/69.M3100
Movement: automatic, Zenith Caliber 3600 "El Primero"; ø 30 mm, height 6.6 mm; 35 jewels; 36,000 vph; 60-hour power reserve
Functions: hours, minutes, subsidiary seconds; chronograph; date
Case: rose gold, ø 41 mm, height 13.6 mm; sapphire crystal; transparent case back; water-resistant to 10 atm
Band: rose gold double folding clasp
Price: $38,200

Chronomaster Sport

Reference number: 18.3101.3600/21.M3100
Movement: automatic, Zenith Caliber 3600 "El Primero"; ø 30 mm, height 6.6 mm; 35 jewels; 36,000 vph; 60-hour power reserve
Functions: hours, minutes, subsidiary seconds; chronograph; date
Case: rose gold, ø 41 mm, height 13.6 mm; sapphire crystal; transparent case back; water-resistant to 10 atm
Band: rose gold double folding clasp
Price: $38,200

Chronomaster Sport

Reference number: 18.3100.3600/69.C920
Movement: automatic, Zenith Caliber 3600 "El Primero"; ø 30 mm, height 6.6 mm; 35 jewels; 36,000 vph; 60-hour power reserve
Functions: hours, minutes, subsidiary seconds; chronograph; date
Case: rose gold, ø 41 mm, height 13.6 mm; ceramic bezel; sapphire crystal; transparent case back; water-resistant to 10 atm
Band: calfskin, triple folding clasp
Price: $22,400

Chronomaster Sport

Reference number: 51.3100.3600/69.M3100
Movement: automatic, Zenith Caliber 3600 "El Primero"; ø 30 mm, height 6.6 mm; 35 jewels; 36,000 vph; 60-hour power reserve
Functions: hours, minutes, subsidiary seconds; chronograph; date
Case: stainless steel, ø 41 mm, height 13.6 mm; bezel in rose gold; sapphire crystal; transparent case back; rose-gold crown and pusher; water-resistant to 10 atm
Band: stainless steel with rose gold elements, double folding clasp
Price: $17,000

Chronomaster Sport

Reference number: 03.3100.3600/69.M3100
Movement: automatic, Zenith Caliber 3600 "El Primero"; ø 30 mm, height 6.6 mm; 35 jewels; 36,000 vph; 60-hour power reserve
Functions: hours, minutes, subsidiary seconds; chronograph; date
Case: stainless steel, ø 41 mm, height 13.6 mm; ceramic bezel; sapphire crystal; transparent case back; water-resistant to 10 atm
Band: stainless steel, double folding clasp
Price: $11,000
Variations: with rubber strap ($10,500)

Chronomaster Sport

Reference number: 03.3100.3600/21.C822
Movement: automatic, Zenith Caliber 3600 "El Primero"; ø 30 mm, height 6.6 mm; 35 jewels; 36,000 vph; 60-hour power reserve
Functions: hours, minutes, subsidiary seconds; chronograph; date
Case: stainless steel, ø 41 mm, height 13.6 mm; ceramic bezel; sapphire crystal; transparent case back; water-resistant to 10 atm
Band: rubber with textile layer, double folding clasp
Price: $10,500
Variations: with stainless steel bracelet ($11,000)

Chronomaster Open

Reference number: 18.3300.3604/69.C922
Movement: automatic, Zenith Caliber 3604; ø 30 mm, height 6.6 mm; 35 jewels; 36,000 vph; movement partially skeletonized under the regulator; 60-hour power reserve
Functions: hours, minutes, subsidiary seconds; chronograph
Case: rose gold, ø 39.5 mm, height 12.6 mm; sapphire crystal; transparent case back; water-resistant to 10 atm
Band: calfskin, folding clasp
Price: $21,300

Chronomaster Open

Reference number: 18.3300.3604/21.M3300
Movement: automatic, Zenith Caliber 3604; ø 30 mm, height 6.6 mm; 35 jewels; 36,000 vph; movement partially skeletonized under the regulator; 60-hour power reserve
Functions: hours, minutes, subsidiary seconds; chronograph
Case: stainless steel, ø 39.5 mm, height 12.6 mm; sapphire crystal; transparent case back; water-resistant to 10 atm
Band: stainless steel, folding clasp
Price: $10,000

Chronomaster Open

Reference number: 18.3300.3604/69.C823
Movement: automatic, Zenith Caliber 3604; ø 30 mm, height 6.6 mm; 35 jewels; 36,000 vph; movement partially skeletonized under the regulator; 60-hour power reserve
Functions: hours, minutes, subsidiary seconds; chronograph
Case: stainless steel, ø 39.5 mm, height 12.6 mm; sapphire crystal; transparent case back; water-resistant to 10 atm
Band: stainless steel, folding clasp
Price: $9,500

Chronomaster Original

Reference number: 03.3200.3600/69.C902
Movement: automatic, Zenith Caliber 3600 "El Primero"; ø 30 mm, height 6.6 mm; 35 jewels; 36,000 vph; 60-hour power reserve
Functions: hours, minutes, subsidiary seconds; chronograph; date
Case: stainless steel, ø 38 mm, height 12.6 mm; sapphire crystal; transparent case back; water-resistant to 5 atm
Band: calfskin, triple folding clasp
Price: $9,000

Chronomaster Original

Reference number: 03.3200.3600/69.M3200
Movement: automatic, Zenith Caliber 3600 "El Primero"; ø 30 mm, height 6.6 mm; 35 jewels; 36,000 vph; 60-hour power reserve
Functions: hours, minutes, subsidiary seconds; chronograph; date
Case: stainless steel, ø 38 mm, height 12.6 mm; sapphire crystal; transparent case back; water-resistant to 5 atm
Band: stainless steel, folding clasp
Price: $9,500

Chronomaster Original

Reference number: 16.3200.3600/02.C907
Movement: automatic, Zenith Caliber 3600 "El Primero;" ø 30 mm, height 6.6 mm; 35 jewels; 36,000 vph; 60-hour power reserve
Functions: hours, minutes, subsidiary seconds; chronograph; date
Case: stainless steel set with 56 diamonds, ø 38 mm, height 12.6 mm; sapphire crystal; transparent case back; water-resistant to 5 atm
Band: calfskin, triple folding clasp
Remarks: dial set with 9 brilliant-cut diamonds
Price: $13,000

Caliber 9004 El Primero

Automatic; independent chronograph mechanism with separate escapement (360,000 vph) and power management; COSC-certified chronometer; 2 hairsprings of nanotube carbon matrix, impervious to magnetic fields and temperature fluctuations; single spring barrel, 50-hour power reserve; Timelab-certified chronometer
Functions: hours, minutes, subsidiary seconds; power reserve indicator (for chronograph functions); chronograph displays 1/100th of a second
Diameter: 32.8 mm
Height: 7.9 mm
Jewels: 53

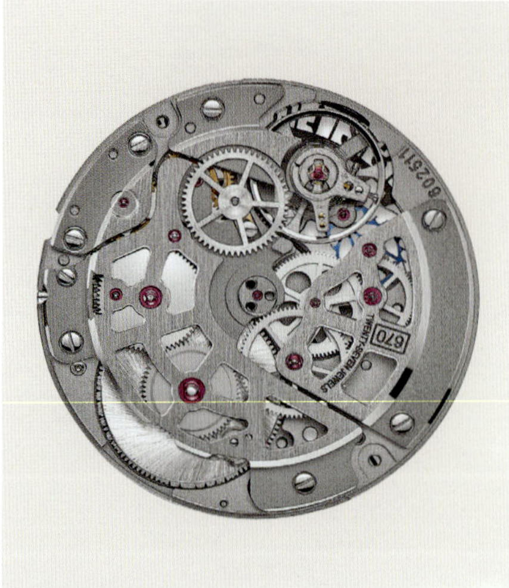

Caliber 670 Elite

Automatic; skeletonized movement; single spring barrel, 50-hour power reserve
Functions: hours, minutes, sweep seconds; date
Diameter: 25.6 mm
Height: 3.88 mm
Jewels: 27
Balance: glucydur
Frequency: 28,800 vph
Balance spring: flat hairspring
Shock protection: Kif
Remarks: 187 parts

Caliber 3600 El Primero

Automatic; silicon pallet and escape wheel; column wheel control of chronograph functions; single spring barrel, 60-hour power reserve, COSC-certified chronometer
Functions: hours, minutes, subsidiary seconds; chronograph; date
Diameter: 30 mm
Height: 6,6 mm
Jewels: 35
Balance: Glucydur Frequency: 36,000 vph
Balance spring: flat
Shock protection: Kif

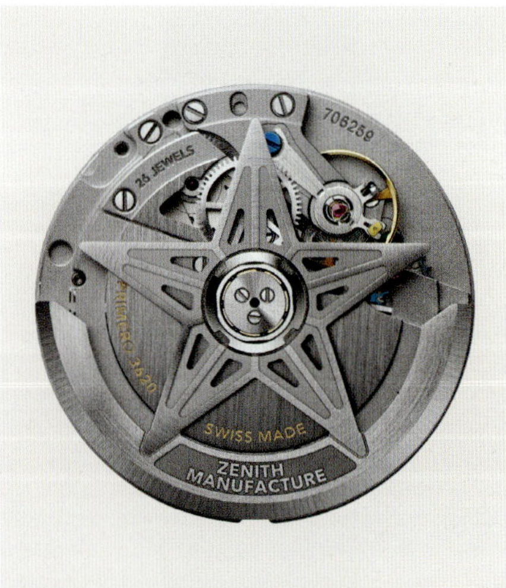

Caliber 3620 El Primero

Automatic; silicon pallet lever and escape wheel; single spring barrel, 60-hour power reserve; COSC-certified chronometer
Functions: hours, minutes, subsidiary seconds; date
Diameter: 30 mm
Jewels: 26
Balance: glucydur
Frequency: 36,000 vph
Balance spring: flat hairspring
Shock protection: Kif

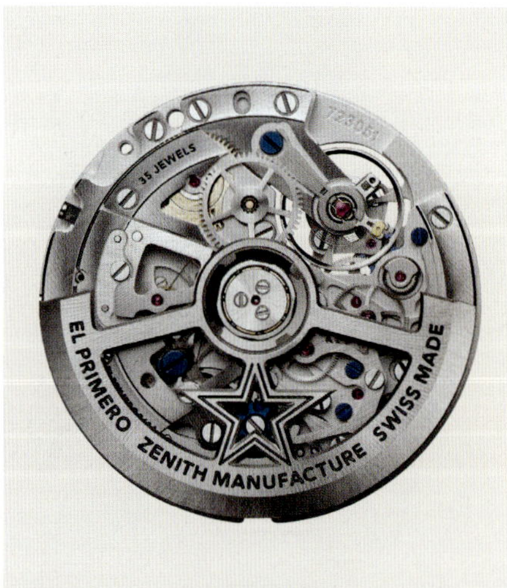

Caliber 3604 El Primero

Automatic; silicon pallet lever and escape wheel; single spring barrel, 60-hour power reserve;
Functions: hours, minutes, subsidiary seconds; chronograph
Diameter: 30 mm
Height: 7.9 mm
Jewels: 26
Balance: glucydur
Frequency: 36,000 vph
Balance spring: flat hairspring
Shock protection: Kif
Remarks: movement partially skeletonized under the regulator

Caliber 679 Elite

Automatic; single spring barrel, 50-hour power reserve
Functions: hours, minutes, sweep seconds
Diameter: 25.6 mm
Height: 3.85 mm
Jewels: 27
Balance: glucydur
Frequency: 28,800 vph
Balance spring: flat hairspring
Shock protection: Kif
Remarks: perlage on plate, rotor (removed for image) and bridges finely finished with côtes de Genève; 126 parts

Zero West LTD
41 Bridgefoot Path
Emsworth
Hampshire
PO10 7EB
United Kingdom

Tel.:
+44 (0)1243-376 676

E-mail:
time@zerowest.co.uk

Website:
www.zerowest.watch

Founded:
2015

Number of employees:
5

Distribution:
Contact the manufacturer directly

Most important collections:
Aviation (Spitfire S1/S2/S3), (Hurricane H1); Marine (Longitude L2; Motorsport (TT-58R, CR-2 Café Racer Chronograph, LS-2 Land Speed Bullhead)

ZERO WEST

Time, place, and history are the reference points for Zero West, a company founded in 2015 by Andrew Brabyn and Graham Collins, a leading graphic designer and an aerospace engineer, respectively. The company name itself refers to the coordinates of the Greenwich Royal Observatory. Their first watch was a statement. The Longitude L1 paid homage to an icon of British (even world) horology: John Harrison's remarkable H4 maritime clock that managed to keep accurate time on a ship in 1761 and contributed to the establishment of the Greenwich prime meridian by George Airy in 1851.

Meanwhile, the company has defined three core collections for their brand: automotive, aviation, and marine. Their latest aviation model, for example, celebrates an absolute icon: the Lancaster DB-1. The design recalls the plane's altimeter dial, and inside is a smelted disc from the bodywork of ED825, which was along for the famous "Dambusters" raid in 1943, during which the RAF ricocheted special bombs on dams in the Ruhgr region to try and cripple Nazi Germany's industrial production.

The automotive portfolio includes the TT-58R motorsport-inspired watch, featuring a machined disc cut from the drive shaft of the 1958 race winning Aston Martin DBR1 driven by Stirling Moss and Tony Brooks. A rare watch at only fifty-eight builds. The LS 2 Land Speed remembers Daytona Beach, March 29, 1927, when Henry Segrave broke the 200-mph barrier in his Sunbeam. The chronograph comes in a beautifully engineered bullhead case, with the pushers at 11 and 1 o'clock.

The watches are designed and assembled at the company's workshop and headquarters on the South Coast of England. It is where the two founders do their historical research and brainstorm each new watch dial. It is also where Graham Collins makes the straps for the collections. Low volume ensures high quality. The geographical location on the dials and case back relates to the watch's theme. Each watch is powered by tried-and-true Swiss calibers, like the ETA 2824, and Valjoux 7750 for the chronographs.

DB-1 Lancaster

Reference Number: DB-1 Lancaster
Movement: automatic, Sellita SW200-1; ø 25.60, height 4.5 mm; 28,800 vph, 26 jewels; 41-hour power reserve
Functions: hours, minutes, sweep seconds
Case: stainless steel, with eight polished vertically cut ball-nose flutes, ø 44 mm, height 14.1 mm; sapphire crystal; transparent case back; water-resistant to 10 atm
Band: fluroelastomer rubber strap, buckle
Remarks: case back displays smelted bodywork from Lancaster ED825
Price: $4,190; limited to 100 pieces
Variations: DB-1 Blackout, with black PVD

LS-2 Landspeed

Reference Number: LS-2
Movement: automatic Valjoux caliber 7750; ø 30 mm, height 7.9 mm; 25 jewels; 28,800vph; decorated movement with custom rotor; 48-hour power reserve
Functions: hours, minutes, subsidiary seconds; chronograph
Case: stainless steel "bullhead," ø 44 mm, height 15.7 mm; transparent case back; water-resistant to 10 atm
Remarks: case style references in-car rally timers; date and coordinates reference Sir Henry Seagrave's Daytona Beach land speed record of 203.79 mph in 1927
Price: $4,785; limited to 50 pieces

CR-2 Café Racer

Reference Number: CR-2 Café Racer
Movement: automatic, Valjoux 7750; ø 30 mm, height 13.25; 28,800 vph, 25 jewels custom red rotor; 48-hour power reserve
Functions: hours, minutes, subsidiary seconds; chronograph; day, date
Case: stainless steel, ø 44 mm, height 16.3 mm; sapphire crystal, transparent case back; water-resistant to 10 atm
Band: fluroelastomer rubber strap, buckle
Remarks: front dial design based on vintage Norton motorcycle styling
Price: $4,785; limited to 50 pieces

CONCEPTO

The Concepto Watch Factory, founded in 2006 in La Chaux-de-Fonds, is the successor to the family-run company Jaquet SA, which changed its name to La Joux-Perret a little while ago and then moved to a different location on the other side of the hub of watchmaking. In 2008, Valérien Jaquet, son of the company founder Pierre Jaquet, began systematically building up a modern movement and watch component factory on an empty floor of the building.

Today, the Concepto Watch Factory employs eighty people in various departments, such as Development/Prototyping, Decoparts (partial manufacturing using lathes, machining, or wire erosion), Artisia (production of movements and complications in large series), as well as Optimo (escapements). In addition to the standard family of calibers, the C2000 (based on the Valjoux) and the vintage chronograph movement C7000 (the evolution of the Venus Caliber), the company's product portfolio includes various tourbillon movements (Caliber C8000) and several modules for adding onto ETA movements (Caliber C1000). A brand-new caliber series, the C3000, features a retrograde calendar and seconds, a power reserve indicator, and a chronograph. The C4000 chronograph caliber with automatic winding is currently in pre-series testing.

One of Concepto's greatest assets is its flexibility. Most of the company's movements are not sold off the shelf, as it were, but rather designed according to the specific requirements of the customer with regard to form or technical DNA. Complicated movements are assembled entirely and tested by the company's watchmakers, while others are sold as kits for assembly by the watchmakers. Annual production is somewhere between 30,000 and 40,000 units, with additional hundreds of thousands of components made for contract manufacturing.

Caliber 1053

Automatic; inverted construction with dial-side escapement; bidirectional off-center winding rotor; single spring barrel; 42-hour power reserve
Functions: hours, minutes, subsidiary seconds (all off-center)
Diameter: 33 mm
Height: 3.75 mm
Jewels: 31
Balance: glucydur
Frequency: 28,800 vph
Balance spring: flat hairspring
Remarks: black finishing on movement

Caliber 2904 (dial side)

Inverted construction with dial-side escapement; single spring barrel; 48-hour power reserve
Functions: hours, minutes, subsidiary seconds
Diameter: 30.4 mm
Height: 4.6 mm
Jewels: 31
Balance: screw balance
Frequency: 28,800 vph
Balance spring: flat hairspring

Caliber 3041 Skeleton (dial side)

Manually wound; skeletonized symmetrical construction; single spring barrel; 48-hour power reserve
Functions: hours, minutes
Diameter: 32.6 mm
Height: 5.5 mm
Jewels: 21
Balance: screw balance
Frequency: 28,800 vph
Balance spring: flat hairspring
Remarks: extensive personalization options for finishing and accessories

Caliber 2000-RAC

Automatic; column wheel control of chronograph functions; stop-second system; single spring barrel; 48-hour power reserve
Functions: hours, minutes, subsidiary seconds; chronograph
Diameter: 30.4 mm; **Height:** 8.4 mm
Jewels: 26; **Balance:** screw balance
Frequency: 28,800 vph
Balance spring: flat hairspring
Shock protection: Incabloc
Remarks: related calibers: 2000 (without control wheel); with two or three totalizers ("tricompax") with or without date; various additional displays (moon phase, retrograde date hand, additional 24-hour sweep hand, power reserve indicator)

Caliber 8500

Manually wound; 1-minute tourbillon; column wheel control of chronograph functions; single spring barrel; 50-hour power reserve
Functions: hours, minutes, subsidiary seconds; split-seconds chronograph
Diameter: 31.3 mm
Height: 7.2 mm
Jewels: 31
Balance: screw balance
Frequency: 21,600 vph
Balance spring: flat hairspring
Remarks: very fine movement finishing

Caliber 8950-A

Automatic; 1-minute tourbillon; single spring barrel; 60-hour power reserve
Functions: hours, minutes
Diameter: 30.4 mm
Height: 6.7 mm
Jewels: 27
Balance: glucydur
Frequency: 28,800 vph
Balance spring: flat hairspring
Remarks: related caliber: 8950-M (manual winding); extensive personalization options for the finishing, accessories, and functions

Caliber 8000 (dial side)

Manually wound; 1-minute tourbillon; single spring barrel; 72-hour power reserve
Functions: hours, minutes
Diameter: 32.6 mm
Height: 5.7 mm
Jewels: 19
Balance: screw balance
Frequency: 21,600 vph
Balance spring: flat hairspring
Remarks: extensive personalization options for the finishing, accessories, and functions

Caliber 8152

Automatic; 1-minute tourbillon; bridges and plate made of sapphire crystal; off-center, bidirectional rotor; single spring barrel; 72-hour power reserve
Functions: hours, minutes
Diameter: 32.6 mm
Height: 8.5 mm
Jewels: 25
Balance: screw balance
Frequency: 21,600 vph
Balance spring: flat hairspring
Remarks: extensive personalization options for the finishing, accessories, and functions

Caliber 8600 (dial side)

Manually wound; 1-minute tourbillon; double spring barrel; 72-hour power reserve
Functions: hours, minutes; minute repeater with carillon (3 gongs)
Diameter: 34.6 mm
Height: 6.45 mm
Jewels: 36
Balance: screw balance
Frequency: 21,600 vph
Hairspring: flat hairspring
Remarks: many customization options for finishing, equipment and functions

ETA

This Swatch Group movement manufacturer produces more than five million movements a year. And after the withdrawal of Richemont's Jaeger-LeCoultre as well as Swatch Group sisters Nouvelle Lémania and Frédéric Piguet from the business of selling movements on the free market, most watch brands can hardly help but beat down the door of this full-service manufacturer.

ETA offers a broad spectrum of automatic movements in various dimensions with different functions, chronograph mechanisms in varying configurations, pocket watch classics (Calibers 6497 and 98), and manually wound calibers of days gone by (Calibers 1727 and 7001). This company truly offers everything that a manufacturer's heart could desire—not to mention the sheer variety of quartz technology from inexpensive three-hand mechanisms to highly complicated multifunctional movements and futuristic ETAquartz featuring autonomous energy creation using a rotor and generator.

The almost stereotypical accusation of ETA being "mass goods" is not justified, however, for it is a real art to manufacture filigreed micromechanical technology in consistently high quality. This is certainly one of the reasons why there have been very few movement factories in Europe that can compete with ETA, or that would want to. Since the success of Swatch—a pure ETA product—millions of Swiss francs have been invested in new development and manufacturing technologies. ETA today owns more than twenty production locales in Switzerland, France, Germany, Malaysia, and Thailand.

In 2002, ETA's management announced it would discontinue providing half-completed component kits for reassembly and/or embellishment to specialized workshops, and from 2010 only offer completely assembled and finished movements for sale. The Swiss Competition Commission, however, studied the issue, and a new deal was struck in 2013, phasing out sales to customers over a period of six years. ETA is already somewhat of a competitor of independent reassemblers such as Soprod, Sellita, La Joux-Perret, Dubois Dépraz, and others thanks to its diversification of available calibers, which has led the rest to counter by creating their own base movements.

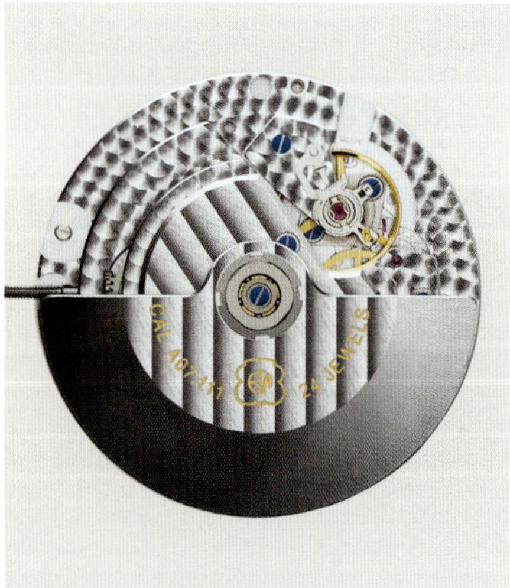

Caliber A07.111

Automatic; ETACHRON regulating system with fine-timing device, rotor on ball bearings, stop-second system; single spring barrel; 48-hour power reserve
Functions: hours, minutes, sweep seconds
Diameter: 37.2
Height: 7.9 mm
Jewels: 24
Frequency: 28,800 vph
Balance spring: flat hairspring
Shock protection: Incabloc
Remarks: related calibers: A07.161 (with power reserve display)

Caliber A07.171 (dial side)

Automatic; ETACHRON regulating system with fine-timing device, rotor on ball bearings, stop-second system; single spring barrel; 48-hour power reserve
Functions: hours, minutes, sweep seconds; 2nd time zone, additional 24-hour display (2nd time zone); quick-set date window
Diameter: 37.2 mm
Height: 7.9 mm
Jewels: 24
Frequency: 28,800 vph
Balance spring: flat hairspring
Shock protection: Incabloc

Caliber A07.211 (dial side)

Automatic; ETACHRON regulating system with fine-timing device, rotor on ball bearings, stop-second system; single spring barrel; 48-hour power reserve
Functions: hours, minutes, subsidiary seconds; chronograph; quick-set date window
Diameter: 37.2 mm
Height: 7.9 mm
Jewels: 25
Frequency: 28,800 vph
Balance spring: flat hairspring
Shock protection: Incabloc

Caliber 2000-1

Automatic; ball bearing-mounted rotor; stop-seconds, ETACHRON regulating system; single spring barrel; 40-hour power reserve
Functions: hours, minutes, sweep seconds; quick-set date window
Diameter: 20 mm
Height: 3.6 mm
Jewels: 20
Balance: glucydur
Frequency: 28,800 vph
Balance spring: flat hairspring
Shock protection: Incabloc

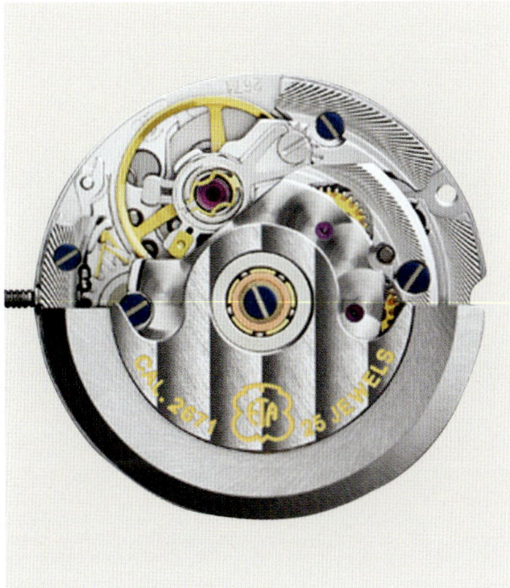

Caliber 2671

Automatic; ball bearing-mounted rotor; stop-seconds, ETACHRON regulating system; single spring barrel; 38-hour power reserve
Functions: hours, minutes, sweep seconds; date window
Diameter: 17.5 mm
Height: 4.8 mm
Jewels: 25
Balance: glucydur
Frequency: 28,800 vph
Balance spring: flat hairspring
Shock protection: Incabloc
Remarks: related calibers: 2678 (additional weekday window, height 5.35 mm)

Caliber 2681 (dial side)

Automatic; ball bearing-mounted rotor; stop-seconds, ETACHRON regulating system; single spring barrel; 38-hour power reserve
Functions: hours, minutes, sweep seconds; quick-set date window
Diameter: 20 mm
Height: 4.8 mm
Jewels: 25
Balance: glucydur
Frequency: 28,800 vph
Balance spring: flat hairspring
Shock protection: Incabloc

Caliber 2801-2

Manually wound; ETACHRON regulating system; 42-hour power reserve
Functions: hours, minutes, sweep seconds
Diameter: 26 mm
Height: 3.35 mm
Jewels: 17
Frequency: 28,800 vph
Related caliber: 2804-2 (with date window and quick set)

Caliber 2824-2

Automatic; ball bearing-mounted rotor; stop-seconds, ETACHRON regulating system; 38-hour power reserve
Functions: hours, minutes, sweep seconds; quick-set date window at 3 o'clock
Diameter: 26 mm
Height: 4.6 mm
Jewels: 25
Frequency: 28,800 vph
Related calibers: 2836-2 (additional day window at 3 o'clock, height 5.05 mm); 2826-2 (with large date, height 6.2 mm)

Caliber 2834-2 (dial side)

Automatic; ball bearing-mounted rotor; stop-seconds, ETACHRON regulating system; single spring barrel; 38-hour power reserve
Functions: hours, minutes, sweep seconds; quick-set date window, quick-set weekday
Diameter: 29.4 mm
Height: 5.05 mm
Jewels: 25
Balance: glucydur
Frequency: 28,800 vph
Balance spring: flat hairspring
Shock protection: Incabloc

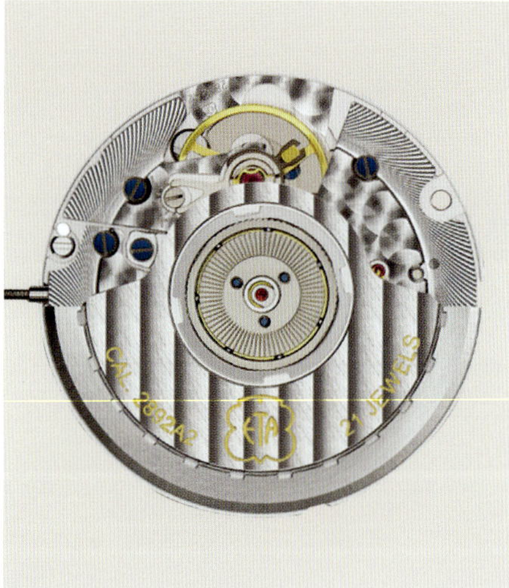

Caliber 2892-A2

Automatic; ball bearing–mounted rotor; stop-seconds, ETACHRON regulating system; single spring barrel; 42-hour power reserve
Functions: hours, minutes, sweep seconds; quick-set date window
Diameter: 26.2 mm
Height: 3.6 mm
Jewels: 21
Balance: glucydur
Frequency: 28,800 vph
Balance spring: flat hairspring
Shock protection: Incabloc

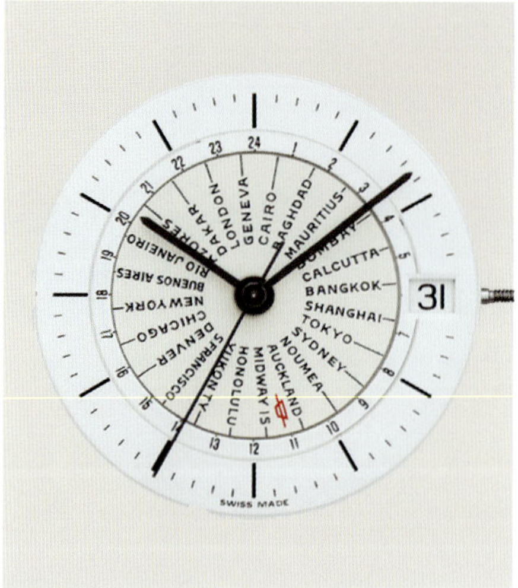

Caliber 2893-1 (dial side)

Automatic; ball bearing rotor; stop-seconds, ETACHRON regulating system; 42-hour power reserve
Functions: hours, minutes, sweep seconds; quick-set date window at 3 o'clock; world time display via central disk
Diameter: 25.6 mm
Height: 4.1 mm
Jewels: 21
Frequency: 28,800 vph
Related calibers: 2893-2 (24-hour hand; 2nd time zone instead of world time disk); 2893-3 (only world time disk without date window)

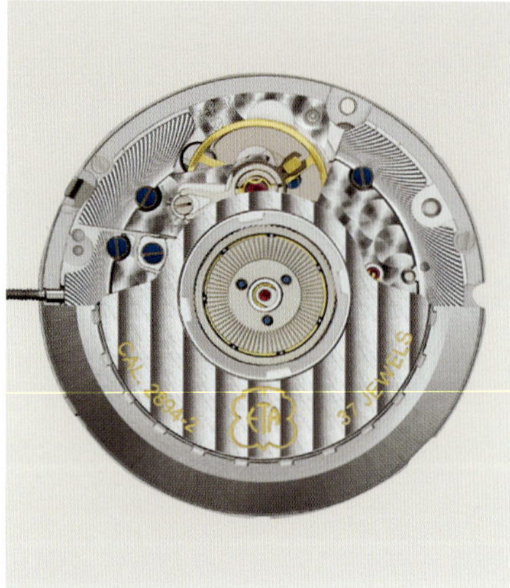

Caliber 2894-2

Automatic; ball bearing–mounted rotor; stop-seconds, ETACHRON regulating system; single spring barrel; 42-hour power reserve
Functions: hours, minutes, subsidiary seconds; chronograph; quick-set date window
Diameter: 28.6 mm
Height: 6.1 mm
Jewels: 37
Balance: glucydur
Frequency: 28,800 vph
Balance spring: flat hairspring
Shock protection: Incabloc
Related caliber: 2094 (diameter 23.9 mm, height 5.5 mm, 33 jewels)

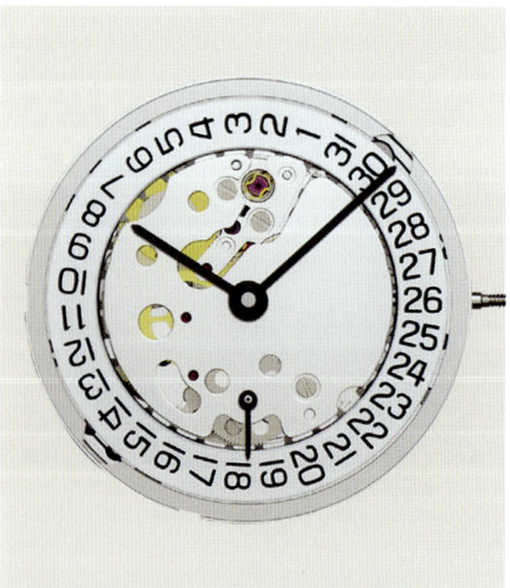

Caliber 2895-2 (dial side)

Automatic; ball bearing–mounted rotor; stop-seconds, ETACHRON regulating system; single spring barrel; 42-hour power reserve
Functions: hours, minutes, subsidiary seconds, at 6 o'clock; quick-set date window
Diameter: 26.2 mm
Height: 4.35 mm
Jewels: 27
Balance: glucydur
Frequency: 28,800 vph
Balance spring: flat hairspring
Shock protection: Incabloc

Caliber 2896 (dial side)

Automatic; ball bearing rotor; stop-seconds, ETACHRON regulating system; 42-hour power reserve
Functions: hours, minutes, sweep seconds; power reserve display at 3 o'clock
Diameter: 25.6 mm
Height: 4.85 mm
Jewels: 21
Frequency: 28,800 vph

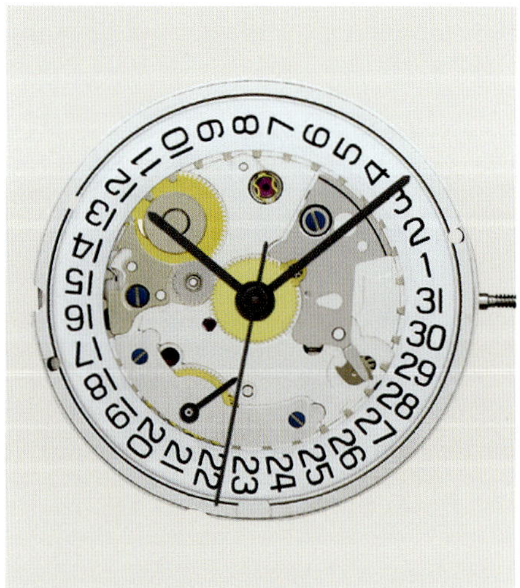

Caliber 2897 (dial side)

Automatic; ball bearing–mounted rotor; stop-seconds, ETACHRON regulating system; single spring barrel; 42-hour power reserve
Functions: hours, minutes, sweep seconds; power reserve indicator; quick-set date window
Diameter: 26.2 mm
Height: 4.85 mm
Jewels: 21
Balance: glucydur
Frequency: 28,800 vph
Balance spring: flat hairspring
Shock protection: Incabloc

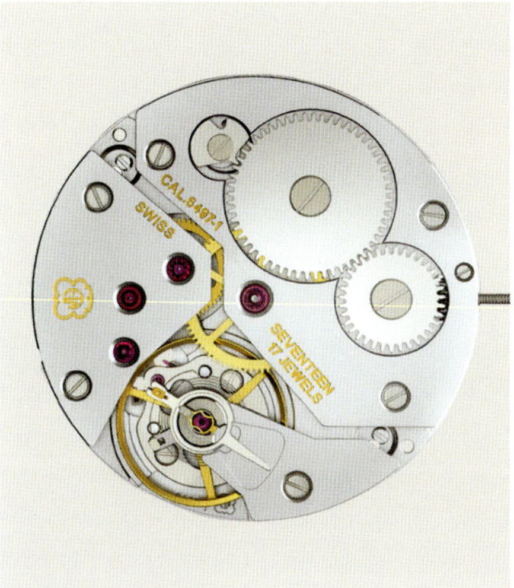

Caliber 6497-1

Manually wound; ETACHRON regulating system; single spring barrel; 46-hour power reserve
Functions: hours, minutes, subsidiary seconds
Diameter: 37.2 mm
Height: 4.5 mm
Jewels: 17
Frequency: 18,000 vph
Balance spring: flat hairspring
Remarks: pocket watch movement (Unitas model) in Lépine version with subsidiary seconds extending from the winding stem); as Caliber 6497-2 with 21,600 vph and 53-hour power reserve

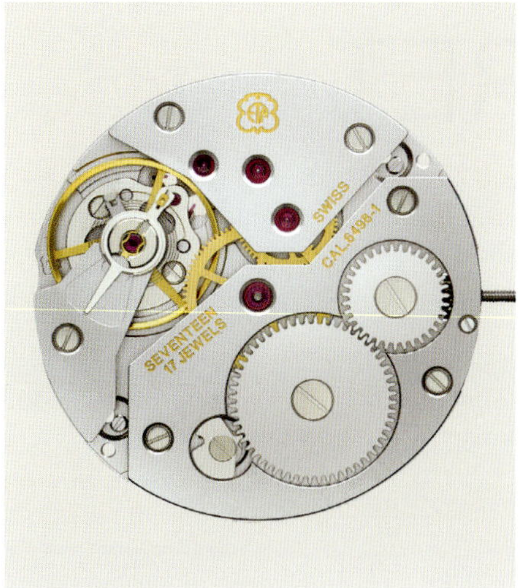

Caliber 6498-1

Manually wound; ETACHRON regulating system; single spring barrel; 46-hour power reserve
Functions: hours, minutes, subsidiary seconds
Diameter: 37.2 mm
Height: 4.5 mm
Jewels: 17
Frequency: 18,000 vph
Balance spring: flat hairspring
Remarks: pocket watch movement (Unitas model) in savonette version (subsidiary seconds at right angle to the winding stem); as Caliber 6498-2 with 21,600 vph and 53-hour power reserve

Caliber 7001

Manually wound; ultrathin construction; single spring barrel; 42-hour power reserve
Functions: hours, minutes, subsidiary seconds
Diameter: 23.7 mm
Height: 2.5 mm
Jewels: 17
Frequency: 21,600 vph
Balance spring: flat hairspring

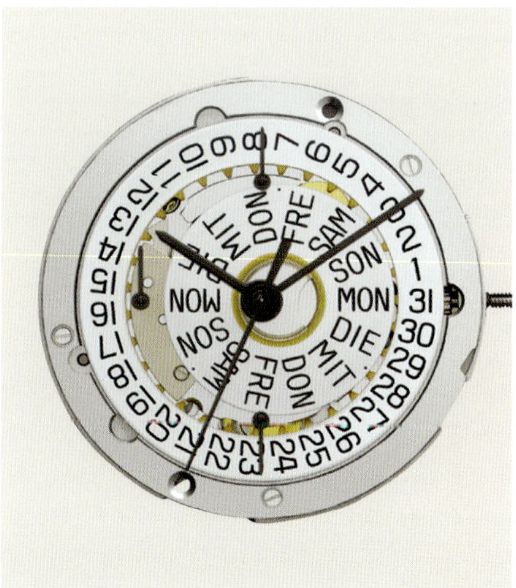

Caliber 7750 (dial side)

Automatic; stop-second system; single spring barrel; 42-hour power reserve
Functions: hours, minutes, subsidiary seconds; chronograph; quick-set date and weekday window
Diameter: 30.4 mm
Height: 7.9 mm
Jewels: 25
Balance: glucydur
Frequency: 28,800 vph
Balance spring: flat hairspring
Shock protection: Incabloc

Caliber 7751 (dial side)

Automatic; stop-second system; single spring barrel; 42-hour power reserve
Functions: hours, minutes, subsidiary seconds; additional 24-hour display; chronograph; full calendar with date, weekday, month, moon phase
Diameter: 30.4 mm
Height: 7.9 mm
Jewels: 25
Balance: glucydur
Frequency: 28,800 vph
Balance spring: flat hairspring
Shock protection: Incabloc
Remarks: related caliber: 7754 with sweep 24-hour hand (2nd time zone)

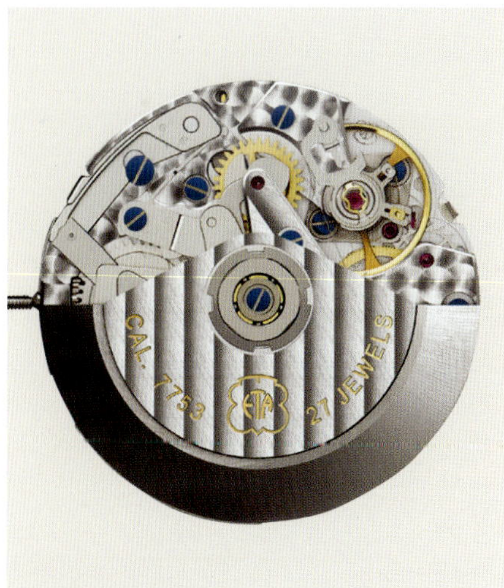

Caliber 7753

Automatic; stop-second system; single spring barrel; 42-hour power reserve
Functions: hours, minutes, subsidiary seconds; chronograph; quick-set date window with pusher
Diameter: 30.4
Height: 7.9 mm
Jewels: 25
Balance: glucydur
Frequency: 28,800 vph
Balance spring: flat hairspring
Shock protection: Incabloc
Remarks: variation of the Valjoux chronograph caliber with symmetrical "tricompax" layout of the totalizers

MANUFACTURE LA JOUX-PERRET

The re-industrialization of the caliber segment in Switzerland, brought about by some very confusing signals from Swatch Group and the Swiss government's Competition Commission, has created a number of opportunities for caliber builders who had until recently been operating in the shadow of ETA. Among them is Manufacture La Joux-Perret (MLJP), known primarily for its bespoke complication calibers for prestigious brands. It has now decided to enter the ready-to-wear caliber market in 2021 with the revised G100 three-hand automatic movement and the L100 automatic chronograph.

Due to their dimensions and specifications, both movements are suitable as replacements for the widely used 2824 and 7750 ("Valjoux") models, which will no longer be available to the watch industry in sufficient quantities after the expiry of the general supply obligation on the part of Swatch Group subsidiary ETA. The two MLJP calibers compete with Sellita's own high-volume movements SW200 and SW500, but they offer a greater amount of power reserve (68 and 60 hours, respectively) and partly better equipment (column-wheel control). Also in the standard portfolio of this caliber specialist is a classic-a manually wound movement with the caliber number D100, whose architecture is strongly reminiscent of the pocket watch "Unitas" caliber. Its diameter, however, is only 23.3 millimeters.

MLJP has been part of the Citizen Group (Japan) for five years, but the company's headquarters and production facilities are located in La Chaux-de-Fonds, in the heart of watch country.

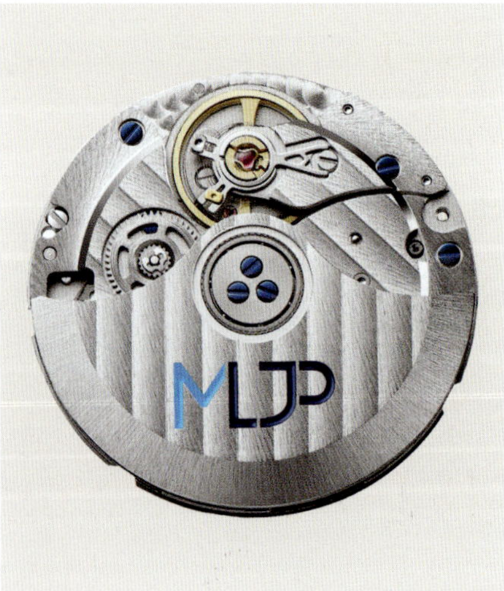

G100

Automatic; rotor on ball bearing, second stop; single spring barrel, 68-hour power reserve
Functions: hours, minutes, sweep seconds; date aperture
Diameter: 26 mm
Height: 4.45 mm
Jewels: 24
Balance: glucydur
Frequency: 28,800 vph
Hairspring: flat hairspring
Shock protection: Kif
Remarks: functionality and parts compatibility with ETA 2824-2; various display options, many customization options

L100

Automatic; column wheel control of chronograph functions; second stop; single spring barrel, 60-hour power reserve
Functions: hours, minutes, subsidiary seconds; chronograph; date and weekday aperture with rapid correction
Diameter: 30.4 mm
Height: 7.9 mm
Jewels: 26
Balance: Glucydur
Frequency: 28,800 vph
Hairspring: flat hairspring
Shock protection: Incabloc
Remarks: functionality and parts compatibility with ETA 7750; various display options, many customization options

D100

Manually wound; single spring barrel, 50-hour power reserve
Functions: hours, minutes, subsidiary seconds
Diameter: 23.3 mm
Height: 2.5 mm
Jewels: 18
Frequency: 21,600 vph
Hairspring: flat hairspring
Shock protection: Incabloc
Remarks: many customization options

RONDA

Ronda is a Swiss company with a long tradition. It was founded by William Mosset, born in 1909 in the village of Hölstein, a man whose gift for micro-engineering declared itself early on when he invented a way to drill thirty-two holes in a metal plate in one operation and with great accuracy. The company was founded in 1946 in Lausen, a little town in the hinterlands of German-speaking Switzerland near Basel, where the first factory was built.

In the meantime the company has turned into a group with multiple subsidiaries: There are two production sites in Ticino, one in the Jura Mountains, and an operation in Thailand. Overall, Ronda employs around 1,800 people in Switzerland and Asia.

The shareholders of the family enterprise, which is now in its second generation, value the company's absolute independence. This is undoubtedly a key advantage for the customer, since Ronda can continue defining its own strategy and can react decisively to customer needs.

That is why the company, which had already made a name for itself with quartz movements, decided to add a portfolio of automatic mechanical movements. The first product batches arrived on the market in early 2017; in the medium term, the mechanical Ronda Caliber R150 is to be produced in batches of six figures per year.

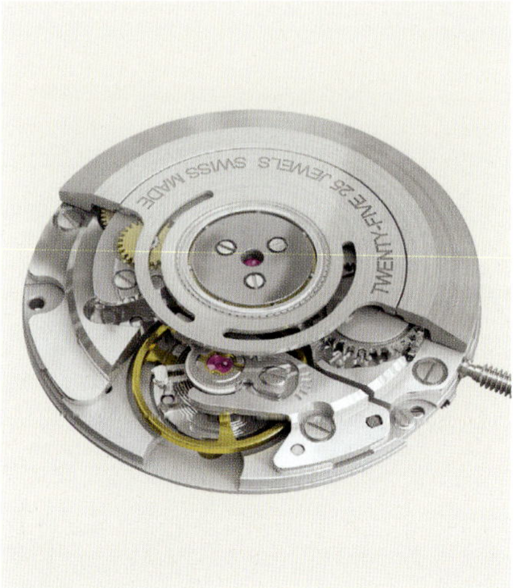

Caliber R150

Automatic; ball bearing-mounted rotor; stop-seconds, index for fine adjustment; single spring barrel; 40-hour power reserve
Functions: hours, minutes, sweep seconds; quick-set date
Diameter: 25.6 mm
Height: 4.4 mm
Jewels: 25
Frequency: 28,800 vph
Balance spring: flat hairspring
Shock protection: Incabloc

Caliber 5040.B

Quartz; 54-month power reserve; single spring barrel
Functions: hours, minutes, subsidiary seconds; chronograph, with add and split function; large date
Diameter: 28.6 mm
Height: 4.4 mm
Jewels: 13

Caliber 7004.P

Quartz; 48-month power reserve; single spring barrel
Functions: hours, minutes, subsidiary seconds; large date and weekday (retrograde)
Diameter: 34.6 mm
Height: 5.6 mm
Jewels: 6

SELLITA

Sellita, founded in 1950 by Pierre Grandjean in La Chaux-de-Fonds, is one of the biggest reassemblers and embellishers in the mechanical watch industry. On average, Sellita embellishes and finishes about one million automatic and hand-wound movements annually—a figure that represents about 25 percent of Switzerland's mechanical movement production, according to Miguel García, Sellita's president.

Reassembly can be defined as the assembly and regulation of components to make a functioning movement. This is the type of work that ETA loved to give to outside companies back in the day in order to concentrate on manufacturing complete quartz movements and individual components for them.

Reassembly workshops like Sellita refine and embellish components purchased from ETA according to their customers' wishes and can even successfully fulfill smaller orders made by the company's estimated 350 clients.

When ETA announced that it would only sell ébauches to companies outside the Swatch Group until the end of 2010, García, who has owned Sellita since 2003, reacted by shifting production to the development and manufacturing of new in-house products.

He planned and implemented a new line of movements based on the dimensions of the most popular ETA calibers, whose patents had expired. The company now has a line of manually wound or automatic movements with little complications, like a date, weekday, GMT, or a second time zone, as well as chronographs with different display constellations. The new design types are all based on mature models. A whole new line of automatic movements was launched, the Caliber SW1000, which has no ETA parts at all. The way to identify these movements will simply be the four digits. The price range will be similar to that of other products offered by the company.

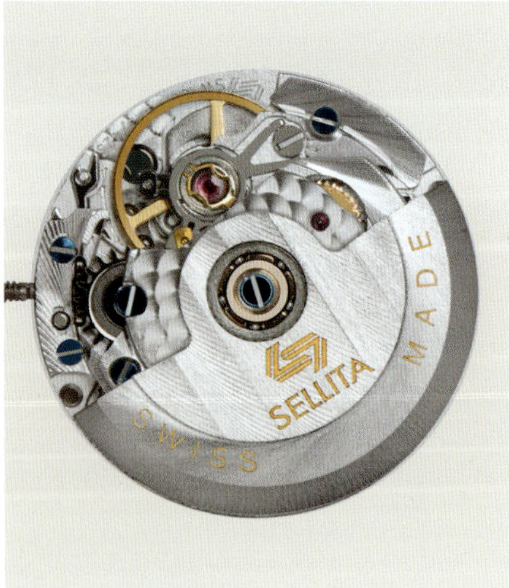

Caliber SW100-1

Automatic; ball-bearing mounted rotor, stop second mechanism; single spring barrel, 38-hour power reserve
Functions: hours, minutes, sweep seconds; date , with rapid correction
Diameter: 17.2 mm
Height: 4.8 mm
Jewels: 25
Balance: nickel or Glucydur Frequency: 28,800 vph
Hairspring: Nivaflex
Shock protection: Novodiac or Incabloc

Caliber SW200-1

Automatic; ball-bearing mounted rotor, stop-second mechanism; single spring barrel, 38-hour power reserve
Functions: hours, minutes, sweep seconds; date, with rapid correction
Diameter: 25.6 mm
Height: 4.6 mm
Jewels: 26
Balance: nickel or glucydur
Frequency: 28,800 vph
Hairspring: Nivaflex
Shock protection: Novodiac or Incabloc
Related calibers: SW260-1 and SW261-1 (with subsidiary seconds at 6 o'clock); SW290-1 (with subsidiary seconds at 9 o'clock)

Caliber SW215-1

Manually wound; stop-second mechanism; single spring barrel, 42-hour power reserve
Functions: hours, minutes, sweep seconds; date
Diameter: 25.6 mm
Height: 3.35 mm
Jewels: 19
Balance: nickel
Frequency: 28,800 vph
Hairspring: Nivaflex
Shock protection: Novodiac or Incabloc
Related caliber: SW210-1 (without date); SW216-1 (with small second and date)

Caliber SW220-1 M

Manually wound; stop-second mechanism; single spring barrel, 42-hour power reserve
Functions: hours, minutes, sweep seconds; date and weekday with rapid correction
Diameter: 25.6 mm
Height: 3.8 mm
Jewels: 19
Balance: nickel or Glucydur
Frequency: 28,800 vph
Hairspring: flat hairspring, Nivaflex
Shock protection: Novodiac or Incabloc
Related calibers: SW221-1 M (with date hand); SW240-1 M with larger mainplate (ø 29 mm)

Caliber SW300-1

Automatic; ball bearing-mounted rotor; stop-second system; single spring barrel; 42-hour power reserve
Functions: hours, minutes, sweep seconds; quick-set date
Diameter: 25.6 mm
Height: 3.6 mm
Jewels: 25
Balance: glucydur
Frequency: 28,800 vph
Balance spring: flat hairspring, Nivaflex
Shock protection: Incabloc
Remarks: related caliber: SW360-1 (with subsidiary seconds, height 4.35 mm, 31 jewels); SW330-2 (with additional 24-hour hand for 2nd time zone)

Caliber SW400-1

Automatic; ball-bearing mounted rotor, stop-second mechanism; single spring barrel, 38-hour power reserve
Functions: hours, minutes, sweep seconds; date with rapid correction
Diameter: 31 mm
Height: 4.67 mm
Jewels: 26
Balance: nickel or glucydur
Frequency: 28,800 vph
Hairspring: Nivaflex
Shock protection: Novodiac or Incabloc
Related Caliber: SW461-1 (with subsidiary second)

Caliber SW500-1

Automatic; ball-bearing mounted rotor, stop-second; single spring barrel, 48-hour power reserve
Functions: hours, minutes, subsidiary seconds; chronograph; date and weekday with rapid correction
Diameter: 30 mm
Height: 7.9 mm
Jewels: 25
Frequency: 28,800 vph
Shock protection: Incabloc
Related calibers: SW500 M (manually wound version, height 7 mm, 21 jewels); SW500 BV (bicompax without subsidiary seconds); SW510 (tricompax with symmetrical totalizers); SW510 BH (bicompax without hour totalizer); SW500/510 MP (monopusher); SW500/510 MPC (crown pusher)

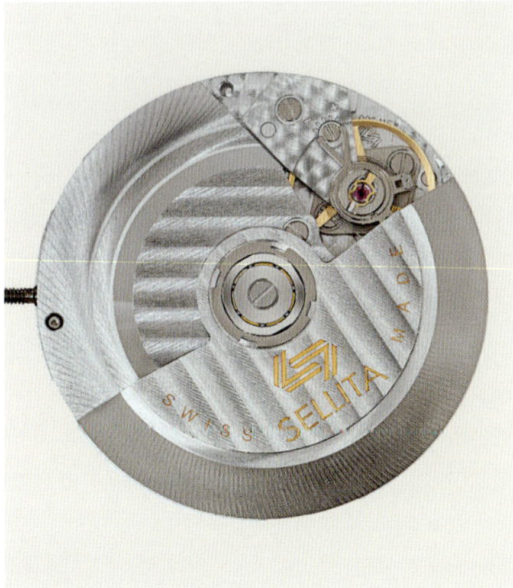

Caliber SW600

Automatic; ball-bearing mounted rotor, stop-second; single spring barrel, 48-hour power reserve
Functions: hours, minutes, sweep seconds; date and weekday with rapid correction
Diameter: 30 mm
Height: 7.9 mm
Jewels: 24
Balance: nickel or glucydur
Frequency: 28,800 vph
Hairspring: Nivaflex
Shock protection: Incabloc
Related caliber: SW690 (with subsidiary seconds)

Caliber SW1000-1

Automatic; ball-bearing mounted rotor, stop second mechanism; single spring barrel, 38-hour power reserve
Functions: hours, minutes, sweep seconds; date with rapid correction
Diameter: 20 mm
Height: 3.9 mm
Jewels: 18
Balance: nickel or glucydur
Frequency: 28,800 vph
Hairspring: Nivaflex
Shock protection: Incabloc

SOPROD

The name Soprod stands for "Société de Production Horlogère" and refers to a company with a fairly long tradition of movement-building, though, admittedly, mostly in quartz. It was originally founded in 1966, though its later reputation rested on its laurels as an external assembly company for ETA movements. Soprod continued enlarging its portfolio, adding customized decorations and finishings as a service and then building modules that could be used to enhance base movements. Around the turn of the millennium, the company finally began to seriously develop its own calibers. This development was accelerated by ETA's announcement that in the foreseeable future, they would no longer supply movement parts kits to external assemblers but would supply end-customers directly.

In the meantime, Soprod had slipped under the wing of the Swiss Festina Group and supplemented the existing capacities in the field of inexpensive quartz movements. But their mechanical division was growing steadily with two caliber lines (M and C) with over fifteen iterations. In 2011, at Baselworld, they presented their Alternance 10, or A10, which had the look and feel of the very popular ETA 2892. As a base movement, it could serve in many cases, and Soprod already had a wide range of modules on tap to supplement it, like large dates, GMT, power reserves, and moon phases.

Soprod continued expanding its production capacities and today, besides a range of calibers, it manufactures its own escapement parts such as anchors, escape wheels, balance wheels, and hairsprings at its founding site in Les Reussilles in the Jura. It is completely self-sufficient.

M100SQ

Automatic; skeletonized plate and bridges; bidirectional winding rotor, stop-second mechanism; single spring barrel, 42-hour power reserve
Functions: hours, minutes, sweep seconds; date with rapid correction
Diameter: 25.6 mm
Height: 3.6 mm
Jewels: 25
Frequency: 28,800 vph
Shock protection: Incabloc
Related calibers: M100 (standard version without skeletonization); M100 Balancier Visible (with openworked plate under the escapement parts)

M100

Automatic; bidirectional winding rotor, stop-second mechanism; single spring barrel, 42-hour power reserve
Functions: hours, minutes, sweep seconds; date with rapid correction
Diameter: 25.6 mm
Height: 3.6 mm
Jewels: 25
Frequency: 28,800 vph
Shock protection: Incabloc
Remarks: various regulation options (COSC, among others); various finishings (Optimal, Excellence, Manufacture)

Newton

Automatic; in-house escapement and hairspring; unidirectional winding rotor, stop-second mechanism; single spring barrel, 44-hour power reserve
Functions: hours, minutes, sweep seconds; date, with rapid correction
Diameter: 25.6 mm
Height: 4.6 mm
Jewels: 23
Frequency: 28,800 vph
Shock protection: Incabloc
Remarks: with/without côtes de Genève

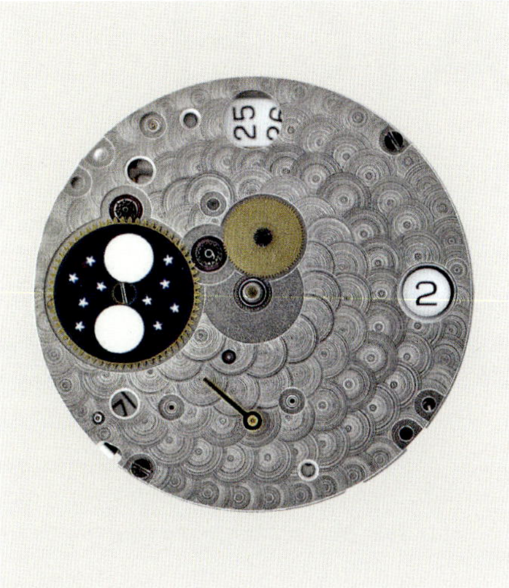

C105

Automatic; bidirectional winding rotor, stop-second mechanism; single spring barrel, 42-hour power reserve
Functions: hours, minutes, subsidiary seconds; date with rapid correction, moon phase Diameter: 25.6 mm
Height: 5.1 mm
Jewels: 33
Frequency: 28,800 vph
Shock protection: Incabloc

C110

Automatic; bidirectional winding rotor, stop-second mechanism; single spring barrel, 42-hour power reserve
Functions: hours, minutes, subsidiary seconds; date with rapid correction
Diameter: 25.6 mm
Height: 5.1 mm
Jewels: 29
Frequency: 28,800 vph
Shock protection: Incabloc

C115

Automatic; bidirectional winding rotor, stop-second mechanism; single spring barrel, 42-hour power reserve
Functions: hours, minutes, sweep seconds; additional 24-hour display (second time zone), power reserve display; date with rapid correction
Diameter: 25.6 mm
Height: 5.1 mm
Jewels: 33
Frequency: 28,800 vph
Shock protection: Incabloc

C125

Automatic; bidirectional winding rotor, stop-second mechanism; single spring barrel, 42-hour power reserve
Functions: hours, minutes, sweep seconds; additional 12-hour display (second time zone), day/night indication (with hour and minute at 6 o'clock); large date with rapid correction
Diameter: 25.6 mm
Height: 5.1 mm
Jewels: 25
Frequency: 28,800 vph
Shock protection: Incabloc

C120

Automatic; bidirectional winding rotor, stop-second mechanism; single spring barrel, 42-hour power reserve
Functions: hours, minutes, sweep seconds; additional 24-hour display (sweep second time zone); date, with rapid correction
Diameter: 25.6 mm
Height: 4.1 mm
Jewels: 25
Frequency: 28,800 vph
Shock protection: Incabloc

C130

Automatic; bidirectional winding rotor, stop-second mechanism; single spring barrel, 42-hour power reserve
Functions: hours, minutes, sweep seconds; power reserve display; large date with rapid correction
Diameter: 25.6 mm
Height: 5.1 mm
Jewels: 27
Frequency: 28,800 vph
Shock protection: Incabloc
Related calibers: C135 (with additional sweep 24-hour hand and date aperture); C140 (power reserve display und date aperture)

WATCH YOUR WATCH

Mechanical watches are not only by and large more expensive and complex than quartzes, they are also a little high-maintenance, as it were. The mechanism within does need servicing occasionally—perhaps a touch of oil and an adjustment. Worse yet, the complexity of all those wheels and pinions engaged in reproducing the galaxy means that a user will occasionally do something perfectly harmless like wind his or her watch up only to find everything grinding to a halt. Here are some tips for dealing with these mechanical beauties for new watch owners and reminders for the old hands.

1. DATE CHANGES

Do not change the date manually (via the crown or pusher) on any mechanical watch—whether manual wind or automatic—when the time indicated on the dial reads between 10 and 2 o'clock. Although some better watches are protected against this horological quirk, most mechanical watches with a date indicator are engaged in the process of automatically changing the date between the hours of 10 p.m. and 2 a.m. Intervening with a forced manual change while the automatic date shift is engaged can damage the movement. Of course, you can make the adjustment between 10 a.m. and 2 p.m. in most cases—but this is just not a good habit to get into. When in doubt, roll the time past 12 o'clock and look for an automatic date change before you set the time and date. The Ulysse Nardin brand is notable, among a very few others, for in-house mechanical movements immune to this effect.

Bovet's barrier to pressing the wrong pusher.

2. CHRONOGRAPH USE

On a simple chronograph, start and stop are almost always the same button. Normally located above the crown, the start/stop actuator can be pressed at will to initiate and end the interval timing. The reset button, normally below the crown, is only used for resetting the chronograph to zero, but only when the chronograph is stopped—never while engaged. Only a "flyback" chronograph allows safe resetting to zero while running. With the chronograph engaged, you simply hit the reset button and all the chronograph indicators (seconds, minutes, and hours) snap back to zero and the chronograph begins to accumulate the interval time once again. In the early days of air travel this was a valuable complication as pilots would reset their chronographs when taking on a new heading—without having to fumble about with a three-step procedure with gloved hands.

Nota bene: Don't actuate or reset your chronograph while your watch is submerged—even if you have one of those that are built for such usage, like Omega, IWC, and a few other brands. Feel free to hit the buttons before submersion and jump in and swim while they run; just don't push anything while in the water.

3. CHANGING TIME BACKWARD

Don't adjust the time on your watch in a counterclockwise direction—especially if the watch has calendar functions. A few watches can tolerate the abuse, but it's better to avoid the possibility of damage altogether. Change the dates as needed (remembering the 10 and 2 rule above).

4. SHOCKS

Almost all modern watches are equipped with some level of shock protection. Best practices for the Swiss brands allow for a three-foot fall onto a hard wood surface. But if your watch is running poorly—or even worse has stopped entirely after an impact—do not shake, wind, or bang it again to get it running; take it to an expert for service as you may do even more damage. Sports like tennis, squash, or golf can have a deleterious effect on your watch, including flattening the pivots, overbanking, or even bending or breaking a pivot.

5. OVERWINDING

Most modern watches are fitted with a mechanism that allows the mainspring to slide inside the barrel—or stops it completely once the spring is fully wound—for protection against overwinding. The best advice here is just don't force it. Over the years, a winding crown may start to get "stickier" and more difficult to turn even when unwound. That's a sure sign it is due for service.

6. JACUZZI TEMPERATURE

Don't jump into the Jacuzzi—or even a steaming hot shower—with your watch on. Better-built watches with a deeper water-resistance rating typically have no problem with this scenario. However, take a 3 or 5 atm water-resistant watch into the Jacuzzi, and there's a chance the different rates of expansion and contraction of the metals and sapphire or mineral crystals may allow moisture into the case.

Panerai makes sure you think before touching the crown.

Do it yourself at your own risk.

7. SCREW THAT CROWN DOWN (AND THOSE PUSHERS)!

Always check and double-check to ensure a watch fitted with a screwed-down crown is closed tightly. Screwed-down pushers for a chronograph—or any other functions—deserve the same attention. This one oversight has cost quite a few owners their watches. If a screwed-down crown is not secured, water will likely get into the case and start oxidizing the metal. In time, the problem can destroy the watch.

8. MAGNETISM

If your watch is acting up, running faster or slower, it may have become magnetized. This can happen if you leave your timepiece near a computer, cell phone, or some other electronic device. Many service centers have a so-called degausser to take care of the problem. A number of brands also make watches with a soft iron core to deflect magnetic fields, though this might not work with the stronger ones.

9. TRIBOLOGY

Keeping a mechanical timepiece hidden away in a box for extended lengths of time is not the best way to care for it. Even if you don't wear a watch every day, it is a good idea to run your watch at regular intervals to keep its lubricating oils and greases viscous. Think about a can of house paint: Keep it stirred and it stays liquid almost indefinitely; leave it still for too long and a skin develops. On a smaller level the same thing can happen to the lubricants inside a mechanical watch.

10. SERVICE

Most mechanical watches call for a three- to five-year service cycle for cleaning, oiling, and maintenance. Some mechanical watches can run twice that long and have functioned within acceptable parameters, but if you're not going to have your watch serviced at regular intervals, you do run the risk of having timing issues. Always have your watch serviced by a qualified watchmaker (see box), not at the kiosk in the local mall. The best you can expect there is a quick battery change.

Gary Girdvainis is the founder of Isochron Media LLC, publishers of WristWatch *and* AboutTime *magazines.*

WATCH REPAIR SERVICE CENTERS

RGM
www.rgmwatches.com/repair

Stoll & Co.
www.americaswatchmaker.com

Swiss Watchmakers & Company
www.swisswatchland.com

Universal Watch Repair
www.universalwatch.net

Watch Repairs USA
www.watchrepairsusa.com

Glossary

ANNUAL CALENDAR

The automatic allowances for the different lengths of each month of a year in the calendar module of a watch. This type of watch usually shows the month and date, and sometimes the day of the week (like this one by Patek Philippe) and the phases of the moon.

ANTIMAGNETIC

Magnetic fields found in common everyday places affect mechanical movements, hence the use of anti- or non-magnetic components in the movement. Some companies encase movements in antimagnetic cores such as Sinn's Model 756, the Duograph, shown here.

ANTIREFLECTION

A film created by steaming the crystal to eliminate light reflection and improve legibility. Antireflection functions best when applied to both sides of the crystal, but because it scratches, some manufacturers prefer to have it only on the interior of the crystal. It is mainly used on synthetic sapphire crystals. Dubey & Schaldenbrand applies antireflection on both sides for all of the company's wristwatches, such as this Aquadyn model.

AUTOMATIC WINDING

A rotating weight set into motion by moving the wrist winds the spring barrel via the gear train of mechanical watch movement. Automatic winding was invented during the pocket watch era in 1770 but the breakthrough automatic winding movement via rotor began with the ball bearing Eterna-Matic in the late 1940s. Today we speak of unidirectional winding and bidirectionally winding rotors, depending on the type of gear train used. Shown is IWC's automatic Caliber 50611.

BALANCE

The beating heart of a mechanical watch movement is the balance. Fed by the energy of the mainspring, a tirelessly oscillating little wheel, just a few millimeters in diameter and possessing a spiral-shaped balance spring, sets the rhythm for the escape wheel and pallets with its vibration frequency. Today the balance is usually made of one piece of antimagnetic glucydur, an alloy that expands very little when exposed to heat.

BAR OR COCK

A metal plate fastened to the base plate at one point, leaving room for a gear wheel or pinion. The balance is usually attached to a bar called the balance cock. Glashütte tradition dictates that the balance cock be decoratively engraved by hand like this one by Glashütte Original.

BEVELING

To uniformly file down the sharp edges of a plate, bridge, or bar and give it a high polish. The process is also called *anglage.* Edges are usually beveled at a 45° angle. As the picture shows, this is painstaking work that needs the skilled hands and eyes of an experienced watchmaker or *angleur.*

BRIDGE

A metal plate fastened to the base plate at two points leaving room for a gear wheel or pinion. This vintage Favre-Leuba movement illustrates the point with three individual bridges.

CARBON FIBER

A very light, tough composite material, carbon fiber is composed of filaments comprised of several thousand seven-micron carbon fibers held together by resin. The arrangement of the filaments determines the quality of a component, making each unique. Carbon fiber is currently being used for dials, cases, and even movement components.

CALIBER

A term, similar to type or model, that refers to different watch movements. Pictured here is Heuer's Caliber 11, the legendary automatic chronograph caliber from 1969. This movement was a coproduction jointly researched and developed for four years by Heuer-Leonidas, Breitling, and Hamilton-Büren. Each company gave the movement a different name after serial production began.

CHAMPLEVÉ

A dial decoration technique, whereby the metal is engraved, filled with enamel, and baked, as in this cockatoo on a Cartier Tortue, enhanced with mother-of-pearl slivers.

CERAMIC

An inorganic, nonmetallic material formed by the action of heat and practically unscratchable. Pioneered by Rado, ceramic is a high-tech material generally made from aluminum and zirconia oxide. Today, it is used generally for cases and bezels and now comes in many colors.

CHRONOGRAPH

From the Greek *chronos* (time) and *graphein* (to write). Originally a chronograph literally wrote, inscribing the time elapsed on a piece of paper with the help of a pencil attached to a type of hand. Today this term is used for watches that show not only the time of day, but also certain time intervals via independent hands that may be started or stopped at will. Stopwatches differ from chronographs because they do not show the time of day. This exploded illustration shows the complexity of a Breitling chronograph.

CHRONOMETER

Literally, "measurer of time." As the term is used today, a chronometer denotes an especially accurate watch (one with a deviation of no more than 5 seconds a day for mechanical movements). Chronometers are usually supplied with an official certificate from an independent testing office such as the COSC. The largest producer of chronometers in 2008 was Rolex, with 769,850 officially certified movements. Chopard came in sixth with more than 22,000 certified L.U.C mechanisms, like the 4.96 in the Pro One model shown here.

COLUMN WHEEL

The component used to control chronograph functions within a true chronograph movement. The presence of a column wheel indicates that the chronograph is fully integrated into the movement. In the modern era, modules are generally used that are attached to a base caliber movement. This particular column wheel is made of blued steel.

CONSTANT FORCE MECHANISM

Sometimes called a constant force escapement, it isn't really: in most cases this mechanism is "simply" an initial tension spring. It is also known in English by part of its French name, the *remontoir*, which actually means "winding mechanism." This mechanism regulates and portions the energy that is passed on through the escapement, making the rate as even and precise as possible. Shown here is the constant force escapement from A. Lange & Söhne's Lange 31—a mechanism that gets as close to its name as possible.

COSC

The Contrôle Officiel Suisse de Chronomètrage, the official Swiss testing office for chronometers. The COSC is the world's largest issuer of so-called chronometer certificates, which are only otherwise given out individually by certain observatories (such as the one in Neuchâtel, Switzerland). For a fee, the COSC tests the rate of movements that have been adjusted by watchmakers. These are usually mechanical movements, but the office also tests some high-precision quartz movements. Those that meet the specifications for being a chronometer are awarded an official certificate as shown here.

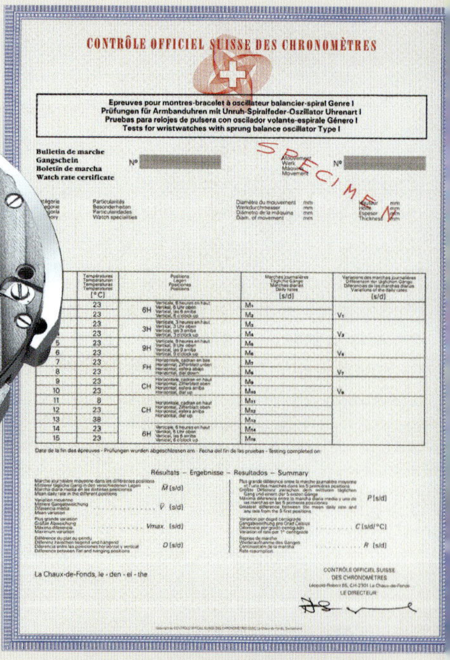

CONTRÔLE OFFICIEL SUISSE DES CHRONOMÈTRES

Epreuves pour montres-bracelet à oscillateur balancier-spiral Genre I
Prüfungen für Armbanduhren mit Unruh-Spiralfeder-Oszillator Uhrenart I
Pruebas para relojes de pulsera con oscilador volante-espiral Género I
Tests for wristwatches with sprung balance oscillator Type I

SPECIMEN

CÔTES DE GENÈVE

Also called *vagues de Genève* and Geneva stripes. This is a traditional Swiss surface decoration comprising an even pattern of parallel stripes, applied to flat movement components with a quickly rotating plastic or wooden peg. Glashütte watchmakers have devised their own version of *côtes de Genève* that is applied at a slightly different angle, called Glashütte ribbing.

CROWN

The crown is used to wind and set a watch. A few simple turns of the crown will get an automatic movement started, while a manually wound watch is completely wound by the crown. The crown is also used for the setting of various functions, almost always including at least the hours, minutes, seconds, and date. A screwed-down crown like the one on the TAG Heuer Aquagraph pictured here can be tightened to prevent water entering the case or any mishaps while performing extreme sports such as diving.

EQUATION OF TIME

The mean time that we use to keep track of the passing of the day (24 hours evenly divided into minutes and seconds) is not equal to true solar time. The equation of time is a complication devised to show the difference between the mean time shown on one's wristwatch and the time the sun dictates. The Équation Marchante by Blancpain very distinctly indicates this difference via the golden sun-tipped hand that also rotates around the dial in a manner known to watch connoisseurs as *marchant*. Other wristwatch models, such as the Boreas by Martin Braun, display the difference on an extra scale on the dial.

ESCAPEMENT

The combination of the balance, balance spring, pallets, and escape wheel, a subgroup which divides the impulses coming from the spring barrel into small, accurately portioned doses. It guarantees that the gear train runs smoothly and efficiently. The pictured escapement is one newly invented by Parmigiani, containing pallet stones of varying colors, though they are generally red synthetic rubies. Here one of them is a colorless sapphire, or corundum, the same geological material that ruby is made of.

FLINQUÉ

A dial decoration in which a guilloché design is given a coat of enamel, softening the pattern and creating special effects, as shown here on a unique Bovet.

FLYBACK CHRONOGRAPH

A chronograph with a special dial train switch that makes the immediate reuse of the chronograph movement possible after resetting the hands. It was developed for special timekeeping duties such as those found in aviation, which require the measurement of time intervals in quick succession. A flyback may also be called a *retour en vol*. An elegant example of this type of chronograph is Corum's Classical Flyback Large Date shown here.

GEAR TRAIN

A mechanical watch's gear train transmits energy from the mainspring to the escapement. The gear train comprises the minute wheel, the third wheel, the fourth wheel, and the escape wheel.

GLUCYDUR

Glucydur is a functional alloy of copper, beryllium, and iron that has been used to make balances in watches since the 1930s. Its hardness and stability allow watchmakers to use balances that were poised at the factory and no longer required adjustment screws.

GUILLOCHÉ

A surface decoration usually applied to the dial and the rotor using a grooving tool with a sharp tip, such as a rose engine, to cut an even pattern onto a level surface. The exact adjustment of the tool for each new path is controlled by a device similar to a pantograph, and the movement of the tool can be controlled either manually or mechanically. Real *guillochis* (the correct term used by a master of guilloché) are very intricate and expensive to produce, which is why most dials decorated in this fashion are produced by stamping machines. Breguet is one of the very few companies to use real guilloché on every one of its dials.

INDEX

A regulating mechanism found on the balance cock and used by the watchmaker to adjust the movement's rate. The index changes the effective length of the balance spring, thus making it move more quickly or slowly. This is the standard index found on an ETA Valjoux 7750.

JEWEL

To minimize friction, the hardened steel tips of a movement's rotating gear wheels (called pinions) are lodged in synthetic rubies (fashioned as polished stones with a hole) and lubricated with a very thin layer of special oil. These synthetic rubies are produced in exactly the same way as sapphire crystal using the same material. During the pocket watch era, real rubies with hand-drilled holes were still used, but because of the high costs involved, they were only used in movements with especially quickly rotating gears. The jewel shown here on a bridge from A. Lange & Söhne's Double Split is additionally embedded in a gold chaton secured with three blued screws.

LIGA

The word LIGA is actually a German acronym that stands for lithography *(Lithografie)*, electroplating *(Galvanisierung)*, and plastic molding *(Abformung)*. It is a lithographic process exposed by UV or X-ray light that literally "grows" perfect micro components made of nickel, nickel-phosphorus, or 23.5-karat gold in a plating bath. The components need no finishing or trimming after manufacture.

LUMINOUS SUBSTANCE

Tritium paint is a slightly radioactive substance that replaced radium as a luminous coating for hands, numerals, and hour markers on watch dials. Watches bearing tritium must be marked as such, with the letter *T* on the dial near 6 o'clock. It has now for the most part been replaced by nonradioactive materials such as Superluminova. Traser technology (as seen on these Ball timepieces) uses tritium gas enclosed in tiny silicate glass tubes coated on the inside with a phosphorescing substance. The luminescence is constant and will hold around twenty-five years.

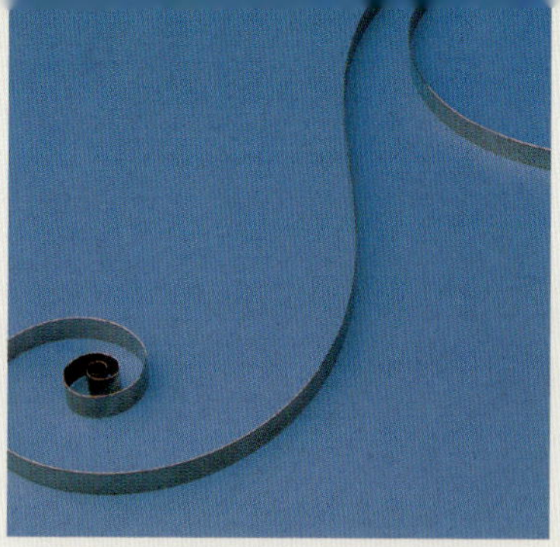

MAINSPRING

The mainspring, located in the spring barrel, stores energy when tensioned and passes it on to the escapement via the gear train as the tension relaxes. Today, mainsprings are generally made of Nivaflex, an alloy invented by Swiss engineer Max Straumann at the beginning of the 1950s. This alloy basically comprises iron, nickel, chrome, cobalt, and beryllium.

MINUTE REPEATER

A striking mechanism with hammers and gongs for acoustically signaling the hours, quarter hours, and minutes elapsed since noon or midnight. The wearer pushes a slide, which winds the spring. Normally a repeater uses two different gongs to signal hours (low tone), quarter hours (high and low tones in succession), and minutes (high tone). Some watches have three gongs, called a carillon. The Chronoswiss Répétition à Quarts is a prominent repeating introduction of recent years.

PERPETUAL CALENDAR

The calendar module for this type of timepiece automatically makes allowances for the different lengths of each month as well as leap years until the next secular year, which will occur in 2100. A perpetual calendar usually shows the date, month, and four-year cycle, and may show the day of the week and moon phase as well, as does this one introduced by George J von Burg at Baselworld 2005. Perpetual calendars need much skill to complete.

PERLAGE

Surface decoration comprising an even pattern of partially overlapping dots, applied with a quickly rotating plastic or wooden peg, as shown here on the plates of Frédérique Constant's *manufacture* Caliber FC 910-1

PLATE

A metal platform having several tiers for the gear train. The base plate of a movement usually incorporates the dial and carries the bearings for the primary pinions of the "first floor" of a gear train. The gear wheels are made complete by tightly fitting screwed-in bridges and bars on the back side of the plate. A specialty of the so-called Glashütte school, as opposed to the Swiss school, is the reverse completion of a movement not via different bridges and bars, but rather with a three-quarter plate. Glashütte Original's Caliber 65 (shown) displays a beautifully decorated three-quarter plate.

POWER RESERVE DISPLAY

A mechanical watch contains only a certain amount of power reserve. A fully wound modern automatic watch usually possesses between 36 and 42 hours of energy before it needs to be wound again. The power reserve display keeps the wearer informed about how much energy his or her watch still has in reserve, a function that is especially practical on manually wound watches with several days of possible reserve. The Nomos Tangente Power Reserve pictured here represents an especially creative way to illustrate the state of the mainspring's tension. On some German watches the power reserve is also displayed with the words "auf" and "ab."

PULSOMETER

A scale on the dial, flange, or bezel that, in conjunction with the second hand, may be used to measure a pulse rate. A pulsometer is always marked with a reference number—if it is marked with *gradué pour 15 pulsations*, for example, then the wearer counts fifteen pulse beats. At the last beat, the second hand will show what the pulse rate is in beats per minute on the pulsometer scale. The scale on Sinn's World Time Chronograph (shown) is marked simply with the German world *Puls* (pulse), but the function remains the same.

QUALITÉ FLEURIER

This certification of quality was established by Chopard, Parmigiani Fleurier, Vaucher, and Bovet Fleurier in 2004. Watches bearing the seal must fulfill five criteria, including COSC certification, passing several tests for robustness and precision, top-notch finishing, and being 100 percent Swiss-made (except for the raw materials). The seal appears here on the dial of the Parmigiani Fleurier Tonda 39.

RETROGRADE DISPLAY

A retrograde display shows the time linearly instead of circularly. The hand continues along an arc until it reaches the end of its scale, at which precise moment it jumps back to the beginning instantaneously. This Nienaber model not only shows the minutes in retrograde form, it is also a regulator display.

ROTOR

The rotor is the component that keeps an automatic watch wound. The kinetic motion of this part, which contains a heavy metal weight around its outer edge, winds the mainspring. It can either wind unilaterally or bilaterally (to one or both sides) depending on the caliber. The rotor from this Temption timepiece belongs to an ETA Valjoux 7750.

SAPPHIRE CRYSTAL

Synthetic sapphire crystal is known to gemologists as aluminum oxide (Al_2O_3) or corundum. It can be colorless (corundum), red (ruby), blue (sapphire), or green (emerald). It is virtually scratchproof; only a diamond is harder. The innovative Royal Blue Tourbillon by Ulysse Nardin pictured here features not only sapphire crystals on the front and back of the watch, but also actual plates made of both colorless and blue corundum within the movement.

SCREW BALANCE

Before the invention of the perfectly weighted balance using a smooth ring, balances were fitted with weighted screws to get the exact impetus desired. Today a screw balance is a subtle sign of quality in a movement due to its costly construction and assembly utilizing minuscule weighted screws.

SEAL OF GENEVA

Since 1886 the official seal of this canton has been awarded to Genevan watch *manufactures* who must follow a defined set of high-quality criteria that include the following: polished jewel bed drillings, jewels with olive drillings, polished winding wheels, quality balances and balance springs, steel levers and springs with beveling of 45 degrees and *côtes de Genève* decoration, and polished stems and pinions. The list was updated in 2012 to include the entire watch and newer components. Testing is done on the finished piece. The Seal consists of two, one on the movement, one on the case. The pictured seal was awarded to Vacheron Constantin, a traditional Genevan *manufacture*.

SILICIUM/SILICON

Silicon is an element relatively new to mechanical watches. It is currently being used in the manufacture of precision escapements. Ulysse Nardin's Freak has lubrication-free silicon wheels, and Breguet has successfully used flat silicon balance springs.

SKELETONIZATION

The technique of cutting a movement's components down to their weight-bearing basic substance. Th is generally done by hand in painstaking hours of microscopic work with a small handheld saw, though machines can skeletonize parts to a certain degree, such as the version of the Valjoux 7750 that was created for Chronoswiss's Opus and Pathos models. This tourbillon created by Christophe Schaffo is additionally—and masterfully—hand-engraved.

SONNERIE

A variety of minute repeater that—like a tower clock—sounds the time not at the will of the wearer, but rather automatically *(en passant)* every hour *(petite sonnerie)* or quarter hour *(grande sonnerie)*. Gérald Genta designed the most complicated sonnerie back in the early nineties. Shown is a recent model from the front and back.

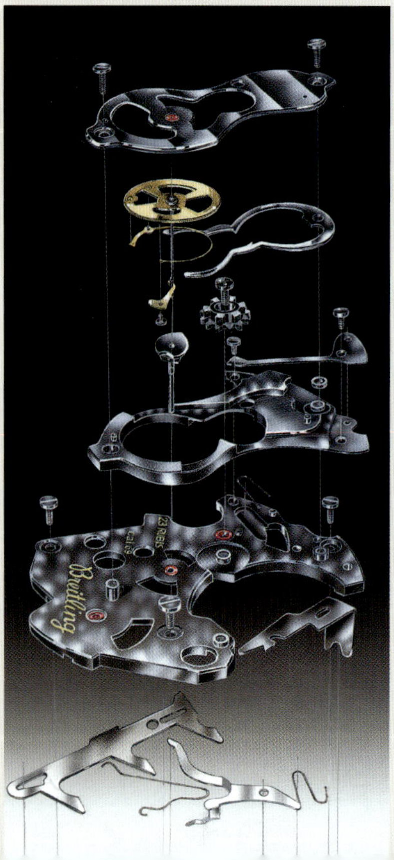

SPLIT-SECONDS CHRONOGRAPH

Also known in the watch industry by its French name, the *rattrapante* (exploded view at left). A watch with two second hands, one of which can be blocked with a special dial train lever to indicate an intermediate time while the other continues to run. When released, the split-seconds hand jumps ahead to the position of the other second hand. The PTC by Porsche Design illustrates this nicely.

SPRING BARREL

The spring barrel contains the mainspring. It turns freely on an arbor, pulled along by the toothed wheel generally doubling as its lid. This wheel interacts with the first pinion of the movement's gear train. Some movements contain two or more spring barrels for added power reserve.

SWAN-NECK FINE ADJUSTMENT

A regulating instrument used by the watchmaker to adjust the movement's rate in place of an index. The swan neck is especially prevalent in fine Swiss and Glashütte watchmaking (here, Lang & Heyne's Moritz model). Mühle Glashütte has varied the theme with its woodpecker's neck.

TACHYMETER

A scale on the dial, flange, or bezel of a chronograph that, in conjunction with the second hand, gives the speed of a moving object. A tachymeter takes a value determined in less than a minute and converts it into miles or kilometers per hour. For example, a wearer could measure the time it takes a car to pass between two mile markers on the highway. When the car passes the marker, the second hand will be pointing to the car's speed in miles per hour on the tachymetric scale.

TOURBILLON

A technical device invented by Abraham-Louis Breguet in 1801 to compensate for the influence of gravity on the balance of a pocket watch. The entire escapement is mounted on an epicyclic train in a "cage" and rotated completely on its axis over regular periods of time. This superb horological highlight is seen as a sign of technological know-how in the modern era. Harry Winston's Histoire de Tourbillon 4 is a spectacular example.

VIBRATION FREQUENCY (VPH)

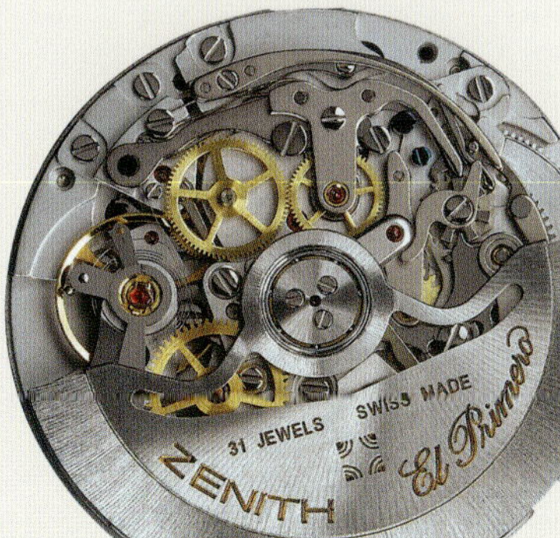

The spring causes the balance to oscillate at a certain frequency measured in hertz (Hz) or vibrations per hour (vph). Most of today's wristwatches tick at 28,800 vph (4 Hz) or 21,600 vph (3 Hz). Less usual is 18,000 vph (2.5 Hz). Zenith's El Primero was the first serial movement to beat at 36,000 vph (5 Hz), and the Breguet Type XXII runs at 72,000 vph.

WATER RESISTANCE

Water resistance is an important feature of any timepiece and is usually measured in increments of one atmosphere (atm or bar, equal to 10 meters of water pressure) or meters and is often noted on the dial or case back. Watches resistant to 100 meters are best for swimming and snorkeling. Timepieces resistant to 200 meters are good for scuba diving. To deep-sea dive there are various professional timepieces available for use in depths of 200 meters or more. The Hydromax by Bell & Ross (shown) is water-resistant to a record 11,000 meters.

Editor-in-chief: Peter Braun
Editor: Marton Radkai
Production manager: Louise Kurtz
Copy Editors: Cynthia K. Barton, Stephanie Sarkany, Katherine Macedon
Composition: Erin Morris, Evergreen Design Studio
Project Management: Kourtnay King, Layman Poupard Publishing

Printed and bound in China.

ISBN 978-0-7892-1456-0

Twenty-fourth edition
10 9 8 7 6 5 4 3 2 1

Library of Congress Cataloging-in-Publication Data available upon request

For bulk and premium sales and for text adoption procedures, write to Customer Service Manager,
Abbeville Press, 655 Third Avenue, New York, NY 10017, or call 1-800-ARTBOOK.

Visit Abbeville Press online at www.abbeville.com.

ISBN 978-0-7892-1456-0 U.S. $39.95
53995
EAN
9 780789 214560